MECHANISMS OF SOCIAL CONNECTION

MECHANISMS OF SOCIAL CONNECTION

From Brain to Group

Edited by Mario Mikulincer and Phillip R. Shaver

American Psychological Association • Washington, DC

Published by
American Psychological Association
750 First Street, NE
Washington, DC 20002
www.apa.org

To order
APA Order Department
P.O. Box 92984
Washington, DC 20090-2984
Tel: (800) 374-2721; Direct: (202) 336-5510
Fax: (202) 336-5502; TDD/TTY: (202) 336-6123
Online: www.apa.org/pubs/books
E-mail: order@apa.org

In the U.K., Europe, Africa, and the Middle East, copies may be ordered from
American Psychological Association
3 Henrietta Street
Covent Garden, London
WC2E 8LU England

Typeset in Goudy by Circle Graphics, Inc., Columbia, MD

Printer: Edwards Brothers, Inc., Lillington, NC
Cover Designer: Mercury Publishing Services, Inc., Rockville, MD

Cover art: Brian Kershisnik (American, b. 1962), *Many Reunions*, 2010, Oil on Canvas, 66″ × 84″

The opinions and statements published are the responsibility of the authors, and such opinions and statements do not necessarily represent the policies of the American Psychological Association.

Library of Congress Cataloging-in-Publication Data

Mechanisms of social connection : from brain to group / edited by Mario Mikulincer and Phillip R. Shaver. — First edition.
     pages cm. — (The Herzliya series on personality and social psychology)
     Includes bibliographical references and index.
     ISBN 978-1-4338-1415-0 — ISBN 1-4338-1415-3 1. Social interaction—Psychological aspects. 2. Interpersonal relations—Psychological aspects. 3. Social psychology.
I. Mikulincer, Mario editor of compilation. II. Shaver, Phillip R. editor of compilation.
     HM1111.M43 2014
     302—dc23   2013003490

British Library Cataloguing-in-Publication Data
A CIP record is available from the British Library.

Printed in the United States of America
First Edition

http://dx.doi.org/10.1037/14250-000

THE HERZLIYA SERIES ON PERSONALITY
AND SOCIAL PSYCHOLOGY

Mario Mikulincer and Phillip R. Shaver, Series Editors

Series Titles

Prosocial Motives, Emotions, and Behavior: The Better Angels of Our Nature
    Edited by Mario Mikulincer and Phillip R. Shaver

Human Aggression and Violence: Causes, Manifestations, and Consequences
    Edited by Phillip R. Shaver and Mario Mikulincer

The Social Psychology of Morality: Exploring the Causes of Good and Evil
    Edited by Mario Mikulincer and Phillip R. Shaver

Meaning, Mortality, and Choice: The Social Psychology of Existential Concerns
    Edited by Phillip R. Shaver and Mario Mikulincer

Mechanisms of Social Connection: From Brain to Group
    Edited by Mario Mikulincer and Phillip R. Shaver

CONTENTS

CONTRIBUTORS

Bianca P. Acevedo, PhD, Department of Public Health, Weill Cornell Medical College, New York, NY

Arthur P. Aron, PhD, Department of Psychology, Stony Brook University, Stony Brook, NY

Karen L. Bales, PhD, Department of Psychology, University of California; National Primate Research Center, Davis, CA

Lane Beckes, PhD, Department of Psychology, University of Virginia, Charlottesville

Gurit E. Birnbaum, PhD, School of Psychology, Interdisciplinary Center (IDC) Herzliya, Herzliya, Israel

Rechele Brooks, PhD, Institute for Learning & Brain Sciences, Department of Psychiatry & Behavioral Sciences, University of Washington, Seattle

Casey L. Brown, BA, Department of Psychology, University of Virginia, Charlottesville

Jude Cassidy, PhD, Department of Psychology, Maryland Child and Family Development Laboratory, University of Maryland, College Park

Justin V. Cavallo, PhD, Department of Psychology, Wilfrid Laurier University, Waterloo, Ontario, Canada

James A. Coan, PhD, Department of Psychology, University of Virginia, Charlottesville

Volker A. Coenen, MD, Department of Stereotactic and Functional Neurosurgery/Department of Neurosurgery, University Hospital Freiburg, Freiburg, Germany

Nancy L. Collins, PhD, Department of Psychological and Brain Sciences, University of California, Santa Barbara

W. Andrew Collins, PhD, Institute of Child Development, University of Minnesota, Minneapolis

Carsten K. W. De Dreu, PhD, Department of Psychology, University of Amsterdam, Amsterdam, the Netherlands

Jean Decety, PhD, Department of Psychology, University of Chicago, Chicago, IL

Katherine B. Ehrlich, PhD, Institute for Policy Research, Northwestern University, Evanston, IL

Tsachi Ein-Dor, PhD, School of Psychology, Interdisciplinary Center Herzliya, Herzliya, Israel

Naomi Ellemers, PhD, Department of Social Psychology, the Leiden Institute for Brain and Cognition, Leiden University, Leiden, the Netherlands

Brooke C. Feeney, PhD, Department of Psychology, Carnegie Mellon University, Pittsburgh, PA

Ruth Feldman, PhD, Department of Psychology and the Gonda Brain Sciences Center, Bar-Ilan University, Ramat-Gan, Israel

Peter Fonagy, PhD, Research Department of Clinical, Educational, and Health Psychology, University College London, London, England

Valeria Gazzola, PhD, Social Brain Lab, Netherlands Institute for Neuroscience, Amsterdam, the Netherlands; Department of Neuroscience, University of Groningen, University Medical Center Groningen, the Netherlands

John G. Holmes, PhD, Psychology Department, University of Waterloo, Waterloo, Ontario, Canada

Lauren H. Howard, MA, Department of Psychology, University of Chicago, Chicago, IL

Tatsuya Kameda, PhD, Department of Behavioral Science, Hokkaido University, Sapporo, Japan

Christian Keysers, PhD, Social Brain Lab, Netherlands Institute for Neuroscience, Amsterdam, the Netherlands; Department of Neuroscience, University of Groningen, University Medical Center Groningen, the Netherlands

Nina Koren-Karie, PhD, School of Social Work and Center for the Study of Child Development, University of Haifa, Haifa, Israel

Andrew N. Meltzoff, PhD, Institute for Learning & Brain Sciences, Department of Psychology, University of Washington, Seattle

Mario Mikulincer, PhD, School of Psychology, Interdisciplinary Center Herzliya, Herzliya, Israel

Sandra L. Murray, PhD, Psychology Department, University at Buffalo, State University of New York, Buffalo

David Oppenheim, PhD, Department of Psychology and Center for the Study of Child Development, University of Haifa, Haifa, Israel

Jaak Panksepp, PhD, Department of Veterinary and Comparative Anatomy, Pharmacology and Physiology, Washington State University, Pullman

Harry T. Reis, PhD, Department of Clinical & Social Sciences in Psychology, University of Rochester, Rochester, NY

Jessica E. Salvatore, PhD, Department of Psychiatry, School of Medicine, Virginia Commonwealth University, Richmond

Daan Scheepers, PhD, Institute of Psychology, Leiden University, Leiden, the Netherlands

Thomas E. Schläpfer, MD, Department of Psychiatry and Psychotherapy, Bonn University Medical Center, Bonn, Germany; Department of Psychiatry and Behavioral Sciences, The Johns Hopkins University School of Medicine, Baltimore, MD

Dana Shai, PhD, School of Psychology, Interdisciplinary Center Herzliya, Herzliya, Israel

Phillip R. Shaver, PhD, Department of Psychology, University of California, Davis

Laura J. Sherman, MS, Department of Psychology, University of Maryland, College Park

Jeffry A. Simpson, PhD, Department of Psychology, University of Minnesota, Minneapolis

Mark Solms, PhD, Department of Psychology, University of Cape Town, Rondebosch, South Africa

Sooyeon Sung, MA, Department of Psychology, University of Minnesota, Minneapolis

Félice van Nunspeet, MS, Social and Organizational Psychology Unit, Leiden Institute for Brain and Cognition, Leiden University, Leiden, the Netherlands

Mark van Vugt, PhD, Department of Social and Organizational Psychology, VU University Amsterdam, Amsterdam, the Netherlands; Institute for Cognitive and Evolutionary Anthropology, University of Oxford, Oxford, England

PREFACE

Why are human beings so eager to form social bonds, and why do they suffer so grievously when those bonds are disrupted or broken? How does a person overcome fear of rejection and distrust to become emotionally invested in and attached to others? How do we become identified with other members of a social group to the extent that we include them in our self-concept and rely on them to supply our sense of value? Why do they contribute so powerfully to our sense of meaning and our feelings of vitality, on the one hand, and—at times—to our anguish and despair, on the other? What neural and hormonal processes are involved in the formation and maintenance of social bonds? How do our social experiences in infancy and childhood influence our relational behavior and the quality of our social bonds in adulthood? How are our social connections influenced by biological and evolutionary processes and sociocultural contexts?

These important questions about human connections have attracted the attention of researchers from diverse disciplines, such as social psychology, developmental psychology, communication studies, sociology, and neuroscience. But there is too little dialogue between the different disciplines, and this has resulted in a lack of integration of insights and findings.

In the first four volumes of our Herzliya Series on Personality and Social Psychology, we focused on prosocial motives, emotions, and behavior; aggression, violence, and their effects; morality ("good and evil"); and existential concerns such as mortality, meaning, and freedom. In this, the fifth volume, we deepen our analysis of human social behavior by surveying some of the latest developments in theory and research concerning the physiological and psychological mechanisms underlying the formation of social connections at neural, dyadic, and group levels. We do this with the entire human life span in mind, beginning with infant–parent relationships.

This new volume contains 21 chapters organized into four main sections: the brain level (focusing on the neural underpinnings of social connections and the hormonal processes that contribute to forming connections); the developmental level (focusing especially on child–parent relationships); the dyadic relationship level (focusing especially on romantic and marital relationships); and the group level (considering both evolutionary and physiological bases of group processes). Each section describes state-of-the-art theories and research from the disciplines of social psychology, developmental psychology, and social neuroscience.

The chapter authors, all experts in their fields, generously agreed to come to Herzliya and deliver lectures at the 2012 Herzliya Symposium on Personality and Social Psychology. They participated in hours of formal lectures and discussions, spent many informal hours together, and then returned home and prepared chapters based on the lectures and discussions. The meeting was cohosted by the two editors of this volume. We worked with the chapter authors to make the resulting book as accessible, coherent, and readable as possible so it would be suitable for researchers and application-oriented professionals as well as for university classes and the educated public. The book provides a lively, engaging, readable, and up-to-the-moment review of social psychological, developmental, and neuroscientific approaches to understanding the formation and quality of social connections across the life span.

We are grateful to everyone who made the preparation of this book possible and enjoyable. We first thank all of the chapter authors—an amazing group of scholars and admirable human beings who care about science and the betterment of human life. We also especially thank Uriel Reichmann, president of the Interdisciplinary Center Herzliya, who provided financial and staff support for an annual series of conferences on personality and social psychology. We thank the staff of the Interdisciplinary Center Herzliya—Keren Mifano, Reut Kramer, Shulli Sardes, and Adi Peri—who handled all of the arrangements for the conference, dealt effectively with the many on-site details, and coped masterfully with the inevitable glitches and emergencies. We also thank Maureen Adams, senior acquisitions editor at American Psychological Association (APA) Books, for seeing the value of this book and the series in which it appears and for being a generous, thoughtful, and supportive friend during this book's preparation. Finally, we thank Robin Easson and Mark Winter at APA Books for their careful reviewing and copyediting and the anonymous academic reviewer who made many helpful suggestions.

MECHANISMS OF SOCIAL CONNECTION

INTRODUCTION

MARIO MIKULINCER AND PHILLIP R. SHAVER

During most of our lives, we are in the presence of other people, and most of our behavior takes place in the context of relationships with other people and social groups. Moreover, "my relationships" is the most frequent response when people are asked what makes their lives meaningful and happy. In fact, we are wired by evolution to form social connections, feel pleased when new bonds are formed, become angry or sad when social bonds are broken, and devote much of our cognitive processing capacity to interpreting others' behavior in our social interactions, dyadic relationships, and groups. Social connections are crucial for psychological growth, well-being, mental health, and social functioning across the life span, beginning from the first hours of life.

Given the importance of social connections, it isn't surprising that researchers have devoted a great deal of time and effort to understanding the formation and maintenance of social connections across the life span and the affective, cognitive, and behavioral effects of these connections. One of the most exciting recent developments in social psychology is the incorporation of

http://dx.doi.org/10.1037/14250-001
Mechanisms of Social Connection: From Brain to Group, M. Mikulincer and P. R. Shaver (Editors)
Copyright © 2014 by the American Psychological Association. All rights reserved.

neural, physiological, evolutionary, and developmental concepts and methods into the study of social connections. Although such integration is obviously desirable from a scientific standpoint, it has been rare in a field based largely on behavioral experiments involving American or European college students. In this book, we survey some of the latest developments in theory and research concerning the physiological and psychological mechanisms underlying the formation of social connections at the neural, dyadic, and group levels—considering such processes across the life span, beginning with infant–parent relationships.

Our main goal in the volume is to provide an opportunity for discussion among proponents of various theories and research paradigms relevant to the nature and formation of social connections investigated at different levels of analysis. The book is organized in terms of four levels of analysis. The first section includes six chapters that provide a neuroscientific analysis of the physiological underpinnings of social connections and of the various brain mechanisms underlying the formation of these connections, the subjective experience of being connected, and the core relational affects and cognitions involved in being connected (e.g., love, empathy). The second section of the book includes six chapters devoted to a developmental analysis of the formation of social connections and the physiological and psychological mechanisms that affect the quality of primary human connections during infancy and childhood (i.e., parent–infant relationships) and the developmental trajectory of social connections in later stages of life. The third section includes five chapters that offer a relational analysis of some central emotional ties in adulthood (romantic and marital relationships) and the intraindividual and dyadic mechanisms that affect the formation and quality of these bonds, with a special emphasis on attachment, caregiving, and sex. The fourth section includes four chapters that provide a group-level analysis of social connections and the physiological and psychological processes that play a part in intra- and intergroup relations.

THE NEURAL BASIS OF SOCIAL BONDS

The first section of the book is devoted to brain mechanisms underlying the formation of social connections and the emotions, cognitions, and behaviors that occur within close relationships. In Chapter 1, Karen L. Bales focuses on two neuropeptide hormones, oxytocin and vasopressin, that play important roles in the development of social behaviors including maternal and paternal behavior, pair-bonding, aggression, and sex. Bales reviews what is known about the roles of oxytocin and vasopressin across species and stages of development, from the level of the brain to the level of social groups. She reviews comparative data on these two hormones; explains her research on monogamous titi monkeys (*Callicebus cupreus*), one of the first nonhuman primate models for studying the neurobiology of social connections; and discusses how early experiences and the oxytocin and vasopressin systems interact to affect the quality of social connections over time.

In Chapter 2, Jaak Panksepp, Mark Solms, Thomas E. Schläpfer, and Volker A. Coenen consider the neural circuits underlying primary emotions that arise in social relationships and relate these circuits to psychiatric disorders, focusing especially on neuropsychological states and neurochemical processes that contribute to depressive feelings. They consider two main neural systems: the SEEKING system, which mediates appetitive behaviors in close relationships, and the GRIEF/PANIC system, which mediates the psychological pain of separation distress. They describe two contributions to depression: overactivity of the PANIC/GRIEF system and underactivity of the SEEKING system. Panksepp et al. suggest new treatments for depression, including both neurochemical and psychotherapeutic methods, based on the psychological pain and deactivation of "brain reward" networks that occur when an important social bond is lost or disrupted.

In Chapter 3, Bianca P. Acevedo and Arthur P. Aron present a neuroscientific analysis of love and review evidence from functional magnetic resonance imaging (fMRI) studies of romantic love and human pair-bonds, or attachments. Acevedo and Aron discuss diverse findings, including ones from their own research programs, showing that the brain's mesolimbic dopamine system, which is involved in reward processing and implicated in a variety of behaviors, from eating to responding to monetary rewards and addictive substances, is also deeply involved in the formation of human pair-bonds, the experience of romantic love, and reactions to the loss of a loved one. They conclude by highlighting issues ripe for further research on the integration of knowledge about the reward system that mediates love, pair-bonding, and addiction and the ways in which such integration may suggest new interventions for substance abuse and pathological grief.

In Chapter 4, Christian Keysers and Valeria Gazzola discuss the brain's mirror neuron system and the role of this system in the formation of social bonds. They review evidence that neurons and brain regions involved in controlling one's own actions become activated when one observes or listens to others. Keysers and Gazzola present new findings from their own research program showing that brain regions involved in sensing one's own body become active when one observes movements and evidence of tactile sensations of others. According to the authors, these regions form a "vicarious brain" in which the actions, sensations, and emotions of others are represented by a projection of one's own motor, somatosensory, and limbic states. They argue that these vicarious representations are acquired through Hebbian learning processes (often summarized in the phrase "neurons that fire together wire together") and that this vicarious brain accounts for our intuition that the people around us are fundamentally like us, which makes it easier to form social connections with them.

In Chapter 5, James A. Coan, Casey L. Brown, and Lane Beckes draw on the biological principle of economy of action to present what they call social baseline theory. Their theory is designed to explain the importance of social connections for survival and adaptation. They argue (a) that the primary ecology to which human beings are adapted is one rich with other humans; (b) that familiarity involves the inclusion of individuals with whom individuals are familiar in their neural representation of self; (c) that this expanded self affects the brain's evaluation of currently available metabolic and material resources; and (d) that the perceived increase in available resources helps individuals actually conserve important and often metabolically costly somatic and neural resources. Coan et al. review recent neuroimaging and peripheral psychophysiological evidence from their own research program concerning how the proximity of relationship partners regulates brain responses to threats, self/other overlap in neural representations of threats, and associations between blood glucose concentration and the avoidance of social connections.

In the last chapter of the first section (Chapter 6), Jean Decety and Lauren H. Howard provide a neuroscience perspective on empathy and the development of morality; they consider in particular whether empathy is necessary for morality. They argue that empathy involves a number of interacting and partially dissociable neurobiological systems that evolved in the context of social bonds. They argue further that the interaction of empathic arousal, emotional awareness, and empathic concern is intertwined with social, contextual, and motivational contingencies. They examine the neurodevelopment of morality with reference to early signs of sensitivity, fairness, and concern for others and discuss data from a series of fMRI and evoked-related potential studies showing that empathic arousal plays an important and perhaps necessary role in the development of morality. Decety and Howard conclude their chapter by stressing the importance of affective processing in the development of morality and underscoring the importance of adopting a multisystem approach to understanding individual differences that contribute to adaptive and maladaptive trajectories of socioemotional functioning.

THE DEVELOPMENT OF SOCIAL CONNECTIONS DURING INFANCY AND CHILDHOOD

The second section of the book is devoted to analyses of the physiological and psychological mechanisms underlying the formation and quality of primary bonds with parental figures during infancy and childhood. In the first chapter of this section (Chapter 7), Jude Cassidy, Katherine B. Ehrlich, and Laura J. Sherman describe the physiological regulatory processes that shape infants' developing emotional bonds with caregivers. During the past 30 years, the study of infant–parent attachment has been focused on the mental representations that infants form during their first year of life—"working models" of caregivers, of self, and of close relationships. Cassidy et al. add significantly to this work by considering the nonrepresentational, physiological mechanisms that underlie infant–parent attachments, focusing mainly on the physiological regulators of infants' responses to threats and to caregivers' provision of a safe haven from threats. They also discuss ways in which representational and nonrepresentational processes may interact to influence the developmental trajectory of a person's social connections across the life span.

In Chapter 8, Ruth Feldman considers the biobehavioral synchrony involved in the formation of an infant–parent attachment bond. Synchrony is the process by which physiological and behavioral cues are exchanged between parent and infant during social interactions, leading to a dyadic unit based on shared experiences. Feldman presents a model of biobehavioral synchrony and explains how physiological and microbehavioral systems become integrated in infant–parent attachment. Feldman discusses three kinds of systems: (a) hormonal systems, especially oxytocin, the neurohormonal foundation for social connections; (b) brain systems that support parenting and bond formation, including limbic-motivational and cortical-social neural networks; and (c) the autonomic nervous system, with its sympathetic and parasympathetic branches.

In Chapter 9, Rechele Brooks and Andrew N. Meltzoff discuss two behavioral mechanisms—joint attention and gaze following—that develop during infancy and play an important role in social interactions and the formation of mental representations of others. Brooks and Meltzoff argue that gaze following is an entry point for understanding other people's minds and that infants use their own visual experiences as a basis for interpreting the visual experiences of others. They review studies showing that the experience of infants with their own visual systems colors their understanding of others' gaze and provides information relevant to understanding other people. The chapter concludes with a theoretical discussion connecting gaze following to broader issues in the development of interpersonal relations, including the human tendency to divide the social world into ingroups and outgroups.

Whereas Chapters 7 through 9 focus on physiological and psychological mechanisms within infants that contribute to the formation of infant–parent bonds, Chapters 10 and 11 consider parents' contributions to these bonds, with an emphasis on parents' abilities to sensitively interpret and respond to infants' inner states. In Chapter 10, Dana Shai and Peter Fonagy explain how parental embodied mentalizing—the capacity to accurately interpret infants' mental states though nonverbal modalities, such as head movements, paralinguistic speech, touch, posture, and facial expressions—contributes to infant–parent attachment. Thus far, parental mentalizing has been conceptualized and assessed in terms of verbal representations of others' mental states. In their chapter, Shai and Fonagy extend the domain of parental mentalizing to include the dynamic whole-body interaction process in which mental states of infants and parents are expressed kinesthetically. The authors articulate the construct of parental embodied mentalizing, describe an observational measure that captures the meeting of parents' and infants' minds in embodied forms, and review findings linking parental embodied mentalizing to individual differences in children's development including the emergence of attachment security.

In Chapter 11, David Oppenheim and Nina Koren-Karie focus on two aspects of parenting that are particularly relevant for the quality of child–parent attachment and children's well-being: (a) parents' insightfulness—their capacity to "see things from the child's point of view"—and (b) parents' sensitive guidance of dialogues concerning emotional experiences. Oppenheim and Koren-Karie argue that when these parental processes include coherent, organized, and child-centered affective meaning making, they promote secure child–parent attachments and children's flexible and adaptive coping strategies, emotion regulation, and well-being. They explain throughout the chapter the theoretical basis for considering these two aspects of parenting, the methods used to assess them, and findings showing the contribution of the two processes to children's attachment security and emotional well-being.

In the last chapter in this section (Chapter 12), Jeffry A. Simpson, W. Andrew Collins, Jessica E. Salvatore, and Sooyeon Sung build a bridge between Section 2 of the volume and the subsequent section and examine the long-term effects of infant–parent attachment on the quality of romantic relationships in adulthood. They use data from the very rich Minnesota Longitudinal Study of Risk and Adaptation to show how interpersonal experiences early in life predict how individuals resolve relationship conflicts; recover from conflicts; and achieve stable, satisfying relationships with their romantic partners in early adulthood. Simpson et al. reveal specific interpersonal experiences during middle childhood and adolescence that mediate the connection between early emotion regulation in interactions with parents at age 1 and later emotion regulation in romantic relationships in the early 20s. The chapter concludes with a discussion of the advantages of adopting an organizational view of social development as it unfolds across the life span.

ROMANTIC AND MARITAL RELATIONSHIPS IN ADULTHOOD

The third section of the book deals with psychological processes and mechanisms underlying the formation and quality of romantic and marital relationships in adulthood. In Chapter 13, Justin V. Cavallo, Sandra L. Murray, and John G. Holmes offer an interdependence analysis of close relationships in adulthood and show how risk regulation processes shape the quality of these relationships. Establishing meaningful social connections often requires one to balance the motivation to seek intimacy with the need to protect oneself from potential rejection. Cavallo et al. propose a regulatory system that reconciles motivational tension between connectedness and self-protection, and they review recent evidence concerning the operation of this system. They show that trust in a partner's regard for oneself plays an important role in determining whether one overrides unconsciously activated rules in the service of pursuing connectedness goals or self-protection goals. The chapter concludes with a discussion of the ways in which risk regulation processes foster patterns of mutual responsiveness between romantic partners.

In Chapter 14, Harry T. Reis highlights the role of responsiveness as a cardinal process in close relationships. *Responsiveness* refers to the processes by which relationship partners attend to and respond supportively to each other's needs, wishes, and concerns, thereby promoting each other's welfare. Reis describes a theoretical model of responsiveness and reviews evidence concerning (a) the role of perceived partner responsiveness in self-regulation; (b) how partners help each other to build upon shared positive events; and (c) the role of partners in promoting movement toward personal goals. In each case, Reis considers the role of actual and perceived partner responsiveness and discusses the role of each in promoting relationship well-being.

In Chapter 15, Phillip R. Shaver and Mario Mikulincer provide an adult attachment theory perspective on the formation of romantic bonds. We explain how a close relationship partner in adolescence or adulthood can become a person's main attachment figure. We review extensive research showing that interactions with such a partner affect distress regulation and psychological growth. We also discuss research showing that the potential or actual loss of a partner often causes severe emotional dysregulation until a bereaved individual's hierarchy of attachment figures is reorganized. The chapter focuses mainly on normative aspects of romantic relationships, but we also pay some attention to well-studied individual differences connected with adult attachment patterns.

In Chapter 16, Brooke C. Feeney and Nancy L. Collins focus on the effects of adult relationships on "thriving," as manifested in indices of physical and psychological health and well-being, and on the social interaction patterns or dyadic processes that contribute to these effects. They develop a theory of thriving through relationships and posit that there are two life contexts in which people may potentially thrive: coping successfully with life's adversities and actively pursuing life's opportunities for growth and development. (These contexts are similar to what has been called the safe haven and secure base functions of attachment relationships.) Feeney and Collins review evidence concerning interpersonal processes that promote thriving in these relational contexts.

In closing this section, Gurit E. Birnbaum (Chapter 17) highlights the role of sexuality in the formation and maintenance of romantic relationships. She reviews evidence indicating that sex promotes emotional bonds between partners and discusses the role of attachment processes in linking sexuality with relationship quality. She presents new findings concerning the functional significance of sex in different stages of relationship development—for example, in evaluating the suitability of a potential partner at the stage of acquaintance and in keeping partners committed to each other in later stages of relationship development. The chapter concludes with ideas for future research on the ways in which sexuality contributes to relationship development, maintenance, and dissolution.

THE FORMATION AND FUNCTIONING OF SOCIAL GROUPS

In the chapter opening the book's final section, Mark van Vugt and Tatsuya Kameda (Chapter 18) consider group processes from the perspective of evolutionary psychology. According to this perspective, human sociality is a biological adaptation, and group living is an adaptive strategy that enabled humans to cope with threats and take advantage of opportunities over the course of evolutionary history. Van Vugt and Kameda discuss the adaptive challenges associated with group living, such as social coordination, cooperation, status, cohesion, group decision making, and intergroup relations. They then review evidence showing that cognitive adaptations evolved to deal with these challenges. The chapter concludes with a discussion of conceptual and practical implications of an evolutionary perspective on group dynamics.

In Chapter 19, Tsachi Ein-Dor introduces social defense theory as an extension of attachment theory useful for analyzing group processes and effectiveness in solving problems and dealing with threats. According to the theory, the value of a person's responses to threat, which are based partly on dispositional variables, can be fully understood only at the group level. Each kind of response can be beneficial to the group, even when it may look dysfunctional at the individual level. Ein-Dor shows that attachment-anxious individuals, who often create problems for themselves and their partners in couple relationships, are useful to a group in some situations because of their sensitivity and vigilance to threats and dangers. Avoidant individuals, who also have well-studied problems with intimate, couple relationships, can be useful in a group because of their self-reliance and ability to take self-protective actions rapidly and effectively; these traits often help other group members find a way out of a threatening situation. Secure individuals are likely to help others and to coordinate and manage collective efforts. Ein-Dor reviews research evidence showing that groups containing all three kinds of people are more effective in dealing with threats and dangers than are less heterogeneous groups. Implications of this theory for understanding and facilitating group functioning are discussed at the end of the chapter.

Drawing on social identity theory, Naomi Ellemers, Félice van Nunspeet, and Daan Scheepers (Chapter 20) focus on social identification—the tendency to associate oneself with particular others or groups—and on its effects on neurophysiological and behavioral responses in group contexts. Ellemers et al. explain how social identification processes result in a group-level conception of self and specify the methodological challenges associated with studying these processes empirically. They also review recent evidence from their research program showing that social identification processes affect cardiovascular and brain responses (a) to threats and challenges to one's group, (b) to problems and challenges during group performance, and (c) to information concerning how one is regarded by other members of one's group.

In closing this book, Carsten K. W. De Dreu (Chapter 21) considers the neurohormonal bases of group cohesion and intergroup competition. He shows that hypothalamic release (or experimenter infusion) of the neuro-peptides oxytocin and vasopressin regulates a range of social behaviors that promote the functioning of a group, including the tendency to protect one's ingroup through competitive reactions to threatening outsiders. De Dreu explains how oxytocin modulates two critical processes involved in within-group cooperation: ingroup trust and concern for members of the ingroup. He also reviews new evidence that oxytocin can motivate non-cooperation and aggression toward rival outgroups. In other words, as Bales also explains in the book's first chapter, oxytocin is not simply a "love" chemical. Its various functions make sense only when they are considered in a broad evolutionary perspective on social connections and social competition.

CONCLUSION

As we hope can be gleaned from these thumbnail sketches of the 21 chapters, the chapter authors cover an incredible array of fascinating theories and bodies of research concerning the nature, formation, and disruption of social connections. The authors illuminate the neural structures and physiological and psychological mechanisms underlying dyadic, group, and intergroup relationships across the life span. They delineate the core intrapsychic and interpersonal processes that contribute to the formation and quality of primary relationships with caregivers during infancy and childhood and of romantic and marital relationships in adulthood. They also shed light on physiological and psychological processes involved in group membership, social identity, and intergroup relations. Given the depth and complexity of their research, it is remarkable how clearly and compellingly they have explained their pioneering work and related it to the work of other chapter authors. The book offers several avenues into an emerging integrative perspective on social psychology, developmental psychology, and neuroscience that will be essential for anyone hoping to understand the amazing human, very social, mind.

I

BRAIN

1

COMPARATIVE AND DEVELOPMENTAL PERSPECTIVES ON OXYTOCIN AND VASOPRESSIN

KAREN L. BALES

When infants and parents become emotionally bonded to each other and when adolescent and adult lovers become similarly attached, there is presumably something systematic going on at the physiological—that is, neurological and neurochemical—level that helps to explain the subjectively perceivable and behaviorally observable changes in feelings of safety, trust, love, and connection. Because the process of childbirth involves a unique endocrine environment for a human mother, the neurohormone oxytocin was identified early on as a possible factor in the formation of mother–infant bonds and the emergence of maternal behavior (Pedersen, Ascher, Monroe, & Prange, 1982; Pedersen & Prange, 1979). And because of similarities in chemical structure and sex differences in typical levels of production, the closely related hormone arginine vasopressin was hypothesized to serve a similar bonding function in fathers of infants (Winslow, Hastings, Carter, Harbaugh, & Insel, 1993; Winslow & Insel, 1991).

http://dx.doi.org/10.1037/14250-002

Mechanisms of Social Connection: From Brain to Group, M. Mikulincer and P. R. Shaver (Editors)

These neuropeptide hormones, now well studied in rodents, are less understood in human and nonhuman primates. Researchers know, however, that they are likely to play a crucial role in the development of social behavior including maternal and paternal behavior, pair-bonding, aggression, and sexual behavior, and it is likely that their operation is affected by factors such as stress and early experiences. Researchers are beginning to understand the long-term effects of early stressors and experiences on the oxytocin and vasopressin systems and the consequences of human health-related practices (e.g., administration of drugs) on these systems and on their behavioral sequelae. For instance, physicians have for decades exposed perinatal infants to oxytocin in the form of pitocin administered to induce labor. Moreover, chronic intranasal oxytocin spray is now being proposed as a treatment for developmental disorders including autism and schizophrenia.

In this chapter, I review what is known regarding the role of oxytocin and vasopressin across species and development, from brain to social group. I begin with a review of the central and peripheral actions of oxytocin and vasopressin. I then examine comparative data on these two hormones. As their role in social bonding was first examined in a comparative fashion, this is also a review of the history of the field. I cover work that my colleagues, my students, and I have initiated in titi monkeys (*Callicebus cupreus*), one of the first nonhuman primate models for the neurobiology of social bonding. Next, I review how interactions between early experience and the oxytocin and vasopressin systems shape behavior in the long term, including our studies on early oxytocin manipulation in prairie voles. I conclude the chapter with a discussion of human developmental manipulations of oxytocin and vasopressin and their potential long-term consequences.

OXYTOCIN AND VASOPRESSIN

Oxytocin (OT) and arginine vasopressin (AVP) are nine-amino-acid peptides produced in the paraventricular and supraoptic nuclei of the hypothalamus; they differ by only two amino acids (du Vigneaud, Ressler, Swan, Roberts, & Katsoyannis, 1954; Verney, 1946; Wang, Young, De Vries, & Insel, 1998; Zingg, 2002). They are capable of binding to each other's receptors (Barberis & Tribollet, 1996; Gimpl & Fahrenholz, 2001), and many pharmacological agents have effects on both OT and AVP receptors (Bankowski, Manning, Seto, Haldar, & Sawyer, 1980; Manning et al., 1995; Manning, Stoev, Cheng, Wo, & Chan, 2001).

AVP is also produced in several other brain areas, including some that are sexually dimorphic. Males of many species have AVP-producing cell bodies in the medial amygdala and bed nucleus of the stria terminalis, with fibers extending to the lateral septum (De Vries & Villalba, 1997), whereas females do not. AVP production in these areas is androgen dependent (De Vries & Villalba, 1997).

OT has one currently known receptor type, whereas AVP has three (V1a, V1b, and V2) (Barberis & Tribollet, 1996; Gimpl & Fahrenholz, 2001). In addition, OT is produced peripherally (away from the brain) by organs such as the ovaries (Churchland & Winkielman, 2011), and it is possible that peripheral OT can act on the brain.

OT AND AVP IN COMPARATIVE PERSPECTIVE

Whereas infant–mother bonding is widespread among mammals, the existence of attachments between adults is less common. But the role of OT and AVP in regulation of adult social bonding has been confirmed in voles, a taxonomic group of rodents that includes many closely related species with varied patterns of social bonding. For instance, pine and prairie voles (*Microtus pinetorum* and *Microtus ochrogaster*) are monogamous, whereas meadow and montane voles (*Microtus pennsylvanicus* and *Microtus montanus*) have polygynous social structures (Getz & Hofmann, 1986; Winslow, Shapiro, Carter, & Insel, 1993). OT and AVP receptor distribution in the brain varies between monogamous and polygynous vole species (Insel, Wang, & Ferris, 1994; Shapiro & Insel, 1992; Witt, Carter, & Insel, 1991). In particular, monogamous voles have higher OT receptor binding in the nucleus accumbens and higher AVP V1a binding in the ventral pallidum, areas in which there are also many dopamine D2 receptors. The current understanding is that coordinated activation of OT/AVP receptors and D2 receptors in these areas leads to the formation of adult pair-bonds in monogamous vole species (Lim, Hammock, & Young, 2004; Lim & Young, 2004; Pitkow et al., 2001; Ross, Cole, et al., 2009; Ross, Freeman, et al., 2009).

The structure and distribution of OT and AVP peptide themselves are highly conserved across mammals (Acher, Chauvet, & Chauvet, 1995), including most primates (Ragen & Bales, 2012). However, it was recently discovered that some (but not all) New World primates have variations in the OT gene that result in a different form of OT, which may have functional consequences (Lee et al., 2011). A study investigating the role of intranasal OT (normal sequence) in pair-bonding in a species of marmoset with the altered OT sequence found only minimal effects of the conserved peptide on the demonstration of a partner preference in that species (Smith, Agmo, Birnie, & French, 2010).

OT and AVP are also involved in social bonds in nonmonogamous species, although their role may depend on whether bonds are actually attachments, as defined by Bowlby (1969) in his theoretical book on human attachments (see also Chapter 15, this volume). These kinds of relationships are characterized by a preference for one other individual, distress upon separation, and the ability of the attachment figure to serve as a buffer against stress (Mason & Mendoza, 1998). In species such as mice, rats, and rhesus monkeys, adults are unlikely to form attachment bonds to other adults. Experimentally administered extra OT or AVP (or the addition of receptors in areas such as the nucleus accumbens and ventral pallidum) usually increases general affiliative behavior without making these species "monogamous."

For instance, increased AVP V1a expression in the ventral pallidum of mice increased affiliation but did not induce a preference for a particular familiar partner (Young, Nilsen, Waymire, MacGregor, & Insel, 1999). The story is somewhat different, however, for closely related polygynous vole species, which may form partner preferences under certain conditions (Parker, Phillips, & Lee, 2001). For example, although increasing OT receptors in the nucleus accumbens of female meadow voles did not induce a partner preference (Ross, Freeman, et al., 2009), increasing AVP V1a receptor expression in the ventral pallidum of male meadow voles did induce a partner preference (Lim, Wang, et al., 2004).

The structure of the OT and AVP V1a receptor genes may be important in determining receptor distributions and thereby affecting social structures, although it is likely that the details of these genetic variations differ across species (Babb, Fernandez-Duque, & Schurr, 2010; Hammock & Young, 2005; Rosso, Keller, Kaessmann, & Hammond, 2008; Walum et al., 2008). The prairie vole V1a receptor gene has a number of tandem repeats not present in the meadow vole gene, and introducing the prairie vole gene into the meadow vole ventral pallidum increases partner preference (Lim et al., 2004). Within prairie voles, males selectively bred for an increased number of repeats in the V1a promoter region form pair-bonds more quickly (Hammock & Young, 2005). However, when a larger number of rodent species is considered, longer promoter regions are not associated with social monogamy (Fink, Excoffier, & Heckel, 2006). Humans exhibit a different polymorphism in the V1a receptor gene, the RS3 polymorphism, which has been associated with marital satisfaction in men (Walum et al., 2008). This polymorphism is not present in a socially monogamous New World monkey, the owl monkey (*Aotus azarai*; Babb et al., 2010). One genetic sequence in the OT receptor was recently associated with pair-bonding in human females (Walum et al., 2012), but this requires further investigation.

Recent studies of more unusual rodent species support the view that although OT and AVP are probably widely involved in mammalian sociality, the mechanisms are probably different in each species (see the review in Beery, Lacey, & Francis, 2008). For instance, a social species of tuco-tuco

(*Ctenomys sociabilis*, a South American rodent) exhibited quite different patterns of OT and AVP V1a receptor binding than did a solitary species (*Ctenomys haigi*; Beery et al., 2008). Likewise, two species of singing mice (*Scotinomys teguina* and *Scotinomys xerampelinus*) differed in level of vocality as well as some aspects of social behavior. *S. xerampelinus*, the species with higher maternal investment (indicated by smaller litter size, larger pups, etc.), displayed higher V1a receptor binding in many areas including the medial amygdala and many thalamic areas, as well as higher OT receptor binding in the nucleus accumbens and central amygdala. In contrast, the more vocal species (*S. teguina*) had higher V1a receptor binding in the anterior hypothalamus and periaqueductal gray of the midbrain (an area associated with vocalizations; Campbell, Ophir, & Phelps, 2009). The eusocial mole rat (*Fukomys anselli*), which lives in monogamous, multigenerational families, also has OT cell bodies in the supramammillary nucleus, something not found in other rodents (Valesky, Burda, Kaufmann, & Oeslschlager, 2012). The naked mole rat (*Heterocephalus glaber*), also eusocial (a term that usually refers to a behavioral and reproductive division of labor and cooperative breeding of young, as seen in many bee species), shows higher OT binding in the nucleus accumbens than does the solitary Cape mole rat (*Georychus capensis*; Kalamatianos et al., 2010). This pattern of differences is similar to that found in monogamous versus polygynous vole species.

Although the neurobiology of social bonding is a subject of broad interest, the only animal model studied in any depth has been the prairie vole. In my laboratory, my colleagues, my students, and I have begun to develop, as well, the titi monkey (*Callicebus cupreus*) as a nonhuman primate model for the neurobiology of social bonding. Titi monkeys are socially monogamous, arboreal New World monkeys that live in small family groups consisting of a pair-bonded male and female and their offspring (Mason, 1966, 1975). They display a strong emotional bond, which includes all of the characteristics of a human attachment bond (Mason, 1974; Mason & Mendoza, 1998; Mendoza & Mason, 1986, 1997), so they provide an ideal nonhuman primate model for human sociality.

EMOTIONAL BONDING IN THE TITI MONKEY

When titi monkey males are given intranasal AVP, they increase their contact with a partner more than with a female stranger (Jarcho, Mendoza, Mason, Yang, & Bales, 2011). They also experience a decrease in gene expression of pro-inflammatory cytokines, suggesting reduced stress. It is possible that the interaction with the mate provides increased social support following a stressful experience, thus inhibiting the inflammatory response. In any case, the direction of the AVP effects on behavior is consistent with those reported previously in the rodent literature.

Titi monkey males have regional and global changes in brain activity with the formation of pair-bonds, including many regions that contain OT and AVP receptors or that produce OT and AVP. In a cross-sectional positron emission tomography (PET) study, which used glucose uptake as a proxy for brain activity because glucose is the only fuel usable by the brain, males in long-term pair-bonded relationships exhibited higher whole-brain glucose metabolism and lower adjusted regional glucose uptake in the nucleus accumbens, ventral pallidum, medial amygdala, medial preoptic area, supraoptic nucleus, and lateral septum (Bales, Mason, Catana, Cherry, & Mendoza, 2007). Within 24 hours of pairing, males already experienced changes in glucose metabolism (in the nucleus accumbens and ventral pallidum), which were in the same direction demonstrated in long-term paired males. All of these regions either produce OT and AVP (e.g., supraoptic nucleus) or have OT/AVP receptors; all have also been implicated in studies of rodent pair-bonding. In a more recent longitudinal study with age-matched control males, the paraventricular and supraoptic nuclei continued to show significantly elevated glucose uptake a week following pairing (Maninger et al., 2011). In summary, the OT and AVP systems are clearly involved in pair-bonding in nonhuman primates as well as in prairie voles, although the details may differ. For instance, the nucleus accumbens and caudate may play a more prominent role in male pair-bonding in primates than in rodents, a viewpoint supported by studies in humans (see Chapter 3, this volume).

Recent human studies have focused on intranasally delivered OT as an experimental methodology for manipulating central OT. (The OT is delivered from a nasal spray bottle of the kind used in over-the-counter treatments for allergies and cold symptoms.) It is important to realize that the study often cited to support central nervous system penetrance of intranasal OT (Born et al., 2002) did not actually examine OT; it examined AVP and several other peptides. It is possible, as these citations imply, that OT is acting on the brain via peripheral input (Churchland & Winkielman, 2011), but it is important not to simply assume this is happening.

Intranasal OT has been shown to affect reactions to facial expressions (Domes et al., 2007, 2010; Goldman, Gomes, Carter, & Lee, 2011; Marsh, Yu, Pine, & Blair, 2010), as well as facial recognition memory (Savaskan, Ehrhardt, Schulz, Walter, & Schachinger, 2008), trust (Baumgartner, Heinrichs, Vonlanthen, Fischbacher, & Fehr, 2008; Kosfeld, Heinrichs, Zak, Fischbacher, & Fehr, 2005), and perceptions of trustworthiness (Theodoridou, Rowe, Penton-Voak, & Rogers, 2009). These are obviously important to the formation of close relationships between adult humans. In subsets of the population (e.g., people who score high on measures of attachment anxiety;

see Chapters 15, 17, and 19, this volume), however, intranasal OT can have different, even opposite, effects (Bartz et al., 2010, 2011). For instance, Bartz et al. (2010) found that though intranasal OT increased warm memories of the mother in securely attached people, it decreased warm memories of the mother in anxiously attached people. It will be important in future studies to carefully integrate experimental manipulations of OT with measurements of endogenous OT levels in plasma, saliva, or cerebrospinal fluid (Schneiderman, Zagoory-Sharon, Leckman, & Feldman, 2012; Zak, Kurzban, & Matzner, 2005; see also Chapter 8, this volume). For instance, do humans with naturally high baseline levels of OT react differently to intranasal OT than do humans with low baseline levels?

OT AND AVP IN DEVELOPMENTAL PERSPECTIVE

The OT and AVP systems are present and functional very early in the lives of rodents (Barberis & Tribollet, 1996; Tribollet, Charpak, Schmit, Dubois-Dauphin, & Dreifuss, 1989; Tribollet, Goumaz, Raggenbass, Dubois-Dauphin, & Dreifuss, 1991), although there are some age-related changes in the distribution of receptors. A large variety of early experiences, pharmacological and more naturally occurring, has been shown to have long-term effects on the OT and AVP systems and on social bonding behaviors (reviewed in Bales and Perkeybile, 2012). One well-known example in rats is the division of mothers into high licking and grooming and low licking and grooming categories (Meaney, 2001). High licking and grooming mothers produce offspring that are less responsive to stress (Liu et al., 1997), that function better as mothers (Francis, Diorio, Liu, & Meaney, 1999), and that have higher levels of OT receptors in the medial preoptic area of the brain (Champagne, Diorio, Sharma, & Meaney, 2001; Francis, Young, Meaney, & Insel, 2002).

Prairie voles make particularly good models for the study of developmental effects on social behavior, because in addition to studying female–offspring relationships, one can study long-term developmental effects on adult male–female bonding and father care of offspring. In my laboratory, both early OT and early experiences have been manipulated to examine their long-term effects on social behavior and the OT and AVP systems.

Neonatal treatment with OT results in long-term changes in many social behaviors. Pitocin (artificial OT) is used to induce labor in many delivery rooms (Zhang et al., 2011). Given that stress results in increased permeability of barriers such as the placental barrier and the infant blood–brain barrier (Laudanski & Pierzynski, 2003), this practice is likely to expose an infant's brain to some level of exogenous OT. We found in a series of experiments that neonatal administration of OT to prairie vole pups resulted in a dose-dependent facilitation or disruption of partner preference in both males and females (Bales, Van Westerhuyzen, et al., 2007; Carter, Boone, & Bales, 2008). Aggression was increased in OT-treated females that had been exposed to males (Bales & Carter, 2003), but treatment with either OT or the OT antagonist resulted in changes in male sexual behavior and lower success in getting sperm into the female reproductive tract (Bales, Abdelnabi, Cushing, Ottinger, & Carter, 2004). OT-antagonist treatment in males also resulted in lower alloparental behavior (nurturing behavior directed toward a strange pup) and more attacks on the pup (Bales, Pfeifer, & Carter, 2004). The behavioral changes were mediated through changes in AVP V1a receptors in multiple brain areas (Bales, Plotsky, et al., 2007), with OT up-regulating V1a in the cingulate cortex in males and OT antagonist down-regulating V1a in the medial preoptic area, bed nucleus of the stria terminalis, and lateral septum. These results suggest that large doses of OT and OT antagonist given to the developing brain flood the OT receptors and bind to the V1a receptors. Pitocin administration in humans could therefore represent a potent manipulation of both OT and AVP systems in the developing human brain, and it could possibly have long-term neurobiological and/or behavioral effects.

Other early treatments also affect social behavior and the OT/AVP systems. Handling of rodent pups is known to have long-term effects on their later stress reactivity (Denenberg & Whimbey, 1963; Levine, 2002; Levine & Lewis, 1959), possibly through modification of the mother's behavior upon return of the pups (Denenberg, 1999; Smotherman & Bell, 1980) and/or to pup exposure to novelty (Tang, Akers, Reeb, Romeo, & McEwen, 2006). In prairie voles, variations in handling of both parents result in long-term changes in male alloparenting and female pair-bonding (Bales, Lewis-Reese, Pfeifer, Kramer, & Carter, 2007). Animals whose parents experienced reduced handling compared with normal colony animals displayed social deficits later in life. Males were less alloparental, and females failed to form pair-bonds even when given six times the amount of time that control females would normally take. These changes in behavior were accompanied by up-regulation of OT receptors in several brain areas (particularly in females) and lower production of OT in the supraoptic nucleus (Bales, Boone, Epperson, Hoffman, & Carter, 2011). One key point demonstrated by this study, as well as by studies of human grief (Taylor et al., 2006) and rodent social isolation (Grippo et al., 2007), is that high OT or more OT receptors may not be equal to ideal social circumstances. In fact, the OT system may up-regulate in response to poor early environments or challenges to attachments.

Other forms of early experience affect later behavior and possibly the OT and AVP systems as well. For instance, the experience of having cared for younger siblings leads to more effective parenting—spending less time with pups yet having the pups gain significantly more weight (Stone, Mathieu,

Griffin, & Bales, 2010). Just as in rats, offspring of high-contact prairie vole parents display higher levels of social behavior and lower anxiety; in addition, they display altered behavior in an experimental setup designed to measure which animals are more likely to explore away from or possibly leave their natal group (Bales, Perkeybile, & Arias del Razo, unpublished data).

Researchers are also studying the manipulation of developmental OT in clinical contexts with humans by means other than pitocin administration. For example, there are a number of clinical trials in progress to evaluate the use of chronic intranasal OT for treating autism and other psychological disorders (see http://www.clinicaltrials.gov). In addition to OT being administered exogenously, drugs that cause the brain to release OT endogenously are being tested. All of these treatments could result in the formation of physiological tolerance via down-regulation and internalization of OT receptors (Ancellin et al., 1999; Gimpl & Fahrenholz, 2001), processes that result in reduction of receptor availability and thus decreased effectiveness of any OT produced by the brain itself. Potentially, this could result in the opposite behavioral results than those desired: Decreased availability of OT receptors could result in long-term decreases in social behaviors. It is therefore very important to test long-term interventions in animal models before applying them to humans.

CONCLUSION

The OT and AVP systems are closely involved in the neurobiological regulation of social behavior. This has been shown in a wide variety of mammals, although specific details of the mechanisms differ across species. Some of the effects appear to be species wide, but their expression may differ based on the age at which interventions are introduced. Some of the effects are clearly different in different species and even in different individuals within a species, including humans. Early experiences of many kinds, including human health practices, affect the OT and AVP systems and their behavioral output. The discovery of these neurohormones and of their fascinating implications for human relationships has spurred both new research and theoretical and journalistic extrapolations beyond current scientific evidence. It will be important to continue this research without jumping to conclusions about the hoped-for beneficial effects on human welfare.

REFERENCES

Acher, R., Chauvet, J., & Chauvet, M. T. (1995). Man and the chimaera: Selective versus neutral oxytocin evolution. *Advances in Experimental Medicine and Biology*, *395*, 615–627.

Ancellin, N., Preisser, L., Le Maout, S., Barbado, M., Creminon, C., Corman, B., & Morel, A. (1999). Homologous and heterologous phosphorylation of the vasopressin V1a receptor. *Cellular Signalling, 11*, 743–751. doi:10.1016/S0898-6568(99)00035-2

Babb, P. L., Fernandez-Duque, E., & Schurr, T. G. (2010). *AVPR1A* sequence variation in monogamous owl monkeys (*Aotus azarai*) and its implications for the evolution of platyrrhine social behavior. *Journal of Molecular Evolution, 71*, 279–297. doi:10.1007/s00239-010-9383-6

Bales, K. L., Abdelnabi, M., Cushing, B. S., Ottinger, M. A., & Carter, C. S. (2004). Effects of neonatal oxytocin manipulations on male reproductive potential in prairie voles. *Physiology & Behavior, 81*, 519–526. doi:10.1016/j.physbeh.2004.02.016

Bales, K. L., Boone, E., Epperson, P., Hoffman, G., & Carter, C. S. (2011). Are behavioral effects of early experience mediated by oxytocin? *Frontiers in Psychiatry, 2*(24). doi:10.3389/fpsyt.2011.00021

Bales, K. L., & Carter, C. S. (2003). Sex differences and developmental effects of oxytocin on aggression and social behavior in prairie voles (*Microtus ochrogaster*). *Hormones and Behavior, 44*, 178–184. doi:10.1016/S0018-506X(03)00154-5

Bales, K. L., Lewis-Reese, A. D., Pfeifer, L. A., Kramer, K. M., & Carter, C. S. (2007). Early experience affects the traits of monogamy in a sexually dimorphic manner. *Developmental Psychobiology, 49*, 335–342. doi:10.1002/dev.20216

Bales, K. L., Mason, W. A., Catana, C., Cherry, S. R., & Mendoza, S. P. (2007). Neural correlates of pair-bonding in a monogamous primate. *Brain Research, 1184*, 245–253. doi:10.1016/j.brainres.2007.09.087

Bales, K. L., & Perkeybile, A. M. (2012). Developmental experiences and the oxytocin receptor system. *Hormones and Behavior, 61*, 313–319. doi:10.1016/j.yhbeh.2011.12.013

Bales, K. L., Perkeybile, A. M., & Arias del Razo, R. (2012). [Effects of parenting on offspring dispersal in prairie voles]. Unpublished raw data.

Bales, K. L., Pfeifer, L. A., & Carter, C. S. (2004). Sex differences and effects of manipulations of oxytocin on alloparenting and anxiety in prairie voles. *Developmental Psychobiology, 44*, 123–131. doi:10.1002/dev.10165

Bales, K. L., Plotsky, P. M., Young, L. J., Lim, M. M., Grotte, N. D., Ferrer, E., & Carter, C. S. (2007). Neonatal oxytocin manipulations have long-lasting, sexually dimorphic effects on vasopressin receptors. *Neuroscience, 144*, 38–45. doi:10.1016/j.neuroscience.2006.09.009

Bales, K. L., Van Westerhuyzen, J. A., Lewis-Reese, A. D., Grotte, N. D., Lanter, J. A., & Carter, C. S. (2007). Oxytocin has dose-dependent developmental effects on pair-bonding and alloparental care in female prairie voles. *Hormones and Behavior, 52*, 274–279. doi:10.1016/j.yhbeh.2007.05.004

Bankowski, K., Manning, M., Seto, J., Haldar, J., & Sawyer, W. H. (1980). Design and synthesis of potent in vivo antagonists of oxytocin. *International Journal of Peptide and Protein Research, 16*, 382–391. doi:10.1111/j.1399-3011.1980.tb02962.x

Barberis, C., & Tribollet, E. (1996). Vasopressin and oxytocin receptors in the central nervous system. *Critical Reviews in Neurobiology, 10*, 119–154. doi:10.1615/CritRevNeurobiol.v10.i1.60

Bartz, J., Simeon, D., Hamilton, H., Kim, S., Crystal, S., Braun, A., . . . Hollander, E. (2011). Oxytocin can hinder trust and cooperation in borderline personality disorder. *Social Cognitive and Affective Neuroscience, 6*, 556–563. doi:10.1093/scan/nsq085

Bartz, J. A., Zaki, J., Ochsner, K. N., Bolger, N., Kolevzon, A., Ludwig, N., & Lydon, J. E. (2010). Effects of oxytocin on recollections of maternal care and closeness. *Proceedings of the National Academy of Sciences, USA, 107*, 21371–21375. doi:10.1073/pnas.1012669107

Baumgartner, T., Heinrichs, M., Vonlanthen, A., Fischbacher, U., & Fehr, E. (2008). Oxytocin shapes the neural circuitry of trust and trust adaptation in humans. *Neuron, 58*, 639–650. doi:10.1016/j.neuron.2008.04.009

Beery, A. K., Lacey, E. A., & Francis, D. D. (2008). Oxytocin and vasopressin receptor distributions in a solitary and a social species of tuco-tuco (*Ctenomys haigi* and *Ctenomys sociabilis*). *Journal of Comparative Neurology, 507*, 1847–1859. doi:10.1002/cne.21638

Born, J., Lange, T., Kern, W., McGregor, G. P., Bickel, U., & Fehm, H. L. (2002). Sniffing neuropeptides: A transnasal approach to the human brain. *Nature Neuroscience, 5*, 514–516. doi:10.1038/nn0602-849

Bowlby, J. (1969). *Attachment and loss: Vol. 1. Attachment.* New York, NY: Basic Books.

Campbell, P., Ophir, A. G., & Phelps, S. M. (2009). Central vasopressin and oxytocin receptor distributions in two species of singing mice. *Journal of Comparative Neurology, 516*, 321–333. doi:10.1002/cne.22116

Carter, C. S., Boone, E. M., & Bales, K. L. (2008). Early experience and the developmental programming of oxytocin and vasopressin. In R. S. Bridges (Ed.), *Neurobiology of the parental brain* (pp. 417–434). New York, NY: Academic Press. doi:10.1016/B978-012374285-8.00027-5

Champagne, F., Diorio, J., Sharma, S., & Meaney, M. J. (2001). Naturally occurring variations in maternal behavior in the rat are associated with differences in estrogen-inducible central oxytocin receptors. *Proceedings of the National Academy of Sciences, USA, 98*, 12736–12741. doi:10.1073/pnas.221224598

Churchland, P. S., & Winkielman, P. (2012). Modulating social behavior with oxytocin: How does it work? What does it mean? *Hormones and Behavior, 61*, 392–399. doi:10.1016/j.yhbeh.2011.12.003

Denenberg, V. H. (1999). Commentary: Is maternal stimulation the mediator of the handling effect in infancy? *Developmental Psychobiology, 34*, 1–3. doi:10.1002/(SICI)1098-2302(199901)34:1<1::AID-DEV2>3.0.CO;2-U

Denenberg, V. H., & Whimbey, A. E. (1963). Infantile stimulation and animal husbandry: A methodological study. *Journal of Comparative and Physiological Psychology, 56*, 877–878. doi:10.1037/h0043211

De Vries, G. J., & Villalba, C. (1997). Brain sexual dimorphism and sex differences in parental and other social behaviors. *Annals of the New York Academy of Sciences, 807,* 273–286.doi:10.1111/j.1749-6632.1997.tb51926.x

Domes, G., Heinrichs, M., Glascher, J., Buchel, C., Braus, D. F., & Herpertz, S. C. (2007). Oxytocin attenuates amygdala responses to emotional faces regardless of valence. *Biological Psychiatry, 62,* 1187–1190. doi:10.1016/j.biopsych.2007.03.025

Domes, G., Lischke, A., Berger, C., Grossmann, A., Hauenstein, K., Heinrichs, M., & Herpetz, S. C. (2010). Effects of intranasal oxytocin on emotional face processing in women. *Psychoneuroendocrinology, 35,* 83–93. doi:10.1016/j.psyneuen.2009.06.016

du Vigneaud, V., Ressler, C., Swan, J. M., Roberts, C. S., & Katsoyannis, P. G. (1954). The synthesis of oxytocin. *Journal of the American Chemical Society, 76,* 3115–3121. doi:10.1021/ja01641a004

Fink, S., Excoffier, L., & Heckel, G. (2006). Mammalian monogamy is not controlled by a single gene. *Proceedings of the National Academy of Sciences, USA, 103,* 10956–10960. doi:10.1073/pnas.0602380103

Francis, D., Diorio, J., Liu, D., & Meaney, M. J. (1999, November 5). Nongenomic transmission across generations of maternal behavior and stress responses in the rat. *Science, 286,* 1155–1158. doi:10.1126/science.286.5442.1155

Francis, D. D., Young, L. J., Meaney, M. J., & Insel, T. R. (2002). Naturally occurring differences in maternal care are associated with the expression of oxytocin and vasopressin (V1a) receptors: Gender differences. *Journal of Neuroendocrinology, 14,* 349–353. doi:10.1046/j.0007-1331.2002.00776.x

Getz, L. L., & Hofmann, J. E. (1986). Social organization in free-living prairie voles, *Microtus ochrogaster. Behavioral Ecology and Sociobiology, 18,* 275–282. doi:10.1007/BF00300004

Gimpl, G., & Fahrenholz, F. (2001). The oxytocin receptor system: Structure, function, and regulation. *Physiological Reviews, 81,* 629–683.

Goldman, M. B., Gomes, A. M., Carter, C. S., & Lee, R. (2011). Divergent effects of two different doses of intranasal oxytocin on facial affect discrimination in schizophrenic patients with and without polydipsia. *Psychopharmacology, 216,* 101–110. doi:10.1007/s00213-011-2193-8

Grippo, A. J., Gerena, D., Huang, J., Kumar, N., Shah, M., Ughreja, R., & Carter, C. S. (2007). Social isolation induces behavioral and neuroendocrine disturbances relevant to depression in female and male prairie voles. *Psychoneuroendocrinology, 32,* 966–980. doi:10.1016/j.psyneuen.2007.07.004

Hammock, E. A., & Young, L. J. (2005, June 10). Microsatellite instability generates diversity in brain and sociobehavioral traits. *Science, 308,* 1630–1634. doi:10.1126/science.1111427

Insel, T. R., Wang, Z. X., & Ferris, C. F. (1994). Patterns of brain vasopressin receptor distribution associated with social organization in microtine rodents. *Journal of Neuroscience, 14,* 5381–5392.

Jarcho, M. R., Mendoza, S. P., Mason, W. A., Yang, X., & Bales, K. L. (2011). Intranasal vasopressin affects pair bonding and peripheral gene expression in male *Callicebus cupreus*. *Genes, Brain and Behavior, 10*, 375–383. doi:10.1111/j.1601-183X.2010.00677.x

Kalamatianos, T., Faulkes, C. G., Oosthuizen, M. K., Poorun, R., Bennett, N. C., & Coen, C. W. (2010). Telencephalic binding sites for oxytocin and social organization: A comparative study of eusocial naked mole-rats and solitary Cape mole-rats. *Journal of Comparative Neurology, 518*, 1792–1813. doi:10.1002/cne.22302

Kosfeld, M., Heinrichs, M., Zak, P. J., Fischbacher, U., & Fehr, E. (2005, June 2). Oxytocin increases trust in humans. *Nature, 435*, 673–676. doi:10.1038/nature03701

Laudanski, T., & Pierzynski, P. (2003). Oxytocin and fetal membranes in preterm labor: Current concepts and clinical implication. *Gynecological Endocrinology, 17*, 261–267.

Lee, A. G., Cool, D. R., Grunwald, W. C., Jr., Neal, D. E., Buckmaster, C. L., Cheng, M. Y., . . . Parker, K. J. (2011). A novel form of oxytocin in New World monkeys. *Biology Letters, 7*, 584–587. doi:10.1098/rsbl.2011.0107

Levine, S. (2002). Enduring effects of early experience on adult behavior. In D. W. Pfaff, A. P. Arnold, A. M. Etgen, S. E. Fahrbach, & R. T. Rubin (Eds.), *Hormones, brain, and behavior* (pp. 535–542). New York, NY: Academic Press. doi:10.1016/B978-012532104-4/50075-5

Levine, S., & Lewis, G. W. (1959). The relative importance of experimenter contact in an effect produced by extra-stimulation in infancy. *Journal of Comparative and Physiological Psychology, 52*, 368–369. doi:10.1037/h0044637

Lim, M. M., Hammock, E. A. D., & Young, L. J. (2004). The role of vasopressin in the genetic and neural regulation of monogamy. *Journal of Neuroendocrinology, 16*, 325–332. doi:10.1111/j.0953-8194.2004.01162.x

Lim, M. M., Wang, Z., Olazabal, D. E., Ren, X., Terwilliger, E. F., & Young, L. J. (2004, June 17). Enhanced partner preference in a promiscuous species by manipulating the expression of a single gene. *Nature, 429*, 754–757. doi:10.1038/nature02539

Lim, M. M., & Young, L. J. (2004). Vasopressin-dependent neural circuits underlying pair bond formation in the monogamous prairie vole. *Neuroscience, 125*, 35–45. doi:10.1016/j.neuroscience.2003.12.008

Liu, D., Diorio, J., Tannenbaum, B., Caldji, C., Francis, D., Freedman, A., . . . Meaney, M. J. (1997, September 12). Maternal care, hippocampal glucocorticoid receptors, and hypothalamic-pituitary-adrenal responses to stress. *Science, 277*, 1659–1662. doi:10.1126/science.277.5332.1659

Maninger, N., Hinde, K., Mendoza, S. P., Mason, W. A., Cherry, S. R., & Bales, K. L. (2011). Functional imaging of pair-bond formation in the coppery titi monkey (*Callicebus cupreus*). *American Journal of Primatology, 73*(Suppl. 1), 45.

Manning, M., Miteva, K., Pancheva, S., Stoev, S., Wo, N. C., & Chan, W. Y. (1995). Design and synthesis of highly selective *in vitro* and *in vivo* uterine receptor antagonists of oxytocin: Comparisons with Atosiban. *International Journal of Peptide and Protein Research, 46,* 244–252. doi:10.1111/j.1399-3011.1995.tb00596.x

Manning, M., Stoev, S., Cheng, L. L., Wo, N. C., & Chan, W. Y. (2001). Design of oxytocin antagonists, which are more selective than Atosiban. *Journal of Peptide Science, 7,* 449–465. doi:10.1002/psc.339

Marsh, A. A., Yu, H. H., Pine, D. S., & Blair, R. J. R. (2010). Oxytocin improves specific recognition of positive facial expressions. *Psychopharmacology, 209,* 225–232. doi:10.1007/s00213-010-1780-4

Mason, W. A. (1966). Social organization of the South American monkey, *Callicebus moloch:* A preliminary report. *Tulane Studies in Zoology, 13,* 23–28.

Mason, W. A. (1974). Comparative studies of *Callicebus* and *Saimiri:* Behavior of male–female pairs. *Folia Primatologica, 22,* 1–8. doi:10.1159/000155614

Mason, W. A. (1975). Comparative studies of social behavior of *Callicebus* and *Saimiri:* Strength and specificity of attraction between male–female cagemates. *Folia Primatologica, 23,* 113–123. doi:10.1159/000155664

Mason, W. A., & Mendoza, S. P. (1998). Generic aspects of primate attachments: Parents, offspring, and mates. *Psychoneuroendocrinology, 23,* 765–778. doi:10.1016/S0306-4530(98)00054-7

Meaney, M. J. (2001). Maternal care, gene expression, and the transmission of individual differences in stress reactivity across generations. *Annual Review of Neuroscience, 24,* 1161–1192. doi:10.1146/annurev.neuro.24.1.1161

Mendoza, S. P., & Mason, W. A. (1986). Contrasting responses to intruders and to involuntary separation by monogamous and polygynous New World monkeys. *Physiology & Behavior, 38,* 795–801. doi:10.1016/0031-9384(86)90045-4

Mendoza, S. P., & Mason, W. A. (1997). Attachment relationships in New World primates. *Annals of the New York Academy of Sciences, 807,* 203–209. doi:10.1111/j.1749-6632.1997.tb51921.x

Parker, K. J., Phillips, K. M., & Lee, T. M. (2001). Development of selective partner preferences in captive male and female meadow voles. *Microtus pennsylvanicus. Animal Behaviour, 61,* 1217–1226. doi:10.1006/anbe.2000.1707

Pedersen, C. A., Ascher, J. A., Monroe, Y. L., & Prange, A. J., Jr. (1982, May 7). Oxytocin induces maternal behavior in virgin female rats. *Science, 216,* 648–650. doi:10.1126/science.7071605

Pedersen, C. A., & Prange, A. J., Jr. (1979). Induction of maternal behavior in virgin rats after intracerebroventricular administration of oxytocin. *Proceedings of the National Academy of Sciences, USA, 76,* 6661–6665. doi:10.1073/pnas.76.12.6661

Pitkow, L. J., Sharer, C. A., Ren, X. L., Insel, T. R., Terwilliger, E. F., & Young, L. J. (2001). Facilitation of affiliation and pair-bond formation by vasopressin receptor gene transfer into the ventral forebrain of a monogamous vole. *Journal of Neuroscience, 21,* 7392–7396.

Ragen, B. R., & Bales, K. L. (2012). Oxytocin and vasopressin in non-human primates. In E. Choleris & M. Kavaliers (Eds.), *Oxytocin, vasopressin, and related peptides in the regulation of behavior* (pp. 288–306). Cambridge, MA: Cambridge University Press.

Ross, H. E., Cole, C. D., Smith, Y., Neumann, I. D., Landgraf, R., Murphy, A. Z., & Young, L. J. (2009). Characterization of the oxytocin system regulating affiliative behavior in female prairie voles. *Neuroscience, 162,* 892–903. doi:10.1016/j.neuroscience.2009.05.055

Ross, H. E., Freeman, S. M., Spiegel, L. L., Ren, X., Terwilliger, E. F., & Young, L. J. (2009). Variation in oxytocin receptor density in the nucleus accumbens has differential effects on affiliative behaviors in monogamous and polygamous voles. *Journal of Neuroscience, 29,* 1312–1318. doi:10.1523/JNEUROSCI.5039-08.2009

Rosso, L., Keller, L., Kaessmann, H., & Hammond, R. L. (2008). Mating system and *avpr1a* promoter variation in primates. *Biology Letters, 4,* 375–378. doi:10.1098/rsbl.2008.0122

Savaskan, E., Ehrhardt, R., Schulz, A., Walter, M., & Schachinger, H. (2008). Post-learning intranasal oxytocin modulates human memory for facial identity. *Psychoneuroendocrinology, 33,* 368–374. doi:10.1016/j.psyneuen.2007.12.004

Schneiderman, I., Zagoory-Sharon, O., Leckman, J. F., & Feldman, R. (2012). Oxytocin during the initial stages of romantic attachment: Relation to couples' interactive reciprocity. *Psychoneuroendocrinology, 37,* 1277–1285. doi:10.1016/j.psyneuen.2011.12.021

Shapiro, L. E., & Insel, T. R. (1992). Oxytocin receptor distribution reflects social organization in monogamous and polygynous voles. *Annals of the New York Academy of Sciences, 652,* 448–451. doi:10.1111/j.1749-6632.1992.tb34380.x

Smith, A. S., Agmo, A., Birnie, A. K., & French, J. A. (2010). Manipulation of the oxytocin system alters social behavior and attraction in pair-bonding primates, *Callithrix penicillata. Hormones and Behavior, 57,* 255–262. doi:10.1016/j.yhbeh.2009.12.004

Smotherman, W. P., & Bell, R. W. (1980). Maternal mediation of early experience. In W. P. Smotherman & R. W. Bell (Eds.), *Maternal influence and early behavior* (pp. 201–210). New York, NY: Spectrum. doi:10.1007/978-94-011-6287-6_8

Stone, A. I., Mathieu, D., Griffin, L., & Bales, K. L. (2010). Alloparenting experience affects future parental behavior and reproductive success in prairie voles (*Microtus ochrogaster*). *Behavioural Processes, 83,* 8–15. doi:10.1016/j.beproc.2009.08.008

Tang, A. C., Akers, K. G., Reeb, B. C., Romeo, R. D., & McEwen, B. S. (2006). Programming social, cognitive, and neuroendocrine development by early exposure to novelty. *Proceedings of the National Academy of Sciences, USA, 103,* 15716–15721. doi:10.1073/pnas.0607374103

Taylor, S. E., Gonzaga, G. C., Klein, L. C., Hu, P., Greendale, G. A., & Seeman, T. E. (2006). Relation of oxytocin to psychological stress responses and hypothalamic-pituitary-adrenal axis activity in older women. *Psychosomatic Medicine, 68,* 238–245. doi:10.1097/01.psy.0000203242.95990.74

Theodoridou, A., Rowe, A. C., Penton-Voak, I. S., & Rogers, P. J. (2009). Oxytocin and social perception: Oxytocin increases perceived facial trustworthiness and attractiveness. *Hormones and Behavior, 56,* 128–132. doi:10.1016/j.yhbeh. 2009.03.019

Tribollet, E., Charpak, S., Schmit, A., Dubois-Dauphin, M., & Dreifuss, J. J. (1989). Appearance and transient expression of oxytocin receptors in fetal, infant, and peripubertal rat brain studied by autoradiography and electrophysiology. *Journal of Neuroscience, 9,* 1764–1773.

Tribollet, E., Goumaz, M., Raggenbass, M., Dubois-Dauphin, M., & Dreifuss, J. J. (1991). Early appearance and transient expression of vasopressin receptors in the brain of rat fetus and infant: An autoradiographical and electrophysiological study. *Developmental Brain Research, 58,* 13–24. doi:10.1016/0165-3806(91)90232-8

Valesky, E. M., Burda, H., Kaufmann, R., & Oeslschlager, H. H. A. (2012). Distribution of oxytocin- and vasopressin-immunoreactive neurons in the brain of the eusocial mole rat (*Fukomys anselli*). *Anatomical Record, 295,* 474–480. doi:10.1002/ar.22414

Verney, E. B. (1946). Absorption and excretion of water: The antidiuretic hormone. *Lancet, 248,* 781–783. doi:10.1016/S0140-6736(46)91092-6

Walum, H., Lichtenstein, P., Neiderhiser, J. M., Reiss, D., Ganiban, J. M., Spotts, E. L., . . . Westberg, L. (2012). Variation in the oxytocin receptor gene is associated with pair-bonding and social behavior. *Biological Psychiatry, 71,* 419–426. doi:10.1016/j.biopsych.2011.09.002

Walum, H., Westberg, L., Henningsson, S., Neiderhiser, J. M., Reiss, D., Igl, W., . . . Lichtenstein, P. (2008). Genetic variation in the vasopressin receptor 1a gene (*AVPR1a*) associates with pair-bonding behavior in humans. *Proceedings of the National Academy of Sciences, USA, 105,* 14153–14156. doi:10.1073/pnas. 0803081105

Wang, Z., Young, L. J., De Vries, G. J., & Insel, T. R. (1998). Voles and vasopressin: A review of molecular, cellular, and behavioral studies of pair bonding and paternal behaviors. *Progress in Brain Research, 119,* 483–499. doi:10.1016/S0079-6123 (08)61589-7

Winslow, J., & Insel, T. R. (1991). Vasopressin modulates male squirrel monkeys' behavior during social separation. *European Journal of Pharmacology, 200,* 95–101. doi:10.1016/0014-2999(91)90671-C

Winslow, J. T., Hastings, N., Carter, C. S., Harbaugh, C. R., & Insel, T. R. (1993, October 7). A role for central vasopressin in pair bonding in monogamous prairie voles. *Nature, 365,* 545–548. doi:10.1038/365545a0

Winslow, J. T., Shapiro, L., Carter, C. S., & Insel, T. R. (1993). Oxytocin and complex social behavior: Species comparisons. *Psychopharmacology Bulletin, 29,* 409–414.

Witt, D. M., Carter, C. S., & Insel, T. R. (1991). Oxytocin receptor binding in female prairie voles: Endogenous and exogenous estradiol stimulation. *Journal of Neuroendocrinology, 3,* 155–161. doi:10.1111/j.1365-2826.1991.tb00258.x

Young, L. J., Nilsen, R., Waymire, K. G., MacGregor, G. R., & Insel, T. R. (1999, August 19). Increased affiliative response to vasopressin in mice expressing the V-1a receptor from a monogamous vole. *Nature, 400,* 766–768. doi:10.1038/23650

Zak, P. J., Kurzban, R., & Matzner, W. T. (2005). Oxytocin is associated with human trustworthiness. *Hormones and Behavior, 48,* 522–527. doi:10.1016/j.yhbeh.2005.07.009

Zhang, J., Branch, D. W., Ramirez, M. M., Laughon, S. K., Reddy, U., Hoffman, M., . . . Hibbard, J. U. (2011). Oxytocin regimen for labor augmentation, labor progression, and perinatal outcomes. *Obstetrics & Gynecology, 118,* 249–256. doi:10.1097/AOG.0b013e3182220192

Zingg, H. H. (2002). Oxytocin. In D. Pfaff, A. P. Arnold, A. M. Etgen, S. E. Fahrbach, & R. T. Rubin (Eds.), *Hormones, brain, and behavior* (pp. 779–802). New York, NY: Academic Press. doi:10.1016/B978-012532104-4/50059-7

2

PRIMARY-PROCESS SEPARATION-DISTRESS (PANIC/GRIEF) AND REWARD EAGERNESS (SEEKING) PROCESSES IN THE ANCESTRAL GENESIS OF DEPRESSIVE AFFECT AND ADDICTIONS

JAAK PANKSEPP, MARK SOLMS, THOMAS E. SCHLÄPFER, AND VOLKER A. COENEN

Decades of research with preclinical (animal) models in the field of affective neuroscience has clarified the functional neuroanatomy of seven primary-process (i.e., genetically provided) emotional systems in mammalian brains. The emotional primes consist of the following processes (capitalized, to highlight the noncolloquial, primary-process referents of the terms): SEEKING, RAGE, FEAR, sexual LUST, maternal CARE, separation-distress PANIC/GRIEF (henceforth, simply PANIC), and joyful PLAY. All are subcortically situated (for summaries, see Panksepp, 1998; Panksepp & Biven, 2012). This allows animal models to guide the needed behavioral and neuroscientific analyses at levels of causal detail that cannot be achieved through human research, even work highlighting many interesting correlates based on modern brain imaging. We are interested in how such knowledge interfaces with psychiatric issues and the implications for human development and the evolutionary understanding of our cross-mammalian social nature.

We appreciate support of this work by grants from the Hope for Depression Research Foundation to Volker A. Coenen, Jaak Panksepp, Thomas E. Schläpfer, and Mark Solms.

http://dx.doi.org/10.1037/14250-003
Mechanisms of Social Connection: From Brain to Group, M. Mikulincer and P. R. Shaver (Editors)

Several of these systems figure heavily in social bonding and drug addictions—processes that are intimately interrelated within the lower reaches of the brain. So far, mammalian brain research has not revealed any primal social "attachment system" dedicated exclusively to the formation of social bonds. What it has revealed is a series of affective–emotional systems from which attachments emerge as a function of social learning. Among the most important systems are (a) those that mediate separation-distress vocalizations (PANIC), which promote affectively painful psychological states during social isolation, and (b) those that promote the SEEKING of reunion with caretakers, which, if successful, arouses (c) opioid- and oxytocin-mediated relief and social pleasure (Panksepp, 1981, 1992). This reward can be fully engendered in youngsters only by primary caretakers whose nurturant CARE systems are engaged in sustained, positive-affect-generating ways. This cultivates brain systems needed for future social bonds.

As children mature, they increasingly utilize the developmentally emergent brain processes of the PLAY system to enthusiastically and positively engage with others and thereby establish friendships. These systems are of great importance in leading to the final package that we call *social attachments*. When such processes are derailed during development, the probability of mental disorders such as depression is increased (for overviews, see Panksepp & Watt, 2011; Watt & Panksepp, 2009).

In this chapter, we focus especially on the genesis of depression, highlighting two antecedent emotional mechanisms. One is sustained overactivity of the separation-distress PANIC/GRIEF system (typically reflecting severed social bonds and, at higher cognitive levels, intrapsychic alienation). If sustained, this overactivity can lead to a downward cascade of psychological depletion of positive affective resources and the ascendancy of negative emotions (as originally formulated by John Bowlby, 1973). The second antecedent mechanism is the despair phase that follows the acute PANIC response. This shift seems to be characterized by abnormally low activity of the SEEKING system (and its so-called brain reward networks), leading to the amotivational states that characterize depression.

Both mechanisms can promote drug addictions, often acquired in an effort to restore psychic homeostasis (for a psychobiological overview, see Zellner, Watt, Solms, & Panksepp, 2011). Separation distress promotes opioid addiction (because opioids alleviate the psychic pain of loss), and the emptiness of diminished desire (depletion of SEEKING urges) promotes the amotivational aspect of depression, which can be temporarily alleviated by psychostimulants. Depressive affect is promoted by these brain mechanisms of social loss and depleted desire (for a full analysis of the underlying dynamics, see Watt & Panksepp, 2009, and accompanying commentaries).

Such an affective neuroscience perspective can begin to answer age-old questions: Why does depression feel so bad? What are the specific negative-affect-generating networks of the mammalian brain whose excessive activities initiate and sustain the cascades of brain–mind changes that characterize depression? As Bowlby (1973) well recognized, separation distress—the panicky "protest" that promptly follows social loss, especially in young animals—feels bad in a special way: It is a variant of psychic pain, which if prolonged, promotes psychic emptiness. Understanding these neural processes can help clinicians craft new psychotherapeutic approaches, including better utilization of positive effects that arise from the SEEKING and PLAY systems and including new pharmacological and other brain–mind treatments. Here, we briefly summarize the role of these systems in psychiatrically significant distress and discuss new psychiatric modalities in treatment-resistant depressive disorders based on deep brain stimulation (DBS; Coenen, Schläepfer, Mäedler, & Panksepp, 2011; Schläepfer et al., 2008).

AFFECTIVE NEUROSCIENCE APPROACHES TO UNDERSTANDING EMOTIONAL MINDS

The affective neuroscience approach to understanding the emotional minds of all mammals (Panksepp, 1998, 2004) makes two key assumptions. These allow us to address important and difficult questions in both basic psychological research and clinical practice and to do so in novel and productive ways. First, primal emotions and their associated feelings evolved to do something specific in relation to biologically significant and life-challenging situations. They are not mere epiphenomena. Second, felt aspects of primary-process emotions—specific kinds of affects that have been built into the brain and are shared homologously by all mammals—serve three key adaptive purposes: (a) They highlight key survival and reproductive issues in the ambient environment, with positive affects indexing situations that increase and negative affects indexing situations that decrease an animal's chances of surviving to reproduce. (b) They motivate organisms to behave in ways that promote survival and reproduction, providing a psychobehavioral compass that leads to individual safety and reproductive success. (c) They promote memory construction through neural systems that reinforce learned behaviors by yet unfathomed laws of affect. These laws should replace the behaviorist law of effect, which was based on rewards and punishments (identified as increasing and decreasing rates of a behavior) without considering the inner psychological lives of humans or other animals. They are effective codes with which to anticipate biological survival issues.

In contrast, the behaviorist approach led to a scientifically solid—perhaps rigid—outsider's view of the psychological life of nonhuman animals and, for a while, humans. We instead advance an inner emotional-affective view of all mammalian species, without neglecting the outer behavioral view. The reason these perspectives can be brought together is that everywhere in the brain one can evoke coherent instinctual emotional behaviors using DBS, and one can demonstrate that the evoked internal states are rewarding and punishing (for summaries, see Panksepp 1982, 1998, 2004; Panksepp & Biven, 2012).

Affects are functional. Positive affects automatically signal to animals that they are on paths likely to increase their fitness. Negative affects inform them that they are in life-diminishing/threatening situations and provide neural reinforcement for unconditional escape and learned avoidance strategies. Among the emotional primes, four mediate affectively positive behavioral urges: namely, SEEKING, LUST, CARE, and PLAY, with the last three heavily utilizing the SEEKING urge. And three mediate affectively negative emotions: RAGE, FEAR and PANIC. There are others primal affects, but we ignore the sensory and homeostatic ones here. Because the primal emotion systems are probably important for the genesis of depression and other psychiatric disorders, we have developed a personality test to evaluate the strengths and weaknesses of the primal emotions in humans (Davis & Panksepp, 2011; Davis, Panksepp, & Normansell, 2003). This measure may be of value to psychologists, providing a common metric to estimate the status of the primal emotions in the lives of their subjects and clients.

FLAWS WITH CURRENT PRECLINICAL
AND MEDICINAL APPROACHES TO DEPRESSION

For about 30 years, there has been a vigorous movement to produce animal (aka preclinical) models of depression. Practically all have used sustained administration of various stressors, including repeated restraint, social stress, and a large variety of aversive stimuli. Although the general stress-induced preclinical models of depression have many shortcomings, one is especially problematic: Global stressors influence practically everything the brain does, providing little of the specificity necessary to help researchers track down the precise emotional pathways that figure most heavily in depression. This problem could be solved through the development of more refined approaches based on current understanding of basic emotional systems. However, few researchers have sought to specifically and directly evoke and measure depression by modifying and monitoring the activities of the most relevant affective networks of the brain (PANIC and SEEKING, as noted previously). Likewise, most models use rather general behavioral outcome measures (changes in open-field exploration, enforced swimming, and a vast array of traditional behavioral models of fearfulness) that have little clear functional relationship to human affective and interpersonal issues—issues that are of foremost importance for social psychologists and clinical practitioners. These models disregard the underlying psychological issues most relevant to feelings of social loss and defeat in the genesis of both depression and drug addiction (see Solms & Panksepp, 2010, and Zellner et al., 2011, for psychodynamic discussions of those perspectives).

As a result of the neglect of brain emotional circuitry in behavioral analyses, depression research during the last 4 decades of the 20th century focused most heavily on the consequences of global stress (de Kloet, Joels, & Holsboer, 2005; McEwen, 2007) and brain norepinephrine and serotonin dynamics (articles ranging from Schildkraut, 1965, to Harro & Oreland, 2001)—generalized neurochemical pathways that modulate everything that animals do. Because it was considered scientifically inappropriate to discuss emotional feelings of other animals, one key question was neglected: Why specifically does depression feel so bad? Our answer is that the negative feelings of PANIC are amplified and the euphoric potentials of SEEKING are depleted.

Authors of generalized behavioral analyses were excessively impressed by the capacity of very generalized brain neurochemical systems, such as serotonin, to dampen all emotional behaviors. Thus, it is no great surprise that serotonin-specific reuptake inhibitors can treat so many psychiatric problems but have had only modest effects when evaluated across large cohorts of individuals (highlighted well by the disappointing recent STAR*D findings of Rush, Trivedi, and Fava, 2003, and Rush, 2007). But few were seeking to understand more specific affective changes. As noted, our answer is that this is largely because of the sustained negative affect—psychological pain—arising from the psychic pain of PANIC arousal and gradual depletion of resources of the many joys promoting by SEEKING, including LUST, CARE, and PLAY.

General brain serotonergic and/or noradrenergic changes, which regulate everything animals do, certainly regulate general arousal (Delgado et al., 1990), which influences all emotions and cognitive processes. However, it is becoming ever harder to believe that such changes can specifically explain the morbid moods of depression. More recent preclinical work has usefully focused on various neurotrophic factors (Koziesk, Middlemas, & Bylund, 2008), stress-induced hippocampal shrinkage and central nervous system inflammation (Miller, Maletic, & Raison, 2009), and various genetic underpinnings of such autonomic, psychophysiological problems (Levinson, 2006), but those approaches have not yet generated new medicines. Perhaps this is because such strategies provide no specific insight into the affective feelings that characterize depression. Here, our goal is to address how more specific affective neuroscience approaches may yield more specific understanding of the causal underpinnings of depressive affect (e.g., as addressed by Burgdorf, Panksepp, & Moskal, 2011; Kroes, Burgdorf, Otto, Panksepp, & Moskal, 2007; Watt & Panksepp, 2009).

We believe that more specific emotional-systems analyses not only will help promote the needed interdisciplinary dialogues but also will lead to the development of more focused kinds of therapeutic interventions than are currently available in biological psychiatry or in psychotherapeutics. Cognitive-behavioral regulatory strategies are emphasized in such interventions, often at the expense of more immediately affect-oriented therapies (but see Fosha, Siegel, & Solomon, 2009, for such interventions, and especially Shedler, 2010, which summarizes impressive evidence in support of the efficacy of emotionally based psychodynamic approaches).

In contrast to general behavioral approaches, the affective neuroscience view promotes the use of preclinical models that seek to instigate depressive cascades by directly stimulating the relevant negative affective systems of the brain, while monitoring chronic changes in affect with validated measures of declining capacities to sustain positive social affect (Wright & Panksepp, 2012). The development of new medicinals is facilitated by the emerging understanding of changes in the relevant genetics and brain neurochemical systems (e.g., Burgdorf et al., 2011; Moskal, Burgdork, Kroes, Brudzynski, & Panksepp, 2011; Normansell & Panksepp, 2011), which also help to illuminate the fact that drug addictions often emerge from individuals trying to achieve emotional homeostasis through the intake of mood-altering drugs (Panksepp, 1981; Panksepp, Herman, Vilberg, Bishop, & DeEskinazi, 1980). On the psychotherapeutic front, affective neuroscience concepts and approaches can help promote more effective use of positive emotions in psychotherapy and provide a rationale for the use of DBS of the relevant affective circuits in treatment-resistant depressions (Bewernick et al., 2010; Coenen et al., 2011; Mayberg, 2009; Schläepfer et al., 2008).

AN AFFECTIVE NEUROSCIENTIFIC PERSPECTIVE ON WHY DEPRESSION FEELS SO BAD

The PANIC system (see Figure 2.1), which engenders psychological pain, has been proposed as the primary emotional system indexing social loss (Panksepp, 2003a, 2003b, 2005a, 2005b, 2010), the epidemiological stressor that most commonly leads to depression (Bowlby, 1980; Heim & Nemeroff, 1999). The PANIC circuitry originates in midbrain central gray regions, commonly called the periaqueductal gray. It ascends through medial diencephalic structures, especially the dorsomedial thalamus, and terminates in more ventral

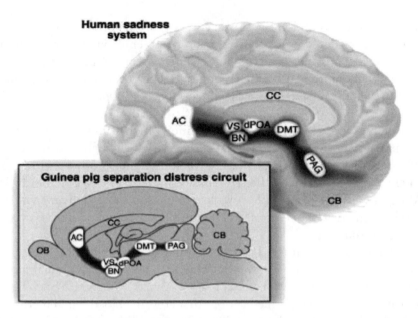

Figure 2.1. Human and animal sadness of sadness and separation-distress systems. The anatomical areas shared in these cross-species analyses were in the anterior cingulate (AC), the dorsomedial thalamus (DMT), the periaqueductal gray (PAG), and also regions in the most ancient parts of the cerebellum (CB). Animals showed remarkably similar anatomies, including the ventral septal area (VS), dorsal preoptic area (dPOA), and the bed nucleus of the stria terminalis (BN). From "Feeling the Pain of Social Loss" by J. Panksepp, 2003, *Science, 302,* pp. 237–239. Copyright by American Association for the Advancement of Science. Reprinted with permission.

or subcallosal anterior cingulate forebrain regions. Inhibition of this system with DBS may have already figured positively in the modulation of treatment-resistant depressions (Mayberg et al., 2005).

Based on pharmacological studies, the key neurochemistries that promote separation calls (which Bowlby [1973] called *protest*) are declining opioid and oxytocin and elevated corticotropin-releasing factor, combined with increased glutamatergic drive in PANIC circuits of the brain, with the neuropeptides probably being more important than the excitatory amino acids in controlling the specific social-affective responses of the brain. Still, inhibition of both neuropeptide and excitatory amino acid (e.g., glutamatergic) promoters of PANIC (e.g., Normansell & Panksepp, 2011; Panksepp, Normansell, Herman, Bishop, & Crepeau, 1988) should help to alleviate the bad feelings of depression. Recent work along these lines has been very promising (Holsboer, 2000; Zarate et al., 2006).

The key brain chemistries that can specifically reduce separation distress are opioids that activate mu-receptors, as well as molecules that activate oxytocin and prolactin receptors (Panksepp, 1981, 1998). Each could be considered as a potential vector for beneficially countering the affective changes that promote depression. Of course, modern clinicians reasonably hesitate to use addictive opioids, even though they were widely used to treat depression before the modern era of pharmacotherapy, beginning in the mid-1950s (Tenore, 2008). Still, as discussed below, safe opioids such as ultra-low-dose buprenorphine (which stimulates only opioid receptors at low doses but becomes antagonistic at high doses) are very effective antidepressants for individuals for whom no other medications have provided sustained relief (Bodkin, Zornberg, Lukas, & Cole, 1995). With the advent of possible low-dose buprenorphine delivery via skin patches, any development of a behaviorally mediated addictive cycle is further minimized.

Centrally administered oxytocin is also remarkably effective in alleviating separation distress and promoting social bonding in animal models (Nelson & Panksepp, 1998; Panksepp, 1992; Uvnäs-Moberg, 1998). Whether nonpeptide oxytocinergic medications that cross the blood–brain barrier, yet to be developed, can be harnessed to help reestablish affective homeostasis during excessively aroused PANIC in human beings has not been determined (but psychological effects observed in intranasal studies are promising; e.g., Heinrichs & Domes, 2008; Insel, 2010). In this context, we note that one of the rarely considered effects of this neuropeptide is its capacity to sustain the activity of endogenous opioid processes, thereby sustaining positive social feelings, by inhibiting the development of tolerance and, hence, loss of positive affect to opioids (Kovács, Sarnyai, & Szabó, 1998).

SEPARATION DISTRESS/PANIC IS ONE GATEWAY TO DEPRESSION

The PANIC system probably evolved from general pain mechanisms (Panksepp 1981, 1998, 2003b), probably over two hundred million years ago (birds possess a homologous system). This critical opioid- and oxytocin-modulated system promotes social connection, helps forge social attachments and dependencies between infants and mothers, probably fortifies sexual relationships, and may ultimately promote group solidarity among group-living species. As an index of its role in attachment, we argue, when one misses someone with whom one is bonded, through separation, this system is aroused. If someone is never missed, this suggests that one does not have an attachment to the absent individual. Thus, the affective consequences of severed attachment bonds make individuals suffer in distinctly aversive ways, which, if prolonged, can lead to depression.

The acute separation-distress response, although instigating affective pain that can promote depression, does not constitute depression on its own. For that, other neuroaffective changes have to be set in motion to generate feelings of lassitude and despair, and the neuroscientific account of this cascade remains incomplete. One line of research suggests that immune modulators (e.g., cytokines such as Interleukin (IL) 1, IL-6, and TNF-α) can instigate sickness-like affective states that may promote the sustained despair of depression (Hennessy, Deak, & Schiml-Webb, 2001). Another promising possibility, which we focus on here, is that sustained separation distress cascades into despair because of the ensuing diminution of SEEKING urges (see Figure 2.2).

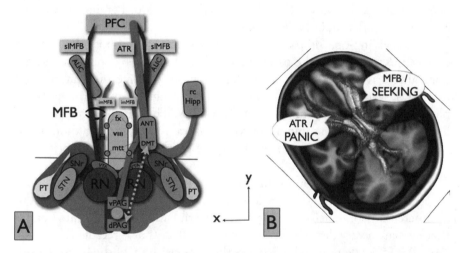

Figure 2.2. Anatomy of the SEEKING and PANIC systems. Left: A conceptual sketch of the relevant SEEKING and PANIC anatomies on a horizontal anatomical section depicting the upper mesencephalic (midbrain) cross-section from which various transdiencephalic pathways ascend within midline regions of the brain. These pathways form the caudal level of the third ventricle (vIII), with the following anatomical designations from lateral to medial regions: PT = pyramidal tract; STN = subthalamic nucleus; SNr = substantia nigra pars reticulata; RN = red nucleus; VTA = ventral tegmental area; dPAG and vPAG = dorsal and ventral periaqueductal gray. The more rostral anatomical designations are mtt = mamillo-thalamic tracts; vIII = third ventricle; fx = fornix; MFB = medial forebrain bundle; imMFB = inferiomedial limb of the medial forebrain bundle; DMT = dorsomedial thalamus; ANT = anterior nucleus of thalamus; ALIC = anterior limb of the internal capsule; rcHipp = retrocommissural hippocampus; ATR = anterior thalamic radiations; slMFB = superiolateral limb of the medial forebrain bundle; PFC = prefrontal cortex. Right: On a horizonal diffusion tensor imaging rendition of the human brain, the PANIC system, represented by the anterior thalamic radiations (ATR), runs dorsal to the more ventral trajectories of the medial forebrain bundle (MFB)-based SEEKING system, with abundant possibilities of direct interactions at the level of the VTA. From "Human Medial Forebrain Bundle (MFB) and Anterior Thalamic Radiation (ATR): Imaging of Two Major Subcortical Pathways That May Promote a Dynamic Balance of Opposite Affects Relevant for Understanding Depression" by V. A. Coene, J. Paksepp, T. A. Hurwitz, H. Urbcah, and B. Madler, 2002, *Journal of Neuropsychiatry and Clinical Neurosciences, 24,* pp. 223–236. Copyright by American Neuropsychiatric Association. Adapted with permission.

When protest fails to achieve social reunion, a gradual behavioral and psychological shutdown process occurs. At this critical transition from protest to despair, a sustained negative affect emerges that constitutes a fully developed depressive phenotype. This negative affect of despair contributes to "giving up" as the responsiveness of the SEEKING-euphoria system diminishes. This state is characterized by a diminished positive attitude to life and by reduced pursuit of rewards, both real and imagined. In animal models this was highlighted by Anisman and Matheson's (2005) discovery that stressors that promote depressive profiles in animal models are accompanied by elevated thresholds in brain reward-SEEKING arousal. Similar views have been advocated by others (Nestler & Carlezon, 2006; Pereira Do Carmo, Stevenson, Carlezon, & Negus, 2009).

This giving-up, "despair" phase can be counteracted not only by brain chemistries that reduce the psychic pain of loss but also by ones that elevate dopamine-driven SEEKING urges that promote positive motivations and interest. Low doses of opioids can do both, yielding dopamine-independent pleasures as well as dopamine-SEEKING urges. Thus, in the emergence of depressive affect, it is as important to emphasize the lassitude of diminished SEEKING as it is to focus on the lingering psychic pain and emptiness of separation distress.

What specifically causes this reduction in SEEKING urges is currently a hot topic in preclinical depression research. A key candidate is the gradually increasing influence of dynorphins, powerful and pervasive brain opioids that mediate a very distinct form of negative affect that is recruited by social loss. This affect demonstrably reduces the responsivity of the brain reward-SEEKING system (McLaughlin, Li, Valdez, Chavkin, & Chavkin, 2006), both at synaptic terminals (Mu, Neumann, Panksepp, Schlüter, & Dong, 2011) and in relevant neuropeptide modulators of affect such as orexin (Nocjar, Zhang, Feng, & Panksepp, 2012).

Besides the neurochemistries highlighted here, there will be many brain growth factors and other neurochemical cascades that are bound to promote or retard this downward spiral (e.g., Feder, Nestler, & Charney, 2009). As in psychotherapeutic disciplines, the goal of psychopharmacology is to counteract and reverse this downward cascade. In our estimation, new therapeutic approaches that take advantage of the positive hedonics of social CARE systems (the primal foundation of empathy) and PLAY systems (the primal source of social joy) may be especially important for better therapeutic outcomes. However, rather than to develop psychotherapeutic concepts for treatment of acute depressive episodes by promoting social reconnection and reattachment of depressed individuals, our remaining goal here will be to (a) introduce and flesh out new, emerging concepts in pharmacotherapeutics of depression; (b) provide a synopsis of how the neural trajectories of the above PANIC and SEEKING systems are being analyzed in human beings; and (c) provide a description of how modern DBS approaches in humans are providing dramatic support for the efficacy of direct manipulations of these systems, further affirming the importance of basic affective systems in human mental health.

NEW PSYCHOPHARMACOTHERAPEUTIC APPROACHES

In addition to the discovery of new uses for old chemistries such as D-cycloserine, an indirect glutamate facilitator, for the consolidation of psychotherapeutic outcomes in various disorders (e.g., Wilhelm et al., 2008), other beneficial mind–brain influences from our emerging understanding of the primary-process social affective systems of the brain can now be envisioned (Panksepp, 2004, 2006, 2009). With respect to cardinal brain chemistries of social bonding and alleviation of separation distress, we can envision direct antidepressant effects of existing positive-affect-facilitation neurochemistries. Here, because of limited space we discuss only the antidepressant effects of moderate doses of the safe opioid buprenorphine. We also highlight how positive-affect-facilitating pharmacotherapeutic agents may emerge from the genetic analysis of the SEEKING and PLAY systems.

With regard to buprenorphine, as noted, prior to the modern era of psychopharmacology, psychiatrists used opioids only for treating mental suffering (Tenore, 2008). Although opioids were very effective antidepressants in the short term, their addictive potential discouraged long-term use, especially after the discovery of non-opioid antidepressants (Panksepp, 2006). The mixed mu-opioid receptor agonist/antagonist buprenorphine solves most of these problems, and open trials have highlighted the substantial and sustained efficacy of low doses in depressed clients who have had no relief from many accepted antidepressants (Bodkin et al., 1995). This drug also has the uniquely desirable effect of blocking the dynorphin receptors that are so widespread in the brain, which directly inhibit brain dopamine-mediated SEEKING urges. This effect should promote SEEKING urges. Also, because high doses of buprenorphine actually block addictive mu-opioid receptors, the drug has a fail-safe mechanism that limits addictive escalations and the ensuing abuse that characterizes pure opiate-receptor stimulants, with the ever-present risk of respiratory arrest. One reason this medication has been badly neglected in research (there has been no proper follow-up to Bodkin et al.'s 1995 provocative findings in the treatment of refractory depression) is its low profit margin (it is off-patent) and the resulting lack of financial investments for expensive clinical trials required for medical approval.

However, in terms of new drug development, analysis of the genetic changes in animals engaged in abundant social PLAY, which operates in part through the mesolimbic dopamine-energized function of the medial forebrain bundle SEEKING system (Burgdorf, Wood, Kroes, Moskal, & Panksepp, 2007; Panksepp & Moskal, 2008), has yielded diverse targets for new antidepressant drug development (see Moskal et al., 2011; see also Krishnan & Nestler, 2008, for related work). A top candidate is the glutamate-receptor-related family of regulatory systems. These systems were found to facilitate positive affect in our preclinical models, and a medicinal vector that is a partial agonist for the glycine receptor yielded an antidepressive, prohedonic profile. Indeed, GLYX-13 has passed both animal and human toxicology tests (with no adverse effects observed). It has completed Phase 2 clinical testing (Burgdorf et al., 2011), exhibiting antidepressant effects stronger than placebos and a standard serotonin-specific reuptake inhibitor antidepressant.

We also believe it is important that the "power of PLAY" in psychotherapy remains almost completely untapped, at least in any systematic way. There are good reasons to believe that the long-term recruitment of such mental energies could be effective for the amelioration of various recalcitrant childhood problems, such as childhood impulsivity, through the capacity of such prosocial activities to promote both socialization and brain maturation (Panksepp, 2007). For instance, play can "fertilize" the brain by promoting gene expression leading to growth factors such as brain-derived neurotrophic factor within the brain (Gordon, Burke, Akil, Watson, & Panksepp, 2003). In preclinical models, brain-derived neurotrophic factor promotes antidepressant genetic cascades in the brain that oppose the hippocampal dysgenesis that often accompanies depression (McEwen, 2007).

In this context, it is noteworthy that animal models of positive affect that we developed (i.e., by systematic tickling of rats, which can bring hedonic 50-kHz ultrasonic vocalizations under experimental control and can be used as a positive affective psychoassay) have demonstrated antidepressant-type hippocampal neuronal proliferation in rats (Wöhr et al., 2009). Indeed, these 50-kHz ultrasonic vocalizations, intensely exhibited during social play, have been mapped within the brain to the mesolimbic dopamine system. This provides investigators with direct readouts of aroused social SEEKING (e.g., euphoric eagerness), which can counteract depressive affect (Burgdorf et al., 2007). These affectively positive vocalizations, along with the negative 22-kHz ultrasonic vocalizations, can be used to index social affective shifts that illuminate the underlying affective changes that characterize depression and its amelioration (Kroes et al., 2007).

Indeed, the robust effects of play on cortical gene expression (Moskal et al., 2011) have led to the identification of other growth factors that may prove to be affectively positive adjuncts to playful psychotherapy. One of the biggest gene-expression changes we have seen in the neocortex (Burgdorf, Kroes, Beinfeld, Panksepp, & Moskal, 2010) is in the elevated expression of insulin-like growth factor-1 (IGF-1). When this growth factor was tested for functional changes in relevant social behaviors, with direct intracerebral injections of an IGF-1 receptor antagonist as well as inhibition of IGF-1 brain activity, it yielded convergent evidence for the role of IGF-1 in promoting positive affect (Burgdorf et al., 2010). However, because of the capacity of IGF-1 to promote tumor growth, further development of that medicinal concept was abandoned. In any event, further research on the positive social-affect systems of the mammalian brain should yield new ways to promote feelings of secure affective well-being that may counteract depressive cascades.

We believe the SEEKING system of the human brain could be even more directly targeted as a way to alleviate depression with DBS. Since a first report of mania during the inadvertent activation of the human medial forebrain bundle during subthalamic nucleus DBS in a patient with Parkinson's disease (Coenen et al., 2009) and depiction of its anatomical trajectory with diffusion tensor imaging, we have envisioned how the SEEKING system interacts with anterior thalamic radiations that may represent the PANIC system and thereby generated ideas concerning how direct DBS might be used to alleviate depressive despair in patients (Coenen et al., 2011; Coenen, Panksepp, Hurwitz, Urbach, & Mädler, 2012).

STIMULATION OF THE MEDIAL FOREBRAIN BUNDLE AS A THERAPEUTIC MODALITY FOR DEPRESSION

As summarized above, it was proposed that functional interactions between the two primal emotional systems—overarousal of the PANIC (or GRIEF) system and underarousal of the SEEKING system—promote feelings of psychological pain or separation distress. This diminishes the possibility of social joy, a psychological state that surely plays a major role in counteracting depression (for summaries of related human work, see Coenen et al., 2011, 2012). Because the SEEKING system finds its anatomical expression in the medial forebrain bundle, we have suggested, DBS applied to this anatomical system should result in clinically significant alleviation of depression. In a previous study we were able to show that four distinct forms of brain damage, which had yielded antidepressant effects during the historical era of psychosurgery, converged on the above brain regions, which are therefore potential targets for the clinical benefits that were observed (Schoene-Bake et al., 2010).

Moreover, we were able to demonstrate in another study (Coenen et al., 2011) that the medial forebrain bundle plays a key role in the effectiveness of two (if not all) of the current experimentally stimulated DBS targets for depression (nucleus accumbens and anterior limb of the internal capsule). Thus, in an ethically approved trial, the medial forebrain bundle was targeted for direct stimulation in a preliminary group of very treatment-resistant patients with depression. Effects in seven individuals have been evaluated to date. With the help of diffusion tensor imaging of this system, the area of the most densely packed medial forebrain bundle fibers was the anatomical target for stereotactically implanted electrodes, with subsequent chronic "pacemaker" stimulation at low levels of electrical current. The acute effects that were seen intraoperatively with unilateral high-frequency stimulation were consistent with what would be expected from acute activation of the SEEKING system: All seven patients showed clear effects of increased appetitive motivation, including a general anticipation of rewarding activities but not directly reported feelings of reward (pleasure) itself. All patients showed increased exploratory behavior accompanied by active turning of their heads toward the interviewer, which they had not done in the previous, unstimulated phases of observation. They visually searched the room promptly upon initiation of test stimulation and reported elevated motivations such as increased interest in travels or other life-engaging activities, which they had not pursued for years. These are clear signs of SEEKING behavior. However, none of the patients reported any sign of hypomania/mania or elevated mood, an effect that has been reported in some individuals with Parkinson's disease (Coenen et al., 2009). It was clear that in our depressed subjects, acute stimulation induced anticipation of future reward and not a feeling of reward itself. This corresponds with what has been described as the primary mode of action of the SEEKING system (euphoric drive; Panksepp 1998).

CONCLUSION

Our analysis of the social brain supplements the psychological insights of John Bowlby (1980), who originally conjectured that depression arises from protracted separation distress that is followed, if sustained for too long, by chronic depressive despair. We now have abundant data on the brain mechanisms of separation distress—the protest phase that may lead to depression—and novel affective neuroscience hypotheses concerning how diminished SEEKING urges tend to promote depressive despair. The separation-distress-mediating PANIC system in the brain is regulated by various prosocial neuropeptides that also promote CARE and PLAY behaviors (e.g., endogenous opioids, oxytocin, and prolactin). The ability of these systems to consolidate social bonds (Panksepp, 1981, 1998) may help to explain why depression is almost twice as common in females as in males: Female brains may be intrinsically more responsive than male brains to prosocial emotions (Swain, Loberbaum, Kose, & Strathearn, 2007).

The pain of depression—often arising from social loss and social defeat—can be the price we mammals pay for the evolutionary advantages of social bonds, which enormously enhance our survival chances and enrich our affective lives. Although animal research cannot directly inform us about the complex cognitive-affective amalgams (especially the ruminations and the "darkening" of cognition) that emerge in humans during depression, they can inform us about the evolutionarily conserved brain–mind affective mechanisms that generate our social attachments, which, when dysregulated, can lead to depressive despair. Accordingly, the potential for depression is intimately linked to the pain of social loss and the resulting diminution of engagement with the world that is an intrinsic vulnerability of the primal affective programs of our prosocial brains.

The primary-process emotion-generating systems are all situated in ancient, medially situated subcortical brain regions that all mammals share; they comprise large, longitudinally coursing systems, such as the medial forebrain bundle. These affective systems of the brain get connected to many life experiences through learning, but their affectivity itself is an evolutionary birthright of all mammalian minds. This makes the study of comparative neurophenomenology critically important for unraveling the affective processes that make life worth living and the emotional problems of the brain that can make it so horrible.

In conclusion, why does depression feel bad? It feels bad, in our view, for two reasons, both related to diminished feelings of internal security: First, because of their intrinsic relationship to separation distress, the PANIC and SEEKING systems encourage us to form and maintain addictive attachments, particularly to early caregivers but also to our mates and children, as well as to extended social groups. We should not forget that in primates, social grooming releases brain opioids (Keverne, Martensz, & Tuite, 1989; Keverne, Nevison, & Martel, 1997), and human voices are, in part, a way for our species to groom. Second, depression persuades us to abandon hope if our attempts to reunite with such figures or groups do not succeed within a limited period of time, and thereby we become psychologically detached from the world. This sustained loss of affective energy, which depletes cognitive meaning, may be intimately linked to diminished SEEKING, which is the epicenter of all major forms of drug addiction. In short, at the neurochemical level, we are all addicted to the ones we love and can become addicted to drugs that ease the pain of loss (Panksepp, 1981).

In light of the existence of brain systems that generate such feelings, it seems reasonable to hypothesize that the linchpin of at least one major form of depression is not the things that have preoccupied contemporary psychiatric researchers over the past three decades but rather the evolutionarily conserved brain states that mediate the transition from protest to despair in the wake of social loss. The final result is intimately linked to reduced arousal of the dopamine-energized SEEKING urges. In other words, the core brain basis of depression may revolve around the processes by which PANIC is aroused and SEEKING urges are shut down, possibly by diminished dopamine arousal, declining mu- and delta-opioids, and increasing kappa-opioids (dynorphin) receptor activities. Dysphoria may be enhanced further by various inflammatory cytokines, which prompt animals and humans to "give up" when the affective mind, which supports the cognitive apparatus, overflows with the psychic pain of separation distress.

REFERENCES

Anisman, H., & Matheson, K. (2005). Stress, depression, and anhedonia: Caveats concerning animal models. *Neuroscience & Biobehavioral Reviews*, 29, 525–546. doi:10.1016/j.neubiorev.2005.03.007

Bewernick, B. H., Hurlemann, R., Matusch, A., Kayser, S., Grubert, C., Hadrysiewicz, B., . . . Schläepfer, T. E. (2010). Nucleus accumbens deep brain stimulation decreases ratings of depression and anxiety in treatment-resistant depression. *Biological Psychiatry*, 67, 110–116. doi:10.1016/j.biopsych.2009.09.013

Bodkin, J. A., Zornberg, G. L., Lukas, S. E., & Cole, J. O. (1995). Buprenorphine treatment of refractory depression. *Journal of Clinical Psychopharmacology*, 15, 49–57. doi:10.1097/00004714-199502000-00008

Bowlby, J. (1973). *Attachment and loss: Vol. 2. Separation: Anxiety and anger*. New York, NY: Basic Books.

Bowlby, J. (1980). *Attachment and loss: Vol. 3. Loss: Sadness and depression*. New York, NY: Basic Books.

Burgdorf, J., Kroes, R. A., Beinfeld, M. C., Panksepp, J., & Moskal, J. R. (2010). Uncovering the molecular basis of positive affect using rough-and-tumble play in rats: A role for insulin-like growth factor 1. *Neuroscience*, 168, 769–777. doi:10.1016/j.neuroscience.2010.03.045

Burgdorf, J., Panksepp, J., & Moskal, J. R. (2011). Frequency-modulated 50 kHz ultrasonic vocalizations: A tool for uncovering the molecular substrates of positive affect. *Neuroscience & Biobehavioral Reviews*, 35, 1831–1836. doi:10.1016/j.neubiorev.2010.11.011

Burgdorf, J., Wood, P. L., Kroes, R. A., Moskal, J. R., & Panksepp, J. (2007). Neurobiology of 50-kHz ultrasonic vocalizations in rats: Electrode mapping, lesion, and pharmacology studies. *Behavioural Brain Research*, 182, 274–283. doi:10.1016/j.bbr.2007.03.010

Coenen, V. A., Honey, C. R., Hurwitz, T., Rahman, A. A., McMaster, J., Bürgel, U., & Mädler, B. (2009). Medial forebrain bundle stimulation as a pathophysiological mechanism for hypomania in subthalamic nucleus deep brain stimulation for Parkinson's disease. *Neurosurgery, 64,* 1106–1114. doi:10.1227/01.NEU. 0000345631.54446.06

Coenen, V. A., Panksepp, J., Hurwitz, T. A., Urbach, H., & Mädler, B. (2012). Human medial forebrain bundle (MFB) and anterior thalamic radiation (ATR): Imaging of two major subcortical pathways that may promote a dynamic balance of opposite affects relevant for understanding depression. *Journal of Neuropsychiatry and Clinical Neurosciences, 24,* 223–236. doi:10.1176/appi.neuropsych.11080180

Coenen, V. A., Schläepfer, T. E., Mäedler, B., & Panksepp, J. (2011). Cross-species affective functions of the medial forebrain bundle: Implications for the treatment of affective pain and depression in humans. *Neuroscience & Biobehavioral Reviews, 35,* 1971–1981. doi:10.1016/j.neubiorev.2010.12.009

Davis, K. L., & Panksepp, J. (2011). The brain's emotional foundations of human personality and the Affective Neuroscience Personality Scales. *Neuroscience & Biobehavioral Reviews, 35,* 1946–1958. doi:10.1016/j.neubiorev.2011.04.004

Davis, K. L., Panksepp, J., & Normansell, L. (2003). The Affective Neuroscience Personality Scales: Normative data and implications. *Neuropsychoanalysis, 5,* 57–69.

de Kloet, E. R., Joels, M., & Holsboer, F. (2005). Stress and the brain: From adaptation to disease. *Nature Reviews Neuroscience, 6,* 463–475. doi:10.1038/nrn1683

Delgado, P. L., Charney, D., Price, L. H., Aghajanian, G. K., Landis, H., & Heninger, G. R. (1990). Serotonin function and the mechanism of antidepressant action: Reversal of antidepressant-induced remission by rapid depletion of plasma tryptophan. *Archives of General Psychiatry, 47,* 411–418. doi:10.1001/archpsyc.1990.01810170011002

Feder, A., Nestler, E. J., & Charney, D. S. (2009). Psychobiology and molecular genetics of resilience. *Nature Reviews Neuroscience, 10,* 446–457. doi:10.1038/nrn2649

Fosha, D., Siegel, D. J., & Solomon, M. F. (Eds.). (2009). *The healing power of emotion: Affective neuroscience, development and clinical practice.* New York, NY: Norton.

Gordon, N. S., Burke, S., Akil, H., Watson, S., & Panksepp, J. (2003). Socially-induced brain "fertilization": Play promotes brain derived neurotrophic factor transcription in the amygdala and dorsolateral frontal cortex in juvenile rats. *Neuroscience Letters, 341,* 17–20. doi:10.1016/S0304-3940(03)00158-7

Harro, J., & Oreland, L. (2001). Depression as a spreading adjustment disorder of monoaminergic neurons: A case for primary implications of the locus coeruleus. *Brain Research Reviews, 38,* 79–128. doi:10.1016/S0165-0173(01)00082-0

Heim, C., & Nemeroff, C. (1999). The impact of early adverse experiences on brain systems involved in the pathophysiology of anxiety and affective disorders. *Biological Psychiatry, 46,* 1509–1522. doi:10.1016/S0006-3223(99)00224-3

Heinrichs, M., & Domes, G. (2008). Neuropeptides and social behaviour: Effects of oxytocin and vasopressin in humans. *Progress in Brain Research, 170,* 337–350. doi:10.1016/S0079-6123(08)00428-7

Hennessy, M. B., Deak, T., & Schiml-Webb, P. A. (2001). Stress-induced sickness behaviors: An alternative hypothesis for responses during maternal separation. *Developmental Psychobiology, 39,* 76–83. doi:10.1002/dev.1031

Herman, B. H., & Panksepp, J. (1981, March 6). Ascending endorphinergic inhibition of distress vocalization. *Science, 211*, 1060–1062. doi:10.1126/science.7466377

Holsboer, F. (2000). The corticosteroid receptor hypothesis of depression. *Neuropsychopharmacology, 23*, 477–501. doi:10.1016/S0893-133X(00)00159-7

Insel, T. R. (2010). The challenge of translation in social neuroscience: A review of oxytocin, vasopressin, and affiliative behavior. *Neuron, 65*, 768–779. doi:10.1016/j.neuron.2010.03.005

Keverne, E. B., Martensz, N., & Tuite, B. (1989). Beta-endorphin concentrations in cerebrospinal fluid of monkeys are influenced by grooming relationships. *Psychoneuroendocrinology, 14*, 155–161. doi:10.1016/0306-4530(89)90065-6

Keverne, E. B., Nevison, C. M., & Martel, F. L. (1997). Early learning and the social bond. *Annals of the New York Academy of Sciences, 807*, 329–339. doi:10.1111/j.1749-6632.1997.tb51930.x

Kovács, G. L., Sarnyai, Z., & Szabó, G. (1998). Oxytocin and addiction: A review. *Psychoneuroendocrinology, 23*, 945–962.

Kozisek, M. E., Middlemas, D., & Bylund, D. B. (2008). Brain-derived neurotrophic factor and its receptor tropomyosin-related kinase B in the mechanism of action of antidepressant therapies. *Pharmacology & Therapeutics, 117*, 30–51. doi:10.1016/j.pharmthera.2007.07.001

Krishnan, V., & Nestler, E. J. (2008, October 16). The molecular neurobiology of depression. *Nature, 455*, 894–902. doi:10.1038/nature07455

Kroes, R. A., Burgdorf, J., Otto, N. J., Panksepp, J., & Moskal, J. R. (2007). Social defeat, a paradigm of depression in rats that elicits 22-kHz vocalizations, preferentially activates the cholinergic signaling pathway in the periaqueductal gray. *Behavioural Brain Research, 182*, 290–300. doi:10.1016/j.bbr.2007.03.022

Levinson, D. F. (2006). The genetics of depression: A review. *Biological Psychiatry, 60*, 84–92. doi:10.1016/j.biopsych.2005.08.024

Mayberg, H. S. (2009). Targeted electrode-based modulation of neural circuits for depression. *Journal of Clinical Investigation, 119*, 717–725. doi:10.1172/JCI38454

Mayberg, H. S., Lozano, A. M., Voon, V., McNeely, H. E., Seminowicz, D., Hamani, C., . . . Kennedy, S. H. (2005). Deep brain stimulation for treatment-resistant depression. *Neuron, 45*, 651–660. doi:10.1016/j.neuron.2005.02.014

McEwen, B. S. (2007). Physiology and neurobiology of stress and adaptation: Central role of the brain. *Physiological Reviews, 87*, 873–904. doi:10.1152/physrev.00041.2006

McLaughlin, J. P., Li, S., Valdez, J., Chavkin, T. A., & Chavkin, C. (2006). Social defeat stress-induced behavioral responses are mediated by the endogenous kappa opioid system. *Neuropsychopharmacology, 31*, 1241–1248. doi:10.1038/sj.npp.1300872

Miller, A. H., Maletic, V., & Raison, C. L. (2009). Inflammation and its discontents: The role of cytokines in the pathophysiology of major depression. *Biological Psychiatry, 65*, 732–741. doi:10.1016/j.biopsych.2008.11.029

Moskal, J. R., Burgdorf, J., Kroes, R. A., Brudzynski, S. M., & Panksepp, J. (2011). A novel NMDA receptor glycine-site partial agonist, GLYX-13, has therapeutic potential for the treatment of autism. *Neuroscience & Biobehavioral Reviews, 35,* 1982–1988. doi:10.1016/j.neubiorev.2011.06.006

Mu, P., Neumann, P. A., Panksepp, J., Schlüter, O. M., & Dong, Y. (2011). Exposure to cocaine alters dynorphin-mediated regulation of excitatory synaptic transmission in nucleus accumbens neurons. *Biological Psychiatry, 69,* 228–235. doi:10.1016/j. biopsych.2010.09.014

Nelson, E. E., & Panksepp, J. (1998). Brain substrates of infant–mother attachment: Contributions of opioids, oxytocin, and norepinephrine. *Neuroscience & Biobehavioral Reviews, 22,* 437–452. doi:10.1016/S0149-7634(97)00052-3

Nestler, E. J., & Carlezon, W. A., Jr. (2006). The mesolimbic dopamine reward circuit in depression. *Biological Psychiatry, 59,* 1151–1159. doi:10.1016/j.biopsych. 2005.09.018

Nocjar, C., Zhang, J., Feng, P., & Panksepp, J. (2012). The social defeat animal model of depression shows diminished levels of orexin in mesocortical regions of the dopamine system, and of dynorphin and orexin in the hypothalamus. *Neuroscience, 218,* 138–153. doi:10.1016/j.neuroscience.2012.05.033

Normansell, L., & Panksepp, J. (2011). Glutamatergic modulation of separation distress: Profound emotional effects of excitatory amino acids in chicks. *Neuroscience & Biobehavioral Reviews, 35,* 1890–1901. doi:10.1016/j.neubiorev.2011.06.004

Panksepp, J. (1981). Brain opioids: A neurochemical substrate for narcotic and social dependence. In S. Cooper (Ed.), *Progress in theory in psychopharmacology* (pp. 149–175). London, England: Academic Press.

Panksepp, J. (1982). Toward a general psychobiological theory of emotions. *Behavioral and Brain Sciences, 5,* 407–467.

Panksepp, J. (1992). Oxytocin effects on emotional processes: Separation distress, social bonding, and relationships to psychiatric disorders. *Annals of the New York Academy of Sciences, 652,* 243–252. doi:10.1111/j.1749-6632.1992.tb34359.x

Panksepp, J. (1998). *Affective neuroscience: The foundations of human and animal emotion.* New York, NY: Oxford University Press.

Panksepp, J. (2003a). Can anthropomorphic analyses of "separation cries" in other animals inform us about the emotional nature of social loss in humans? *Psychological Review, 110,* 376–388. doi:10.1037/0033-295X.110.2.376

Panksepp, J. (2003b, October 10). Feeling the pain of social loss. *Science, 302,* 237–239. doi:10.1126/science.1091062

Panksepp, J. (2004). (Ed.). *Textbook of biological psychiatry.* Hoboken, NJ: Wiley.

Panksepp, J. (2005a). Feelings of social loss: The evolution of pain and the ache of a broken heart. In R. Ellis & N. Newton (Eds.), *Consciousness and emotions* (Vol. 1, pp. 23–55). Amsterdam, the Netherlands: Benjamin.

Panksepp, J. (2005b). Why does separation distress hurt? A comment on MacDonald and Leary (2005). *Psychological Bulletin, 131,* 224–230. doi:10.1037/0033-2909. 131.2.224

Panksepp, J. (2006). Emotional endophenotypes in evolutionary psychiatry. *Progress in Neuro-Psychopharmacology and Biological Psychiatry, 30*, 774–784. doi:10.1016/j.pnpbp.2006.01.004

Panksepp, J. (2007). Can PLAY diminish ADHD and facilitate the construction of the social brain? *Journal of the Canadian Academy of Child and Adolescent Psychiatry, 10*, 56–66.

Panksepp, J. (2009). Brain emotional systems and qualities of mental life: From animal models of affect to implications for psychotherapeutics. In D. Fosha, D. J. Siegel, & M. F. Solomon (Eds.), *The healing power of emotion: Affective neuroscience, development and clinical practice* (pp. 1–26). New York, NY: Norton.

Panksepp, J. (2010). The neurobiology of social loss in animals: Some keys to the puzzle of psychic pain in humans. In G. MacDonald & L. A. Jensen-Campbell (Eds.), *Social pain: Neuropsychological and health implications of loss and exclusion* (pp. 11–52). Washington, DC: American Psychological Association.

Panksepp, J., & Biven, L. (2012). *The archaeology of mind.* New York, NY: Norton.

Panksepp, J., Herman, B. H., Vilberg, T., Bishop, P., & DeEskinazi, F. G. (1980). Endogenous opioids and social behavior. *Neuroscience & Biobehavioral Reviews, 4*, 473–487. doi:10.1016/0149-7634(80)90036-6

Panksepp, J., & Moskal, J. (2008). Dopamine and SEEKING: Subcortical "reward" systems and appetitive urges. In A. Elliot (Ed.), *Handbook of approach and avoidance motivation* (pp. 67–87). New York, NY: Taylor & Francis.

Panksepp, J., Normansell, L. A., Herman, B., Bishop, P., & Crepeau, L. (1988). Neural and neurochemical control of the separation distress call. In J. D. Newman (Ed.), *The physiological control of mammalian vocalizations* (pp. 263–299). New York, NY: Plenum. doi:10.1007/978-1-4613-1051-8_15

Panksepp, J., & Watt, J. (2011). Why does depression hurt? Ancestral primary-process separation-distress (PANIC) and diminished brain reward (SEEKING) processes in the genesis of depressive affect. *Psychiatry, 74*, 5–13. doi:10.1521/psyc.2011.74.1.5

Pereira Do Carmo, G., Stevenson, G. W., Carlezon, W. A., & Negus, S. S. (2009). Effects of pain- and analgesia-related manipulations on intracranial self-stimulation in rats: Further studies on pain-depressed behavior. *Pain, 144*, 170–177. doi:10.1016/j.pain.2009.04.010

Rush, A. J. (2007). STAR*D: What have we learned? *American Journal of Psychiatry, 164*, 201–204. doi:10.1176/appi.ajp.164.2.201

Rush, A. J., Trivedi, M., & Fava, M. (2003). Depression, IV: STAR*D treatment trial for depression. *American Journal of Psychiatry, 160*, 237. doi:10.1176/appi.ajp.160.2.237

Schildkraut, J. J. (1965). The catecholamine hypothesis of affective disorders: A review of supportive evidence. *American Journal of Psychiatry, 122*, 509–522.

Schläepfer, T. E., Cohen, M. X., Frick, C., Kosel, M., Brodesser, D., Axmacher, N., . . . Sturm, V. (2008). Deep brain stimulation to reward circuitry alleviates anhedonia in refractory major depression. *Neuropsychopharmacology, 33*, 368–377. doi:10.1038/sj.npp.1301408

Schoene-Bake, J. C., Parpaley, Y., Weber, B., Panksepp, J., Hurwitz, T. A., & Coenen, V. A. (2010). Tractographic analysis of historical lesion surgery for depression. *Neuropsychopharmacology, 35*, 2553–2563. doi:10.1038/npp.2010.132

Shedler, J. (2010). Efficacy of psychodynamic psychotherapy. *American Psychologist, 65*, 98–109. doi:10.1037/a0018378

Solms, M., & Panksepp, J. (2010). Why depression feels bad. In E. Perry, D. Collerton, F. LeBeau, & H. Ashton (Eds.), *New horizons in the neuroscience of consciousness* (pp. 169–179). Amsterdam, the Netherlands: Benjamin.

Swain, J. E., Lorberbaum, J. P., Kose, S., & Strathearn, L. (2007). Brain basis of early parent–infant interactions: Psychology, physiology, and in vivo functional neuroimaging studies. *Journal of Child Psychology and Psychiatry, 48*, 262–287. doi:10.1111/j.1469-7610.2007.01731.x

Tenore, P. L. (2008). Psychotherapeutic benefits of opioid agonist therapy. *Journal of Addictive Diseases, 27*, 49–65. doi:10.1080/10550880802122646

Uvnäs-Moberg, K. (1998). Oxytocin may mediate the benefits of positive social interaction and emotions. *Psychoneuroendocrinology, 23*, 819–835.

Watt, D., & Panksepp, J. (2009). Depression: An evolutionarily conserved mechanism to terminate separation distress? A review of aminergic, peptidergic, and neural network perspectives. *Neuropsychoanalysis, 11*, 7–51.

Wilhelm, S., Buhlmann, U., Tolin, D. F., Meunier, S. A., Pearlson, G. D., Reese, H. E., . . . Rauch, S. L. (2008). Augmentation of behavior therapy with D-cycloserine for obsessive-compulsive disorder. *American Journal of Psychiatry, 165*, 335–341. doi:10.1176/appi.ajp.2007.07050776

Wöhr, M., Kehl, M., Borta, A., Schänzer, A., Schwarting, R. K., & Höglinger, G. U. (2009). New insights into the relationship of neurogenesis and affect: Tickling induces hippocampal cell proliferation in rats emitting appetitive 50-kHz ultrasonic vocalizations. *Neuroscience, 163*, 1024–1030. doi:10.1016/j.neuroscience.2009.07.043

Wright, J. S., & Panksepp, J. (2012). An evolutionary framework to understand foraging, wanting, and desire: The neuropsychology of the SEEKING system. *Neuropsychoanalysis, 14*, 5–39.

Zarate, C. A., Jr., Singh, J. B., Carlson, P. J., Brutsche, N. E., Ameli, R., Luckenbaugh, D. A., . . . Manji, H. K. (2006). A randomized trial of an N-methyl-D-aspartate antagonist in treatment-resistant major depression. *Archives of General Psychiatry, 63*, 856–864. doi:10.1001/archpsyc.63.8.856

Zellner, M. R., Watt, D. F., Solms, M., & Panksepp, J. (2011). Affective neuroscientific and neuropsychoanalytic approaches to two intractable psychiatric problems: Why depression feels so bad and what addicts really want. *Neuroscience & Biobehavioral Reviews, 35*, 2000–2008. doi:10.1016/j.neubiorev.2011.01.003

3

ROMANTIC LOVE, PAIR-BONDING, AND THE DOPAMINERGIC REWARD SYSTEM

BIANCA P. ACEVEDO AND ARTHUR P. ARON

Romantic love is a multifaceted fundamental human experience. It is a basic drive associated with our physiology, the workings of our minds, our emotions, and our sense of connectedness. Love is also deeply embedded in our social world. This was also true of our ancestors, as evidenced by love's presence in works of art and scriptures dating back thousands of years. Indeed, romantic love is an important part of our evolutionary heritage, and it expands beyond humans to other species that instinctually form and maintain monogamous pair-bonds. Recently, we have garnered evidence of love's universality in humans through brain imaging studies that showed similar neural patterns for romantic love among individuals in Eastern and Western cultures, among those newly in love and in long-term love, and even in the context of romantic rejection. Romantic love is associated with feelings of euphoria, connection, and inspiration. Simultaneously, the attachment features associated with pair-bonds provide couples with a sense of calm, ease, and the feeling that "all is right in the world." Indeed, the drives to love and pair-bond are fundamental human

http://dx.doi.org/10.1037/14250-004
Mechanisms of Social Connection: From Brain to Group, M. Mikulincer and P. R. Shaver (Editors)

drives and powerful natural rewards. As such, when these basic needs are not met, it is common to experience depression and anxiety; emotional, eating, and sleeping disruptions; intrusive thinking; and even suicidal tendencies.

Humans (and other animals) are wired for love and attachment. There are different types of attachment bonds (e.g., pair-bond and parent–infant bonds), and although they differ in key ways (e.g., the presence or absence of sex drive), they do seem to share common behaviors and biological substrates (e.g., C. S. Carter, 1998; Fisher, 1992; Hazan & Shaver, 1987; Mikulincer & Shaver, 2007). This idea has been supported by neuroimaging research showing overlapping patterns of neural activation for different types of love (e.g., Acevedo, Aron, Fisher, & Brown, 2012a; Bartels & Zeki, 2004).

Pair-bonds are unique in that they include sexual attraction and the drive to mate. They support reproduction (in heterosexual couples), biparental care of offspring, familial stability, and the well-being of individuals (Aron & Henkemeyer, 1995; Masuda, 2003; O'Leary, Acevedo, Aron, Huddy, & Mashek, 2012; Simpson, Campbell, & Berscheid, 1986). Lasting pair-bonds seem to be one adaptation to keep humans together. Couples may provide each other with constant love, affection, companionship, support, and care. The pair-bond is also unique because inherent in it are many memories of a life built together—the birth of a child, travels together, a wedding day, quiet moments of walking along the beach, supporting each other through illness. It is clear that our social bonds enrich life in infinite ways. They infuse us with meaning, hope, and revitalization in times of need, celebration, and play.

Increasingly over recent decades, scientists have started to investigate romantic love—a phenomenon that was once relegated to poets and mystics— with sophisticated methodologies, such as functional magnetic resonance imaging (fMRI), neurobiological markers (e.g., hormones), and animal models (e.g., testing relationship processes in nonhuman primates and rodent mammals; see Bales, Mason, Catana, Cherry, & Mendoza, 2007; see also Chapter 1, this volume). In the present chapter, we review fMRI research on romantic love and pair-bonding in humans. We discuss findings related to the brain's mesolimbic dopamine reward system, which sustains behaviors needed for survival of the species (e.g., feeding, mating) but also responds to other stimuli, such as monetary rewards and addictive substances. Finally, we discuss how integrating knowledge concerning reward system processes that mediate romantic love and pair-bonding may elucidate knowledge on addiction.

RESEARCH ON THE NEURAL CORRELATES OF ROMANTIC LOVE

In the past 10 years, several studies have utilized fMRI to investigate the neural basis of romantic love and relationship processes. These studies have shown that romantic love—early-stage, long-term, and even following a breakup—is associated with activation of the brain's reward system (e.g., Acevedo et al., 2012a; Aron et al., 2005; Fisher, Brown, Aron, Strong, & Mashek, 2010).

The first two studies that measured the neural correlates of early-stage romantic love were carried out by research teams in the United States and the United Kingdom (Aron et al., 2005; Bartels & Zeki, 2000). Both studies showed research participants facial images of their romantic partners and friends or familiar acquaintances (who served as controls). The main findings revealed brain activations specific to viewing the partner in key areas of the dopaminergic reward system; namely, the ventral tegmental area, caudate nucleus, and putamen.

Ortigue, Bianchi-Demicheli, Hamilton, and Grafton (2007) measured the neural correlates of early-stage romantic love with fMRI. However, they implemented a different paradigm in which 36 women were subliminally shown concepts that were related to their partner, a male friend, or a life passion (e.g., a hobby). Even with a different experimental paradigm, previous findings were replicated, showing activation of the ventral tegmental area and caudate nucleus specific to the partner (compared with the friend and hobby). In addition, this study suggests that information processing related to a romantic partner may occur rapidly and below the level of conscious perception, as the stimuli were presented subliminally.

Evidence for reward system activation in the context of early-stage romantic love has also been found in cross-cultural samples and for both same-sex and opposite-sex relationships. One study carried out in China replicated procedures used by Aron et al. (2005), recruiting undergraduate couples who had been together for about 7 months on average and who reported intense early-stage romantic love. Participants in China also showed reward system activation in response to facial images of their partners relative to those of a familiar acquaintance (Xu et al., 2011). In a study carried out in Germany, researchers compared brain activations in individuals who had been in love for about 6 months with those of individuals who were experiencing grief following a recent breakup with a romantic partner (Stoessel et al., 2011). Consistent with previous studies, individuals who are happily in love showed significant activation of reward centers, such as the caudate, in response to facial images of their beloved. In yet another study carried out in the United Kingdom, researchers compared brain activity in response to romantic part-ners among individuals in same-sex and opposite-sex relationships of about 3.7 years duration. Results showed that activation of the ventral tegmental area and caudate nucleus for romantic partners did not differ by gender or sexual orientation (Zeki & Romaya, 2010).

Studies have also measured the neural correlates of romantic love in other contexts, such as in long-term pair-bonding, in relationship breakup, and in response to pain. Acevedo et al. (2012a) replicated procedures used by Aron et al. (2005) to examine long-term romantic love in a sample married 20 years on average. The study revealed commonalities in brain activations for early-stage and long-term romantic love in key areas of the dopamine reward system (e.g., the ventral tegmental area and caudate; the mid-insula, which is involved in emotion and visceral processing). In addition, the study revealed commonalities in regions such as the posterior hippocampus, an area implicated in memory of primary rewards, hunger, and satiation (e.g., Fernández & Kroes, 2010). Reward system activations commonly associated with maternal love were also found in the context of long-term relationships in key areas (e.g., the substantia nigra, caudate, putamen, and globus pallidus); in an area rich in serotonin receptors (dorsal raphe region) and important for mood regulation (e.g., anxiety and intrusive thinking); in areas involved in emotion and visceral processing (the mid-insula and the insular cortex); and in areas important for attention, arousal, and pain regulation (the anterior and posterior cingulate).

Researchers have also investigated neural activations in lovers who had recently experienced a breakup (e.g., Fisher et al., 2010; Najib, Loberbaum, Kose, Bohning, & George, 2004). It is known that mammals may experience continued "longing for union" with a beloved in the context of rejection or loss; this is often associated with unwanted physiological states (e.g., depression, anxiety, suicide, sleep disturbances, intrusive thinking) while the attachment system adapts to the absence of the beloved (e.g., Sbarra & Hazan, 2008). We discuss this later in relation to research on addiction.

ROMANTIC LOVE, DOPAMINE, AND REWARD

Dopamine release in the brain's reward system is associated with approach-related behaviors toward a stimulus (e.g., Schultz, 2001). This involves a variety of processes such as learning and motivation to seek out a given reward, regardless of whether it is affectively pleasant or unpleasant. Research by Berridge and Robinson (1998) suggests that brain mechanisms involved in "liking or disliking" something (implicit emotion) and "wanting" something (implicit motivation) are distinct and that "liking" (pleasure) is not necessary for "wanting." Thus, even when lovers experience obstacles, challenges, or rejection, they may continue to crave their beloved and work to be united with him or her.

Numerous studies have shown the importance of the ventral tegmental area and caudate nucleus, not only in romantic love but also in motivation, reinforcement learning, and decision making (e.g., R. M. Carter, MacInnes, Huettel, & Adcock, 2009; D'Ardenne, McClure, Nystrom, & Cohen, 2008). The ventral tegmental area is centrally placed in a motivational/reward network associated with behaviors necessary for survival (e.g., Camara, Rodriguez-

Fornells, Ye, & Munte, 2009). Activation of dopamine-rich sites, such as the ventral tegmental area and caudate, occurs in response to rewards such as food (e.g., Hare, O'Doherty, Camerer, Schultz, & Rangel, 2008), monetary gains (e.g., Delgado, Locke, Stenger, & Fiez, 2003), cocaine and alcohol (e.g., Heinz et al., 2004; Risinger et al., 2005), and other highly motivational stimuli (e.g., Knutson & Greer, 2008). Recruitment of the mesolimbic dopamine reward system for romantic love is consistent with descriptions of romantic love as a desire for union with another person. Activation of the dopamine system suggests that, beyond desire, the romantic partner evokes responses associated with reinforcement learning. Thus, individuals are motivated to approach the relationship partner and engage in behaviors that support relationship maintenance.

The caudate (or dorsal striatum) is another key structure of the meso-limbic dopamine system identified across studies of romantic love. It is associated with motor and cognitive control and with goal-directed behavior (e.g., O'Doherty et al., 2004). The caudate shows increased dopamine release in association with expecting monetary rewards (e.g., Knutson, Fong, Adams, Varner, & Hommer, 2001). Goal-directed behavior is necessary to attain rewards. In the context of romantic love, activation of the caudate may also reflect behaviors, such as seeking proximity, working to make one's partner happy, and rejecting unfamiliar conspecifics (e.g., Fisher, 1998), that are necessary to initiate, form, maintain, and protect a pair-bond (e.g., Aragona, Liu, Curtis, Stephan, & Wang, 2003; Wang, Hulihan, & Insel, 1997; Winslow, Hastings, Carter, Harbaugh, & Insel, 1993).

Activation of the caudate in the context of romantic love is particularly interesting, as it responds to visual information (e.g., Hikosaka, Takikawa, & Kawagoe, 2000). Indeed, research suggests that romantic partners elicit attraction and focused attention, particularly to the face (e.g., Fisher, 1998; Zeki, 2007).

Correlations With the Passionate Love Scale

Numerous studies investigating the neural correlates of romantic love have revealed associations with a well-validated and widely used scale, the Passionate Love Scale (Hatfield & Sprecher, 1986). Studies of early-stage romantic love reported that scores in the Passionate Love Scale were positively correlated with activation in regions including the right anteromedial caudate body and the septum-fornix (Aron et al., 2005) and the ventral tegmental area, caudate nucleus, angular gyrus, insula, parahippocampal gyrus, and frontal gyrus (Ortigue et al., 2007). For long-term romantic love, scores in the Passionate Love Scale were positively associated with activations in the medial caudate, septum-fornix, putamen, posterior cingulate, and posterior hippocampus

(Acevedo et al., 2012a). In the context of romantic rejection, these scores were significantly correlated with activations in the caudate and septum-fornix (Fisher et al., 2010).

The correlations of scores in the Passionate Love Scale and brain activity reported in these studies were striking, given the limited range of these scores among participants selected for being strongly in love. Moreover, the fact that some results replicated across samples, stages of love (early vs. long-term love and even following breakup), and experimental paradigms (facial images vs. subliminal stimuli) provides strong evidence of the association between passionate love scores and activation of specific brain regions, such as the septum-fornix (found in three of the four studies). Acevedo et al. (2012a) carried out further analyses of the Passionate Love Scale, separating obsession-related items (e.g., "I feel I can't control my thoughts, they are obsessively on my partner") from romantic love items ("I will love my partner forever"), and found that activation of the septum-fornix was distinctly related to obsession-related items of the Passionate Love Scale. Lesion studies with rats suggest that the septum-fornix is implicated in anxiety reduction (e.g., Decker, Curzon, & Brioni, 1995; Degroot & Treit, 2004). Human studies suggest that the septum/fornix is implicated in episodic and recall memory (rather than working and recognition memory; e.g., Vann et al., 2008).

Correlations With Marital Satisfaction

Numerous studies have established links between relationship (or marital) satisfaction and health (e.g., Kiecolt-Glaser, Glaser, Cacioppo, & Malarkey, 1998; see Proulx, Helms, & Buehler, 2007, for a meta-analysis). Responsiveness to a close other's needs involves attending to and empathizing with the person, approaching him or her, responding appropriately to the other's emotional or cognitive states, and deriving a sense of reward from such interactions (which enables learning and continuation of the behavior).

Imaging research has begun to show how brain processes mediate the various processes involved in responding to a relationship partner's needs. For example, in an fMRI study of providing support (by holding the partner's arm) to a loved one, 20 individuals in long-term relationships were scanned while their partner (or a stranger) stood beside them receiving unpleasant electric shocks (Inagaki & Eisenberger, 2012). The study showed that participants who provided support to their loved one showed greater activation in the ventral striatum region of the reward system. In addition, the reward activations were stronger for individuals who reported better support-giving and social connection with their partners.

In another fMRI study of support, researchers examined effects of receiving support (Coan, Schaefer, & Davidson, 2006). The study showed that holding a spouse's hand while receiving shocks resulted in attenuation of the threat and stress response. An interesting caveat is that the attenuation-of-threat response was stronger for individuals reporting greater marital satisfaction.

Acevedo, Aron, Fisher, and Brown (2012b) also examined the neural correlates of marital satisfaction in a group of 17 individuals in happy, long-term marriages. They found positive correlations between marital satisfaction and activation of brain regions involved in reward processing and motivation (e.g., the ventral tegmental area). In addition, findings showed stronger activation of regions reflecting stress control, emotion regulation, and empathy and in the mirror system for those reporting greater marital satisfaction. The idea that relationship partners elicit activation of brain areas related to empathy has been supported in other fMRI studies (e.g., Singer et al., 2004, 2006), and these activations appear to be moderated by relationship satisfaction.

Acevedo et al. (2012b) also found that relationship satisfaction was negatively correlated with brain activity in the subcallosal cingulate gyrus, an area that is less active during states of satiation (e.g., Small et al., 2003) and more active during states of major depression (e.g., Lozano et al., 2008). This finding has been replicated in at least two other samples of pair-bonded individuals (newlywed and newly in love; Acevedo, Aron, Gross, Xu, & Ralte, 2010; Xu et al., 2012), and it highlights how brain mechanisms mediate the link between relationship quality and health.

NEURAL CORRELATES OF PAIR-BONDING OVER TIME

Several studies of romantic love have examined regional brain activations as a function of relationship length. These results may reflect the establishment and maintenance of pair-bonds. Fisher et al. (2010) and Aron et al. (2005) both reported time-related activation of the anterior cingulate for their studies assessing romantic love among individuals who were either rejected or newly in love, respectively. The anterior cingulate is implicated in focused attention (e.g., Bush, Luu, & Posner, 2000; Ursu, Stenger, Shear, Jones, & Carter, 2003) and in cocaine craving (e.g., Risinger et al., 2005).

Aron et al. (2005) also reported greater activation of the reward system in the area of the ventral putamen/pallidum associated with longer relationships. Consistent with this finding, Fisher et al. (2010) found weaker activation of the ventral pallidum for individuals with longer times since a relationship breakup. The ventral pallidum is an area that integrates sensory, emotional, and cognitive information and appropriate motor responses. It is rich in receptors for vasopressin, a hormone associated with monogamous pair-bonding in rodents (e.g., Insel, Wang, & Ferris, 1994; Young, Lim, Gingrich, & Insel, 2001). It has also been linked with alcohol consumption and cocaine-seeking behavior (e.g., Childress et al., 2008; Kemppainen, Raivio, Suo-Yrjo, & Kiianmaa, 2012), hunger and satiation signals (e.g., Smith, Tindell, Aldridge, & Berridge, 2009), and mood disorders (e.g., Murrough et al., 2011; Prossin, Love, Koeppe, Zubieta, & Silk, 2010). This suggests that the ventral pallidum may be a key area linking attachment and addiction.

For long-term pair-bonds, correlations with years married were seen in areas of the accumbens and the periacqueductal gray. Activations in nearby regions of the accumbens were found in studies of individuals grieving following a breakup (e.g., Fisher et al., 2010; Najib et al., 2004) or the death of a loved one (O'Connor et al., 2008). Activation in this area has also been associated with cocaine-induced highs (Risinger et al., 2005). Activation in the area of the accumbens in association with years married may reflect the reinforcing properties of the marriage. In other words, it may reflect what keeps spouses coming back for more, even after decades of marriage. Activation of the periacqueductal gray is also interesting in the context of long-term pair-bonds, as it has been found in numerous studies of parental attachment to infants (e.g., Bartels & Zeki, 2004). More important, the periacqueductal gray is part of the brain's pain system and is rich in receptors for oxytocin, vasopressin, and opioids (Jenkins, Ang, Hawthorn, Rossor, & Iversen, 1984; Loup, Tribollet, Dubois-Dauphin, Pizzolato, & Dreifuss, 1989; Peckys & Landwehrmeyer, 1999). As such, activation of the periacqueductal gray as a function of time highlights its association as part of the human attachment system. Although this is highly speculative, it may be that the attachment bond (and calm, ease, and pain-relieving properties associated with the partner) strengthens with time.

The results concerning brain areas associated with relationship length are important for pair-bonding research because they provide clues about the unfolding of human pair-bonding as relationships are initiated (e.g., Aron et al., 2005), dissolved (e.g., Fisher et al., 2010) and sustained over time (e.g., Acevedo et al., 2012a). Moreover, by integrating knowledge of the neural underpinnings of the human attachment system with new discoveries in addiction research, scientists can gain important insights for alleviating problems related to addiction and suffering from the loss of a loved one. For example, as described above, some key neural sites may be critical for emotional bonding (both romantic and parental) and addiction.

Finally, by highlighting the shared neural circuitry between attachment and addiction, we revisit a hypothesis that substance use in mammals may reflect attempts to ameliorate natural neurobiological processes associated with broken or lost attachment bonds (e.g., Flores, 2001; Lewis, Amini, & Lannon, 2000; MacLean, 1990). Other research suggests that human brain development is largely influenced by nurturing attachment (e.g., Siegel, 1999). When adequate nurture is not provided in early childhood, brain development is affected, as reflected in differences in the brain's dopaminergic reward circuits and opioid-rich attachment centers (among others such as serotonin and oxytocin). As such, individuals with disruptions in early attachment often respond to the environment in less adaptive ways. For example, because they have not developed self-soothing and regulatory mechanisms early on, individuals may be more susceptible to substance use to self-regulate. Indeed, there is a critical link between attachment and addiction.

By understanding the similarity in neural circuitry in attachment bonds and addiction, program developers and policymakers may utilize this knowledge in helping individuals overcome unwanted addictions. By increasing their awareness and knowledge of the close tie between addiction and attachment, health care providers, therapists, researchers, funding agencies, and intervention and treatment program developers may put close relationships front and center in their efforts to help individuals overcome addictions, unresolved grief, and trauma.

CONCLUSION

Results from a variety of studies examining romantic love and conducted around the globe consistently show involvement of the brain's dopaminergic reward system, which is important for motivation and approach-related behavior. The findings are robust across procedures, relationship stages, opposite- and same-sex relationships, and cultures. This supports the idea that romantic love is a basic human motive to be united with a specific other person and is a form of "wanting" and "longing" (e.g., Acevedo et al., 2010; Aron & Aron, 1986; Fisher, 1998; Hatfield & Sprecher, 1986). Romantic love is multifaceted. It is associated with behaviors that are necessary for survival and propagation of the species, such as pair-bonding and reproduction, which are associated with states such as euphoria and craving. It is also associated with feelings of calm, acquiescence, and stress buffering.

We also reviewed several studies examining the neural mechanisms mediating the link between pair-bond quality (and relationship satisfaction) and health. These studies suggest that providing support to a loved one is associated with reward-related brain activity (Inagaki & Eisenberger, 2012). Thus, as the support provider experiences some reward, this serves as a reinforcer to continue the behavior. This mechanism serves to promote the well-being of the person in need of support as well as to maintain the pair-bond. Also, receiving support from a loved one is associated with attenuation of stress and neural threat responses. These effects seem to be moderated by perceived relationship quality, such that individuals in more satisfying relationships experience stronger stress buffering (e.g., Coan et al., 2006). Finally, relationship quality is associated with brain regions involved in reward and motivation, stress, emotion regulation, empathy, and mood disorders (Acevedo et al., 2012b). These studies provide a new methodological perspective on human health and highlight mediating processes linking attachment bond quality with physiological, emotional, and psychological well-being. This fits well with previous research linking marital quality and health (e.g., Kiecolt-Glaser et al., 1998) and with earlier observational research on orphaned children and young primates deprived of social bonds (e.g., Bowlby, 1969; Harlow, Dodsworth, & Harlow, 1965; Robertson & Robertson, 1971; Spitz, 1951).

In addition to being implicated in romantic love, pair-bonding, and relationship satisfaction, the dopaminergic reward system is involved in behaviors related to feeding (Hare et al., 2008), monetary gains (D'Ardenne et al., 2008), and consumption of addictive substances such as cocaine and alcohol (e.g., Heinz et al., 2004; Risinger et al., 2005). By highlighting and understanding the shared neural circuitry underlying attachment bonds and addiction, health care providers, researchers, program developers, and policymakers may be positioned to help people recover from addiction, loss, and trauma.

REFERENCES

Acevedo, B. P., Aron, A., Fisher, H., & Brown, L. L. (2012a). Neural correlates of long-term intense romantic love. *Social Cognitive and Affective Neuroscience, 7,* 145–159. doi:10.1093/scan/nsq092

Acevedo, B. P., Aron, A., Fisher, H. E., & Brown, L. L. (2012b). Neural correlates of marital satisfaction and well-being: Reward, empathy, and affect. *Clinical Neuropsychiatry: Journal of Treatment Evaluation, 9,* 20–31.

Acevedo, B. P., Aron, A., Gross, J. J., Xu, X., & Ralte, Z. (2010). *Is love different from "basic" emotions? Valence, complexity, and emotion regulation.* Manuscript under review.

Aragona, B. J., Liu, Y., Curtis, J. T., Stephan, F. K., & Wang, Z. (2003). A critical role for nucleus accumbens dopamine in partner-preference formation in male prairie voles. *Journal of Neuroscience, 23,* 3483–3490.

Aron, A., & Aron, E. (1986). *Love and the expansion of self: Understanding attraction and satisfaction.* New York, NY: Hemisphere.

Aron, A., Fisher, H., Mashek, D. J., Strong, G., Li, H., & Brown, L. I. (2005). Reward, motivation, and emotion systems associated with early-stage intense romantic love. *Journal of Neurophysiology, 94,* 327–337. doi:10.1152/jn.00838.2004

Aron, A., & Henkemeyer, L. (1995). Marital satisfaction and passionate love. *Journal of Social and Personal Relationships, 12,* 139–146. doi:10.1177/0265407595121010

Bales, K. L., Mason, W. A., Catana, C., Cherry, S. R., & Mendoza, S. P. (2007). Neural correlates of pair-bonding in a monogamous primate. *Brain Research, 1184,* 245–253. doi:10.1016/j.brainres.2007.09.087

Bartels, A., & Zeki, S. (2000). The neural basis of romantic love. *NeuroReport, 11*, 3829–3834. doi:10.1097/00001756-200011270-00046

Bartels, A., & Zeki, S. (2004). The neural correlates of maternal and romantic love. *NeuroImage, 21*, 1155–1166. doi:10.1016/j.neuroimage.2003.11.003

Berridge, K. C., & Robinson, T. E. (1998). What is the role of dopamine in reward: Hedonic impact, reward learning, or incentive salience? *Brain Research Reviews, 28*, 309–369. doi:10.1016/S0165-0173(98)00019-8

Bowlby, J. (1969). *Attachment and loss: Vol. 1. Attachment.* London, England: Hogarth.

Bush, G., Luu, P., & Posner, M. I. (2000). Cognitive and emotional influences in anterior cingulate cortex. *Trends in Cognitive Sciences, 4*, 215–222. doi:10.1016/S1364-6613(00)01483-2

Camara, E., Rodriguez-Fornells, A., Ye, Z., & Munte, T. F. (2009). Reward networks in the brain captured by connectivity measures. *Frontiers in Neuroscience, 3*, 350–362. doi:10.3389/neuro.01.034.2009

Carter, C. S. (1998). Neuroendocrine perspectives on social attachment and love. *Psychoneuroendocrinology, 23*, 779–818. doi:10.1016/S0306-4530(98)00055-9

Carter, R. M., MacInnes, J. J., Huettel, S. A., & Adcock, R. A. (2009). Activation in the VTA and nucleus accumbens increases in anticipation of both gains and losses. *Frontiers in Behavioral Neuroscience, 3*.Article 21. doi:10.3389/neuro.08.021.2009

Childress, A. R., Ehrman, R. N., Wang, Z., Li, Y., Sciortino, N., Hakun, J., & O'Brien, C. P. (2008). Prelude to passion: limbic activation by "unseen" drug and sexual cues. *PLoS One, 3*(1), e1506.

Coan, J. A., Schaefer, H. S., & Davidson, R. J. (2006). Lending a hand: Social regulation of the neural response to threat. *Psychological Science, 17*, 1032–1039. doi:10.1111/j.1467-9280.2006.01832.x

D'Ardenne, K., McClure, S. M., Nystrom, L. E., & Cohen, J. D. (2008, February 28). BOLD responses reflecting dopaminergic signals in the human ventral tegmental area. *Science, 319*, 1264–1267. doi:10.1126/science.1150605

Decker, M. W., Curzon, P., & Brioni, J. D. (1995). Influence of separate and combined septal and amygdala lesions on memory, acoustic startle, anxiety, and locomotor activity in rats. *Neurobiology of Learning and Memory, 64*, 156–168. doi:10.1006/nlme.1995.1055

Degroot, A., & Treit, D. (2004). Anxiety is functionally segregated within the septo-hippocampal system. *Brain Research, 1001*, 60–71. doi:10.1016/j.brainres.2003.10.065

Delgado, M. R., Locke, H. M., Stenger, V. A., & Fiez, J. A. (2003). Dorsal striatum responses to reward and punishment: Effects of valence and magnitude manipulations. *Cognitive, Affective, & Behavioral Neuroscience, 3*, 27–38. doi:10.3758/CABN.3.1.27

Fernández, G., & Kroes, M. C. (2010). Protecting endangered memories. *Nature Neuroscience, 13*, 408–410. doi:10.1038/nn0410-408

Fisher, H. E. (1992). *Anatomy of love: The natural history of monogamy, adultery, and divorce*. New York, NY: Norton.

Fisher, H. E. (1998). Lust, attraction, and attachment in mammalian reproduction. *Human Nature, 9*, 23–52. doi:10.1007/s12110-998-1010-5

Fisher, H. E., Brown, L. L., Aron, A., Strong, G., & Mashek, D. (2010). Reward, addiction, and emotion regulation systems associated with rejection in love. *Journal of Neurophysiology, 104*, 51–60. doi:10.1152/jn.00784.2009

Flores, P. J. (2001). Addiction as an attachment disorder: Implications for group therapy. *International Journal of Group Psychotherapy, 51*, 63–81. doi:10.1521/ijgp.51.1.63.49730

Hare, T. A., O'Doherty, J., Camerer, C. F., Schultz, W., & Rangel, A. (2008). Dissociating the role of the orbitofrontal cortex and the striatum in the computation of goal values and prediction errors. *Journal of Neuroscience, 28*, 5623–5630. doi:10.1523/JNEUROSCI.1309-08.2008

Harlow, H. F., Dodsworth, R. O., & Harlow, M. K. (1965). Total social isolation in monkeys. *Proceedings of the National Academy of Sciences of the United States of America, 54*, 90–97.

Hatfield, E., & Sprecher, S. (1986). Measuring passionate love in intimate relations. *Journal of Adolescence, 9*, 383–410. doi:10.1016/S0140-1971(86)80043-4

Hazan, C., & Shaver, P. R. (1987). Romantic love conceptualized as an attachment process. *Journal of Personality and Social Psychology, 52*, 511–524. doi:10.1037/0022-3514.52.3.511

Heinz, A., Siessmeier, T., Wrase, J., Hermann, D., Klein, S., Grüsser-Sinopli, S. M., . . . Bartenstein, P. (2004). Correlation between dopamine D2 receptors in the ventral striatum and central processing of alcohol cues and craving. *American Journal of Psychiatry, 161*, 1783–1789. doi:10.1176/appi.ajp.161.10.1783

Hikosaka, O., Takikawa, Y., & Kawagoe, R. (2000). Role of the basal ganglia in the control of purposeive saccadic eye movements. *Psychological Reviews, 80*, 953–978.

Inagaki, T. K., & Eisenberger, N. I. (2012). Neural correlates of giving support to a loved one. *Psychosomatic Medicine, 74*, 3–7. doi:10.1097/PSY.0b013e3182359335

Insel, T. R., Wang, Z. X., & Ferris, C. F. (1994). Patterns of brain vasopressin receptor distribution associated with social organization in microtine rodents. *Journal of Neuroscience, 14*, 5381–5392.

Jenkins, J. S., Ang, V. T., Hawthorn, J., Rossor, M. N., & Iversen, L. L. (1984). Vasopressin, oxytocin and neurophysins in the human brain and spinal cord. *Brain Research, 291*, 111–117. doi:10.1016/0006-8993(84)90656-5

Kemppainen, H., Raivio, N., Suo-Yrjo, V., & Kiianmaa, K. (2012). Opioidergic modulation of ethanol self-administration in the ventral pallidum. *Alcoholism: Clinical and Experimental Research, 36*, 286–293. doi:10.1111/j.1530-0277.2011.01611.x

Kiecolt-Glaser, J. K., Glaser, R., Cacioppo, C., & Malarkey, W. B. (1998). Marital stress: Immunologic, neuroendocrine, and autonomic correlates. *Annals of the*

New York Academy of Sciences, 840, 656–663. doi:10.1111/j.1749-6632.1998.
tb09604.x

Knutson, B., Fong, G. W., Adams, C. M., Varner, J. L., & Hommer, D. (2001).
Dissociation of reward anticipation and outcome with event-related fMRI.
NeuroReport, 12, 3683–3687. doi:10.1097/00001756-200112040-00016

Knutson, B., & Greer, S. M. (2008). Anticipatory affect: Neural correlates and
consequences for choice. *Philosophical Transactions of the Royal Society of London,
Series B: Biological Sciences, 363,* 3771–3786. doi:10.1098/rstb.2008.0155

Lewis, T., Amini, F., & Lannon, R. (2000). *A general theory of love.* New York, NY:
Random House.

Loup, F. E., Tribollet, E., Dubois-Dauphin, M., Pizzolato, G., & Dreifuss, J. J. (1989).
Localization of oxytocin binding sites in the human brainstem and upper spinal
cord: An auto radiographic study. *Brain Research, 500,* 223–230.

Lozano, A. M., Mayberg, H. S., Giacobbe, P., Hamani, C., Craddock, R. C., &
Kennedy, S. H. (2008). Subcallosal cingulate gyrus deep brain stimulation for
treatment-resistant depression. *Biological Psychiatry, 64,* 461–467. doi:10.1016/
j.biopsych.2008.05.034

MacLean, P. D. (1990). *The triune brain in evolution: Role in paleocerebral functions.*
New York, NY: Plenum Press.

Masuda, M. (2003). Meta-analyses of love scales: Do various love scales measure
the same psychological constructs? *Japanese Psychological Research, 45,* 25–37.
doi:10.1111/1468-5884.00030

Mikulincer, M., & Shaver, P. R. (2007). *Attachment in adulthood: Structure, dynamics,
and change.* New York, NY: Guilford Press.

Murrough, J. W., Henry, S., Hu, J., Gallezot, J.-D., Planeta-Wilson, B., Neumaier, J. F.,
& Neumeister, A. (2011). Reduced ventral striatal/ventral pallidal serotonin1B
receptor binding potential in major depressive disorder. *Psychopharmacology, 213,*
547–553. doi:10.1007/s00213-010-1881-0

Najib, A., Lorberbaum, J. P., Kose, S., Bohning, D. E., & George, M. S. (2004). Regional
brain activity in women grieving a romantic relationship breakup. *American
Journal of Psychiatry, 161,* 2245–2256. doi:10.1176/appi.ajp.161.12.2245

O'Connor, M. F., Wellisch, D. K., Stanton, A. L., Eisenberger, N. I., Irwin, M. R., &
Lieberman, M. D. (2008). Craving love? Enduring grief activates brain's reward
center. *NeuroImage, 42,* 969–972. doi:10.1016/j.neuroimage.2008.04.256

O'Doherty, J., Dayan, P., Schultz, J., Deichmann, R., Friston, K., & Dolan, R. J.
(2004, April 16). Dissociable roles of ventral and dorsal striatum in instrumental conditioning. *Science, 304,* 452–454. doi:10.1126/science.1094285

O'Leary, K. D., Acevedo, B. P., Aron, A., Huddy, L., & Mashek, D. (2012). Is long-term
love more than a rare phenomenon? If so, what are its correlates? *Social Psychological and Personality Science, 3,* 241–249. doi:10.1177/1948550611417015

Ortigue, S., Bianchi-Demicheli, F., Hamilton, A. F., & Grafton, S. T. (2007). The
neural basis of love as a subliminal prime: An event-related fMRI study. *Journal
of Cognitive Neuroscience, 19,* 1218–1230. doi:10.1162/jocn.2007.19.7.1218

Peckys, D., & Landwehrmeyer, G. B. (1999). *Neuroscience, 88*, 1093–1135.

Prossin, A. R., Love, T. M., Koeppe, R. A., Zubieta, J. K., & Silk, K. R. (2010). Dysregulation of regional endogenous opioid function in borderline personality disorder. *American Journal of Psychiatry, 167*, 925–933. doi:10.1176/appi.ajp.2010.09091348

Proulx, C. M., Helms, H. M., & Buehler, C. (2007). Marital quality and personal well-being: A meta-analysis. *Journal of Marriage and Family, 69*, 576–593. doi:10.1111/j.1741-3737.2007.00393.x

Risinger, R. C., Salmeron, B. J., Ross, T. J., Amen, S. L., Sanfilipo, M., Hoffmann, R. G., . . . Stein, E. A. (2005). Neural correlates of high and craving during cocaine self-administration using BOLD fMRI. *NeuroImage, 26*, 1097–1108. doi:10.1016/j.neuroimage.2005.03.030

Robertson, J. & Robertson, J. (1971) Young children in brief separation: A fresh look. *Psychoanalytic Study of the Child, 26*, 264–315.

Sbarra, D. A., & Hazan, C. (2008). Coregulation, dysregulation, self-regulation: An integrative analysis and empirical agenda for understanding adult attachment, separation, loss, and recovery. *Personality and Social Psychology Review, 12*, 141–167. doi:10.1177/1088868308315702

Schultz, W. (2001). Reward signaling by dopamine neurons. *Neuroscientist, 7*, 293–302.

Siegel, D.J. (1999). *The developing mind: Toward a neurobiology of interpersonal experience.* New York, NY: Guilford Press.

Simpson, J. A., B., Campbell, B., & Berscheid, E. (1986). The association between romantic love and marriage: Kephart (1967) twice revisited. *Personality and Social Psychology Bulletin, 12*, 363–372.

Singer, T., Seymour, B., O'Doherty, J., Kaube, H., Dolan, R. J., & Frith, C. D. (2004, February 20). Empathy for pain involves the affective but not sensory components of pain. *Science, 303*, 1157–1162.

Singer, T., Seymour, B., O'Doherty, J. P., Stephan, K. E., Dolan, R. J., & Frith, C. D. (2006, January 26). Empathic neural responses are modulated by the perceived fairness of others. *Nature, 439*, 466–469. doi:10.1038/nature04271

Small, D. M., Gregory, M. D., Mak, Y. E., Gitelman, D., Mesulam, M. M., & Parrish, T. (2003). Dissociation of neural representation of intensity and affective valuation in human gustation. *Neuron, 39*, 701–711. doi:10.1016/S0896-6273(03)00467-7

Smith, K. S., Tindell, A. J., Aldridge, J. W., & Berridge, K. C. (2009). Ventral pallidum roles in reward and motivation. *Behavioural Brain Research, 196*, 155–167. doi:10.1016/j.bbr.2008.09.038

Spitz, R. A. (1951). The psychogenic diseases in infancy: An attempt at their etiologic classification. *Psychoanalytic Study of the Child, 6*, 255–275.

Stoessel, C., Stiller, J., Bleich, S., Boensch, D., Doerfler, A., Garcia, M., . . . Forster, C. (2011). Differences and similarities on neuronal activities of people being happily and unhappily in love: A functional magnetic resonance imaging study. *Neuropsychobiology, 64*, 52–60. doi:10.1159/000325076

Ursu, S., Stenger, V. A., Shear, M. K., Jones, M. R., & Carter, C. S. (2003). Overactive action monitoring in obsessive-compulsive disorder: Evidence from functional magnetic resonance imaging. *Psychological Science, 14*, 347–353. doi:10.1111/1467-9280.24411

Vann, S. D., Denby, C., Love, S., Montaldi, D., Renowden, S., & Coakham, H. B. (2008). Memory loss resulting from fornix and septal damage: Impaired supraspan recall but preserved recognition over a 24-hour delay. *Neuropsychology, 22*, 658–668. doi:10.1037/a0012542

Wang, Z., Hulihan, T. J., & Insel, T. R. (1997). Sexual and social experience is associated with different patterns of behavior and neural activation in male prairie voles. *Brain Research, 767*, 321–332. doi:10.1016/S0006-8993(97)00617-3

Winslow, J. T., Hastings, N., Carter, C. S., Harbaugh, C. R., & Insel, T. R. (1993, October 3). A role of central vasopressin in pair bondings in monogamous prairie voles. *Nature, 365*, 545–548. doi:10.1038/365545a0

Xu, X., Aron, A., Brown, L., Cao, G., Feng, T., & Weng, X. (2011). Reward and motivation systems: A brain mapping study of early-stage intense romantic love in Chinese participants. *Human Brain Mapping, 32*, 249–257. doi:10.1002/hbm.21017

Xu, X., Brown, L., Aron, A., Acevedo, B., Cao, G., Feng, T., & Weng, X. (2012). Brain activations during early-stage intense romantic love associated with relationship outcomes 40 months later. *Neuroscience Letters, 526*, 33-38.

Young, L. J., Lim, M. M., Gingrich, B., & Insel, T. R. (2001). Cellular mechanisms of social attachment. *Hormones and Behavior, 40*, 133–138. doi:10.1006/hbeh.2001.1691

Zeki, S. (2007). The neurobiology of love. *FEBS Letters, 581*, 2575–2579. doi:10.1016/j.febslet.2007.03.094

Zeki, S., & Romaya, J. P. (2010). The brain reaction to viewing faces of opposite- and same-sex romantic partners. *PLoS ONE, 5*, e15802. doi:10.1371/journal.pone.0015802

4

THE VICARIOUS BRAIN

CHRISTIAN KEYSERS AND VALERIA GAZZOLA

Social skills are key to the success of the human species. During homi-nization, the brain was therefore under great pressure to develop mechanisms that enable humans to connect with the minds of other humans and learn from and interact and communicate with them. Here, we explore one specific family of neuronal mechanisms that seem deeply engrained in the architecture of the human brain and make humans intuitively able to connect with the minds of others. In the first section, we review evidence that viewing the actions of others triggers neural representations of one's own actions as if one were actually performing similar actions. We call these visual activations *vicarious motor activations*; the term *vicarious* reflects the fact that one's actions are triggered as if one were in the stead of the person observed. In the second section, we show that viewing others in situations that would make one feel somatosensory sensations vicariously activates brain regions normally involved

The research was supported by a VENI grant (451-09-006) to Valeria Gazzola and a National Initiative for Brain and Cognition grant (056-13-017) to Christian Keysers.

http://dx.doi.org/10.1037/14250-005
Mechanisms of Social Connection: From Brain to Group, M. Mikulincer and P. R. Shaver (Editors)

71

in feeling corresponding somatosensory sensations of one's own. In the third section, we show how brain regions involved in feeling emotions get vicariously activated while one views the emotions of others. We then tie these sections together to show how combining vicarious motor, somatosensory, and emotional activations allows one empathically to get under other people's skin. We explain (a) that these systems do not allow people to truly feel what others feel but rather to project their own states onto others; (b) that Hebbian learning can explain their development; and (c) that they interact with more cognitive brain regions involved in attention, mentalizing, and cognitive control.

VICARIOUS MOTOR ACTIVATIONS

For decades scientists believed that the premotor cortices were exclusively involved in programming an individual's own actions. These motor programs would then be sent to the primary motor cortex, which would execute the programs and make the individual move. On the other hand, scientists believed that the visual system together with areas involved in mentalizing would process the actions of others to code the goals and intentions of others. The discovery of neurons within the premotor cortex that also processed the actions of others was therefore revolutionary. Because it remains generally impossible to study single neurons in humans, single-cell recordings in monkeys remain the foundation upon which human work is interpreted.

Mirror Neurons in Macaque Monkeys

The first evidence for vicarious activations in the primate brain came with the discovery of mirror neurons in monkeys (Gallese, Fadiga, Fogassi, & Rizzolatti, 1996). These neurons, originally found in premotor region F5 of the macaque brain, respond both when the monkey performs a goal-directed action (e.g., grasping) and when it observes another individual perform a similar action (Keysers, 2009). Each neuron in F5 has a restricted set of actions that it programs, with one particular neuron responding when the monkey grasps an object with its hand and another responding when the monkey grasps an object with its hand or mouth. The set of effective motor actions determines the motor tuning. Electrical stimulation of area F5 in monkeys triggers the execution of complex motor behaviors—for example, grasping an object and taking it to the mouth—indicating that this region is indeed involved in motor control of complex actions (Graziano, Taylor, & Moore, 2002). About 10% of the neurons in F5 also respond when the monkey sees or hears similar actions being performed by others (Kohler et al., 2002). The set of observed actions that triggers activity in an F5 neuron can be called its sensory tuning.

In mirror neurons, the sensory and motor tunings must overlap: At least one action must be associated with a discharge in the mirror neuron both when the monkey performs the action and when the monkey sees or hears another individual perform a similar action. How tightly the sensory and motor tunings correspond differs from mirror neuron to mirror neuron. A minority of mirror neurons (about 30%) seem to have very similar tuning during execution and observation, and they are therefore called *strictly congruent* (Gallese et al., 1996). For the majority (about 60%) of mirror neurons, however, the correspondence is less tight, and they are called *broadly congruent* (Gallese et al., 1996; Rozzi, Ferrari, Bonini, Rizzolatti, & Fogassi, 2008). A broadly congruent mirror neuron might, for instance, respond only during the execution of a precision grasp with the hand, but during observation, it might respond to grasping with the hand and the mouth. The effective observed actions in broadly congruent mirror neurons are often actions that have the same goal as the effective executed action (e.g., grasping and therefore obtaining the object).

The combination of broadly and strictly congruent mirror neurons ensures that the premotor cortex of an observing monkey has information about the goal of observed actions, through the activity of both broadly and strictly congruent mirror neurons, and about the specific means associated with the movement, through the activity of strictly congruent mirror neurons (Thioux, Gazzola, & Keysers, 2008). The firing pattern of a mirror neuron can discriminate which of two actions was performed with over 90% accuracy, independently of whether the action was performed by the monkey itself or by another individual (heard or seen; Keysers et al., 2003).

More recent studies have shown that neurons in the inferior parietal lobe have similar properties (Rozzi et al., 2008). In addition, neurons in the dorsal premotor cortex of the monkey seem to respond both when the monkey uses a joystick to move a cursor to a target position and when another monkey does so, with the observer merely witnessing the movement of the cursor (Cisek & Kalaska, 2004). Some neurons in parietal region LIP respond both when a monkey moves its own eyes and when it sees another monkey perform similar eye movements (Shepherd, Klein, Deaner, & Platt, 2009). Most of the brain, however, has not yet been explored for the presence of mirror neurons, so it is possible that mirror neurons exist elsewhere in the monkey's brain (Keysers & Gazzola, 2009). Mirror neurons also exist in songbirds (Prather, Peters, Nowicki, & Mooney, 2008).

Detecting Vicarious Activations in Humans

A number of techniques have been used to explore whether humans exhibit brain activity that suggests the presence of mirror neurons. The most prominent among these techniques are functional magnetic resonance imaging (fMRI), transcranial magnetic stimulation (TMS), and electroencephalography (EEG). A smaller number of studies have also used neurological lesions and single-cell recordings in patients with intractable epilepsy.

fMRI

The most prominent technique for examining a potential human mirror neuron system is fMRI, which is used to measure brain activity when participants perform actions or witness others performing similar actions. Results obtained to date indicate a broad network of voxels (small neural regions) in which participants showed vicarious motor activations. The network includes the ventral premotor cortex and the anterior inferior parietal lobule, regions thought to correspond to areas F5 and PFG in the monkey; the primary somatosensory cortex; the dorsal premotor area; the supplementary motor area; and the cerebellum (Gazzola & Keysers, 2009). This suggests that mirror neurons exist in more brain regions than previously expected (Keysers & Gazzola, 2009), a possibility confirmed by a recent meta-analysis (Caspers, Zilles, Laird, & Eickhoff, 2010). Pattern-classification fMRI has further confirmed not only that the same brain regions are active during action perception and execution but also that they are activated in a similar spatial pattern, providing evidence that the same neural population code is used during perception and execution of movements (Etzel, Gazzola, & Keysers, 2009). When measuring the brain activity of a gesturer and an observer, we found that the brain activity of the observer's mirror neuron system indeed resonates with the brain activity of the gesturer (Schippers, Roebroeck, Renken, Nanetti, & Keysers, 2010).

TMS

TMS has been used in two ways to explore the existence of vicarious motor activations in humans. When single pulses of TMS are given over the primary motor cortex, they trigger muscle activity in the corresponding body parts. This muscle activity is increased when listening to or viewing the actions of others, and it is specifically activated for the muscles involved in the observed actions (Fadiga, Craighero, & Olivier, 2005). To explore which brain regions are necessary for action observation to recruit motor programs, one can also use TMS to interfere with the functioning of particular brain regions. Results suggest that the ventral premotor cortex and the somatosensory cortex are necessary for the sight of actions to modulate the muscle twitch evoked by single pulses of TMS (Avenanti, Bolognini, Maravita, & Aglioti, 2007). Moreover, the perception of actions is impaired after TMS interference with premotor brain regions (Pobric & Hamilton, 2006).

Mu-Suppression

EEG and magnetoencephalography (MEG) measure, through the scalp, electrical currents generated by synchronous activity of populations of neurons. Two rhythms have been associated with the motor system: the mu (8–12 Hz) and beta (~20 Hz) rhythms. Both rhythms have more power when a study participant is at rest than when he or she performs an action. The power in these frequency bands is thus an indicator of how active the sensorimotor system is. Perceiving the actions of others is linked with changes in the power spectrum of the EEG and MEG signals that resemble those associated with executing similar actions. Simultaneous EEG/fMRI experiments have shown that the dorsal premotor and primary somatosensory cortices, which we have suggested are part of the mirror neuron system, are the most likely sources of this mu-suppression (Arnstein, Cui, Keysers, Maurits, & Gazzola, 2011), whereas the ventral premotor cortex is not tightly correlated with trial-by-trial mu-suppression.

Single-Cell Recordings

Rare recordings in the supplementary motor area, presupplementary motor area, and medial temporal lobe of individuals with epilepsy have revealed a small number of neurons that respond specifically when an individual performs one of several actions and also when he or she observes the same action (Mukamel, Ekstrom, Kaplan, Iacoboni, & Fried, 2010). This confirms our claim that the vicarious motor activations extend beyond the ventral premotor and posterior parietal lobes (Gazzola & Keysers, 2009). Some neurons in the supplementary motor area show activation during action execution but show inhibition during action observation. Such neurons may allow a person to suppress automatic imitation of observed actions.

Neurological Lesions

Participants with apraxia and lesions in the premotor cortex have difficulty recognizing the actions of others (Pazzaglia, Smania, Corato, & Aglioti, 2008). The ventral premotor cortex is also involved in mirroring a very specific type of action: facial expressions (van der Gaag, Minderaa, & Keysers, 2007a). Lesions to this area impair the recognition of facial expressions (Adolphs, Damasio, Tranel, Cooper, & Damasio, 2000).

VICARIOUS SOMATOSENSATION

Somatosensation involves the processing of tactile, proprioceptive, and nociceptive (pain) information. In humans and monkeys, the term *somatosensory cortices* has traditionally referred to the anterior parietal cortex and the upper bank (operculum) of the lateral sulcus, two areas that process tactile, proprioceptive, and nociceptive information (Kaas, 2004). The anterior parietal cortex consists of four parallel sectors: cytoarchitectonic Brodmann areas (BAs) 3a, 3b, 1, and 2. In humans, BAs 3a and 3b correspond roughly to the posterior bank of the central sulcus, BA 1 to the crown of the postcentral gyrus, and BA 2 to the anterior bank of the postcentral gyrus. Each of these four areas is known to constitute a separate representation with different connections and functions (see Kaas, 2004, for a review). The primary somatosensory cortex refers to BAs 3a + 3b + 1 + 2.

BA 3a receives proprioceptive information and has close anatomical connections with the motor cortex. BA 3b is the primary area for tactile processing, and it receives its major activating inputs from the ventroposterior nucleus of the thalamus. BA 3b also receives input from nociceptive neurons in the spinal cord and brain stem. BA 1 receives strong activating inputs from BA 3b, and thus it is thought to be involved in a secondary cortical stage of tactile processing. BA 2 receives inputs from BAs 3a, 3b, and 1 and therefore constitutes a third level of cortical processing of tactile and proprioceptive information. This tactile information is combined with proprioceptive inputs from the thalamus. Thus, neurons in BA 2 are especially responsive when objects are actively explored or manipulated with the hands.

The connections between the different areas of the primary somatosensory cortex are reciprocal. BA 2 has direct, reciprocal connections with regions of the fundus of the intraparietal sulcus (area VIP) and the inferior parietal lobule (areas PF/PFG in particular) that combine visual, auditory, and somatosensory information. Some cells in area VIP respond both when a monkey is touched and when it sees another individual being touched in a similar way (Ishida, Nakajima, Inase, & Murata, 2010), whereas some neurons in areas PF/PFG respond both when a monkey performs a goal-directed action and when it sees another individual perform a similar action (Rozzi et al., 2008). Moreover, these posterior parietal regions are thought to constitute the main source of visual and auditory information to mirror neurons in the premotor cortex (Keysers & Perrett, 2004). The fact that these regions also project to BA 2 makes it plausible that BA 2 could demonstrate vicarious activations in response to other individuals' goal-directed actions. From the primary somatosensory cortex, somatosensory information is sent to the secondary somatosensory cortex, which lies in the parietal operculum. Secondary somatosensory cortex also receives inputs from a number of brain regions with cells that respond to visual and auditory input (Keysers, Kaas, & Gazzola, 2010).

For nociception, classically, the primary and secondary somatosensory cortices are thought to process the sensory discriminative aspects (i.e., the intensity and location) of pain. This occurs in parallel with the more affective/

motivational processing of nociceptive input that is thought to take place in the insula and the rostral cingulate gyrus.

Vicarious Tactile Activations

A number of fMRI studies now show that somatosensory cortices might be vicariously activated while an individual watches another individual being touched. In the first such experiment, we touched the legs of participants in a scanner after those participants had watched movie clips either of other people's legs being touched by a rod or, as control stimuli, of the same rod moving too far away from the other people's legs to touch them. Being touched activated the leg representations in both primary and secondary somatosensory cortices. Viewing other people being touched (compared to the control condition) also activated the secondary somatosensory cortex (but not the primary one; Keysers et al., 2004). The secondary somatosensory cortex was also activated when participants watched objects (e.g., rolls of paper) instead of legs being touched (Keysers et al., 2004). Other studies also revealed secondary somatosensory cortex activity in participants seeing film clips of the hands (Ebisch et al., 2008; Schaefer, Xu, Flor, & Cohen, 2009) or the neck and face (Blakemore, Bristow, Bird, Frith, & Ward, 2005) of other people being touched. Vicarious activation in secondary somatosensory cortex could convey a simulation of the quality of touch one would feel if one were touched in a similar way. In contrast to the secondary somatosensory cortex, BA 3 was never activated during the observation of touch, and BA 2 and BA 1 were activated only if the stimulus films showed a human hand delivering the touch (Blakemore et al., 2005) or if the task focused attention on the action of touching (Schaefer et al., 2009). It is likely that this activation vicariously represented the hand delivering the touch rather than the sensations of the person being touched.

The fact that BA 3a and BA 3b are recruited only when we ourselves are being touched could account for why participants who see other people being touched can vicariously activate the secondary somatosensory cortex, as if they themselves were being touched, without being confused about who is actually being touched. About 1% of people, however, experience a vivid sensation of touch on their own body when they see the body of another being touched (Banissy, Kadosh, Maus, Walsh, & Ward, 2009), and these participants also activate their primary somatosensory cortex (probably including BA 3) and secondary somatosensory cortex more strongly than do controls when seeing film clips of other people being touched (Blakemore et al., 2005). This suggests that the degree of vicarious activations in somatosensory brain regions and in particular the involvement of BA 3 can determine the vividness with which one empathically shares what other people are experiencing.

Vicarious Haptics and Proprioceptive Activations

Does the primary somatosensory cortex also help us perceive the actions of other people? As mentioned above, fMRI experiments have shown that BA 2 in particular is consistently activated when a person executes actions and while a person listens to or views the actions of others (Gazzola, Aziz-Zadeh, & Keysers, 2006; Gazzola & Keysers, 2009; Keysers et al., 2010). In contrast to BA 2, the more anterior sectors of the primary somatosensory cortex are rarely and only weakly recruited during the observation of other people's actions. Seeing hand movements with more joint stretching activates BA 2 more strongly (Costantini et al., 2005), and deactivating BA 2 with TMS reduces motor evoked potentials in the hand when seeing such extreme joint stretching (Avenanti et al., 2007). BA 2 is more active when viewing hands manipulate objects (e.g., grasping a cup) than when viewing actions that do not involve objects (Buccino et al., 2001; Pierno et al., 2009). Together, and in accordance with the convergence of tactile and proprioceptive input in BA 2, BA 2 may be particularly involved in vicariously representing the haptic combination of tactile and proprioceptive signals that would arise if the participant manipulated the object in the observed way. This vicarious representation of haptic aspects of actions in BA 2 adds to the vicarious representations of passive touch in the secondary somatosensory cortex. Additionally, executing hand and mouth actions causes activity in dorsal and ventral areas of the primary somatosensory cortex, respectively, and perceiving mouth and hand actions triggers vicarious activity in the corresponding locations (Gazzola et al., 2006). Multivoxel pattern classification of activity data in primary somatosensory cortex during action perception can identify the body part that was used for an observed action performed by another individual (Etzel, Gazzola, & Keysers, 2008). Together, these data suggest that vicarious BA 2 activity can provide fine-grained, somatotopically specific representations of other people's actions.

The simulation of actions would thus involve both simulating the motor output that would be necessary to perform the observed action (as represented in the classic premotor and posterior parietal mirror neuron containing regions) and simulating the haptic somatosensory input that would accompany performance of those actions.

Facial expressions are a special type of action. Experiments that have examined the neural structures involved in both the observation and the execution of dynamic facial expressions concur that, akin to observing hand actions, observing the facial expressions of others also vicariously activates ventral sectors of BA 2 and/or secondary somatosensory cortex that are involved in sensing self-produced facial expressions (van der Gaag, Minderaa, & Keysers, 2007b). Real and virtual TMS lesions in these somatosensory face representations also impair the recognition of facial expressions (Adolphs et al., 2000; Pitcher, Garrido, Walsh, & Duchaine, 2008). This suggests that vicarious somatosensory representations of what it feels like to move the face in the observed way contribute to the recognition of other people's facial expressions.

Vicarious Nociceptive Activations

If we see our partner's face expressing intense pain, we feel deeply distressed. If we see her cut her finger with a sharp kitchen knife, we not only feel distress but often feel compelled to grasp our own finger. About a third of people feel pain on the corresponding part of their own body when they see certain injuries of other people (Osborn & Derbyshire, 2010). Neuroimaging research is now starting to shed light on this multifaceted nature of empathic pain. In brief, this research shows that if all we know is that another person is in pain, we vicariously recruit brain regions involved in the affective experience of pain: the anterior insula and rostral cingulate cortex. Whenever our attention is directed to the somatic cause of the pain of others, BA 1 and BA 2 within primary and secondary somatosensory cortices also become vicariously activated in most experiments (Lamm, Decety, & Singer, 2011).

When observing photographs of injuries (e.g., an athlete breaking his leg), about one third of the population reports feeling pain in the corresponding body part. The remainder reports negative feelings without a sense of somatic pain. An fMRI study showed that primary and secondary somatosensory cortices' vicarious activity was significantly triggered by such images only in those participants experiencing localized vicarious pain (Osborn & Derbyshire, 2010). This finding provides further support for the notion that vicarious activity of primary and secondary somatosensory cortices adds a somatic dimension to social perception.

Taken together, these data indicate that we can share the pain of others in two ways. If all we know is that the observed person is in pain, we share the affective aspects of his or her distress through vicarious activity in the anterior insula and rostral cingulate cortex. If, on the other hand, we focus on the somatic causes of that pain, we additionally share its somatic consequences by vicarious recruitment of BA 1, BA 2, or secondary somatosensory cortex.

VICARIOUS EMOTIONAL ACTIVITY

Brain regions associated with emotions have been found to be vicariously activated while participants perceive the emotional states of others. Viewing facial expressions that signal an emotion, be it disgust (Jabbi, Swart, & Keysers,

2007; Wicker et al., 2003), happiness (Hennenlotter et al., 2005; Jabbi et al., 2007), or a combination of different emotions (Carr, Iacoboni, Dubeau, Mazziotta, & Lenzi, 2003), activates regions of the anterior insula and adjacent frontal operculum (jointly referred to as IFO) involved in experiencing similar emotions. These findings dovetail with findings that viewing stimuli that suggest other people's pain (e.g., facial expressions of pain, symbols indicating that someone else is in pain, or body parts in painful configurations) triggers activity in this region (Lamm et al., 2011). Together, these findings suggest that representations of emotional bodily states in the IFO can be triggered by many sources of information that signal that another individual is experiencing similar emotional states.

Emotional empathy seems not to be restricted to primates. In the late 1950s, Church exposed rats to other rats receiving electrical shocks and found that this disrupted witnessing behavior (Church, 1959). Recently, we came to a similar conclusion. We split rats into four groups, based on having experienced electroshocks in the past or not and on now witnessing another rat receive an electroshock or not. We found that rats previously exposed to electroshocks showed (vicarious) freezing behavior, a sign of fear, when they witnessed another rat experiencing an electroshock (Atsak et al., 2011). This behavior was not simply triggered by distress vocalizations (the playback of which failed to trigger a similar effect) but was triggered by perceiving the complex behavior of a rat that reacts to electroshocks. None of the other groups showed such elevated freezing. This suggests that prior experience is a necessary condition for vicarious fear in rats and that vicarious emotional representations exist in rodents. Rice and Gainer (1962) showed that a rat would vigorously press a lever to release another rat from a distressing situation, suggesting that vicarious distress might motivate prosocial behavior in rodents.

Unlike the actions of other individuals, which can be directly perceived by an observer, the emotions of others cannot be directly seen but must be deduced from expressions and actions (e.g., facial expressions, screams), visible causes (e.g., a syringe penetrating a hand), or more arbitrary cues such as language (e.g., "I'm very sad today"). Anatomically, the IFO receives input from the prefrontal cortex, the motor system, and all sensory modalities. Functional connectivity analyses are now increasingly being used to disentangle which of these sources of input trigger vicarious activity in the IFO in particular cases. While facial expressions are viewed, premotor brain regions involved in producing similar facial expressions (Carr et al., 2003; Hennenlotter et al., 2005; van der Gaag et al., 2007a) seem to play an important role in triggering activity in the IFO (Jabbi & Keysers, 2008). While pain is being deduced from viewing of bodily causes, the superior temporal sulcus seems to play a dominant role (Zaki, Ochsner, Hanelin, Wager, & Mackey, 2007). When one reads about emotions, Broca's area, the temporal pole, and the supplementary motor area play critical roles (Jabbi, Bastiaansen, & Keysers, 2008). Neurological studies confirm that disrupting activity in the IFO or the premotor cortex impairs the recognition of other people's emotions from facial expressions (Adolphs et al., 2000; Adolphs, Tranel, & Damasio, 2003; Calder, Keane, Manes, Antoun, & Young, 2000). Studies also confirm that impairing the primary and secondary somatosensory representations of the face that become active when we feel the consequences of our own facial expressions (Hennenlotter et al., 2005; van der Gaag et al., 2007a) impairs facial affect recognition. Together, these data suggest that the IFO may work in concert with brain regions involved in the mirror neuron system and vicarious somatosensory activations to trigger representations of emotions that match those of the people around us.

In this kind of research, participants often view the emotions of people they have never met, and they activate representations of their own emotions. This suggests that the brain spontaneously triggers vicarious representations when seeing the emotions of others. The strength of these vicarious representations correlates with how empathic participants report being in their everyday lives (Jabbi et al., 2007; Singer et al., 2004), suggesting that the vicarious activations are a neural correlate of what people call empathy. A number of factors can reduce this spontaneously occurring vicarious activation. If one knows that the other person has been unfair (Singer et al., 2006), belongs to another race (Avenanti, Sirigu, & Aglioti, 2010), or supports a rival football team (Hein, Silani, Preuschoff, Batson, & Singer, 2010), vicarious activations are reduced.

VICARIOUS MOTOR, SOMATOSENSORY, AND EMOTIONAL ACTIVATIONS AND COGNITION

The evidence reviewed so far suggests that humans, monkeys, and birds vicariously activate their own actions when they see or hear those of others. Humans and perhaps other animals additionally activate representations of their own sensations and emotions when they perceive those of others. In other words, when we perceive what others do or what they experience, we not only recruit visual and auditory brain regions that encode what we see and hear but additionally trigger representations of how we would perform similar actions or feel similar sensations and emotions. In a way, we slip under the skin of the people we witness and share their actions, sensations, and emotions. Lesions in brain regions that show such vicarious activations impair people's capacity to optimally feel what others do and feel, suggesting that these vicarious representations are an important mechanism of social cognition.

Of course, we cannot magically sense what goes on in other people. Instead, vicarious activations are a projection onto others of what we would do or feel. The projective nature of this process becomes particularly striking when looking at cases in which participants view robotic actions. Our human participants knew that the robot we showed them in videos was not endowed with a premotor cortex or somatosensory regions resembling those of humans (Gazzola, Rizzolatti, Wicker, & Keysers, 2007). Hence, an accurate representation of what goes on in the robot's CPU should not involve the recruitment of premotor or somatosensory brain regions in a viewer. If, on the other hand, viewers project their own intentional actions and sensations onto others, one would expect to see brain activation in the viewers' premotor and somatosensory regions, and this activity should be as strong as when viewing humans performing actions similar to those of the robot. Our evidence fully supported the projection hypothesis, with premotor and somatosensory activity being as strong when viewing robots as when viewing humans perform certain actions (Gazzola et al., 2007). Hence, vicarious activations should be considered heuristics, in which people use the only motor programs, somatosensory representations, and emotions they have ever experienced, namely, their own, to perceive and understand those of others (Keysers, 2011).

How do vicarious activations develop? Because an actor is also a spectator and auditor of his or her own actions, during hand actions for instance, parietal and premotor neurons controlling the action fire at the same time as neurons in the visual and auditory cortex that respond to the observation and sound of this specific hand action. These sensory and motor neurons that fire together would, as Donald Hebb (1949) famously proposed, wire together—that is, strengthen their connections through synaptic potentiation (Keysers & Perrett, 2004). After repeated self-observation or self-audition, the motor neurons in the premotor and parietal regions would receive such strong synaptic input from sensory neurons that they would become a mirror. The same pairing between execution and observation would also occur in cases in which an individual is imitated by another (Del Giudice, Manera, & Keysers, 2009). For instance, a child cannot observe its own facial expressions, but the adult who imitates the child's expression serves as a mirror, triggering in the child's superior temporal sulcus an activity pattern representing what the expression sounds and looks like. This then becomes associated with the premotor cortex activity producing the expression that was imitated. Hebbian learning could explain the emergence of the motor neuron system in infants and its plasticity in adulthood. This perspective does not preclude the possibility that some genetic factors guide its development. It suggests that the motor neuron system is not a specific social adaptation that evolved to permit action understanding but is a simple consequence of sensorimotor learning that has to occur for an individual to be able to visually control his or her own actions. Note that, due to sensorimotor latencies, there is a systematic time lag between motor activity and sensory consequences that endows this Hebbian learning circuit with predictive properties.

Vicarious activations in the motor, somatosensory, and emotional systems interact and sometimes depend on other, more cognitive brain systems involved in attention, mentalizing, and cognitive control: (a) Directing attention toward or away from actions modulates activity in vicarious motor representations (Shmuelof & Zohary, 2005). (b) Asking participants to reflect on the intentions behind observed actions triggers activity in mentalizing and motor brain regions, suggesting that motor simulation provides an input to mentalizing brain regions (Keysers & Gazzola, 2007). (c) If people are asked to switch from doing the same thing another person is doing to doing the opposite of that action to achieve a common goal, cognitive control brain regions are activated along with mirror regions (Kokal, Gazzola, & Keysers, 2009). These regions are probably necessary to determine, based on current goals, whether mirror representations of the observed actions will be executed or whether representations of complementary actions are executed. In addition, empathy with the emotions of others can be modulated by prior knowledge about the fairness of the victim and by other forms of cognitive appraisal and perspective taking (see Hein & Singer, 2008, for a review). Finally, in a recent experiment analyzing the information flow between two communicating brains, we could see that regions involved in vicarious motor activations and those involved in mentalizing cooperate to represent information about the state of the sender's brain (Schippers et al., 2010).

CONCLUSION

In recent years, there has been an explosion of evidence suggesting that vicarious brain activations are not restricted to monkeys, to actions, or to the premotor cortex: (a) humans and birds have mirror neurons; (b) many other brain regions involved in motor execution seem to be vicariously activated during the observation of other people's actions; and (c) in addition to triggering motor representations, our brain seems to vicariously trigger somatosensory and emotional representations when we watch others being touched, performing actions, or experiencing emotions. Instead of supporting a model in which the ventral premotor cortex is a singular brain region endowed with a unique mirror property that can single-handedly shed light on the inner lives of others, recent findings paint a less monochromatic picture: Vicarious activity can be measured in many brain regions, including motor, somatosensory, and emotional cortices. The flexible interplay of these circuits with brain regions associated with attention, cognitive control, and mentalizing may be what allows us to feel and empathize with the inner lives of others. In support of this idea, lesions in somatosensory, insular, and premotor regions all seem to impair our capacity to empathically feel others' emotions (Adolphs et al.,

2000, 2003; Calder et al., 2000). Understanding the precise function of each of the many vicariously recruitable brain regions used in social perception remains an important challenge for future research.

REFERENCES

Adolphs, R., Damasio, H., Tranel, D., Cooper, G., & Damasio, A. R. (2000). A role for somatosensory cortices in the visual recognition of emotion as revealed by three-dimensional lesion mapping. *Journal of Neuroscience, 20,* 2683–2690.

Adolphs, R., Tranel, D., & Damasio, A. R. (2003). Dissociable neural systems for recognizing emotions. *Brain and Cognition, 52,* 61–69. doi:10.1016/S0278-2626 (03)00009-5

Arnstein, D., Cui, F., Keysers, C., Maurits, N. M., & Gazzola, V. (2011). μ-suppression during action observation and execution correlates with BOLD in dorsal premotor, inferior parietal, and SI cortices. *Journal of Neuroscience, 31,* 14243–14249. doi:10.1523/JNEUROSCI.0963-11.2011

Atsak, P., Orre, M., Bakker, P., Cerliani, L., Roozendaal, B., Gazzola, V., . . . Keysers, C. (2011). Experience modulates vicarious freezing in rats: A model for empathy. *PLoS ONE, 6,* e21855. doi:10.1371/journal.pone.0021855

Avenanti, A., Bolognini, N., Maravita, A., & Aglioti, S. M. (2007). Somatic and motor components of action simulation. *Current Biology, 17,* 2129–2135. doi:10.1016/j.cub.2007.11.045

Avenanti, A., Sirigu, A., & Aglioti, S. M. (2010). Racial bias reduces empathic sensorimotor resonance with other-race pain. *Current Biology, 20,* 1018–1022. doi:10.1016/j.cub.2010.03.071

Banissy, M. J., Kadosh, R. C., Maus, G. W., Walsh, V., & Ward, J. (2009). Prevalence, characteristics and a neurocognitive model of mirror-touch synaesthesia. *Experimental Brain Research, 198,* 261–272. doi:10.1007/s00221-009-1810-9

Blakemore, S.-J., Bristow, D., Bird, G., Frith, C., & Ward, J. (2005). Somatosensory activations during the observation of touch and a case of vision–touch synaesthesia. *Brain, 128,* 1571–1583. doi:10.1093/brain/awh500

Buccino, G., Binkofski, F., Fink, G. R., Fadiga, L., Fogassi, L., Gallese, V., . . . Freund, H. J. (2001). Action observation activates premotor and parietal areas in a somatotopic manner: An fMRI study. *European Journal of Neuroscience, 13,* 400–404.

Calder, A. J., Keane, J., Manes, F., Antoun, N., & Young, A. W. (2000). Impaired recognition and experience of disgust following brain injury. *Nature Neuroscience, 3,* 1077–1078. doi:10.1038/80586

Carr, L., Iacoboni, M., Dubeau, M. C., Mazziotta, J. C., & Lenzi, G. L. (2003). Neural mechanisms of empathy in humans: A relay from neural systems for imitation to limbic areas. *Proceedings of the National Academy of Sciences, USA, 100,* 5497–5502. doi:10.1073/pnas.0935845100

Caspers, S., Zilles, K., Laird, A. R., & Eickhoff, S. B. (2010). ALE meta-analysis of action observation and imitation in the human brain. *NeuroImage, 50*, 1148–1167. doi:10.1016/j.neuroimage.2009.12.112

Church, R. M. (1959). Emotional reactions of rats to the pain of others. *Journal of Comparative and Physiological Psychology, 52*, 132–134. doi:10.1037/h0043531

Cisek, P., & Kalaska, J. F. (2004, October 21). Neural correlates of mental rehearsal in dorsal premotor cortex. *Nature, 431*, 993–996. doi:10.1038/nature03005

Costantini, M., Galati, G., Ferretti, A., Caulo, M., Tartaro, A., Romani, G. L., & Aglioti, S. M. (2005). Neural systems underlying observation of humanly impossible movements: An FMRI study. *Cerebral Cortex, 15*, 1761–1767. doi:10.1093/cercor/bhi053

Del Giudice, M., Manera, V., & Keysers, C. (2009). Programmed to learn? The ontogeny of mirror neurons. *Developmental Science, 12*, 350–363. doi:10.1111/j.1467-7687.2008.00783.x

Ebisch, S. J., Perrucci, M. G., Ferretti, A., Del Gratta, C., Romani, G. L., & Gallese, V. (2008). The sense of touch: Embodied simulation in a visuotactile mirroring mechanism for observed animate or inanimate touch. *Journal of Cognitive Neuroscience, 20*, 1611–1623. doi:10.1162/jocn.2008.20111

Etzel, J. A., Gazzola, V., & Keysers, C. (2008). Testing simulation theory with cross-modal multivariate classification of fMRI data. *PLoS ONE, 3*, e3690. doi:10.1371/journal.pone.0003690

Etzel, J. A., Gazzola, V., & Keysers, C. (2009). An introduction to anatomical ROI-based fMRI classification analysis. *Brain Research, 1282*, 114–125. doi:10.1016/j.brainres.2009.05.090

Fadiga, L., Craighero, L., & Olivier, E. (2005). Human motor cortex excitability during the perception of others' action. *Current Opinion in Neurobiology, 15*, 213–218. doi:10.1016/j.conb.2005.03.013

Gallese, V., Fadiga, L., Fogassi, L., & Rizzolatti, G. (1996). Action recognition in the premotor cortex. *Brain, 119*, 593–609. doi:10.1093/brain/119.2.593

Gazzola, V., Aziz-Zadeh, L., & Keysers, C. (2006). Empathy and the somatotopic auditory mirror system in humans. *Current Biology, 16*, 1824–1829. doi:10.1016/j.cub.2006.07.072

Gazzola, V., & Keysers, C. (2009). The observation and execution of actions share motor and somatosensory voxels in all tested subjects: Single-subject analyses of unsmoothed fMRI data. *Cerebral Cortex, 19*, 1239–1255. doi:10.1093/cercor/bhn181

Gazzola, V., Rizzolatti, G., Wicker, B., & Keysers, C. (2007). The anthropomorphic brain: The mirror neuron system responds to human and robotic actions. *NeuroImage, 35*, 1674–1684. doi:10.1016/j.neuroimage.2007.02.003

Graziano, M. S., Taylor, C. S., & Moore, T. (2002). Complex movements evoked by microstimulation of precentral cortex. *Neuron, 34*, 841–851. doi:10.1016/S0896-6273(02)00698-0

Hebb, D. O. (1949). *The organization of behavior*. New York, NY: Wiley.

Hein, G., Silani, G., Preuschoff, K., Batson, C. D., & Singer, T. (2010). Neural responses to ingroup and outgroup members' suffering predict individual differences in costly helping. *Neuron, 68*, 149–160. doi:10.1016/j.neuron.2010.09.003

Hein, G., & Singer, T. (2008). I feel how you feel but not always: The empathic brain and its modulation. *Current Opinion in Neurobiology, 18*, 153–158. doi:10.1016/j.conb.2008.07.012

Hennenlotter, A., Schroeder, U., Erhard, P., Castrop, F., Haslinger, B., Stoecker, D., . . . Ceballos-Baumann, A. O. (2005). A common neural basis for receptive and expressive communication of pleasant facial affect. *NeuroImage, 26*, 581–591. doi:10.1016/j.neuroimage.2005.01.057

Ishida, H., Nakajima, K., Inase, M., & Murata, A. (2010). Shared mapping of own and others' bodies in visuotactile bimodal area of monkey parietal cortex. *Journal of Cognitive Neuroscience, 22*, 83–96. doi:10.1162/jocn.2009.21185

Jabbi, M., Bastiaansen, J., & Keysers, C. (2008). A common anterior insula representation of disgust observation, experience and imagination shows divergent functional connectivity pathways. *PLoS ONE, 3*, e2939. doi:10.1371/journal.pone.0002939

Jabbi, M., & Keysers, C. (2008). Inferior frontal gyrus activity triggers anterior insula response to emotional facial expressions. *Emotion, 8*, 775–780. doi:10.1037/a0014194

Jabbi, M., Swart, M., & Keysers, C. (2007). Empathy for positive and negative emotions in the gustatory cortex. *NeuroImage, 34*, 1744–1753. doi:10.1016/j.neuroimage.2006.10.032

Kaas, J. H. (2004). Somatosensory system. In G. Paxinos & J. K. Mai (Eds.), *The human nervous system* (2nd ed., pp. 1059–1092). London, England: Elsevier. doi:10.1016/B978-012547626-3/50029-6

Keysers, C. (2009). Mirror neurons. *Current Biology, 19*, R971–R973. doi:10.1016/j.cub.2009.08.026

Keysers, C. (2011). *The empathic brain*. New York, NY: Social Brain Press.

Keysers, C., & Gazzola, V. (2007). Integrating simulation and theory of mind: From self to social cognition. *Trends in Cognitive Sciences, 11*, 194–196. doi:10.1016/j.tics.2007.02.002

Keysers, C., & Gazzola, V. (2009). Expanding the mirror: Vicarious activity for actions, emotions, and sensations. *Current Opinion in Neurobiology, 19*, 666–671. doi:10.1016/j.conb.2009.10.006

Keysers, C., Kaas, J. H., & Gazzola, V. (2010). Somatosensation in social perception. *Nature Reviews Neuroscience, 11*, 417–428. doi:10.1038/nrn2833

Keysers, C., Kohler, E., Umilta, M. A., Nanetti, L., Fogassi, L., & Gallese, V. (2003). Audiovisual mirror neurons and action recognition. *Experimental Brain Research, 153*, 628–636. doi:10.1007/s00221-003-1603-5

Keysers, C., & Perrett, D. I. (2004). Demystifying social cognition: A Hebbian perspective. *Trends in Cognitive Sciences, 8,* 501–507. doi:10.1016/j.tics.2004.09.005

Keysers, C., Wicker, B., Gazzola, V., Anton, J.-L., Fogassi, L., & Gallese, V. (2004). A touching sight: SII/PV activation during the observation and experience of touch. *Neuron, 42,* 335–346. doi:10.1016/S0896-6273(04)00156-4

Kohler, E., Keysers, C., Umilta, M. A., Fogassi, L., Gallese, V., & Rizzolatti, G. (2002, August 2). Hearing sounds, understanding actions: Action representation in mirror neurons. *Science, 297,* 846–848. doi:10.1126/science.1070311

Kokal, I., Gazzola, V., & Keysers, C. (2009). Acting together in and beyond the mirror neuron system. *NeuroImage, 47,* 2046–2056. doi:10.1016/j.neuroimage.2009.06.010

Lamm, C., Decety, J., & Singer, T. (2011). Meta-analytic evidence for common and distinct neural networks associated with directly experienced pain and empathy for pain. *NeuroImage, 54,* 2492–2502. doi:10.1016/j.neuroimage.2010.10.014

Mukamel, R., Ekstrom, A. D., Kaplan, J., Iacoboni, M., & Fried, I. (2010). Single-neuron responses in humans during execution and observation of actions. *Current Biology, 20,* 750–756. doi:10.1016/j.cub.2010.02.045

Osborn, J., & Derbyshire, S. W. (2010). Pain sensation evoked by observing injury in others. *Pain, 148,* 268–274. doi:10.1016/j.pain.2009.11.007

Pazzaglia, M., Smania, N., Corato, E., & Aglioti, S. M. (2008). Neural underpinnings of gesture discrimination in patients with limb apraxia. *Journal of Neuroscience, 28,* 3030–3041. doi:10.1523/JNEUROSCI.5748-07.2008

Pierno, A. C., Tubaldi, F., Turella, L., Grossi, P., Barachino, L., Gallo, P., & Castiello, U. (2009). Neurofunctional modulation of brain regions by the observation of pointing and grasping actions. *Cerebral Cortex, 19,* 367–374. doi:10.1093/cercor/bhn089

Pitcher, D., Garrido, L., Walsh, V., & Duchaine, B. C. (2008). Transcranial magnetic stimulation disrupts the perception and embodiment of facial expressions. *Journal of Neuroscience, 28,* 8929–8933. doi:10.1523/JNEUROSCI.1450-08.2008

Pobric, G., & Hamilton, A. F. (2006). Action understanding requires the left inferior frontal cortex. *Current Biology, 16,* 524–529. doi:10.1016/j.cub.2006.01.033

Prather, J. F., Peters, S., Nowicki, S., & Mooney, R. (2008, January 17). Precise auditory–vocal mirroring in neurons for learned vocal communication. *Nature, 451,* 305–310. doi:10.1038/nature06492

Rice, G. E., & Gainer, P. (1962). "Altruism" in the albino rat. *Journal of Comparative and Physiological Psychology, 55,* 123–125. doi:10.1037/h0042276

Rozzi, S., Ferrari, P. F., Bonini, L., Rizzolatti, G., & Fogassi, L. (2008). Functional organization of inferior parietal lobule convexity in the macaque monkey: Electrophysiological characterization of motor, sensory and mirror responses and their correlation with cytoarchitectonic areas. *European Journal of Neuroscience, 28,* 1569–1588. doi:10.1111/j.1460-9568.2008.06395.x

Schaefer, M., Xu, B., Flor, H., & Cohen, L. G. (2009). Effects of different viewing perspectives on somatosensory activations during observation of touch. *Human Brain Mapping, 30,* 2722–2730. doi:10.1002/hbm.20701

Schippers, M. B., Roebroeck, A., Renken, R., Nanetti, L., & Keysers, C. (2010). Mapping the information flow from one brain to another during gestural communication. *Proceedings of the National Academy of Sciences, USA, 107,* 9388–9393. doi:10.1073/pnas.1001791107

Shepherd, S. V., Klein, J. T., Deaner, R. O., & Platt, M. L. (2009). Mirroring of attention by neurons in macaque parietal cortex. *Proceedings of the National Academy of Sciences, USA, 106,* 9489–9494. doi:10.1073/pnas.0900419106

Shmuelof, L., & Zohary, E. (2005). Dissociation between ventral and dorsal fMRI activation during object and action recognition. *Neuron, 47,* 457–470. doi:10.1016/j.neuron.2005.06.034

Singer, T., Seymour, B., O'Doherty, J., Kaube, H., Dolan, R. J., & Frith, C. D. (2004, February 20). Empathy for pain involves the affective but not sensory components of pain. *Science, 303,* 1157–1162. doi:10.1126/science.1093535

Singer, T., Seymour, B., O'Doherty, J. P., Stephan, K. E., Dolan, R. J., & Frith, C. D. (2006, January 26). Empathic neural responses are modulated by the perceived fairness of others. *Nature, 439,* 466–469. doi:10.1038/nature04271

Thioux, M., Gazzola, V., & Keysers, C. (2008). Action understanding: How, what and why. *Current Biology, 18,* R431–R434. doi:10.1016/j.cub.2008.03.018

van der Gaag, C., Minderaa, R. B., & Keysers, C. (2007a). The BOLD signal in the amygdala does not differentiate between dynamic facial expressions. *Social Cognitive and Affective Neuroscience, 2,* 93–103. doi:10.1093/scan/nsm002

van der Gaag, C., Minderaa, R.B., & Keysers, C. (2007b). Facial expressions: What the mirror neuron system can and cannot tell us. *Social Neuroscience, 2,* 179–222. doi:10.1080/17470910701376878

Wicker, B., Keysers, C., Plailly, J., Royet, J.-P., Gallese, V., & Rizzolatti, G. (2003). Both of us disgusted in *my* insula: The common neural basis of seeing and feeling disgust. *Neuron, 40,* 655–664. doi:10.1016/S0896-6273(03)00679-2

Zaki, J., Ochsner, K. N., Hanelin, J., Wager, T. D., & Mackey, S. C. (2007). Different circuits for different pain: Patterns of functional connectivity reveal distinct networks for processing pain in self and others. *Social Neuroscience, 2,* 276–291. doi:10.1080/17470910701401973

5

OUR SOCIAL BASELINE: THE ROLE OF SOCIAL PROXIMITY IN ECONOMY OF ACTION

JAMES A. COAN, CASEY L. BROWN, AND LANE BECKES

Apart from primary physiological needs, social relationships may be the most powerful factor related to human health and well-being. Social isolation brings emotional pain and increased risk for illness and death (House, Landis, & Umberson, 1988), but proximity to rich social networks attenuates stress-related autonomic and hypothalamic–pituitary–adrenal axis activity (Eisenberger, Taylor, Gable, Hilmert, & Lieberman, 2007; Flinn & England, 1997; Lewis & Ramsay, 1999) and lowers the risk for both physical and psychological maladies (Moak & Agrawal, 2010). These positive effects are strongest in high-functioning romantic and family relationships characterized by high levels of trust, positive affect, and interdependence (Coan, Schaefer, & Davidson, 2006; Kiecolt-Glaser, Glaser, Cacioppo, & Malarkey, 1998; Robles & Kiecolt-Glaser, 2003). Indeed, when close personal relationships rupture, the negative emotional and physiological sequelae can be catastrophic (Sbarra, Law, & Portley, 2011). Although there are likely to be many mechanisms linking social relationships to health, a major factor

http://dx.doi.org/10.1037/14250-006
Mechanisms of Social Connection: From Brain to Group, M. Mikulincer and P. R. Shaver (Editors)

is the perception of social resources—a perception that can literally make the world look less demanding (Schnall, Harber, Stefanucci, & Proffitt, 2008) and safer (Coan et al., 2006). When we perceive ourselves to be embedded in a rich social network, we tend to believe that the network's resources are shared with us. This allows us to adjust our level of personal effort accordingly. Humans have a unique and powerful ability to forge and maintain networks of social interdependence characterized by shared goals, joint attention, and cooperative, even altruistic, behavior (Herrmann, Call, Hernandez-Lloreda, Hare, & Tomasello, 2007). The regulatory effects of social relationships are a major human adaptation—one that forms part of the foundation of the human habitat, which can itself be found, more than any specific terrestrial niche or diet, in the company of other humans.

In this chapter, we review the ways in which social relationships help offset the cost of many of life's effortful activities, including the activities of the human brain. In our discussion, we emphasize the management by social proximity and interaction of prefrontal resources devoted to vigilance, working memory, and self-regulation. We then contrast two models—the down-regulation model and the social baseline model—of potential neural mechanisms linking the social regulation of emotion to decreased threat responding, and we review the evidence supporting the two views. The down-regulation model emphasizes regulatory circuits within the prefrontal cortex and elsewhere that mediate associations between social contact and decreased subcortical threat responding. The social baseline model views social contact as closer to the human brain's "baseline" state of relative calm, positing no mediation by regulatory circuits of the decrease in threat-related processing during social contact. In discussing the social baseline model, we review principles of human behavioral ecology, such as economy of action, budgeting, risk distribution, and load sharing, which may have shaped human perceptual and regulatory capabilities to be intensely social in nature. Finally, we discuss the possible roles of oxytocin, the dorsal anterior cingulate cortex, and endogenous opioids in the social regulation of emotion.

THE PREFRONTAL CORTEX IS POWERFUL AND COSTLY

The human prefrontal cortex provides humans with a distinct advantage over other animals. Across a wide variety of contexts, humans are capable of anticipating future rewards, planning detailed contingencies, thinking in abstractions, executing very complex communication, and controlling their impulses and emotions. Indeed, humans are even capable of using prefrontal processing to soothe themselves in a variety of ways and for a variety of purposes, as when, for example, they tell themselves that the violence they are observing is "only a movie" (Gross & Thompson, 2007). Moreover, individual differences in these capabilities are highly consequential. In children, the ability to inhibit emotional impulses—as when gratification is delayed—is associated with a host of early social, cognitive, and academic advantages (Mischel, Shoda, & Rodriguez, 1989); fewer externalizing problems such as aggression, conduct disorder, and oppositional defiant disorder (e.g., Beauchaine, Gatzke-Kopp, & Mead, 2007; Crowe & Blair, 2008; Hill, Degnan, Calkins, & Keane, 2006; Rydell, Berlin, & Bohlin, 2003); and decreased risk for affective disorders (Buckner, Mezzacappa, & Beardslee, 2009; Dennis, Brotman, Huang, & Gouley, 2007). Effective self-regulation is no less beneficial to adults, in whom it is similarly associated with enhanced life satisfaction, decreased affective psychopathology, happier relationships, and better overall health (Haga, Kraft, & Corby, 2009; Smyth & Arigo, 2009). Many psychotherapeutic interventions emphasize self-regulation. In particular, cognitive-behavioral therapy and mindfulness meditation help individuals develop their capacity to regulate their own emotional responses (Lykins & Baer, 2009; Smyth & Arigo, 2009; Suveg, Sood, Comer, & Kendall, 2009).

Human self-regulation capabilities are so powerful that we find it is useful to think of humans as the cheetahs of self-control. Just as the cheetah is the earth's fastest land animal (capable of reaching speeds of up to 75 miles per hour), no species on the planet other than humans is capable of crafting a regulatory cognition that even approximates the phrase "it's only a movie." Less appreciated, however, is that the cheetah analogy extends to another important aspect of self-control: Its use is constrained by the perception of available resources. Just as the cheetah can sustain its top speed for only short bursts of time, human self-regulation abilities are difficult to sustain for long periods (Gailliot & Baumeister, 2007). Several experiments by Baumeister and colleagues suggest that self-control depletes some kind of computational or physiological resource. In these experiments, the deployment of self-control in one situation appears to decrease or compromise its use in another. For example, when compared to simply solving math problems, engaging in a thought-suppression task makes people more likely to drink a free alcoholic beverage before a driving evaluation (Muraven, Collins, & Nienhaus, 2002). Some have argued that this limitation is a function of blood glucose concentration, which is thought to diminish as a function of neural—particularly prefrontal—activity (Gailliot & Baumeister, 2007). But this isn't likely. First, blood glucose levels in the brain probably do not change enough during self-control tasks to account for the apparent depletion effects that many have observed (Kurzban, 2010). Second, simple experimental manipulations—such as presenting participants with a gift (Tice, Baumeister, Shmueli, & Muraven, 2007) or simply persuading participants that willpower is an unlimited resource (Job, Dweck, & Walton, 2010)—can apparently reduce or eliminate these depletion effects.

All of this suggests to us (a) that self-control is indeed costly (or depletion effects would not so commonly obtain); (b) that the cost of self-control is unlikely to be a function of a specifically proximal resource limitation (meaning that apparent depletion effects can in essence be overridden when needed; see Chapter 15, this volume, for an example); (c) that in any case, because self-control is apparently costly in some important if poorly understood way, the brain tends to avoid engaging in self-control efforts whenever possible; and (d) that the brain probably reflexively uses a variety of heuristic cues to decide when it is reasonable to conserve its regulatory capabilities instead of deploying them. In this way, rather than being beholden to a specific quantity of a metabolic resource (e.g., glucose; cf. Gailliot & Baumeister, 2007), the brain is probably designed to update its "budget" for self-regulatory resources, with an eye toward conservation, as a person moves through the uncertain world. Budgeting is a broad principle governing how the human body manages its resources. This is why we feel hungry and eat long before we are in danger of starvation and why we feel fatigued long before we run out of metabolic resources—even when engaged in a physically demanding task such as running a marathon (Noakes, 2012; Swart, Lindsay, Lambert, Brown, & Noakes, 2012). Below, we argue that one of the human brain's primary sources of information for economizing its cognitive and regulatory activity is the degree of proximity to social resources (Beckes & Coan, 2011; Coan, 2008). We frame our argument in terms of our own empirical work and a conceptual frame borrowed from behavioral ecology and the study of perception/action links.

SOCIAL REGULATION OF THE NEURAL RESPONSE TO THREAT

Many mammals regulate emotion through social contact and proximity (Fogel, 1993). Social contact has a significant impact on health and well-being, enhancing immune functioning (Lutgendorf et al., 2005; see Uchino, 2006, for a review), minimizing salivary cortisol responses (Turner-Cobb, Sephton, Koopman, Blake-Mortimer, & Spiegel, 2000), lowering resting blood pressure (Uchino, Holt-Lunstad, Uno, Betancourt, & Garvey, 1999), and decreasing risk for carotid artery atherosclerosis (Knox et al., 2000). Higher levels of social integration even reduce age-adjusted risk of death (House et al., 1988).

Our lab has begun to systematically explore social affect regulation with functional magnetic resonance imaging (fMRI). In the first of several studies (Coan et al., 2006), functional brain images were collected from 16 married women, selected for very high marital satisfaction, who we placed under the threat of mild shock during each of three conditions: holding the hand of their relational partner, holding the hand of a stranger, or lying alone in the scanner. We were interested both in the subjective experience of unpleasantness and arousal during these tasks and in any modulations of the brain's threat response as a function of hand-holding. Self-reported unpleasantness was indeed lowest during the partner hand-holding condition, relative to either stranger hand-holding or no hand-holding, whereas subjective arousal was reduced in both stranger and relational partner hand-holding relative to the alone condition.

Analyses of threat-related brain activity suggested that the brain was highly active when threats were faced alone, significantly less active during either stranger or partner hand-holding, and least active during partner hand-holding. Regions of the brain involved in the modulation of arousal and bodily preparation for action, such as the ventral anterior cingulate cortex, posterior cingulate cortex, postcentral gyrus, and supramarginal gyrus, were all less responsive to threat cues during any hand-holding. But partner hand-holding also attenuated threat responding in the dorsolateral prefrontal cortex, superior colliculus, caudate, and nucleus accumbens—all regions associated with threat vigilance and self-regulation.

Given that the sample consisted of highly satisfied couples, it was surprising that relationship quality (as measured by the Dyadic Adjustment Scale; Spanier, 1976) was negatively correlated with threat responding in brain regions critical to the status and regulation of the body in response to stress, such as the right anterior insula ($r = -.47$), the left superior frontal gyrus ($r = -.59$), and the hypothalamus ($r = -.46$). More surprising still was that these negative correlations were observed only during the partner hand-holding condition. Taken together, these findings provide strong evidence that most threat-responsive brain areas are less active when individuals are experiencing physical contact with another person. Moreover, the effect is larger and more widespread when that other person is a relational partner, and it is larger still among individuals in the highest quality relationships.

The Down-Regulation Model

The down-regulation model is in many ways the implicitly assumed model of emotion regulation, including social emotion regulation. This model postulates a regulatory circuit that inhibits circuits automatically responsive to a threat. In the context of the hand-holding study discussed above, the down-regulation model would suggest (a) that the threat cue activated a widespread threat system and (b) that hand-holding activated an additional regulatory system that exerted an inhibitory influence on the already active threat system. For this model to be correct, of course, evidence for both systems must obtain, as must evidence that activation in one is inversely proportional to activation in the other. Indeed, because additional regulatory effects were observed as hand-holders changed from strangers to familiar partners and, within partners, from lower to higher quality relationships, it may be necessary to postulate additional down-regulatory mechanisms associated with these moderating variables.

If the down-regulation model is correct, it is possible and perhaps likely that the brain would be most active when one faces a threat while receiving support from a close relational partner with whom a very high quality relationship is shared. This is because both excitatory and inhibitory activity would necessarily occur more or less simultaneously across a variety of threat-responsive regions, an effect that would resemble pressing on the accelerator of a car and simultaneously pressing on the brake. Indeed, this is precisely the kind of effect one finds during self-regulation tasks, and it may in turn contribute to the fatigue that self-regulation tasks frequently cause (Gailliot & Baumeister, 2007). But what we actually observed in the hand-holding study did not resemble self-regulation. In fact, in that study, absolutely no neural circuits were identified that were, independent of the presence of a threat cue, simply more active during hand-holding, during hand-holding associated with a relational partner, or during hand-holding as a function of relationship quality. The brain was simply more active when one faced threat alone, relative to when one faced threat coupled with social support. Thus, the down-regulation model of social support was not supported by our data.

The Social Baseline Model

The social baseline model questions the core assumption of the down-regulation model by suggesting that the brain assumes proximity to social networks and relational partners (Coan, 2008). If this is the case, social proximity—not the alone condition—is closer to the brain's baseline, and social support acts not by exerting a regulatory force so much as by returning an organism to its baseline or default state. From this perspective, being alone is the special case; the social support condition is in fact normative. The social baseline model requires a seemingly subtle but actually powerful change of perspective, much like a figure–ground illusion. It encourages a change of focus from a process of decreasing threat sensitivity via social proximity to a process of increasing threat sensitivity by being alone—two perspectives that are no more identical than the famous Rubin vase and the two faces that frame it (Rubin, 1921). It is easy to expect that more is going on in a participant's environment when the participant is with a close friend—especially during a threatening situation—because there are literally more perceivable stimuli with the friend included. But from the brain's perspective, there may actually be fewer perceived costs associated with the threat when the close friend is present, and this reduction in cost may allow the brain to engage in less action.

Indeed, the social baseline model appeals to the *economy of action* principle (Proffitt, 2006), which states that organisms must conserve more energy than they consume in order to survive, an imperative that leads to the conservation of resources whenever possible (Krebs & Davies, 1993; Proffitt, 2006). We already know that perception is not an entirely passive process but rather is influenced by a number of factors—goals, emotions, physiological states— related to an organism's situation (Proffitt, 2006). It is similarly true that an organism's perceptions are closely aligned with its unique adaptations and, by extension, its unique environment. In this way, perceptions are tightly linked to the actions that environments afford. Proffitt and colleagues (Schnall et al., 2008) have argued that these perception–action links are often highly "economical" in the sense that they tend toward the optimization of return on investment. For example, an individual perceives hills to be steeper and distances farther away if he or she is wearing a heavy backpack. According to Proffitt (2006), the bodily perception of the heavy backpack translates to increased perceived physiological load, which causes a perceptual shift in the geographical features with which the individual must cope. All of this perceptual information updates the perceived cost of engaging in the corresponding actions—climbing a steep hill or walking a long distance. Thus, when the individual has increased weight to carry, the hill appears steeper; the brain perceives a greater investment in added tasks, effort, or both; and commensurably more motivation must be marshaled if the hill is going to be climbed. Put another way, without the backpack, a simple curiosity in what the top of the hill looks like may be sufficient to motivate climbing it. With the backpack on, however, simple curiosity might not provide sufficient motivation—a payoff commensurate with the additional cost is required. Because energy management is a critical aspect of daily living and a major pressure in evolution, organisms have evolved to calculate (in mostly implicit ways) the perceived cost–benefit ratio of any given action or investment of resources, including, we believe, self-regulation.

Social baseline theory (SBT; Beckes & Coan, 2011; Coan, 2010) suggests that, for humans, being alone is like carrying a heavy backpack. The fundamental premise of SBT is that, more than any specific terrestrial environment or diet, social proximity and interaction constitute the baseline human habitat; thus, socially mediated regulatory influences are sufficiently powerful, widespread, economical, and unconditioned to be considered the default human regulation strategy. From the perspective of SBT, just as salamanders are born with physiological (and obviously implicit) expectations of finding moist, cool, dark spaces to inhabit, humans are born with physiological and psychological expectations of human contact through touch and affective expression—of individuals with whom to share resources, goals, attention, and regulation (Kudo & Dunbar, 2001; Sbarra & Hazan, 2008; Tomasello, 2009).

We use social cues to guide us in making decisions about the economy of certain actions, which in turn guide the activation of neural circuits commensurate with carrying out those actions. If social proximity is a baseline human situation, less effort should be needed in terms of vigilance for potential threats and emotion regulation when we are actually in reasonably close proximity to individuals with whom we share familiarity, interdependence, and trust. When it comes to emotion regulation in particular, our efforts may be normatively outsourced to close others who decrease our need for regulatory effort, either by obviating the need for an affective response altogether or by engaging in regulatory behavior for us (e.g., by noticing our discomfort and holding our hand), effectively loaning us prefrontal cortex processing. This would allow us to achieve regulatory benefits at a greatly reduced cost. SBT refers to this process as *load sharing* and argues that it is largely a function of familiarity, interdependence, and interpersonal conditioning. With a moment's reflection, load sharing is very easy to illustrate and understand. If an individual is confronted with four problems in his immediate environment, he must solve all of those problems himself if no one is there to help him. If a stranger is present, it may be that at least some of the load—say, a single one of those problems—can be "contracted out" to the stranger, leaving only three problems. If the social resource is familiar and predictable, the number of problems may be reduced to two, and if the social resource is someone with whom a high-quality relationship is shared, only a single problem of the possible four may require an independent solution.

Examples of social affect regulation are most obvious in infancy, where the regulation of physiological needs (hunger, thirst, warmth) is achieved through caregiver responses to the infant's negative affect (Polan & Hofer, 2008). As the infant develops through toddlerhood and beyond, however, the regulation of physiological needs via the child's affect gradually evolves into the regulation of the child's affect per se (Hofer, 2006; Nelson & Panksepp, 1998). All of this occurs in a context of rich and rapid neural development within the infant brain, which, through these years, is characterized by both the rapid expansion and the pruning of synaptic connections. In this putatively (though not indisputably) critical period, the child is beginning to form expectations and implicit beliefs about the environment it can expect to face as it develops toward independence.

One of the least developed regions of the brain immediately following birth is the prefrontal cortex, a broad region of the brain powerfully associated with self-regulation, including the self-regulation of emotion (Ochsner,

Bunge, Gross, & Gabrieli, 2002; Ochsner & Gross, 2005). Human infants are physiologically dependent upon adult caregivers, but even as they develop the means to be relatively independent, they continue to rely on adults for many years because of underdeveloped reasoning and regulatory abilities yoked to similarly underdeveloped prefrontal cortices. Thus, although a child of 7 years is physically capable of navigating, for example, a cross-country trip on public transportation, most of us would not be willing to let her (or him) do so unaccompanied. The base of knowledge required for such a trip is minimal and probably well within her grasp, but we would not expect her to be particularly good at regulating her anxiety along the way; nor would we trust her judgment about how best to respond to unexpected dangers. According to SBT, adult caregivers assist with these needs by loaning their children prefrontal effort. If a boy is incapable of regulating himself at a frightening movie, for example, his parent can hold his hand and do the regulatory work for him by reminding him that the action in the movie isn't real and that he is any case safe because the parent will protect him. At both the experiential and neural levels, regulatory work is effortful and (as many parents well know) even potentially exhausting. This is because the parent is exercising his or her own prefrontal effort to maintain vigilance for the child's state and to respond to the child's state with alternative interpretations of the situation—both activities that involve a great deal of cortical, including prefrontal, processing (Chudasama, 2011; Ochsner & Gross, 2005; Pardo, Fox, & Raichle, 1991).

Mediating Mechanisms of Social Regulation

As we reviewed above, we do not think the down-regulation model does the best job of explaining the results of the previously reviewed hand-holding study because we did not observe any neural activation positively correlated with hand-holding per se and through which the social regulation effects were mediated. Nevertheless, there must be some mechanism capable of identifying the presence of conspecifics, particularly relational partners, as well as a mechanism linking the general perception of plentiful social resources to attenuated threat reactivity.

One obvious potential mechanism mediating the decreased responsiveness to threat during social contact is the neuropeptide oxytocin (OT). OT plays a central role in social behavior in a variety of species, including humans (see Chapter 1, this volume). Indeed, OT is released during pleasurable social contact; it may be necessary for establishing and maintaining social bonds, particularly among monogamous species, and it appears to be sufficient in many cases for increasing feelings of trust and inhibiting feelings of fear (Insel & Fernald, 2004; Taylor, 2006). These findings make it a natural candidate mechanism for the social regulation of neural threat responding.

In fact, Kirsch et al. (2005) reported direct evidence for OT's role in the regulation of human amygdala function. Half their participants were given a placebo, and the other half were given OT via a nasal spray. Participants who received OT showed significantly less bold response in the amygdala to negative emotional pictures than did those in the placebo condition, indicating a reduced threat response as a function of OT administration. This suggests that OT may reduce threat vigilance. Given OT's tendency to be released in the presence of social stimuli, social contact may reduce an individual's need to self-regulate in a manner consistent with SBT. If this is correct, people should rely less on the prefrontal cortex to regulate their emotion when social resources are high, and this should be mediated by increased OT activity in the amygdala and elsewhere.

Another possibility is that endogenous opioids, particularly in the dorsal anterior cingulate cortex, inhibit activation of threat-related emotional responses in part by modulating threat detection (see Chapter 2, this volume). Eisenberger et al. (2007) observed that the dorsal anterior cingulate cortex is highly sensitive to the availability of social resources, with important implications for how individuals respond to threatening stimuli. They reported that higher daily levels of perceived social support were associated with lower levels of threat-related activity in the dorsal anterior cingulate cortex. Although this is not direct evidence, Eisenberger et al. suggested that positive social experience may desensitize the dorsal anterior cingulate cortex through repeated exposure to endogenous opioids. This brain area does in fact have a high density of opioid receptors, and endogenous opioids are unconditionally released in response to positive social experiences (Panksepp, 1998; Panksepp, Nelson, & Siviy, 1994). Moreover, abundant evidence suggests that opioid activity inhibits both central and peripheral stress responses, not only in the midst of a perceived stressor but also by a process of building "opioid tone" via opioid activity during nonstress states (Zubieta et al., 2003). Although a detailed understanding of these potential mechanisms of social support awaits additional research, OT activity in regions such as the hypothalamus, nucleus accumbens, and amygdala as well as endogenous opioid activity in the dorsal anterior cingulate cortex are exciting possibilities.

SUMMARY AND CONCLUSIONS

Human beings possess powerful attention and self-regulation capabilities, owing in large measure to their large and commensurably powerful prefrontal cortices. But sustained activation of these prefrontal capabilities is exhausting and probably metabolically costly in ways that are only beginning to be understood. In any case, vigilance and self-regulation are likely to be most effective over relatively short periods of time, with longer term demands resulting in steadily diminishing returns. Social contact and proximity appear to manage this potential problem by attenuating the demands for self-initiated attention and regulation. We have suggested that this dynamic creates a pressure to stay in close proximity to social resources and that close social proximity is by extension a baseline state for human beings.

This line of thinking presents new opportunities for research and theory development. A critical prediction of SBT, for example, is that computational or metabolic resources devoted to attention and self-regulation are indeed conserved through social proximity and interaction. Although our initial hand-holding/fMRI study provides some glimpses of such conservation, future research should test this position in more specific ways. For example, according to Alquist and Baumeister (2012), we might expect smaller changes in circulating blood glucose following a stressful self-regulation task in the presence of active social support. Failing such a direct impact on circulating blood glucose (an uncertain and in any case disputed potential proxy measure of cognitive effort), stress may lead to greater consumption of resources (concretely, eating more food) reflecting a change in resource "budgeting" as a result of increased self-regulatory demand. All of this may be mitigated by reliable social support. Alternatively, it seems likely that self-regulation exerts a measurable negative influence on concomitant or competing cognitive activities—one that might be offset by, again, close proximity to social resources.

SBT holds a number of implications for applied fields as well. It may be possible, for example, to develop a neural assay of social support by imaging the social regulation of hypothalamic activity during stress. Such information may lead to significant progress in predicting the effect of a person's social support network on a variety of health outcomes, including response to medical treatment, risk of depression, and physical resilience to disease. Access to reliable social resources may prove critical in determining people's abilities to manage pain related to arthritis, cancer treatment, and a variety of other health problems. Interventions could be used to potentiate the impact of social proximity, such as interdependence training for couples or social capital development for communities. More can be done to understand how social resources can be mobilized to reduce the stress and health impact of major life transitions such as going to college, becoming a parent, or beginning retirement.

Real-world anecdotes point to the potential for social regulation. For example, in the midst of data collection for the original hand-holding study, one participant exited the scanner in tears. When asked what was wrong, she reported that the combination of threat and soothing hand-holding caused her to remember holding her husband's hand during labor with their first child—a memory that brought her tears of joy. In another example, an individual who hadn't participated in the hand-holding study but had read about it in the popular press sent a letter to the laboratory describing her experience of coping with her husband's cancer. In it, she noted that "he never holds my hand, it is not like him. But, after this surgery and all the time in the hospital, he constantly wants me to hold his hand. He reaches for me all the time."

REFERENCES

Alquist, J. & Baumeister, R.F. (2012). Self-control: limited resources and extensive benefits. *Wiley Interdisciplinary Reviews: Cognitive Science, 3*, 419–423. Retrieved from http://dx.doi.org/10.1002/wcs.1173

Beauchaine, T. P., Gatzke-Kopp, L., & Mead, H. K. (2007). Polyvagal theory and developmental psychopathology: Emotion dysregulation and conduct problems from preschool to adolescence. *Biological Psychology, 74*, 174–184. doi:10.1016/j.biopsycho.2005.08.008

Beckes, L., & Coan, J. A. (2011). Social baseline theory: The role of social proximity in emotion and economy of action. *Social and Personality Psychology Compass, 5*, 976–988. doi:10.1111/j.1751-9004.2011.00400.x

Buckner, J. C., Mezzacappa, E., & Beardslee, W. R. (2009). Self-regulation and its relations to adaptive functioning in low-income youths. *American Journal of Orthopsychiatry, 79*, 19–30. doi:10.1037/a0014796

Chudasama, Y. (2011). Animal models of prefrontal executive function. *Behavioral Neuroscience, 125*, 327–343. doi:10.1037/a0023766

Coan, J. A. (2008). Toward a neuroscience of attachment. In J. Cassidy & P. R. Shaver (Eds.), *Handbook of attachment: Theory, research, and clinical applications* (2nd ed., pp. 241–265). New York, NY: Guilford Press.

Coan, J. A. (2010). Adult attachment and the brain. *Journal of Social and Personal Relationships, 27*, 210–217. doi:10.1177/0265407509360900

Coan, J. A., Schaefer, H. S., & Davidson, R. J. (2006). Lending a hand: Social regulation of the neural response to threat. *Psychological Science, 17*, 1032–1039. doi:10.1111/j.1467-9280.2006.01832.x

Crowe, S. L., & Blair, R. J. R. (2008). The development of antisocial behavior: What can we learn from functional neuroimaging studies? *Development and Psychopathology, 20*, 1145–1159. doi:10.1017/S0954579408000540

Dennis, T. A., Brotman, L. M., Huang, K. Y., & Gouley, K. K. (2007). Effortful control, social competence, and adjustment problems in children at risk for psychopathology. *Journal of Clinical Child and Adolescent Psychology, 36*, 442–454. doi:10.1080/15374410701448513

Eisenberger, N. I., Taylor, S. E., Gable, S. L., Hilmert, C. J., & Lieberman, M. D. (2007). Neural pathways link social support to attenuated neuroendocrine stress responses. *NeuroImage, 35*, 1601–1612. doi:10.1016/j.neuroimage.2007.01.038

Flinn, M. V., & England, B. G. (1997). Social economics of childhood gluco-corticoid stress response and health. *American Journal of Physical Anthropology*, *102*, 33–53. doi:10.1002/(SICI)1096-8644(199701)102:1<33::AID-AJPA4>3.0. CO;2-E

Fogel, A. (1993). *Developing through relationships: Communication, self, and culture in early infancy*. Hemel Hempstead, England: Harvester-Wheatsheaf.

Gailliot, M. T., & Baumeister, R. F. (2007). The physiology of willpower: Linking blood glucose to self-control. *Personality and Social Psychology Review*, *11*, 303–327. doi:10.1177/1088868307303030

Gross, J. J., & Thompson, R. A. (2007). Emotion regulation: Conceptual foundations. In J. J. Gross (Ed.), *Handbook of emotion regulation* (pp. 3–24). New York, NY: Guilford Press.

Haga, S. M., Kraft, P., & Corby, E.-K. (2009). Emotion regulation: Antecedents and well-being outcomes of cognitive reappraisal and expressive suppression in cross-cultural samples. *Journal of Happiness Studies*, *10*, 271–291. doi:10.1007/s10902-007-9080-3

Herrmann, E., Call, J., Hernandez-Lloreda, M. V., Hare, B., & Tomasello, M. (2007, September 10). Humans have evolved specialized skills of social cognition: The cultural intelligence hypothesis. *Science*, *317*, 1360–1366. doi:10.1126/science.1146282

Hill, A. L., Degnan, K. A., Calkins, S. D., & Keane, S. P. (2006). Profiles of externalizing behavior problems for boys and girls across preschool: The roles of emotion regulation and inattention. *Developmental Psychology*, *42*, 913–928. doi:10.1037/0012-1649.42.5.913

Hofer, M. A. (2006). Psychobiological roots of early attachment. *Current Directions in Psychological Science*, *15*, 84–88. doi:10.1111/j.0963-7214.2006.00412.x

House, J. S., Landis, K. R., & Umberson, D. (1988, July 29). Social relationships and health. *Science*, *241*, 540–545. doi:10.1126/science.3399889

Insel, T. R., & Fernald, R. D. (2004). How the brain processes social information: Searching for the social brain. *Annual Review of Neuroscience*, *27*, 697–722. doi:10.1146/annurev.neuro.27.070203.144148

Job, V., Dweck, C. S., & Walton, G. M. (2010). Ego depletion—Is it all in your head? Implicit theories about willpower affect self-regulation. *Psychological Science*, *21*, 1686–1693. doi:10.1177/0956797610384745

Kiecolt-Glaser, J. K., Glaser, R., Cacioppo, J. T., & Malarkey, W. B. (1998). Marital stress: Immunologic, neuroendocrine, and autonomic correlates. *Annals of the New York Academy of Sciences*, *840*, 656–663. doi:10.1111/j.1749-6632.1998. tb09604.x

Kirsch, P., Esslinger, C., Chen, Q., Mier, D., Lis, S., Siddhanti, S., . . . Meyer-Lindenberg, A. (2005). Oxytocin modulates neural circuitry for social cognition and fear in humans. *Journal of Neuroscience*, *25*, 11489–11493. doi:10.1523/JNEUROSCI.3984-05.2005

Knox, S. S., Adelman, A., Ellison, R. C., Arnett, D. K., Siegmund, K. D., Weidner, G., & Province, M. A. (2000). Hostility, social support, and carotid artery atherosclerosis in the National Heart, Lung, and Blood Institute Family Heart Study. *American Journal of Cardiology, 86,* 1086–1089. doi:10.1016/S0002-9149(00)01164-4

Krebs, J. R., & Davies, N. B. (1993). *An introduction to behavioural ecology* (3rd ed.). Malden, MA: Blackwell.

Kudo, H., & Dunbar, R. I. M. (2001). Neocortex size and social network size in primates. *Animal Behaviour, 62,* 711–722. doi:10.1006/anbe.2001.1808

Kurzban, R. (2010). Does the brain consume additional glucose during self-control tasks? *Evolutionary Psychology, 8,* 244–259.

Lewis, M., & Ramsay, D. S. (1999). Effect of maternal soothing on infant stress response. *Child Development, 70,* 11–20. doi:10.1111/1467-8624.00002

Lutgendorf, S. K., Sood, A. K., Anderson, B., McGinn, S., Maiseri, H., Dao, M., . . . Lubaroff, D. M. (2005). Social support, psychological distress, and natural killer cell activity in ovarian cancer. *Journal of Clinical Oncology, 23,* 7105–7113. doi:10.1200/JCO.2005.10.015

Lykins, E. L. B., & Baer, R. A. (2009). Psychological functioning in a sample of long-term practitioners of mindfulness meditation. *Journal of Cognitive Psychotherapy, 23,* 226–241. doi:10.1891/0889-8391.23.3.226

Mischel, W., Shoda, Y., & Rodriguez, M. I. (1989, May 26). Delay of gratification in children. *Science, 244,* 933–938. doi:10.1126/science.2658056

Moak, Z. B., & Agrawal, A. (2010). The association between perceived interpersonal social support and physical and mental health: Results from the National Epidemiological Survey on Alcohol and Related Conditions. *Journal of Public Health, 32,* 191–201. doi:10.1093/pubmed/fdp093

Muraven, M., Collins, R. L., & Nienhaus, K. (2002). Self-control and alcohol restraint: A test of the self-control strength model. *Psychology of Addictive Behaviors, 16,* 113–120. doi:10.1037/0893-164X.16.2.113

Nelson, E. E., & Panksepp, J. (1998). Brain substrates of infant–mother attachment: Contributions of opioids, oxytocin, and norepinephrine. *Neuroscience & Biobehavioral Reviews, 22,* 437–452. doi:10.1016/S0149-7634(97)00052-3

Noakes, T. D. (2012). The central governor model in 2012: Eight new papers deepen our understanding of the regulation of human exercise performance. *British Journal of Sports Medicine, 46,* 1–3. doi:10.1136/bjsports-2011-090811

Ochsner, K. N., Bunge, S. A., Gross, J. J., & Gabrieli, J. D. (2002). Rethinking feelings: An fMRI study of the cognitive regulation of emotion. *Journal of Cognitive Neuroscience, 14,* 1215–1229. doi:10.1162/089892902760807212

Ochsner, K. N., & Gross, J. J. (2005). The cognitive control of emotion. *Trends in Cognitive Sciences, 9,* 242–249. doi:10.1016/j.tics.2005.03.010

Panksepp, J. (1998). *Affective neuroscience: The foundations of human and animal emotions.* New York, NY: Oxford University Press.

Panksepp, J., Nelson, E., & Siviy, S. (1994). Brain opioids and mother–infant social motivation. *Acta Paediatrica, 83*, 40–46. doi:10.1111/j.1651-2227.1994.tb13264.x

Pardo, J. V., Fox, P. T., & Raichle, M. E. (1991, January 3). Localization of a human system for sustained attention by positron emission tomography. *Nature, 349*, 61–64. doi:10.1038/349061a0

Polan, H. J., & Hofer, M. A. (2008). Psychobiological origins of infant attachment and its role in development. In J. Cassidy & P. R. Shaver (Eds.), *Handbook of attachment: Theory, research, and clinical applications* (pp. 158–172). New York, NY: Guilford Press.

Proffitt, D. R. (2006). Embodied perception and the economy of action. *Perspectives on Psychological Science, 1*, 110–122. doi:10.1111/j.1745-6916.2006.00008.x

Robles, T. F., & Kiecolt-Glaser, J. K. (2003). The physiology of marriage: Pathways to health. *Physiology & Behavior, 79*, 409–416. doi:10.1016/S0031-9384(03)00160-4

Rubin, E. (1921). *Visuell wahrgenommene Figuren* [Visually perceived figures]. Copenhagen, Denmark: Gyldendals.

Rydell, A.-M., Berlin, L., & Bohlin, G. (2003). Emotionality, emotion regulation, and adaptation among 5- to 8-year-old children. *Emotion, 3*, 30–47. doi:10.1037/1528-3542.3.1.30

Sbarra, D. A., & Hazan, C. (2008). Co-regulation, dysregulation, self-regulation: An integrative analysis and empirical agenda for understanding adult attachment, separation, loss, and recovery. *Personality and Social Psychology Review, 12*, 141–167. doi:10.1177/1088868308315702

Sbarra, D. A., Law, R. W., & Portley, R. M. (2011). Divorce and death. *Perspectives on Psychological Science, 6*, 454–474. doi:10.1177/1745691611414724

Schnall, S., Harber, K. D., Stefanucci, J. K., & Prof?tt, D. R. (2008). Social support and the perception of geographical slant. *Journal of Experimental Social Psychology, 44*, 1246–1255. doi:10.1016/j.jesp.2008.04.011

Smyth, J. M., & Arigo, D. (2009). Recent evidence supports emotion-regulation interventions for improving health in at-risk and clinical populations. *Current Opinion in Psychiatry, 22*, 205–210. doi:10.1097/YCO.0b013e3283252d6d

Spanier, G. B. (1976). Measuring dyadic adjustment: New scales for assessing the quality of a marriage and similar dyads. *Journal of Marriage and the Family, 38*, 15–28. doi:10.2307/350547

Suveg, C., Sood, E., Comer, J. S., & Kendall, P. C. (2009). Changes in emotion regulation following cognitive-behavioral therapy for anxious youth. *Journal of Clinical Child and Adolescent Psychology, 38*, 390–401. doi:10.1080/15374410902851721

Swart, J., Lindsay, T. R., Lambert, M. I., Brown, J. C., & Noakes, T. D. (2012). Perceptual cues in the regulation of exercise performance—Physical sensations of exercise and awareness of effort interact as separate cues. *British Journal of Sports Medicine, 46*, 42–48. doi:10.1136/bjsports-2011-090337

Taylor, S. E. (2006). Tend and befriend: Biobehavioral bases of affiliation under stress. *Current Directions in Psychological Science, 15,* 273–277. doi:10.1111/j.1467-8721.2006.00451.x

Tice, D. M., Baumeister, R. F., Shmueli, D., & Muraven, M. (2007). Restoring the self: Positive affect helps improve self-regulation following ego depletion. *Journal of Experimental Social Psychology, 43,* 379–384. doi:10.1016/j.jesp.2006.05.007

Tomasello, M. (2009). *Why we cooperate.* Cambridge, MA: MIT Press.

Turner-Cobb, J. M., Sephton, S. E., Koopman, C., Blake-Mortimer, J., & Spiegel, D. (2000). Social support and salivary cortisol in women with metastatic breast cancer. *Psychosomatic Medicine, 62,* 337–345.

Uchino, B. N. (2006). Social support and health: A review of physiological processes potential underlying links to disease outcomes. *Journal of Behavioral Medicine, 29,* 377–387. doi:10.1007/s10865-006-9056-5

Uchino, B. N., Holt-Lunstad, J., Uno, D., Betancourt, R., & Garvey, T. S. (1999). Social support and age-related differences in cardiovascular function: An examination of potential mediators. *Annals of Behavioral Medicine, 21,* 135–142. doi:10.1007/BF02908294

Zubieta, J. K., Ketter, T. A., Bueller, J. A., Xu, Y., Kilbourn, M. R., Young, E. A., & Koeppe, R. A. (2003). Regulation of human affective responses by anterior cingulate and limbic μ-opioid neurotransmission. *Archives of General Psychiatry, 60,* 1145–1153. doi:10.1001/archpsyc.60.11.1145

6

EMOTION, MORALITY,
AND THE DEVELOPING BRAIN

JEAN DECETY AND LAUREN H. HOWARD

Whereas most people would likely agree that they know a good person when they meet one, there is decidedly less agreement as to what centrally defines *morality*. Psychoanalytic models tend to focus on internalized societal norms of behavior (i.e., superego) and the corresponding emotions of self-reproach (e.g., guilt). Developmental psychologists focus on overt behavior as the core of psychological morality (e.g., early signs of concerns for others, helping, sharing), and sociocultural theorists highlight the role of cultural transmission of values and personality traits (moral character). Cognitive psychologists emphasize the link between moral reasoning and decision making, and biologists tend to focus on evolutionary functions and genetic selection of moral characteristics (Berkowitz & Grych, 1998). Interestingly, most fields agree that an intuitive sense of fairness, concern for others, and observance of cultural norms seem to permeate human social existence.

The writing of this chapter was supported by a National Science Foundation award to Jean Decety (BCS-0718480).

http://dx.doi.org/10.1037/14250-007
Mechanisms of Social Connection: From Brain to Group, M. Mikulincer and P. R. Shaver (Editors)

Over the past decade, an explosion of interdisciplinary research in psychology, anthropology, biology, economics, and neuroscience has resulted in an attempt to define more clearly the concept of morality across domains. Work in these fields of study suggests that human social sensibilities emerge from a sophisticated integration of emotional, cognitive, and motivational mechanisms that are shaped through cultural exposure. The mechanisms can therefore be seen as a product of our biological, evolutionary, and cultural history that provides an important adaptive contribution to social cohesion and cooperation. Another development in contemporary morality research has been the placing of increased weight on the role of affect in moral judgment, as distinct from rationality or social duty. Although past research on moral cognition drew from cognitive theories rooted in Kantian philosophy, more recent work in psychology and cognitive neuroscience emphasizes the crucial relationship between emotion and moral judgment. New findings from developmental science indicate that infants are able to evaluate a range of interactions as positive or negative (Wynn, 2011), and they can use these evaluations to adapt their own social behavior. Such evaluations, along with early prosocial tendencies, are a prerequisite for moral thought.

Our primary goal in this chapter is to highlight the relations among affective processes and moral cognition by integrating developmental research with burgeoning work on the neurobiological underpinnings of empathy and morality. We begin by defining the constructs of empathy and morality within a naturalized (i.e., scientifically testable) framework. Next, the neurodevelopment of morality is examined with reference to early signs of sensitivity, fairness, and concern for others, abilities posited as precursors to a more mature morality. Functional neuroimaging studies focusing on the developmental changes in the perception of others' distress are then presented in support of the role of empathic arousal in moral reasoning, followed by neurodevelopmental empirical data indicating that the affective, cognitive, and regulatory aspects of morality involve interacting neural circuits with distinct developmental trajectories. We conclude by stressing the importance of affective processing in the development of morality, underscoring the importance of a multisystem approach to understanding individual differences that may contribute to maladaptive socioemotional functioning.

NATURALIZING EMPATHY AND MORALITY

To naturalize a construct is to bring it under the purview of science, confining theories to claims that research is able to countenance. Methodologically, it involves attempting to limit philosophical inquiry to empirical methods whose scientific validity can be demonstrated. Both empathy and morality have extensive research histories dating back to the earliest philosophers. But it is only with clear definitions, sound methodologies, and an understanding of evolutionary history that we are able to take these abstract ideas and examine them with scientific methods. Furthermore, it is important to consider the complex relationship between empathy and morality, focusing on the individual contributions and interconnected nature of these prosocial constructs.

The ability to empathize with another has been defined in multiple ways using various criteria. Although to most people empathy means feelings of concern for others (known as *empathic concern*, a motivational state aimed at improving another's welfare), the definition can include the awareness of other conspecifics and their subjective experiences—their feelings, desires, beliefs, and intentions. Including these abilities in the definition of empathy likens the construct to abilities such as having a theory of mind (the metacognitive capacity to explain, predict, and interpret behavior by attributing mental states such as desires, beliefs, intentions and emotions to oneself and to other people) or cognitive empathy (putting oneself into the mental shoes of another to perceive and understand what he or she feels). Another important element of empathy involves the capacity to either share or become affectively aroused by others' emotions, commonly referred to as *emotion contagion* or *empathic arousal*, arguably the evolutionarily oldest component of empathy and the earliest one to develop in ontogeny (Decety & Svetlova, 2012).

Empathic understanding, which encompasses self/other awareness and metacognition, is probably specific to humans, but empathic arousal and empathic concern are shared with other primates and mammals and depend on evolutionarily ancient systems adapted for intersubjectivity. Rooted in emotional bonding, attachment to kin, and motivation to care for their well-being (see Chapters 1, 7, and 8, this volume), these systems rely on subcortical neural pathways (brain stem, hypothalamus, amygdala, and basal ganglia) and hormonal processes highly conserved across species (Decety, 2011).

Whereas empathy tends to encompass our emotional and motivational reactivity to others, morality has been defined as possessing and acting on prescriptive norms regarding how people should treat one another, including concepts such as justice, fairness, and rights (Killen & Rutland, 2011). Haidt and Kesebir (2010) offered an additional definition, which encompasses the full array of psychological mechanisms that are active in the moral lives of people across cultures. Rather than specifying the content of moral issues (e.g., justice and welfare), this definition specifies the function of moral systems as interlocking sets of values, virtues, norms, practices, identities, and evolved psychological mechanisms that work together to suppress or regulate selfishness and make cooperative social life possible. What seems clear is that all definitions of morality minimally include judgment of the rightness or wrongness of acts or behaviors that knowingly cause harm to people other than the agent.

Regardless of how they define morality, many scholars, from Darwin (1871) to D. S. Wilson (2002; see also E. O. Wilson, 2012), have claimed that it is an evolved aspect of human nature. Such a claim is well supported when it comes to the role of emotion in moral cognition. It is highly plausible that some moral emotions (e.g., guilt, shame, empathy) have an evolutionary history, because social emotions contribute to fitness in shaping decisions and actions when living in complex social groups (see Chapters 19, 20, and 21, this volume). For example, associating in groups rather than living a solitary existence improves the chances of survival, reinforcement of moral behaviors minimizes criminal behavior and social conflict, and moral norms provide safeguards against possible safety or health infringements.

As with empathic arousal, some components of moral cognition (e.g., fairness and inequity aversion) are found in nonhuman primates. For example, capuchin monkeys respond negatively to unequal reward distribution in exchanges with a human experimenter. In a study by Brosnan and de Waal (2003), monkeys refused to participate if they witnessed a conspecific obtain a more attractive reward for equal effort. The effect was amplified if the partner received such a reward without any effort at all. Such findings across species highlight the need for an evolutionary model of morality.

Although the prosocial activities of other species provide strong evidence for the biological and evolutionary roots of morality, the social environment continues to play a large role in how such constructs are shaped. Even within a country or culture, differences in what constitutes a moral transgression can vary according to socioeconomic status or political affiliations (Haidt & Graham, 2007). This suggests that an individual's definition of morality is a highly socialized construct. Though morality relies on an emotional foundation (shame and guilt when one has performed an immoral action and anger and disgust when an action is performed by someone else), some have argued that these responses are inculcated by culture and not hardwired through natural selection (Prinz, 2007). In this case, emotional conditioning and social learning are the essential tools for acquiring moral values and explain variability both across and within cultures.

Empathetic abilities are often associated with morality, but research in social psychology suggests that empathic concern does not necessarily produce moral behavior. In fact, empathy may lead one to act in a way that violates the moral principle of justice when, for instance, allocating resources preferentially to the person for whom empathy was felt (Batson, Klein, Highberger, & Shaw, 1995). On the other hand, a lack of empathic concern for the welfare of others is considered a risk factor for amoral behavior; individuals with psychopathy constitute a paradigmatic case (Hawes & Dadds, 2012). In short, relations between empathy and morality are complex. Basic emotional processes such as empathic arousal may be necessary for developing some aspects of moral reasoning, such as care-based morality, but empathy alone is insufficient for mature moral cognition.

EARLY SIGNS OF MORAL SENSITIVITY

In the last decade, developmental psychologists have shown a renewed interest in the social evaluations and seemingly moral behavior of babies and young children. As demonstrated through a variety of techniques such as preferential looking time, violation-of-expectation tasks, and behavioral observations, children under the age of 3 appear to act in and prefer a prosocial manner. These results suggest that precursors to a more mature morality appear very early in development, though the nature of these prosocial propensities is debatable (Warneken & Tomasello, 2009; Wynn, 2011).

The foundation for later moral behavior and understanding may lie in infants' propensity to prefer social stimuli from the first days of life. For example, newborns are drawn to social stimuli such as the human face (e.g., Johnson, Dziurawiec, Ellis, & Morton, 1991). Furthermore, neonates can socially imitate facial emotional expressions despite never having seen their own (e.g., Field, Woodson, Greenberg, & Cohen, 1982). This behavior may stem from a primitive desire for interpersonal contact.

Although the preference for social partners may serve to enhance social bonds or focus an infant on relevant stimuli in the environment, it may also result in negative arousal and distress. For example, neonates contagiously cry in response to the distress of conspecifics in their proximity, a reaction that is specific to another's crying as opposed to the infant's own crying (Dondi, Simion, & Caltran, 1999). A lack of emotional expression on an interaction partner's face and noncontingent interactions may also arouse feelings of distress in an infant. Starting around 1.5 months, infants decrease their gaze and positive affect toward a disengaged experimenter displaying a "still face" expression after she had acted as a social partner (Bertin & Striano, 2006). By 3 to 6 months, this decrease in gaze is accompanied by other signs of frustration and self-soothing, such as crying or grasping at oneself, suggesting that a still and neutral face is quite distressing for young babies (Toda & Fogel, 1993). Furthermore, babies as young as 3 months of age appear to respond to the affective state of their caregiver, expressing negative emotions if their mother shows signs of depression (Cohn, Campbell, Matias, & Hopkins, 1990). These results suggest that infants react to both negative social stimuli and a lack of positive social stimuli in ways that may contribute later to moral understanding.

Although research on early infancy often focuses on the emotional reactions of young babies, infants quickly begin to use social information as a way to evaluate and distinguish the people around them. For example, 3-month-olds preferentially attend to a character who previously acted in a prosocial manner (Hamlin, Wynn, & Bloom, 2010), suggesting a partiality towards those who "do good things." By 6 months of age, this visual preference is expanded to the realm of behaviors; participants not only selectively attend to prosocial agents but also selectively approach them when there is a choice between them and antisocial or neutral characters (Hamlin & Wynn, 2011; Hamlin, Wynn, & Bloom, 2007). One series of studies showed that 6- to 10-month-old babies could evaluate a range of social behaviors (e.g., a character helping or hindering another character's progress up a hill) as either prosocial or antisocial in the same way that adults do (Bloom, 2012). These premoral evaluations are also associated with emotional expressions. Babies are more likely to smile, clap, and so on when viewing prosocial interactions and to frown, shake their heads, and look sad or otherwise upset while watching an antisocial interaction (Bloom, 2012); this suggests an emotional response to the good or bad deeds of others. Babies have no experience with the repercussions of such actions, which makes it difficult to assume that their judgments of "good" or "bad" are based on specific personal experiences (see Wynn, 2011).

As children progress through the second year of life, their reactions to social stimuli evolve from personal affective arousal to more empathetic behavior such as helping, sharing, and consoling. Early signs of helping behavior include informing someone who seems to need further information; for example, children as young as 12 months of age point to an object for which an experimenter is searching (Liszkowski, Carpenter, & Tomasello, 2008). Fourteen- to 18-month-olds help by fetching objects that an experimenter seems to want but cannot reach (Warneken & Tomasello, 2006). Children between 1 and 2 years of age comfort others who are in distress and may go so far as to give up their own favorite objects empathically to comfort another (Svetlova, Nichols, & Brownell, 2010). Toddlers exhibit more concern for the victim of a moral transgression than for the transgressor, even if the victim did not show any behavioral signs of distress (Vaish, Carpenter, & Tomasello, 2009). Hence, 18- to 25-month-olds are reacting not simply to emotional displays but to the intentions and desires of others.

Empathic responses increase throughout infancy, with the earliest forms of empathy appearing around 8 to 16 months and continuing to develop into the second year of life (Roth-Hanania, Davidov, & Zahn-Waxler, 2011). Between the ages of 18 and 36 months, empathic arousal becomes more specific, with children showing more emotional distress and engaging in more distress behavior in response to another's sadness than to another's pain (Bandstra, Chambers, McGrath, & Moore, 2011). Older children are more likely to show empathic concern than personal distress in reaction to another in pain, but no effect of age is found in reactions to another's sadness.

As children enter the preschool years, their reactions to moral stimuli continue to shift from personal distress to more proactive empathic behaviors. For example, preschoolers are better than their younger counterparts at assuming another person's perspective, and they respond to the distress of others not just with emotional discomfort but also with feelings of sympathy and a need to help (Hoffman, 2007). Of course, preschoolers have significantly more experience than infants with socially and culturally appropriate moral behaviors. In fact, they are quite adept at explaining verbally how to respond correctly to a peer's distress, even if they do not act on their knowledge behaviorally (Caplan & Hay, 1989). In general, their increase in social understanding does not always lead to an increase in prosocial behaviors, because children become increasingly selective in their sharing of objects and in their responsiveness to others' distress (Demetriou & Hay, 2004).

Although there is obviously considerable development in prosocial and moral abilities between infancy and childhood, it is less clear what motivates this change. There is evidence that an improvement in one prosocial ability may correlate with increased abilities in other prosocial areas. For example, 15-month-old infants who chose to share a toy they preferred (compared with a nonpreferred toy or no toy at all) with an experimenter also attended significantly longer to a third-party interaction in which the allocation of resources among conspecifics was unequal (Schmidt & Sommerville, 2011). Infants who behaved altruistically also expected others to do the same.

One neurological system that may be particularly influential in moral development is the executive system. Executive functions (including working memory, inhibition, planning, and attentional control), underpinned by the prefrontal cortex, are often associated with moral understanding and moral behavior. Although executive function research involving infants and young children is still rare, results so far suggest that the development of these abilities occurs in tandem with increased moral understanding. For example, the ability to inhibit one action in favor of another improves drastically during the second year of life (Kochanska, Murray, & Harlan, 2000), around the same time that children begin to inhibit their own emotional arousal in a distressing situation in favor of helping others. By the preschool years, executive functions are highly correlated with increased theory-of-mind abilities, skills thought to be necessary for mature moral understanding (Carlson, Moses, & Breton, 2002).

Social learning and cultural socialization also play an important part in children's moral development. The concept of moral socialization was originally made popular by Kohlberg's (1984) stage theory of moral reasoning, and recent work has confirmed the importance of more socialization, especially in the family. For example, parenting practices have long been known to play an important role in children's moral development (Dunn,

2006; Smetana, 1999). Moral development is more advanced in toddlers who come from homes in which mothers talk more about conflict resolution (Laible & Thompson, 2002), and higher levels of altruism are observed in children who come from families that show high degrees of emotional warmth (Brody & Shaffer, 1982). Abused infants often respond to peers with anger, whereas securely attached infants attend to others' distress and display empathy (Main & George, 1985). In general, early social experience may affect how well children understand and regulate their own emotions, which in turn affects their ability to empathize with others.

BRAIN RESPONSES TO PERCEIVING OTHERS IN DISTRESS

As mentioned, the capacity to understand and to resonate emotionally with the affective states of others is a foundational step toward experiencing empathy (Decety & Svetlova, 2012). Human infants are biologically predisposed to be sensitive to others' emotional expressions, especially when the expressions are vocalized. Neonates appear to possess a neural mechanism for discriminating vocalizations associated with emotions: They exhibit a mismatched electroencephalographic response over the right hemisphere in response to emotionally laden syllables (happy or fearful vs. neutral) within the first few days of life (Cheng, Lee, Chen, Wang, & Decety, 2012). In 3- to 7-month-olds, another person's sad vocalizations are associated with a selective increase of hemodynamic activity in brain regions involved in processing affective stimuli, such as the orbitofrontal cortex and insula (Blasi et al., 2011). These results suggest remarkably early functional specialization for processing negative emotions expressed in the human voice.

When adults' brains are imaged while the adults are presented with stimuli conveying another person's distress or pain, numerous studies have revealed reliable activation of a neural network involved in pain perception, including the anterior midcingulate cortex, anterior insular cortex, supplementary motor area, and periaqueductal gray area. Activation in this network has been reported in response to seeing facial expressions of pain, seeing body parts being injured, imagining the pain of others, or simply observing a signal indicating that someone will receive painful stimulation (see Lamm, Decety, & Singer, 2011, for a meta-analysis). These vicariously instigated activations of the pain matrix may not be specific to the sensory qualities of pain but instead might be associated with more general survival mechanisms, such as aversion and withdrawal when exposed to danger and threat (Decety, 2010).

Due to the methodological constraints of functional magnetic resonance imaging (fMRI), no study involving this technique has investigated morally relevant reactions in very young children. However, one cross-sectional developmental fMRI study tested participants ranging from 7 to 40 years of age while they were exposed to visual stimuli depicting individuals being physically injured by accident or intentionally by another person (Decety & Michalska, 2010). Subjective evaluations of the stimuli, collected after scanning, indicated a gradual decrease in the judgment of pain intensity for both conditions (accidental vs. intentional) across age, with younger participants rating the scenarios as significantly more painful than older participants did. An interesting developmental finding was that the younger the participants, the more strongly the amygdala, posterior insula, and medial orbitofrontal cortex were recruited when watching others in painful situations. A significant negative correlation between age and degree of neurohemodynamic response was found in the posterior insula. In contrast, a positive correlation was found in the anterior portion of the insula. A posterior-to-anterior progression of increasingly complex re-representations in the human insula is thought to provide a foundation for the sequential integration of the individual homeostatic condition with one's sensory environment and motivational condition (Craig, 2003). The posterior insula receives inputs from the ventromedial nucleus of the thalamus, an area highly specialized to convey emotional and homeostatic information, and it serves as a primary sensory cortex for both of these distinct interoceptive feelings from the body. The fact that, in response to others' physical distress, younger participants recruited the posterior portion of the insula, in conjunction with the amygdala and medial orbitofrontal cortex, more than adults did may speak to the children's tendency to be aroused by the perception of others' distress in a more direct sense. This in turn may lead to a heightened experience of discomfort associated with a visceral response to a potential threat, whereas adult participants tend to use more abstract secondary representations of pain when perceiving others in distress.

Decety and Michalska (2010) also found that age correlated with a larger signal change in prefrontal regions such as the dorsolateral prefrontal cortex and right inferior frontal gyrus, areas that are involved in cognitive control and response inhibition (Aron, Robbins, & Poldrack, 2004). This developmental pattern reflects the frontalization of regulatory capacities by providing increased top-down modulation of emotion processing, especially of amygdala reactivity to aversive stimuli (Yurgelun-Todd, 2007). The engagement of the amygdala, periaqueductal gray, insula, and medial orbitofrontal cortex in children during the perception of others' distress is consistent with the timing of their structural maturation. These reciprocally interconnected regions come online much earlier in ontogeny than other neural structures do; they underlie rapid and prioritized processing of emotion signals and are involved in affective arousal and somatovisceral resonance. In contrast, the dorsal prefrontal cortex and lateral orbitofrontal cortex undergo considerable maturation during the childhood years, becoming progressively specialized for the evaluation of social stimuli (Paus, 2011). These latter regions of the prefrontal cortex are vital for more advanced forms of empathy, such as those associated with perspective taking and theory of mind.

Taken together, emotional arousal in response to another's distress seems to be a necessary part of normal moral development. This affective response is present as early as childhood and becomes increasingly modulated by higher order neural regions with age. A lack of emotional response to the distress of others is associated with psychopathy and antisocial tendencies, suggesting an important link between emotional arousal and empathy (Cheng, Hung, & Decety, 2012).

BRAIN CIRCUITS UNDERPINNING MORAL COGNITION

Our knowledge of the brain circuits involved in moral cognition is based on converging results from lesion studies (e.g., Gleichgerrcht, Torralva, Roca, Pose, & Manes, 2011) and fMRI studies (Young & Dungan, 2012). These studies indicate the specific roles of the orbitofrontal cortex, anterior cingulate cortex, amygdala, ventromedial prefrontal cortex, medial prefrontal cortex, and posterior superior temporal sulcus in moral cognition. At first glance, moral reasoning might seem to be underpinned by specific neural circuitry, but in fact these circuits are not unique to morality. Rather, morality involves regions and systems that underlie various states of feelings, cognition, and motivation. Morality depends on an emotional learning system (mediated by the amygdala) and a system for making decisions on the basis of reinforcement expectations (mediated by the ventromedial prefrontal cortex), both of which are crucial for cuing morally appropriate behavior and for acquiring moral knowledge during childhood (Blair & Fowler, 2008).

Only two neuroimaging studies have investigated developmental changes in responses to morally relevant stimuli. In one study, involving a large sample of individuals ages 4 to 37 years, moral evaluations, eye tracking, and fMRI measures were used to assess reactions to brief animated scenarios (Decety, Michalska, & Kinzler, 2012). The scenarios depicted either people or objects being injured, with these injuries occurring via intentional or unintentional actions. Intentionality is a critical issue in this design because its detection is the decisive cue in determining whether an action is or is not malicious. After scanning, participants were presented with the same stimuli they saw in the scanner and were asked to judge whether the action performed by the perpetrator in the video clip was or was not intentional. Participants were also asked to respond to a set of questions probing moral judgment (wrongness and deserved punishment), empathic concern for the victim, personal distress, and understanding of the perpetrator's mental state. In all participants, perceived intentional harm to people (as opposed to accidental harm) was associated with increased activation in brain regions sensitive to the perception, prediction, and interpretation of others' intentions, such as the right posterior superior temporal sulcus (Blakemore et al., 2003). There was also activation in regions for processing the affective consequences of these actions; namely, the temporal poles, insula, ventromedial prefrontal cortex, and amygdala. The more participants reported being personally distressed about a harmful action, the greater the activity in the amygdala. Developmental trends were also examined. Age was negatively correlated with empathic sadness for the victims of harm in the video clips, with the youngest participants exhibiting the greatest sadness. Ratings of sadness for the victim correlated with activity in the insula, thalamus, and subgenual prefrontal cortex. The latter region has extensive connections with circuits implicated in emotional behavior and autonomic/neuroendocrine responses to stressors, including the amygdala, lateral hypothalamus, and brain stem serotonergic, noradrenergic, and dopaminergic nuclei (Drevets et al., 1997).

The signal change in the amygdala appeared to follow a curvilinear function, being greatest at the youngest ages, decreasing rapidly through childhood and early, and asymptoting in late adolescence through adulthood. The age-dependent signal change in the amygdala and correlations with ratings of empathic distress imply a role for this region in the normal development of empathic understanding (Decety & Michalska, 2010). Conversely, the neurohemodynamic signal in older participants increased in the medial prefrontal cortex and ventromedial prefrontal cortex, regions associated with metacognitive representations and decision making that enable a person to reflect on the values linked to outcomes and actions.

Patterns of functional connectivity during the perception of intentional harm (compared with perceptions of accidental harm) provided complementary evidence for increased integration between prefrontal cortex and the amygdala during development. Older participants displayed significant coactivation in these regions during the perception of intentional harm (relative to accidental harm), whereas the youngest children exhibited significant covariation only between the ventromedial prefrontal cortex and periaqueductal gray. Furthermore, adult participants showed stronger connectivity between ventromedial prefrontal cortex and posterior superior temporal sulcus while viewing moral (relative to nonmoral) actions than the younger participants did, suggestive of developmental changes in functional integration within the mentalizing system.

Neurodevelopmental changes during the perception of morally relevant situations are clearly seen in structures that are implicated in emotion saliency (amygdala and insula), with a gradual decrease in activation with age.

Conversely, activity in regions of the medial and ventral prefrontal cortex that are reciprocally connected with the amygdala and involved in decision making and evaluation increases with age, and these regions become more functionally coupled. This pattern of developmental change is reflected in the participants' moral evaluations, which require the capacity to integrate a representation of the mental states of others with the consequences of their actions (Leslie, Knobe, & Cohen, 2006). Although judgments of wrongness did not change across age—all participants rated intentional harm as more wrong than accidental harm—when participants were asked about the malevolence of the agent, their evaluations indicated a more differentiated appraisal with age. Whereas young children considered all agents malicious, irrespective of intention and targets (i.e., people or objects), older participants perceived the perpetrator as clearly less immoral (mean) when carrying out an accidental action, especially when the target was an object. Ratings of deserved punishment changed similarly with age. As age increased, participants punished an agent who damaged an object less severely than they did an agent who harmed a person. Although even young children attend to both intentionality and target, which affect their empathic responses and judgments of wrongness, the age-related increase in the discrimination of intentionality and target when determining moral culpability is consistent with the developmental shift in moral judgment dominated by a focus on the cognitive integration of both intent to harm and consequences.

In another study, 51 healthy male participants ages 13 to 53 were scanned while viewing International Affective Picture System pictures that did or did not depict situations considered to represent moral violations. They were also asked to rate the severity of moral violations (Harenski, Harenski, Shane, & Kiehl, 2012). These severity ratings were associated with increased activity in the amygdala, right inferior frontal gyrus, posterior superior temporal sulcus, and posterior cingulate cortex activity in both adolescents and adults, and the magnitude of activity in the posterior superior temporal sulcus was positively correlated with age. Given the role of the posterior superior temporal sulcus in mentalizing and the fact that its underlying neural substrates undergo extensive developmental changes from adolescence to adulthood, Harenski et al. hypothesized that adolescents use theory-of-mind inferences less than adults do when making moral judgments.

Overall, the results of these developmental studies highlight the importance of both affect and cognition in the development of morality, and this dual aspect of moral reactions has implications for broad theories of morality. The fact that morally relevant stimuli evoke stronger empathic sadness in younger participants, combined with a stronger response in neural networks coding affective saliency in young children, supports the notion that emotion plays a critical role in guiding the developmental trajectory of humans' moral capacities. Thus, what develops is not just one's theory of mind but also the ability to integrate knowledge about others' thoughts with information about behavioral consequences and one's own emotional reactions when making moral judgments.

CONCLUSION

Moral evaluations and decision making are fundamental aspects of social cognition that have evolved through natural selection. Although certain aspects of moral judgments may differ across cultures and individuals, experts in different disciplines and ordinary people from different cultures agree that physically harming others and violating considerations of fairness are central to the moral domain. The development of care-based morality is one of the building blocks from which cultures create moralities that are unique yet constrained in their variations (Haidt & Kesebir, 2010). Understanding the cognitive processes and neural mechanisms underlying empathy and morality and examining how they develop is not only a fascinating intellectual endeavor; it is important for understanding psychopathological conditions that lead to breakdowns in moral behavior.

Developmental research indicates that some initial cognitive structures and computations necessary for evaluations or interactions between social entities appear to emerge very early during development and are often associated with affective responses (Bloom, 2012; Hamlin & Wynn, 2011). These preverbal cognitive and emotional capacities do not seem to be the product of social learning; such capacities are evident in infants before they are able to experience the range of behaviors and outcomes that they are capable of evaluating. Burgeoning developmental neuroscience research highlights the importance of emotion in our earliest moral interactions, demonstrating that children's emotional reactions are mediated by ancient evolutionary circuits that connect brain stem regions with the hypothalamus, amygdala, insula, and orbitofrontal cortex. These circuits organize sustained responses to rewarding and aversive stimuli and regulate bodily states, providing a quick, efficient, and implicit understanding of the relationship between the social world and oneself. Abundant descending and ascending anatomical and functional connectivity gradually matures during development, coordinating and integrating instinctual emotional reactions with neurocognitive systems that underlie metacognitive representations. This increase in connectivity allows for more complex and deliberative moral judgments and decision making. The ventromedial prefrontal cortex, through its extensive reciprocal connections with amygdala, striatum, sensory cortices, and various regions of the prefrontal cortex, plays a pivotal role in integrating bodily responses with affective representations in the service of moral decision making and empathy.

Without input from the affective system (empathic arousal), moral behavior is understandably difficult to develop. This is best exemplified in children who do not respond emotionally to others' suffering and in adult psychopaths, who understand what is right or wrong in a given situation but do not seem to care (Cheng, Hung, & Decety, 2012). Individuals such as these, with impaired aversive emotion processing, often show display impaired moral judgment, suggesting that cognitive understanding is not sufficient to guide moral behavior.

REFERENCES

Aron, A. R., Robbins, T. W., & Poldrack, R. A. (2004). Inhibition and the right inferior frontal cortex. *Trends in Cognitive Sciences, 8,* 170–177. doi:10.1016/j.tics.2004.02.010

Bandstra, N. F., Chambers, C. T., McGrath, P., & Moore, C. (2011). The behavioural expression of empathy to others' pain versus others' sadness in young children. *Pain, 152,* 1074–1082. doi:10.1016/j.pain.2011.01.024

Batson, C. D., Klein, T. R., Highberger, L., & Shaw, L. L. (1995). Immorality from empathy-induced altruism: When compassion and justice conflict. *Journal of Personality and Social Psychology, 68,* 1042–1054. doi:10.1037/0022-3514.68.6.1042

Berkowitz, M. W., & Grych, J. (1998). Fostering goodness: Teaching parents to facilitate children's moral development. *Journal of Moral Education, 27,* 371–391. doi:10.1080/0305724980270307

Bertin, E., & Striano, T. (2006). The still-face response in newborn, 1.5-, and 3-month-old infants. *Infant Behavior & Development, 29,* 294–297. doi:10.1016/j.infbeh.2005.12.003

Blair, R. J. R., & Fowler, K. (2008). Moral emotions and moral reasoning from the perspective of affective cognitive neuroscience: A selective review. *European Journal of Developmental Science, 2,* 303–323.

Blakemore, S. J., Boyer, P., Pachot-Clouard, M., Meltzoff, A., Segebarth, C., & Decety, J. (2003). The detection of contingency and animacy from simple animations in the human brain. *Cerebral Cortex, 13,* 837–844. doi:10.1093/cercor/13.8.837

Blasi, A., Mercure, E., Lloyd-Fox, S., Thomson, A., Brammer, M., Sauter, D., . . . Murphy, D. G. M. (2011). Early specialization for voice and emotion processing in the infant brain. *Current Biology, 21,* 1220–1224. doi:10.1016/j.cub.2011.06.009

Bloom, P. (2012). Moral nativism and moral psychology. In M. Mikulincer & P. R. Shaver (Eds.), *The social psychology of morality: Exploring the causes of good and evil* (pp. 71–89). Washington, DC: American Psychological Association.

Brody, G., & Shaffer, D. (1982). Contributions of parents and peers to children's moral socialization. *Developmental Review, 2,* 31–75. doi:10.1016/0273-2297(82)90003-X

Brosnan, S. F., & de Waal, F. B. M. (2003). Monkeys reject unequal pay. *Nature, 425,* 297–299. doi:10.1038/nature01963

Caplan, M. Z., & Hay, D. F. (1989). Preschoolers' response to peers' distress and beliefs about bystander intervention. *Journal of Child Psychology and Psychiatry, 30,* 231–242. doi:10.1111/j.1469-7610.1989.tb00237.x

Carlson, S. M., Moses, L. J., & Breton, C. (2002). How specific is the relation between executive function and theory of mind? Contributions of inhibitory control and working memory. *Infant and Child Development, 11,* 73–92. doi:10.1002/icd.298

Cheng, Y., Hung, A., & Decety, J. (2012). Dissociation between affective sharing and emotion understanding in juvenile psychopaths. *Development and Psychopathology, 24,* 623–636. doi:10.1017/S095457941200020X

Cheng, Y., Lee, S. Y., Chen, H. Y., Wang, P., & Decety, J. (2012). Voice and emotion processing in the human neonatal brain. *Journal of Cognitive Neuroscience, 24,* 1411–1419. doi:10.1162/jocn_a_00214

Cohn, J. F., Campbell, S. B., Matias, R., & Hopkins, J. (1990). Face-to-face interactions of postpartum depressed and nondepressed mother–infant pairs at 2 months. *Developmental Psychology, 26,* 15–23. doi:10.1037/0012-1649.26.1.15

Craig, A. D. (2003). Interoception: The sense of the physiological condition of the body. *Current Opinion in Neurobiology, 13,* 500–505. doi:10.1016/S0959-4388(03)00090-4

Darwin, C. (1871). *The descent of man and selection in relation to race* (2nd ed.). London, England: Murray.

Decety, J. (2010). The neurodevelopment of empathy in humans. *Developmental Neuroscience, 32,* 257–267. doi:10.1159/000317771

Decety, J. (2011). The neuroevolution of empathy. *Annals of the New York Academy of Sciences, 1231,* 35–45. doi:10.1111/j.1749-6632.2011.06027.x

Decety, J., & Michalska, K. J. (2010). Neurodevelopmental changes in the circuits underlying empathy and sympathy from childhood to adulthood. *Developmental Science, 13,* 886–899. doi:10.1111/j.1467-7687.2009.00940.x

Decety, J., Michalska, K. J., & Kinzler, K. D. (2012). The contribution of emotion and cognition to moral sensitivity: A neurodevelopmental study. *Cerebral Cortex, 22,* 209–220. doi:10.1093/cercor/bhr111

Decety, J., & Svetlova, M. (2012). Putting together phylogenetic and ontogenetic perspectives on empathy. *Developmental Cognitive Neuroscience, 2,* 1–24. doi:10.1016/j.dcn.2011.05.003

Demetriou, H., & Hay, D. F. (2004). Toddlers' reactions to the distress of familiar peers: The importance of context. *Infancy, 6,* 299–318. doi:10.1207/s15327078in0602_9

Dondi, M., Simion, F., & Caltran, G. (1999). Can newborns discriminate between their own cry and the cry of another newborn infant? *Developmental Psychology, 35*, 418–426. doi:10.1037/0012-1649.35.2.418

Drevets, W. C., Price, J. L., Simpson, J. R., Jr., Todd, R. D., Reich, T., Vannier, M., & Raichle, M. E. (1997). Subgenual prefrontal cortex abnormalities in mood disorders. *Nature, 386*, 824–827. doi:10.1038/386824a0

Dunn, J. (2006). Moral development in early childhood and social interaction in the family. In M. Killen & J. Smetana (Eds.), *Handbook of moral development* (pp. 331–350). Mahwah, NJ: Erlbaum.

Field, T. M., Woodson, R., Greenberg, R., & Cohen, D. (1982). Discrimination and imitation of facial expressions by neonates. *Science, 218*, 179–181. doi:10.1126/science.7123230

Gleichgerrcht, E., Torralva, T., Roca, M., Pose, M., & Manes, F. (2011). The role of social cognition in moral judgment in frontotemporal dementia. *Social Neuroscience, 6*, 113–122. doi:10.1080/17470919.2010.506751

Haidt, J., & Graham, J. (2007). When morality opposes justice: Conservatives have moral intuitions that liberals may not recognize. *Social Justice Research, 20*, 98–116. doi:10.1007/s11211-007-0034-z

Haidt, J., & Kesebir, S. (2010). Morality. In S. Fiske, D. Gilbert, & G. Lindzey (Eds.), *Handbook of social psychology* (5th ed., pp. 797–832). Hoboken, NJ: Wiley.

Hamlin, J. K., & Wynn, K. (2011). Five- and 9-month-old infants prefer prosocial to antisocial others. *Cognitive Development, 26*, 30–39. doi:10.1016/j.cogdev.2010.09.001

Hamlin, J. K., Wynn, K., & Bloom, P. (2007). Social evaluation by preverbal infants. *Nature, 450*, 557–559. doi:10.1038/nature06288

Hamlin, J. K., Wynn, K., & Bloom, P. (2010). Three-month-olds show a negativity bias in their social evaluations. *Developmental Science, 13*, 923–929. doi:10.1111/j.1467-7687.2010.00951.x

Harenski, C. L., Harenski, K. A., Shane, M. S., & Kiehl, K. A. (2012). Neural development of mentalizing in moral judgment from adolescence to adulthood. *Developmental Cognitive Neuroscience, 2*, 162–173. doi:10.1016/j.dcn.2011.09.002

Hawes, D. J., & Dadds, M. R. (2012). Revisiting the role of empathy in childhood pathways to antisocial behavior. In R. Langdon & C. Mackenzie (Eds.), *Emotions, imagination, and moral reasoning* (pp. 45–70). New York, NY: Psychology Press.

Hoffman, M. L. (2007). The origins of empathic morality in toddlerhood. In C. Brownell & C. Kopp (Eds.), *Socioemotional development in the toddler years: Transitions and transformations* (pp. 132–145). New York, NY: Guilford Press.

Johnson, M. H., Dziurawiec, A., Ellis, H., & Morton, J. (1991). Newborns' preferential tracking of face-like stimuli and its subsequent decline. *Cognition, 40*, 1–19. doi:10.1016/0010-0277(91)90045-6

Killen, M., & Rutland, A. (2011). *Children and social exclusion: Morality, prejudice, and group identity*. New York, NY: Wiley-Blackwell. doi:10.1002/9781444396317

Kochanska, G., Murray, K. T., & Harlan, E. (2000). Effortful control in early childhood: Continuity and change, antecedents, and implications for social development. *Developmental Psychology, 36*, 220–232. doi:10.1037/0012-1649.36.2.220

Kohlberg, L. (1984). *Essays in moral development: Vol. 2. The psychology of moral development.* New York, NY: Harper & Row.

Laible, D. J., & Thompson, R. A. (2002). Mother–child conflict in the toddler years: Lessons in emotion, morality, and relationships. *Child Development, 73*, 1187–1203. doi:10.1111/1467-8624.00466

Lamm, C., Decety, J., & Singer, T. (2011). Meta-analytic evidence for common and distinct neural networks associated with directly experienced pain and empathy for pain. *NeuroImage, 54*, 2492–2502. doi:10.1016/j.neuroimage.2010.10.014

Leslie, A. M., Knobe, J., & Cohen, A. (2006). Acting intentionally and the side-effect effect: Theory of mind and moral judgment. *Psychological Science, 17*, 421–427. doi:10.1111/j.1467-9280.2006.01722.x

Liszkowski, U., Carpenter, M., & Tomasello, M. (2008). Twelve-month-olds communicate helpfully and appropriately for knowledgeable and ignorant partners. *Cognition, 108*, 732–739. doi:10.1016/j.cognition.2008.06.013

Main, M., & George, C. (1985). Responses of young abused and disadvantaged toddlers to distress in agemates: A study in the day care setting. *Developmental Psychology, 21*, 407–412. doi:10.1037/0012-1649.21.3.407

Paus, T. (2011). Brain development during childhood and adolescence. In J. Decety & J. T. Cacioppo (Eds.), *The Oxford handbook of social neuroscience* (pp. 293–313). New York, NY: Oxford University Press.

Prinz, J. (2007). *The emotional construction of morals.* New York, NY: Oxford University Press.

Roth-Hanania, R., Davidov, M., & Zahn-Waxler, C. (2011). Empathy development from 8 to 16 months: Early signs of concerned for others. *Infant Behavior & Development, 34*, 447–458. doi:10.1016/j.infbeh.2011.04.007

Schmidt, M. F. H., & Sommerville, J. A. (2011). Fairness expectations and altruistic sharing in 15-month-old human infants. *PLoS ONE, 6*, e23223. doi:10.1371/journal.pone.0023223

Smetana, J. G. (1999). The role of parents in moral development: A social domain analysis. *Journal of Moral Education, 28*, 311–321. doi:10.1080/030572499103106

Svetlova, M., Nichols, S. R., & Brownell, C. A. (2010). Toddlers' prosocial behavior: From instrumental to empathic to altruistic helping. *Child Development, 81*, 1814–1827. doi:10.1111/j.1467-8624.2010.01512.x

Toda, S., & Fogel, A. (1993). Infant response to the still-face situation at 3 and 6 months. *Developmental Psychology, 29*, 532–538. doi:10.1037/0012-1649.29.3.532

Vaish, A., Carpenter, M., & Tomasello, M. (2009). Sympathy through affective perspective taking and its relation to prosocial behavior in toddlers. *Developmental Psychology, 45*, 534–543. doi:10.1037/a0014322

Warneken, F., & Tomasello, M. (2006). Altruistic helping in human infants and young chimpanzees. *Science, 311,* 1301–1303. doi:10.1126/science.1121448

Warneken, F., & Tomasello, M. (2009). The roots of human altruism. *British Journal of Psychology, 100,* 455–471. doi:10.1348/000712608X379061

Wilson, D. S. (2002). *Darwin's cathedral: Evolution, religion and the nature of society.* Chicago, IL: University of Chicago Press.

Wilson, E. O. (2012). *The social conquest of earth.* New York, NY: Norton.

Wynn, K. (2011). Some innate foundations of social and moral cognition. In P. Carruthers, S. Laurence, & S. Stich (Eds.), *The innate mind* (Vol. 3, pp. 330–346). New York, NY: Oxford University Press.

Young, L., & Dungan, J. (2012). Where in the brain is morality? Everywhere and maybe nowhere. *Social Neuroscience, 7,* 1–10. doi:10.1080/17470919.2011.569146

Yurgelun-Todd, D. (2007). Emotional and cognitive changes during adolescence. *Current Opinion in Neurobiology, 17,* 251–257. doi:10.1016/j.conb.2007.03.009

II

INFANCY AND DEVELOPMENT

7

CHILD–PARENT ATTACHMENT AND RESPONSE TO THREAT: A MOVE FROM THE LEVEL OF REPRESENTATION

JUDE CASSIDY, KATHERINE B. EHRLICH, AND LAURA J. SHERMAN

During the past 30 years, the study of individual differences in the quality of infant–parent attachment has focused on the mental representations that infants form of their caregivers, themselves, and relationships during their first year of life. John Bowlby, the developer of attachment theory, sometimes called these *representational models* (Bowlby, 1973) and sometimes *internal working models* (the latter to emphasize the active nature of these representations; Bowlby, 1973, 1988). Representational models of attachment are thought to center on the extent to which the parent serves as a secure base from which the infant can explore and as a safe haven to which the infant can return when distressed or threatened. Following the pioneering empirical work

Portions of this paper were presented at the Attachment Pre-Conference of the meetings of the Society for Research in Child Development, Denver, Colorado, in March 2009. Preparation of this manuscript was supported by a grant from the National Institute on Drug Abuse (DA25550) to Jude Cassidy, by a Ruth L. Kirschstein National Research Service Award (DA027365) to Katherine Ehrlich, and by an Ann G. Wylie Dissertation Fellowship to Laura Sherman. We are grateful for the thoughtful comments that Inge Bretherton and Joan Stevenson-Hinde provided on a previous draft of this chapter.

http://dx.doi.org/10.1037/14250-008
Mechanisms of Social Connection: From Brain to Group, M. Mikulincer and P. R. Shaver (Editors)

of Mary Ainsworth (e.g., Ainsworth, Blehar, Waters, & Wall, 1978) and later of Mary Main (e.g., Main, Kaplan, & Cassidy, 1985), there has been an explosion of research related to these representations. Above all else, the notion that representations derive from experiences was central to Bowlby's conceptualizations.

At the same time that these experiences with caregivers are contributing to the formation of infant representations, they are also likely to set into motion a variety of nonrepresentational, physiological regulatory processes that play important roles in children's developing attachment systems. The fact that Bowlby paid relatively little attention to these infant physiological processes is surprising, given that he studied medicine as an undergraduate student at Cambridge and that the education about ethology that he received, largely from the ethologist Robert Hinde, was so central to his early theorizing about why humans become attached to their caregivers. Yet, Bowlby's focus on representations is understandable considering that much of his writing took place during a time when many branches of science were focused on the "cognitive revolution." Moreover, most of the research related to physiology in the mother–infant relationship was not yet available.

The aspect of infant and child functioning on which we focus in this chapter is the response to threat. Understanding children's response to threat is fundamental to understanding virtually all aspects of children's well-being, including social, emotional, cognitive, and physiological, as well as the development of psychopathology and physical disease. One of the core propositions of attachment theory is that proximity to an attachment figure reduces fearfulness in the face of possible or actual threat and that a central mechanism explaining this link is children's experience-based representations of the availability of the attachment figure. Moreover, individual differences in the nature of these representations are thought to predict individual differences in children's response to threat. Yet, in species that do not possess the representational capacities that humans possess, the link between attachment and response to threat nonetheless clearly exists. Our goal in this chapter is to consider what is known about this link that does not involve the highly cognitive representational processes usually discussed in the attachment literature.

We begin this chapter with Bowlby's (1969/1982, 1973) thinking about the link between attachment and responses to threat, which is best understood within the context of what he referred to as the *secure base/safe haven* construct. Bowlby drew on the research available at the time to focus on behavioral response to threat. We describe briefly the nature of attachment-related representations and how they are thought to mediate the link between child–parent attachment and child behavioral response to threat. We then focus on the ways in which the same experiences with caregivers that contribute to infant representations are also likely to contribute to nonrepresentational regulatory processes that reflect response to threat at the physiological level. In this way, we discuss how early experiences within the attachment relationship can contribute directly to infant and child response to threat without involving representational processes, as is surely the case in some nonhuman mammals. Next, we discuss the ways in which representational and nonrepresentational processes may interact to influence development in humans. We conclude with a brief summary and consideration of additional topics that could be examined within a broader model of cognitive and physiological responses to threat.

THE SECURE BASE/SAFE HAVEN CONSTRUCT: UNDERSTANDING THE LINK BETWEEN ATTACHMENT AND CHILDREN'S RESPONSE TO THREAT

Attachment theory contains key propositions about the link between attachment and children's response to threat. In fact, much of the early development of attachment theory grew from observations that children appeared to view separations from their mothers as threats to which they responded with considerable distress. Bowlby (1988), along with his colleague Ainsworth (1963), proposed what has come to be known as the secure base/safe haven construct, and it is their thinking about this construct that lies at the center of understanding the link between attachment and response to threat.

The secure base/safe haven construct is based on the notion that an attachment figure's two principal roles in the life of an infant are (a) serving as a secure base from which the child can explore and (b) providing a haven of safety to which the child can return in times of threat or distress (*haven of safety* is a term originally used by Harlow, 1958). As such, the secure base/safe haven construct rests on a conceptualization of the interrelations among three behavioral systems: the attachment, exploration, and fear systems. Bowlby (1969/1982) borrowed the behavioral system concept from ethologists to describe a species-specific system of behaviors that leads to certain predictable outcomes, at least one of which contributes to reproductive fitness.

When formulating attachment theory, Bowlby (1958) initially observed that infants engage in a series of behaviors that have the predictable outcome of gaining or maintaining proximity to caregivers. He called them *attachment behaviors* (e.g., crying, following, signaling). Bowlby (1969/1982) argued that attachment behaviors are organized into an attachment behavioral system that evolved because of its biological function of protection from harm. According to Bowlby, the exploratory system contributes to a child's survival in a different way by providing important information about the workings of the environment. Yet, unbridled exploration with no attention to potential hazards can be dangerous. The complementary yet mutually inhibiting nature of the exploratory and attachment systems is thought to have evolved to ensure that while the child is protected by maintaining proximity to attachment figures, he or she nonetheless gradually learns about the environment through exploration. According to Ainsworth (1972), "equilibrium between these two behavioral systems is even more significant for development (and for survival) than either in isolation" (p. 118).

The fear system, with its close links to both exploration and attachment, is another behavioral system particularly important to understanding children's responses to threat. For Bowlby (1973), the biological function of the fear system, like that of the attachment system, is protection. The evolutionary advantage of the fear system stems from the fact that it is biologically adaptive for children to be frightened of certain stimuli. Without such fear, survival and reproduction would be less likely. Bowlby described "natural clues to danger"—stimuli that are not inherently dangerous but that increase the likelihood of danger (e.g., darkness, loud noises, being alone). Because the attachment and fear systems are intertwined, infants who find these stimuli frightening are considered more likely to seek protection from caregivers and thus to survive to pass on their genes.

Most infants balance these three behavioral systems, responding flexibly to a specific situation after assessing both the environment's characteristics and the caregiver's availability and likely behavior. For our purposes in this chapter, it is most important to note that experiences related to the attachment figure's availability and responsiveness are thought to play an important role in the activation of an infant's fear system, such that an available and responsive attachment figure makes the infant much less susceptible to fear. According to Bowlby (1973), "the degree to which each of us is susceptible to fear turns in great part on whether our attachment figures are present or absent" (p. 201). Bowlby (1973) described as important not only the physical presence of an attachment figure but also the infant's confidence that the attachment figure will be available if needed. The evolutionary advantage derived from this linkage is that when the child is under threat and therefore most vulnerable, he or she has most to gain from contact with and protection from the attachment figure. In sum, for Bowlby (1988), the secure base/safe haven concept was at the heart of attachment theory: "No concept within the attachment framework is more central to developmental psychiatry than that of the secure base" (pp. 163–164).

INTERNAL REPRESENTATIONAL MODELS AND THEIR ROLE AS MEDIATORS OF THE LINK BETWEEN ATTACHMENT AND RESPONSE TO THREAT

In addition to the normative links between attachment and responses to threats, individual differences in the quality of attachment relate in important ways to variation in children's response to threat. Although virtually all children become attached to their primary caregivers, the quality of the attachment varies as a function of the nature of the specific infant–caregiver relationship. Some infants, labeled *securely attached,* are able to use their caregivers effectively as a secure base from which to explore and a safe haven to return to in times of need, whereas other infants, labeled *insecurely attached,* are unable to do so effectively (Ainsworth et al., 1978). Several studies of infants and young children have reported links between attachment quality and behavioral response to threat, with children securely attached to their mothers showing less fearfulness than one subgroup of insecurely attached children (insecure/ambivalent children; e.g., Stevenson-Hinde, Shouldice, & Chicot, 2011).

Attempts to explain how attachment and early attachment-related caregiving experiences are linked to behavioral response to threat in humans have centered in large part on infant mental representations as the causal mechanism. According to attachment theory, infants develop experience-based mental models of their caregivers' likely behavior (Bowlby, 1969/1982, 1973, 1979, 1980, 1988). The models, which develop early in life, begin as simple sensorimotor expectations and become more complex, flexible, and extendable over time. These models contain information about "how [an infant's] mother and other significant persons may be expected to behave, how he himself may be expected to behave, and how each interacts with the other" (Bowlby, 1969/1982, p. 354). These models then operate like cognitive schemas and scripts, allowing individuals to efficiently predict, interpret, and guide their interactions with others (see Bretherton & Munholland, 2008). For instance, securely attached infants have representations of their caregivers as effective secure bases, and these representations can be conceptualized as predictive scripts, for example, "If I'm upset, then my father will comfort me." In contrast, insecure infants may have predictive scripts, for example, "If I'm upset, then my father will push me away." These models also allow infants to interpret their caregivers' behavior in new situations. Finally, these models guide how infants behave with caregivers. Securely attached infants, as compared to insecurely attached infants, are more likely to approach their caregiver when distressed because they have an expectation that the caregiver will respond and will be an effective aid.

What are the precursors of representational models? According to Bowlby, these representational models are experience based. He viewed them as "tolerably accurate reflections of the experiences those individuals have actually had" with their caregivers (Bowlby, 1973, p. 202) rather than as projections of the child's internal drives, as psychoanalysts had proposed. Securely attached infants represent their caregiver as a secure base and a safe haven because past experiences during attachment-related interactions provided information that their caregiver was available, responsive, and sensitive. This information is stored as part of the child's mental model and is used as the basis from which to create expectations for the caregiver's future behavior. As such, individual differences in the content of these representations are based on the caregiver's parenting behavior during day-to-day attachment-related interactions. To the extent that caregiving experiences remain stable, children's attachment representations remain stable as well, and they become increasingly resistant to change (Bowlby, 1988). If, however, caregiving experiences change, either for the better or for the worse, children's attachment representations will change accordingly (Weinfield, Sroufe, & Egeland, 2000).

That Bowlby viewed representations as playing an important role in predicting children's response to threat is clear. In his discussion of representational models, Bowlby (1973) noted that

> intimately linked to the type of [representational] forecast a person makes of the probable availability of his attachment figures, moreover, is his susceptibility to respond with fear whenever he meets any potentially alarming situation during the ordinary course of his life. (p. 203)

In particular, it is because securely attached infants are more likely than insecurely attached infants to predict caregiver availability and responsiveness that they are able to interpret the threat as manageable and respond to it with less fear and anxiety.

A MOVE FROM THE LEVEL OF REPRESENTATIONS: A FOCUS ON PHYSIOLOGY

Two important and related advances since the time of Bowlby's (1958, 1969/1982, 1973) initial writings about infant attachment and response to separation have greatly extended scientists' understanding of the link between attachment and response to threat. One important advance originated in the research of Myron Hofer, which began to emerge in the 1970s. Hofer, a developmental psychobiologist, noticed defensive vocal protest responses to maternal separation in infant rat pups and asked what nonrepresentational process could account for these responses. This work has facilitated researchers' consideration of processes beyond the level of representations (see Main, 1999). A second and related advance has been an extensive examination of response to threat beyond the behavioral and emotional levels to an examination of response to threat at the physiological level, largely outside the range of conscious experience. The increase in research on stress reactivity has greatly enriched our understanding of the links between early attachment experiences and response to threat at multiple levels of analysis.

We begin this section with a review of Hofer's seminal work on the physiological subsystems that become disrupted in response to maternal separation, as well as the work of Seymour Levine, who examined the effects of maternal separation on rat pups' physiological threat response system. Next, we discuss the important work of Michael Meaney and colleagues, who identified how maternal caregiving experiences influence gene expression and response to threat in rats. We then describe evidence from studies of primates, again showing how attachment experiences shape responses to threat in mammals without fully developed representational systems. We conclude this section with a brief review of caregiving influences on the threat response system in humans, highlighting evidence that suggests the presence of underlying physiological systems that serve regulatory functions in response to threat.

Hidden Regulators in Mother–Infant Interactions: The Case of the Rat

Hofer's (1970) observations that rat pups responded with significant distress when separated from their mothers—similar to distress signals in humans—led him to wonder about the mechanisms of separation distress in nonhuman mammals. After all, rat pups lack the capacity for human-like mental representations, and these signals of distress could not, therefore, be rooted in representational processes. To explore this question, Hofer conducted a series of tightly controlled experiments to identify what physiological subsystems might be disrupted when mothers were removed from their pups (for reviews, see Hofer, 1994, 2002, 2006). These studies revealed a number of "hidden regulators" that no longer function properly if rat pups are separated from their mothers. These regulators are hidden because they are not immediately visible; they operate "under the skin." Hofer found that when rat pups were removed from their mothers, they showed changes in multiple physiological and behavioral systems, such as those controlling heart rate, body temperature, food intake, and exploratory behavior. Hofer argued that maternal separation resulted in the removal of the important regulatory functions that the mother served for her offspring, and the absence of these regulatory components resulted in rat pups' visible behavioral distress. These studies led Hofer to conclude that mother–infant interactions have embedded within them a number of vital physiological regulatory functions that are negatively affected by separation from maternal care and that presumably do not require cognitive representations as triggers or mediators.

New evidence that the environment can influence an infant's developing stress response system came from Levine's (1957) paradigm-shifting research. This and subsequent work revealed the influence of maternal care on rat pups' developing physiology, identifying ways in which mothers serve as regulators of their infants' pituitary-adrenal stress response systems (see Levine, 2005, for a review). In one study, for example, feeding rat pups helped buffer their corticosterone response to maternal separation, suggesting that one regulator of the rats' stress response system is mothers' regulation of infant feeding (Suchecki, Rosenfeld, & Levine, 1993).

But how do mother–infant interactions have such a profound effect on rat pup stress physiology? What is it about maternal behavior that gets under the skin? The work of Meaney and colleagues sheds light on this question. Meaney found that certain caregiving experiences early in infancy were associated with long-term changes in rats' stress response physiology (Liu et al., 1997). Rat pups that received high levels of maternal licking and grooming and arched-back nursing positions showed attenuated responses to threat and increased exploratory behavior—effects that lasted into adulthood (Liu et al., 1997; see Meaney, 2001, for a review). Meaney and his colleagues further found that these individual differences in maternal behavior led to differences in gene expression in offspring (Weaver et al., 2004). Although the genes themselves did not differ between rats treated differently, the ways in which the genes operated differed as a function of maternal behavior (see Weaver et al., 2004, for more information).

Attachment and Response to Threat in Nonhuman Primates

Just as rodent mothers serve as regulators of their pups' physiology, so too do nonhuman primate mothers (Levine & Wiener, 1988; see Suomi, 2008, for a review). For example, following an initial state of hyperarousal, infant pig-tail macaque monkeys who were separated from their mothers showed declines in heart rate and body temperature (Reite, Kaufman, Pauley, & Stynes, 1974). Similarly, infant behaviors changed as a result of maternal separation: The youngest infants exhibited characteristic depressed behaviors (e.g., slouched posture and motor coordination problems), and the older infants showed decreased play behavior. These findings suggest that mothers' absence is a threatening experience, and the lack of maternal availability leads to the dysregulation of behavioral and physiological systems.

Additional evidence for maternal regulation of infant physiological systems comes from studies of nonhuman primates' endocrine dysregulation in response to separation. Rhesus macaque infants who were separated physically from their mothers but who could still see, hear, and smell their mothers showed a lower cortisol stress response than did those who were completely isolated from their mothers (Levine, Johnson, & Gonzalez, 1985). In another study, infant rhesus monkeys who had been repeatedly separated from their mothers between 3 and 6 months of age exhibited long-term changes in cortisol stress reactivity during an acoustic startle paradigm (Sánchez et al., 2005). These effects on the regulation of infant biology appear to be specific to contact with the mother, as evidenced by findings that infant monkeys who accidentally sought contact from another monkey experienced increases, rather than decreases, in physiological arousal (Suomi, 1979).

In addition, a number of studies have documented connections between the quality of maternal care and infants' biological and behavioral responses to threat. Coplan et al. (1996) created a stressful caregiving environment for a sample of bonnet macaque infants and their mothers by varying the stability of the available food supply. Monkeys who had been raised by mothers in the variable food condition had elevated corticotropin-releasing factor in their cerebrospinal fluid in adulthood. In comparison, monkeys who were raised in consistent, predictable environments—characterized by either low or high levels of effort required to obtain food—had lower corticotropin-releasing factor levels. Thus, these long-term changes in the biological stress system were not due simply to the availability of food but rather to the stress of uncertainty in the caregiving environment. Similarly, monkeys who had been abused by their mothers showed dysregulation in hypothalamic–pituitary–adrenal (HPA) axis functioning (see Suomi, 2008, for a review). In summary, it is clear that variations in early caregiving experiences play an important role in regulating nonhuman primates' physiological responses to threat.

Early Attachment-Related Experiences and Human Infant Biological Response to Stress

As discussed earlier, an infant's experiences with an attachment figure contribute to the development of representations about the availability of support when needed. The same experiences also contribute to the development of a number of biologically based regulatory processes. Our focus is on evidence of connections between infants' interactions with their mothers and HPA axis physiology, but we note that caregiving interactions also influence other physiological systems that are beyond the scope of this chapter.

A fully developed human stress response system is present at birth (see Adam, Klimes-Dougan, & Gunnar, 2007). This system becomes activated in response to stressful events, ultimately leading to the production of cortisol. The HPA axis is sensitive to environmental and contextual perturbations in humans as it is in rats and some nonhuman primates, and a growing body of research suggests that differences in the quality of early caregiving experiences contribute to variations in the initial calibration and continued regulation of this system. The regulation of the HPA axis in turn plays an important role in shaping behavioral responses to threat (Jessop & Turner-Cobb, 2008).

Researchers have examined the connections between caregiving experiences and infant stress physiology by comparing infants' cortisol levels before and after a stressful task (e.g., the laboratory Strange Situation paradigm, which contains two brief episodes of infant–mother separation; Ainsworth et al., 1978). For example, Nachmias, Gunnar, Mangelsdorf, Parritz, and Buss (1996) found that inhibited toddlers who were insecurely attached to their caregivers exhibited elevated cortisol following exposure to novel stimuli. Additional evidence for the role of maternal influences in shaping an infant's stress response comes from experimental evidence showing that mothers' touch buffered infants' cortisol stress response typically associated with a stressful experience (in this case, during the still-face laboratory procedure in which mothers are asked to cease interacting with their infants; Feldman, Singer, & Zagoory, 2010).

Children living in violent families endure particularly stressful caregiving environments, and such exposure is extremely dysregulating for children. The constant uncertainty and turmoil of these environments have consequences for children's stress reactivity (Taylor, Repetti, & Seeman, 1997). A number of studies have documented the disrupted stress response of maltreated children (e.g., Davies, Sturge-Apple, Cicchetti, & Cummings, 2007). Even living in a family in which the violence does not involve them directly has negative consequences for children, and some evidence suggests that the quality of caregiving in these hostile environments plays an important role in modifying the stress response. For example, in a longitudinal study of intimate partner violence and children's adrenocortical responses to stress, Hibel, Granger, Blair, Cox, and the FLP Investigators (2011) found that children who were exposed to intimate partner violence but whose mothers demonstrated high levels of sensitivity were buffered from heightened cortisol reactivity, compared to children who were exposed to intimate partner violence and low maternal sensitivity.

ATTACHMENT AS A REGULATOR OF INFANT STRESS REACTIVITY: EVOLUTIONARY UNDERPINNINGS

In the species discussed in this chapter, the stress reactivity system helps an animal to mobilize protective resources in times of threat and to devote metabolic and psychological resources elsewhere (e.g., food gathering, exploration) in the absence of threat. It seems reasonable, therefore, that the most evolutionarily adaptive stress reactivity system would include a component that can extract information about the organism's environment, gauge the level of environmental threat, and prompt an appropriate response. With high environmental threat, greatest adaptation entails a stress reactivity system that is calibrated to recognize, attend to, and respond to threat quickly. Importantly, one central factor that demarks the extent of environmental threat is the presence or absence of a reliably responsive caregiver; an environment lacking a protective attachment figure is an environment of increased risk. Thus, for an infant without a responsive attachment figure, adaptation means being vigilant to threat and ready for a quick response.

Just as infants are thought to have evolved with the capacity to use experience-based information about the availability of a protective caregiver to calibrate their attachment behavioral system (Main, 1990), and given the close intertwining of the attachment and fear systems as described above, it is likely that infants evolved with the capacity to use information about the availability of an attachment figure to calibrate their threat response system at both the behavioral and physiological levels (Cassidy, 2009). This thinking about the role of attachment in the calibration of the infant's stress reactivity emerges directly from Bowlby's (1969/1982, 1973) theories of attachment and fear, Hinde's (1986) evolutionary thinking about parental signaling about the state of the environment, and Main's (1990) ideas about attachment strategies, as well as from the thinking of contemporary evolutionary biologists (e.g., West-Eberhard, 2003).

INTERACTION OF REPRESENTATIONAL AND NONREPRESENTATIONAL PROCESSES IN PREDICTING CHILDREN'S RESPONSE TO THREAT

Just as the study of the correlates of attachment security at multiple levels of analysis is important, so too will be the examination of how cognitive processes interact with physiological processes to influence child outcomes. An important set of questions emerges: How are representational and physiological processes linked, and how do they influence each other? How do these two sets of processes work together to predict child functioning? Does the nature of the interaction vary across particular aspects of child functioning and across developmental periods? How do these processes interact during initial attachment formation and during maintenance of an attachment? How can we understand these interactions in relation to both normative development and individual differences? The growth of knowledge since the time of Bowlby's initial writings, including findings from the studies described here, has brought many scientists to a working assumption: Anything that influences representations influences many parts of the body and brain.

The most fundamental question relates to how representational and nonrepresentational processes are linked. In humans, each process is thought to initiate the other in ways unlikely to be the case in other species. Sapolsky (2004) noted that in humans, representational processes—the anticipation of threat when none currently exists—can launch a stress response: "A stressor can also be the *anticipation* of [something] happening. Sometimes we are smart enough to see things [threats] coming and, based only on anticipation, can turn on a stress-response as robust as if the event had actually occurred" (p. 6). Relatedly, Bowlby (1973), focusing on the link between attachment and fear, specified representational "forecasts of availability or unavailability" of the attachment figure as "a major variable that determines whether a person is or is not alarmed by any potentially alarming situation" (p. 204). Thus, the representations that others will be unavailable or rejecting when needed— that is, representations that characterize insecure attachment—could contribute to chronic activation of physiological stress response systems, as could the associated representations of others as having hostile intentions (see Dykas & Cassidy, 2011, for a review of the social information-processing patterns associated with secure and insecure attachment). Just as representational processes are useful in the anticipation of threats, so are they useful in anticipating protective resources that will dampen the stress reactivity system. Thus, in times of both anticipated and actual threat, the capacity to represent a responsive attachment figure can reduce physiological responses associated with threatening or painful experiences (for evidence of reduced neural responses to painful stimuli when participants viewed pictures of their attachment figure, see Eisenberger et al., 2011). Consideration of the linkage between representational and nonrepresentational processes must also contain a recognition not only that can representations lead to both increases and decreases in physiological stress reactivity but that pathways of influence can run in the opposite direction: Physiological stress responses can lead an individual to engage in higher level cognitive process to understand, justify, or change the stressor (Festinger, 1957; Schachter & Singer, 1962).

When and how do young children come to use attachment-related representations as regulators of stress? Neither the normative trajectories nor individual differences in the developmental course of the use of representations to influence stress reactivity have been examined extensively. Evidence that stress dysregulation can lead to the conscious engagement of representational processes comes from children as young as age 4, who are able to describe cognitive mechanisms for alleviating distress (e.g., changing thoughts, reappraising the situation, mental distraction; Sayfan & Lagattuta, 2009). Younger children may possess these capacities without being able to verbalize them. Moreover, there is behavioral evidence of representations dampening distress in young children: Representations of their mothers (in the form of photographs) were calming to 24-month-olds experiencing a brief laboratory separation (inferred from greater engagement in play; Passman & Longeway, 1982) and to young children experiencing extended separations of several days (Robertson & Robertson, 1989).

Hofer (Polan & Hofer, 2008) and Suomi (2008) converge in their thinking about the biological advantages of the ways in which representational and nonrepresentational processes work together in relation to human attachment. Hofer proposed that mechanisms wherein parents are early physiological regulators of infant stress reactivity (which prepare infants for the environment they are likely to face; he referred to this as the "predictive role of parenting"; see the initial thinking of Hinde, 1986) will be most effective when they allow a means for "corrective effects" (i.e., input from later environments, some of which will involve representations) if the later environment differs substantially from that predicted by earlier parent–child interaction. Furthermore, Hofer (2006) called for future research to understand how specific components of mother–infant interaction, such as touch, voice, and imitation, link both to representational and to neural and hormonal processes other than representation and how these processes interact to predict later functioning. Hofer's (1994) proposition that hidden regulators constitute some of the building blocks of representations has a compelling basis in the animal research literature and merits examination in humans.

Suomi's (2008) speculations about how physiological mechanisms and cognitive representations interact included the notion that advanced levels of cognition are not needed for the complex workings of the attachment system within most primates and that humans have higher level cognitions superimposed on these other biological processes. Suomi (2008) further described representational processes and underlying biology in relation to both continuity and change:

> Working models . . . may represent a luxury for humans that enables individuals to cognitively reinforce the postulated underlying biological foundation, in which case the predicted developmental continuity may actually be strengthened. On the other hand, the existence of a working model that has the potential to be altered by specific experiences (and/or insights) in late childhood, adolescence, or adulthood may provide a basis for breaking an otherwise likely continuity between one's early attachment experiences and subsequent performance as a parent. These important issues deserve not only further theoretical consideration, but empirical investigation as well. (pp. 186–187)

From a historical perspective, it is interesting to note that Bowlby's early work (e.g., 1958), focusing on the evolutionary basis of the initial formation of the attachment bond, contained no mention of representational processes—an understandable state of affairs given that Bowlby's initial search for experimental data led him to Harlow's studies of infant rhesus monkeys separated from their mothers (Harlow, 1958, 1960; see van der Horst, 2011). In fact, Bowlby clarified his "wish to distinguish [his theory about separation anxiety] from states of anxiety dependent on foresight [i.e., representations]" (Bowlby, 1961, p. 267, cited in van der Horst, 2011, p. 120). It was only later, when Bowlby turned his attention to individual differences in attachment quality throughout the early years of human life, that he highlighted the role of children's representations as a mechanism linking attachment and later functioning.

SUMMARY AND ADDITIONAL CONSIDERATIONS

In this chapter, we have described the ways in which the same experiences with caregivers that contribute to infant attachment representations contribute also to nonrepresentational regulatory processes, some of which reflect responses to threat at the physiological level; in this way, early caregiving experiences contribute to child response to threat directly, without involving complex cognitive or representational processes. Since the time of Bowlby's original writing, research examining these nonrepresentational processes has burgeoned. The idea that early caregiving experiences influence both immediate and long-term behavioral and physiological response to threat is well replicated and is widely accepted with respect to some rodents, nonhuman primates, and humans (Meaney, 2001; Suomi, 2008).

Several important topics are beyond the scope of this chapter; we mention a few of these here briefly. First, the focus of this chapter is on the early years of life. Bowlby, however, emphasized that attachment characterizes humans "from the cradle to the grave" (1969/1982, p. 208). Hofer (1984) proposed that hidden regulators continue to function throughout life and suggested that the withdrawal of hidden regulators may account for bereavement processes in adulthood. Moreover, recent evidence suggests that hidden regulators play a role not only in adult bereavement but also in more daily adult attachment processes (e.g., accounting for alterations in sleep/wake patterns when a long-term romantic partner is away on a business trip; see Diamond, Hicks, & Otter-Henderson, 2008). Furthermore, if evolution has provided organisms with the capacity to extract information from their environments about the level of likely threat, it seems reasonable that this capacity would be present as early in development as possible, including during the prenatal period (e.g., the fetal-programming model; Ellison, 2010). Second, we have focused on the ways in which maternal caregiving experiences contribute to the calibration and regulation of infant neuroendocrine responses to threat, but it is likely that the same caregiving experiences also manifest themselves in a number of other physiological changes. For example, variations in caregiving quality have been associated with telomere length (Drury et al., 2012), inflammatory profiles (Chen, Miller, Kobor, & Cole, 2011), and sympathetic nervous system activity (Moore et al., 2009).

Third, we discuss only the behavioral and physiological levels of response to threat in this chapter; other levels should be considered as well (e.g., the information-processing level). Fourth, a rich set of questions about clinical implications emerges from consideration of the issues discussed in this chapter. Given the extent to which many forms of psychopathology reflect problems of self-regulation in the face of stress (e.g., internalizing problems, externalizing problems, substance abuse; Kring & Sloan, 2010), what can hidden regulators embedded within human infant–mother interactions tell us about the precursors of psychopathology? What about hidden regulators embedded within the relationship with a therapist (who, according to Bowlby, 1988, comes to serve as an attachment figure within the context of long-term psychotherapy)? When change occurs following long-term therapy, does this change emerge through representations, physiological regulation, or both (see also Stern, 2004)?

We end by noting that the theory and data reviewed here are fully compatible with the earliest thinking of Bowlby, whose scientific roots were in biology. Yet, in Bowlby's lifetime, many of the tools for examining neural and physiological processes that scientists now possess were unavailable—as was even the concept of experiential effects on gene expression. We imagine that Bowlby would have found these newest developments enormously exciting.

REFERENCES

Adam, E. K., Klimes-Dougan, B., & Gunnar, M. R. (2007). Social regulation of the adrenocortical response to stress in infants, children, and adolescents. In D. Coch, G. Dawson, & K. W. Fischer (Eds.), *Human behavior and the developing brain: Atypical development* (2nd ed., pp. 264–304). New York, NY: Guilford Press.

Ainsworth, M. D. S. (1963). The development of infant–mother interaction among the Ganda. In B. M. Foss (Ed.), *Determinants of infant behavior* (pp. 67–104). New York, NY: Wiley.

Ainsworth, M. D. S. (1972). Attachment and dependency: A comparison. In J. L. Gewirtz (Ed.), *Attachment and dependency* (pp. 97–137). Washington, DC: Winston.

Ainsworth, M. D. S., Blehar, M. C., Waters, E., & Wall, S. (1978). *Patterns of attachment: A psychological study of the strange situation*. Hillsdale, NJ: Erlbaum.

Bowlby, J. (1958). The nature of the child's tie to his mother. *International Journal of Psycho-Analysis, 39*, 350–373.

Bowlby, J. (1973). *Attachment and loss: Vol. 2. Separation: Anxiety and anger*. New York, NY: Basic Books.

Bowlby, J. (1979). *The making and breaking of affectional bonds*. London, England: Tavistock.

Bowlby, J. (1980). *Attachment and loss: Vol. 3. Loss: Sadness and depression*. New York, NY: Basic Books.

Bowlby, J. (1982). *Attachment and loss: Vol. 1. Attachment* (2nd ed.). New York, NY: Basic Books. (Original work published 1969)

Bowlby, J. (1988). *A secure base: Parent–child attachment and healthy human development*. New York, NY: Basic Books.

Bretherton, I., & Munholland, K. A. (2008). Internal working models in attachment relationships: Elaborating a central construct in attachment theory. In J. Cassidy & P. R. Shaver (Eds.), *Handbook of attachment: Theory, research, and clinical applications* (2nd ed., pp. 102–127). New York, NY: Guilford Press.

Cassidy, J. (2009, March). *New directions in attachment research*. Paper presented at the Attachment Pre-Conference of the Society for Research in Child Development, Denver, CO.

Chen, E., Miller, G. E., Kobor, M. S., & Cole, S. W. (2011). Maternal warmth buffers the effects of low early-life socioeconomic status on pro-inflammatory signaling in adulthood. *Molecular Psychiatry, 16*, 729–737. doi:10.1038/mp.2010.53

Coplan, J. D., Andrews, M. W., Rosenblum, L. A., Owens, M. J., Friedman, S., Gorman, J. M., & Nemeroff, C. B. (1996). Persistent elevations in cerebrospinal fluid concentrations of corticotrophin-releasing factor in adult nonhuman primates exposed to early-life stressors: Implications for the pathophysiology of mood and anxiety disorders. *Proceedings of the National Academy of Sciences, USA, 93*, 1619–1623. doi:10.1073/pnas.93.4.1619

Davies, P. T., Sturge-Apple, M. L., Cicchetti, D., & Cummings, E. M. (2007). The role of child adrenocortical functioning in pathways between interparental conflict and child maladjustment. *Developmental Psychology, 43*, 918–930. doi:10.1037/0012-1649.43.4.918

Diamond, L. M., Hicks, A. M., & Otter-Henderson, K. D. (2008). Every time you go away: Changes in affect, behavior, and physiology associated with travel-related separations from romantic partners. *Journal of Personality and Social Psychology, 95*, 385–403. doi:10.1037/0022-3514.95.2.385

Drury, S. S., Theall, K., Gleason, M. M., Smyke, A. T., DeVivo, I., Wong, J. Y. Y., . . . Nelson, C. A. (2012). Telomere length and early severe social deprivation: Linking early adversity and cellular aging. *Molecular Psychiatry, 17*, 719–727. doi:10.1038/mp.2011.53

Dykas, M. J., & Cassidy, J. (2011). Attachment and the processing of social information across the life span: Theory and evidence. *Psychological Bulletin, 137*, 19–46. doi:10.1037/a0021367

Eisenberger, N. I., Master, S. L., Inagaki, T. K., Taylor, S. E., Shirinyan, D., Lieberman, M. D., & Naliboff, B. D. (2011). Attachment figures activate a safety signal-related neural region and reduce pain experience. *Proceedings of the National Academy of Sciences, USA, 108*, 11721–11726. doi:10.1073/pnas.1108239108

Ellison, P. (2010). Fetal programming and fetal psychology. *Infant and Child Development, 19*, 6–20. doi:10.1002/icd.649

Feldman, R., Singer, M., & Zagoory, O. (2010). Touch attenuates infants' physiological reactivity to stress. *Developmental Science, 13*, 271–278. doi:10.1111/j.1467-7687.2009.00890.x

Festinger, L. (1957). *A theory of cognitive dissonance.* Stanford, CA: Stanford University Press.

Harlow, H. F. (1958). The nature of love. *American Psychologist, 13*, 673–685. doi:10.1037/h0047884

Harlow, H. F. (1960). Primary affectional patterns in primates. *American Journal of Orthopsychiatry, 30*, 676–684. doi:10.1111/j.1939-0025.1960.tb02085.x

Hibel, L. C., Granger, D. A., Blair, C., Cox, M. J., & the FLP Investigators. (2011). Maternal sensitivity buffers the adrenocortical implications of intimate partner violence exposure during early childhood. *Development and Psychopathology, 23*, 689–701. doi:10.1017/S0954579411000010

Hinde, R. A. (1986). Some implications of evolutionary theory and comparative data for the study of human prosocial and aggressive behavior. In D. Olweus, J. Block, & M. Radke-Yarrow (Eds.), *Development of antisocial and prosocial behavior* (pp. 13–32). Orlando, FL: Academic Press.

Hofer, M. A. (1970). Physiological responses of infant rats to separation from their mothers. *Science, 168*, 871–873. doi:10.1126/science.168.3933.871

Hofer, M. A. (1984). Relationships as regulators: A psychobiologic perspective on bereavement. *Psychosomatic Medicine, 46*, 183–197.

Hofer, M. A. (1994). Hidden regulators in attachment, separation, and loss. *Monographs of the Society for Research in Child Development, 59*, 192–207.

Hofer, M. A. (2002). The riddle of development. In D. J. Lewkowicz & R. Lickliter (Eds.), *Conceptions of development* (pp. 5–30). Philadelphia, PA: Psychology Press.

Hofer, M. A. (2006). Psychobiological roots of early attachment. *Current Directions in Psychological Science, 15*, 84–88. doi:10.1111/j.0963-7214.2006.00412.x

Jessop, D. S., & Turner-Cobb, J. M. (2008). Measurement and meaning of salivary cortisol: A focus on health and disease in children. *Stress, 11*, 1–14. doi:10.1080/10253890701365527

Kring, A., & Sloan, D. (Eds.). (2010). *Emotion regulation and psychopathology: A transdiagnostic approach to etiology and treatment.* New York, NY: Guilford Press.

Levine, S. (1957). Infantile experience and resistance to physiological stress. *Science, 126*, 405. doi:10.1126/science.126.3270.405

Levine, S. (2005). Developmental determinants of sensitivity and resistance to stress. *Psychoneuroendocrinology, 30*, 939–946. doi:10.1016/j.psyneuen.2005.03.013

Levine, S., Johnson, D. F., & Gonzalez, C. A. (1985). Behavioral and hormonal responses to separation in infant rhesus monkeys and mothers. *Behavioral Neuroscience, 99*, 399–410. doi:10.1037/0735-7044.99.3.399

Levine, S., & Wiener, S. G. (1988). Psychoendocrine aspects of mother–infant relationships in nonhuman primates. *Psychoneuroendocrinology, 13*, 143–154. doi:10.1016/0306-4530(88)90011-X

Liu, D., Diorio, J., Tannenbaum, B., Caldji, C., Francis, D., Freedman, A., . . . Meaney, M. J. (1997, September 12). Maternal care, hippocampal glucocorticoid receptors, and hypothalamic-pituitary-adrenal responses to stress. *Science, 277*, 1659–1662. doi:10.1126/science.277.5332.1659

Main, M. (1990). Cross-cultural studies of attachment organization: Recent studies, changing methodologies, and the concept of conditional strategies. *Human Development, 33*, 48–61. doi:10.1159/000276502

Main, M. (1999). Attachment theory: Eighteen points with suggestions for future studies. In J. Cassidy & P. R. Shaver (Eds.), *Handbook of attachment* (pp. 845–887). New York, NY: Guilford Press.

Main, M., Kaplan, N., & Cassidy, J. (1985). Security in infancy, childhood, and adulthood: A move to the level of representation. *Monographs of the Society for Research in Child Development, 50*, 66–104.

Meaney, M. J. (2001). Maternal care, gene expression, and the transmission of individual differences in stress reactivity across generations. *Annual Review of Neuroscience, 24*, 1161–1192. doi:10.1146/annurev.neuro.24.1.1161

Moore, G. A., Hill-Soderlund, A. L., Propper, C. B., Calkins, S. D., Mills-Koonce, W. R., & Cox, M. J. (2009). Mother–infant vagal regulation in the face-to-face still-face paradigm is moderated by maternal sensitivity. *Child Development, 80*, 209–223. doi:10.1111/j.1467-8624.2008.01255.x

Nachmias, M., Gunnar, M., Mangelsdorf, S., Parritz, R. H., & Buss, K. (1996). Behavioral inhibition and stress reactivity: The moderating role of attachment security. *Child Development, 67*, 508–522. doi:10.2307/1131829

Passman, R. H., & Longeway, K. P. (1982). The role of vision in maternal attachment: Giving 2-year-olds a photograph of their mother during separation. *Developmental Psychology, 18*, 530–533. doi:10.1037/0012-1649.18.4.530

Polan, J., & Hofer, M. (2008). Psychobiological origins of infant attachment and its role in development. In J. Cassidy & P. R. Shaver (Eds.), *The handbook of attachment: Theory, research, and clinical applications* (pp. 158–172). New York, NY: Guilford Press.

Reite, M., Kaufman, C., Pauley, D., & Stynes, A. J. (1974). Depression in infant monkeys: Physiological correlates. *Psychosomatic Medicine, 36*, 363–367.

Robertson, J., & Robertson, J. (1989). *Separation and the very young.* Oxford, England: Free Association Books.

Sánchez, M. M., Noble, P. M., Lyon, C. K., Plotsky, P. M., Davis, M., Nemeroff, C. B., & Winslow, J. T. (2005). Alterations in diurnal cortisol rhythm and acoustic startle response in nonhuman primates with adverse rearing. *Biological Psychiatry*, *57*, 373–381. doi:10.1016/j.biopsych.2004.11.032

Sapolsky, R. M. (2004). *Why zebras don't get ulcers* (3rd ed.). New York, NY: Holt.

Sayfan, L., & Lagattuta, K. (2009). Scaring the monster away: What children know about managing fears of real and imaginary creatures. *Child Development, 80*, 1756–1774. doi:10.1111/j.1467-8624.2009.01366.x

Schachter, S., & Singer, J. (1962). Cognitive, social, and physiological determinants of emotional state. *Psychological Review, 69*, 379–399. doi:10.1037/h0046234

Stern, D. (2004). *The present moment in psychotherapy and everyday life*. New York, NY: Norton.

Stevenson-Hinde, J., Shouldice, A., & Chicot, R. (2011). Maternal anxiety, behavioral inhibition, and attachment. *Attachment & Human Development, 13*, 199–215. doi:10.1080/14616734.2011.562409

Suchecki, D., Rosenfeld, P., & Levine, S. (1993). Maternal regulation of the hypothalamic-pituitary-adrenal axis in the infant rat: The roles of feeding and stroking. *Developmental Brain Research, 75*, 185–192. doi:10.1016/0165-3806 (93)90022-3

Suomi, S. J. (1979). Differential development of various social relationships by rhesus monkey infants. In M. Lewis & L. A. Rosenblum (Eds.), *Genesis of behavior: The child and its family* (Vol. 2, pp. 219–244). New York, NY: Plenum Press. doi:10.1007/978-1-4684-3435-4_12

Suomi, S. J. (2008). Attachment in rhesus monkeys. In J. Cassidy & P. R. Shaver (Eds.), *Handbook of attachment: Theory, research, and clinical applications* (2nd ed., pp. 173–191). New York, NY: Guilford Press.

Taylor, S. E., Repetti, R. L., & Seeman, T. E. (1997). Health psychology: What is an unhealthy environment and how does it get under the skin? *Annual Review of Psychology, 48*, 411–447. doi:10.1146/annurev.psych.48.1.411

van der Horst, F. C. P. (2011). *John Bowlby: From psychoanalysis to ethology*. Chichester, England: Wiley-Blackwell. doi:10.1002/9781119993100

Weaver, I. C. G., Cervoni, N., Champagne, F. A., D'Alessio, A. C., Sharma, S., Seckl, J. R., . . . Meaney, M. J. (2004). Epigenetic programming by maternal behavior. *Nature Neuroscience, 7*, 847–854. doi:10.1038/nn1276

Weinfield, N. S., Sroufe, L., & Egeland, B. (2000). Attachment from infancy to early adulthood in a high-risk sample: Continuity, discontinuity, and their correlates. *Child Development, 71*, 695–702. doi:10.1111/1467-8624.00178

West-Eberhard, M. J. (2003). *Developmental plasticity and evolution*. New York, NY: Oxford University Press.

8

SYNCHRONY AND THE NEUROBIOLOGICAL BASIS OF SOCIAL AFFILIATION

RUTH FELDMAN

Affiliation, from the Medieval Latin word *affiliatus*—to adopt as a son—is defined as "to bring or receive into close connection" ("Affiliation," 2002). The definition seems to contain two elements; it refers to a close interpersonal bond, such as that between a parent and child, and it involves a process or action needed for that bond to be established. During the mid-20th century, authors such as Bowlby (1958), Harlow (1958), and Spitz and Wolf (1946) began to draw attention to the primary role of love as a central motivating force for psychological development and a critical ingredient in the survival, safety, and well-being of the young. Affiliative bonds, defined as selective and enduring attachments, were conceptualized as providing the foundation for an infant's ability to function competently within an ecosocial niche, grow to form intimate bonds with nonkin members of society, and eventually nurture

Research at Ruth Feldman's lab is supported by the Israel Science Foundation (1318/08), the U.S.–Israel Binational Science Foundation (2005-273), the NARSAD Foundation, the German–Israel Science Foundation, the Irving B. Harris Foundation, and the Katz Family Foundation.

http://dx.doi.org/10.1037/14250-009
Mechanisms of Social Connection: From Brain to Group, M. Mikulincer and P. R. Shaver (Editors)

the next generation. This paradigm shift, which transported "love" from the realm of the literary to the domain of science, drew on several lines of concurrent inquiry in biology, philosophy, and the social sciences. These fields not only introduced novel ideas but also advocated new methodologies for scientific progress. Most important were the works of the early ethologists (Lorenz, 1950; Tinbergen, 1963), who designated bonding as the central process supporting mammalian adaptation, emphasized behavior as the lens through which science should approach the study of social maturation, and argued that meticulous documentation of behaviors that emerge or intensify during periods of bond formation is a necessary precondition for any theory of human nature.

By focusing on concrete behaviors related to bonding, these researchers advocated a bottom-up, behavior-based approach, thus opposing the two central perspectives of the time: psychoanalysis, which was based on a theory of imagined internal processes; and Skinnerian behaviorism, which focused on the behavior of individuals rather than relational units. The new ethological approach altered the conceptualization of human affiliation in three ways. First, it suggested that bonding is expressed through a set of species-specific caregiving (and care-receiving) behaviors that appear immediately after birth and provide a foundation for neurobehavioral maturation—a critical-period viewpoint on attachment. Second, it indicated that bond formation is supported by unique neurohormonal systems and brain circuits, hence linking specific biology to specific behavior. Third, it offered a lifetime perspective on bonding, suggesting that the three prototypical forms of affiliation in mammals—parental, romantic/sexual, and filial—share underlying physiological mechanisms and overt behavioral expressions and that patterns formed in early infancy shape the way individuals function within their various attachment relationships throughout life.

Several large-scale studies that followed children from infancy onward, as well as animal studies of mother–infant relations, provided support for these hypotheses. For instance, Hofer (1994) demonstrated that a mother's physical presence includes a set of biobehavioral regulators, such as maternal touch, odor, movements, and body rhythms, each of which regulates a specific physiological system in the pup. The work of Meaney and colleagues (Kappeler & Meaney, 2010; Meaney, 2010) later specified some of the neuroendocrine basis of social affiliation and its cross-generational transmission. The studies highlighted the role of oxytocin (OT)—a nine-amino-acid neuropeptide synthesized in the hypothalamus—in maternal care and the role of cortisol receptors in the hippocampus that help to down-regulate stress responses. This research program showed that the amount of maternal caregiving, particularly the licking-and-grooming behaviors of rat mothers (dams), shaped the stress responses of their offspring and organized their OT-mediated affiliation systems. Moreover, the intergenerational transmission of parental behavior was mediated by behavioral rather than genetic mechanisms and was related to the amount of touch and contact the mother received as an infant (Champagne, 2008).

Over the past decade, research in my lab has followed up these lines of inquiry in humans, in an attempt to describe the neurobiological bases of human social affiliation. Working from our model of biobehavioral synchrony, other researchers and I examined the way physiological and microlevel behavioral systems integrate to form the basis for selective and enduring attachment bonds. The following sections of this chapter detail such integration in three systems: (a) hormonal systems, with a particular emphasis on OT as the neuro-hormonal foundation for social affiliation; (b) brain systems that support parenting and bond formation, including limbic-motivational and cortical-social neural networks; and (c) the autonomic system and its sympathetic and parasympathetic branches.

BIOBEHAVIORAL SYNCHRONY

Our model of biobehavioral synchrony provides a theoretical frame for the findings presented below. It builds on the concept of synchrony, which emphasizes the temporal concordance of biological and social processes (Feldman, 2007d, 2012a, 2012b). Synchrony is a concept developed by the first researchers who studied parenting in social animals, beginning with research on social insects nearly a century ago (Wheeler, 1928). Prompted by the question of what enables a group of ants to jointly carry a grain of wheat or, broadly speaking, collaborate to achieve a social goal, researchers described the process of biobehavioral synchrony. Among members of a social group, such as flocks of birds synchronizing their journey toward warm climates or fish moving in perfectly synchronous cycles to ward off a shark, there is a temporal concordance between the behavioral patterns of various group members and their physiological processes, such as neural firing or hormonal release. In this way, the physiology of one group member is synchronized with the behavior of another group member. These synchronous processes create a continuously time-locked relationship between the physiology and behavior of group members that is critical for the survival of the group and each individual's adaptation to the social milieu.

Biobehavioral synchrony, in other words, is the process by which organisms become members of a social group and function collaboratively within it. The evolution of mammals, which are nursed by their mother early in life, resulted in individual members of an ecosocial niche that are no longer initiated directly into large social groups but are ushered into social life through intimate, one-on-one reciprocal relationships with a caregiver. That is, mammalian young receive their training for social reciprocity not within the large group but in the context of the nursing dyad, and they do so by means of finely tuned biobehavioral adaptations (Rosenblatt, 1965; Schneirla, 1946). Across mammalian species, dyad-specific maternal–infant bonds are built on repeatedly experienced patterns of sensorimotor and behavioral cues in each partner. Over time and repeated experience these discrete, synchronized biobehavioral events coordinate to form a unique bond that characterizes the rhythms, content, focus, and pace of a specific attachment relationship (Feldman, 2012a, 2012b).

In this context, it is important to note that the construct of synchrony refers only to the temporal concordance between processes that occur simultaneously or sequentially; it postulates no heuristic system of symbols and makes no a priori assumptions. As such, the concept of synchrony provides an optimal framework for a bottom-up model that centers on discrete building blocks that gradually cohere to form a relational bond. Recent perspectives in neuroscience underscore synchrony as the mechanism that underlies consciousness and supports the brain's capacity to form a unitary event out of the simultaneous activity of discrete brain regions (Damasio, 2003; Edelman, 2004, 2006). This change in conceptual focus from mechanisms of a "central organizer" to those of temporal synchrony highlights the importance of a bottom-up perspective and parallels the shift of emphasis advocated long before by the early ethologists. In the following section, I focus on studies that demonstrate biobehavioral synchrony in physiological systems and matched dyadic behavior within attachment relationships: synchrony within each partner, among partners, and between the physiology of one partner and the behavior of the other.

In addition to having relevance for social affiliation, the biobehavioral synchrony model has implications for the conceptualization of emotions and the current debate about whether emotions are discrete hardwired networks or constructed cognitive appraisals. I suggest that emotions are based on microlevel units of biobehavioral experiences epigenetically wired from repeated experiences within the mother–infant relationship, which then gain sophistication, differentiation, linguistic labels, and symbolic meanings. I argue that the basis of emotional experiences is feeling states (or, in Damasio's 2003 terminology, *background emotions*) that do not define a concrete "basic emotion"; rather, they provide a framework for the perception and expression of emotions by describing the contour, tempo, and sensorimotor envelopes of nonverbal, biologically based affective states. Hence, emotions are rooted in biosocial, discrete, and repetitive experiences that gain complexity, specificity, and meaning within specific cultural contexts and symbolic frameworks in the context of dyad-specific attachment relationships (Feldman, 2007b). Such microlevel background emotions are irreducible and provide the building blocks, color, and depth of our emotional life. This perspective accords with the philosophical writings of Bergson (1907), Merleau-Ponty (1945), and Mead (1934).

Like other mammals, human mothers and infants engage in a species-typical repertoire of postpartum behaviors, which include gazing at the infant's face or body, "motherese" (high-pitched, rhythmic vocalizations), expressions of positive affect, and affectionate touch, a behavior akin to the licking and grooming seen in other mammals. Human mothers express these maternal behaviors as soon as the first postpartum day. They enact approximately 70% of their behaviors during the 7% of the time that their newborns spend in an alert-scanning state, creating temporal contingencies between infant state and maternal social behavior as soon as the first postbirth hours (Feldman & Eidelman, 2007). These social contingencies are supported by physiological periodicities maturing in the fetus during the third trimester of pregnancy, including the "biological clock" and cardiac pacemaker (Feldman, 2006). Thus, as soon as human infants are born, they can experience a temporal match between their own state and the response of the social environment mediated by their mother. This early concordance between maternal and infant readiness for social engagement is a critical human addition to the physiological provisions supplied by other mammalian mothers, and it provides a foundation for the development of human-specific social, emotional, empathic, and symbolic competencies.

At approximately 3 months of age, infants enter the social world as active partners and begin to engage in synchronous exchanges with their caregivers. These sequences contain coordinated gaze patterns, covocalizations, mutual expressions of positive affect, and loving touch. Synchrony experienced during the critical period between 3 and 9 months has been shown to predict children's later self-regulation (Feldman, Greenbaum, & Yirmiya, 1999), symbol use (Feldman, 2007b), a capacity for empathy throughout childhood (Feldman, 2007a), and more optimal social adaptation and lower rates of depression in adolescence (Feldman, 2010). These longitudinal findings support the sensitive period perspective suggested by ethological models.

From the end of the first year of life on, interactions between close partners contain two parallel lines: (a) a nonverbal line of synchrony between the partners' gaze patterns, affective expressions, vocal qualities, body orientations, movements, and proximity position; and (b) a verbal line of synchrony between levels of communicative intimacy (e.g., the degrees of self-disclosure between close friends or romantic partners; Feldman, 2007c). In the first stages of romantic attachment, for instance, couples' interactions are similarly built on affect sharing, mutual gaze, touch, joint positive arousal, and warm voice (Schneiderman, Zagoory-Sharon, Leckman, & Feldman, 2012). Similarly, interactions between young children and their first "best friends" at 3 years of age are marked by affective matching, social reciprocity, mutual gazing, joint tool use, and consideration of the other's goals and intentions (Feldman, Gordon, Influs, Gutbir, & Ebstein, 2013). Synchrony, therefore, is a critical component of close relationships that builds on familiarity with the partner's style, manner, affective patterns, rhythms, behavioral preferences, and pace of intimacy.

It is worth noting that fathers create a unique kind of synchrony with their infants, which, as with other biparental mammals, builds on stimulatory contact, high positive arousal, and exploratory focus. Similar to mother–child synchrony, father–infant synchrony provides critical inputs for children's social adaptation across childhood and into adolescence. In a longitudinal study in which we followed parents and infants from 5 months to 13 years, we found that father–infant reciprocity uniquely predicted children's social competence and lower aggression with peers in the preschool years, as well as children's dialogical skills during interactions with best friends in adolescence. Whereas father–child synchrony predicted adolescents' capacity to handle conflicts in dialogical ways, mother–child synchrony uniquely contributed to adolescents' ability to jointly plan and engage in positive interactions with their best friends. Each parent, therefore, constructs a unique type of synchrony with the child, which remains stable across childhood, is mutually shaped between parents through processes of coparenting, and supports different social skills for later intimate relationships throughout life.

Finally, interactive synchrony is also observed in triadic mother–father–infant contexts beginning in the first months of life. Four-month-old infants can coordinate their behavior with both mother and father during triadic sessions, and they respond within a few seconds to signals between their parents and shift their interactive focus from mother to father (Gordon & Feldman, 2008). Microlevel triadic synchrony between the mother–father and parent–child subsystems during family interactions—particularly coordination of gazing, physical proximity, and affective touch—is supported by affiliation hormones, provides infants their first collaborative participation in a group experience, and predicts better emotion regulation and adaptation to the peer group in later childhood (Feldman, Masalha, & Alony, 2006).

In summary, parents and infants shape each other's behavior in the modalities of gaze, touch, affect, vocalization, and proximity, and they do so in both dyadic and group contexts. Such interactive synchrony is supported by hormonal, brain, and autonomic functioning within each partner. Biological synchrony in each of these systems is observed, indicating that partners shape each other's hormonal, brain, and autonomic responses by means of social contact. Links are charted between behavioral and biological synchrony, suggesting that affiliation-related physiology and microlevel social behavior in each partner are mutually shaped through repeated social interactions.

BIOBEHAVIORAL SYNCHRONY: THE COORDINATION OF NEUROENDOCRINE, BRAIN, AND AUTONOMIC RESPONSES BETWEEN ATTACHED PARTNERS

In the following subsections, expressions of biobehavioral synchrony in hormones, brains, and behavior are described.

Affiliation-Related Hormones: Oxytocin and Biobehavioral Synchrony

Studies of nonhuman mammals and emerging data from humans suggest that the formation of dyad-specific affiliative bonds is underpinned by the extended OT system (Gimpl & Fahrenholz, 2001; Insel, 1997; Ross & Young, 2009). Yet, because the distribution of OT receptors in the brain and the links between maternal behaviors and OT expression are substantially different in different species (Insel, 2010; Ross et al., 2009), it is critical that the specific associations between OT and processes of social bonding be studied in humans, notwithstanding the limitations of human neuroendocrine and molecular research. In the present context, it is impossible to provide an in-depth discussion of the oxytocinergic system, but suffice it to say that OT is widely distributed throughout the body and brain; dynamically interacts with the hypothalamic–pituitary–adrenal (HPA) axis and the dopaminergic and immunological systems; and is inherently epigenetic, implying that it is shaped in extrauterine life through patterns of parental care. Such an overarching behavior- and environment-sensitive system provides the neurobiological substrate for processes of biobehavioral synchrony, which bind members of a social unit into a time-locked unit, and affords ongoing physiological and behavioral support for dyad-specific attachments.

OT and Mothering and Fathering

Several studies in our lab have documented the involvement of OT in processes of bond formation. In the first study to evaluate OT and the development of maternal behavior in humans, we measured maternal plasma OT and cortisol, a biomarker of the HPA axis stress response. We conducted the measurements repeatedly from the first trimester of pregnancy and up through the first postpartum month. Postpartum mothers were observed interacting with their infants and were interviewed about attachment-related processes. We found that OT increased during periods of bond formation compared to periods of no parental or romantic involvement (Gordon et al., 2008). OT levels were highly stable within individuals, and the mother's OT levels in the first trimester predicted the amount of maternal postpartum behavior, including gaze, positive affect, motherese vocalizations, and affectionate touch.

This suggests that OT during gestation primes mothers for the expression of maternal behavior, consistent with what has been observed in other mammals (Feldman, Weller, Zagoory-Sharon, & Levine, 2007). Maternal bonding to the fetus in the third trimester of pregnancy was predicted by the increase in plasma OT from the first to the third trimester, indicating dynamic associations between OT and bond formation (Levine, Zagoory-Sharon, Feldman, & Weller, 2007).

To examine the associations between OT and both fathering and mothering, we observed 160 mothers and fathers (80 couples) and their firstborn child, microcoded maternal and paternal social behavior, and measured the parents' plasma OT and salivary cortisol in the first postpartum month and again 6 months later. Counter to expectations, comparable levels of OT were found in fathers and mothers across the first 6 months of parenting, and the levels were higher than those in nonparents. Consistent with our model, OT in mothers and fathers exhibited biological synchrony; that is, maternal and paternal levels were interrelated both in the postpartum period and 6 months later, suggesting a process of endocrine fit in which partners shape each other's neuropeptide response through marital and coparental attachment. Similar to what happens in other biparental mammals, maternal OT correlated with a social-affective repertoire including maternal gaze, affect, vocalizations, and affectionate touch, whereas father OT correlated with object-oriented stimulatory play, positive arousal, and stimulatory touch (Gordon, Zagoory-Sharon, Leckman, & Feldman, 2010a).

We examined whether the parent-specific form of touch induces an OT response in a subsequent study. OT functions as part of a biobehavioral feedback loop: More touch and contact within attachment relationships increases OT levels and vice versa. Plasma and salivary OT were collected from mothers and fathers at baseline and following a 15-minute "play-and-touch" session in which parents were asked to play with their infants with any form of touch they typically used. Consistent with the distinction between high- and low-licking-and-grooming rodents (Champagne, 2008), mothers who provided high levels of affectionate touch (> 66% of the time) showed an increase in salivary OT from pre- to postinteraction, but no such increase was observed among mothers providing minimal touch (< 33%). Similarly, fathers who provided high levels of stimulatory contact, such as moving the infant's limbs, throwing the infant in the air, or moving him or her across the room, increased their OT levels, but there was no such rise in fathers who engaged in minimal stimulatory touch (Feldman, Gordon, & Zagoory-Sharon, 2010). These findings indicate that active parental touch can trigger an OT response in parents, which supports the hypothesis that OT functions as a biobehavioral feedback loop. These findings suggest that touch-based interventions could be used when OT is dysfunctional, such as in cases of postpartum maternal depression or following premature birth.

Another of our studies examined maternal and paternal plasma, salivary, and urinary OT in relation to parent–infant synchrony, romantic attachment, and bonding to a parent's own parents (Feldman, Gordon, & Zagoory-Sharon, 2011). We found that parental plasma and salivary OT were interrelated, and both correlated with the degree of affect matching and the number of positive communicative sequences in parent–infant play, in addition to memories of better care by one's own parents and more secure attachment to romantic partners. Urinary OT was associated with relationship anxiety and greater parental stress in mothers only.

OT and the Cross-Generational Transmission of Human Affiliation

To assess cross-generational transmission of OT as mediated by parenting behavior, we measured salivary OT in mothers and fathers and in their 6-month-old infants at baseline and following the play-and-touch paradigm. We also microcoded partners' interaction synchrony. When the infant was 4 months of age, OT levels in infant and parent were already correlated, and this cross-generational link was mediated by parent–infant synchrony: When synchrony was high, the degree of concordance between the parent's and infant's OT levels was high, but this was not the case when synchrony was low. Thus, behavioral coordination appears to be the mechanism through which parental OT shapes a child's hormonal system and its long-term effects on attachment (Feldman, Gordon, Schneiderman, Weisman, & Zagoory-Sharon, 2010).

Central and Peripheral OT and Biobehavioral Synchrony

Among the central difficulties in human OT research is the inability to test OT at the brain-neurochemical level and to chart the degree to which central (brain) and peripheral activity of the system are coordinated. To address this issue, we used a neurogenetic biobehavioral design and tested the links between plasma OT, variations in the OT receptor (*OXTR*) and *CD38* genes, synchronous parenting, and memories of parental care in a large group of 352 mothers, fathers, and nonparents. Variations in *OXTR* have been associated with multiple social and emotional processes, and risk alleles on the *OXTR* rs2254298 and rs1042778 single nucleotide polymorphisms (SNPs) have been linked with increased risk for disorders characterized by social dysfunctions, such as autism and major depression.

We also measured allelic variations on the *CD38* gene, an ectoenzyme that mediates the release of OT through the mobilization of calcium and has been linked with autism. We found that individuals with high-risk alleles on the OXTR rs2254298 or the OXTR rs1042778 SNPs or on the CD38 rs3796863 SNP had lower levels of plasma OT. The effects were similar in mothers, fathers, and nonparents, demonstrating that peripheral levels of OT partially reflect OT in neuropathways. Reduced plasma OT and risk alleles on the OXTR and CD38 genes were each related to lower frequencies of parental touch during parent–infant interactions, and episodes of parent–infant gaze synchrony were longest among parents who had both high levels of plasma OT and the low-risk CD38 allele. These findings provide initial evidence that human attachment is mediated by the extended oxytocinergic system, including (a) peripheral levels of plasma OT; (b) the CD38 gene, which is essential for OT release; and (c) OXTR, the single receptor encoding for this neuropeptide.

Individuals who reported more favorable care from their parents also had low-risk alleles, had higher levels of plasma OT, and provided more touch to their own infants. Consistent with findings for other mammals, therefore, the cross-generational transmission of optimal parenting is related to patterns of maternal care (Feldman et al., 2012).

OT Administration and Parenting

In addition to assessing peripheral levels of OT and genetic variability in the OT system in relation to synchronous parenting behavior, researchers have employed an intranasal OT procedure and have documented its effects on a host of social and affiliative processes. For example, in Weisman, Zagoory-Sharon, and Feldman (2012), fathers and their 6-month-old infants participated in a double-blind, placebo-controlled crossover study. Fathers inhaled either OT or placebo, and salivary OT from father and infant was measured four times: at baseline and in 20-minute intervals following administration. Respiratory sinus arrhythmia was recorded from father and child during play, and paternal and infant social behaviors were microcoded. Following OT administration, father's salivary OT increased dramatically and respiratory sinus arrhythmia was higher, indicating greater physiological readiness for social engagement. Fathers showed more frequent touch and longer durations of engagement behavior in the OT condition. Surprisingly, however, and consistent with our model's predictions, OT administration to the father had a parallel effect on the physiology and behavior of the infant. Infant salivary OT rose dramatically in the father OT condition, although infants did not inhale OT; they also had higher respiratory sinus arrhythmia and exhibited social gaze and toy exploration for longer periods. These findings are the first to demonstrate that OT administration to a parent can lead to alterations in the physiology and behavior of the parent's infant.

They should lead to interventions for infants at risk for social dysfunctions—interventions that do not include administering a drug to a young infant (Weisman, Zagoory-Sharon, & Feldman, 2012).

OT and Romantic Attachment

Animal studies point to the role of OT in mammalian pair bonding (Carter, 1998), as seen, for instance, in pair-bond formation in monogamous prairie voles (Insel & Hulihan, 1995; see also Chapter 1, this volume). Human studies similarly highlight the involvement of OT in pair bonding. OT administration increases couples' positive communication (Ditzen et al., 2009), and plasma OT is related to positive communication, affiliation, and emotional support between partners (Gonzaga, Turner, Keltner, Campos, & Altemus, 2006; Grewen, Girdler, Amico, & Light, 2005; Holt-Lunstad, Birmingham, & Light, 2008). But results concerning associations between OT and romantic love have been mixed, and few studies have found correlations between OT and negative emotions, anxiety, or distress in romantic couples. In a recent study, we assessed the role of OT in romantic attachment in a group of 163 young adults, including 120 new lovers (60 couples) 3 months after the initiation of a romantic relationship and 43 nonattached singles (Schneiderman et al., 2012). Of the 36 couples who stayed together, 25 were seen again 6 months later. In ways similar to those used in our studies of parents and infants, couples were observed in dyadic interactions and were separately interviewed regarding relationship-related thoughts.

We found that OT was much higher in new lovers than in singles, suggesting increased activity of the OT system during the period of falling in love. OT in new lovers was even higher than in new parents, suggesting that the early period of romantic love, with its typical euphoria, is associated with the greatest increase in OT production. During the 6 months between our first and second assessments, the high OT levels did not drop and were stable within individuals. Plasma OT was correlated with a couple's interactive synchrony, including behaviors such as social focus, positive affect, affectionate touch, and synchronized dyadic states, as well as with new lovers' preoccupations and worries regarding their partner and relationship. These findings support our model's hypothesis concerning the consistency among the three prototypical kinds of attachment in humans. The findings further indicate that parental and romantic attachment are supported by similar OT-based neuroendocrine mechanisms and are expressed in similar behavioral repertoires including gaze, touch, affect, and vocalizations, all of which involve interpartner coordination (Schneiderman et al., 2012).

Finally, in the largest study of plasma OT to date, involving 473 adults measured twice within a 6-month interval, we examined associations between

OT, on the one hand, and trait and attachment anxiety, on the other, in both women and men (Weisman, Zagoory-Sharon, Schneiderman, Gordon, & Feldman, 2012). Associations between OT and stress have been inconsistent and controversial, with some studies stressing the anxiolytic effects of OT and others linking it with relationship distress. We found gender-specific associations between OT and trait and attachment anxiety. Higher attachment anxiety was correlated with higher OT levels in women but with lower OT levels in men. Similarly, OT was associated with lower trait anxiety in men but not in women. However, women with extreme values of OT (greater than 2.5 standard deviations above the mean) also tended to be highly anxious. These findings suggest that the neurobiological basis of attachment may have evolved differently in women—who needed to maintain constant vigilance for infant survival—than in men, for whom romantic relationships were associated with increased calmness.

Biobehavioral Synchrony and Other Hormonal Systems

We measured OT and prolactin in the plasma of fathers and microcoded their behaviors during two play sessions: a social play session and an object-exploration toy session. OT and prolactin were interrelated but were differentially associated with paternal behavior in the two play sessions. OT correlated with the father's behavior during social play, whereas prolactin correlated with the father's play during a session that called for the introduction of specific toys and coordinating exploration with the infant (Gordon et al., 2010c). Consistent with much research on the links between OT and heightened social focus in humans, OT appears to be particularly associated with early parental behavior in contexts that focus on social exchanges. In a study that examined OT and cortisol in relation to parents' and infant's behavior during a triadic mother–father–infant interaction (Gordon et al., 2010b), triadic synchrony—when parents and child were all in physical contact and coordinated their social gaze—was predicted by both mothers' and fathers' OT and was negatively related to the parents' cortisol level (Gordon et al., 2010b).

Endocrine fit, concordance between parental and child's hormonal levels, has also been found for cortisol. In a study assessing mother's and infant's cortisol response to a still-face paradigm (wherein the mother shows no emotional expression), we found concordance between mother's and child's cortisol levels at baseline, postchallenge, and recovery, and these concordances were related to the degree of dyssynchrony and intrusiveness during free play. Infant cortisol levels were attenuated when mothers provided touch while maintaining a still face, which further points to the associations between bonding-related hormones and maternal touch and contact (Feldman, Singer, & Zagoory, 2010).

Cortisol and salivary alpha amylase, a biomarker of the sympathetic–adrenal–medullary system, were also measured in a group of mothers and preschool-age children exposed to war-related trauma (Feldman, Vengrober, Eidelman-Rothman, & Zagoory-Sharon, in press). Both biomarkers showed endocrine fit between mothers and children, and the degree of fit was associated with the degree of reciprocity between mother and child during social interactions. Finally, in the aforementioned study of romantic partners, we also measured cortisol, prolactin, dehydroepiandrosterone, and testosterone in relation to partners' behavior during a conflict discussion (Schneiderman, Zagoory-Sharon, & Feldman, 2012). A couple's empathic resolution of interpersonal conflict was independently predicted by higher prolactin, lower cortisol, and higher dehydroepiandrosterone. On the other hand, hostile conflict resolution was predicted by higher cortisol and the interaction of testosterone and gender. Women, but not men, with higher testosterone levels engaged in more hostile conflict interactions. Overall, these findings highlight the close links between biological synchrony across multiple hormonal systems within attachment relationships, specific behavior between attached partners, and the mutual influence of partners' hormones as they are mediated by affiliative behaviors during social contact.

Brain Responses and Biobehavioral Synchrony

Studies of the parental brain demonstrate the utility of the biobehavioral synchrony model in relation to brain activations.

Maternal Brain and Mother–Infant Synchrony

Animal studies of maternal behavior have implicated motivational and OT-rich brain areas in the expression of maternal behavior. In particular, the nucleus accumbens, part of the mesolimbic dopaminergic reward circuit that receives OT projections, provides motivation for maternal behavior; the amygdala, a central node of the limbic affective system that also receives OT projections, has also been implicated in maternal attachment. The nucleus accumbens and amygdala work in concert with several cortical areas, including the medial preoptic area, an OT-rich site that integrates infant sensory cues; the anterior cingulate cortex; and the dorsomedial prefrontal cortex. It thus appears that the neural basis of mothering integrates subcortical limbic areas with higher level networks implicated in emotion modulation, social cognition, and empathy. Together, these networks allow a mother to read her infant's signals and plan adequate parental behavior.

In a recent study that integrated behavioral synchrony, OT, and the maternal brain (Atzil, Hendler, & Feldman, 2011), we examined mothers' brain responses to dynamic, ecologically valid infant stimuli (an infant video). Two groups of mothers were recruited on the basis of their social behavior: synchronous mothers, those who coordinated their social behavior with their infant's signals; and intrusive mothers, those who provided excessive parenting when their infant signaled a need for rest. Whole-brain analyses showed that synchronous mothers exhibited greater activation in the left nucleus accumbens, indicating that parenting in these mothers was underlain by reward-related motivational mechanisms; intrusive mothers activated the right amygdala, suggesting anxious and stress-related mechanisms underlying maternal care. Functional connectivity analysis showed that among the synchronous mothers, left nucleus accumbens and right amygdala were functionally correlated with emotion modulation, theory of mind, and empathy networks, whereas among intrusive mothers, left nucleus accumbens and right amygdala were functionally correlated with premotor areas, such as the right premotor cortex and the left orbitofrontal cortex. Sorting points into neighborhoods (SPIN) analysis, a technique used to measure the temporal coherence of activity in a brain nucleus over time, indicated that in the synchronous group, left nucleus accumbens and right amygdala activations displayed clearer organization over time, whereas in the intrusive group, activations were less well organized. Finally, correlations between OT, on the one hand, and nucleus accumbens and amygdala activations, on the other, emerged in the synchronous group only. Overall, these findings suggest that synchronous parenting is underlain by reward-related motivational mechanisms; temporal organization of brain and behavior; and concordance between maternal brain, interactive behavior, and OT system.

Synchrony in the Maternal and the Paternal Brain

Biological synchrony at the brain level between attachment partners was tested with a functional magnetic resonance imaging paradigm in which mothers and fathers were scanned while observing the same video of the attachment target—their own infant engaged in solitary play. Thirty mothers and fathers (15 married couples with young infants) were scanned while observing their own infant, compared to standard-infant videos, and correlations between the voxel-by-voxel activations of mother's and father's brains were computed with a specifically tailored algorithm. Online synchrony of activations in mothers' and fathers' brains emerged in social-cognitive cortical networks implicated in empathy, theory of mind, and mirror functions. It did not emerge in limbic networks, including the medial prefrontal cortex, superior temporal sulcus, insula, and inferior frontal gyrus, which are areas that support parents' intuitive understanding of infant signals. Mothers showed greater limbic activations than did fathers, and maternal limbic activations correlated with maternal OT. Fathers showed greater activations in emotion-regulatory circuits (e.g., the medial prefrontal cortex), which were linked with paternal arginine vasopressin.

These findings show that parents synchronize online brain activity in social-cognitive networks that support intuitive understanding of their infant's communications and the planning of appropriate caregiving. The data provide further evidence for our biobehavioral synchrony model and suggest that brain synchrony may support the emergence of human attachment within the matrix of neurobiological attunement between social partners (Atzil, Hendler, Zagoory-Sharon, Winetraub, & Feldman, 2012).

Autonomic Response and Biobehavioral Synchrony

The autonomic nervous system (ANS), which controls visceral functions and regulates the body's physiological homeostasis, is divided into two branches, sympathetic and parasympathetic. Both neural systems originate in the brain stem and regulate automatic bodily functions, including heart rate, digestion, respiration rate, salivation, perspiration, diameter of the pupils, and urination. Each function is the result of the interplay of the two systems (Beauchaine, 2001). The sympathetic nervous system mobilizes the body's resources under stress, increases arousal and energy, and induces the fight-or-flight response, whereas the parasympathetic nervous system engages in energy preservation; relaxation of vital organs at rest; and reduction of arousal, heart rate, and vagal tone reactivity (Porges, 2003). Alterations in ANS activity, particularly in parasympathetic response, have been noted during periods of bonding, such as becoming a parent and falling in love.

Parents' Sympathetic Arousal and Infant Reminders

Using a biobehavioral experimental design, we tested 140 new parents (70 couples) of 6-month-old infants (Mosek-Eilon, Hirschberger, Kanat-Maymon, & Feldman, 2012). While parents engaged in a conflict interaction, eight indices of sympathetic arousal were assessed from each parent and were used to create a measure of sympathetic arousal. Parents' ongoing dialogue was microcoded for hostility and empathy. Parents were randomly divided into an experimental group, in which a picture of their own infant appeared on a screen halfway into the interaction, and a control group, in which members observed a neutral stimulus. Infant reminders altered parents' sympathetic reactivity. Mothers' sympathetic reactivity decreased following exposure to infant cues, consistent with the possibility that mothering behavior evolved in such a way that it requires calm states. Fathers reacted by maintaining vigilance and preserving sympathetic arousal, suggesting an evolved role as a protector of mother and young. For both parents, infant reminders decreased marital hostility in a synchronous way. Much research has shown that marital hostility has long-term negative consequences for infant emotional development, and our findings suggest that even a short exposure to infant reminders during the sensitive postbirth period activates the parents' biological goal to protect their infant from harm and to control their own disagreements for the baby's benefit. Consistent with our model's predictions, findings show that physiological and microlevel social behaviors in mothers and fathers are altered online to provide a more optimal context for parent–infant bonding and to protect the infant from harm (Mosek-Eilon et al., 2012).

Parasympathetic Response and Parental and Romantic Attachment

To examine dynamic synchrony between maternal and infant autonomic and behavioral responses, we observed face-to-face interactions between mothers and their 3-month-old infants while cardiac output was measured from both mother and child (Feldman, Magori-Cohen, Galili, Singer, & Louzoun, 2011). Using bootstrapping modeling, we found that mothers and infants synchronize their heart rhythms within lags of less than 1 second, an effect that is specific to a mother's own infant. During moments of vocal and affect synchrony, biological synchrony between mother's and infant's heart rhythms increased substantially. These findings highlight the links between biological and social synchrony and their mutual adaptation between members of a dyad.

Finally, we compared the respiratory sinus arrhythmia of new lovers in the first 3 months of their relationship, as well as of a group of nonattached singles, in response to relationship-related and unrelated affectively negative and positive films. We found that love attenuated parasympathetic responses to negative-relationship-related films, suggesting that during periods of bond formation the ANS is altered to buffer an individual against stress and negative emotionality (Schneiderman, Zilberstain-Kra, Leckman, & Feldman, 2011).

Overall, the findings described here concerning the hormonal, brain, and autonomic systems support our conceptual model. They suggest that periods of bond formation are associated with significant alterations in behavioral and biological systems that involve coordination between relationship partners' biology and behavior.

CONCLUSION

Our biobehavioral synchrony model highlights the behavioral building blocks of social bonding, including gaze, touch, and vocal, bodily, and affective expressions; considers the ways in which these microsocial behaviors coalesce to form unique affiliative bonds with a specific pace, rhythm, pattern, and interpersonal focus starting in the first day of life; and addresses how hormonal, brain, and autonomic systems realign between attachment partners to accommodate the formation of affiliative bonds.

According to the well-known neuroscientist Gerald Edelman (2006), the central unresolved issue in current neuroscience is that of subjectivity. After countless studies, there is still no way science can bridge the "subjectivity gap" and measure how cognitions and emotions are felt by a self-aware individual. This is not merely a problem to be resolved by more sophisticated methods but may indicate an inherently unbridgeable gap that would require a paradigm shift. While acknowledging the gravity of the subjectivity problem, I would like to tentatively suggest that one way to approach the issue of subjectivity is through the lens of intersubjectivity. According to the phenomenological philosophy of Husserl (1911), the human capacity to "know" about things in the outside world is never categorical but always involves a relationship between the perceiving self and the external object. Our biobehavioral synchrony model suggests that the human capacity to perceive such relations is formed within the parent–child dyad and is supported by neurohormonal and brain systems that maintain infant involvement with attachment partners. The role of these partners, in turn, is to become intimately familiar with the infant's social signals and to escort the child gradually into the world in a manner that resonates with the child's subjectivity at both biological and behavioral levels. Within such finely tuned attachments, a human infant can send signals that are reciprocated. Within this process, the infant's subjective experiences are transformed into interpersonal events that turn subjectivity into intersubjectivity. Synchronous processes (e.g., the coactivation of brain response between attachment partners) can thus transform subjective experiences into intersubjective events. At this moment, when the subjective experience turns into an interpersonal event, it also becomes available for scientific scrutiny and can be open for "objective" assessment that is shared among partners.

Synchronous processes, therefore, through their integration of physiology and behavior within a social context, can transform an intrapsychic private brain experience into an interpersonal shared brain event that is open to objective measurement without losing its emotional quality. Such synchrony may provide a new language to a deeper understanding of consciousness and humanity and may begin to chart the terrain for the formation of what Edelman called a "brain-based epistemology."

REFERENCES

Affiliation. (2002). In *Merriam-Webster's online dictionary*. Retrieved from http://www.merriam-webster.com

Atzil, S., Hendler, T., & Feldman, R. (2011). Specifying the neurobiological basis of human attachment: Brain, hormones, and behavior in synchronous and intrusive mothers. *Neuropsychopharmacology, 36*, 2603–2615. doi:10.1038/npp.2011.172

Atzil, S., Hendler, T., Zagoory-Sharon, O., Winetraub, Y., & Feldman, R. (2012). Synchrony and specificity in the maternal and the paternal brain: Relations to oxytocin and vasopressin. *Journal of the American Academy of Child & Adolescent Psychiatry, 51*, 798–811. doi:10.1016/j.jaac.2012.06.008

Beauchaine, T. (2001). Vagal tone, development, and Gray's motivational theory: Toward an integrated model of autonomic nervous system functioning in psychopathology. *Development and Psychopathology, 13*, 183–214. doi:10.1017/S0954579401002012

Bergson, H. (1907). *L'evolution creatice* [Creative evolution]. Paris, France: Les Presses Universitaires de France.

Bowlby, J. (1958). The nature of the child's tie to his mother. *International Journal of Psycho-Analysis, 39*, 350–373.

Carter, C. S. (1998). Neuroendocrine perspectives on social attachment and love. *Psychoneuroendocrinology, 23*, 779–818. doi:10.1016/S0306-4530(98)00055-9

Champagne, F. A. (2008). Epigenetic mechanisms and the transgenerational effects of maternal care. *Frontiers of. Neuroendocrinology, 29*, 386–397. doi:10.1016/j.yfrne.2008.03.003

Damasio, A. R. (2003). *Looking for Spinoza: Joy, sorrow and the feeling brain.* New York, NY: Harcourt.

Ditzen, B., Schaer, M., Gabriel, B., Bodenmann, G., Ehlert, U., & Heindrichs, M. (2009). Intranasal oxytocin increases positive communication and reduces cortisol levels during couple conflict. *Biological Psychiatry, 65*, 728–731. doi:10.1016/j.biopsych.2008.10.011

Edelman, G. M. (2004). *Wider than the sky: The phenomenal gift of consciousness.* New Haven, CT: Yale University Press.

Edelman, G. M. (2006). *Second nature: Brain science and human knowledge.* New Haven, CT: Yale University Press.

Feldman, R. (2006). From biological rhythms to social rhythms: Physiological precursors of mother–infant synchrony. *Developmental Psychology, 42*, 175–188. doi:10.1037/0012-1649.42.1.175

Feldman, R. (2007a). Mother–infant synchrony and the development of moral orientation in childhood and adolescence: Direct and indirect mechanisms of developmental continuity. *American Journal of Orthopsychiatry, 77*, 582–597. doi:10.1037/0002-9432.77.4.582

Feldman, R. (2007b). On the origins of background emotions: From affect synchrony to symbolic expression. *Emotion, 7*, 601–611. doi:10.1037/1528-3542.7.3.601

Feldman, R. (2007c). Parent–infant synchrony: Biological foundations and developmental outcomes. *Current Directions in Psychological Science, 16*, 340–345. doi:10.1111/j.1467-8721.2007.00532.x

Feldman, R. (2007d). Parent–infant synchrony and the construction of shared timing; Physiological precursors, developmental outcomes, and risk conditions. *Journal of Child Psychology and Psychiatry, 48*, 329–354. doi:10.1111/j.1469-7610.2006.01701.x

Feldman, R. (2010). The relational basis of adolescent adjustment: Trajectories of mother–child interactive behaviors from infancy to adolescence shape adolescents' adaptation. *Attachment & Human Development, 12,* 173–192. doi:10.1080/14616730903282472

Feldman, R. (2012a). Oxytocin and social affiliation in humans. *Hormones and Behavior, 61,* 380–391. doi:10.1016/j.yhbeh.2012.01.008

Feldman, R. (2012b). Parent–infant synchrony: A biobehavioral model of mutual influences in the formation of affiliative bonds. *Monographs of the Society for Research in Child Development, 77*(2), 42–51. doi:10.1111/j.1540-5834.2011.00660.x

Feldman, R., & Eidelman, A. I. (2007). Maternal postpartum behavior and the emergence of infant–mother and infant–father synchrony in preterm and full-term infants: The role of neonatal vagal tone. *Developmental Psychobiology, 49,* 290–302. doi:10.1002/dev.20220

Feldman, R., Gordon, I., Influs, M., Gutbir, T., & Ebstein, R.P. (2013). Parental oxytocin and early caregiving jointly shape children's oxytocin response and social reciprocity. *Neuropsychopharmacology.* Advance online publication. doi:10.1038/npp.2012.22

Feldman, R., Gordon, I., Schneiderman, I., Weisman, O., & Zagoory-Sharon, O. (2010). Natural variations in maternal and paternal care are associated with systematic changes in oxytocin following parent–infant contact. *Psychoneuroendocrinology, 35,* 1133–1141. doi:10.1016/j.psyneuen.2010.01.013

Feldman, R., Gordon, I., & Zagoory-Sharon, O. (2010). The cross-generation transmission of oxytocin in humans. *Hormones and Behavior, 58,* 669–676. doi:10.1016/j.yhbeh.2010.06.005

Feldman, R., Gordon, I., & Zagoory-Sharon, O. (2011). Maternal and paternal plasma, salivary, and urinary oxytocin and parent–infant synchrony: Considering stress and affiliation components of human bonding. *Developmental Science, 14,* 752–761. doi:10.1111/j.1467-7687.2010.01021.x

Feldman, R., Greenbaum, C. W., & Yirmiya, N. (1999). Mother–infant affect synchrony as an antecedent to the emergence of self-control. *Developmental Psychology, 35,* 223–231. doi:10.1037/0012-1649.35.1.223

Feldman, R., Magori-Cohen, R., Galili, G., Singer, M., & Louzoun, Y. (2011). Mother and infant coordinate heart rhythms through episodes of interaction synchrony. *Infant Behavior & Development, 34,* 569–577. doi:10.1016/j.infbeh.2011.06.008

Feldman, R., Masalha, S., & Alony, D. (2006). Microregulatory patterns of family interactions: Cultural pathways to toddlers' self-regulation. *Journal of Family Psychology, 20,* 614–623. doi:10.1037/0893-3200.20.4.614

Feldman, R., Singer, M., & Zagoory, O. (2010). Touch attenuates infants' physiological reactivity to stress. *Developmental Science, 13,* 271–278. doi:10.1111/j.1467-7687.2009.00890.x

Feldman, R., Vengrober, A., Eidelman-Rothman, M., & Zagoory-Sharon, O. (in press). Stress reactivity in war-exposed young children with and without PTSD:

Multi-level effects of biology, parenting, and child emotionality and regulation. *Development and Psychopathology*.

Feldman, R., Weller, A., Zagoory-Sharon, O., & Levine, A. (2007). Evidence for a neuroendocrinological foundation of human affiliation: Plasma oxytocin levels across pregnancy and the postpartum period predict mother–infant bonding. *Psychological Science, 18*, 965–970. doi:10.1111/j.1467-9280.2007.02010.x

Feldman, R., Zagoory-Sharon, O., Maoz, R., Weisman, O., Gordon, I., Schneiderman, I., & Ebstein, R. P. (2012). Sensitive parenting is associated with plasma oxytocin and polymorphisms in the *OXTR* and *CD38* genes. *Biological Psychiatry, 72*, 175–181. doi:10.1016/j.biopsych.2011.12.025

Gimpl, G., & Fahrenholz, F. (2001). The oxytocin receptor system: Structure, function, and regulation. *Physiological Reviews, 81*, 629–683.

Gonzaga, G. C., Turner, R. A., Keltner, D., Campos, B., & Altemus, M. (2006). Romantic love and sexual desire in close relationships. *Emotion, 6*, 163–179. doi:10.1037/1528-3542.6.2.163

Gordon, I., & Feldman, R. (2008). Synchrony in the triad: A microlevel process model of coparenting and parent–child interactions. *Family Process, 47*, 465–479. doi:10.1111/j.1545-5300.2008.00266.x

Gordon, I., Zagoory-Sharon, O., Leckman, J. F., & Feldman, R. (2010a). Oxytocin and the development of parenting in humans. *Biological Psychiatry, 68*, 377–382. doi:10.1016/j.biopsych.2010.02.005

Gordon, I., Zagoory-Sharon, O., Leckman, J. F., & Feldman, R. (2010b). Parental oxytocin and triadic family interactions. *Physiology & Behavior, 101*, 679–684. doi:10.1016/j.physbeh.2010.08.008

Gordon, I., Zagoory-Sharon, O., Leckman, J. F., & Feldman, R. (2010c). Prolactin, oxytocin, and the development of paternal behavior across the first six months of fatherhood. *Hormones and Behavior, 58*, 513–518. doi:10.1016/j.yhbeh.2010.04.007

Gordon, I., Zagoory-Sharon, O., Schneiderman, I., Leckman, J. F., Weller, A., & Feldman, R. (2008). Oxytocin and cortisol in romantically unattached young adults: Associations with bonding and psychological distress. *Psychophysiology, 45*, 349–352. doi:10.1111/j.1469-8986.2008.00649.x

Grewen, K. M., Girdler, S. S., Amico, J., & Light, K. C. (2005). Effects of partner support on resting oxytocin, cortisol, norepinephrine, and blood pressure before and after warm partner contact. *Psychosomatic Medicine, 67*, 531–538. doi:10.1097/01.psy.0000170341.88395.47

Harlow, H. F. (1958). The nature of love. *American Psychologist, 13*, 673–685. doi:10.1037/h0047884

Hofer, M. A. (1994). Hidden regulators in attachment, separation, and loss. *Monographs of the Society for Research in Child Development, 59*, 192–207.

Holt-Lunstad, J., Birmingham, W. A., & Light, K. C. (2008). Influence of a "warm touch" support enhancement intervention among married couples on ambulatory blood pressure, oxytocin, alpha amylase, and cortisol. *Psychosomatic Medicine, 70*, 976–985. doi:10.1097/PSY.0b013e318187aef7

Husserl, E. (1911). Philosophie als strenge Wissenschaft [Philosophy as rigorous science]. *Logos, 1*, 289–341.

Insel, T. R. (1997). A neurobiological basis of social attachment. *American Journal of Psychiatry, 154*, 726–735.

Insel, T. R. (2010). The challenge of translation in social neuroscience: A review of oxytocin, vasopressin, and affiliative behavior. *Neuron, 65*, 768–779. doi:10.1016/j.neuron.2010.03.005

Insel, T. R., & Hulihan, T. J. (1995). A gender-specific mechanism for pair bonding: Oxytocin and partner preference formation in monogamous voles. *Behavioral Neuroscience, 109*, 782–769. doi:10.1037/0735-7044.109.4.782

Kappeler, L., & Meaney, M. J. (2010). Epigenetics and parental effects. *BioEssays, 32*, 818–827. doi:10.1002/bies.20100015

Levine, A., Zagoory-Sharon, O., Feldman, R., & Weller, A. (2007). Oxytocin during pregnancy and early postpartum: Individual patterns and maternal–fetal attachment. *Peptides, 28*, 1162–1169. doi:10.1016/j.peptides.2007.04.016

Lorenz, K. Z. (1950). The comparative method in studying innate behavior patterns. *Symposia of the Society for Experimental Biology 4: Physiological mechanisms in animal behavior* (pp. 221–268). Oxford, England: Academic Press.

Mead, G. H. (1934). *Mind, self, and society*. Chicago, IL: University of Chicago Press.

Meaney, M. J. (2010). Epigenetics and the biological definition of gene × environment interactions. *Child Development, 81*, 41–79. doi:10.1111/j.1467-8624.2009.01381.x

Merleau-Ponty, M. (1945). *Phenomenologie de la perception* [Phenomenology of perception]. Paris, France: Gallimard.

Mosek-Eilon, V., Hirschberger, G., Kanat-Maymon, Y., & Feldman, R. (2012). Infant reminders alter sympathetic reactivity and reduce couple hostility at the transition to parenthood. *Developmental Psychology*. Advance online publication. doi:10.1037/a0030088

Porges, S. W. (2003). Social engagement and attachment: A polygenetic perspective. *Annals of the New York Academy of Sciences, 1008*, 31–47. doi:10.1196/annals.1301.004

Rosenblatt, J. S. (1965). The basis of synchrony in the behavioral interaction between the mother and her offspring in the laboratory rat. In B. M. Foss (Ed.), *Determinants of infant behavior* (pp. 3–45). London, England: Methuen.

Ross, H. E., Freeman, S. M., Spiegel, L. L., Ren, X., Terwilliger, E. F., & Young, L. J. (2009). Variation in oxytocin receptor density in the nucleus accumbens has differential effects on affiliative behaviors in monogamous and polygamous voles. *Journal of Neuroscience, 29*, 1312–1318. doi:10.1523/JNEUROSCI.5039-08.2009

Ross, H. E., & Young, L. J. (2009). Oxytocin and the neural mechanisms regulating social cognition and affiliative behavior. *Frontiers in Neuroendocrinology, 30*, 534–547. doi:10.1016/j.yfrne.2009.05.004

Schneiderman, I., Zagoory-Sharon, O., & Feldman, R. (2012). *Hormonal change and conflict dialogue at the first stages of romantic love.* Manuscript submitted for publication.

Schneiderman, I., Zagoory-Sharon, O., Leckman, J. F., & Feldman, R. (2012). Oxytocin at the first stages of romantic attachment: Relations to couples' interactive reciprocity. *Psychoneuroendocrinology, 37,* 1277–1285. doi:10.1016/j.psyneuen. 2011.12.021

Schneiderman, I., Zilberstain-Kra, Y., Leckman, J. F., & Feldman, R. (2011). Love alters autonomic reactivity to emotions. *Emotion, 11,* 1314–1321. doi:10.1037/a0024090

Schneirla, T. C. (1946). Problems in the biopsychology of social organizations. *Journal of Abnormal and Social Psychology, 41,* 385–402. doi:10.1037/h0055210

Spitz, R. A., & Wolf, K. M. (1946). Anaclitic depression—An inquiry into the genesis of psychiatric conditions in early childhood. *Psychoanalytic Study of the Child, 2,* 313–342.

Tinbergen, N. (1963). On aims and methods in ethology. *Zeitschrift für Tierpsychologie, 20,* 410–433. doi:10.1111/j.1439-0310.1963.tb01161.x

Weisman, O., Zagoory-Sharon, O., & Feldman, R. (2012). Oxytocin administration to parent enhances infant physiological and behavioral readiness for social engagement. *Biological Psychiatry, 72,* 982–989. doi:10.1016/j.biopsych. 2012.06.011

Weisman, O., Zagoory-Sharon, O., Schneiderman, I., Gordon, I., & Feldman, R. (2012). Plasma oxytocin distributions in a large cohort of women and men and their gender-specific associations with anxiety. *Psychoneuroendocrinology.* Advance online publication. doi:10.1016/j.psyneuen.2012.08.011

Wheeler, W. M. (1928). *The social insects.* New York, NY: Harcourt.

9

GAZE FOLLOWING: A MECHANISM FOR BUILDING SOCIAL CONNECTIONS BETWEEN INFANTS AND ADULTS

RECHELE BROOKS AND ANDREW N. MELTZOFF

From the first smile to the first word, infants' social acts are greeted with joy and awe by parents. Regardless of the reason for a smile, parents are hooked—and so are the researchers who study these acts. Parents socially connect with their infants in moments of eye contact and face-to-face inter-action; researchers see in these behaviors the foundation of intersubjectivity and reciprocity. However, these joyful, dyadic interactions are destined not to last, because third parties come onto the scene. The mother's eyes stray from her infant to other people and objects, and the infant begins to notice where the mother is looking. Instead of being part of a simple dyad, infants become part of a triangle involving self, mother, and object. This is the birth of what scientists term *triadic exchanges*, in which an external object (whether person or thing) becomes a part of the interaction. The external

This work was supported by grants from the University of Washington Royalty Research Fund to Rechele Brooks and from the National Science Foundation (OMA-0835854) and the Office of Naval Research (N00014-09-1-0097) to Andrew N. Meltzoff.

http://dx.doi.org/10.1037/14250-010
Mechanisms of Social Connection: From Brain to Group, M. Mikulincer and P. R. Shaver (Editors)

167

world intrudes on the dyad and expands the primordial relationship between mother and child.

Adults smoothly shift between dyadic and triadic interactions. From a dyadic perspective, when an adult sees his or her social partner look away, this could suggest that the partner is thinking about something, avoiding intimacy, or losing interest (Argyle & Cook, 1976; Kendon, 1990). From a triadic standpoint, adults often make the attribution that the social partner glanced away to look at an important object in the room and perhaps even to communicate interest in it to bring in a new, shared external referent into the interpersonal exchange. The ontogenesis of triadic social interaction is the subject of this chapter.

For adults, shifts of eye gaze are salient social-communicative signals. When a person on the street or in a group suddenly turns to look up in the sky, others in the group tend to follow his or her gaze. The observers are prompted to catch a glimpse of what the other is looking at. Adult observers interpret looking in a certain direction as more than a simple bodily movement; instead, they regard it as a perceptual/psychological act through which they can glean information about the gazer's perceptions, desires, emotions, and intentions.

Gaze following is an entry point for understanding other people's minds. For adults, a person's eye gaze is understood as giving the viewer perceptual access to and/or referring to something in the external world. For example, a person might look at an object with a disgusted facial expression while saying, "I don't like *that*!" or "That's so annoying!" Adults viewing this act can follow her gaze and discover what disgusted or irritated her. Adults follow gaze to help understand what their social partner's emotion is about, and recent work showed that young children do this as well (e.g., Repacholi & Meltzoff, 2007).

Infants begin to notice others' gaze by their first birthdays. This much is uncontroversial. But it is highly controversial how they come to understand gaze as a social-referential signal. Eyes may attract the attention of the newborn: Newborns may be compelled to look at the quickly moving orbs, but do they interpret these movements as indicating mental processes (perception) in the gazer? Do they know that the eyes are pointing to an object that is at the end of the person's line of regard? When does the infant interpret an eye movement as being more than mere movement and as being more a psychological act connecting a viewer to an object?

We hypothesize that infants' own first-person experiences with vision play a vital role in their developing this more sophisticated, psychological notion of gaze. We suggest that infants use their own visual experiences as a lever to help interpret the visual experiences of others like them. We call this the *like-me* developmental theory, and we show in this chapter how it can be applied to a range of issues beyond gaze following itself (Meltzoff, 2007, 2013).

We begin this chapter by making conceptual distinctions between gaze following and other forms of joint engagement that are both broader and narrower than gaze following per se. Next, we discuss the ontogenesis of infant gaze following. Then, we marshal evidence showing that infants' self-experience with their own visual system colors their understanding of others' gaze. The core of this argument is that humans, even preverbal ones, do not come to social relationships as blank slates; rather, infants interpret social interactions through their own past experiences. We conclude with a theoretical discussion that connects gaze following to broader issues concerning the development of interpersonal relations. We theorize that the like-me perceptions that begin in infancy are the developmental origin of the human tendency to divide the social world into ingroups and outgroups. We draw connections between developmental science, social psychology, and neuroscience and argue that the study of infant development can provide foundations for a science of social learning (Meltzoff, Kuhl, Movellan, & Sejnowski, 2009).

Our focus on gaze following complements other approaches in this volume that emphasize (a) the physiological and neural mechanisms supporting social interaction (mirror neurons, oxytocin, and neural reward systems, as discussed in Chapters 1, 3, and 4, this volume) and (b) the individual's psychological and behavioral contributions to harmonious dyadic interactions (synchrony, proximity, and mentalization, as discussed in Chapters 5, 8, and 10). The current chapter brings to the table a developmental viewpoint, showing how seemingly simple behaviors, such as gaze following, illuminate how infants develop an understanding of other people as social agents with perceptions and emotions just "like me." By studying gaze following, we are uncovering a key avenue by which early social connections are formed prior to language.

LOOKING FOR CONNECTIONS: PUTTING GAZE FOLLOWING INTO A LARGER CONTEXT

The literature uses an array of terms and behavioral measures to indicate when a parent and a child share attention toward an external object. These include, among others, *joint engagement, gaze following,* and *manual pointing.* In this section, we differentiate and clarify terms to set the stage for the rest of the chapter.

Joint Engagement

Joint engagement occurs when two individuals jointly attend to the same object. For infants, this often happens when they are playing with an object and their parent is watching them. Infants may interrupt their play to look up and check what the parent is doing or watching. Some researchers have argued that infants are attempting to share visual attention when they initiate eye contact with the adult and shift their own gaze back and forth between the object and the adult, as if to make it a topic of nonverbal "discussion." This type of gaze alternation is often called *coordinated joint engagement* (Bakeman & Adamson, 1984) because it happens at the behavioral rather than the linguistic level. Key to the term's application is that the infant initiates eye contact with an adult rather than looking up in response to the adult's verbal comment. It is the infant who possesses the object and tries to share it with the adult (Carpenter, Nagell, & Tomasello, 1998).

Young infants' alternation of gaze varies as a function of the context. In formal clinical assessments, when infants are already facing an adult tester and an object, 9- to 18-month-old infants consistently make eye contact with the adult and alternate gaze to the object (Mundy et al., 2007). In contrast, in studies of unstructured play with their mothers, infants have only fleeting moments of coordinated joint engagement at 9 months of age, but after they reach 12 months they become more consistent (Carpenter et al., 1998). However, even 18-month-olds spend less than 30% of their unstructured play in coordinated engagement, and these instances occur more often with their parents than with their peers (Bakeman & Adamson, 1984).

The support or scaffolding provided by a social partner may induce joint engagement. When a mother observes her child look back and forth from a toy to her face, the mother may verbally label that toy (i.e., follow-in labeling). This type of parental support prompts infants to alternate gaze before they fully recognize that visual attention connects viewers to objects. In this way, infants may alternate their own gaze between object and parent, without trying to follow their parent's gaze toward objects that lie outside the immediate interaction. (The latter would involve true gaze following, and we will shortly come to this.)

Pointing

Infants can direct others' attention by pointing to objects or events. The prototypical version of this gesture involves extending one's arm and index finger toward an object, although other hand gestures (e.g., using the whole hand as a pointer) are seen in social interactions. Infants usually begin pointing to things or events in their surroundings between 9 and 12 months of age (Butterworth, 2003; Camaioni, Perucchini, Bellagamba, & Colonnesi, 2004).

Bates, Camaioni, and Volterra (1975) distinguished between the types of messages conveyed by pointing, dividing points into proto-imperative meanings ("I want that") and proto-declarative meanings ("Look at that").

Some theorists argue that proto-imperative points do not require infants to appreciate others' visual attention. Rather, it has been argued that infants are simply trying to obtain something by directing the adult's behavior rather than the adult's attention (Colonnesi, Stams, Koster, & Noom, 2010). With respect to proto-declarative points, theorists suggest that infants demonstrate this ability when they point in order to direct and share attention to distal objects (Camaioni et al., 2004; Liszkowski, Carpenter, Henning, Striano, & Tomasello, 2004). Researchers have coded whether or not infants look at others as they point. As pointing emerges near 1 year of age, infants are likely first to point at the event and then to look at the adult (Liszkowski et al., 2004). After 15 months, they are more likely to look at the adult before pointing to the event (Franco & Butterworth, 1996). This change may be relevant to the issue of when the infant is pointing to convey information to the adult.

An interesting way of testing infants' use of pointing as a proto-declarative act of communicating and visual sharing is to assess whether infants change their pointing in relation to what others can see. With a bit of prompting (e.g., with a moving puppet), by 12 to 15 months of age, infants point to a nearby event when the adult did not appear to see it spontaneously (Camaioni et al., 2004). Similarly, Brooks and Meltzoff (2002) reported that 12- to 18-month-old infants were more likely to point to an object when the adult had her eyes open (rather than closed) and thus could observe the infant's point. In situations in which an adult seems to be actively searching for an object after accidentally dropping it on the floor (e.g., a pen falls off a table), 12-month-olds point to the object's location (Tomasello, Carpenter, & Liszkowski, 2007). In this way, infants' use of pointing may indicate some primitive sensitivity to the adult's perspective.

Conceptual Issues in Gaze Following

Gaze following refers to the act of following another person's line of regard. Adult observers seek to catch a glimpse of what a nearby gazer is seeing. But this seemingly simple act involves understanding a number of components. For example, it is not gaze following if a loud plane prompts both the child and the mother to look at the object at the same time, because the synchronized looking would be due to a common third cause (the noise) rather than the infant's perception of the mother's looking behavior. Nor is it gaze following if an infant simply tracks an adult's head movement or bodily orientation and does not process the adult's gaze. In its most sophisticated forms, as shown by adults, the act of gaze following also includes an inference about perception: The observer follows to see what the gazer perceives. In analyzing gaze following and its development, it is useful to distinguish it from other closely aligned phenomena that may seem like gaze following.

Salience of Eyes

Detecting eye gaze is not gaze following per se but is sometimes confused with it. In studies in which faces are presented to infants, even newborns distinguish whether eyespots are directed forward toward them or averted to the side (Farroni, Massaccesi, Pividori, & Johnson, 2004; Johnson, Grossmann, & Farroni, 2008). However, infants may differentiate these displays on the basis of physical properties of the displays, such as whether high-contrast stimuli are centered or lateral, not by understanding gaze per se.

Gaze Detection

In another line of research, shifts of eye gaze have been used to cue the location of nearby targets on a screen (Hood, Willen, & Driver, 1998; Johnson et al., 2008). The classic stimulus in this cuing procedure is a digitized face with eyes that shift to one side before a target appears slightly to the left or the right of the face. The two-dimensional face usually vanishes from the screen before the close-in peripheral targets appear. Adults and infants typically shift their gaze more rapidly to the target that has been cued: If the cue shifts to the right side, they look to a target that appears on the right faster than to one that appears on the left (Frischen, Bayliss, & Tipper, 2007). Under specialized conditions, this cuing effect is seen with newborns (Farroni et al., 2004).

Though interesting, these findings do not provide evidence about following gaze in real-world social interactions. In the real world, when a mother looks at an object, her face does not disappear—yet in the gaze-cuing research that is the procedure used (to allow the infant to disengage from the face and look to the peripheral target). Indeed, if the gaze-cuing procedure is slightly changed so that the face remains on the screen, the face attracts young infants' attention more often than the target and disrupts this specialized effect (Hood et al., 1998). Moreover, in the cuing studies, it is not necessarily the eyes that provide the directional signal to infants: When the whole head and face is artificially displaced laterally (e.g., to the left) and the eyes remain fixed in their original spot on the screen, the apparent motion of the head cues infants to the left (Farroni, Johnson, Brockbank, & Simion, 2000, Experiment 2). This raises the possibility of motion following and not gaze following. Furthermore, in this cuing paradigm the peripheral targets pop into view (after the face vanishes), and this sudden appearance of a target again contrasts with real-world social interactions. In social interchanges, the world remains stable and the adult's gaze spotlights an existing object. In short, infants' sensitivity to directional shifts in the cuing paradigm does not ensure that infants follow the gaze of actual people, and the underlying mechanisms that support these two behaviors may be different.

TESTS OF INFANT GAZE FOLLOWING

In the typical gaze-following paradigm, an adult makes eye contact with the infant and then turns to a distal object that is often outside of peripheral view. This situation gives infants an opportunity to follow the adult's line of regard to the distant object. However, when we are tracking where the person turns, how do we know that infants are following the looker's eye gaze?

Heading Toward Targets

Early reports suggested that infants seem to follow an adult's line of regard by 3 to 6 months of age under certain conditions (see Moore, 2008, for a review). A difficulty in interpreting these findings is that the adult turns his or her eyes and head toward a target. The adult's salient head motion may draw infants' gaze in the correct direction without the infants processing the adult's gaze at all. Empirical evidence and computational models support the claim that salient head movements often drive where infants look (Corkum & Moore, 1995; Triesch, Teuscher, Deák, & Carlson, 2006), which of course is not gaze following at all.

To the extent that this is the case, infants may be pulled in the correct direction by the adult's head turn and then coincidentally notice the object the adult was viewing. This is not gaze following. First, infants are simply following the directional signal of the head motion and not necessarily processing the gaze. Second, although infants are responding to the adult, they are not searching for the target; infants come across an interesting object by coincidence. Third, infants need not make any effort to infer what the adult sees, because the motion is sufficient to attract the infants' attention. Following body or head motion can shift infants' eyes without the infants taking into account the adult's gaze or visual experience.

Following Others' Gaze

We developed a test to determine whether or not infants truly follow gaze (Brooks & Meltzoff, 2002). In this paradigm, an adult turned toward one of two identical targets (situated off to the left and the right side of the infant). The adult's head motion was controlled. Infants were randomly assigned to one of two groups: For one, the adult silently turned toward a target with open eyes, and for the other she turned with closed eyes.

The reason such a manipulation is theoretically crucial is that our eyes are our means of visual perception. We see with our eyes and not our head. An important step toward gaining the adult psychological interpretation of "seeing" is to recognize that the eyes are critical. If infants understand that the eyes are relevant for connecting the adult and the object, they should differentiate the two conditions and look at the target object only when the adult has open eyes. If, however, infants respond to head movements, they should turn in response to both actions.

Brooks and Meltzoff (2002) tested 12-, 14-, and 18-month-old infants in this eyes open/closed experimental protocol. Infants' reactions were scored with respect to whether infants looked at the correct target (the same target as the adult vs. the opposite target). Infants of all ages looked significantly more often at the target when the adult turned toward it with open rather than closed eyes.

Because we were interested in gaze following as a component of social connectedness to others, we also examined a broader network of social acts (pointing, vocalizing) during the gaze-following tests. First, we measured infants' average duration of correct looking to examine how long the infants stared at a correct target (i.e., the adult's target) once they gaze followed. We discovered that infants inspected the target longer when the adult turned with open rather than closed eyes. We also found that infants vocalized toward the correct target more in the open-eyes than in the closed-eyes group. Finally, significantly more infants pointed to the correct target in the open-eyes group than in the closed-eyes group. The results indicate that infants notice others' eye status and selectively look, vocalize, and point at the target when the adult can see it.

These findings are important because they help us interpret gaze following. The leanest interpretation has been that an adult's movement attracts infants' attention to a hemifield of space where the infants (by chance) see an interesting object. This could not explain the results from our study, however, because head motion was controlled. Moreover, infants marshal other target-directed acts in a selective manner, such as pointing at the target and vocalizing toward it when the adult can see the target. The infants are not imitating the adult because they are generating communicative acts that the adult herself did not produce. Infants cannot be pointing solely because they are interested in the colorful targets, because the objects are equally available in both conditions. Infants point when the social partner can see the objects but refrain when the partner cannot see them.

Finally, the duration measure also helps make sense of infants' behavior within a social context. If the conservative proposal that the adult's head movement simply brings the infant's attention to the object were correct, this would not explain why infants inspect the object longer when the adult's eyes are open rather than closed. The object itself is the same whether the adult turns toward it with open or closed eyes. However, the infants treat the target object as if it has a special value once the social partner has looked at it. It is as though the adult has shone a psychological spotlight on it, motivating intense infant inspection of it. Infants' selective looking, pointing, and vocalizing when the adult's eyes are open suggests that infants are treating others as social agents who see and whose visual perception can be directed.

Developmental Roots of Infant Gaze Following

The work reviewed so far shows that 12-month-old infants follow others' gaze. A pressing question concerns younger infants. Because there are changes in social interactions near 9 months of age (Bråten, 2007), we selected children of that age for study. Brooks and Meltzoff (2005) recruited infants for a visit within 1 week of becoming 9, 10, or 11 months of age. Infants were randomly assigned to either the open- or the closed-eyes condition.

The results showed that 9-month-olds did not discriminate between the open- and closed-eyes conditions. They turned equally often in the two cases. It is important to note that 9-month-olds did not fail to follow the adult. In fact, they turned frequently even when the adult turned with closed eyes, as if they did not process their social partner's ability to see. However, there was a developmental transition. By 10 months, infants tended not to follow the turns of the closed-eyed adult. For the 10- and 11-month-olds, the gaze-following scores in the open-eyes group were significantly greater than those in the closed-eyes group. By 10 months, but not by 9 months, infants were genuinely following the gaze of their social partners.

These results are theoretically important because of claims that gaze following starts as early as 3 or 4 months of age. At first, these reports seem to contradict our assertion that the development of gaze following occurs at 10 to 11 months of age. But there is no contradiction. We believe that infants turn to follow the direction of head movements and postural changes at 9 months and younger. These young infants turn even if the adult cannot possibly be looking at the target, and thus they are not truly gaze following. We think that infants 9 months old and younger construe others as "body orienters" and are sensitive to the postural changes of adults in relation to objects. The first evidence for exhibiting true gaze following and treating the social partner as a psychological, visually perceptive agent is at 10 to 11 months.

In sum, by 10 to 12 months, following head motion alone does not explain why infants look at an adult's visual target. The 10- to 11-month-old infants selectively follow the turns of an adult with open eyes and rarely follow the turns of an adult with closed eyes, even though the head motion is the same for the two types of head turns (Brooks & Meltzoff, 2005). Older infants begin to understand others as visually connected to the external world and turn to follow another person's gaze. This is an important step in understanding another person as an intentional perceiver (a looker, a gazer). Recent work with "social robots" has extended this work to investigate in detail what constitutes an entity whose gaze the child will follow (Meltzoff, Brooks,

Shon, & Rao, 2010). Infants were more likely to follow the "gaze" of a robot after they had seen a person and the robot engage in a social interchange (e.g., imitating each other) than when this social connection was not built up. This finding underscores that gaze following is part of a larger network of ideas that the infant is developing about social cognition.

Links Between Gaze Following and Language

Gaze following gives infants a nonverbal means to connect to and interact with their social partners. However, verbal exchanges soon expand infants' social repertoire. From a theoretical perspective, following gaze could provide important social-cognitive support for acquiring language (e.g., Baldwin, 2000; Carpenter et al., 1998; Kuhl, 2004; Mundy, Sullivan, & Mastergeorge, 2009). For example, when a parent says, "There's the ball," the parent is likely staring at a ball. An infant who gaze follows can learn what visual object goes with the verbal label.

To empirically test this idea, Brooks and Meltzoff (2008) conducted a longitudinal study of the children who had come into the lab at 10 to 11 months of age (the youngest ages with clear evidence of gaze following). Parents reported their infants' productive vocabulary for the ages of 10–11, 14, 18, and 24 months. We tested whether the gaze-following behavior of infants (before they started talking) predicted the rate of their subsequent vocabulary growth. The hypothesis was that early social understanding would be positively correlated with subsequent language development, showing the interweaving of social development and language development.

The results showed that infants with better gaze-following ability had faster vocabulary growth. In particular, the duration measure of gaze following was a significant predictor of the number of words infants produced through 24 months of age. Infants who had extended looks at the target were the infants who had larger vocabularies, whereas infants with short (or no) glances at the adult's target had smaller vocabularies by 24 months of age. Infants' gaze-following ability was still a significant predictor of language outcome, even after controlling for background parental factors such as maternal education.

The empirical findings confirm the theoretical position that gaze following supports and indeed accelerates word learning. Longer looks seem to indicate that the target acquired a special valence when another person looked at it, arousing the infants' curiosity and desire to visually inspect it. Infants who tend to react in this way may have great opportunities to learn the names of objects. They linger on an object long enough to hear a verbal label applied to it by the adult. This work fits well with other findings that infants more readily learn language during social exchanges with human social partners than from TV, which does not afford social interactivity in the same way that a flesh-and-blood person does (see Meltzoff et al., 2009, for a review).

MECHANISM OF CHANGE: INFANTS' OWN EXPERIENCES WITH SEEING

The difference between open eyes and closed eyes is not the only distinction that infants need to make if they are to understand social exchanges in the real world. People can look through a window but cannot see through a wall. Do infants realize that barriers, such as walls and other inanimate objects, block one's line of sight?

We have used a procedure similar to the open/closed eyes paradigm to explore what infants understand about inanimate occluders (Brooks & Meltzoff, 2002). In these studies, for one group of infants, an adult turned with a cloth (blindfold) blocking her view. For infants in the other group, she had a clear view because the cloth was worn on her forehead as a headband. This at first seemed like a minor variation, but the results were surprisingly different from those in the study with open or closed eyes.

The 12-month-olds mistakenly followed the adult's turn when she wore the blindfold. They turned equally as much when the adult was wearing the headband as when she was wearing the blindfold (Brooks & Meltzoff, 2002, Experiment 2). In contrast, the infants at 14 and 18 months distinguished between the two conditions. The older infants rarely followed the turns of the blindfolded adult, whereas they did follow the turns when the cloth was on her forehead as a headband. It seems that 1-year-olds know that eye closure blocks an adult's vision, but they do not know that inanimate occluders do.

Why do infants understand eye closure at an earlier age than they do blindfolds? A theory based on salience of head motion cannot explain why there would be this difference because both actions used the same head motion. Further, infants do not seem to use a general rule, such as "I can (or cannot) see your eyes," to solve this problem: The adult's eyes were not visible in either the blindfold or the eyes-closed condition, yet those conditions prompted different responses from the 12-month-old infants.

We propose that the difference between eye closure and a blindfold is infants' own experience and sense of agency. Infants amass visual experience by opening and closing their own eyes; when they close their eyes, they can no longer see. We believe that infants use their own phenomenological experience gained by closing their eyes to give meaning to the corresponding acts of others.

If this hypothesis is correct, giving infants experience that blindfolds block their view should make a difference. Meltzoff and Brooks (2008) conducted the relevant experiment with 12-month-olds. Infants sat at a table and played with an object. Next, the adult gently raised a blindfold to block infants' vision. The adult then lowered the cloth and play resumed. This process was repeated in a game-like fashion with other objects for about 7 minutes. This provided infants with first-person, self-experience about how the blindfold blocked their own view. Our question was whether this self-experience changed the infants' understanding of their social partners. To test this, we then had, for the first time, the adult wear the blindfold, and we administered the standard gaze-following test.

The self-experience changed infants' interpretation of the adult's behavior. Infants no longer followed the blindfolded adult's "gaze" to the object, whereas the 12-month-olds without blindfold experience still followed (Meltzoff & Brooks, 2008). We thus discovered that infants could generalize from their own experience to that of their social partner. Because they could not see when a blindfold was in front of their eyes, they inferred that the adult could not see in a similar situation.

In the typical course of development, infants change their understanding of visual perception. By 14 to 18 months of age, infants do not act as though adults can see through opaque barriers, and they refrain from gaze following if an opaque barrier blocks the adult's view (e.g., Butler, Caron, & Brooks, 2000; Dunphy-Lelii & Wellman, 2004).

To press the self-experience idea one step further, Meltzoff and Brooks (2008, Experiment 2) provided 18-month-olds with novel experience that countered their expectation about opaque occluders. We designed a trick blindfold that looked opaque from the outside but that was made of special material that could be seen through when held close to the eyes. Infants were randomly assigned to one of three groups: experience with this trick blindfold, experience with the opaque blindfold, and a baseline control condition (familiarity with the blindfold lying flat on the table). After training, infants saw the adult wear the blindfold in the standard test. We discovered that infants who had first-person experience with the trick see-through blindfold followed the adult's head turns significantly more often than did infants in the other two groups.

The effects of training demonstrate that infants' own visual experiences have a powerful effect on their interactions with others. The information infants learned through self-experience was immediately applied to social others. As infants gain firsthand experience, they transform their understanding of others who are "like me." This "like-me" mechanism allows infants to use their own experiences to give meaning to the acts of other social agents (Meltzoff, 2007).

CONCLUSION

Gaze following is fundamental to everyday social-cognitive understanding. For adults, it is not simply that the other person turns his or her head to the side; rather, the other person's eye gaze is interpreted as an act of perception, a psychological link between viewer and object. For this reason, developmental scientists have considered gaze following a front-end ability that helps promote the development of understanding other minds. Individual differences in following gaze are important partly because they predict language development (Brooks & Meltzoff, 2008; Mundy et al., 2007). Gaze-following deficits are of particular concern for children with autism spectrum disorders. It has been argued that these deficits in decoding the meaning of people's looking at objects may contribute to downstream deficits in language and social understanding (Baron-Cohen, 1995; Mundy et al., 2009; Toth, Munson, Meltzoff, & Dawson, 2006) including deficits in more sophisticated aspects of perspective taking (e.g., Moll & Meltzoff, 2011), which can be thought of as developmental sequelae of infant gaze following.

Gaze following is itself a developmental accomplishment, and it helps illuminate changes in infants' social cognition. Infants begin to follow the gaze of others before their first birthdays. By 10 to 12 months, infants distinguish between open and closed eyes, as shown by their selectively following turns of an adult with open eyes. They begin to treat their eye-orienting partner as making a perceptual act and to treat gaze as a psychological connection between the gazer and a distal object. The ontogenesis of gaze following gives infants an emerging means to interpret the behavior of others and thus facilitate the formation of interpersonal connections.

We come now to a crucial argument about infants using their own first-person experience to understand others. When infants explore their surroundings, they have opportunities to play with their visual experiences, such as closing their eyes to shut out unwanted stimulation. These experiences help infants develop resources for interpreting the acts of others who are "like me" (Meltzoff, 2007, 2013). As infants open and close their eyes—seeing versus shutting out the world—they learn about the consequences of eye closure and can rapidly generalize this experience to other social agents "like them." We provided an experimental test of this idea of interpersonal projection. We systematically manipulated infants' experience that a blindfold could block their own view of the external world; next, we tested whether this changed their interpretation of how the blindfold affected the visual experience of a social partner (Meltzoff & Brooks, 2008). These studies provided empirical evidence to support the claim that infants' own experiences with occlusion and vision color how they interpret the visual experiences of others. This pattern of findings fits well with the "like-me" theory of infant social-cognitive development (Meltzoff, 2007), which holds that infants use their own bodily experiences to give meaning to others' acts and reciprocally rely on their observations of others' acts to change themselves.

Meltzoff (2013) theorized that the infantile proclivity to see others as "like me" is the foundation for the ontogenesis of ingroup affinities. Social psychologists have long been interested in the psychological processes by which we develop the "us" versus "them" distinction (e.g., Heider, 1958; Tajfel, 1981), but the origins have been little explored. The "like-me" attributions made by infants in gaze-following experiments may reveal the developmental origins of people's tendency to identify with others and their sense of belonging to certain social groups (e.g., Cheryan, Meltzoff, & Kim, 2011; Cvencek, Greenwald, & Meltzoff, 2011). We have begun to explore the neuroscience correlates of this powerful "like-me" judgment in young children (Marshall & Meltzoff, 2011; Saby, Marshall, & Meltzoff, 2012) in an effort to connect developmental science, social psychology, and neuroscience (e.g., Jackson, Meltzoff, & Decety, 2005; Lamm, Meltzoff, & Decety, 2010), a grand challenge also explored by many others, such as Decety and Howard (see Chapter 6, this volume) and Ellemers, van Nunspeet, and Scheepers (see Chapter 20).

In summary, the study of gaze following contributes to an interdisciplinary examination of key building blocks for social cognition and begins to illuminate mechanisms of early developmental change. The eyes and the actions of adults provide a foundation on which infants can build social connections between self and other, and they reciprocally provide adult scientists a way of understanding the minds and hearts of infants, who are too young to speak for themselves.

REFERENCES

Argyle, M., & Cook, M. (1976). *Gaze and mutual gaze*. Cambridge, England: Cambridge University Press.

Bakeman, R., & Adamson, L. B. (1984). Coordinating attention to people and objects in mother–infant and peer–infant interaction. *Child Development, 55*, 1278–1289. doi:10.2307/1129997

Baldwin, D. A. (2000). Interpersonal understanding fuels knowledge acquisition. *Current Directions in Psychological Science, 9*, 40–45. doi:10.1111/1467-8721.00057

Baron-Cohen, S. (1995). *Mindblindness: An essay on autism and theory of mind*. Cambridge, MA: MIT Press.

Bates, E., Camaioni, L., & Volterra, V. (1975). The acquisition of performatives prior to speech. *Merrill-Palmer Quarterly, 21*, 205–226.

Bråten, S. (Ed.). (2007). *On being moved: From mirror neurons to empathy*. Philadelphia, PA: Benjamins.

Brooks, R., & Meltzoff, A. N. (2002). The importance of eyes: How infants interpret adult looking behavior. *Developmental Psychology, 38*, 958–966. doi:10.1037/0012-1649.38.6.958

Brooks, R., & Meltzoff, A. N. (2005). The development of gaze following and its relation to language. *Developmental Science, 8*, 535–543. doi:10.1111/j.1467-7687. 2005.00445.x

Brooks, R., & Meltzoff, A. N. (2008). Infant gaze following and pointing predict accelerated vocabulary growth through two years of age: A longitudinal, growth curve modeling study. *Journal of Child Language, 35*, 207–220. doi:10.1017/ S030500090700829X

Butler, S. C., Caron, A. J., & Brooks, R. (2000). Infant understanding of the referential nature of looking. *Journal of Cognition and Development, 1*, 359–377. doi:10.1207/S15327647JCD0104_01

Butterworth, G. (2003). Pointing is the royal road to language for babies. In S. Kita (Ed.), *Pointing: Where language, culture, and cognition meet* (pp. 9–33). Mahwah, NJ: Erlbaum.

Camaioni, L., Perucchini, P., Bellagamba, F., & Colonnesi, C. (2004). The role of declarative pointing in developing a theory of mind. *Infancy, 5*, 291–308. doi:10.1207/s15327078in0503_3

Carpenter, M., Nagell, K., & Tomasello, M. (1998). Social cognition, joint attention, and communicative competence from 9 to 15 months of age. *Monographs of the Society for Research in Child Development, 63*(4, Serial No. 255). doi:10.2307/ 1166214

Cheryan, S., Meltzoff, A. N., & Kim, S. (2011). Classrooms matter: The design of virtual classrooms influences gender disparities in computer science classes. *Computers & Education, 57*, 1825–1835. doi:10.1016/j.compedu.2011.02.004

Colonnesi, C., Stams, G. J. J. M., Koster, I., & Noom, M. J. (2010). The relation between pointing and language development: A meta-analysis. *Developmental Review, 30*, 352–366. doi:10.1016/j.dr.2010.10.001

Corkum, V., & Moore, C. (1995). Development of joint visual attention in infants. In C. Moore & P. J. Dunham (Eds.), *Joint attention: Its origins and role in development* (pp. 61–83). Hillsdale, NJ: Erlbaum.

Cvencek, D., Greenwald, A. G., & Meltzoff, A. N. (2011). Measuring implicit attitudes of 4-year-olds: The Preschool Implicit Association Test. *Journal of Experimental Child Psychology, 109*, 187–200. doi:10.1016/j.jecp.2010.11.002

Dunphy-Lelii, S., & Wellman, H. M. (2004). Infants' understanding of occlusion of others' line-of-sight: Implications for an emerging theory of mind. *European Journal of Developmental Psychology, 1*, 49–66. doi:10.1080/17405620444000049

Farroni, T., Johnson, M. H., Brockbank, M., & Simion, F. (2000). Infants' use of gaze direction to cue attention: The importance of perceived motion. *Visual Cognition, 7*, 705–718. doi:10.1080/13506280050144399

Farroni, T., Massaccesi, S., Pividori, D., & Johnson, M. H. (2004). Gaze following in newborns. *Infancy, 5*, 39–60. doi:10.1207/s15327078in0501_2

Franco, F., & Butterworth, G. (1996). Pointing and social awareness: Declaring and requesting in the second year. *Journal of Child Language, 23*, 307–336. doi:10.1017/ S0305000900008813

Frischen, A., Bayliss, A. P., & Tipper, S. P. (2007). Gaze cueing of attention: Visual attention, social cognition, and individual differences. *Psychological Bulletin*, *133*, 694–724. doi:10.1037/0033-2909.133.4.694

Heider, F. (1958). *The psychology of interpersonal relations*. New York, NY: Wiley. doi:10.1037/10628-000

Hood, B. M., Willen, J. D., & Driver, J. (1998). Adults' eyes trigger shifts of visual attention in human infants. *Psychological Science*, *9*, 131–134. doi:10.1111/1467-9280.00024

Jackson, P. L., Meltzoff, A. N., & Decety, J. (2005). How do we perceive the pain of others? A window into the neural processes involved in empathy. *NeuroImage*, *24*, 771–779. doi:10.1016/j.neuroimage.2004.09.006

Johnson, M. H., Grossmann, T., & Farroni, T. (2008). The social cognitive neuro-science of infancy: Illuminating the early development of social brain functions. In R. V. Kail (Ed.), *Advances in child development and behavior* (Vol. 36, pp. 331–372). San Diego, CA: Elsevier. doi:10.1016/S0065-2407(08)00008-6

Kendon, A. (1990). *Conducting interaction: Patterns of behavior in focused encounters*. Cambridge, England: Cambridge University Press.

Kuhl, P. K. (2004). Early language acquisition: Cracking the speech code. *Nature Reviews Neuroscience*, *5*, 831–843. doi:10.1038/nrn1533

Lamm, C., Meltzoff, A. N., & Decety, J. (2010). How do we empathize with someone who is not like us? A functional magnetic resonance imaging study. *Journal of Cognitive Neuroscience*, *22*, 362–376. doi:10.1162/jocn.2009.21186

Liszkowski, U., Carpenter, M., Henning, A., Striano, T., & Tomasello, M. (2004). Twelve-month-olds point to share attention and interest. *Developmental Science*, *7*, 297–307. doi:10.1111/j.1467-7687.2004.00349.x

Marshall, P. J., & Meltzoff, A. N. (2011). Neural mirroring systems: Exploring the EEG mu rhythm in human infancy. *Developmental Cognitive Neuroscience*, *1*, 110–123. doi:10.1016/j.dcn.2010.09.001

Meltzoff, A. N. (2007). "Like me": A foundation for social cognition. *Developmental Science*, *10*, 126–134. doi:10.1111/j.1467-7687.2007.00574.x

Meltzoff, A. N. (2013). Origins of social cognition: Bidirectional mapping between self and other and the "Like-Me" hypothesis. In M. Banaji & S. Gelman (Eds.), *Navigating the social world: What infants, children, and other species can teach us* (pp. 139–144). New York, NY: Oxford University Press.

Meltzoff, A. N., & Brooks, R. (2008). Self-experience as a mechanism for learning about others: A training study in social cognition. *Developmental Psychology*, *44*, 1257–1265. doi:10.1037/a0012888

Meltzoff, A. N., Brooks, R., Shon, A. P., & Rao, R. P. N. (2010). "Social" robots are psychological agents for infants: A test of gaze following. *Neural Networks*, *23*, 966–972. doi:10.1016/j.neunet.2010.09.005

Meltzoff, A. N., Kuhl, P. K., Movellan, J., & Sejnowski, T. J. (2009, July 17). Founda-tions for a new science of learning. *Science*, *325*, 284–288. doi:10.1126/science.1175626

Moll, H., & Meltzoff, A. N. (2011). How does it look? Level 2 perspective-taking at 36 months of age. *Child Development, 82*, 661–673. doi:10.1111/j.1467-8624.2010.01571.x

Moore, C. (2008). The development of gaze following. *Child Development Perspectives, 2*, 66–70. doi:10.1111/j.1750-8606.2008.00052.x

Mundy, P., Block, J., Delgado, C., Pomares, Y., Van Hecke, A. V., & Parlade, M. V. (2007). Individual differences and the development of joint attention in infancy. *Child Development, 78*, 938–954. doi:10.1111/j.1467-8624.2007.01042.x

Mundy, P., Sullivan, L., & Mastergeorge, A. M. (2009). A parallel and distributed-processing model of joint attention, social cognition and autism. *Autism Research, 2*, 2–21. doi:10.1002/aur.61

Repacholi, B. M., & Meltzoff, A. N. (2007). Emotional eavesdropping: Infants selectively respond to indirect emotional signals. *Child Development, 78*, 503–521. doi:10.1111/j.1467-8624.2007.01012.x

Saby, J. N., Marshall, P. J., & Meltzoff, A. N. (2012). Neural correlates of being imitated: An EEG study in preverbal infants. *Social Neuroscience, 7*, 650–661. doi:10.1080/17470919.2012.691429

Tajfel, H. (1981). *Human groups and social categories: Studies in social psychology.* Cambridge, England: Cambridge University Press.

Tomasello, M., Carpenter, M., & Liszkowski, U. (2007). A new look at infant pointing. *Child Development, 78*, 705–722. doi:10.1111/j.1467-8624.2007.01025.x

Toth, K., Munson, J., Meltzoff, A. N., & Dawson, G. (2006). Early predictors of communication development in young children with autism spectrum disorder: Joint attention, imitation, and toy play. *Journal of Autism and Developmental Disorders, 36*, 993–1005. doi:10.1007/s10803-006-0137-7

Triesch, J., Teuscher, C., Deák, G. O., & Carlson, E. (2006). Gaze following: Why (not) learn it? *Developmental Science, 9*, 125–147. doi:10.1111/j.1467-7687.2006.00470.x

10

BEYOND WORDS: PARENTAL EMBODIED MENTALIZING AND THE PARENT–INFANT DANCE

DANA SHAI AND PETER FONAGY

How does the sense of a subjective self develop in humans? Cutting through philosophy and passing through psychoanalytic psychology to reach contemporary developmental psychology and neuroscience, one finds everywhere the premise that the self can emerge fully only in the presence of and in relation to another self. That is, an infant's subjectivity and mind can emerge, at least in their normal forms, only through the infant's interactions with a responsive, reciprocal, and mentalizing caregiver. In this chapter, we explore the possibility that a human infant's full development as a subjective being depends, more specifically, on the quality of embodied experiences with a caregiver. We introduce the concept of parental embodied mentalizing and show how it can be operationalized to detect individual differences. We present preliminary findings showing that these individual differences among parents predict a variety of children's developmental achievements, including attachment security.

http://dx.doi.org/10.1037/14250-011
Mechanisms of Social Connection: From Brain to Group, M. Mikulincer and P. R. Shaver (Editors)
Copyright © 2014 by the American Psychological Association. All rights reserved.

THE IMPORTANCE OF PARENTAL MENTALIZING TO CHILD DEVELOPMENT

What parental relational capacities affect an infant's development? Attachment theorists have traditionally focused on maternal sensitivity as a key factor in the formation and establishment of attachment security and related developmental outcomes (e.g., Ainsworth, Blehar, Waters, & Wall, 1978; see Cassidy & Shaver, 2008, for a review of the attachment literature). More recently, scholars have discovered that a crucial parental capacity that influences child development is *mentalizing*—the capacity to consider and treat a child as a psychological agent motivated by mental states (Fonagy, Gergely, Jurist, & Target, 2002; Slade, 2005). For example, higher parental capacity for mentalizing has been shown to be associated with greater likelihood of infant secure attachment (e.g., Arnott & Meins, 2007; see also Chapter 11, this volume), even in the presence of trauma and deprivation (Fonagy et al., 1995). Moreover, parental mentalizing has been shown to predict attachment security above and beyond maternal sensitivity, suggesting that parental mentalizing underlies the capacity of a parent to respond sensitively to his or her infant (Kelly, Slade, & Grienenberger, 2005; Koren-Karie, Oppenheim, Dolev, Sher, & Etzion-Carasso, 2002; Laranjo, Bernier, & Meins, 2008). Higher parental mentalizing also predicts a child's more optimal socioemotional development, including more adaptive social behavior and lower psychopathology symptomatology (Fonagy et al., 1995, 2002; Katz & Windecker-Nelson, 2004; Meins et al., 2003; Sharp, Fonagy, & Goodyer, 2006).

There are currently three approaches to assessing parental mentalizing: the Parental Reflective Functioning measure (Slade, 2002), the Maternal Mind-Mindedness measure (Meins, 1999), and the Insightfulness Assessment (Oppenheim, Koren-Karie, & Sagi, 2001; see also Chapter 11, this volume). The term *parental reflective functioning* refers to parents' capacity to make sense of their own and their child's mental states, and this capacity is assessed by analyzing the 45-item semistructured clinical Parental Development Interview (Slade, Aber, Bresgi, Berger, & Kaplan, 2004). The interview was designed to assess a parent's representations of his or her relationship with a child, and it specifically emphasizes representations of internal experiences of both the parent and the child at times of heightened affective arousal. *Mind-mindedness* refers to the parent's proclivity to treat the child as an individual with a mind, rather than merely as an entity with physical needs that must be met. Parents are video-recorded while interacting with their infants for 20 minutes during a free-play session, and the recordings are coded for parents' appropriate mind-minded comments about their infants (Meins et al., 2003). *Insightfulness* refers to parents' "capacity to consider the motives underlying their children's behaviors and emotional experiences in a complete, positive, and child-focused manner while taking into consideration their children's perspectives" (Koren-Karie et al., 2002, p. 534). Insightfulness assessment involves parents being interviewed about their perceptions of their own thoughts and feelings and those of their child during a video-recorded parent–child interaction (see Chapter 11, this volume).

Despite their differences, these three approaches conceptualize and measure parental representations of children's intentionality (i.e., parental mentalizing) in terms of verbal expressions, and they portray parental mentalizing as a reflective, semantic, and declarative capacity. However, because these measures either necessitate reflection and measure abstract mental representations (in the Parental Reflective Functioning or the Insightfulness Assessment) or examine a parent's mentalizing capacity via language (in the Maternal Mind-Mindedness), they remain limited in their ability to illuminate how this verbal content can shape a preverbal infant's mind. That is, these measures fail to explain how parental mentalizing actually comes to influence an infant's mind and psychosocial development.

Recognizing this limitation, the first author created a measure of parental embodied mentalizing (Shai, 2011). In its creation, a theoretical and operational approach was adopted to assessing the meeting of parental and infant minds through an explicit focus on the whole-body movements that unfold during dyadic interactions rather than on verbal content. Our discussion of parental embodied mentalizing in this chapter is divided into two parts. The first part outlines support for the premise that parental mentalizing is partly an embodied phenomenon. The second part of the chapter discusses preliminary findings linking parental embodied mentalizing capacities to individual differences in children's developmental trajectories, including the emergence of attachment security.

PARENTAL MENTALIZING IS AN EMBODIED PHENOMENON

There are abundant data showing that preverbal infants have rather sophisticated capacities for social communication and have at their disposal a rich and subtle nonverbal language that they use to express internal states (e.g., pleasure, excitement, curiosity, frustration) and to engage their parents' interest and support. Infants use their faces, voices, hands, and entire bodies to display their varying internal states, their seeking of interpersonal contact, and their monitoring of changes in their environment (Trevarthen, 2004; Tronick, 2007). Parents have been shown to be highly sensitive to these nonverbal communicative signals (e.g., Beebe et al., 2010; Tronick, 1989) and to use nonverbal communication to engage with and relate to their infants. These nonverbal modalities include head movements, paralinguistic speech, touch, posture, and facial expressions, all of which can convey the degree to which they are emotionally available to their infant's varying internal states (Stern, 1985; Trevarthen, 2004).

Indeed, young infants are highly sensitive to parents' emotional and intentional signals expressed in the form and intensity of communicative gestures in different modalities (e.g., Emde, 1988; Malloch, 1999). And infants are capable of modifying their affective and attentional bodily displays in a reciprocally coordinated manner (e.g., Beebe, 2000; Tronick, Als, & Brazelton, 1977). They appear to have remarkable capacities for detecting regularities in events, temporal relations between environmental events, and contingencies between their own behavior and environmental consequences and for anticipating when certain events will occur (e.g., Beebe et al., 2010; Watson, Futo, Fonagy, & Gergely, 2011).

Pipp (1990), among others, stated early on that the bodily self and the bodily other are the sources of action that come together in coordinated sequences of infant–parent interaction. A considerable body of evidence indicates that nonverbal parent–infant interactions are characterized by bidirectional mutual influence, with parent and infant responding to each other's nonverbal behavior (Beebe, 2000; Tronick, 2007). And the quality of this multimodal dialogue—nonverbal, reciprocal, rhythmic, and temporal exchanges between parent and infant—is associated with crucial developmental achievements, including forming attachment relationships, developing a sense of agency, and improving in self-regulation (e.g., Beebe et al., 2000).

During nonverbal dialogues, in which both parent and infant reveal what is in their mind and respond to the other's mind mainly without awareness, parents' ability to make sense of the infant's nonverbally expressed internal world (i.e., the parents' capacity to mentalize) is of critical importance. The nature of each partner's contingent coordination with the other affects the infant's ability to attend, process information, and modulate behavior and emotions. These processes are essential to the creation of infants' and parents' social expectancies and collaborative interactions and to infants' cognitive development (Stern, 1985).

Considering the sophistication and implications of this nonverbal reciprocal encounter between parents and infants, and keeping in mind the importance of parental mentalizing for the child's socioemotional development, it is surprising that parental mentalizing is currently conceptualized and measured solely through linguistic means. In line with Stolorow and Atwood's (1992) assertion that "the caregiver's affect attunement is communicated primarily through sensorimotor contact with the infant's body" (p. 46), Shai and Belsky (2011a, 2011b) have suggested investigating the observable aspects of parent–infant interactions to further elucidate the mechanisms through which parental mentalizing is transmitted to the infant and thus can affect the infant's development. They proposed considering parental mentalizing as an embodied phenomenon and investigating the embodied "dance" the parent and infant implicitly choreograph together via their dynamic, interactive kinesthetics.

This dance is probably based on an innate capacity of the human infant to experience some of a caregiver's experiences, communicated largely unconsciously and nonverbally. Initially, experience is primarily somatic (bodily). It begins with somatic experiences in the womb, where the infant's movements and emotions are closely coordinated with the mother's movements and emotions. In other words, infants begin their psychological development with a form of embodied intersubjectivity even before they have emerged into what is usually thought of as the social world. This connection of bodily experience with what might be called "lived experience" (i.e., the experience of movements and sounds external to us) provides an embodied foundation for interpersonal relatedness. What an infant sees or hears is given meaning through its relationship to bodily experience within interpersonal interactions with a caregiver.

PARENTAL EMBODIED MENTALIZING

In our view, the richness of early nonverbal parent–infant interactions calls for revisiting parental mentalizing and expanding its domain beyond linguistic communication guided by explicit reflection. The broader domain includes implicit, body-based interactive processes between parent and infant. Indeed, recent studies make the restriction of mentalizing to the declarative (explicit) domain inconsistent with neurological evidence. Recent studies reveal a differentiation between implicit (automatic, unconscious, and nonverbal) mentalizing, on the one hand, and controlled (explicit, verbal, and reflective) mentalizing, on the other (e.g., Keysers & Gazzola, 2006, 2007; see also Chapter 4, this volume).According to these studies, implicit mentalizing relies chiefly on the external, observable features of nonverbal bodily actions that do not necessitate reflection. Gallese (2006) argued as follows:

> Social cognition is not only "social metacognition," that is, explicitly thinking about the contents of someone else's mind by means of abstract representations. There is also an *experiential* dimension of interpersonal relationships, which enables a direct grasping of the sense of the actions performed by others, and of the emotions, and sensations they experience. This dimension of social cognition is *embodied* in that it mediates between the multimodal experiential knowledge we hold of our lived body and the experience we make of others. (p. 16, emphasis added)

In fact, consideration of the original definition of mentalizing reveals no requirement that it be restricted to such metacognitive manifestations (e.g., Fonagy et al., 2002; Meins, 1999; Slade, 2002). *Reflective functioning*, for instance, is defined as the "overt manifestation, in narrative, of an individual's mentalizing capacity" (Slade, 2005, p. 269). This definition implies that mentalizing capacity could manifest itself in myriad ways, including implicit and nonreflective ones. Indeed, Fonagy and Target (1997) stated that "the caregiver's recognition of the child's intentional stance . . . is communicated nonverbally, beginning at birth" (p. 682).

Shai and Belsky (2011a, 2011b) have suggested that parental mentalizing capacities are reflected in and can be assessed by considering a parent's use of the communicative means that infants employ—the nonverbal, kinesthetic mode. Thus, *parental embodied mentalizing* refers to parents' capacity (a) to implicitly, not necessarily consciously, conceive, comprehend, and extrapolate their infant's mental states (e.g., wishes, interests, desires, or preferences) from the infant's whole-body kinesthetic expressions (e.g., changes in body movement and posture) and (b) to adjust their own kinesthetic patterns accordingly. Parental kinesthetic behavior is not considered in isolation but, reflecting a relational perspective, always in reference to that of the infant.

Tronick's (2003) detailed and specific model of the way meaning and coherence emerge out of interactive processes focused on mutual regulation provides a comprehensive and rigorous way to approach the process whereby parental mentalizing influences an infant and shapes his or her mind. Tronick's (1989, 2007) mutual regulation model of infant–adult interaction focuses on the subtle, nonverbal, microregulatory, and social-emotional processes that unfold in infant–mother interactions. Tronick conceptualized the infant as taking part in an open thermodynamic system that must constantly take in energy and work toward coherence in order to stave off dissipation. According to this model, infants have "self-organizing neurobehavioral capacities" and "biopsychological processes" that allow them to organize behavioral states and make sense of themselves and their place in the world (Tronick, 2007).

At the same time, Tronick (2007) pointed out that infants' self-organizing capacities must be supplemented by a "larger dyadic regulatory system" (p. 17) in which the infant participates with the caregiver. In this way, Tronick suggested, regulation is accomplished through the operation of a communication system in which the infant communicates his or her regulatory status to the caregiver, who responds appropriately to the meaning of the communication. This communication is expressed through the totality of the infant's and caregiver's biopsychological processes—including the "shape" (intonation contours) of words, other sounds that each uses, momentary changes in facial expression, the quality of their touch, body movements, and even changes in their bodily odors.

Mentalizing could be assumed to emerge out of successful mutual regulation between the partners, which in turn is probably achieved when an infant and caregiver together generate, communicate, and integrate meaningful elements of their respective experiences. This creates an experience of implicit relational knowing, meaning that each can anticipate and "know" the moves of the other. This "knowing" is initially of a pattern of physiological responses rather than of intentional states, although quite clearly it can be the platform on which understanding intentions builds in a subsequent developmental stage. The parent–infant collaboration results in an organized dyadic state that is believed to be more than the sum of its parts. A 6-month-old infant is likely to be capable of apprehending another's state of consciousness, allowing a mutual mapping of each other's states of mind, as Tronick (2007) suggested. Each individual's sense of self is augmented by the bodily derived meanings, representations of the other, and representations of the relationship as a whole. This leads to what Tronick (2003) called a state of *co-creativity*, a state in which infant and caregiver shape their relationship through a process of mutual physical regulation. Focusing on the parental contribution to the creation of these moments of meeting of minds, we suggest that parental embodied mentalizing facilitates the formation and maintenance of such significant relational moments. Because an infant's mind is very much based on bodily processes, actions, and kinesthetic feedback, a parent's embodied mentalizing is the chief means of achieving a meeting of minds with the infant. The process of assessing parental embodied mentalizing involves focusing precisely on such moments and examining the degree to which a parent's ability to appreciate his or her infant's kinesthetically manifested mental state is translated into the parent's modifying her or his own kinesthetics in an attempt to fulfill the infant's intentions, even beyond the infant's own abilities.

Tronick also suggested that miscommunication and "messiness" lie at the heart of the development of self and self-regulation. Miscommunication creates negative affect, but when interactive errors are repaired, the negative affect is replaced by positive affect in both infant and parent. These intense experiences generate "coherence" of mother and infant, deepening their dyadic state of consciousness. We believe, in line with Tronick's ideas, that a parent's capacity for embodied mentalizing does not require the parent's initial behavior to magically suit the infant's mental state. Indeed, high parental embodied mentalizing capacities involve parents' ability to repair interactive errors. Recall that mentalizing does not imply being able to magically read the minds of others but rather to appreciate the opaque nature of minds, with the understanding that the mental states of another cannot be known with certainty (Fonagy et al., 2002). From this standpoint, misunderstandings and miscoordinations should be frequent. And indeed, during the first year, fewer than 30% of parent–infant face-to-face interactions are coordinated (Tronick, 1989). Intriguingly, interactive repairs in the first months of life, far more than interactive miscoordination, play a key role in establishing secure attachment. Therefore, a parent's ability to repair dyadic miscoordination is central to the concept of parental embodied mentalizing and to its assessment.

Relational disruptions and repair of ongoing regulations, where expectations are violated and ensuing efforts to resolve these breaches are made, are hypothesized to underpin the promotion of self-organization (Blatt & Luyten, 2009). Early on, Winnicott (1949), for instance, emphasized the importance of a mother's ordinary, everyday failures for the development of the infant's mind. It is her deficiencies that allow for the infant's mental activity. In fact, one of the mother's functions is to provide graduated failures of adaptation. In this way, "the mental activity of the infant turns a good-enough environment into a perfect environment, that is to say, turns a relative failure of adaptation into adaptive success" (Winnicott, 1949, p. 245). The parental mismatching of the infant's abilities, needs, or desires is inherent in the infant's environment and provides the infant with an expanded environment within which he or she can develop.

According to Trevarthen (2008), "human feelings about intentions, and about contents and relationships that arise between us, are signalled as changing tensions and contours of muscular energy in vocalisations and gestures" (p. 12). Furthermore, the nonverbal information exchanged through various qualities of movement is informative about the mover's feelings and intentions (Trevarthen, 2008). Central to the measurement of parental embodied mentalizing, then, is the explicit consideration of and the exclusive focus on how interactive bodily actions are performed and coordinated rather than on which actions are performed. What makes this argument most compelling is the synesthesia that appears to run through all aspects of the perceptual experience of the infant. In careful psychophysical studies of newborns, Lewkowicz and Turkewitz (1980) demonstrated that neonates readily transfer learning from the auditory to the visual modality. So, habituation to either a bright or a dimmed light reduces neonates' responsivity to correspondingly intense or soft sounds. Mondloch and Maurer (2004) showed that most young toddlers systematically perceive that a higher pitched sound goes with a brighter color or that the letter A goes with the color red, a conjunction also manifested by the 5% of adults who are synesthetic. As we describe below, researchers who study parent–infant communication implicitly note this phenomenological correspondence across modalities for infants. It appears that embodied intentionality may be rooted in the ability we possess at birth to orient toward the shared qualities of phenomena across differences in modality and setting. We argue that this capacity of human infants enables them to discern the attitude or intention behind a specific action. Thus, the ability to sense sameness in things that are ontologically different (Rochat, 2010) contributes directly to the development of future social competencies.

Focusing on an act's style or manner calls attention to the shading of behavior rather than to its color. This is evident in Stern's (1985) key notion of *vitality affects*—qualities of processes in several different modalities that reflect forms of affect, rather than content. These qualities can be described in dynamic, kinetic terms, such as *exploding* or *fleeting*. According to Stern (2002), vitality affects are present in all subjective experiences, including those related to any goal-directed mental activity such as thinking, feeling, interacting, or dialoguing. Vitality affects are constantly present in experiences, whether or not one is conscious of them, and infants are especially sensitive to them. According to Stern (1985), "the social world experienced by the infant is primarily one of vitality affects before it is a world of formal acts" (p. 57). Stern (1985) proposed that vitality affects—the temporal progression, the dynamics, and movement of any mental process (be they memories, thoughts, or feelings)—imbue experiences with meaning.

The kinesthetic communication of both infants and adults follows the principle of equipotentiality; that is, the same type of touch or movement is capable of expressing very different meanings or intentions, especially in combination with other kinesthetic qualities (Cicchetti & Rogosch, 1996). Conversely, different patterns of movement and touch by either the parent or the infant can convey the same emotional communicative outcome, thus following the principle of equifinality (Hertenstein, 2002).

Weinberg and Tronick (1994) stipulated that this expressive flexibility serves important functions. An infant capable of expressing the same message in multiple ways may maximize the chance that the caregiver will eventually interpret the message correctly and respond to it in an appropriate manner. As Weinberg and Tronick (1994) noted, "the infant makes an initial communicative attempt using a particular affective configuration or sequence of configurations and then, based on the caregiver's response, makes another and somewhat different type of communicative effort" (p. 1513). Hence, it is the assembly of kinesthetic qualities in the moment-to-moment interaction that reveals their mentalistic meaningfulness (Stern, 1985; Tronick, 2005).

Clearly, then, any simplistic taxonomy of the mental meanings of particular body movements would be misleading. Nonetheless, various movement analysis paradigms offer valuable means of characterizing human movement, although of individuals rather than dyads (e.g., Kestenberg, 1965; Laban & Lawrence, 1947). Drawing on but not being restricted to these paradigms, we can identify several kinesthetic patterns as of prime importance when considering parent–infant interactions (Shai, 2010, 2011; Shai & Belsky, 2011b), and these kinesthetic patterns often reflect a mental state that can be reliably interpreted by an observer. Indeed, evaluating parent–infant interaction through such a kinesthetic prism affords the careful account of the interactive mentalistic exchanges taking place between parent and infant on the embodied level.

THE PARENTAL EMBODIED MENTALIZING CODING SYSTEM

The parental embodied mentalizing coding system is an observational coding system in which video-recorded parent–infant interactions are used as a basis for assessing a parent's embodied mentalizing capacities. When this system is used, the focus is on the dyad, with the aim of capturing the quality of parental mentalizing as it unfolds on the somatic and kinesthetic level during the interactions with one's infant. The parental embodied mentalizing coding system focuses on the degree to which the parent is kinesthetically responsive to the infant's kinesthetically manifested mental states during an interaction. When this system is used, it should be assumed that the patterns visible in the parent–infant dance reflect the meeting of their mental states.

When focusing on whole-body kinesthetic expressions, we do not consider gaze patterns, facial expressions, or any verbal behavior. To code a parent's embodied mentalizing capacity, we play back the video-recorded interactions at normal speed, although frequent pausing is permitted for viewing the interaction in frame-by-frame mode. The first stage of coding involves identifying episodes of parental embodied mentalizing, termed *embodied circles of communication*, including their onset and termination times. The second stage involves describing the kinesthetic sequence of each embodied circle of communication in terms of movement qualities, such as tempo, direction of movement, where the interaction occurs in space, its pacing and pathway in space, and how much muscle tension is used to execute it. The third and final stage involves rating the overall quality of parental embodied mentalizing capacity in each embodied circle of communication and then creating a summary, global parental embodied mentalizing score. We now describe the movement qualities used to depict each embodied circle of communication, continue to outline how a parental embodied mentalizing rating is ascribed, and conclude with an illustrative example of an embodied circle of communication event.

Movement Qualities

Describing each step of an embodied circle of communication in kinesthetic terms affords an account of the subtle kinesthetic components that constitute the embodied interaction between the parent and the infant. Any given movement is likely to be characterized by a number of co-occurring movement qualities, and the following qualities are used to describe kinesthetic actions in the parental embodied mentalizing coding system (for further details, see Shai, 2011).

Tempo

Tempo refers to how fast or slow the movement is or the frequency of the pulse of the movement within a time unit (e.g., velocity), with a range from low to high tempo.

Space

Space refers to where in space the movement is taking place, with the individual's body serving as a point of reference. For the purposes of parental embodied mentalizing coding, a distinction is made between personal and interpersonal space. *Personal space,* referred to as kinesphere or orbit, is the personal three-dimensional sphere surrounding the body, the periphery of which is reachable by extending one's limbs while staying in a still position (Tortora, 2006). *Interpersonal space* refers to the interactive, changing spatial distances between two individuals in a given environment (Scheflen & Ashcraft, 1976), which involves how overlapping or separate the kinespheres of two individuals are. Also considered are the relative distance of the movement from the mover's body (near, intermediate, or far) and the movement's orientation in relation to the ground (horizontal, vertical, or sagittal).

Pathways

This term refers to goal-directed movements that cut through space and make clear and intentional connections between the individual and his or her surroundings (Tortora, 2006). It concerns the imaginary line that a movement creates in space. This can be a straight, direct, linear path, as in a gesture describing a triangle; it can also be a curvy, indirect, circular, or rounded path, as in a gesture describing a balloon moving in the air.

Pacing

This term refers specifically to the velocity of changes or alterations in movement. Pacing ranges from abrupt and rushed to gradual and sustained. In abrupt pacing there is no clear sequence of fluent connections between movements (Davis, 1975), which is likely to provoke a staccato-like sense of fragmentation and unpredictability. Gradual pacing, on the other hand, is characterized by a clear sequence of fluent connections between movements. The change in movement appears to be planned, controlled, composed, and continuous.

Directionality

Directionality concerns the growing or shrinking movement of bodily dimensions in relation to the body center and is associated with different degrees of pleasure (Kestenberg-Amighi, Loman, Lewis, & Sossin, 1999). A *growing movement*—widening (horizontal), lengthening (vertical), bulging (sagittal)—creates open bodily shapes as a result of moving away from the body's center, and it exposes the body to the environment. A *shrinking movement*—narrowing (horizontal), shortening (vertical), hollowing (sagittal)—creates closed bodily shapes as a result of moving toward the body's center, and it reduces exposure of the body to contact or interaction with the external world. When observing the kinesthetic quality of directionality, the coder distinguishes whether the movement is performed with the torso alone, extremities (or head) alone, or some combination of the two. The varying degrees of participation of the body in the directional movement reflect the degree or intensity of the desire to move away or toward a stimulus.

Tension Flow

This term refers to the muscular tone involved in the movement and more specifically to sequences of fluency and restraint in the state of the muscles in various parts of the body. Tension flow concerns alterations between free and bound movements (Kestenberg, 1965). A contraction of an agonistic muscle initiates movement. When the agonistic muscle moves the body with little opposition or resistance of its antagonistic muscle, the movement flows freely and is fairly unrestrained. The greater the contraction and resistance of the antagonistic muscle, the more the movement is restrained and controlled, thus exhibiting the quality of bound tension flow (Kestenberg, 1965). Bound tension-flow movements appear stiff or tensed, with rigid holding of body parts, torso, or the full body attitude.

Rating Parental Embodied Mentalizing

Once an embodied circle of communication has been temporally identified and depicted in kinesthetic terms, the quality of parental mentalizing, as this is manifested in the interactive movement, can be assessed. The parental embodied mentalizing rating reflects the degree to which the parent was able to demonstrate, in his or her movement, an appreciation of the infant's mind and to respond to it via means of modifying his or her own movement to better suit the infant's mental state. Assessing the parent's embodied mentalizing capacity in a given embodied circle of communication involves many considerations. We outline here only some of the chief considerations: (a) How clear is the infant's kinesthetically manifested mental state? That is, when the infant's movement qualities are examined, how easy or difficult is it to understand the infant's need, desire, or interest? (b) To what extent can observers confidently assume that the parent detected the infant's movement? (c) How fast or slowly is the parent able to adjust his or her own movement to better suit the infant's kinesthetically manifest mental state? (d) Does the infant need to resort to self-affective regulation (e.g., thumb sucking) during the interaction with the parent, and how does the parent respond to these signals of distress and overarousal? (e) Was the parent able to follow the infant's kinesthetically manifested mental state and lead it to completion without interruption?

The parental embodied mentalizing rating for each circle of communication requires coders to pay careful attention to each circle, and the global rating is based on the set of circle ratings. The global rating is not based on some formal, algebraic compositing of component ratings given to each individual circle of communication event; rather, it reflects the degree to which the parent typically manifests a kinesthetic appreciation of the infant as a mental agent and implicitly uses this appreciation to continuously modify his or her own kinesthetic patterns and qualities to better suit those of the infant.

An Example of Coding Parental Embodied Mentalizing

Let us use a typical interaction between a parent and an infant to illustrate how parental embodied mentalizing is assessed. A mother offers her baby a toy by extending her arm forward, away from her body center (directionality) in a fast movement (pacing), in a linear direction toward (pathway) and close to the baby's face (space). In response, the infant pulls his torso back (directionality) in a sudden movement (pacing) while his fists tense up (tension flow). To rate the mother's embodied mentalizing capacities in this embodied circle of communication, observers have to examine how she responds to this behavioral sequence enacted by her baby. If the mother responds by withdrawing her arm that is holding the toy (directionality) and perhaps also by moving her torso back (directionality) to create more space between her and the baby (space), she would be rated high on the parental embodied mentalizing measure. Another interactive possibility is that the mother persists in holding the toy close to the infant's face (space). The infant moves further back and twists his body away from the mother (directionality) and tenses up not only his fists but also his arms (tension flow). The mother, in response, starts shaking the toy at high speed (tempo) and moves it even closer into the infant's face (space). This persistent behavior on the part of the mother continues even when the infant inserts a thumb into his mouth (affect regulation) and loses his upright body posture (tension flow). A mother interacting this way would be rated very low on the parental embodied mentalizing measure.

Preliminary Evidence Regarding Parental Embodied Mentalizing

Although the concept of parental embodied mentalizing is in its infancy, there are a number of promising findings pertaining to the importance of the parent's embodied mentalizing capacity for the quality of parent–infant interaction, as well as its effects on a child's development. First, in two independent studies, one with an American sample and the other with a high-risk South African sample, higher parental embodied mentalizing capacities were found to correlate with higher maternal sensitivity ratings. This was found whether the latter was measured with the Home Observation for Measurement of the Environment (Caldwell & Bradley, 1984; $r = .39$), Play Sensitivity (National Institute of Child Health and Human Development Early Child Care Research Network, 1997; $r = .33$), or Emotional Availability (Biringen, Robinson, & Emde, 2000; $r = .49$). Moreover, higher ratings of parental embodied mentalizing were significantly correlated with higher verbal parental mentalizing, as measured with the Parental Development Interview. The parental embodied mentalizing rating was not related to infant birth order (which should be an indication of more or less experience on the part of mothers) or temperament.

We recently found that parents' embodied mentalizing, measured 6 months after the child's birth during a free-play interaction at home, predicted infant attachment security at 15 months (Shai & Belsky, 2013). Mothers who scored higher on parental embodied mentalizing were significantly more likely to have secure infants than avoidant or resistant infants. This correlation remained when we controlled for traditional, robust measures of parental care, such as maternal sensitivity. Moreover, parental embodied mentalizing capacities measured at 6 months significantly predicted individual differences in children's' social skills, social competence, and internalizing and externalizing problems at 54 months: Children of mothers with higher parental embodied mentalizing ratings were significantly more likely to have improved social skills, and they were less likely to have internalizing or externalizing problems than were children of mothers with lower ratings on the parental embodied mentalizing measure.

CONCLUDING REMARKS

The concept of parental embodied mentalizing represents an attempt to conceptualize nonverbal parental capacities that are meaningful and influential in parent–infant interactions and that involve the entire body (rather than just the head or face). This kind of mentalizing is an active part of the rich communication of mental states between parents and infants. The concept and measurement of parental embodied mentalizing capacities are in their infancy, and the findings sketched in this chapter are preliminary and in need of replication and elaboration. Future research would benefit from (a) investigating the unique movement patterns that fathers, in comparison with mothers, exhibit when interacting with their infants and how these contribute to a child's development; (b) examining cultural similarities and differences in nonverbal interactions between parents and their infants; and (c) comparing behavioral manifestations of embodied mentalizing with physiological and brain activity. The concept of embodied mentalizing is, of course, closely tied to other bodily processes, and these processes, mental and physical, are the foundation of the developing minds of young children. Measuring and understanding these processes will provide a better and fuller understanding of the social foundations of the human mind.

REFERENCES

Ainsworth, M. D. S., Blehar, M., Waters, E., & Wall, S. (1978). *Patterns of attachment: A psychological study of the Strange Situation.* Hillside, NJ: Erlbaum.

Arnott, B., & Meins, E. (2007). Links between antenatal attachment representations, postnatal mind-mindedness, and infant attachment security: A preliminary study of mothers and fathers. *Bulletin of the Menninger Clinic, 71,* 132–149. doi:10.1521/bumc.2007.71.2.132

Beebe, B. (2000). Coconstructing mother–infant distress: The microsynchrony of maternal impingement and infant avoidance in the face-to-face encounter. *Psychoanalytic Inquiry, 20,* 421–440. doi:10.1080/07351692009348898

Beebe, B., Jaffe, J., Lachmann, F., Feldstein, S., Crown, C., & Jasnow, M. (2000). Systems models in development and psychoanalysis: The case of vocal rhythm coordination and attachment. *Infant Mental Health Journal, 21,* 99–122. doi:10.1002/(SICI)1097-0355(200001/04)21:1/2<99::AID-IMHJ11>3.0.CO;2-#

Beebe, B., Jaffe, J., Markese, S., Buck, K., Chen, H., Cohen, P., . . . Feldstein, S. (2010). The origins of 12-month attachment: A microanalysis of 4-month mother–infant interaction. *Attachment & Human Development, 12,* 6–141. doi:10.1080/14616730903338985

Biringen, Z., Robinson, J. L., & Emde, R. N. (2000). Appendix B: The Emotional Availability Scales (3rd ed.; an abridged Infancy/Early Childhood Version). *Attachment & Human Development, 2,* 256–270.

Blatt, S. J., & Luyten, P. (2009). A structural–developmental psychodynamic approach to psychopathology: Two polarities of experience across the life span. *Development and Psychopathology, 21,* 793–814. doi:10.1017/S0954579409000431

Caldwell, B. M., & Bradley, R. H. (1984). *Home observation for measurement of the environment.* Little Rock: University of Arkansas Press.

Cassidy, J., & Shaver, P. R. (2008). *Handbook of attachment: Theory, research, and clinical applications* (2nd. ed.). New York, NY: Guilford Press.

Cicchetti, D., & Rogosch, F. (1996). Equifinality and multifinality in developmental psychopathology. *Development and Psychopathology, 8,* 597–600. doi:10.1017/S0954579400007318

Davis, M. (1975). *Towards understanding the intrinsic in body movement.* New York, NY: Arno Press.

Emde, R. N. (1988). Development terminable and interminable: I. Innate and motivational factors from infancy. *International Journal of Psycho-Analysis, 69,* 23–42.

Fonagy, P., Gergely, G., Jurist, E. L., & Target, M. (2002). *Affect regulation, mentalization, and the development of the self.* London, England: Karnac.

Fonagy, P., Steele, M., Steele, H., Leigh, T., Kennedy, R., Mattoon, G., & Target, M. (1995). Attachment, the reflective self, and borderline states: The predictive specificity of the Adult Attachment Interview and pathological emotional development. In S. Goldberg, R. Muir, & J. Kerr (Eds.), *Attachment theory: Social, developmental and clinical perspectives* (pp. 233–278). Hillsdale, NJ: Analytic Press.

Fonagy, P., & Target, M. (1997). Attachment and reflective function: Their role in self-organization. *Development and Psychopathology, 9,* 679–700. doi:10.1017/S0954579497001399

Gallese, V. (2006). Intentional attunement: A neurophysiological perspective on social cognition and its disruption in autism. *Brain Research, 1079,* 15–24. doi:10.1016/j.brainres.2006.01.054

Hertenstein, M. J. (2002). Touch: Its communicative functions in infancy. *Human Development, 45,* 70–94. doi:10.1159/000048154

Katz, L. F., & Windecker-Nelson, B. (2004). Parental meta-emotion philosophy in families with conduct-problem children: Links with peer relations. *Journal of Abnormal Child Psychology, 32,* 385–398. doi:10.1023/B:JACP.0000030292.36168.30

Kelly, K., & Slade, A., & Grienenberger, J. F. (2005). Maternal reflective functioning, mother–infant affective communication, and infant attachment: Exploring the link between mental states and observed caregiving behavior in the intergenerational transmission of attachment. *Attachment & Human Development, 7,* 299–311. doi:10.1080/14616730500245963

Kestenberg, J. S. (1965). The role of movement patterns in development. I. Rhythms of movement. *Psychoanalytic Quarterly, 34,* 1–36.

Kestenberg-Amighi, J., Loman, S., Lewis, P., & Sossin, M. K. (1999). *The meaning of movement: Developmental and clinical perspectives of the Kestenberg Movement Profile.* New York, NY: Routledge.

Keysers, C., & Gazzola, V. (2006). Towards a unifying neural theory of social cognition. *Progress in Brain Research, 156,* 379–401. doi:10.1016/S0079-6123(06)56021-2

Keysers, C., & Gazzola, V. (2007). Integrating simulation and theory of mind: From self to social cognition. *Trends in Cognitive Sciences, 11,* 194–196. doi:10.1016/j.tics.2007.02.002

Koren-Karie, N., Oppenheim, D., Dolev, S., Sher, E., & Etzion-Carasso, A. (2002). Mothers' insightfulness regarding their infants' internal experience: Relations with maternal sensitivity and infant attachment. *Developmental Psychology, 38,* 534–542. doi:10.1037/0012-1649.38.4.534

Laban, R., & Lawrence, F. C. (1947). *Effort: A system analysis, time motion study.* London, England: MacDonald & Evans.

Laranjo, J., Bernier, A., & Meins, E. (2008). Associations between maternal mind-mindedness and infant attachment security: Investigating the mediating role of maternal sensitivity. *Infant Behavior & Development, 31,* 688–695. doi:10.1016/j.infbeh.2008.04.008

Lewkowicz, D. J., & Turkewitz, G. (1980). Cross-modal equivalence in early infancy: Auditory-visual intensity matching. *Developmental Psychology, 16,* 597–607. doi:10.1037/0012-1649.16.6.597

Malloch, S. (1999). Mothers and infants and communicative musicality. *Musicae Scientiae, Special Issue, 1999–2000,* 29–57.

Meins, E. (1999). Sensitivity, security, and internal working models: Bridging the transmission gap. *Attachment & Human Development, 1,* 325–342. doi:10.1080/14616739900134181

Meins, E., Fernyhough, C., Wainwright, R., Clark-Carter, D., Das Gupta, M., Fradley, E., & Tuckey, M. (2003). Pathways to understanding mind: Construct validity and predictive validity of maternal mind-mindedness. *Child Development, 74,* 1194–1211. doi:10.1111/1467-8624.00601

Mondloch, C. J., & Maurer, D. (2004). Do small white balls squeak? Pitch–object correspondences in young children. *Cognitive, Affective & Behavioral Neuroscience, 4,* 133–136. doi:10.3758/CABN.4.2.133

National Institute of Child Health and Human Development Early Child Care Research Network. (1997). The effects of infant child care on infant–mother attachment security: Results of the NICHD Study of Early Child Care. *Child Development, 68,* 860–879.

Oppenheim, D., Koren-Karie, N., & Sagi, A. (2001). Mother's insightfulness of their preschoolers' internal experience: Relations with early attachment. *International Journal of Behavioral Development, 25,* 16–26. doi:10.1080/01650250042000096

Pipp, S. (1990). Sensorimotor and representational internal working models of self, other and relationship: Mechanisms of connection and separation. In D. C. M. Beeghly (Ed.), *Topics in transition in development: Self-development* (pp. 243–264). Chicago, IL: University of Chicago Press.

Rochat, P. (2010). Me and mine in early development. In T. Fuchs, H. Sattel, & P. Henningsen (Eds.), *The embodied self: Dimensions, coherence and disorders* (pp. 175–182). Stuttgart, Germany: Schattauer.

Scheflen, A. E., & Ashcraft, N. (1976). *Human territories: How we behave in space–time.* Englewood Cliffs, NJ: Prentice-Hall.

Shai, D. (2010). Introducing parental embodied mentalising: Exploring moments of meeting of mind of parents and infants from a relational whole-body kinaesthetic perspective. In S. Bender (Ed.), *Movement analysis of interaction* (pp. 107–124). Berlin, Germany: Logos Verlag.

Shai, D. (2011). *Beyond words: Introducing parental embodied mentalising and its links with maternal sensitivity and attachment security* (Unpublished doctoral dissertation). Birkbeck University of London, London, England.

Shai, D., & Belsky, J. (2011a). Parental embodied mentalising: Let's be explicit about what we mean by implicit. *Child Development Perspectives, 5,* 187–188. doi:10.1111/j.1750-8606.2011.00195.x

Shai, D., & Belsky, J. (2011b). When words just won't do: Introducing parental embodied mentalising. *Child Development Perspectives, 5,* 173–180. doi:10.1111/j.1750-8606.2011.00181.x

Shai, D., & Belsky, J. (2013). *Beyond words: Whole-body parent–infant interaction predicts child's socioemotional development.* Manuscript in preparation.

Sharp, C., Fonagy, P., & Goodyer, I. M. (2006). Imaging your child's mind: Psychosocial adjustment and mothers' ability to predict their children's attributional response styles. *British Journal of Developmental Psychology, 24,* 197–214. doi:10.1348/026151005X82569

Slade, A. (2002). Keeping the baby in mind: A critical factor in perinatal mental health. *Zero to Three, 22*(6), 10–16.

Slade, A. (2005). Parental reflective functioning: An introduction. *Attachment & Human Development, 7,* 269–281. doi:10.1080/14616730500245906

Slade, A., Aber, J. L., Bresgi, I., Berger, B., & Kaplan, M. (2004). *The Parent Development Interview—Revised.* Unpublished manuscript, City University of New York.

Stern, D. N. (1985). *The interpersonal world of the infant.* London, England: Karnac.

Stern, D. N. (2002). *The first relationship: Infant and mother.* Cambridge, MA: Harvard University Press.

Stolorow, R., & Atwood, G. (1992). *Contexts of being: The intersubjective foundations of psychological life.* Hillsdale, NJ: Analytic Press.

Tortora, S. (2006). *The dancing dialogue: Using the communicative power of movement with young children.* Baltimore, MD: Brookes.

Trevarthen, C. (2004). Intimate contact from birth: How we know one another by touch, voice, and expression in movement. In K. White (Ed.), *Touch: Attachment and the body* (pp. 1–16). London, England: Karnac.

Trevarthen, C. (2008). The musical art of infant conversation: Narrating in the time of sympathetic experience, without rational interpretation, before words. *Musicae Scientiae, Special Issue, 2008,* 15–46.

Tronick, E., Als, H., & Brazelton, T. (1977). Mutuality in mother–infant interaction. *Journal of Communication, 27,* 74–79. doi:10.1111/j.1460-2466.1977.tb01829.x

Tronick, E. Z. (1989). Emotions and emotional communication in infants. *American Psychologist, 44,* 112–119. doi:10.1037/0003-066X.44.2.112

Tronick, E. Z. (2003). "Of course all relationships are unique": How co-creative processes generate unique mother–infant and patient–therapist relationships and change other relationships. *Psychoanalytic Inquiry, 23,* 473–491. doi:10.1080/07351692309349044

Tronick, E. Z. (2005). Why is connection with others so critical? The formation of dyadic states of consciousness: Coherence governed selection and the co-creation of meaning out of messy meaning making. In J. Nadel & D. Muir (Eds.), *Emotional development* (pp. 293–315). Oxford, England: Oxford University Press.

Tronick, E. Z. (2007). *The neurobehavioral and social-emotional development of infants and children.* New York, NY: Norton.

Watson, J. S., Futo, J., Fonagy, P., & Gergely, G. (2011). Gender and relational differences in sensitivity to internal and external cues at 12 months. *Bulletin of the Menninger Clinic, 75,* 64–93. doi:10.1521/bumc.2011.75.1.64

Weinberg, M. K., & Tronick, E. Z. (1994). Beyond the face: An empirical study of infant affective configurations of facial, vocal, gestural, and regulatory behavior. *Child Development, 65,* 1503–1515. doi:10.2307/1131514

Winnicott, D. W. (1958). Mind and its relation to the psyche-soma. In *Collected papers: Through paediatrics to psycho-analysis* (pp. 243–254). Oxford, England: Basic Books.

11

PARENTAL INSIGHTFULNESS AND CHILD–PARENT EMOTION DIALOGUES: THEIR IMPORTANCE FOR CHILDREN'S DEVELOPMENT

DAVID OPPENHEIM AND NINA KOREN-KARIE

A long-held premise of child development researchers and clinicians is that the impact of experience on children's development is mediated through the affective meaning ascribed to the experience: The same event may have very different implications for the child's development depending on its emotional meaning for the child. Such meanings are not solitary child creations, however, but are co-constructed by children and their parents (as well as other significant persons in their lives). Both parents and children contribute to the co-construction process, with the parent—the more mature, resourceful, and experienced partner in the relationship—having a particularly important role in shaping the interactions with the child and, ultimately the affective meaning the child constructs.

This chapter focuses on two aspects of parenting that are particularly relevant for children's affective meaning-making process: parents' insightfulness—their capacity to "see things from the child's point of view"—and parents' sensitive guidance of dialogues about emotional experiences. Insightfulness

http://dx.doi.org/10.1037/14250-012
Mechanisms of Social Connection: From Brain to Group, M. Mikulincer and P. R. Shaver (Editors)

is assessed by interviewing parents about the child, and sensitive guidance is assessed through observations of parents talking with the child. Our studies propose that when these parental processes involve coherent, organized, and child-centered affective meaning making, they promotes children's flexible and adaptive coping, emotion regulation, and well-being.

In this chapter, we review our research on parental insightfulness and on parent–child dialogues. Both assessments are deeply rooted in attachment theory, particularly its expansion by Main into the level of representations and construction of meaning (Main, Kaplan, & Cassidy, 1985). We present the theoretical basis for each of these constructs, the methods used to assess them, and the findings that support these methods. In addition we discuss the commonalties underlying the capacity for both insightfulness and sensitive guidance of dialogues. We turn first to a review of parental insightfulness.

PARENTAL INSIGHTFULNESS: BACKGROUND

The concept of insightfulness is rooted in the work of clinicians and developmental researchers who have argued that a full understanding of parent–child relationships requires an appreciation of the parent's internal representation of the child, including the specific and unique emotional meaning the child holds for the parent. Perhaps the best known expression of this point of view was presented over three decades ago by Fraiberg, Adelson, and Shapiro (1975), who described how the mother's representations of her child can be so intensely colored by trauma and unmet needs from her own history that she cannot, in effect, "see" the child. In such situations, mothers experience difficulties in developing insight into the motives, thoughts, and goals underlying the child's behavior and in responding empathically to the child's signals and the emotional needs that underlie them.

On the basis of Fraiberg et al. (1975) as well as Bowlby's concept of internal working models (Bowlby, 1982), several researchers have developed assessments of parents' representations of their children in which interviews are used (see George & Solomon, 2008, for a review). This body of research has shown that mothers of secure children are flexible, balanced, and integrated in their interviews about their children. Their interviews reflect their commitment, trust, cooperation, knowledge of self and child as individuals, and joy in the parenting experience.

But how do parents apply such representations when they try to understand specific, concrete moments in the life of their child? To assess this process we developed the Insightfulness Assessment (Oppenheim & Koren-Karie, 2009), in which parents are shown several video segments of their child interacting with a parent and are asked about the child's thoughts and feelings during the segments. The goal in this procedure is to simulate moments from everyday life in which parents try to make sense of their children's behavior and understand the motives and emotions that may underlie the behavior. Unlike "real-life" moments, however, in which these meaning-making processes are implicit and operate mostly outside of awareness, the Insightfulness Assessment requires parents to make these processes explicit. Insightful parents show insight regarding the motives for child's behaviors, an emotionally complex view of the child, and openness to new and sometimes unexpected information regarding the child.

Insight refers to the parent's capacity to think about the motives that underlie the child's behavior. Considering such motives is based on accepting the child as a separate person with plans, needs, and wishes of his or her own. The parent understands the motives underlying the child's behavior and accompanies such understanding with acceptance of these motives. This stance is thought to provide the basis for appropriate parental responses, especially toward challenging or unrewarding child behavior. An emotionally complex view of the child involves a full and integrated portrayal of him or her as a whole person with both positive and negative features. Positive features, which typically outweigh negative features, are described openly and are supported by convincing examples from everyday life. Frustrating, unflattering, and upsetting aspects of the child are discussed within an accepting framework and in the context of attempts to find reasonable and appropriate explanations for the child's negative behavior. Finally, *openness* refers to parents' capacity not only to see the familiar and comfortable aspects of their children but also to see, without distortion, unexpected behaviors and to update the view of the child as they talk.

THE INSIGHTFULNESS ASSESSMENT PROCEDURE

In the Insightfulness Assessment procedure, parents and children are first videotaped in three interactions. Parents subsequently watch short segments from the videotaped interactions and are asked to reflect upon their child's thoughts and feelings during the segment and describe how they felt when they watched the video. Throughout the Insightfulness Assessment procedure, parents are asked to support their statements with examples from the observations of the videotaped segments and from everyday life. Interview transcripts are rated on 10 scales and, based on the profile of the scales, are classified into one of four groups. The first of the four groups, called positively insightful, indicates the capacity for insightfulness, whereas the remaining three (one-sided, disengaged, and mixed) indicate a lack of insightfulness (Koren-Karie, Oppenheim, Dolev, Sher, & Etzion-Carasso, 2002).

Positively insightful parents are able to see various experiences through their child's eyes and to try to understand the motives underlying their child's behavior. They are flexible when viewing their child on the video segments, and they may gain new insights as they talk. They convey acceptance of the child, and they talk openly about both positive and negative aspects of their child's personality and behavior as well as of their own caregiving. *One-sided* parents have a preset conception of their child that they impose on the video-taped segments, and this conception does not appear open to change. These parents often find it difficult to maintain the focus of their speech on the child and switch to discussing their own feelings or to other, irrelevant issues. *Disengaged* parents are characterized by their lack of emotional involvement during the interview. Their answers are short and limited. The idea of under-standing what is on their child's mind appears new to them, and they do not seem to find the prospect pleasurable or valuable. When asked what their child might be feeling in the video segment they viewed, they provide answers like "I don't know." *Mixed* parents do not show one style of narration as defined in the above categories. Rather, such parents may respond to one video segment in one style and to another segment with a different style, and the researcher cannot judge which of the styles is dominant.

EMPIRICAL SUPPORT FOR THE INSIGHTFULNESS ASSESSMENT PROCEDURE

Insightfulness Assessment and Attachment

The conceptual foundations of the Insightfulness Assessment procedure are strongly rooted in attachment theory, particularly in Ainsworth's description of sensitive mothers as those who are able to "see things from the child's point of view" (Ainsworth, Blehar, Waters, & Wall, 1978, p. 142) and her pioneering research showing the contribution of sensitive caregiving to children's secure attachment. Therefore, the goal in our initial studies with the Insightfulness Assessment procedure was to establish its links with children's attachment to their parents. First, we hypothesized that positively insightful parents will have children with secure attachment, because insightfulness facilitates correct interpretations and empathic responses to children's signals. Insightfulness also facilitates open examination of the appropriateness (or inappropriateness) of the parent's caregiving behavior based on the child's reactions. Such caregiving is likely to be experienced by the child as matched to his or her emotional needs and thus will contribute to a secure infant–mother attachment (Ainsworth et al., 1978; Weinfield, Sroufe, Egeland, & Carlson, 1999).

Second, we hypothesized that one-sided parents will have children with insecure-ambivalent attachments. The unidimensional view of the child characteristic of one-sided parents is likely to be associated with inconsistent care: When the child's behavior is congruent with the mother's expectations, she may respond appropriately, whereas when the child's behavior is not congruent with the mother's expectations, she may ignore or respond in a way that is not matched to the child's needs. In addition, mothers classified as one-sided are often preoccupied with their own emotional issues; consequently, their availability and capacity to focus on the child's inner world may be impaired. The parenting of mothers classified as one-sided may be experienced by the child as frustrating and confusing—the kind of caregiving found to lead to ambivalent attachment (Cassidy & Berlin, 1994).

Third, we hypothesized that disengaged parents will have children with insecure-avoidant attachment. The lack of emotional engagement characteristic of the disengaged parent may lead to minimizing or even ignoring the child's bids for closeness and protection, which is experienced by the child as rejection. Disengaged parenting may leave children with the feeling that although their external behavior may be acknowledged, their emotional and psychological needs are unrecognized (Slade, 1999). These experiences are likely to lead to the child's inhibition of his or her emotional expression, particularly of negative affect and vulnerability, which is the hallmark of children with avoidant attachment (Zeanah, Benoit, Hirshberg, Barton, & Regan, 1994). Finally, we hypothesized that parents classified as mixed will have children with insecure-disorganized attachment. The lack of a coherent strategy for understanding the child's motives and feelings may be reflected in competing or contradictory caregiving behaviors when interacting with the child. Such strategies have been described by Lyons-Ruth, Bronfman, and Atwood (1999) as being expressed in disruptive parental affective communication and leading to disorganized attachment.

Two studies of mothers and their typically developing infants supported the associations between insightfulness and infant–mother attachment (Koren-Karie et al., 2002; Oppenheim, Koren-Karie, & Sagi, 2001). In both studies, as expected, mothers classified as positively insightful had secure children, mothers classified as one-sided had insecure-ambivalent children, and mothers classified as mixed had children classified as insecure-disorganized. Unexpectedly, no associations were found between the disengaged classification and children's attachment, perhaps because the samples (like all those based on studies conducted in Israel; van IJzendoorn & Sagi, 1999) included very few children classified as avoidant. However, mothers classified as disengaged were rated as less sensitive than those classified as insightful, providing support for the validity of the disengaged classification at least with regard to its linkage to maternal behavior (Koren-Karie et al., 2002).

Two studies of mothers and their atypically developing children also supported the associations between insightfulness and attachment (Oppenheim, Feniger-Shaal, & Koren-Karie, 2010; Oppenheim, Koren-Karie, Dolev, & Yirmiya, 2009). Due to the limited size of the samples in both studies, the associations were examined only dichotomously, linking insightfulness versus noninsightfulness with security versus insecurity. In a sample of preschool-age boys with autistic spectrum disorder, maternal insightfulness was associated with child attachment: Mothers who were insightful had securely attached children, and mothers who were noninsightful had children with insecure attachments (Oppenheim et al., 2009). Additionally, no association was found between insightfulness and either the severity of the child's diagnosis on the autism spectrum or the child's intelligence. This suggests that insightfulness is more a reflection of the parent's meaning-making process and is less sensitive to characteristics of the child, such as the level of the child's impairment. We found similar associations in a sample of children with intellectual disability: Mothers who were insightful had children with secure attachments, and mothers who were noninsightful had children with insecure attachments (Oppenheim et al., 2010).

Association Between Insightfulness and Parental Caregiving Behavior

Because insightfulness is thought to be expressed in sensitive and emotionally regulating caregiving behavior, we investigated associations between insightfulness and maternal sensitivity. In our study of typically developing infants, mothers classified as insightful were more sensitive in their interactions with infants in both home and laboratory observations than were those mothers not classified as insightful, suggesting that insightfulness has its effects on child attachment through sensitive caregiving behavior (Koren-Karie et al., 2002). We replicated the insightfulness–sensitivity link in the sample of children with autistic spectrum disorder described earlier (Oppenheim et al., 2009). Similar results were reported by Hutman, Siller, and Sigman (2009), who found that mothers of children with autistic spectrum disorder classified as positively insightful were more synchronous in their interactions with their children than were mothers classified as noninsightful; Kuhn (2007), who also studied mothers of children with autistic spectrum disorder, failed to replicate the insightfulness–synchrony association. Finally, in a study of children with intellectual disability we found, as expected, that insightful mothers were rated as more sensitive than noninsightful mothers during their interactions with their children (Oppenheim et al., 2010).

A recent study of foster mothers (Koren-Karie, Oppenheim, Yuval-Adler, & Mor, 2012) revealed a link between insightfulness and mothers' sensitive guidance of emotional dialogues with their children. The mothers, each of whom fostered several children, were observed with both the most and the least challenging child in their care while co-constructing a conversation about emotional themes. Insightful mothers guided the conversation more sensitively than did noninsightful mothers, and this was true of their interactions with both the least challenging and the most challenging child. Thus, like the studies reviewed above, this study linked insightfulness to the quality of mother–child interactions, supporting the idea that insightfulness has its effects on the child through maternal behavior. In addition, our foster care study showed that insightfulness was not associated with the child's status as most or least challenging. This finding was similar to the lack of association between insightfulness and level of child impairment in our study of children with autistic spectrum disorder, described above. This suggests again that insightfulness appears to be more a reflection of the parent's meaning-making process and is less sensitive to individual differences among children—in this case, the level of challenge the child presented.

In sum, studies of insightfulness have shown that it is associated with caregiving behavior that is sensitive to the child's emotional signals and that children benefit from parental insightfulness in terms of their security and emotion and behavior regulation. It is noteworthy that the assessment of insightfulness is not based on the specific behaviors or characteristics the parents describe or on the accuracy of their judgments regarding the motives underlying their children's behavior. Rather, it is the flexible, open, and emotionally coherent way in which parents organize their thought process when asked to make meaning of their children's behavior that appears to be critical for insightfulness.

In the next body of research that we describe, we proposed that these parental capacities are significant not only when parents talk about their children but also when they talk with them, particularly when focusing on the children's emotional experiences. In particular, they support dialogues that provide children with a psychological "secure base." We describe our research on this issue next.

Parent–Child Emotion Dialogues: The Psychological Secure Base

The secure base, a core construct in attachment theory (Bowlby, 1988), consists of the dynamic balance between children's attachment and exploratory behaviors. When children feel secure they are likely to distance themselves from their parent and explore the environment, but when their sense of security is threatened, they increase their proximity to the caregiver. The hallmarks of a secure attachment are smooth transitions between exploratory and attachment behavioral systems, in which the child flexibly moves from one to the other in accordance with his or her needs (Main, 1996). For the secure-base pattern to operate optimally, parents are expected to match their behavior to the fluctuations in the child's exploratory and attachment behaviors and to the child's emotional signals.

The secure base is considered pertinent not only in infancy but throughout development (Ainsworth, 1989). The child's emotional needs continue to be as important as in the early years, when exploration of the physical world was the focus. But now exploration expands to new arenas beyond the child's immediate environment. It involves the psychological exploration of the past and the future, not only the present, of real worlds but also of worlds that are imagined—of events that are hoped and yearned for but also those that are dreaded and feared (Wolf, 2003). Such exploration is promoted in parent–child emotion dialogues in which the entire spectrum of the child's emotional signals is accurately perceived and sensitively responded to by the parent (Bretherton, 1990, 1993).

To study how mother–child dialogues provide a secure base, we observed mothers and children reminiscing about emotional events experienced by the child (following Fivush, 1991). In this task, referred to as the Autobiographical Emotional Event Dialogue, mothers and children are presented with five cards with a name and a pictorial representation of a feeling. The feelings are happy, mad, sad, scared, and secure. Dyads are asked to remember an event in which the child felt each of the feelings and to jointly construct a story about each of the events. Transcripts of the dialogues are rated on seven maternal and seven parallel child scales as well as two scales pertaining to the narrative produced by mother and child. On the basis of these scales, transcripts are classified into an emotionally matched category reflecting the psychological secure base or one of three nonemotionally matched categories (excessive, flat, or inconsistent) showing lack of a psychological secure base (Koren-Karie, Oppenheim, Haimovich, & Etzion-Carasso, 2003). *Emotionally matched* dyads tell, in a comfortable and accepting atmosphere, coherent stories with a clear and believable link between the emotion requested and the story provided. The stories can be short, but the reader understands how the event evoked the feeling in the child. When discussing a negative event, the mother guides the child toward a story ending that promotes feelings of strength, self-confidence, and being in control. The partners show patience and acceptance of each other's ideas and suggestions, although the content of their dialogues may involve difficult or conflictual moments in their relationship. *Nonemotionally matched–excessive* dyads are characterized by stories that are poorly organized and hard to follow. These studies may be flooded with negative emotional themes. There are frequent shifts to irrelevant details, repetitiveness, digressions, and excessive and overdramatized talk. Mothers in these dyads often fail to pace their contributions to the child's rhythm. In most cases there is inappropriate closure of the stories and no resolution for negative themes. *Nonemotionally matched–flat* dyads are characterized by limited dialogue and poor development of the stories. In addition, lack of involvement and lack of interest in the task are central features. Both mother and child may mention the names of emotions or events that happened, but there is almost no development of the idea or the story. Finally, *nonemotionally matched–inconsistent* dyads show a significant gap between the styles of talk of the partners. For example, one of the partners adheres to the instructions and is cooperative and coherent, whereas the other partner blocks the dialogue, directs the conversation to irrelevant details, confuses matters, or expresses hostility and anger.

Empirical Research on Mother–Child Emotion Dialogues

Studies on Attachment and Mother–Child Emotion Dialogues

Because we conceptualized mother–child dialogues as reflections of the secure base, our first research steps were to examine longitudinally the associations between attachment in infancy and such dialogues, hypothesizing that secure attachment would be associated with emotionally matched dialogues. We assessed children's attachment at the age of 1 year with the Strange Situation procedure (Ainsworth et al., 1978), and we assessed mother–child autobiographical emotional event dialogues at ages 4.5 and 7.5 years (Oppenheim, Koren-Karie, & Sagi-Schwartz, 2007). The results showed that, controlling for children's vocabulary, children who were securely attached as infants were likely to engage in emotionally matched dialogues, and those who were insecurely attached were likely to engage in nonemotionally matched dialogues. This was true at both child ages, 4.5 and 7.5 years. Somewhat surprisingly, the prediction to age 7.5 dialogues was even stronger than the prediction to age 4.5 dialogues, perhaps because the maturity of linguistic and conversational skills of 7-year-olds permitted a more accurate assessment of the dialogue as a secure base.

Would similar findings emerge if other types of emotion dialogues were observed, or is there something unique to dialogues involving reminiscing? One way to address this question is to compare reminiscing dialogues with other emotion dialogues not involving reminiscing. For this purpose we observed the dyads from the Oppenheim et al. (2007) study in two additional dialogues. The first was a separation–reunion narrative co-construction task (Oppenheim, Nir, Warren, & Emde, 1997), in which mothers and children were asked to jointly develop a play narrative, using dolls and props, about parents leaving their children for the weekend and then returning (for full details, see Oppenheim et al., 2007). The second was the joint storytelling task, in which mothers and children were asked to jointly develop a narrative based on a wordless picture book that showed a child returning home after school, discovering that the door is locked, and discovering that the mother who was supposed to be at home is not there (Gini, Oppenheim, & Sagi-Schwartz, 2007).

The same attachment–dialogue associations that we found when we used the autobiographical emotional event dialogue task were obtained with the separation–reunion narrative co-construction task and the joint storytelling task. Children who were securely attached as infants were more likely to be partners in dyads classified as emotionally matched in the separation–reunion narrative co-construction task (Oppenheim et al., 2007) and as mutual-balanced in the joint storytelling task (a classification similar to emotionally matched; see Gini et al., 2007). These findings suggest that the associations we found between early attachment and later mother–child reminiscing dialogues are not unique to such dialogues. Perhaps this commonality was found because all three assessments involved conversations about emotional themes and focused on the co-constructive dialogic process between parent and child rather than on the specific content of the dialogue.

Mother–Child Dialogues and Parental and Child Risk Status

Although it was important, as a first step, to establish the link between early attachment and later mother–child dialogues in order to support the idea that such dialogues reflect the psychological secure base, we contended that mother–child emotion dialogues are interesting and important not only as outcomes of early attachment. Open, coherent, and emotionally regulated dialogues are of importance because they form a psychological secure base and can contribute to children's emotional and behavioral regulation. Thus, we would expect, for example, that children experiencing behavioral and emotional problems might have difficulties engaging in emotionally matched dialogues with their mothers and that an intervention might increase their capacity to engage in such dialogues. This was examined in our study of young children enrolled in a therapeutic preschool (Oppenheim et al., 2004).

The sample consisted of children manifesting high levels of behavioral and emotional symptoms. Many of the children had been expelled from several preschools and had a history of abuse and/or exposure to violence. Many of the mothers were single and had experienced multiple stressors involving poverty, physical and sexual abuse, and drug abuse. The intervention involved a therapeutic preschool program based on attachment principles. The program was designed to enhance children's feelings of security and their capacity to express their positive and negative emotions while challenging their negative expectations about others (Oppenheim, Goldsmith, & Koren-Karie, 2004). In addition, mothers met with therapists to discuss parenting issues and strategies to support children's therapeutic progress.

There was a significant increase in the number of dyads showing emotionally matched dialogues following treatment (Oppenheim & Koren-Karie, 2009). The main improvements were in shifts from the excessive classification to the emotionally matched classification, indicating improved organization, emotional regulation, and coherence in the dialogues. There are limitations to this study: Because both children and mothers received an intervention, we do not know whether improvements in the mothers or improvements in the children led to the increase in the number of emotionally matched dialogues. And because this study did not employ a control group, we do not know if the improvements are a function of treatment or other factors. Nonetheless, the results are consistent with our expectations that when the parent–child relationship is disturbed, such as when the child experiences significant behavioral and emotional disturbances, the capacity to engage in emotionally matched dialogues is very limited. With treatment, this capacity improves.

In this study the focus was on children being at high risk, but what happens if the risk is associated with the parent? We examined this issue in a study of mothers in treatment for the sexual abuse they experienced as children. The mothers were recruited from agencies specializing in the treatment of adults with a history of sexual abuse. They were observed in the Autobiographical Emotional Event Dialogue task with one of their children. The mothers completed several questionnaires assessing the extent to which they had resolved the trauma they endured; their general psychiatric symptoms; and symptoms of dissociation, intrusion, and avoidance of the trauma that are characteristic of many adults who have experienced trauma.

The goal in the study was to examine whether the degree to which mothers resolved the trauma they experienced would moderate the effect of the trauma on mother–child emotional dialogues (Koren-Karie, Oppenheim, & Getzler-Yosef, 2008). Thus, the impact of the trauma was expected to be less evident among mothers who were more resolved and more evident among mothers who were less resolved with respect to the trauma. We found, as hypothesized, that, compared with those of mothers who were less resolved, mothers who were more resolved guided the dialogues more sensitively, had children who were more cooperative and exploratory, and produced with their children narratives that were more emotionally coherent. These results appeared specific to resolution of the trauma. They were not explained by mothers' symptomatology, dissociation, intrusion, or avoidance, which were all unrelated to the dialogues.

Finally, in the foster care study mentioned earlier (Koren-Karie et al., 2012), in which mothers who fostered several children were assessed with the most and least challenging child under their care, we observed the mothers during emotion dialogues with the children. We hypothesized that because emotion dialogues are strongly influenced by the parent's capacity to sensitively guide the dialogue in a way that is matched to the child's emotions, needs, and competencies, mothers' guidance of the dialogues with both children would be similar, even though the children were selected to present different and contrasting levels of challenge. The findings supported this hypothesis by showing an association between mothers' sensitive guidance of the most challenging child and the least challenging child and by showing no differences in the level of sensitive guidance as a function of the challenge the child presented. These findings highlight the importance of the parent matching his or her input to the specific characteristics of the child and the resulting possibility of establishing emotionally matched dialogues even with children who are challenging.

CONCLUSION

We highlighted two parental capacities—insightfulness regarding the child's inner world and sensitive guidance of emotion dialogues—and presented assessment methods designed to measure these capacities. We also reviewed a body of research that supports their validity and demonstrates their implications for children's socioemotional development. We would like to conclude by speculating with regard to common parenting processes that underlie both assessments, based on attachment theory's relational and organizational view of parenting (Bowlby, 1988; George & Solomon, 2008; Main et al., 1985).

In both assessments, the level of organization (often referred to as the "how") appears to be more important than the specific contents or themes that emerge (the "what"). In the Insightfulness Assessment the parent may describe various behaviors or characteristics, including positive and challenging behaviors of the child vis-à-vis the parent, but this tells us little about the parent's insightfulness. The parent may even describe symptomatic behavior, such as temper tantrums, separation difficulties, or—in the case of children with disabilities—various symptoms related to the child's disorder. But we do not make inferences about parental insightfulness from the description of the child's behavior, including the behavior toward the parent. It is only when we begin to look at the "how" of parental talk and the thought processes that underlie the talk that we can begin to assess insightfulness: Can the parent talk about thoughts, feelings, wishes, and fears that underlie the child's behavior, and are these convincingly linked to the behavior? Or is the parent limited to describing surface behavior or, alternatively, to invoking thoughts and feelings that are not tied to the behavior they are supposed to explain? Can the parent link general statements about the child to specific examples from the video segments? Or does the parent fail to provide the link? Can the parent bring examples from everyday life that match the characteristics the parent attributes to the child? Or, alternatively, does the parent claim that the behavior in the segment is not typical but fail to explain the discrepancy? Can the parent acknowledge unexpected child behavior in the video segment and accommodate his or her view of the child to match the actual, observed behavior? Or does the parent impose a preset view of the child, dismissing the behavior on the tape as "atypical"? These are but a few examples of the emphasis on what we mean by the "how"—the way parental talk is organized.

Similarly, in the context of mother–child dialogues, the themes that parents and children choose to bring up when discussing memories of different emotions, tell us little about the degree to which the dialogue functions as a secure base. Rather, the way the dialogue is organized is much more indicative. In judging whether the dialogues are emotionally matched we do not infer from the content of the story (e.g., a conflict between parent and child) what kind of relationship the parent and child have. Rather, we look at how they discuss the memory: Does the episode match the emotion they are supposed to talk about? Do both partners contribute to the dialogue, or is it dominated by one of the partners? Does the dialogue remain focused on the child and the child's experience, or does it get derailed to other topics including the mother's experience? And, in the case of memories that involve distress, does the parent guide the dialogue to emphasize the child's successful coping with the challenge or difficulty, or does the dialogue end with the child's unresolved experience of distress?

As we illustrated, the two assessments we developed share common elements: Promoting security and emotion regulation in the child depends on the parents focusing on the child's experience in a nondefensive, open way in which the entire spectrum of behaviors and emotions can be brought up, thought about, discussed, and accepted, with a focus on the child's successful coping. "Goodness of fit" between parent and child is crucial in both assessments. It involves matching the descriptions of the child (in the Insightfulness Assessment) or the responses to the child (in the emotion dialogues assessment) to the specific and unique characteristics and needs of the child, with the goal of creating an experience that puts the child's needs in center stage. It follows that our approach does not offer a parenting "prescription" for insightful talk or sensitive guidance of dialogues—at least not in a simple form that can be generalized across children. Rather, our approach is fundamentally relational. It emphasizes the parent's capacity to perceive the child's signals openly and match the parent's thoughts and behaviors to the rhythm, needs, and capacities of the child. We believe that, in such an emotional climate, children can develop a sense of security not only at the level of being protected and comforted in times of distress but in feeling that their inner world is meaningful and that their thoughts and feelings are appreciated, understood, and accepted.

REFERENCES

Ainsworth, M. D. S. (1989). Attachment beyond infancy. *American Psychologist, 44,* 709–716. doi:10.1037/0003-066X.44.4.709

Ainsworth, M. D. S., Blehar, M. C., Waters, E., & Wall, S. (1978). *Patterns of attachment: A psychological study of the Strange Situation.* Hillsdale, NJ: Erlbaum.

Bowlby, J. (1982). *Attachment and loss: Vol. 1. Attachment.* New York, NY: Basic Books.

Bowlby, J. (1988). *A secure base*. London, England: Routledge.

Bretherton, I. (1990). Open communication and internal working models: Their role in attachment relationships. In R. A. Thompson (Ed.), *Nebraska Symposium on Motivation: Vol. 36. Socioemotional development* (pp. 57–113). Lincoln: University of Nebraska Press.

Bretherton, I. (1993). From dialogue to representation: The intergenerational construction of self in relationships. In C. A. Nelson (Ed.), *Minnesota Symposia on Child Psychology: Vol. 26. Memory and affect in development* (pp. 237–263). Hillsdale, NJ: Erlbaum.

Cassidy, J., & Berlin, L. J. (1994). The insecure/ambivalent pattern of attachment: Theory and research. *Child Development, 65,* 971–991. doi:10.2307/1131298

Fivush, R. (1991). The social construction of personal narratives. *Merrill-Palmer Quarterly, 37,* 59–81.

Fraiberg, S., Adelson, E., & Shapiro, V. (1975). Ghosts in the nursery: A psychoanalytic approach to the problems of impaired infant–mother relationships. *Journal of the American Academy of Child Psychiatry, 14,* 387–421. doi:10.1016/S0002-7138 (09)61442-4

George, C., & Solomon, J. (2008). The caregiving system: A behavioral system approach to parenting. In J. Cassidy & P. R. Shaver (Eds.), *Handbook of attachment: Theory, research, and clinical applications* (2nd ed., pp. 833–856). New York, NY: Guilford Press.

Gini, M., Oppenheim, D., & Sagi-Schwartz, A. (2007). Negotiation styles in mother–child narrative co-construction in middle childhood: Associations with early attachment. *International Journal of Behavioral Development, 31,* 149–160. doi:10.1177/0165025407074626

Hutman, T., Siller, M., & Sigman, M. (2009). Mothers' narratives regarding their child with autism predict maternal synchronous behavior during play. *Journal of Child Psychology and Psychiatry, 50,* 1255–1263. doi:10.1111/j.1469-7610.2009.02109.x

Koren-Karie, N., Oppenheim, D., Dolev, S., Sher, E., & Etzion-Carasso, A. (2002). Mothers' empathic understanding of their infants' internal experience: Relations with maternal sensitivity and infant attachment. *Developmental Psychology, 38,* 534–542. doi:10.1037/0012-1649.38.4.534

Koren-Karie, N., Oppenheim, D., & Getzler-Yosef, R. (2008). Shaping children's internal working models through mother–child dialogues: The importance of resolving past maternal trauma. *Attachment & Human Development, 10,* 465–483. doi:10.1080/14616730802461482

Koren-Karie, N., Oppenheim, D., Haimovich, Z., & Etzion-Carasso, A. (2003). Dialogues of seven-year-olds with their mothers about emotional events: Development of a typology. In R. N. Emde, D. P. Wolf, & D. Oppenheim (Eds.), *Revealing the inner worlds of young children: The MacArthur Story Stem Battery and parent–child narratives* (pp. 338–354). New York, NY: Oxford University Press.

Koren-Karie, N., Oppenheim, D., Yuval-Adler, S., & Mor, H. (2012). *Insightfulness and emotion dialogues of foster caregivers with two of their children: The role of the caregivers in shaping the interactions*. Unpublished manuscript, University of Haifa, Haifa, Israel.

Kuhn, J. C. (2007). *Maternal synchrony predicts joint attention and language gains in toddlers with autism.* Unpublished doctoral dissertation. University of Massachusetts, Boston.

Lyons-Ruth, K., Bronfman, E., & Atwood, G. (1999). A relational diathesis of hostile-helpless states of mind: Expressions in mother–infant interaction. In J. Solomon & C. George (Eds.), *Attachment disorganization* (pp. 33–70). New York, NY: Guilford Press.

Main, M. (1996). Introduction to the special section on attachment and psychopathology: Overview of the field of attachment. *Journal of Consulting and Clinical Psychology, 64,* 237–243. doi:10.1037/0022-006X.64.2.237

Main, M., Kaplan, N., & Cassidy, J. (1985). Security in infancy, childhood, and adulthood: A move to the level of representation. *Monographs of the Society for Research in Child Development, 50,* 66–104. doi:10.2307/3333827

Oppenheim, D., Feniger-Shaal, R., & Koren-Karie, N. (2010). [Insightfulness of mothers of young children with intellectual disability]. Unpublished raw data.

Oppenheim, D., Goldsmith, D., & Koren-Karie, N. (2004). Maternal insightfulness and preschoolers' emotion and behavior problems: Reciprocal influences in a day-treatment program. *Infant Mental Health Journal, 25,* 352–367.

Oppenheim, D., & Koren-Karie, N. (2009). Parents' insightfulness regarding their children's internal worlds: Assessment, research, and clinical implications. In C. Zeanah (Ed.), *Handbook of infant mental health* (3rd ed., pp. 266–280). New York, NY: Guilford Press.

Oppenheim, D., Koren-Karie, N., Dolev, S., & Yirmiya, N. (2009). Maternal insightfulness and resolution of the diagnosis are related to secure attachment in preschoolers with autism spectrum disorders. *Child Development, 80,* 519–527. doi:10.1111/j.1467-8624.2009.01276.x

Oppenheim, D., Koren-Karie, N., & Sagi, A. (2001). Mothers' empathic understanding of their preschoolers' internal experience: Relations with early attachment. *International Journal of Behavioral Development, 25,* 16–26. doi:10.1080/01650250042000096

Oppenheim, D., Koren-Karie, N., & Sagi-Schwartz, A. (2007). Emotion dialogues between mothers and children at 4.5 and 7.5 years: Relations with children's attachment at 1 year. *Child Development, 78,* 38–52. doi:10.1111/j.1467-8624.2007.00984.x

Oppenheim, D., Nir, A., Warren, S., & Emde, R. N. (1997). Emotion regulation in mother–child narrative co-construction: Associations with children's narratives and adaptation. *Developmental Psychology, 33,* 284–294. doi:10.1037/0012-1649.33.2.284

Slade, A. (1999). Representation, symbolization, and affect regulation in the concomitant treatment of a mother and a child: Attachment theory and child psychotherapy. *Psychoanalytic Inquiry, 19,* 797–830. doi:10.1080/07351699909534277 van IJzendoorn, M. H., & Sagi, A. (1999). Cross-cultural patterns of attachment: Universal and contextual determinants. In J. Cassidy & P. R. Shaver (Eds.), *Handbook of attachment: Theory, research, and clinical applications* (pp. 713–734). New York, NY: Guilford Press.

Weinfield, N. S., Sroufe, L. A., Egeland, B., & Carlson, E. A. (1999). The nature of individual differences in infant–caregiver attachment. In J. Cassidy & P. R. Shaver (Eds.), *Handbook of attachment: Theory, research, and clinical applications* (pp. 68–88). New York, NY: Guilford Press.

Wolf, D. P. (2003). Making meaning from emotional experience in early narratives. In R. N. Emde, D. P. Wolf, & D. Oppenheim (Eds.), *Revealing the inner worlds of young children: The MacArthur Story Stem Battery and parent–child narratives* (pp. 27–54). New York, NY: Oxford University Press.

Zeanah, C. H., Benoit, D., Hirshberg, L., Barton, M. L., & Regan, C. (1994). Mothers' representations of their infants are concordant with infant attachment classifications. *Developmental Issues in Psychiatry and Psychology, 1*, 9–18.

12

THE IMPACT OF EARLY INTERPERSONAL EXPERIENCE ON ADULT ROMANTIC RELATIONSHIP FUNCTIONING

JEFFRY A. SIMPSON, W. ANDREW COLLINS,
JESSICA E. SALVATORE, AND SOOYEON SUNG

Early social experiences have long been assumed to affect the later developmental trajectory of individuals, especially how they think, feel, and behave in subsequent close relationships. In fact, this premise is common to several major theorists, ranging from Freud (1940), to Erikson (1963), to Bowlby (1969, 1973). For the past several years, we have used data from the Minnesota Longitudinal Study of Risk and Adaptation to investigate how certain interpersonal experiences encountered very early in life (at age 1) systematically predict how people think, feel, and behave in their adult romantic relationships approximately 20 years later.

This research was supported by grants from the National Institute of Mental Health (NIMH) to Byron Egeland, L. Alan Sroufe, and W. Andrew Collins (R01-MH40864) and to Jeffry A. Simpson (R01-MH49599) and by a National Institute of Child Health and Human Development grant to W. Andrew Collins, Byron Egeland, and L. Alan Sroufe (R01-HD054850). Jessica E. Salvatore's work on this chapter was supported by an NIMH predoctoral training grant (T32-MH015755-32) and by a grant to Danielle M. Dick (R01-AA015416).

http://dx.doi.org/10.1037/14250-013
Mechanisms of Social Connection: From Brain to Group, M. Mikulincer and P. R. Shaver (Editors)

Our goal has been to identify and understand how and why early attachment experiences—some of which occurred before individuals could form episodic memories of these events—affect the ways in which the adult romantic relationships of these individuals function and the interpersonal pathways through which transmission patterns may have occurred. We have also examined the powerful role that romantic partners can and often do play in buffering certain people (e.g., those who were insecurely attached as children) from the vulnerabilities posed by their very early negative relationship histories.

Our studies have generated three core insights. First, early experiences associated with attachment security versus insecurity in relation to one's caregivers have small but apparently lasting effects on how people think, feel, and behave in their adult romantic relationships many years later. Second, there appear to be interpersonal pathways through which early life attachment experiences affect adult romantic relationship functioning. Third, certain kinds of romantic partners can buffer individuals who have early life vulnerabilities, such as insecure attachment histories, from experiencing negative relationship outcomes in adulthood.

We begin the chapter by describing the organizational perspective on social development that has guided much of our thinking and research to date. Following this, we discuss the unique longitudinal data set we have used to test a series of predictions concerning how attachment patterns very early in life (during the first 1–1.5 years) are systematically associated with other salient relationship experiences at different points in development, culminating in relationships with romantic partners approximately 20 years later. We then highlight the principal findings of two studies that examined how secure versus insecure attachment patterns very early in life presage (a) the ways in which individuals experience and express positive and negative emotions in their romantic relationships, especially during conflict discussions with their partners; and (b) how well individuals are able to "recover" emotionally from conflict discussions with their romantic partners, along with the critical role that partners assume in this process and in predicting the future stability of a relationship. Following this, we discuss a study that highlights the role of romantic relationships in prompting developmental change and consider how functioning outside of the family earlier in development may allow individuals to form secure and high-quality adult romantic relationships (or secure representations of a romantic partner), independent of early caregiving experiences. We conclude the chapter by discussing several of the advantages to the study of relationships of adopting an organizational perspective on social development, and we suggest some promising directions for future work.

AN ORGANIZATIONAL PERSPECTIVE
ON SOCIAL DEVELOPMENT

Our program of research has been guided by an organizational perspective on social development that is based on four principles (Salvatore, Collins, & Simpson, 2012; Sroufe, Egeland, Carlson, & Collins, 2005). First, the meaning of a given behavior depends on how it fits with other behaviors in a specific social context. For example, disengaging from conflict with a romantic partner when it is appropriate to do so is likely to protect people from the damaging effects of further conflict (Gottman, 1994), whereas failure to do so—especially when continued conflict is futile and issues cannot be resolved at the moment—may undermine future relationship functioning (see Gottman & Levenson, 1999).

Second, the ways in which individuals regulate their emotions in adult relationships should be associated with how they regulated their emotions with their caregivers earlier in life (Sroufe & Fleeson, 1986; Thompson, 2008; see also Chapter 15, this volume). Synchronous and supportive relationships with early caregivers are the first context in which good, functional emotion-regulation skills are learned (Sroufe et al., 2005; see also Chapter 7, this volume). Attachment security, which is an indicator of both well-calibrated interaction synchrony and effective emotion regulation in early childhood (Schore, 2005; see also Chapter 8, this volume), predicts better emotion-regulation skills at later points in life (Thompson, 2008).

Third, mental representations (working models) of self and others formed early in life guide interaction patterns in later relationships (Roisman, Collins, Sroufe, & Egeland, 2005; Sroufe & Fleeson, 1986). This is particularly true of long-term romantic partners, who often serve as attachment figures in most romantic relationships (Hazan & Zeifman, 1994; see also Chapter 15, this volume). Bowlby (1973) claimed that the quality of caregiving provided by early caregivers acts as a template for what can be expected in later relationships, which influences how people think, feel, and behave in their later relationships.

Fourth, experiences in early relationships (with parents) and in later relationships (with adult romantic partners) should jointly affect what happens at later points in development (Carlson, Sroufe, & Egeland, 2004; Sroufe, Egeland, & Kreutzer, 1990). For instance, positive relationship experiences encountered later in life (e.g., getting involved with a devoted, emotionally well-adjusted partner) can counteract and alter the negative working models stemming from negative relationship experiences earlier in life (e.g., experiencing less responsive or inconsistent parenting during childhood; see Ainsworth, 1989; Sroufe et al., 2005). In addition, romantic partners may be able to buffer "developmentally vulnerable" individuals, such as those with insecure attachment histories, from experiencing poor outcomes in their romantic relationships (see Rönkä, Oravala, & Pulkkinen, 2002; Tran & Simpson, 2009).

THE MINNESOTA LONGITUDINAL STUDY
OF RISK AND ADAPTATION

In our research, we have tested how early interpersonal experiences—especially those resulting in patterns of secure versus insecure attachment early in life—are systematically related to adult romantic relationship functioning. We have done this by following a sample of participants from birth into adulthood (Simpson, Collins, & Salvatore, 2011; Simpson, Collins, Tran, & Haydon, 2007). The sample comes from the Minnesota Longitudinal Study of Risk and Adaptation (Sroufe et al., 2005). In 1976–77, first-time mothers who were receiving free prenatal services at Minneapolis public health clinics were recruited for the study. The firstborn children of these mothers, whom we will refer to as *target* participants, became the primary focus of the study. From birth, targets ($N = 174$) have been assessed at regular intervals at each stage of development with multimethod measures (e.g., interviews, questionnaires, teacher and parent ratings, behavioral observations). Our research has focused on approximately 75 targets (and their romantic partners) who were involved in an established romantic relationship when they were 20–21 years old. The target participants in our romantic relationships subsample are demographically representative of the larger sample.

Assessments were conducted at several pivotal points when the targets were negotiating salient socioemotional developmental issues, such as forming attachments with early caregivers, navigating the peer environment in middle childhood, establishing close friendships in adolescence, and forming and maintaining romantic relationships in early adulthood. Competence in these domains was assessed with multiple methods. For children, assessments tapped how effective the parent–child dyad was in modulating the emotional arousal of the child during stressful situations. For example, when the targets were 12 and 18 months old, they were videotaped in the Strange Situation (Ainsworth, Blehar, Waters, & Wall, 1978), a stressful laboratory procedure that involves a series of separations and reunions with caregivers (in our case, each target's mother). Trained observers then viewed the videotapes and classified each target as having a secure or an insecure (anxious or avoidant) relationship with his or her caregiver (mother). In the Strange Situation, securely attached children use their caregivers as a source of comfort and base of security to lower their negative affect and regulate their emotions. This allows them to engage in other life tasks, such as exploring the environment.

Insecurely attached children in the Strange Situation do not use and act as if they cannot rely on their caregivers to dissipate negative affect and manage their negative emotions. As a result, their attachment systems remain activated, and they remain distressed throughout the Strange Situation procedure. There are two primary types of insecure children. Anxiously attached children express their distress and emotional dysregulation overtly by being inconsolable, whereas avoidantly attached children contain or suppress overt manifestations of their distress, yet remain physiologically aroused throughout the procedure (Sroufe & Waters, 1977).

When the targets were in elementary school (ages 6–8), they were rated by their classroom teachers with respect to how socially competent they were in organized classroom situations compared with their classmates. When the targets were age 16, they completed an hour-long interview during which they described the nature and quality of their relationship with their best friend, including how secure their relationship was and how conflicts were resolved with their best friend. When the targets were 20–21 years old, they and their romantic partners came to our laboratory and participated in a videotaped conflict resolution task, which was immediately followed by a conflict recovery task (see below). Each of these tasks assessed how well each target regulated her or his emotions with significant others at different points of social development in different types of stressful situations. When the targets were 23 years old, we assessed whether they were still dating the same romantic partner with whom they were videotaped at age 20 or 21. In addition, at age 23, targets who were in romantic relationships of 4 months or longer were interviewed about their relationship, including feelings of closeness, acceptance, approaches to conflict resolution, and commitment. Interviews were coded on a series of scales tapping the overall quality of the relationship.

Emotion Regulation During Conflict

In an initial study examining emotion regulation during romantic relationship conflict, Simpson et al. (2007) found that if targets had an insecure attachment relationship with their mothers at 12 months of age (assessed in the Strange Situation), they reported and behaviorally expressed more negative emotions when trying to resolve a major relationship conflict with their romantic partner at age 20–21. But this early attachment effect was mediated by targets' degree of social competence in elementary school (rated by their grade-school teachers) and the quality of their relationship with their best friend at age 16 (e.g., the extent to which targets felt they could share all personal feelings with their best friend, regardless of the content and how much they trusted and could count on their best friend). This partial mediation pattern, which fit the data better than several other possible models, is shown in

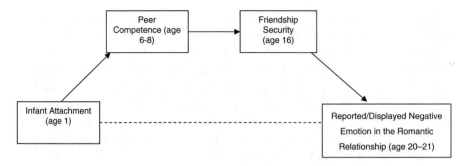

Figure 12.1. The best-fitting model showing the interpersonal pathway through which attachment security versus insecurity at age 1 is associated with greater reported and displayed negative emotions in adult romantic relationships at age 20–21. From "Attachment and the Experience and Expression of Emotions in Adult Romantic Relationships: A Developmental Perspective," by J. A. Simpson, W. A. Collins, S. Tran, and K. C. Haydon, 2007, *Journal of Personality and Social Psychology, 92,* p. 363. Copyright 2007 by the American Psychological Association.

Figure 12.1. These findings reflect one interpersonal pathway through which attachment security versus insecurity very early in life is probabilistically associated with the nature and quality of emotion regulation in adult romantic relationships approximately 20 years later.

Recovering From Conflict

In a second study, Salvatore, Kuo, Steele, Simpson, and Collins (2011) examined whether and how attachment patterns early in life are related to the way in which individuals recover from romantic relationship conflicts. *Conflict recovery* refers to how quickly, well, and completely individuals are able to shift, emotionally and behaviorally, from a negative interaction (e.g., discussing a major relationship problem) to achieving another important dyadic goal (e.g., discussing topics on which both partners agree). Recovering from conflict most likely involves a different set of skills and abilities than does resolving conflicts in a constructive and fair fashion (Gottman & Levenson, 1999; Salvatore et al., 2011). Targets who were securely attached early in life rebounded from conflicts with their romantic partners better at age 20–21, statistically controlling for how difficult the conflict discussion had been. Their romantic partners also recovered better if the targets had been securely attached earlier in life. Moreover, having a romantic partner who recovered better from conflict predicted higher self-reported relationship satisfaction as well as more positive relationship emotions. Finally, targets who had been insecurely attached early in life were significantly more likely to still be involved with the same romantic partners 2 years later (at age 23) if their partners had

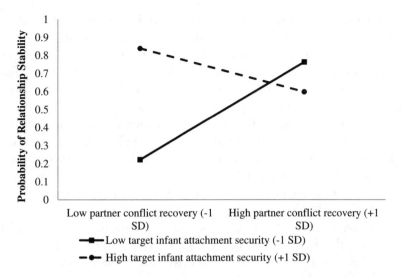

Figure 12.2. The probability of relationship stability over a 2-year period as a function of target participant infant attachment security and partner conflict reform. From "Recovering From Conflict in Romantic Relationships: A Developmental Perspective," by J. E. Salvatore, S. I. Kuo, R. D. Steele, J. A. Simpson, and W. A. Collins, 2011, *Psychological Science, 22,* p. 381. Copyright 2011 by the Authors. Adapted with permission.

displayed better conflict recovery 2 years earlier (at age 20–21; see Figure 12.2). Emotionally well-regulated romantic partners, therefore, appear to "protect" individuals with insecure attachment histories from romantic relationship difficulties in adulthood.

It is important to emphasize that in both of these studies all of the longitudinal effects described above remained statistically significant when assorted measures of current romantic relationship quality and functioning were statistically controlled. The effects reported above, therefore, are not attributable either to the targets' early temperament dispositions or to the quality of the targets' current romantic relationships.

Evidence for Change

As the findings reviewed above suggest, the early parent–child relationship sets the stage for later romantic functioning in important ways. However, those who experienced an insecure attachment are not necessarily doomed for a lifetime to dissatisfying or conflictual interpersonal relationships. A focal point in Bowlby's attachment theory is that later social relationships provide an important opportunity for change in working models of self and others that should, in turn, be related to behavioral and emotional outcomes (Bowlby, 1988). Similarly, an organizational–developmental perspective asserts that individual adaptation is best understood as the combination of one's developmental history in conjunction with current life circumstances (Sroufe et al., 1990). That is, one's present circumstances can take on a different meaning in light of the past and vice versa.

We recently examined this with respect to anxious-depressed symptoms over a 9-year period in young adulthood (measured at ages 23, 26, and 32) as a function of early caregiving (measured at five times between ages 1 and 4) in combination with young adult romantic quality (measured at age 23). Low-quality early caregiving is a risk factor for internalizing symptoms in adulthood (Moffitt et al., 2007); likewise, low-quality or dissatisfying relationships are also associated with adult internalizing symptoms (Whisman, 2001). Consistent with the idea that later interpersonal experiences may alter the consequences of earlier interpersonal experiences, the objective in this study was to test whether the quality of young adult romantic relationship experiences moderated the effects of early caregiving experiences to predict anxious-depressed symptoms across this 9-year period (Salvatore, Haydon, Simpson, & Collins, in press).

The study found evidence for inoculation, amplification, and compensation effects. The anxious-depressed symptoms of those who experienced higher quality early caregiving did not vary much as a function of their young adult romantic relationship quality. This suggests that positive early caregiving experiences may have buffered (i.e., inoculated) these individuals against declines in mental health typically associated with a low-quality romantic relationship (Mikulincer & Florian, 1998; Mikulincer, Shaver, & Pereg, 2003). In contrast, the anxious-depressed symptoms of those who experienced lower quality early caregiving varied greatly as a function of their young adult romantic relationship quality. Those with lower quality early caregiving and a lower quality romantic relationship had the most symptoms (amplification), whereas those with lower quality early caregiving and a higher quality romantic relationship had the fewest symptoms (compensation).

How is it that some individuals are able to form secure and high-quality romantic relationships despite less than optimal early experiences with caregivers? Such findings suggest that romantic relationship functioning may have some developmental origins that are distinct from the parent–child relationship (see Sroufe et al., 2005). Recent findings from our longitudinal project, in which our group examined the shared and distinctive origins of adult participants' attachment representations of experiences both with early caregivers and with a specific romantic partner in early adulthood (Haydon, Collins, Salvatore, Simpson, & Roisman, 2012), provide further evidence for this principle. Representations of early caregiving experiences and the current romantic partner were measured with the Adult Attachment Interview (George, Kaplan,

& Main, 1985) and the Current Relationship Interview (Crowell & Owens, 1996), respectively. Classifications of secure/autonomous versus insecure/ nonautonomous (dismissing or preoccupied) on each of these interviews were made based on the quality of each participant's discourse (rather than his or her description of early caregiving or romantic relationship experiences and events).

The results indicated that early parenting quality (measured at 24 months) predicted secure-autonomous classifications on both the Adult Attachment Interview and the Current Relationship Interview. However, preschool ego resiliency (a measure of attentional and affective flexibility; Block & Block, 1973) uniquely predicted secure classifications on the Current Relationship Interview. Thus, functioning outside the family of origin may be another pathway through which individuals with poor early caregiving experiences (or insecure representations of early caregiving experiences) can form and maintain high-quality romantic relationships (or secure representations of romantic partners, which should in turn predict better romantic functioning).

Summary of the Findings

From an organizational perspective on social development, these findings indicate that adult romantic relationship experiences are embedded in social processes that begin with early parental caregiving. Moreover, the quality of early caregiving is carried forward through subsequent relationship experiences and salient developmental periods, especially critical developmental transitions (see Collins & Sroufe, 1999; Sroufe, 1989). This carry-forward process is complex, and it probably involves the continuous interplay of internal working models and relationship experiences that occur in different developmental periods from infancy through early adulthood (Carlson et al., 2004).

THE ADVANTAGES OF AN ORGANIZATIONAL PERSPECTIVE
ON SOCIAL DEVELOPMENT

Mental representations or "working models" of prior relationships are carried forward into new relationships. This can alter how current partners and relationships are viewed, depending in part on how individuals are being treated in their current relationships (Bowlby, 1973; Carlson et al., 2004). By adopting an organizational view on social development, one can generate unique predictions about an individual's future relationship functioning on the basis of knowledge of his or her past relationships as well as his or her current relationship status (Sroufe et al., 2005). For example, two different people can arrive at the same current relationship outcome (e.g., they can both report the same high level of satisfaction with their current relationship), but they have arrived at this good place from very different starting points. One individual may have had a series of warm and supportive prior relationships starting very early in life and simply be continuing this pleasant trajectory with a current romantic partner. The other individual may have had a series of rocky, difficult, and rather unsupportive past relationships beginning early in life but have found a romantic partner who is very loving and compatible.

In addition, two individuals can arrive at different relationship outcomes from the same early starting point. Both individuals, for example, may have had a history of tumultuous, unsupportive prior relationships starting early in life, but one individual has a very loving, compatible, and emotionally well-regulated romantic partner with whom she or he is very happy, whereas the other individual has a more difficult, emotionally dysregulated romantic partner with whom she or he is unhappy.

Consider a concrete example. Both Sarah and Jennifer feel and display strong negative emotions when they interact with their current romantic partners. Sarah has a secure attachment history, but she recently discovered that her partner was cheating on her. Sarah and her partner are trying to repair the damage to their relationship in therapy, but the emotional strains of the betrayal continue to be reflected in Sarah's negative feelings and tense interactions with her partner. Jennifer also recently learned about her partner's infidelity, and she is also in therapy with her partner trying to mend the relationship. Jennifer, however, has an insecure attachment history and, therefore, is carrying considerable emotional baggage from her prior insecure, unsupportive relationships into her current romantic relationship.

Sarah's and Jennifer's relationships look fairly similar when viewed at a single time point. Each woman is having problems with her current romantic partner. A nondevelopmental perspective might anticipate that Sarah and Jennifer will have rather similar relationship trajectories and outcomes in the near future. But different predictions follow when Sarah's and Jennifer's current adaptation is considered in combination with the women's divergent developmental histories. If Sarah's therapy is successful and she is able to trust her partner once again, her relationship is likely to show better and more rapid improvement than Jennifer's relationship, based on Sarah's secure working models. Jennifer's relationship, in contrast, will probably show poorer and slower improvement than Sarah's even if therapy is helpful, given her insecure working models (see Johnson, 2008).

FUTURE DIRECTIONS AND CONCLUSIONS

There are several important directions for future research. For example, the field needs to learn more about how early social experiences accumulate during development to influence adult relationship outcomes, including nonromantic ones. Little remains known about whether or how certain social experiences that occur at specific time points (e.g., during the first 5 years of life) are uniquely associated with specific types of adult relationship outcomes, such as how partners attempt to resolve relationship conflicts, how they support each other (or fail to do so), and how they share in each other's joys and happy life events. In addition, the field is just beginning to understand how current relationship variables such as satisfaction, commitment, and investments statistically interact with working models of relationships earlier in life to affect adult relationship experiences and outcomes, either within romantic relationships or in other relationship contexts (Salvatore et al., 2012). Finally, future research might determine whether and how specific gene by early environment interactions are associated with specific relationship outcomes in adulthood.

In conclusion, an organizational perspective on social development accentuates the relative coherence of social behavior in different relationships across development. The pattern of relationship-relevant thoughts, feelings, and actions—and especially their representation in working models—is what links early interpersonal experiences with caregivers to later interpersonal experiences with young peers, close friends, and eventually adult romantic partners. Although the behavioral characteristics of good versus poor emotion regulation look somewhat different at each developmental stage, their underlying functions and meaning tend to remain stable across time. Our program of research has documented that important adult romantic outcomes are, in fact, systematically tied to relationship experiences that occurred remarkably early in life, long before individuals formed and retained conscious memories. This link, however, also depends on what transpires in different types of relationships at intervening stages of social development, including relationships with romantic partners in early adulthood.

REFERENCES

Ainsworth, M. D. S. (1989). Attachments beyond infancy. *American Psychologist*, *44*, 709–716. doi:10.1037/0003-066X.44.4.709

Ainsworth, M. D. S., Blehar, M. C., Waters, E., & Wall, S. (1978). *Patterns of attachment: A psychological study of the strange situation*. Hillsdale, NJ: Erlbaum.

Block, J., & Block, J. H. (1973). *Ego development and the provenance of thought: A longitudinal study of ego and cognitive development in young children*. Berkeley: University of California.

Bowlby, J. (1969). *Attachment and loss: Vol. 1. Attachment*. New York, NY: Basic Books.

Bowlby, J. (1973). *Attachment and loss: Vol. 2. Separation: Anxiety and anger*. New York, NY: Basic Books.

Bowlby, J. (1988). *A secure base: Parent–child attachment and healthy human development*. New York, NY: Basic Books.

Carlson, E. A., Sroufe, L. A., & Egeland, B. (2004). The construction of experience: A longitudinal study of representation and behavior. *Child Development, 75*, 66–83. doi:10.1111/j.1467-8624.2004.00654.x

Collins, W. A., & Sroufe, L. A. (1999). Capacity for intimate relationships: A developmental construction. In W. Furman, B. B. Brown, & C. Feiring (Eds.), *The development of romantic relationships in adolescence* (pp. 125–147). New York, NY: Cambridge University Press.

Crowell, J. A., & Owens, G. (1996). *Current Relationship Interview and scoring system*. Unpublished manuscript, State University of New York at Stony Brook.

Erikson, E. (1963). *Childhood and society*. New York, NY: Norton.

Freud, S. (1940). *An outline of psychoanalysis*. New York, NY: Hogarth Press.

George, C., Kaplan, N., & Main, M. (1985). *The Adult Attachment Interview*. Unpublished manuscript, University of California, Berkeley.

Gottman, J. M. (1994). *What predicts divorce? The relationship between marital processes and marital outcomes*. Hillsdale, NJ: Erlbaum.

Gottman, J. M., & Levenson, R. W. (1999). Rebound from marital conflict and divorce prediction. *Family Process, 38*, 287–292. doi:10.1111/j.1545-5300.1999.00287.x

Haydon, K. C., Collins, W. A., Salvatore, J. E., Simpson, J. A., & Roisman, G. I. (2012). Shared and distinctive origins and associations of adult attachment representations: The developmental organization of romantic functioning. *Child Development, 83*, 1689–1702. doi: 10.1111/j.1467-8624.2012.01801.x

Hazan, C., & Zeifman, D. (1994). Sex and the psychological tether. In K. Bartholomew & D. Perlman (Eds.), *Advances in personal relationships: Vol. 5. Attachment processes in adulthood* (pp. 151–178). London, England: Kingsley.

Johnson, S. M. (2008). Couple and family therapy: An attachment perspective. In J. Cassidy & P. R. Shaver (Eds.), *Handbook of attachment: Theory, research, and clinical applications* (2nd ed., pp. 811–829). New York, NY: Guilford Press.

Mikulincer, M., & Florian, V. (1998). The relationship between adult attachment styles and emotional and cognitive reactions to stressful events. In J. A. Simpson & W. S. Rholes (Eds.), *Attachment theory and close relationships* (pp. 143–165). New York, NY: Guilford Press.

Mikulincer, M., Shaver, P. R., & Pereg, D. (2003). Attachment theory and affect regulation: The dynamics, development, and cognitive consequences of attachment-related strategies. *Motivation and Emotion, 27*, 77–102. doi:10.1023/A:1024515519160

Moffitt, T. E., Caspi, A., Harrington, H., Milne, B. J., Melchior, M., Golderberg, D., & Poulton, R. (2007). Generalized anxiety disorder and depression: Childhood risk factors in a birth cohort followed to age 32. *Psychological Medicine, 37*, 441–452. doi:10.1017/S0033291706009640

Roisman, G. I., Collins, W. A., Sroufe, L. A., & Egeland, B. (2005). Predictors of young adults' representations of and behavior in their current romantic relationship: Prospective tests of the prototype hypothesis. *Attachment & Human Development, 7,* 105–121. doi:10.1080/14616730500134928

Rönkä, A., Oravala, S., & Pulkkinen, L. (2002). "I met this wife of mine and things got onto a better track": Turning points in risk development. *Journal of Adolescence, 25,* 47–63. doi:10.1006/jado.2001.0448

Salvatore, J. E., Collins, W. A., & Simpson, J. A. (2012). An organizational–developmental perspective on functioning in adult romantic relationships. In L. Campbell & T. J. Loving (Eds.), *Interdisciplinary research on close relationships: The case for integration* (pp. 155–177). Washington, DC: American Psychological Association. doi:10.1037/13486-007

Salvatore, J. E., Haydon, K. C., Simpson, J. A., & Collins, W. A. (in press). The distinctive role of romantic relationships in moderating the effects of early caregiving on adult anxious-depressed symptoms over nine years. *Development and Psychopathology.*

Salvatore, J. E., Kuo, S. I., Steele, R. D., Simpson, J. A., & Collins, W. A. (2011). Recovering from conflict in romantic relationships: A developmental perspective. *Psychological Science, 22,* 376–383. doi:10.1177/0956797610397055

Schore, A. N. (2005). Back to basics: Attachment, affect regulation, and the developing right brain: Linking developmental neuroscience to pediatrics. *Pediatrics in Review, 26,* 204–217. doi:10.1542/pir.26-6-204

Simpson, J. A., Collins, W. A., & Salvatore, J. E. (2011). The impact of early interpersonal experience on adult romantic relationship functioning: Recent findings from the Minnesota Longitudinal Study of Risk and Adaptation. *Current Directions in Psychological Science, 20,* 355–359. doi:10.1177/0963721411418468

Simpson, J. A., Collins, W. A., Tran, S., & Haydon, K. C. (2007). Attachment and the experience and expression of emotions in adult romantic relationships: A developmental perspective. *Journal of Personality and Social Psychology, 92,* 355–367. doi:10.1037/0022-3514.92.2.355

Sroufe, L. A. (1989). Relationships, self, and individual adaptation. In A. J. Sameroff & R. N. Emde (Eds.), *Relationship disturbances in early childhood: A developmental approach* (pp. 70–94). New York, NY: Basic Books.

Sroufe, L. A., Egeland, B., Carlson, E. A., & Collins, W. A. (2005). *The development of the person: The Minnesota Study of Risk and Adaptation from Birth to Adulthood.* New York, NY: Guilford Press.

Sroufe, L. A., Egeland, B., & Kreutzer, T. (1990). The fate of early experience following developmental change: Longitudinal approaches to individual adaptation in childhood. *Child Development, 61,* 1363–1373. doi:10.2307/1130748

Sroufe, L. A., & Fleeson, J. (1986). Attachment and the construction of relationships. In W. W. Hartup & Z. Rubin (Eds.), *Relationships and development* (pp. 51–71). Hillsdale, NJ: Erlbaum.

Sroufe, L. A., & Waters, E. (1977). Heart rate as a convergent measure in clinical and developmental research. *Merrill-Palmer Quarterly, 23*, 3–27.

Thompson, R. (2008). Early attachment and later development: Familiar questions, new answers. In J. Cassidy & P. R. Shaver (Eds.), *Handbook of attachment: Theory, research, and clinical applications* (2nd ed., pp. 348–365). New York, NY: Guilford Press.

Tran, S., & Simpson, J. A. (2009). Prorelationship maintenance behaviors: The joint roles of attachment and commitment. *Journal of Personality and Social Psychology, 97*, 685–698. doi:10.1037/a0016418

Whisman, M. A. (2001). The association between depression and marital dissatisfaction. In S. R. H. Beach (Ed.), *Marital and family processes in depression: A scientific foundation for clinical practice* (pp. 3–24). Washington, DC: American Psychological Association. doi:10.1037/10350-001

III

ADULT CLOSE
RELATIONSHIPS

13

RISK REGULATION IN CLOSE RELATIONSHIPS

JUSTIN V. CAVALLO, SANDRA L. MURRAY, AND JOHN G. HOLMES

Romantic relationships often present people with a fundamental approach–avoidance dilemma. From the early stages of relationship initiation to the midst of marriage, people are motivated to behave in ways that increase closeness and intimacy with romantic partners. However, establishing a meaningful connection that satisfies fundamental belongingness needs (Baumeister & Leary, 1995) often requires that people think and behave in ways that give their partners great control over their outcomes. That is, they must often forgive a partner for his or her bad behavior (e.g., Rusbult, Verette, Whitney, Slovik, & Lipkus, 1991), seek emotional support for distressing events (e.g., Collins & Feeney, 2000), or sacrifice their own goals for the sake of their partner's (e.g., Van Lange et al., 1997). Although such actions may ultimately facilitate a loving and caring relationship, they also heighten immediate vulnerability to a painful and potentially devastating rejection experience. A partner might exploit forgiveness by continuing to behave badly, rebuff or reject solicitations for social support, or pursue his or her goals

http://dx.doi.org/10.1037/14250-014
Mechanisms of Social Connection: From Brain to Group, M. Mikulincer and P. R. Shaver (Editors)
Copyright © 2014 by the American Psychological Association. All rights reserved.

single-mindedly without acknowledging or reciprocating the other's sacrifice. Given the pain that accompanies rejection (Baumeister & Leary, 1995; MacDonald & Leary, 2005; see also Chapter 2, this volume) and the fact that this pain is intensified as interdependence increases, people are motivated to think and behave in ways that minimize their risk.

Thus, interdependent relationships put these two fundamental motivations at odds. People must continually balance the motivation to pursue intimacy and connection with a partner and the motivation to protect themselves from the pain of potential rejection. How do people reconcile these competing goals? In the present chapter, we detail the operation of a risk regulation system that prioritizes connectedness or self-protection as relationship circumstances warrant, in order to assure that people are safe from potential rejection. We begin by describing how situations of interpersonal risk afford opportunities for both connection and self-protection and review empirical support indicating that perceptions of trust shape which of these competing goals is prioritized. Next, we explore how automatic and controlled processes independently and interactively shape motivated responses to risk. In outlining this dual-process model, we suggest that trust has both an impulsive and a reflective basis, and that these in concert allow people to negotiate the risks of interdependence by motivating them to approach their partners in the face of risk or, instead, to act in ways that allow them to avoid the hurt that might accompany interdependence. We conclude the chapter by elaborating on the role of automatic processes in directing self-regulation in risky interpersonal contexts.

RISKY SITUATIONS AND THE ROLE OF TRUST

Although the self-regulatory dilemma between connection and self-protection goals broadly underlies interdependent relationships, it is most acute in risky situations—that is, in situations that arouse concerns about a partner's caring and responsiveness. People's perception of the extent to which their romantic partner values them, cares for them, and will attend to their needs (see Chapter 14) is central in allowing people to prioritize connection over self-protection. Concerns about a partner's responsiveness arise when people are made to question the extent to which their partner will be responsive to them and can be elicited directly (e.g., during relationship conflict) or indirectly (e.g., when people are confronted with the general costs of interdependence). For example, when partners disagree on the best way to spend a Saturday afternoon, or when a partner's penchant for generosity conflicts with a person's own frugality, the person becomes aware that interdependence constrains autonomy. These situations lead people to question how much their partner truly values them, and this in turn motivates one of two possible responses: People may draw their partner closer in the hope of assuring themselves that their partner is in fact responsive and thus that their dependence is justifiable. Alternatively, they may withdraw and distance themselves from their partner in the service of minimizing the sting of rejection that may come from an unresponsive partner.

These goals compete with each other for motivational priority because both offer compelling incentives and costs. Drawing a partner closer may ultimately restore intimacy but also entails the possibility of even greater hurt if the partner is truly unresponsive. Withdrawing from a partner may dull the impact of anticipated rejection but also lessens the opportunity to establish a more loving and intimate relationship. Because approach-oriented connection goals and avoidance-oriented self-protection goals motivate behavior in opposing directions, they produce a motivational ambivalence that is a poor guide to self-regulation (Cacioppo, Gardner, & Berntson, 1999; Gable, Reis, & Elliot, 2000). To enact a clear response, a person must employ a regulatory system to reconcile the tension (Murray, Holmes, & Collins, 2006). When assessing the level of risk inherent in a given situation and deciding to implement connection or self-protection goals accordingly, a person needs to rely on feelings of trust or distrust. Trust in a partner's responsiveness, caring, and valuation provides assurance that one is safe in depending on one's partner. This gives a person the impetus to prioritize and pursue connection goals when risk arises. People high in trust appear to respond to risk with the procedural rule, "If my partner is accepting, then connect" (Murray & Holmes, 2011). They implement this rule by engaging in cognitive and behavioral strategies that allow them to cast aside potential concerns and deepen their intimacy with their partner.

In contrast, those low in trust have persistent doubts that their partner truly values them and has their best interests at heart. As such, they respond to risk by pursuing self-protection goals, reflecting the procedural contingency rule, "If my partner is rejecting, then self-protect" (Murray & Holmes, 2011). They distance themselves cognitively and behaviorally from their partners, a strategy that allows them to minimize the pain of potential rejection but also entails forgoing the benefits of intimacy. Although people high and low in trust implement different procedural rules and thus prioritize different goals when risk arises, both regulatory strategies allow people to maintain feelings of safety and security in risky situations where their outcomes are largely tied to their partner's thoughts and actions (Murray, Derrick, Leder, & Holmes, 2008; see Chapter 15, this volume).

The divergent prioritization of connectedness and self-protection as a function of trust has been observed in both experimental studies and real-world observational designs. In an example of the latter, Murray, Bellavia, Rose, and Griffin (2003) followed married couples over a period of 21 days. During this time, participants reported events that posed an acute threat to relationship security, such as relationship conflict, or their partner behaved badly. Such events activate concerns about dependence and therefore afford an opportunity for people to respond by pursuing connectedness goals, instead, to act self-protectively. Results revealed that participants' feelings of trust influenced which self-regulatory response they enacted on days following these acute threats. Those who had higher trust that their partner cared about them and would be responsive to their needs reported feeling *closer* to their partners on days following threat. They refrained from retaliating or reciprocating a partner's bad behavior and treated their partner as well as they had the previous day. These cognitions and behaviors reflect a prioritization of connectedness goals; that is, highly trusting people sought to foster intimacy when concerns about interdependence arose. In contrast, those who were less trusting of their partners displayed heightened self-protection goals on days following an acute threat. They reported feeling more distant from their partners and generally treated their partners negatively. They not only reported being more abrupt with their partners but also criticized and insulted them the following day.

Such effects have been observed even when concerns about dependence are activated in less direct ways. People who trust their partner are more willing to support their partner's goals when those goals require a personal sacrifice, thus placing greater control over their outcomes in their partner's hands when they feel it is safe to do so. However, those low in trust are less willing to accommodate their partners, a regulatory strategy that minimizes dependence and thus protects one from being hurt by an uncaring partner (Shallcross & Simpson, 2012).

Many investigations of risk regulation processes have involved measuring individual differences in something other than trust per se, most notably self-esteem, as a proxy for *chronic* trust in shaping responses to risk. Self-esteem is linked with perceptions of relational value and may serve as a suitable proxy for people's chronic trust in their partner's caring (Leary & Baumeister, 2000; Leary, Tambor, Terdal, & Downs, 1995). Those with high self-esteem are confident in their partner's caring and thus have high chronic trust that allows them to seek connectedness when interdependence concerns are salient. In contrast, people with low self-esteem perpetually doubt how much their partner values them and, as a result, prefer to prioritize self-protection goals in risky interpersonal situations. This lack of trust is often unwarranted given partners' actual caring for low-self-esteem people (Murray, Griffin, Rose, & Bellavia, 2003). However, these perceptions often lead low-self-esteem people to behave differently from high-self-esteem people when facing risky interpersonal situations.

In one illustrative study of self-esteem's role in risk regulation, participants and their romantic partners were asked to complete ostensibly identical questionnaires. Those in the experimental condition were tasked with listing aspects of their partner that they disliked. Their partners in the control condition were actually asked instead to describe their dormitory room in detail. The thoroughness with which the control partners completed this task led participants in the experimental condition to believe that their partner found many faults in them, activating responsiveness concerns and thus creating an interpersonally risky situation (Murray, Rose, Bellavia, Holmes, & Kusche, 2002, Experiment 3). Relative to control participants, low-self-esteem people subsequently reported less positive evaluations of their relationship and their partner and reported feeling less close to the partner. When feeling criticized or rejected, they sought to protect themselves by devaluing their relationships and downplaying its importance. High-self-esteem people, in contrast, did not display these self-protective tendencies when faced with an apparently critical partner. Instead, they evaluated their relationship similarly to control participants. In other studies (e.g., Murray et al., 2002, Experiment 2), however, high-self-esteem people facing interpersonal risk actually drew *closer* to their partners. They prioritized connection and intimacy as reflected by more positive evaluations of their partners and greater feelings of closeness.

These differential responses to interpersonal risk as a function of self-esteem appear to be rooted in a broader motivational system that governs sensitivity to risk and reward. That is, interpersonal risk not only leads high- and low-self-esteem people to self-regulate differently in relationship-specific contexts but also affects goal pursuit more broadly outside these contexts. In one illustration of this, participants were exposed to interpersonal risk by having them recall a time when their partner hurt or disappointed them. After activating concerns about a partner's past behavior, participants were asked to evaluate two possible investment opportunities being considered by university officials and were told that the proceeds would be used to provide a tuition rebate. One option was presented as relatively "safe" in that its success was virtually guaranteed, but the return was expected to be relatively small. The alternative option was presented as much less likely to succeed, but also as more lucrative if successful (thus yielding a larger rebate).

Relative to control participants, low-self-esteem participants exposed to relationship risk become more conservative in their decision making, preferring the safer option to the riskier, but potentially more beneficial, option. In contrast, high-self-esteem participants facing relationship risk actually endorsed the riskier investment over the safer one, in hopes of obtaining its potentially larger reward (Cavallo, Fitzsimons, & Holmes, 2009, Study 4). Similar effects emerged when participants indicated their willingness to partake in risky, but potentially rewarding, recreational activities (e.g., skiing;

Cavallo et al., 2009, Study 3). Paralleling traditional risk regulation findings, interpersonal risk led low-self-esteem people to protect themselves from negative outcomes by becoming increasingly cautious, whereas high-self-esteem people became increasingly motivated to pursue rewards and cast aside potential dangers. Thus, the divergent pattern of self-regulation that emerges in the face of interpersonal risk among high- and low-trust people appears to reflect broader motivational orientations that shape goal pursuit both in and outside relationship contexts, perhaps reflecting the fundamental importance of interpersonal risk regulation.

As one might anticipate, self-esteem is but one of the many proxies for gauging chronic feelings of trust. Individual differences in adult attachment styles (see Chapters 15, 17, and 19), for example, have also been shown to moderate the prioritization of self-protection or connection in risky interpersonal contexts. Those who are anxiously attached (less chronically trusting of their partners) respond to threatening relationship situations much in the same way that low-self-esteem people do, prioritizing self-protection goals to guard them from the pain of anticipated rejection. For example, those high in anxiety derogate their partners and their relationships following relationship conflict (Campbell, Simpson, Boldry, & Kashy, 2005; Simpson, Rholes, & Phillips, 1996). They also exhibit greater anger at their partners in situations where they perceive them to be unresponsive (Rholes, Simpson, & Orina, 1999). In contrast, those who are securely attached (i.e., more likely to experience high chronic trust) act much like high-self-esteem people, prioritizing connectedness goals with their partners when the risk of dependence is made salient. They respond to conflict by evaluating their partners more *positively* (Simpson et al., 1996) and otherwise treat their partners at least as positively under risk as they do when such risk is not activated (Campbell et al., 2005).

In sum, there is a large body of evidence suggesting that perceptions of trust shape people's self-regulatory efforts when situations make concerns about a partner's responsiveness salient and thus afford opportunities to pursue conflicting goals. Those high in trust are willing to set aside the risk that they may be subject to a painful rejection experience and assure their safety by drawing their partner closer and deepening intimacy. Those low in trust are less willing to disregard these risks and instead forgo opportunities for intimacy by prioritizing goals that protect against the sting of rejection. However, the role of trust in moderating these responses has largely been examined by investigating people's *explicit* feelings of trust and their deliberative responses to threat. More recently, we have begun to explore the role of automatic processes in shaping risk regulation experiences. This work has illuminated the dual process nature of risk regulation processes that we detail in the next section.

A DUAL PROCESS MODEL OF RISK REGULATION

When goals motivate action in opposing directions, as self-protection and connection are theorized to do, they require reconciliation if a behavioral response is to be enacted. Most models of social cognition indicate that this reconciliation process requires the availability of executive resources (see Chapter 5 for a more detailed discussion). That is, when pursuing a given goal threatens one's ability to pursue an alternative goal—as is the case with connection and self-protection goals—one must exert self-control to prioritize the preferred goal in favor of the competing goal. Controlled self-regulation such as this is dependent on people having sufficient cognitive and regulatory resources to carry out their preferred course or action (Muraven & Baumeister, 2000; see also Chapter 5, this volume). Thus, although feelings of trust may provide the impetus for people to prioritize connection or self-protection motives, *implementing* these goals may be difficult if people lack the ability to exert executive control. Put another way, deliberative feelings of trust may guide risk regulation when people's cognitive resources are unimpeded but have little effect on people's responses to risk when these resources are taxed.

Indeed, it does seem that chronic trust—as operationalized by self-esteem—is most predictive of risk regulation activity when people have sufficient ability to use their executive resources. In one recent investigation, we exposed participants to interpersonal risk by having them read a short passage indicating that people generally overestimate the quality of their relationships (Cavallo, Holmes, Fitzsimons, Murray, & Wood, 2012, Study 2). This tendency to overestimate was illustrated by providing participants with fictitious findings ostensibly derived from prior research suggesting that partners' outward behavior often belied a lack of caring. Following this, participants were asked to learn and rehearse a short or long digit string throughout the experiment, thereby placing them under low or high cognitive load. Participants then indicated their feelings of connectedness to their partners.

Results revealed that when participants had ample executive resources available to them (i.e., were under low cognitive load), high- and low-self-esteem people exhibited divergent patterns of risk regulation similar to those described earlier in this chapter. That is, relative to control participants, high-self-esteem people exposed to relationship risk reported feeling *more* connected to their partners, reflecting the prioritization of connectedness goals over self-protection goals. Conversely, low-self-esteem people in the interpersonal risk condition reported feeling less connected to their partners relative to control participants, reflecting the prioritization of self-protection goals in the presence of doubts about a partner's caring. However, this pattern of results did not emerge when participants' executive resources were taxed.

When cognitive load was high, high- and low-self-esteem participants facing interpersonal risk did not differ from control participants in their feelings of connection to their partners, nor did they differ from each other. Thus, the presence of cognitive load reduced the impact of chronic feelings of trust on risk regulation processes.

A conceptually similar pattern of results was revealed when we examined how chronic working memory capacity influences people's evaluations outside an experimental context (Cavallo et al., 2012, Study 3). Individual differences in working memory capacity are a key determinant of people's ability to control self-regulatory behavior (Hofmann, Gschwendner, Friese, Wiers, & Schmitt, 2008). In a naturalistic study of married couples, we examined how connected participants felt to their partners in the face of general relationship risk, as operationalized by self-reported frequency and intensity of relational conflict. Among participants who had relatively risky relationships, those with high self-esteem believed their partners were more connected to their relationships than low-self-esteem participants, reflecting a relative focus on connection over self-protection. However, this self-esteem difference emerged only among participants who had relatively high chronic working memory capacity. Self-esteem did not predict perceived connectedness among those who had low chronic working memory capacity, nor did it predict these evaluations for participants who had relatively little risk in their relationships (e.g., had relatively infrequent conflict). Again, the availability of executive resources appears to be critical in allowing perceptions of chronic trust to dictate goal prioritization in the face of interpersonal risk.

This finding contributes to emerging evidence indicating that reflective (i.e., conscious) feelings of trust serve a secondary "corrective" function. As we detail in the next section, these deliberative feelings of trust allow people to prioritize goals consistent with their overarching relational motivations when goal conflict arises. This process often involves "overturning" automatic impulses elicited by certain relationship contexts when those impulses run counter to more conscious feelings of trust.

AUTOMATIC AND CONTROLLED RESPONSES TO RISK

Interdependent situations can vary greatly in their relative risk and reward, and as such, the interpersonal mind must remain flexible and efficient (Murray & Holmes, 2011). Accordingly, people often have automatic impulses in relationship situations that motivate connection or self-protection without the need for deliberative control. However, as we have detailed thus far, people also have chronic concerns or feelings of confidence that dictate how comfortable they are in approaching their partner in risky situations. These chronic concerns and stances appear to guide people's self-regulation when people have sufficient ability to employ executive resources, allowing them to reconcile competing goals by shifting priority to the goal that best suits their overall motivational agenda.

Those high in trust have a chronic motivational orientation toward connectedness. Their convictions concerning their partner's caring makes it less risky for them to seek intimacy in precarious situations. Their executive control system ensures that such goals are continually prioritized. This system drives them not only to draw their partners closer in the face of responsiveness concerns, but also to "override" any automatic inclinations that run counter to this overarching goal. That is, when highly risky interpersonal contexts afford greater opportunity to self-protect, highly trusting people appear to correct this impulse and instead remain connected and committed to their partners. In contrast, those low in chronic trust have a chronic motivational orientation toward self-protection. Their perpetual doubt about their partner's caring makes it all the more risky for them to approach their partners when acute concerns arise and, thus, their executive control system ensures that imperative self-protection goals have motivational priority. Even when situational risk is relatively mild and affords greater opportunity to connect with one's partner, low-trust people appear to overturn automatic impulses to connect and instead implement goals that serve their broader motivational agenda to avoid social pain.

These corrective processes have been directly observed by examining how people override nonconsciously activated goals when those goals are incompatible with their more general motivational aims. In one such study, dating participants were primed implicitly with approach goals by completing a word categorization task that contained words associated with connection goals (e.g., *devote, promise*). Following this, participants provided explicit ratings of how close they felt to their partners. Results indicated that people high and low in chronic trust (high- and low-self-esteem people) reacted differently to the goal prime. Relative to control participants, high-self-esteem people reported feeling closer to their partners, thus acting in a prime-congruent way. In contrast, low-self-esteem people who were primed with approach goals reported feeling *less* close to their partners than control participants, suggesting that they "overturned" the experimentally activated goal in favor of implementing their preferred self-regulatory strategy of self-protection (Murray et al., 2008).

This effect was more dramatically demonstrated in a subsequent study in which approach goals were again primed implicitly using a word categorization task. In this iteration, however, participants not only provided explicit feelings of closeness but also completed a measure intended to assess their implicit feelings of connection. This task assessed the speed (i.e., reaction time) with which participants associated positive interpersonal qualities, such as warmth and acceptance, with their partners. When primed with interpersonal approach goals, high-self-esteem people again reported feeling closer to their partners than did control participants. The goal prime also affected their implicit responses in a goal-congruent way, as high-self-esteem people were faster to associate positive traits with their partners. Low-self-esteem people, however, overturned the connection goals that were primed by the experimental manipulation. As in the previous study, low-self-esteem people reported feeling less close than control participants on the explicit self-report measure. However, they were *more positive* than control participants were on the implicit measure of connection. This finding suggests that although the nonconscious goal prime was successful in activating an automatic impulse to draw closer to one's partner, low-self-esteem people overturned this incompatible goal when making explicit responses, and instead acted self-protectively by derogating the importance of their relationships (Murray et al., 2008, Experiment 3).

These corrective processes are evident not just when incongruent goals are activated directly via an experimental manipulation, but also when relationship situations elicit automatic responses that are inconsistent with people's chronic motivational concerns. For example, although becoming close with a partner is highly rewarding, it also imposes constraints on one's autonomy. As interdependence increases, people must, by definition, give up control over their outcomes (Kelley, 1979; Kelley et al., 2003). To maintain commitment in the face of such autonomy concerns, people automatically activate the procedural rule, "If dependent, then justify commitment" (Murray, Holmes, et al., 2009). When such concerns about autonomy are made salient, people automatically seek connection to their partners. For example, participants who were asked to recall a time in which they had concerns about how costly their relationship was to their goal pursuits exhibited faster reaction times when subsequently asked to identity whether or not positive traits (e.g., understanding, warm) were characteristic of their partners. The tendency to heighten positive *implicit* evaluations of romantic partners was not affected by participants' chronic trust.

Again, however, chronic trust seems to moderate the extent to which people deliberately "correct" for this automatic influence at the explicit level. In the same study, high-self-esteem people reported more optimism about their relationships in the autonomy-cost condition relative to control participants, thereby justifying their commitment at the explicit level as well. Because the automatically activated goal was congruent with their chronic motivations to pursue connection with their partners, high-self-esteem people had little need to correct. Thus, their automatic and controlled responses were aligned. Low-self-esteem people, in contrast, did appear to override the influence of automatically activated connection goals. Relative to control participants, low-self-esteem people who recalled autonomy costs reported being *less* optimistic about their relationships. Facing the automatic activation of a goal that is incompatible with chronic self-protective strivings, low-self-esteem people readily seized the opportunity to counteract its influence and derogated their relationship at the explicit level (Murray, Holmes, et al., 2009).

Of course, it is not just low-trust people who utilize an executive control system to prioritize chronic goal strivings. Those high in chronic trust also correct for the influence of automatically activated self-protection goals that sometimes arise in risky relationship contexts. One such instance of this occurs when people are made to feel that they are inferior to their partner. When romantic partners are equitably matched, it is less likely that a partner will attempt to replace one with a more appealing alternative. However, when people feel that they do not match their partner, rejection becomes a very real possibility and presents a great deal of risk. To protect themselves from the doubts that arise with inferiority, people appear to have an automatically activated goal that restores feelings of being irreplaceable, and they often implement this goal by taking action to make their partners more dependent on them. In one illustrative study, concerns about inferiority were aroused implicitly by having participants evaluate the effectiveness of personal ads in which the author of the ad stressed the importance of finding a partner who would be an equitable match. Relative to control participants, those who were exposed to this implicit prime later reported greater feelings of inferiority to their own romantic partners. Moreover, they sought to quell these feelings by behaving in ways that would make them less replaceable, such as assuming responsibility for their partners' day-to-day obligations and duties and restricting their partners' social network, thereby enhancing their importance to their partners and ensuring their partners' continued commitment (Murray, Aloni, et al., 2009).

However, evidence for the "correction" of this automatic impulse as a function of chronic trust was observed in a subsequent study, in which participants were *explicitly* primed with inferiority and thus had greater opportunity to employ corrective processes. That is, when participants were led to believe that partners who matched were more likely to remain married, low-self-esteem people again reported a desire to heighten their partners' dependence and make themselves irreplaceable relative to control participants. Because this self-protective automatic impulse was congruent with their overarching motivational concerns, low-self-esteem people had little impetus to correct. High-self-esteem people, however, did overturn the self-protective impulse aroused by the inferiority prime. Relative to control participants, they reported *less* desire to foster partner dependence when primed with exchange concerns. As their chronic motivational agenda is that of connection, self-protectively making their partners reliant on them is incompatible with these goals, and when they were able to do so, high-self-esteem people overturned this impulse.

Taken together, these results suggest that chronic trust serves an important function in shaping risk regulation processes. Specifically, it serves to ensure that chronic motivational agendas remain prioritized in risky situations. It reconciles motivational conflict in situations that afford pursuit of connection and self-protection relatively equally, and it serves to overturn automatically activated goals when those goals are incongruent with their persistent concerns. However, this process is critically dependent on having sufficient ability to correct. When executive resources are taxed, chronic trust fails to guide risk regulation, and when relationship goals are activated implicitly, the ability to overturn incompatible goals is reduced. This limitation raises an important question: How do people regulate interpersonal risk when they do not have the ability to employ this secondary system? Put another way, how does risk regulation operate at the automatic level?

RISK REGULATION AT THE AUTOMATIC LEVEL

When people are unable to exert executive control, chronic trust has little bearing on their risk regulation behavior. There remains, however, a "smart" unconscious (Murray & Holmes, 2011; Murray, Holmes, & Pinkus, 2010) that guides people toward connection or away from risk as relationship circumstances dictate. As we described in the preceding section, this smart unconscious is sensitive to the relative affordance of connection and self-protection goals in risky interpersonal situations. Situations that pose a relatively high degree of risk afford greater opportunity to pursue self-protection goals and thus are more likely to motivate both high- and low-trust people to guard themselves automatically from hurt. In keeping with this analysis, people who were asked to recall a partner's transgression were faster to identify self-protection words (e.g., *prevent, caution*) on a lexical decision task relative to those in a control condition, indicating greater automatic activation of avoidance-directed goals. This effect was most evident among participants who had not yet forgiven their partners for this transgression, and thus risk was immediate (Murray et al., 2008, Experiment 7).

Similarly, situations that pose a relatively mild degree of risk may afford greater opportunity to afford connectedness goals and allow people to pursue connection and intimacy with their partners automatically, irrespective of chronic trust. In one such study, participants were primed with general interpersonal risk by recalling a time when someone other than their current romantic partner hurt or disappointed them. Although this task may have heightened rejection concerns, such concerns were not immediately tied to the current partner. Participants who completed this task were subsequently faster to respond to words associated with connectedness (e.g., *join, trust*) relative to control participants (Murray et al., 2008, Experiment 1). A second study (Murray et al., 2008, Experiment 2) revealed again that participants exposed to a generalized relationship threat were more willing than control participants to partake in activities that would foster greater interdependence with their current romantic partners, again revealing heightened motivation for connectedness when facing relatively mild interpersonal risk. When the costs of interdependence are low, people seize opportunities to connect with romantic partners and thereby accrue the benefits that accompany connection.

In more ambiguous situations, where risk and reward are commensurate with one another, people may rely on basic associations to direct self-regulatory activity. Evaluative associations that occur at the automatic level generally motivate approach and avoidance behavior. Strong positive associations to specific objects drive people toward those objects, whereas strong negative associations propel people away from those objects (Chen & Bargh, 1999). In a relationship context, more positive associations to one's partner may lead people to automatically pursue connection and intimacy when risk arises, whereas more negative associations may drive people to pursue self-protection goals in the face of risk, especially when they are unable to correct for these impulses by employing executive resources (LeBel & Campbell, 2009; Scinta & Gable, 2007).

Murray et al. (2010) suggested that such implicit associations are formed through actual experience. That is, they proposed that relationship events that escape conscious awareness may nonetheless be encoded by a smart unconscious and that these encodings form the basis of people's automatic evaluative associations with their partners. Relevant evidence was acquired in a longitudinal study of newlywed couples. Murray et al. (2010) examined people's risk regulation behavior over a 14-day span and assessed the frequency with which people found themselves in risky situations (e.g., being criticized by their partner, the partner failing to take one's needs into account). Four years later, the researchers assessed the extent to which people held positive associations toward their partner. Results revealed that the more frequently people found themselves in risky situations, the less positive their associations were 4 years later. However, the way that people responded to such situations also influenced these associations. Those who enacted self-protective behaviors on days following risk (e.g., acting cold and distancing) held more negative automatic associations to their partners 4 years later, whereas those who pursued connectedness on days following risk (e.g., valuing their partner more) had more positive evaluations 4 years later. In addition, explicit feelings of love and satisfaction measured at Time 1 had no bearing on positive associations

4 years later, nor did prior risk regulation behaviors influence these feelings when they were assessed at Time 2. This suggests that risk regulation behavior may have an impact on people's associative evaluations and thereby influence relationship behaviors, even when they appear to have little impact on explicit evaluations.

Because these implicit evaluations are rooted in actual experience, they likely serve as the basis for "impulsive trust" that reflects people's automatic tendency to prioritize connection over self-protection. Indeed, participants who had positive implicit evaluations of a partner established by subliminal conditioning subsequently reported trusting their partners more than control participants did (Murray et al., 2011, Study 2). As unconscious evaluations can diverge from explicit evaluations and have dissociative effects, it is likely that impulsive and reflective trust jointly regulate risk regulation behavior. Specifically, impulsive trust may attenuate the impact of reflective trust in determining how people respond to risk, particularly when people's ability to exert executive control is undermined. This has unique implications for those low in chronic trust. That is, if people low in chronic trust have deliberative concerns about their partner's caring, but at the same time hold incongruent positive attitudes toward their partners, these positive evaluations may drive people toward connection when they are unable to correct for its influence.

Murray et al. (2011) illustrated this joint regulation in a series of studies. In one, participants provided an initial measure of their impulsive trust by completing an implicit association task assessing the extent to which they had positive evaluations of their partners. Following this assessment, participants' reflective trust concerns were undermined by again leading them to believe that they overestimated the quality of their relationships and their partners' responsiveness. Half of the participants then completed a task that reduced their ability to employ executive resources by having them write a story without using the letters *a* or *n* (Schmeichel, 2007), thereby undermining their ability to execute corrective processes. Their automatic motivation to connect with their partners was tapped with an implicit measure that again measured the speed with which they associated partners with positive inter-personal traits.

Results revealed that among participants who had ample executive control, impulsive trust did not predict their automatic tendency to approach their partners in the face of reflective trust concerns. However, among participants whose executive control was undermined by the difficult writing task, impulsive trust overrode reflective trust concerns. Those low in impulsive trust were much less inclined to connect when their reflective trust was threatened relative to control participants, as might be expected. However, those high in impulsive trust actually reported *greater* motivation to approach their partners in the face of reflective trust concerns (relative to control). Thus, impulsive trust served as a resource that minimized the impact of conscious concerns when people had little ability to correct these impulses (Murray et al., 2011, Study 6).

CONCLUSION

Interpersonal risk is a ubiquitous feature of interdependent relationships and thus necessitates a complex regulatory system that governs the pursuit of self-protection and connection goals that satisfy fundamental needs. When people have sufficient cognitive resources, this system employs conscious, deliberative processes to prioritize goals that are congruent with chronic orientations toward connection or self-protection, which vary as a function of chronic trust. However, impulsive trust often provides a basis for directing goal pursuit when people's ability to exert their resources is depleted. Impulsive trust may also shape automatic responses to risk in ways that diverge from more controlled responses. These processes allow the risk regulation system to operate dynamically to assure people that their dependence (or lack thereof) is warranted.

Romantic relationships, perhaps more than other kinds of close relationships, present abundant opportunities for satisfying connection needs (see Chapter 15). Obtaining the rewards, however, often requires people to face substantial risk because a partner's caring can never be absolutely guaranteed. Investigating how people regulate this risk allows us to learn a great deal about how motivation shapes close relationships in unique and sometimes subtle ways. Examining how trust shapes self-regulation at both the automatic and controlled levels of processing, and how these self-regulatory strategies reciprocally shape feelings of trust, will advance our theoretical understanding of interpersonal relationships and perhaps yield a more complete model of how people regulate approach and avoidance conflicts that arise outside relational domains.

REFERENCES

Baumeister, R. F., & Leary, M. R. (1995). The need to belong: Desire for interpersonal attachments as a fundamental human motivation. *Psychological Bulletin, 117*, 497–529. doi:10.1037/0033-2909.117.3.497

Cacioppo, J. T., Gardner, W. L., & Berntson, G. G. (1999). The affect system has parallel and integrative processing components: Form follows function. *Journal of Personality and Social Psychology, 76*, 839–855. doi:10.1037/0022-3514.76.5.839

Campbell, L., Simpson, J. A., Boldry, J. G., & Kashy, D. A. (2005). Perceptions of conflict and support in romantic relationships: The role of attachment anxiety. *Journal of Personality and Social Psychology, 88*, 510–531. doi:10.1037/0022-3514.88.3.510

Cavallo, J. V., Fitzsimons, G. M., & Holmes, J. G. (2009). Taking chances in the face of threat: Romantic risk regulation and approach motivation. *Personality and Social Psychology Bulletin, 35*, 737–751. doi:10.1177/0146167209332742

Cavallo, J. V., Holmes, J. G., Fitzsimons, G. M., Murray, S. L., & Wood, J. V. (2012). Managing motivational conflict: How self-esteem and executive resources influence self-regulatory responses to risk. *Journal of Personality and Social Psychology, 103*, 430–451. doi:10.1037/a0028821

Chen, M. & Bargh, J. A. (1999). Consequences of automatic evaluation: Immediate behavioral predispositions to approach or avoid the stimulus. *Personality and Social Psychology Bulletin, 25*, 215–224. doi:10.1177/0146167299025002007

Collins, N. L., & Feeney, B. C. (2000). A safe haven: Support-seeking and caregiving processes in intimate relationships. *Journal of Personality and Social Psychology, 78*, 1053–1073. doi:10.1037/0022-3514.78.6.1053

Gable, S. L., Reis, H. T., & Elliot, A. J. (2000). Behavioral activation and inhibition in everyday life. *Journal of Personality and Social Psychology, 78*, 1135–1149. doi:10.1037/0022-3514.78.6.1135

Hofmann, W., Gschwendner, T., Friese, M., Wiers, R. W., & Schmitt, M. (2008). Working memory capacity and self-regulatory behavior: Toward an individual differences perspective on behavior determination by automatic versus controlled processes. *Journal of Personality and Social Psychology, 95*, 962–977. doi:10.1037/a0012705

Kelley, H. H. (1979). *Personal relationships: Their structures and processes.* Hillsdale, NJ: Erlbaum.

Kelley, H. H., Holmes, J. G., Kerr, N. L., Reis, H. T., Rusbult, C. E., & Van Lange, P. A. M. (2003). *An atlas of interpersonal situations.* Cambridge, England: Cambridge University Press.

Leary, M. R., & Baumeister, R. F. (2000). The nature and function of self-esteem: Sociometer theory. In M. P. Zanna (Ed.), *Advances in experimental social psychology: Vol. 32* (pp. 1–62). San Diego, CA: Academic Press. doi:10.1016/S0065-2601(00)80003-9

Leary, M. R., Tambor, E. S., Terdal, S. K., & Downs, D. L. (1995). Self-esteem as an interpersonal monitor: The sociometer hypothesis. *Journal of Personality and Social Psychology, 68*, 518–530. doi:10.1037/0022-3514.68.3.518

LeBel, E. P., & Campbell, L. (2009). Implicit partner affect, relationship satisfaction, and the prediction of romantic breakup. *Journal of Experimental Social Psychology, 45*, 1291–1294. doi:10.1016/j.jesp.2009.07.003

MacDonald, G., & Leary, M. R. (2005). Why does social exclusion hurt? The relationship between social and physical pain. *Psychological Bulletin, 131*, 202–223. doi:10.1037/0033-2909.131.2.202

Muraven, M., & Baumeister, R. F. (2000). Self-regulation and depletion of limited resources: Does self-control resemble a muscle? *Psychological Bulletin*, *126*, 247–259. doi:10.1037/0033-2909.126.2.247

Murray, S. L., Aloni, M., Holmes, J. G., Derrick, J. L., Stinson, D. A., & Leder, S. (2009). Fostering partner dependence as trust insurance: The implicit contingencies of the exchange script in close relationships. *Journal of Personality and Social Psychology*, *96*, 324–348. doi:10.1037/a0012856

Murray, S. L., Bellavia, G. M., Rose, P., & Griffin, D. W. (2003). Once hurt, twice hurtful: How perceived regard regulates daily marital interactions. *Journal of Personality and Social Psychology*, *84*, 126–147. doi:10.1037/0022-3514.84.1.126

Murray, S. L., Derrick, J. L., Leder, S., & Holmes, J. G. (2008). Balancing connectedness and self-protection goals in close relationships: A levels-of-processing perspective on risk regulation. *Journal of Personality and Social Psychology*, *94*, 429–459. doi:10.1037/0022-3514.94.3.429

Murray, S. L., Griffin, D. W., Rose, P. & Bellavia, G. M. (2003). Calibrating the sociometer: The relational contingencies of self-esteem. *Journal of Personality and Social Psychology*, *85*, 63–84. doi:10.1037/0022-3514.85.1.63

Murray, S. L., & Holmes, J. G. (2011). *Interdependent minds: The dynamics of close relationships*. New York, NY: Guilford Press.

Murray, S. L., Holmes, J. G., Aloni, M., Pinkus, R. T., Derrick, J. L., & Leder, S. (2009). Commitment insurance: Compensating for the autonomy costs of interdependence in close relationships. *Journal of Personality and Social Psychology*, *97*, 256–278. doi:10.1037/a0014562

Murray, S. L., Holmes, J. G., & Collins, N. L. (2006). Optimizing assurance: The risk regulation system in relationships. *Psychological Bulletin*, *132*, 641–666. doi:10.1037/0033-2909.132.5.641

Murray, S. L., Holmes, J. G., & Pinkus, R. T. (2010). A smart unconscious? Procedural origins of automatic partner attitudes in marriage. *Journal of Experimental Social Psychology*, *46*, 650–656. doi:10.1016/j.jesp.2010.03.003

Murray, S. L., Pinkus, R. T., Holmes, J. G., Harris, B., Gomillion, S., Aloni, M., . . . Leder, S. (2011). Signaling when (and when not) to be cautious and self-protective: Impulsive and reflective trust in close relationships. *Journal of Personality and Social Psychology*, *101*, 485–502. doi:10.1037/a0023233

Murray, S. L., Rose, P., Bellavia, G. M., Holmes, J. G., & Kusche, A. G. (2002). When rejection stings: How self-esteem constrains relationship-enhancement processes. *Journal of Personality and Social Psychology*, *83*, 556–573. doi:10.1037/0022-3514.83.3.556

Rholes, W. S., Simpson, J. A., & Orina, M. M. (1999). Attachment and anger in an anxiety-provoking situation. *Journal of Personality and Social Psychology*, *76*, 940–957. doi:10.1037/0022-3514.76.6.940

Rusbult, C. E., Verette, J., Whitney, G. A., Slovik, L. F., & Lipkus, I. (1991). Accommodation processes in close relationships: Theory and preliminary empirical evidence. *Journal of Personality and Social Psychology, 60,* 53–78. doi:10.1037/0022-3514.60.1.53

Schmeichel, B. J. (2007). Attention control, memory updating, and emotion regulation temporarily reduce the capacity for executive control. *Journal of Experimental Psychology: General, 136,* 241–255. doi:10.1037/0096-3445.136.2.241

Scinta, A., & Gable, S. L. (2007). Implicit attitudes about romantic partners. *Personality and Social Psychology Bulletin, 33,* 1008–1022. doi:10.1177/0146167207301013

Shallcross, S. L., & Simpson, J. A. (2012). Trust and responsiveness in strain-test situations: A dyadic perspective. *Journal of Personality and Social Psychology, 102,* 1031–1044. doi:10.1037/a0026829

Simpson, J. A., Rholes, W. S., & Phillips, D. (1996). Conflict in close relationships: An attachment perspective. *Journal of Personality and Social Psychology, 71,* 899–914. doi:10.1037/0022-3514.71.5.899

Van Lange, P. A. M., Rusbult, C. E., Drigotas, S. M., Arriaga, X. B., Witcher, B. S., & Cox, C. L. (1997). Willingness to sacrifice in close relationships. *Journal of Personality and Social Psychology, 72,* 1373–1395. doi:10.1037/0022-3514.72.6.1373

14

RESPONSIVENESS: AFFECTIVE INTERDEPENDENCE IN CLOSE RELATIONSHIPS

HARRY T. REIS

What makes the behavior of two partners in a close relationship different from the behavior of two independent individuals? The answer to this question, which is fundamental to relationship science, usually involves some sort of mutual influence and interdependence. For example, Kelley (1983) referred to a causal connection between two interacting parties, in the sense that one person's behavior is causally implicated in subsequent changes in the other person. Following this definition, interdependence theorists describe in precise detail how each partner's behavior is affected by the implications of the other's behavior for both of their outcomes (see Rusbult & Van Lange, 1996, for a review). Commonly, studies in this area examine the implications of different types of interdependence for a variety of relationship-relevant behaviors (see Chapters 13, 15, 16, and 17, this volume, for reviews of different types of interdependence).

http://dx.doi.org/10.1037/14250-015
Mechanisms of Social Connection: From Brain to Group, M. Mikulincer and P. R. Shaver (Editors)

Sometimes overlooked in interdependence theorizing is *affective interdependence*—the extent to which emotions and emotional self-regulation are influenced by partners. Yet by almost any definition affective interdependence is a cardinal characteristic of close relationships. Thus, in summing up a series of alternative theoretical positions, Ekman and Davidson (1994) succinctly noted that "emotions are brought into play most often by the actions of others, and, once aroused, emotions influence the course of interpersonal transactions" (p. 139). Reis, Collins, and Berscheid (2000) qualified this conclusion by noting that the others who create these actions and engage in these transactions are usually relationship partners.

Consider these examples of affective interdependence in close relationships. A husband responds angrily when his wife, having had a stressful day at work, barks at him because the house is a mess when she returns home after work. Two parents feel great pride when their child sets a school record in a swimming event. A young woman asks a friend to listen to her describe her feelings about having been dumped by her boyfriend. Two lovers flirt, each taking pleasure in the other's response. An elderly married couple reminisce about life experiences they have shared. A young couple discuss plans for the future, each of them discouraged by the other's lack of interest in his or her most highly valued goals.

What these illustrations have in common is the idea that each person's affective experience is centrally and substantially influenced by the other's behavior. Although a variety of different theoretical models have been proposed to explain these seemingly distinct phenomena, in this chapter, I propose that a common conceptual core links them. I call this core process *perceived partner responsiveness*. The first section of this chapter defines perceived partner responsiveness, explaining how and why it may serve as a core organizing principle for integrating social psychological theories about affective interdependence. In the next section, I illustrate the operation of perceived partner responsiveness with examples from three research programs conducted in our laboratory on (a) the role of perceived partner responsiveness in self-regulation, (b) how partners help each other capitalize on personal positive events, and (c) the role of partners in promoting movement toward personal goals. Throughout this review, for reasons of theoretical clarity, I focus on perceived partner responsiveness and its association with personal and relationship well-being. Nevertheless, because this model considers perceived partner responsiveness to be a product of certain kinds of interpersonal experiences, I also consider actual (or in other words, enacted) partner responsiveness. The chapter concludes with general comments about the value of integrative theoretical models for advancing relationship science.

A GENERAL MODEL OF PERCEIVED PARTNER RESPONSIVENESS

There are many theoretical models in close relationship research that help explain how a partner's behavior influences one's affect. Consider a few selective examples: attachment theory (Mikulincer & Shaver, 2007; see also Chapter 15, this volume); social support (reviewed by Cohen, Underwood, & Gottlieb, 2000); the intimacy process model (Reis & Shaver, 1988); the need to belong (Baumeister & Leary, 1995); communal need satisfaction (Clark & Mills, 2012); the risk regulation model (Murray, Holmes, & Collins, 2006; see also Chapter 13, this volume); trust (Simpson, 2007); partner affirmation, also known as the Michelangelo phenomenon (Rusbult, Finkel, & Kumashiro, 2009); autonomy support (Deci & Ryan, 1987); the temporal interpersonal emotion systems model (Butler, 2011); and emotional acceptance (Jacobson & Christensen, 1998).

Embedded within each of these specific theories is the general idea that when partners are felt to be responding supportively to important needs, goals, values, or preferences in the self-concept, emotional well-being is enhanced and effective emotional self-regulation is facilitated. On the other hand, when partners are seen to be responding critically or when their response is perceived to be controlling or acontingent, emotional well-being suffers and emotional self-regulation is impaired. I refer to these phenomena as perceived partner responsiveness and unresponsiveness.

As Figure 14.1 shows, perceived partner responsiveness is shaped by both intrapersonal and interpersonal forces. The process begins intrapersonally, with a person's own needs, goals, and wishes, such as when one partner in a relationship expresses a need, preference, or aspiration, relates an event for which support or celebration is desired, or otherwise reveals important aspects of the self. (Of course, these intrapersonal factors are often shaped by past relationship experiences; Chen, Boucher, & Tapias, 2006; Mikulincer & Shaver, 2007.) The interpersonal step follows, when the partner enacts a supportive response, which may lead to the perception of responsiveness by the originator. Responses are likely to be perceived as responsive to the extent that they possess three qualities. The first is *understanding*, or whether the partner is believed to have accurately and appropriately "gotten the facts right" about oneself. Understanding matters because it fosters a sense of authenticity (Kernis & Goldman, 2006) and also because the next two factors are predicated on it. The second quality is *validation*, or the belief that a partner values and appreciates one's abilities, traits, and worldview. Validation matters because it conveys the partner's liking for and acceptance of the self (Finkenauer & Righetti, 2011), which supports feelings of belongingness and felt security (Leary & Guadagno, 2008; Murray et al., 2006). The final quality is *caring*, or the confidence that partners will provide help when it

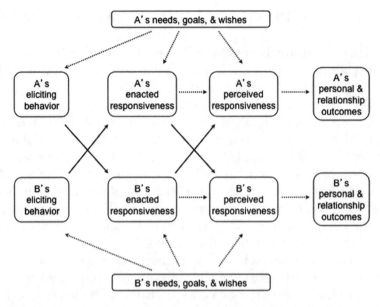

Figure 14.1. The interpersonal model of responsiveness. Interpersonal processes are denoted by solid arrows; intrapersonal process by dotted arrows. From *The Oxford Handbook of Close Relationships* (p. 401), by J. A. Simpson & L. Campbell, 2013. Copyright Oxford University Press. Adapted with permission.

is needed, which demonstrates their concern for one's well-being (Clark & Mills, 2012).

Of course, the process may not unfold as straightforwardly as Figure 14.1 implies. One partner might reveal needs, but the other partner might not respond supportively. More pointedly, even if the responding partner behaves supportively, as an independent observer might verify, the disclosing partner might misperceive this responsiveness, reflecting the impact of motivated biases on social perception. As I argue later in this chapter, there is good reason to believe that both actual responsiveness and motivated interpretation influence perceived partner responsiveness (Reis & Clark, in press). However, from a theoretical standpoint, emotional responses to the sorts of sequences depicted in Figure 14.1 are based on what is perceived, rather than what is enacted. In other words, the emotions that result from the unfolding of the disclosure-and-response process depend on whether the perceiver believes that the partner's response has been understanding, validating, and caring, or misinformed, unappreciative, and uncaring.

In a relationship, this sequence necessarily influences both partners' affects, but I have omitted those links for simplicity. It nevertheless should be acknowledged that successfully providing responsiveness is likely to foster positive emotions in its own right, and will encourage partners to initiate these sequences on their own. Similarly, there is ample evidence that recipients of responsiveness are likely to be responsive when reversing roles with their supporters. The converse is also true: Failed or inadequate attempts to elicit or provide responsiveness are likely to foster negative emotions and to discourage role reversal in subsequent interactions.

PERCEIVED PARTNER RESPONSIVENESS AND SELF-REGULATION

Self-regulation refers to people's attempts to modify or control their own thoughts, feelings, and behavior in order to achieve desired outcomes or to make progress toward valued goals. Of the many factors that affect self-regulation, some of the most influential concern feedback and support from significant others (see Chapter 5, this volume). Theoretically, the self-regulatory value of support can be traced to the intrinsically social nature of our species. The human brain evolved to facilitate bonding as a central means for addressing adaptive problems associated with survival and reproduction (see Chapter 2). Thus, we have been endowed with various specific mechanisms that help us live and work together with other people, coordinating our activities to accomplish mutually desired goals. Among these are several familiar mechanisms from the social psychological literature. For example, the perceived availability of social support facilitates effective coping with stress (Stroebe & Stroebe, 1996). Feeling valued and accepted by others is associated with emotional well-being and persistence on various tasks (Leary & Guadagno, 2008). Particularly well documented is evidence that the actual or symbolic availability of attachment figures engenders better emotional health, greater compassion and caring for others, and more effective exploration (Feeney & Thrush, 2010; Mikulincer & Shaver, 2007; see also Chapters 15 and 16).

Perceived partner responsiveness is central to all of these mechanisms. Knowing that a partner has one's back—in other words, that he or she will be available if needed and is willing to provide nurturance or assistance, even if it were to be costly—gives people the emotional wherewithal to deal with challenges and the security to interact with others confidently and nondefensively. Describing this general sense in terms of perceived partner responsiveness focuses attention on the three components depicted in Figure 14.1. Thus, understanding indicates that the partner has an accurate view of oneself, of one's needs and fears, of what one intends to make happen, and of what one is capable of doing. Validation signifies the partner's esteem, implying that he or she would sacrifice self-interest for the good of the relationship (Murray & Holmes, 2011). Caring directly implicates the partner's active concern for one's well-being. All of these together make the symbolic or actual support of a responsive other credible and trustworthy.

Research conducted in our laboratory over the past decade broadly supports this conclusion. For example, perceived partner responsiveness is associated with better sleep quality in married couples (Carmichael & Reis, 2005) and healthier, more positive attitudes toward sex, especially among women (Birnbaum & Reis, 2006). Both of these can be considered examples of effective self-regulation in a relationship context, inasmuch as anxiety about a partner's acceptance and support would undermine that activity. In the achievement domain, perceived partner responsiveness also predicts better engagement and performance. In a series of studies, Elliot and Reis (2003) showed that college students who felt that attachment figures were responsive and supportive viewed their college courses as challenging more than threatening, and exhibited higher achievement motivation, lower fear of failure, and more approach-oriented (as opposed to avoidance-oriented) motives about school work. In an unpublished study, Caprariello and Reis (2006) found the same pattern with regard to college athletes' participation in competitive athletics.

Responsiveness is usually studied in the context of intimate relationships, but it also applies in less personal relationships. Reis et al. (2008) surveyed 819 individuals in three countries (the United States, Canada, and the United Kingdom) about the extent to which they felt that their primary care physician was responsive to their needs and concerns, and was genuinely interested in their thoughts and feelings. Despite marked differences in the patient–physician relationship in these very different health care systems, perceived physician responsiveness predicted subjective health in each country (even after controlling for gender, age, marital status, years as a patient, and general satisfaction with that physician). This finding meshes well with research on patient-centered communication (i.e., a communication process between physician and patient that emphasizes responsiveness, openness, and active participation by the patient in all decisions), which consistently produces higher patient satisfaction (Epstein & Street, 2007) and lower costs (Epstein et al., 2005).

The most direct research linking perceived partner responsiveness to self-regulation is experimental. Caprariello and Reis (2011) examined the possibility that simply thinking about responsive partners can provide an adaptive resource under threatening circumstances. One of their studies examined self-handicapping, a defensive reaction to the prospect of ego-deflating failure. Participants in this research were led to believe that they would be videotaped in a stressful subtraction race—counting backwards as quickly as possible from 1,978 by a random two-digit number. Beforehand, they were asked to write a brief essay about someone whom they felt was a responsive partner (defined as above), or, in three control conditions, a friend who was not particularly responsive but with whom they had fun, an acquaintance, or an object that helped organize their daily activities. Participants were then given a checklist of 14 external circumstances (e.g., "insufficient rest") that might hamper their performance in the subtraction race, a standard measure of self-handicapping. The more reasons checked off, the more defensive the response—that is, the greater the desire to rationalize in advance the possibility of poor performance. As expected, in the three control conditions, the more threatened participants felt, the more they self-handicapped. But in the responsiveness-priming condition, higher perceptions of threat were associated with lesser self-handicapping, presumably because these participants had readily accessible images of a supportive, caring partner.

This experiment, along with others in a similar vein (Kumashiro & Sedikides, 2005; Mikulincer & Shaver, 2007; Selcuk, Zayas, Günaydin, Hazan, & Kross, 2012), indicates that perceived partner responsiveness provides a valuable resource for adaptive self-regulation.

PERCEIVED PARTNER RESPONSIVENESS AND CAPITALIZING ON POSITIVE EVENTS

Responsiveness is usually studied in the context of negative events—for example, how partners react when one seeks help in coping with a stressful event or how they react to conflict or requests for change or when one partner's sense of felt security has been threatened. Undoubtedly, such circumstances are critical for establishing and maintaining responsiveness in relationships. Nevertheless, the field's emphasis on problems, conflicts, and threat may have obscured the impact of more positive events. Relationships, after all, are not just about fixing problems and dealing with stress, they are also about sharing joy, jointly pursuing valued goals, and promoting growth as an individual and as a couple.

For the past decade or so, we have been exploring a phenomenon we call *capitalization* (see Gable & Reis, 2010, for a review). First described by Langston (1994), capitalization in interpersonal contexts refers to the process of conveying personal good news to other persons. Such conversations initiate a process that has both personal and relational implications. Although on the surface, capitalization attempts focus on the transmission of information to other persons, the interpersonal substance of these interactions depends on the emotions and sense of interdependence experienced during the exchange

(Rimé, 2007). Capitalization attempts do not guarantee responsiveness, of course; they merely create the possibility of an encouraging partner response. After all, partners may or may not display an awareness of, and a willingness to support, the other's aspirations and accomplishments. Partners may experience ambivalence, envy, or indifference; the event may amplify conflicts of interest; or it may threaten stable patterns of interaction (e.g., altering their relative status or availability). In other words, responsiveness to capitalization attempts may be diagnostic of a partner's regard for the self, just as it is in conflictual interactions.

Capitalization attempts can be considered as stimuli that afford partners the opportunity to demonstrate responsiveness. Enthusiastic or otherwise supportive responses signal the listener's interest in the capitalizer's growth and well-being. Such responsiveness begets appreciation and caring, and thereby increases the likelihood of reciprocated propartner behavior. Propartner behaviors are associated with a variety of affective outcomes, such as satisfaction and commitment, and behavioral outcomes, such as trust, accommodation, and the willingness to sacrifice. On the other hand, a partner's nonresponsiveness—for example, emotional disengagement or criticism—implies disinterest in one's well-being and growth and is likely to create distance and *mutual cyclical deterioration* (a mutually self-perpetuating reluctance to enact prorelational behaviors with the partner).

In several studies and experiments, we have shown that responsiveness has clear personal benefit for capitalizers: It enhances the memorability, perceived significance, and emotional appreciation of positive events (Gable, Reis, Impett, & Asher, 2004; Reis et al., 2010). In this chapter, I want to focus on the interpersonal benefits of perceived partner responsiveness to capitalization attempts.

Our earliest studies examined perceptions of how partners generally respond to being told about one's good news, using the Perceived Responses to Capitalization Attempts scale (Gable et al., 2004). This scale presents participants with the stem "When I tell my partner about something good that happened to me" and asks them to rate 12 statements according to how well it describes their relationship. Sample items include *My partner usually reacts to my good fortune enthusiastically* (scored positively) and *Sometimes I get the impression that he/she doesn't care much* (scored negatively). In several college student and middle-aged community samples, the perception of enthusiastic, engaged partners' responses was associated with higher relationship satisfaction, intimacy, and, in a daily diary study, more frequent positive interactions. In contrast, the perception of passive or destructive responses was associated with lower satisfaction and intimacy and fewer positive interactions (Gable et al., 2004; Reis et al., 2010). These findings are unlikely to be due entirely to motivated perception or response bias. In several laboratory-observation studies,

Gable and her colleagues have shown that coding by independent observers of partner responsiveness to capitalization attempts predicted relationship well-being and stability at later times (Gable, Gonzaga, & Strachman, 2006; Gable, Gosnell, Maisel, & Strachman, 2012). Also, in another set of studies from our laboratory, Shannon Smith has shown that responders to capitalization attempts show similar benefits to capitalizers.

Affective interdependence implies something more than good feelings, however. Our model of capitalization and responsiveness suggests that supportive responses should lead to the inference that a partner has one's best interest at heart, an attribution that is central to trust. Reis et al. (2010) tested this idea experimentally. In a capitalization condition, participants described to an interviewer one of the best events to have happened to them in the past few years. The interviewer was trained to respond with interest and enthusiasm (e.g., "Wow, that's really great," "What a great opportunity"). In one control condition, the interviewer simply took notes, offering minimal commentary. In another control condition, participants described a series of Dr. Seuss pictures that the interviewer had to draw (without seeing the picture directly), a highly enjoyable, engaging activity (Fraley & Aron, 2004). Both mood and liking for the interviewer were significantly higher in the capitalization and fun conditions than in the notes condition. More important, trust, responsiveness, and the willingness to disclose sensitive personal information were significantly higher in the capitalization condition than in either of the other two conditions. In short, responsive listening builds trust and intimacy, not just liking.

We obtained conceptually similar results in a daily diary study. Participants in this research nominated a target person—someone with whom they were close and likely to interact every day of the 14-day diary period. Each day, in addition to describing the best thing that happened on that day, participants also reported whether they had informed their target person about those events and, if they had, how the target had responded. Elsewhere in the diary, they described their relationship with the target on that day along several dimensions that indicate willingness to enact *prorelationship transformations*—specifically, how nice, accommodating, and willing to sacrifice they had been toward the target—key markers of constructive interdependence (e.g., Rusbult, Verette, Whitney, Slovik, & Lipkus, 1991). As expected, perceiving the partner's response to one's good news as enthusiastic led to significantly more favorable prorelationship orientations. Because these analyses control for the prior day's orientation, they show how relationships change from one day to the next, rather than describe stable attributes of individuals or relationships.

One final point in this section: Sharing affect about personal positive events is one way that partners can promote positive interdependence in their relationship—in other words, by "including the other in the self," each may share to some extent in the other's positive experiences. Such sharing may be particularly valuable in helping to repair the damage done by annoyances, conflicts, and other threats to relationship security. We reasoned that self-esteem might moderate people's ability to take advantage of this tactic. Prior research has shown that people with low self-esteem react to relationship threats by distancing themselves from their partners, whereas people with high self-esteem attempt to move closer (see Chapter 13 for a review). Consistent with this logic, after priming with relationship threat (in a field experiment) or on days following relationship conflict (in a daily diary study), people with low self-esteem perceived less partner enthusiasm about a personal positive event, but high-self-esteem persons perceived more partner enthusiasm. (Self-esteem had no impact following a neutral prime or no-conflict days.) In other words, the effectiveness of perceived responsiveness to capitalization attempts as a strategy for repairing relationships following threat appears to depend on self-esteem.

RESPONSIVENESS AND INTERDEPENDENCE: MUTUAL CYCLICAL GROWTH

Up to this point, I have focused on perceived partner responsiveness. The model depicted in Figure 14.1 is actually somewhat more interpersonal than this, proposing that the sequence begins when one party expresses a need or desire in which the other might be helpful and continues only when the other party enacts a supportive response. Partners do not always react supportively, of course, and supportive responses are sometimes misperceived. However, for this model to be truly interpersonal and interactional, it must consider how real partner behaviors contribute to perceived partner responsiveness.

Why should actual interactions matter? Perceived partner responsiveness is to some extent an attribution, as Kelley (1979) first suggested: When one partner demonstrates a willingness to set aside his or her own preferences and instead prioritize the other's needs and interests, an observer is led to the logical inference of caring and concern, the fundamental property of a communal relationship (Clark & Mills, 2012). These inferences must have some basis in fact. If motivated perception were fundamentally out of touch with social reality, it would not well serve people's basic goals and motivational purposes. This is what Bowlby (1973) meant when he observed that "the varied expectations of the accessibility and responsiveness of attachment figures that different individuals develop during the years of immaturity are tolerably accurate reflections of the experiences those individuals have actually had" (p. 202). In line with his proposal, many studies show that perceptions of responsiveness and support tend to be grounded in partners' actual behavior (see Reis & Clark, in press, for a summary).

Acknowledging the interactional grounding of perceived partner responsiveness may help us appreciate its role in *mutual cyclical growth*—a process by which, in a close relationship, each partner's support of the other's goals and aspirations builds trust and personal development for both (Wieselquist, Rusbult, Foster, & Agnew, 1999). This is a central concern in any interdependent relationship. Trust develops when each partner feels confident that the other will take his or her best interests into account (Holmes & Rempel, 1989)—in other words, that the partner's motives and behavior toward oneself are benevolent and caring. In turn, perceiving this benevolence motivates reciprocal benevolence and caring, setting off the chain-like sequence of mutual cyclical growth. Perceiving a lack of benevolence of course has the opposite effect. Only by highlighting the interactional components of this process is it possible to see how the process unfolds cyclically, from one partner to the other, and over time.

Responsiveness plays an important role in this process, as depicted in Figure 14.2. People learn to trust their partners when they observe those partners behaving well in diagnostic situations—that is, when partners are perceived to be behaving responsively at some personal cost to themselves (Holmes & Rempel, 1989; Simpson, 2007). Trust fosters commitment, because people are more willing to depend on partners who have exhibited

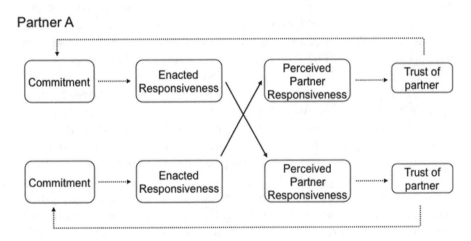

Partner A

Partner B

Figure 14.2. Responsiveness and the process of mutual cyclical growth in close relationships. From *The Oxford Handbook of Close Relationships* (p. 412), by J. A. Simpson & L. Campbell, 2013. Copyright Oxford University Press. Adapted with permission.

concern for their well-being. Commitment, in turn, promotes enactment of responsive behavior for three reasons: because of reciprocity norms, because of the affectionate bond that perceived responsiveness fosters, and because committed partners have a long-term interest in ensuring that their partners' needs are met. Thus, Figure 14.2 proposes that one partner's enacted responsiveness encourages the other's trust and commitment, which leads the other to be open about needs and wishes, and to be reciprocally responsive, and so on.

From an interactional perspective, the key step in this process is the link between enacted and perceived responsiveness. Madoka Kumashiro, Caryl Rusbult, and I investigated this link in three studies: an 18-month longitudinal study in which relevant variables were assessed every 6 months, a 10-day daily diary study, and a laboratory observational study of couples' discussions of their goals for the next 5 to 10 years. In all three studies, we conducted actor–partner interdependence modeling, which controlled for dyadic dependency in the data and, more importantly, allowed us to compare the impact of own behavior and partner behavior on perceived responsiveness. In all three studies, one partner's enacted responsiveness significantly predicted the other's perceived responsiveness. This result was obtained not only for participants' reports of their enacted behaviors but also for coding by independent observers in the laboratory study.

It bears mention that these analyses considered several important alternatives and moderators that have been suggested by other researchers. For example, Lemay, Clark, and Feeney (2007) proposed that perceived responsiveness is influenced by projection—that people infer their partner's responsiveness from their own levels of responsiveness to that partner, presumably reflecting assumed reciprocity. Indeed, we found evidence of projection in all three studies. Nevertheless, even after controlling for projection, the impact of partner's enacted responsiveness on perceived responsiveness was still significant. We also looked for potential moderators, such as sex, marital satisfaction, and social desirability. None of these influenced the basic findings.

A noteworthy feature of these studies is that whereas most studies examine perceived responsiveness in prevention contexts—how partners help each other deal with stress or how they resolve conflict—these studies adopted a promotion context by considering how enacted partner responsiveness helps people make progress toward their valued goals and aspirations. As argued earlier in this chapter, in the ideal case, responsiveness indicates the partner's concern for one's growth and well-being. But does this concern actually help partners accomplish their goals? Two of these studies included measures that tracked goal progress from one assessment to the next. Prospective longitudinal analyses showed that responsiveness at one assessment predicted positive movement toward goals at the next assessment. Mediational analyses indicated that responsiveness helped participants expend greater effort in pursuing their goals, presumably because a responsive partner provides the safety net needed to confidently strive, rather than impelled participants to protect the self against the implications of failure or to devote extra time and effort toward relationship maintenance. It may be, then, that partner responsiveness is an effective strategy for outsourcing the preservation and enhancement of self-regulatory resources (see Chapter 5).

CONCLUSION

Responsiveness is often described as a key contributor to relationship development and maintenance. For example, responsiveness, in the sense of thoughtful appraisal and support of a child's needs and goals, is widely considered a central component of good parenting from infancy on (e.g., Dix, 1992; see also Chapter 7, this volume). Communication studies identify understanding, acceptance, and support as hallmarks of effective communication (e.g., Burleson & MacGeorge, 2002). Communal relationships, which are in many ways the prototype of closeness, are defined by responsiveness to needs (Clark & Mills, 2012). In attachment theory, responsiveness is what makes an attachment figure successful in fulfilling the functions of the attachment behavioral system (see Chapter 15).

It may seem curious to onlookers that these traditions of research have evolved more or less distinctly from one another. Rarely do researchers consider how these various elements might be integrated into a systematic, coherent account. Elsewhere I have argued that for relationship science to take the next step toward becoming a mature, cumulative science, we will need to do a better job of linking our various strands of research to one another— that is, of identifying "core ideas, the principles that make them cohere, and [thereby providing] an organizational framework for understanding how the many empirical pieces interconnect" (Reis, 2007, p. 9). Appreciating how the parts relate to the whole can help establish a nomological network of systematically related constructs, processes, and theories, something that mature sciences have. Relationship research is often described (and taught) as a large, horizontal assemblage of theories and findings, each part conveying something useful about relationships yet remaining separate from other parts. To be sure, specialization and diversity are essential in science, but for our knowledge base to evolve in a more vertical direction, we will need to attend more closely to how our findings and theories connect.

I believe that responsiveness has the potential to be an umbrella construct of this sort. The belief that relationship partners are attentive to and behaviorally supportive of core features of the self, and the foundation of that belief in actual interactions, represents a basic theme in many processes and theoretical models (as I have tried to illustrate by describing three research programs). Responsiveness is an especially clear theme in studies of affect in relationships. Affective interdependence is one of the most striking features of close relationships in everyday life—our emotional lives are intrinsically and often profoundly influenced by the behavior of close others. When we strive to regulate those emotions, our strategies and tactics often revolve around others, notably how we anticipate and perceive their responses to our expression of emotion. Thus, to seek to understand affective interdependence is to consider how responsiveness influences emotional experience.

REFERENCES

Baumeister, R. F., & Leary, M. R. (1995). The need to belong: Desire for interpersonal attachments as a fundamental human motivation. *Psychological Bulletin, 117*, 497–529. doi:10.1037/0033-2909.117.3.497

Birnbaum, G. E., & Reis, H. T. (2006). Women's sexual working models: An evolutionary-attachment perspective. *Journal of Sex Research, 43*, 328–342. doi:10.1080/00224490609552332

Bowlby, J. (1973). *Attachment and loss: Vol. 2. Separation: Anxiety and anger.* New York, NY: Basic Books.

Burleson, B. R., & MacGeorge, E. L. (2002). Supportive communication. In M. L. Knapp & J. A. Daly (Eds.), *Handbook of interpersonal communication* (3rd ed., pp. 374–424). Thousand Oaks, CA: Sage.

Butler, E. A. (2011). Temporal interpersonal emotion systems: The "TIES" that form relationships. *Personality and Social Psychology Review, 15*, 367–393. doi:10.1177/1088868311411164

Caprariello, P., & Reis, H. T. (2006). *Attachment, exploration, and participation in sports.* Unpublished manuscript, University of Rochester, Rochester, NY.

Caprariello, P. A., & Reis, H. T. (2011). Perceived partner responsiveness minimizes defensive reactions to failure. *Social Psychological and Personality Science, 2*, 365–372. doi:10.1177/1948550610391914

Carmichael, C. L., & Reis, H. T. (2005). Attachment, sleep quality, and depressed affect. *Health Psychology, 24*, 526–531. doi:10.1037/0278-6133.24.5.526

Chen, S., Boucher, H. C., & Tapias, M. P. (2006). The relational self revealed: Integrative conceptualization and implications for interpersonal Life. *Psychological Bulletin, 132*, 151–179. doi:10.1037/0033-2909.132.2.151

Clark, M. S., & Mills, J. R. (2012). A theory of communal (and exchange) relationships. In P. A. M. Van Lange, A. W. Kruglanski, & E. T. Higgins (Eds.), *Handbook of theories of social psychology* (Vol. 2, pp. 232–250). Thousand Oaks, CA: Sage.

Cohen, S., Underwood, L. G., & Gottlieb, B. H. (2000). *Social support measurement and intervention: A guide for health and social scientists.* New York, NY: Oxford University Press.

Deci, E. L., & Ryan, R. M. (1987). The support of autonomy and the control of behavior. *Journal of Personality and Social Psychology, 53,* 1024–1037. doi:10.1037/ 0022-3514.53.6.1024

Dix, T. (1992). Parenting on behalf of the child: Empathic goals in the regulation of responsive parenting. In I. E. Sigel, A. V. McGillicuddy-DeLisi, & J. J. Goodnow (Eds.), *Parental belief systems: The psychological consequences for children* (2nd ed., pp. 319–346). Hillsdale, NJ: Erlbaum.

Ekman, P., & Davidson, R. J. (Eds.). (1994). *The nature of emotion: Fundamental questions.* New York, NY: Oxford University Press.

Elliot, A. J., & Reis, H. T. (2003). Attachment and exploration in adulthood. *Journal of Personality and Social Psychology, 85,* 317–331. doi:10.1037/0022-3514. 85.2.317

Epstein, R. M., Franks, P., Shields, C. G., Meldrum, S. C., Miller, K. N., Campbell, T. L., & Fiscella, K. (2005). Patient-centered communication and diagnostic testing. *Annals of Family Medicine, 3,* 415–421. doi:10.1370/afm.348

Epstein, R. M., & Street, R. L. (2007). *Patient-centered communication in cancer care: Promoting healing and reducing suffering.* Bethesda, MD: National Cancer Institute.

Feeney, B. C., & Thrush, R. L. (2010). Relationship influences on exploration in adulthood: The characteristics and function of a secure base. *Journal of Personality and Social Psychology, 98,* 57–76. doi:10.1037/a0016961

Finkenauer, C., & Righetti, F. (2011). Understanding in close relationships: An interpersonal approach. *European Review of Social Psychology, 22,* 316–363. doi:10.1080/10463283.2011.633384

Fraley, B., & Aron, A. (2004). The effect of a shared humorous experience on closeness in initial encounters. *Personal Relationships, 11,* 61–78. doi:10.1111/ j.1475-6811. 2004.00071.x

Gable, S. L., Gonzaga, G. C., & Strachman, A. (2006). Will you be there for me when things go right? Supportive responses to positive event disclosures. *Journal of Personality and Social Psychology, 91,* 904–917. doi:10.1037/0022-3514.91.5.904

Gable, S. L., Gosnell, C. L., Maisel, N. C., & Strachman, A. (2012). Safely testing the alarm: Close others' responses to personal positive events. *Journal of Personality and Social Psychology, 103,* 963–981. doi:10.1037/a0029488

Gable, S. L., & Reis, H. T. (2010). Good news! Capitalizing on positive events in an interpersonal context. In M. P. Zanna (Ed.), *Advances in experimental social psychology* (Vol. 42, pp. 195–257). San Diego, CA: Academic Press. doi:10.1016/ S0065-2601(10)42004-3

Gable, S. L., Reis, H. T., Impett, E. A., & Asher, E. R. (2004). What do you do when things go right? The intrapersonal and interpersonal benefits of sharing positive events. *Journal of Personality and Social Psychology, 87,* 228–245. doi:10.1037/ 0022-3514.87.2.228

Holmes, J. G., & Rempel, J. K. (1989). Trust in close relationships. In C. Hendrick (Ed.), *Review of personality and social psychology: Vol. 10. Close relationships* (pp. 187–220). London, England: Sage.

Jacobson, N. S., & Christensen, A. (1998). *Acceptance and change in couple therapy: A therapist's guide to transforming relationships*. New York, NY: Norton.

Kelley, H. H. (1979). *Personal relationships: Their structures and processes*. Hillsdale, NJ: Erlbaum.

Kelley, H. H. (1983). Analyzing close relationships. In H. H. Kelley, E. Berscheid, A. Christensen, J. H. Harvey, T. L. Huston, G. Levinger, . . . Peterson, D. L. (Eds.), *Close relationships* (pp. 20–67). New York, NY: Freeman.

Kernis, M. H., & Goldman, B. M. (2006). *A multicomponent conceptualization of authenticity: Theory and research*. In M. P. Zanna (Ed.), *Advances in experimental social psychology* (Vol. 38, pp. 283–357). San Diego, CA: Academic Press. doi:10.1016/S0065-2601(06)38006-9

Kumashiro, M., & Sedikides, C. (2005). Taking on board liability-focused feedback: Close positive relationships as a self-bolstering resource. *Psychological Science, 16*, 732–739. doi:10.1111/j.1467-9280.2005.01603.x

Langston, C. A. (1994). Capitalizing on and coping with daily-life events: Expressive responses to positive events. *Journal of Personality and Social Psychology, 67*, 1112–1125. doi:10.1037/0022-3514.67.6.1112

Leary, M. R., & Guadagno, J. (2008). The sociometer, self-esteem, and the regulation of interpersonal behavior. In R. F. Baumeister & K. D. Vohs (Eds.), *Handbook of self-regulation: Research, theory, and applications* (pp. 339–354). New York, NY: Guilford Press.

Lemay, E. P., Jr., Clark, M. S., & Feeney, B. C. (2007). Projection of responsiveness to needs and the construction of satisfying communal relationships. *Journal of Personality and Social Psychology, 92*, 834–853. doi:10.1037/0022-3514.92.5.834

Mikulincer, M., & Shaver, P. R. (2007). *Attachment patterns in adulthood: Structure, dynamics, and change*. New York, NY: Guilford Press.

Murray, S. L., & Holmes, J. G. (2011). *Interdependent minds: The dynamics of close relationships*. New York, NY: Guilford Press.

Murray, S. L., Holmes, J. G., & Collins, N. L. (2006). Optimizing assurance: The risk regulation system in relationships. *Psychological Bulletin, 132*, 641–666. doi:10.1037/0033-2909.132.5.641

Reis, H. T. (2007). Steps toward the ripening of relationship science. *Personal Relationships, 14*, 1–23. doi:10.1111/j.1475-6811.2006.00139.x

Reis, H. T., & Clark, M. S. (in press). Responsiveness. In J. A. Simpson & L. Campbell (Eds.), *The Oxford handbook of close relationships*. New York, NY: Oxford University Press.

Reis, H. T., Clark, M. S., Pereira Gray, D. J., Tsai, F.-F., Brown, J. B., Stewart, M., & Underwood, L. G. (2008). Measuring responsiveness in the therapeutic relationship: A patient perspective. *Basic and Applied Social Psychology, 30*, 339–348. doi:10.1080/01973530802502275

Reis, H. T., Collins, W. A., & Berscheid, E. (2000). The relationship context of human behavior and development. *Psychological Bulletin, 126*, 844–872. doi:10.1037/0033-2909.126.6.844

Reis, H. T., & Shaver, P. R. (1988). Intimacy as an interpersonal process. In S. Duck (Ed.), *Handbook of personal relationships: Theory, research and interventions* (pp. 367–389). Chichester, England: Wiley.

Reis, H. T., Smith, S. M., Carmichael, C. L., Caprariello, P. A., Tsai, F.-F., Rodrigues, A., & Maniaci, M. R. (2010). Are you happy for me? How sharing positive events with others provides personal and interpersonal benefits. *Journal of Personality and Social Psychology, 99*, 311–329. doi:10.1037/a0018344

Rimé, B. (2007). Interpersonal emotion regulation. In J. J. Gross (Ed.), *Handbook of emotion regulation* (pp. 466–485). New York, NY: Guilford Press.

Rusbult, C. E., Finkel, E. J., & Kumashiro, M. (2009). The Michelangelo phenomenon. *Current Directions in Psychological Science, 18*, 305–309. doi:10.1111/j.1467-8721.2009.01657.x

Rusbult, C. E., & Van Lange, P. A. M. (1996). Interdependence processes. In E. T. Higgins & A. Kruglanski (Eds.), *Social psychology: Handbook of basic principles* (pp. 564–596). New York, NY: Guilford Press.

Rusbult, C. E., Verette, J., Whitney, G. A., Slovik, L. F., & Lipkus, I. (1991). Accommodation processes in close relationships: Theory and preliminary empirical evidence. *Journal of Personality and Social Psychology, 60*, 53–78. doi:10.1037/ 0022-3514.60.1.53

Selcuk, E., Zayas, V., Günaydin, G., Hazan, C., & Kross, E. (2012). Mental representations of attachment figures facilitate recovery following upsetting autobiographical memory recall. *Journal of Personality and Social Psychology, 103*, 362–378. doi:10.1037/a0028125

Simpson, J. A. (2007). Foundations of interpersonal trust. In A. W. Kruglanski & E. T. Higgins (Eds.), *Social psychology: Handbook of basic principles* (2nd ed., pp. 587–607). New York, NY: Guilford Press.

Stroebe, W., & Stroebe, M. (1996). The social psychology of social support. In E. T. Higgins & A. W. Kruglanski (Eds.), *Social psychology: Handbook of basic principles* (pp. 597–621). New York, NY: Guilford Press.

Wieselquist, J., Rusbult, C. E., Foster, C. A., & Agnew, C. R. (1999). Commitment, pro-relationship behavior, and trust in close relationships. *Journal of Personality and Social Psychology, 77*, 942–966. doi:10.1037/0022-3514.77.5.942

15

ATTACHMENT BONDS IN ROMANTIC RELATIONSHIPS

PHILLIP R. SHAVER AND MARIO MIKULINCER

In his exposition of attachment theory, Bowlby (1973, 1980, 1982) emphasized the importance to emotion regulation, psychological well-being, and mental health of relational bonds with people who are available, sensitive, and supportive in times of need. (Bowlby called these people *attachment figures*.) Having these relational bonds allows a person of any age to cope constructively with stressful events, maintain self-esteem and emotional stability, and venture into the world confidently in ways that foster autonomy and psychological growth.

Originally, attachment theory (Bowlby, 1982) was formulated to explain infant–parent emotional bonding and its anxiety-buffering and growth-promoting functions in infancy and childhood. However, on the basis of Bowlby's (1979) claim that attachment needs are active "from the cradle to the grave" (p. 129), Shaver, Hazan, and Bradshaw (1988) proposed that romantic relationships in adulthood can be conceptualized as involving attachment bonds that function to regulate distress and provide a secure base for continued

http://dx.doi.org/10.1037/14250-016

Mechanisms of Social Connection: From Brain to Group, M. Mikulincer and P. R. Shaver (Editors)

psychological growth and increasing maturity and autonomy. Our goal in the present chapter is to summarize what has been learned about this extension of attachment theory during the last 25 years and examine in more detail the extent to which romantic relationships serve attachment functions.

We begin the chapter by briefly describing the core concepts of attachment theory and explaining how we think a close relationship partner in adolescence or adulthood can become a person's primary attachment figure. We review research showing that interactions with romantic partners affect distress regulation and psychological growth, as attachment theory would lead us to expect. And we discuss research showing that the potential or actual loss of a romantic relationship often produces severe emotional dysregulation until a person's hierarchy of attachment figures is reorganized. We focus here mainly on the normative aspects of romantic relationships, but we also devote some attention to individual differences arising from differences in people's histories with attachment figures.

ATTACHMENT THEORY: BASIC CONCEPTS

Bowlby (1982) proposed that human infants are born with an innate psychobiological system (which he called the *attachment behavioral system*) that motivates them to seek proximity to supportive others (attachment figures) as a means of protecting themselves from physical and psychological threats and promoting affect regulation, well-being, and increasing self-efficacy. Bowlby speculated that the need to seek and maintain proximity to attachment figures evolved biologically because of children's prolonged dependence on "stronger and wiser" others, usually parents, who can defend children from predators and other dangers while supporting their gradual physical and cognitive development (see Chapter 5, this volume). Although the attachment system is most critical during the early years of life, Bowlby (1988) assumed that it is active over the entire life span and especially within relational bonds in adulthood.

The main goal of the attachment system is to sustain a sense of safety or security (called *felt security* by Sroufe & Waters, 1977), based on beliefs that the world is generally safe, that the self is competent and lovable, and that key others will be available and supportive in times of need. This system is activated by events that threaten the sense of security, such as encountering actual or symbolic threats or noticing that an attachment figure is not sufficiently near, interested, or responsive. In such cases, a person is automatically motivated to seek and reestablish actual or symbolic proximity to an attachment figure (the attachment system's primary operating strategy). These bids for proximity persist until protection and security are attained.

The attachment system is then deactivated, and the person can calmly and coherently return to other activities, which Bowlby thought were motivated by other behavioral systems such as exploration and affiliation.

Beyond describing universal aspects of the attachment system, Bowlby (1973) described individual differences in the system's functioning. Interactions with attachment figures who are generally available in times of need, and who are sensitive and responsive to bids for proximity and support, promote a stable sense of attachment security and result in the construction of positive mental representations of self and others (see Chapter 7). But when a person's attachment figures are not reliably available and supportive, proximity seeking fails to relieve distress, felt security is undermined, negative models of self and others are formed, and the likelihood of establishing insecure orientations toward attachment figures and relationships increases. Research indicates that these attachment insecurities can be measured in adulthood in terms of two independent dimensions: attachment-related anxiety and avoidance (Brennan, Clark, & Shaver, 1998).

A person's position on the anxiety dimension indicates the degree to which he or she worries that a partner will not be available and responsive in times of need. A person's position on the avoidance dimension indicates the extent to which he or she distrusts relationship partners' goodwill and strives to maintain behavioral independence, self-reliance, and emotional distance. The two dimensions are associated in theoretically predictable ways with relationship quality and adjustment (see Mikulincer & Shaver, 2007, for a review).

According to attachment theory, it is important to distinguish between close relationships in general and attachment relationships in particular, and between relationship partners, on the one hand, and attachment figures, on the other. Attachment figures are not just ordinary relationship partners. They are special individuals to whom a person turns when protection and support are needed. Bowlby (1982) specified the provisions that a relationship partner should supply, or the functions this person should serve, if he or she is to be viewed as an attachment figure (see also Hazan & Zeifman, 1994). First, attachment figures are targets of proximity maintenance. Humans of all ages tend to seek and enjoy proximity to their attachment figures in times of need and to experience distress upon separation from them. Second, attachment figures provide a physical and emotional safe haven; they facilitate distress alleviation and are a source of support and comfort. Third, attachment figures provide a secure base from which people can explore and learn about the world and develop their own capacities and personal traits. By accomplishing these functions, a relationship partner becomes a source of attachment security and one's relationship with him or her becomes an attachment bond.

A fourth defining characteristic of an attachment bond is that the real or expected disappearance of an attachment figure evokes strong separation distress; that is, people react with intense distress to actual or potential separations from, or losses of, attachment figures. Bowlby's (1982) ideas about separation distress as a defining feature of an attachment figure were inspired by observations made by Robertson and Bowlby (1952), who noticed that infants and young children who are separated from primary caregivers for extended periods pass through a predictable series of states: separation protest (including crying, clinging, calling, yearning), despair (including depressed mood, decreased appetite, and disturbed sleep), and detachment (emotional withdrawal or anger mixed with excessive vigilance and anxious clinging). According to Bowlby (1982), this sequence of responses is not targeted to every close relationship partner but only to those viewed as attachment figures. Theoretically, separation distress is the normative response to an impending loss of a major source of safety and security.

During infancy, primary caregivers (usually one or both parents, but in many cases other relatives, nannies, and day care providers as well) are likely to serve attachment functions. In later childhood, adolescence, and adulthood, a wider variety of relationship partners can serve as attachment figures, including siblings, other relatives, familiar coworkers, teachers or coaches, close friends, and romantic partners. They form what Bowlby (1982) called a person's "hierarchy of attachment figures." There may also be context-specific attachment figures, such as therapists in therapeutic settings or leaders in organizational settings. Moreover, groups and symbolic personages (e.g., God) can become targets of proximity seeking and sources of safety (Granqvist, Mikulincer, & Shaver, 2010). In our studies, we have found, for example, that the actual presence of a supportive relationship partner in different kinds of relationships (romantic, leader–follower, and therapeutic) has long-term consequences for a person's attachment security, psychological well-being, and mental health (see Shaver & Mikulincer, 2008, for a review).

In the present chapter, we focus mainly on romantic relationships in adulthood and the extent to which they can be conceptualized as involving attachment bonds (Hazan & Shaver, 1987; Shaver et al., 1988). In the next section, we review evidence supporting this conceptualization and indicating that romantic relationships fulfill anxiety-buffering and growth-promoting functions and that a romantic partner or spouse can become a person's principal attachment figure in adulthood.

ATTACHMENT PROCESSES IN ROMANTIC RELATIONSHIPS

In his writings, Bowlby (e.g., 1979) emphasized that the need for comforting figures and the development of emotional attachments to security providers are evident in adult romantic relationships. Following Bowlby's lead, Shaver et al. (1988) proposed that sustained romantic love in adulthood involves an emotional attachment that is conceptually parallel to infants' emotional bonds with their primary caregivers. For example, love in both infancy and adulthood includes eye contact, holding, touching, caressing, smiling, crying, clinging; a desire to be comforted by one's relationship partner when distressed; the experience of anger, anxiety, and sorrow following separation or loss; and the experience of happiness and joy upon reunion. Moreover, formation of a secure relationship with either a primary caregiver or a mate depends on the caregiver's or partner's responsiveness to the attached person's bids for proximity, and this responsiveness causes the attached person to feel safer, more confident, happier, more outgoing, and kinder to others (see Chapter 14). Furthermore, in both kinds of relationships, when the partner is not available and not responsive to the person's bids for proximity, the attached person can become anxious, preoccupied, and hypersensitive to signs of love, approval, or rejection. Separations or nonresponsiveness, up to a point, can increase the intensity of both an infant's and an adult's proximity-seeking behavior, but beyond that point they can instigate defensive distancing from the partner so as to avoid the pain and distress of repeated frustration. All of these parallels led Shaver et al. to conclude that infants' bonds with parents and romantic partners' bonds in adulthood are variants of a single underlying process.

Today, 25 years after Shaver et al.'s (1988) initial statement of their extension of Bowlby's theory, there is ample evidence that romantic relationships can be viewed as attachments and that a mate is often one's principal attachment figure. In the following sections, we review evidence showing that romantic relationships fulfill the four major defining features of attachment and can therefore be viewed as major resources for coping and personal growth.

Romantic Partners as Attachment Figures

One kind of evidence for the claim that romantic relationships involve attachment, in Bowlby's sense of that term, comes from studies examining the identities of people who serve as adults' primary sources of security during adulthood. To explore this issue, Hazan and Zeifman (1994) constructed the WHOTO scale, which identifies a person's primary attachment figures by asking for the names of people who are preferred targets of proximity (e.g., "Whom do you like to spend time with?") and providers of what Bowlby called a safe haven (e.g., "To whom do you turn for comfort when you're feeling down?") and a secure base (e.g., "Whom do you feel you can always count on?"). Hazan and Zeifman administered the WHOTO scale to a sample of young adults and found that they preferred romantic partners rather than parents when they sought closeness or a safe haven. With regard to the secure-base function, they preferred their romantic partner if they were involved in a long-term romantic relationship or marriage. However, if no such relationship existed, adults still preferred parents rather than friends as secure-base providers. These findings have been replicated in subsequent studies (e.g., Schachner, Shaver, & Gillath, 2008).

It is important to note that nominating a romantic partner as the principal attachment figure during adulthood is affected by a variety of relational and individual-differences factors. For example, length of a romantic relationship is associated with choosing the romantic partner as a principal attachment figure (e.g., J. A. Feeney, 2004). In fact, Hazan and Zeifman (1994) found that consolidation of what they called a "full-blown attachment" to a romantic partner (i.e., using the partner for proximity maintenance and as a safe haven and secure base) takes approximately two years. In addition, feelings of trust, intimacy, and commitment in a romantic relationship affect the nomination of a romantic partner as one's principal attachment figure (e.g., J. A. Feeney, 2004). This can explain why young adults scoring higher on attachment anxiety or avoidance—the two principal forms of attachment insecurity that involve deficiencies in trust and intimacy—are less likely to nominate a romantic partner as an attachment figure (e.g., Mayselessx, 2004).

In sum, research conducted to date indicates that romantic partners occupy the top rung in many people's attachment hierarchies during young adulthood, but parents often continue to be primary providers of a secure base for exploration and growth. As adults age, they become increasingly likely to rely on a romantic or marital partner, if they have one, as a principal attachment figure, including as a secure base.

Romantic Partners as a Safe Haven

If romantic relationships involve attachment bonds, people should tend to seek proximity to their romantic partner in times of need, and closeness to this person should alleviate distress and induce comfort and a sense of safety. With regard to proximity seeking, Fraley and Shaver (1998) found many examples of this type of behavior while unobtrusively observing romantic couples waiting in the departure lounges of a public airport. Couples who were about to separate from each other (because one partner was flying to another city) were more likely to seek and maintain physical contact (e.g., by mutually gazing at each other's faces, talking intently, and touching) than couples who were not separating (because they were about to fly somewhere together).

The tendency to seek proximity to a romantic partner in times of need has also been documented in experimental studies of death anxiety following manipulations that make mortality salient (see Mikulincer, Florian, &

Hirschberger, 2003, for a review). For example, Florian, Mikulincer, and Hirschberger (2002) asked people to write briefly about either their own death or a neutral topic (watching TV). Following a common distracter task, all participants then rated the extent to which they were committed to their romantic partner (e.g., "I am completely devoted to my partner") as well as being morally committed to marriage (e.g., "Marriages are supposed to last forever"). People in the mortality salience condition reported greater psychological commitment to their romantic partner than participants in the neutral condition. There was, however, no significant effect of mortality salience on moral commitment to marriage. Florian et al. concluded that death reminders increase the sense of love and closeness to a romantic partner but not the relevance of cultural obligations concerning marriage.

Further evidence for the use of a romantic partner as a safe haven was provided by a diary study tapping within-person variability in support seeking and support provision in dating relationships (Collins & Feeney, 2005). In this study, both members of dating couples completed a diary every evening for 21 consecutive days, noting stressful events, support-seeking efforts, and support provision. Results indicated that individuals sought more support from their partner on days when they experienced more stressful events, and participants responded by providing more support on days when their partner expressed greater need for support. In a more recent diary study, Campa, Hazan, and Wolfe (2009) found that young adults in serious romantic relationships tended to turn to their partner for daily comfort during the 28-day study period even on days when they reported no particular stressor. This level of comfort seeking contrasted with that of participants who were not involved in a romantic relationship. They tended to turn to an attachment figure (usually a parent) for comfort mainly on days when they reported heightened distress. Thus, romantic partners may not only replace parents as a major safe haven but also enjoy closeness and comfort even when there is no special reason for feeling unsafe.

There is also extensive evidence that proximity to a romantic partner alleviates distress. In a naturalistic study of cohabiting and married couples, Gump, Polk, Kamarck, and Shiffman (2001) asked participant partners to wear ambulatory blood pressure monitors for a week and to report what they were doing and feeling and indicate whether anyone was with them every time their blood pressure was recorded. The authors found that blood pressure was lower when participants were interacting with their romantic partner than when they were interacting with other people or were alone. Interestingly, this effect was observed even during nonintimate exchanges with a mate, implying that the partner's mere presence had beneficial effects.

In an observational study of dating couples who were videotaped while one partner disclosed a personal concern to the other, Collins and Feeney

(2000) found that observed (i.e., actual) partner supportiveness reduced the distress experienced by the support recipient. That is, people whose romantic partner provided more responsive support (as judged by independent coders) felt better after disclosing a personal problem than they did beforehand. Moreover, couples who experienced more supportive interactions (as judged by both the couple members themselves and independent coders) reported having better relationships overall. These findings were conceptually replicated by Collins, Ford, Guichard, Kane, and Feeney (2010), who found that spouses who actually received more responsive support from their partner after a stressful speech task (as assessed through self-report and observers' ratings) felt calmer, more secure, and more valued by the partner immediately after the interaction. In addition, spouses who perceived their partner to be a safe haven (i.e., a responsive caregiver) felt more confident of his or her love and commitment.

In addition to these correlational studies, there are a number of experimental studies showing that one's romantic partner can be a stress alleviator. For example, Coan, Schaefer, and Davidson (2006) examined brain responses (using functional magnetic resonance imaging, or fMRI) of married women who underwent a laboratory stressor (threat of electric shock) while they were holding their husband's hand, holding the hand of an otherwise unfamiliar male experimenter, or holding no hand at all. Spousal hand-holding reduced activation in brain regions associated with stress and distress (right anterior insula, superior frontal gyrus, and hypothalamus). The researchers also found that the stress-reducing effects of hand-holding were greater in better functioning marriages, probably because of the greater sense of security induced by physical contact with a responsive and supportive husband (see Chapter 5, this volume, for related studies). In another study, Master et al. (2009) found that holding the hand of a romantic partner or watching his or her photograph reduced perceptions of pain in response to heat stimuli. Younger, Aron, Parke, Chatterjee, and Mackey (2010) replicated these findings in an fMRI study and found that greater analgesia while viewing pictures of a romantic partner was associated with increased activity in several reward-processing brain regions, such as the nucleus accumbens, lateral orbitofrontal cortex, and dorsolateral prefrontal cortex (see Chapter 3).

Following this line of research, Kane, McCall, Collins, and Blascovich (2012) asked young adults to complete a threatening cliff-walking task in an immersive virtual environment. In this virtual world, their romantic partner was, in three experimental conditions, absent from the virtual world, present in the world and attentive to the participant during the task (waving, clapping at successes, nodding their heads, and actively orienting their bodies toward the participant), or present but inattentive (looking away from the participant). Participants in the attentive-partner condition experienced the task as less stressful than those who were alone; they also reported feeling more secure during the task and were less vigilant of their partner's behavior compared with those in the inattentive-partner condition. These findings suggest that a romantic partner can function as a safe haven particularly if he or she acts in an attentive and response manner, that is, as a security-enhancing attachment figure.

Conceptually similar findings were reported by Guichard and Collins (2008), who manipulated the quality of one's romantic partner's support by having the partner send messages (actually written by the researchers) before and after the focal person participated in a stressful speech delivery task. Participants who received highly supportive messages were in a better mood after their speech, had higher state self-esteem, and felt more satisfied with their relationship compared with those who received low-support messages or no message at all from their partner. In a similar study, Collins, Jaremka, and Kane (2009) found that experimentally manipulated supportive messages from a romantic partner during a stressful speech task (as compared with low-support messages) yielded lower cortisol levels and more rapid emotional recovery from the stressful task.

Although all these studies support the notion that a romantic relationship is a place where couple members can find a safe haven in times of need, we should note that the provision of a safe haven can be hampered by attachment insecurities. First, there is evidence that people suffering from attachment insecurity, of either the anxious or the avoidant variety, tend to seek less support from their romantic partners in times of need (see Mikulincer & Shaver, 2007, for a review). Second, several laboratory and field studies (using self-report and observational methods) indicate that relatively insecure people are less likely to be sensitive and responsive to their romantic partner's needs and less likely to provide a safe haven for him or her (for reviews, see Collins et al., 2010; Mikulincer & Shaver, 2012). Taken together, this evidence suggests that the successful operation of the safe-haven function of a romantic relationship depends on the extent to which both the support-seeking partner and the support-providing partner feel secure in attachment relationships (both in general and specifically in the current relationship), trust others, and are confident in their own value and lovability.

Romantic Partners as a Secure Base

Are romantic partners capable of providing a secure base for each other, allowing them to explore the world autonomously and achieve personal goals? According to Bowlby (1988), this is an important function of an attachment figure, allowing people to "make sorties into the outside world" (p. 11) with confidence that they can return for assistance and comfort should obstacles arise. This secure base, which was originally described by Ainsworth, Blehar, Waters, and Wall (1978) in their studies of 1-year-old infants and their mothers, can allow a person of any age to take sensible risks, engage in challenging activities, and pursue new goals. B. C. Feeney and Thrush (2010) further refined the concept of secure-base provision in adulthood and concluded that an attachment figure acts a secure base for a partner's autonomous exploration if he or she (a) is available when this kind of support is needed by a partner, (b) does not interfere with the partner's sorties into the outside world, and (c) accepts and encourages these autonomous sorties. Therefore, if romantic relationships truly involve attachment bonds and processes of the kinds delineated by Bowlby (1982) and Ainsworth et al., adults should seek secure-base support from their romantic partners, and the availability and responsiveness of this partner should facilitate one's efforts at personal growth (see also Chapter 16 for similar ideas).

Unfortunately, there is not yet a probing study of the extent to which people actually seek secure-base support from a romantic partner during exploration or goal pursuit. However, there is evidence that a romantic partner can facilitate autonomous exploration and pursuit of personal goals. For example, B. C. Feeney (2007) found that study participants' perception of their romantic partner's availability and assistance in removing obstacles to goal pursuit were associated with a stronger sense of independence, greater feelings of self-efficacy in goal achievement, and deeper engagement in autonomous exploration. Moreover, during couples' discussions of future personal goals, participants were more likely to engage in exploration of these goals (as coded by external judges) when their partner was coded as communicating more availability and responsiveness to these exploratory inclinations.

Using longitudinal data, B. C. Feeney (2007) also found that individuals whose partners were more responsive to their needs for secure-base support (as reported by the partner or coded by external judges) reported increases in autonomous exploration over 6 months and were more likely to have achieved at least one personal goal that they had identified 6 months earlier. In another laboratory study, B. C. Feeney (2004) found that experimentally manipulated nonintrusiveness of a romantic partner predicted increases in participants' self-esteem and positive mood after an exploration activity.

In a more recent study, B. C. Feeney and Thrush (2010) asked married couples to participate in a videotaped laboratory exploration activity and assessed actual exploratory behavior. The authors found that when spouses were coded by external judges as more available during the exploration task, as less interfering with their partner's exploration, or as more accepting of this activity, the exploring partner persisted longer at the activity and reported heightened self-esteem and a better mood following the exploration task. Conceptually similar findings were reported by Overall, Fletcher, and Simpson

(2010): Study participants whose romantic partners were more available and responsive to their self-improvement desires during a laboratory discussion showed more self-improvement during the next year.

It is important to note, however, that attachment insecurities can reduce or preclude these positive effects of a romantic partner's role as a secure base. In a recent experimental study, Coy, Green, and Davis (2012) asked participants to engage in inner exploration of sensations and feelings alone or in the presence of their romantic partner. Findings indicated that the positive effects of a partner's presence disappeared and were sometimes even reversed among insecurely attached partners. For more avoidant participants, for example, the presence of their partner during the exploration task reduced rather than increased (compared with the alone condition) the time they spent in exploration and their positive mood during the activity. This effect might be attributable to avoidant individuals' dismissal or derogation of their partner's supportiveness (e.g., Collins & Feeney, 2004) or to their partner actually being less responsive to, and less encouraging of, their exploration efforts (B.C. Feeney & Thrush, 2010). Participants with more anxious partners felt less positive after exploring with the partner than when exploring alone. This may be explained by previous research showing that more attachment-anxious individuals (as objectively coded by observers) are more interfering with, and less encouraging of, their romantic partner's autonomous exploration; thus, their presence may increase discomfort rather than provide a secure base (B.C. Feeney & Thrush, 2010).

Responses to Separation and Loss

The distress elicited by separation from, or loss of, a close relationship partner is one of the defining features of an attachment bond. According to Bowlby (1980), the absence of an attachment figure is a threat to a person's sense of security and safety and therefore arouses anxiety, anger, protest, and yearning. An infant, finding itself without an attentive caregiver, cries, thrashes, attempts to reestablish contact with the absent figure by calling and searching, and resists other people's soothing efforts. If the separation is prolonged (e.g., by the mother's extended stay in a hospital or, at worst, by her death), the infant grieves disconsolately, and anxiety and anger gradually give way to despair (Bowlby, 1980).

Similar reactions are often observed in adolescents and adults following the breakup of a romantic relationship (Shaver & Fraley, 2008). For those who are abandoned without warning, the breakup of a love relationship can be devastating, and the reaction can be so intense that it amounts to grief (e.g., Frazier & Cook, 1993). For example, in a diary study of emotions recorded over a 28-day period, Sbarra and Emery (2005) obtained evidence of increased emotional volatility and higher levels of sadness and anger on days following the breakup of a dating relationship than on days before the breakup. Such reactions are especially likely following divorce, which typically evokes intense anxiety, sorrow, loneliness, and despair, especially in a partner who had not prepared in advance for the breakup by gradually detaching him- or herself from the mate (e.g., Birnbaum, Orr, Mikulincer, & Florian, 1997).

Not surprisingly, the most dramatic evidence concerning the effects of breaking or losing an attachment bond is observed following the death of a romantic partner or spouse (see M. S. Stroebe, Hansson, Schut, & Stroebe, 2008, for reviews). This kind of loss is one of the most devastating experiences in most people's lives and is likely to bring forth a torrent of anxiety, sadness, loneliness, guilt, anger, and longing for the deceased (e.g., Shaver & Fraley, 2008). It can cause a person to feel like dying in order to rejoin the lost partner. It can disrupt psychological functioning for months and lead to depression, posttraumatic stress disorder, and impaired physical health (e.g., Boelen, van den Hout, & van den Bout, 2006; W. Stroebe, Abakoumkin, & Stroebe, 2010). In fact, cross-cultural research indicates that despite variations in mourning rituals and expressions of grief across cultures, death of a spouse evokes profound pain and disorientation everywhere in the world and has done so during all periods of recorded history (e.g., Rosenblatt, 2008).

According to attachment theory, these reactions are caused by an upsurge of attachment needs, which are no longer capable of being satisfied by the deceased spouse (Shaver & Fraley, 2008). Therefore, the intensity of grief is a function of the place and importance of the deceased spouse in the bereaved person's hierarchy of attachment figures. Parkes and Weiss (1983) suggested that individuals who lose the person on whom they most depend as a safe haven and secure base are the most vulnerable to despair. In support of this idea, more intense grief is observed among people who describe themselves as having been more strongly attached to the spouse they have lost (e.g., Jerga, Shaver, & Wilkinson, 2011; Wayment & Vierthaler, 2002).

Adaptive coping with the loss of a spouse requires what Bowlby (1980) called "reorganization" of the hierarchy of attachment figures because adults often transfer attachment functions, such as provision of a safe haven and secure base, at least partly, to new relationship partners. But they may not fully detach from the mental representation of the lost spouse. According to Bowlby, adults can rearrange their attachment representations so that the lost spouse continues to serve as a symbolic source of protection while new relationships with living partners are formed and solidified.

Attachment reorganization following the loss of a spouse involves two psychological tasks: (a) accepting the death of the lost partner, returning to mundane activities, and forming new relationships; and (b) maintaining a symbolic bond with the deceased and integrating the lost relationship into a new reality (Mikulincer & Shaver, 2008). This two-part analysis based on attachment theory fits well with various dual process models of bereavement (e.g., M. Stroebe & Schut, 2010).

Of course, the normative process of grieving following the death of a romantic partner or spouse is, like other attachment-related processes, altered by attachment insecurities. Researchers have found that attachment anxiety is associated with complicated grief reactions (see Mikulincer & Shaver, 2008, for a review). For example, Field and Sundin (2001) reported that anxious attachment, assessed 10 months after the death of a spouse, predicted higher levels of psychological distress 14, 25, and 60 months after the loss, and Fraley and Bonanno (2004) found that attachment anxiety assessed 4 months after the loss of a spouse predicted higher levels of anxiety, depression, grief, trauma-related symptoms, and alcohol consumption 18 months following the loss. With regard to avoidant attachment, studies have generally found no significant association between this attachment orientation and depression, grief, or distress immediately following the death of a spouse (see Mikulincer & Shaver, 2008, for a review). But Wayment and Vierthaler (2002) found that avoidance was associated with higher levels of somatic symptoms following the death of spouse, and Jerga et al. (2011) found that avoidant attachment was positively associated with prolonged grief symptoms.

CONCLUDING REMARKS

Although a great deal of adult attachment research has focused on individual differences in attachment security, anxiety, and avoidance, here we have returned to the core idea in Shaver et al.'s (1988) analysis of romantic pair-bonding, which is that long-term couple relationships involve all of the attachment-related processes that Bowlby and Ainsworth originally specified with respect to infant–caregiver relationships. Romantic pair-bonding, or love, involves more than simple familiarity and conscious commitment. It also involves reliance on a partner to serve the attachment-related needs for a safe haven and secure base. It involves an emotional bond that may not be fully recognized until a relationship is threatened, severed, or lost.

Bowlby (1982) imagined that the human brain is equipped with an innate attachment behavioral system, which was assumed to be located somewhere in the brain. As social and affective neuroscience progress, it will be important to reconsider Bowlby's ideas and attempt to specify how the brain accomplishes all of the attachment-related functions researchers have identified. Are the effects of familiarity, supportive caregiving, and continued closeness, as well as the effects of separation and loss, all part of a single neurological system, or—as other authors in this volume (see, e.g., Chapters 3, 4, and 5) have suggested—do these attachment processes occur through more general and pervasive systems, such as mirror neurons and the hypothalamic–pituitary–adrenal axis? This is one of the issues we hope further brain research on the activation and functioning of the attachment system in adulthood will address.

REFERENCES

Ainsworth, M. D. S., Blehar, M. C., Waters, E., & Wall, S. (1978). *Patterns of attachment: A psychological study of the Strange Situation.* Hillsdale, NJ: Erlbaum.

Birnbaum, G. E., Orr, I., Mikulincer, M., & Florian, V. (1997). When marriage breaks up: Does attachment style contribute to coping and mental health? *Journal of Social and Personal Relationships, 14,* 643–654. doi:10.1177/0265407597145004

Boelen, P. A., van den Hout, M. A., & van den Bout, J. (2006). A cognitive-behavioral conceptualization of complicated grief. *Clinical Psychology: Science and Practice, 13,* 109–128. doi:10.1111/j.1468-2850.2006.00013.x

Bowlby, J. (1973). *Attachment and loss: Vol. 2. Separation: Anxiety and anger.* New York, NY: Basic Books.

Bowlby, J. (1979). *The making and breaking of affectional bonds.* London, England: Tavistock.

Bowlby, J. (1980). *Attachment and loss: Vol. 3. Sadness and depression.* New York, NY: Basic Books.

Bowlby, J. (1982). *Attachment and loss: Vol. 1. Attachment* (2nd ed.). New York, NY: Basic Books.

Bowlby, J. (1988). *A secure base: Clinical applications of attachment theory.* London, England: Routledge.

Brennan, K. A., Clark, C. L., & Shaver, P. R. (1998). Self-report measurement of adult romantic attachment: An integrative overview. In J. A. Simpson & W. S. Rholes (Eds.), *Attachment theory and close relationships* (pp. 46–76). New York, NY: Guilford Press.

Campa, M. I., Hazan, C., & Wolfe, J. E. (2009). The form and function of attachment behavior in the daily lives of young adults. *Social Development, 18,* 288–304. doi:10.1111/j.1467-9507.2008.00466.x

Coan, J. A., Schaefer, H. S., & Davidson, R. J. (2006). Lending a hand: Social regulation of the neural response to threat. *Psychological Science, 17,* 1032–1039. doi:10.1111/j.1467-9280.2006.01832.x

Collins, N. L., & Feeney, B. C. (2000). A safe haven: An attachment theory perspective on support-seeking and caregiving in intimate relationships. *Journal of Personality and Social Psychology, 78,* 1053–1073. doi:10.1037/0022-3514.78.6.1053

Collins, N. L., & Feeney, B. C. (2004). Working models of attachment shape perceptions of social support: Evidence from experimental and observational studies.

Journal of Personality and Social Psychology, 87, 363–383. doi:10.1037/0022-3514.87.3.363

Collins, N. L., & Feeney, B. C. (2005). *Attachment processes in intimate relationships: Support-seeking and caregiving behavior in daily interaction.* Paper presented at the annual meeting of the American Psychological Society, Los Angeles, CA.

Collins, N. L., Ford, M. B., Guichard, A. C., Kane, H. S., & Feeney, B. C. (2010). Responding to need in intimate relationships: Social support and caregiving processes in couples. In M. Mikulincer & P. R. Shaver (Eds.), *Prosocial motives, emotions, and behavior: The better angels of our nature* (pp. 367–389). Washington, DC: American Psychological Association.

Collins, N. L., Jaremka, L. M., & Kane, H. (2009). *Social support buffers stress, promotes emotional recovery, and enhances relationship security.* Unpublished manuscript, University of California, Santa Barbara.

Coy, A. E., Green, J. D., & Davis, J. L. (2012). With or without you: The impact of partner presence and attachment on exploration. *Journal of Experimental Social Psychology, 48*, 411–415. doi:10.1016/j.jesp.2011.08.008

Feeney, B. C. (2004). A secure base: Responsive support of goal strivings and exploration in adult intimate relationships. *Journal of Personality and Social Psychology, 87*, 631–648. doi:10.1037/0022-3514.87.5.631

Feeney, B. C. (2007). The dependency paradox in close relationships: Accepting dependence promotes independence. *Journal of Personality and Social Psychology, 92*, 268–285. doi:10.1037/0022-3514.92.2.268

Feeney, B. C., & Thrush, R. L. (2010). Relationship influences on exploration in adulthood: The characteristics and function of a secure base. *Journal of Personality and Social Psychology, 98*, 57–76. doi:10.1037/a0016961

Feeney, J. A. (2004). Transfer of attachment from parents to romantic partners: Effects of individual and relationship variables. *Journal of Family Studies, 10*, 220–238. doi:10.5172/jfs.327.10.2.220

Field, N. P., & Sundin, E. C. (2001). Attachment style in adjustment to conjugal bereavement. *Journal of Social and Personal Relationships, 18*, 347–361. doi:10.1177/0265407501183003

Florian, V., Mikulincer, M., & Hirschberger, G. (2002). The anxiety buffering function of close relationships: Evidence that relationship commitment acts as a terror management mechanism. *Journal of Personality and Social Psychology, 82*, 527–542. doi:10.1037/0022-3514.82.4.527

Fraley, R. C., & Bonanno, G. A. (2004). Attachment and loss: A test of three competing models on the association between attachment-related avoidance and adaptation to bereavement. *Personality and Social Psychology Bulletin, 30*, 878–890. doi:10.1177/0146167204264289

Fraley, R. C., & Shaver, P. R. (1998). Airport separations: A naturalistic study of adult attachment dynamics in separating couples. *Journal of Personality and Social Psychology, 75*, 1198–1212. doi:10.1037/0022-3514.75.5.1198

Frazier, P. A., & Cook, S. W. (1993). Correlates of distress following heterosexual relationship dissolution. *Journal of Social and Personal Relationships, 10,* 55–67. doi:10.1177/0265407593101004

Granqvist, P., Mikulincer, M., & Shaver, P. R. (2010). Religion as attachment: Normative processes and individual differences. *Personality and Social Psychology Review, 14,* 49–59. doi:10.1177/1088868309348618

Guichard, A., & Collins, N. (2008, February). *The influence of social support and attachment style on performance, self-evaluations, and interpersonal behaviors.* Poster presented at the meeting of the Society for Personality and Social Psychology, Albuquerque, NM.

Gump, B. B., Polk, D. E., Kamarck, T. W., & Shiffman, S. M. (2001). Partner interactions are associated with reduced blood pressure in the natural environment: Ambulatory monitoring evidence from a healthy, multiethnic adult sample. *Psychosomatic Medicine, 63,* 423–433.

Hazan, C., & Shaver, P. R. (1987). Romantic love conceptualized as an attachment process. *Journal of Personality and Social Psychology, 52,* 511–524. doi:10.1037/0022-3514.52.3.511

Hazan, C., & Zeifman, D. (1994). Sex and the psychological tether. In K. Bartholomew & D. Perlman (Eds.), *Advances in personal relationships: Vol. 5. Attachment processes in adulthood* (pp. 151–178). London, England: Kingsley.

Jerga, C., Shaver, P. R., & Wilkinson, R. B. (2011). Attachment insecurities and identification of at-risk individuals following the death of a loved one. *Journal of Social and Personal Relationships, 28,* 891–914. doi:10.1177/0265407510397987

Kane, H. S., McCall, C., Collins, N. L., & Blascovich, J. (2012). Mere presence is not enough: Responsive support in a virtual world. *Journal of Experimental Social Psychology, 48,* 37–44. doi:10.1016/j.jesp.2011.07.001

Master, S. L., Eisenberger, N. I., Taylor, S. E., Malinkoff, B. D., Shirnyan, D., & Lieberman, M. D. (2009). A picture's worth: Partner's photographs reduce experimentally induced pain. *Psychological Science, 20,* 1316–1318. doi:10.1111/j.1467-9280.2009.02444.x

Mayselessx, O. (2004). Home leaving to military service: Attachment concerns, transfer of attachment functions from parents to peers, and adjustment. *Journal of Adolescent Research, 19,* 533–558. doi:10.1177/0743558403260000

Mikulincer, M., Florian, V., & Hirschberger, G. (2003). The existential function of close relationships: Introducing death into the science of love. *Personality and Social Psychology Review, 7,* 20–40. doi:10.1207/S15327957PSPR0701_2

Mikulincer, M., & Shaver, P. R. (2007). *Attachment in adulthood: Structure, dynamics, and change.* New York, NY: Guilford Press.

Mikulincer, M., & Shaver, P. R. (2008). An attachment perspective on bereavement. In M. S. Stroebe, R. O. Hansson, H. Schut, & W. Stroebe (Eds.), *Handbook of bereavement research and practice: Advances in theory and intervention* (pp. 87–112). Washington, DC: American Psychological Association.

Mikulincer, M., & Shaver, P. R. (2012). Adult attachment and caregiving: Individual differences in providing a safe haven and secure base to others. In S. L. Brown, R. M. Brown, & L. A. Penner (Eds.), *Moving beyond self-interest: Perspectives from evolutionary biology, neuroscience, and the social sciences* (pp. 39–52). New York, NY: Oxford University Press. doi:10.1093/acprof:oso/9780195388107.003.0018

Overall, N. C., Fletcher, G. J. O., & Simpson, J. A. (2010). Helping each other grow: Romantic partner support, self-improvement, and relationship quality. *Personality and Social Psychology Bulletin, 36,* 1496–1513. doi:10.1177/0146167210383045

Parkes, C. M., & Weiss, R. S. (1983). *Recovery from bereavement.* New York, NY: Basic Books.

Robertson, J., & Bowlby, J. (1952). Responses of young children to separation from their mothers. *Courier of the International Children's Center, Paris, 2,* 131–140.

Rosenblatt, P. C. (2008). Grief across cultures: A review and research agenda. In M. S. Stroebe, R. O. Hansson, H. Schut, & W. Stroebe (Eds.), *Handbook of bereavement research and practice: Advances in theory and intervention* (pp. 207–222). Washington, DC: American Psychological Association.

Sbarra, D. A., & Emery, R. E. (2005). The emotional sequelae of nonmarital relationship dissolution: Analysis of change and intraindividual variability over time. *Personal Relationships, 12,* 213–232. doi:10.1111/j.1350-4126.2005.00112.x

Schachner, D. A., Shaver, P. R., & Gillath, O. (2008). Attachment style and long-term singlehood. *Personal Relationships, 15,* 479–491. doi:10.1111/j.1475-6811.2008.00211.x

Shaver, P., Hazan, C., & Bradshaw, D. (1988). Love as attachment: The integration of three behavioral systems. In R. J. Sternberg & M. L. Barnes (Eds.), *The psychology of love* (pp. 68–99). New Haven, CT: Yale University Press.

Shaver, P. R., & Fraley, R. C. (2008). Attachment, loss, and grief: Bowlby's views and current controversies. In J. Cassidy & P. R. Shaver (Eds.), *Handbook of attachment: Theory, research, and clinical applications* (2nd ed., pp. 48–77). New York, NY: Guilford Press.

Shaver, P. R., & Mikulincer, M. (2008). Augmenting the sense of security in romantic, leader–follower, therapeutic, and group relationships: A relational model of psychological change. In J. P. Forgas & J. Fitness (Eds.), *Social relationships: Cognitive, affective, and motivational processes* (pp. 55–73). New York, NY: Psychology Press.

Sroufe, L. A., & Waters, E. (1977). Attachment as an organizational construct. *Child Development, 48,* 1184–1199. doi:10.2307/1128475

Stroebe, M., & Schut, H. (2010). The dual process model of coping with bereavement: A decade on. *Omega: Journal of Death and Dying, 61,* 273–289. doi:10.2190/OM.61.4.b

Stroebe, M. S., Hansson, R. O., Schut, H., & Stroebe, W. (Eds.). (2008). *Handbook of bereavement research and practice: Advances in theory and intervention.* Washington, DC: American Psychological Association.

Stroebe, W., Abakoumkin, G., & Stroebe, M. (2010). Beyond depression: Yearning for the loss of a loved one. *Omega: Journal of Death and Dying, 61,* 85–101. doi:10.2190/OM.61.2.a

Wayment, H. A., & Vierthaler, J. (2002). Attachment style and bereavement reactions. *Journal of Loss and Trauma, 7,* 129–149. doi:10.1080/153250202753472291

Younger, J., Aron, A., Parke, S., Chatterjee, N., & Mackey, S. (2010). Viewing pictures of a romantic partner reduces experimental pain: Involvement of neural reward systems. *PLoS ONE, 5,* e13309. doi:10.1371/journal.pone.0013309

16

A THEORETICAL PERSPECTIVE ON THE IMPORTANCE OF SOCIAL CONNECTIONS FOR THRIVING

BROOKE C. FEENEY AND NANCY L. COLLINS

Although a great deal of empirical work supports the view that deep and meaningful close relationships play a vital role in human flourishing—by having either a positive or a deleterious effect on psychological well-being and physical health (e.g., Berkman & Syme, 1979; Cohen, 2004; Holt-Lunstad & Smith, 2012; Rook, 1984)—the interpersonal processes by which relationships have their effects are still poorly understood. We recently delineated a theory of thriving through relationships in an effort to provide a conceptual foundation for understanding the importance of social connections for *thriving* (see Feeney & Collins, 2012, for the complete theoretical perspective). Here we summarize the theory in Figure 16.1. As part of this perspective, we address three specific questions: (a) What does it mean to thrive? (b) What social behaviors enable a person to thrive? and (c) What are the mechanisms through which social behaviors have their effects on thriving? Our summary is organized around these three questions.

http://dx.doi.org/10.1037/14250-017
Mechanisms of Social Connection: From Brain to Group, M. Mikulincer and P. R. Shaver (Editors)
Copyright © 2014 by the American Psychological Association. All rights reserved.

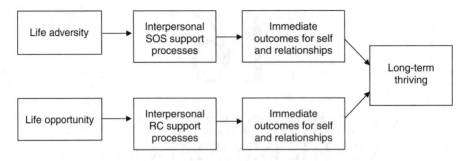

Figure 16.1. Summary of Feeney and Collins's (2012) model of thriving through relationships. SOS = strength of support; RC = relational catalyst.

WHAT DOES IT MEAN TO THRIVE?

Answering this question requires consideration of two important subquestions regarding thriving: (a) What are the life contexts in which individuals may thrive? and (b) What are the indicators of thriving (i.e., what does a thriving person look like)?

Life Contexts in Which Individuals Thrive

One life context in which individuals may thrive is the experience of *life adversity*. Individuals thrive in this context when they are able to cope successfully with life's adversities, not only by being buffered from potentially severe consequences of adversity when it arises but also by emerging from the experience as a stronger or more knowledgeable person in some way (e.g., as a result of learning from the experience, developing new coping mechanisms, or obtaining a new understanding or perspective). Because the word *thriving* implies growth and development, thriving in the face of adversity involves more than simply returning to baseline or maintenance of the status quo. Thriving occurs when people are able to weather the storms of life in ways that enable them to grow from the experience (e.g., perhaps through a heightened sense of mastery, increased self-regard, a greater sense of purpose in life, and deeper and more meaningful social bonds; Ryff & Singer, 1998).

The other life context in which individuals may thrive is the experience of life opportunities for growth in the absence of adversity. Full participation in life opportunities includes active engagement in opportunities for personal growth and development through work, play, socializing, learning, discovery, creating, pursuing hobbies, and making meaningful contributions to community and society (Deci & Ryan, 2000; Ryff & Singer, 1998). These opportunities may be viewed as positive challenges because they frequently involve goal strivings and goal pursuits that require time, effort, and concentration.

Indicators of Thriving Through Adversity and Life Opportunities

Although thriving is both individual and situation specific (because there are many specific ways in which individuals may potentially thrive), we propose that there are 10 core indicators of thriving both through adversity and through life opportunities. All of these indicators involve forms of learning, growth, and prosperity and are consistent with the definition of thriving as flourishing/growing, prospering, and progressing toward or realizing a goal despite or because of circumstances, and consistent with other theorizing regarding optimal well-being (e.g., Ryff & Singer, 2008). We propose that one must function well in both life contexts (in adversity and in pursuing life opportunities) if one is to be a maximally thriving individual, and that functioning in each context makes independent contributions to the prediction of the 10 core thriving outcomes described below.

Development of Skills/Talents

Just as rough seas make skillful sailors, one index of thriving through adversity is the development of skills/talents, or the elicitation of talents that had been dormant in nonadverse times. It sometimes takes adverse circumstances to motivate people to stretch their capacities in ways they otherwise would not. The development of skills/talents is also an index of thriving through participation in life opportunities because people who fully engage in life opportunities (e.g., by trying new things, pursuing meaningful goals, engaging in social activities) are likely to strengthen existing skills, as well as discover and cultivate new abilities.

Self-Discovery/Discovery of One's Life Purpose

Another indicator of thriving through adversity is self-discovery, because individuals can learn a great deal about themselves through adversity: They can learn about what matters most to them in life, about how strong they are with regard to weathering storms, about the type of person they are or want to be, and about their life's purpose. Self-discovery is also an index of thriving through life opportunities because full engagement in life opportunities allows one to obtain a great deal of information about oneself—about one's likes, dislikes, strengths, weaknesses, and untapped abilities.

Accumulation of Life Wisdom

This is an indicator of thriving through adversity because adverse life events often contain nuggets of information about life, people, and the events themselves, and they provide exposure to experiences that one is unlikely to encounter in prosperous times, from which one may glean important insights.

This is also an index of thriving through life opportunities because full engagement in life opportunities provides a variety of experiences that include information (e.g., about life, people, events) that can be obtained only through actual experience in opportunities for growth.

Development of Core Strengths

This includes the development of better coping capacities (e.g., DeLongis & Holtzman, 2005); greater resistance to stress (Seery, Holman, & Silver, 2010); hardiness, which involves a combination of attitudes that motivate individuals to persevere in tough circumstances and turn them into growth opportunities (Dolbier et al., 2001; Eschleman, Bowling, & Alarcon, 2010; Maddi, 2006); better self-regulatory capacities (Baumeister & Vohs, 2004); and growth and development of faith or a positive belief system. The extent to which individuals emerge from adversity with these core strengths would be an indicator of thriving through adversity. This is also an indicator of thriving through life opportunities because individuals who fully embrace life and its opportunities also derive benefits that can form the foundation of core strengths.

Positive Self-Concept

This includes a stable and authentic sense of self-worth (feeling good about one's self, abilities, potential), self-respect and self-acceptance (awareness and acceptance of one's strengths and weakness), and self-compassion. This is an important index of thriving through adversity because adverse circumstances often involve an attack on one's sense of self, and individuals who thrive through adversity not only are buffered from negative effects of life adversity on their self-concept but also develop a stronger, more positive and stable sense of self. A positive self-concept is also a strong indicator of thriving through life opportunities because individuals who fully embrace life and its opportunities are likely to develop skills/talents, to establish a strong and accepting social network, and to know their values and live according to them—all of which underlie a healthy self-concept.

Positive Views of Others/Prosocial Orientation Toward Others

This index of thriving includes general perceptions of others' supportiveness and dependability, optimism about humanity, helping and generativity, and communal motivation (the motivation to respond to others' needs; Clark & Mills, 2012). Because some life adversities involve harm inflicted by others (e.g., betrayal, infidelity, physical injuries, neglect, rejection), these circumstances are especially likely to erode one's positive views of and positive motivation toward others. Individuals who thrive through adversity do not allow particular adverse experiences to taint their overall view of their social network or humanity, or of their concern for the well-being and needs of others. Moreover, because life opportunities include many that are social in nature, and because full engagement in them includes interacting successfully with others, taking others' perspectives, and contributing to others' welfare, thriving through these life opportunities is also indexed by the development of positive views of others and a prosocial orientation toward others.

Movement Toward One's Full Potential

This includes living life to one's full potential; having and progressing toward personally meaningful life goals; showing zest, enthusiasm, and passion in living; being open to experience (e.g., being receptive to inner emotional states, valuing of emotional experience, being inclined to try new things and open to new ideas; McCrae, 1987); being intrinsically motivated to pursue goals (Deci & Ryan, 2000; Emmons, 1991); following one's perceived life purpose; and being genuine and true to oneself. Because adversity has the potential to hinder one's life progress, remaining committed to self-development despite (or because of) the adversity one faces is an indicator of thriving through adversity. Also, movement toward one's full potential is the most obvious indicator of thriving through life opportunities because if an individual is fully engaged in life opportunities for growth, then he or she should be deriving these benefits. This is thriving in terms of being a fully productive and contributing citizen.

Relationship Growth and Prosperity

This includes increases in closeness/intimacy, trust, commitment, feelings of satisfaction with one's relationships, relationship-specific attachment security, relationship stability, healthy interdependence, and positive relations, as well as reduced conflict and negative emotionality in one's relationships. This is an indicator of thriving through adversity because adverse circumstances provide diagnostic contexts in which the behavior of relationship partners can be viewed as indications of caring and commitment (Collins & Feeney, 2004); to the extent that this assessment works out favorably, it should contribute to relationship growth and prosperity over time (Cutrona, 1996b). Also, because individuals' reputations can be built and characters revealed by the way they deal with adverse circumstances, individuals may also experience relationship growth through adversity in terms of respect and admiration from others, and increased positive relations with others. Relationship growth/prosperity is also an index of thriving through life opportunities because full engagement in life opportunities involves creating bonds and connecting with others socially and emotionally, which is important for developing healthy relationships. Engagement in life opportunities should also enhance the quality of relationships by providing opportunities for capitalization within relationships (e.g., celebrating life successes; Gable, Gonzaga, & Strachman, 2006), which has been shown to contribute to relationship prosperity (Gable, Reis, Impett, & Asher, 2004).

Psychological Health

This includes general happiness and life satisfaction, as well as a lack of psychological symptoms of disorders such as depression, anxiety, and hostility (Seery et al., 2010). Individuals who cope with adversity well by not dwelling on or ruminating about negative circumstances, and who experience thriving in the ways previously described, should also thrive in terms of mental health. Positive mental health also includes a special appreciation of good aspects of life that may be taken for granted if individuals never experienced adversity. Psychological health is also an indicator of thriving through engagement in life opportunities because people who fully engage in life opportunities for growth (a) are less likely to have regrets, which should contribute to psychological health and well-being (Morrison & Roese, 2011); (b) are more likely to feel a sense of personal accomplishment, which should reduce feelings of inadequacy, depression, and anxiety; and (c) are more likely to have thriving social relationships, which should also contribute to psychological well-being.

Physical Health

This is an important indicator of thriving through adversity because stress and adverse life events frequently take a negative toll on one's physical health, and although the nature of some adverse life experiences involves physical illnesses, thriving individuals do not experience additional negative health effects that could stem from negative coping. The health of thriving individuals is buffered from the negative effects of stress and perhaps enhanced as a result of experiencing the adversity—for example, if they develop a higher threshold for experiencing subsequent stressors and better coping and self-regulatory capacities. Physical health is also an index of thriving through life opportunities because (a) active engagement in life opportunities should increase one's social network over time, which is likely to provide resources that are health protective (e.g., Cohen, Doyle, Turner, Alper, & Skoner, 2003); (b) variables that represent the opposite of engaging in life opportunities, such as loneliness and social isolation, have been linked with poor physical health outcomes (Hawkley & Cacioppo, 2003; Pressman et al., 2005); (c) the mental health benefits described above have been linked with physical health (e.g., T. Q. Miller, Smith, Turner, Guijarro, & Hallet, 1996; Schulz et al., 2000); (d) increased core strengths and relationship prosperity should have physical health implications (e.g., Cohen, 2004; Newsom, Mahan, Rook, & Krause, 2008; Scheier & Carver, 1992); and (e) active engagement in life opportunities should contribute to physical health via increases in physical activity and mental stimulation (e.g., Warburton, Nicol, & Bredin, 2006).

These 10 indicators of thriving are conceptualized as being additive in the sense that the more of these indicators people have, the more they are thriving. Moreover, the thriving indicators are expected to be complexly interrelated (e.g., the development of skills/talents may contribute to a positive self-concept, which may in turn contribute to movement toward one's full potential, which may contribute to mental health). Although this conceptualization of thriving is consistent with other conceptualizations of optimal well-being (Bundick, Yeager, King, & Damon, 2010; Carver, 1998; Lerner, von Eye, Lerner, Lewin-Bizan, & Bowers, 2010; Ryff & Singer, 2003), other perspectives tend to compartmentalize relationships as an important domain (among other nonrelational domains) in which people have meaning in life. Our theoretical perspective differs not only by viewing relationships as one life domain in which individuals may thrive, but also by viewing relationships as central to enabling all domains of human thriving, as described next.

WHAT SOCIAL BEHAVIORS ENABLE A PERSON TO THRIVE?

A key aspect of this theoretical perspective is that relationships are fundamental to the experience of thriving because they serve two important support functions that correspond to the two life contexts in which people may potentially thrive. The specification of these functions is rooted in the attachment theoretical propositions (Bowlby, 1973, 1982, 1988; Mikulincer & Shaver, 2007) that all individuals enter the world with propensities to seek proximity to close others in times of stress (an attachment system), to explore the environment (an exploration system), and to support the attachment and exploration behavior of close others (a caregiving system). However, the theoretical perspective advanced here differs from attachment theory in its focus on thriving and in its articulation of mechanisms through which relationships contribute to thriving outcomes.

Source of Strength Support

One important function that relationships serve is to support thriving through adversity, not only by buffering partners from the negative effects of stress, but also by helping them to emerge from the stressor in a way that enables them to flourish either because of or despite their circumstances. Relationships serve an important function of not simply helping people return to baseline when they face adversity but also helping them to thrive by exceeding prior baseline levels of functioning. A useful metaphor is that houses destroyed by storms are frequently rebuilt, not into the same houses that existed before the storm but into homes that are better in several respects, including being better able to withstand similar storms in the future. So too are people able to emerge from adverse life circumstances stronger and better off than they were before with the support of relationship partners who fortify and assist them in the rebuilding. In this sense, relationship partners can provide a source of strength, in addition to a refuge, in adverse circumstances. We refer to this relational support function that strengthens/fortifies as well as comforts/protects in times of adversity as *source of strength (SOS) support*. The promotion of thriving through adversity is what differentiates this support function from others that have been considered in the psychological literature.

The proposed features of this support function are as follows: First, the SOS support function must be enacted on a foundation of safe-haven support, which involves providing safety and protection from danger or trouble, as well as relief from the burdens that one experiences during times of adversity (Bowlby, 1982; Collins & Feeney, 2000). Relationship partners can serve this function by accepting the partner's dependency needs in times of stress (Feeney, 2007), providing emotional comfort and reassurance (physical and/or verbal), providing instrumental aid with regard to alleviating the adverse circumstances, and shielding/defending the partner from negative forces related to the stressor.

On this foundation, the SOS support promotes thriving through adversity (instead of just coping with adversity) by assisting a partner in rebuilding after an adverse experience. One process through which support providers may do this is *fortification*—assisting in the development of a partner's strengths and talents in times of adversity. Relationship partners may do this by recognizing, nourishing, and encouraging latent abilities relevant to coping with the adversity that partners might possess. They may point out strengths and abilities that partners already possess but may not recognize or know that they have (i.e., helping the partner learn about the self through the adversity), or they may recognize a strength/ability that is needed for successful coping with the adversity and assist the partner in attaining it. This involves helping the partner to get "fit" for overcoming the adversity.

A related and necessary function of SOS support is actively motivating and assisting the partner in using one's strengths (once developed and noticed) to problem-solve, deal with the adversity in a positive manner, and rebuild after adversity. This involves actively assisting in the reconstruction process once the partner has been fortified with the strength to rebuild. It involves motivating/assisting a partner who has been "knocked down" to get back up, "stay in the game," and use his or her newfound strengths to implement new approaches that take into account the negative forces and opponents identified through the adverse experience. This function of the SOS support also involves motivating positive coping with adversity by encouraging the partner not to dwell on negative circumstances or ruminate on negative aspects of the situation that cannot be changed—and by preventing the partner from reacting to the adversity in behaviorally destructive ways.

Providing effective support in these ways requires cognitive redefinition of the adversity—viewing and using the adverse circumstances as stepping-stones for positive change. Assisting in this process is another function of SOS support. This involves helping to reframe the adverse situation so that it does not seem as threatening or insurmountable as it may have initially seemed. A person may do this by helping his or her relationship partner view the adversity in a positive light or find benefits in the adverse experience. This redefinition of adversity should enable individuals to approach the adversity in a way that will promote thriving.

Relational Catalyst Support

Another important function that relationships serve is to provide support for thriving through full participation in life's opportunities. In the absence of adversity, supportive relationships can help people thrive by promoting engagement in opportunities that enable them to enhance their positive well-being by broadening and building resources (Bowlby, 1982, 1988; Fredrickson, 2001) and finding purpose and meaning in life (Ryff & Singer, 1998). Although most research in the social support literature concerns support in times of stress, our perspective emphasizes that support in the absence of adversity is equally important for thriving. We believe that people must fully embrace life and its opportunities in order to achieve optimal happiness, health, and well-being, and that close relationships are integral to this process and underlie one's ability to embrace opportunities. A useful metaphor is that in order to lift off and successfully accomplish a mission, rockets or spacecraft must have a supportive launchpad, which consists of structures that provide services to the vehicle before and after the launch, as well as connective structures so that services may be provided during the launch. Similarly, close relationship partners can function as launching pads in the pursuit of life opportunities by providing necessary service and connective functions that promote thriving in this context. We refer to this relational support function that promotes full engagement in life opportunities in non-adverse times as *relational catalyst (RC) support* because relationship partners may act as launchpads or catalysts for thriving in this context. This support not only assists an individual in engaging in life opportunities but also promotes thriving through the life opportunities, which is what differentiates this support function from others that have been considered in the psychological literature.

The proposed features of RC support are as follows: First, nurturing a desire to create and/or seize life opportunities for growth is a key feature of RC support. This includes behaviors such as instilling confidence in one's partner, expressing enthusiasm regarding the pursuit of life opportunities, and encouraging the partner to challenge or extend him- or herself and grow as an individual. This category of behaviors also involves communicating the potential benefits of creating/pursuing life opportunities, encouraging a focus on living in the present (instead of the past), and providing encouragement to embrace even small life opportunities that may be stepping-stones to bigger ones. Because opportunities are not always provided by chance, the encouragement to take initiative in creating one's own opportunities is an important part of motivating the pursuit of life opportunities.

Performing this function successfully involves the provision of perceptual assistance in the viewing of life opportunities, which is another feature of RC support. This includes assisting the partner in viewing life opportunities as positive challenges and not as threats to be avoided (Blascovich, 2008). Because a major impediment to full engagement in life opportunities is likely to begin with the recipient's perception of them, individuals who function as relational catalysts help their partners both to notice and to positively evaluate opportunities before they have passed. Assistance in recognizing opportunities is important, as many opportunities are missed because they are not obvious, because they are so plentiful that they are not recognized as opportunities, because the recipient is distracted or not being attentive to opportunities, because the opportunities may not look as expected, or because opportunities do not typically appear with a list of benefits attached.

A third function of RC support is to facilitate preparation for full engagement in life opportunities by providing preparatory assistance in the development of plans, strategies, skills/talents, and resources for approaching opportunities. This includes behaviors such as encouraging the development of necessary skills related to opportunities/goals that one would like to pursue (and giving necessary space to do so), providing instrumental or informational assistance in attaining necessary resources, praising/complimenting preparation efforts, accommodating plans/strategies for pursuing goals, providing direct teaching/instruction or feedback if one has relevant expertise for doing so, encouraging one to perform to his or her capabilities (and to challenge oneself to stretch his or her capabilities), encouraging the setting of attainable goals (Wrosch, Scheier, Miller, Schulz, & Carver, 2003), and communicating that one values the preparation efforts. A relationship partner may also see a "special" quality in an individual that others cannot yet see and so can help to nurture its development (Drigotas, Rusbult, Wieselquist, & Whitton, 1999).

The final function of RC support is to provide the launching function during a partner's actual engagement in life opportunities for growth. This involves the provision of a secure base (Bowlby, 1982, 1988) during the seizing of life opportunities (extended to apply to both novel/exploratory and nonnovel/nonexploratory opportunities). In prior work, we have identified three core features of a secure base (Feeney & Thrush, 2010). These include (a) providing encouragement during the engagement (e.g., complimenting/ praising the partner's progress); (b) not unnecessarily interfering, as the primary function of a base is a waiting one (Bowlby, 1988); and (c) being available in the event that the base is needed while the partner is engaging in life opportunities (e.g., to assist in removing obstacles, provide protection against potential threats, remove burdens that might distract the partner from his or her mission, and stay connected to the partner and his or her world). This is the connective function of RC support that ties the rocket to the launchpad, and it is important because individuals who are confident in the availability of their base do not have to cling to that base to the extent that individuals who lack such confidence do (Feeney, 2007). The other part of this launching function that is particularly important for the promotion of thriving through engagement in life opportunities is assisting in tune-ups and adjustments (e.g., in perceptions, skills, and strategies) that may be necessary during and after engagement in life opportunities for growth, as well as supporting and encouraging capitalization (celebrating successes and participating in the social sharing of good news; Gable et al., 2006, 2004), which should function to encourage continued engagement in life opportunities for growth.

WHAT ARE THE MECHANISMS THROUGH WHICH SOCIAL BEHAVIORS HAVE THEIR EFFECTS ON THRIVING

We have proposed eight broad categories of mechanisms through which SOS and RC support are expected to have their effects on thriving by leading to changes in one's emotional state; self-evaluations and self-perceptions; appraisals of the situation or event; motivational state; situation-relevant behaviors and outcomes; relational outcomes, attitudes, and expectations; neural activation and physiological functioning; and lifestyle behaviors (Feeney & Collins, 2012). These mechanisms are immediate outcomes of receiving SOS and RC support. They are expected to be relatively circumscribed to the particular situation, and to precede the core thriving outcomes, which develop over time and represent long-term outcomes. Although each support function influences all categories of mechanisms, the specific manifestation of each category is expected to differ for each support function. Next, we summarize predictions regarding the proposed influence of each support function on each category of mechanisms.

Emotional State

SOS Support

Because a variety of negative emotions are associated with the experience of adversity, an important immediate outcome of receiving SOS support is decreased or alleviated feelings of immediate negative emotions including fear, anxiety, doubt, distress, sadness, guilt, shame, anger, discouragement, loss/grief, embarrassment, humiliation, resentment, hurt/broken-heartedness, loneliness, frustration, despair, depression, jealousy, and envy—as well as faster recovery from negative emotional states generated by stressors. Increases in some positive emotions should also result from receiving SOS support, including increased feelings of love, hope, gratitude, forgiveness, amusement, serenity/peace/calm, and relief. Increased felt security, which involves a feeling of safety from threats (Bowlby, 1982; Sroufe & Waters, 1977), should be another immediate consequence of receiving SOS support. These predictions are consistent with evidence indicating that acts of caring from a partner in a stressful situation can result in increases in positive mood (Collins & Feeney, 2000; Collins, Jaremka, & Kane, 2012), increases in feeling calm and secure (Simpson, Rholes, & Nelligan, 1992), decreases in depression and anger (Cutrona, 1996a; Winstead & Derlega, 1985), and decreases in anxiety (Kane, McCall, Collins, & Blascovich, 2012).

RC Support

RC support is expected to activate a much broader range of positive emotions than SOS support. These positive emotions include felt enthusiasm/excitement regarding the pursuit of the life opportunity, as well as increases in feelings of interest, happiness, joy, amusement, pride, curiosity, surprise, wonder, and awe—emotions that are likely to be linked with the anticipation and pursuit of life opportunities. RC support may also lead one to feel inspired, lively, energetic, and invigorated. These emotions are in addition to the positive feelings of love, hope, and gratitude that are likely immediate outcomes of receiving both RC and SOS support functions. Consistent with these predictions, research has shown that responsive secure base support is linked with greater expressed enthusiasm during exploration activities and increases in positive mood after engaging in exploration activities (Feeney, 2004; Feeney & Thrush, 2010).

Although RC support is expected to act most strongly on positive emotions, it is also expected to decrease negative emotions that may result from anticipatory concerns regarding engagement in life opportunities: It should decrease feelings of fear, anxiety, doubt, and release one from concerns about failure or from feelings of guilt regarding the opportunity or an obligation to desist in pursuing the opportunity (e.g., because it takes time and resources away from other pursuits). Instilling excitement and enthusiasm for the pursuit of life opportunities and releasing a partner from feelings of guilt or anxiety are primary functions of RC support that should assist the individual in making challenge versus threat appraisals (Blascovich, 2008) regarding the life opportunity and increase the likelihood of one pursuing the opportunity.

Self-Evaluations and Self-Perceptions

SOS Support

Receipt of SOS support should predict increased state self-esteem, self-confidence, and empowerment to the extent that the support has invested the recipient with power/courage or equipped the recipient with skills to overcome the adverse circumstance. Specific self-evaluations/perceptions that should emerge from the receipt of SOS support include views that the self is capable of overcoming adversity, views that the self is strong and resilient, and views that the self is loved and valued.

RC Support

Because the provision of RC support involves instilling confidence and courage in one's partner, assisting the partner in viewing life opportunities as positive challenges, providing preparatory assistance in the development of skills/talents, and promoting successful engagement in life opportunities for growth, natural consequences of receiving this type of support should include increased state self-esteem (an immediate sense of personal worth), self-confidence, and empowerment involving feelings of perceived competency and self-efficacy (power to produce desired effects). Specific self-evaluations that should emerge from the receipt of RC support include views of the self as capable of accomplishing goals, and views that the self is accomplished, skilled, and engaged in life. These predictions are consistent with evidence indicating that variables representing components of RC support are associated with increases in state self-esteem after engaging in exploration (Feeney, 2004; Feeney & Thrush, 2010), as well as greater perceived self-efficacy, perceived ability to achieve one's goals, self-confidence, and perceived capability (Feeney, 2004, 2007).

Appraisals of the Situation or Event

SOS Support

Receipt of SOS support should predict optimism and positive expectancies/appraisals about the likely outcome of the adverse event. This includes appraisals that one's resources outweigh the demands of the situation (Lazarus & Folkman, 1984), appraisals of the problem as only temporary and not as the way circumstances always will be, an expectation that one will emerge from the adversity better than before, and appraisals of the experience as important for positive change. These are active expectations that convey an unshakable assurance either that the adverse circumstance will provide a stepping-stone for positive change or that one can deal successfully with a situation that cannot be changed.

RC Support

Receipt of RC support should also predict optimism and positive expectancies/appraisals about likely outcomes of engaging in the life opportunity. This includes expectations that engagement in the life opportunity will be successful (e.g., that one's goals will be accomplished), as well as appraisals of the experience as enjoyable and worth one's time and effort. Depending on the nature of the opportunity, it may also include appraisals of the experience as meaningful and as having the potential to impact others. Corroborating these predictions, initial research in this area has shown that responsive secure base support provision is linked with greater perceptions that exploration is enjoyable and that one is smart and competent to engage in it (Feeney & Thrush, 2010).

Motivational State

SOS Support

Because SOS support is not just about minimizing negative effects of adversity but is also about thriving through the experience, switching from a prevention or avoidance orientation to a promotion or approach orientation should be an immediate outcome of receiving SOS support. Although people have evolved to approach pleasurable/hedonistic opportunities and avoid unpleasant circumstances in order to promote growth, avoid painful experiences, and protect themselves from harm (Elliot & Covington, 2001), our model predicts that SOS support results in an approach motivation in adverse circumstances that may lead to growth through adversity. Receiving SOS support should motivate individuals to make positive changes in their lives, to work toward rebuilding, and to avoid giving up; it motivates individuals by expectations of what can be instead of what the situation currently is.

RC Support

Because RC support encourages pursuit of life opportunities and releases one from constraints that may hinder these pursuits, a natural immediate consequence of this support function should be an approach (vs. avoidance) motivation toward the opportunity for growth. This motivational state involves beliefs that it is important and worthwhile to pursue the opportunity and beliefs that one should stretch to new levels in life and not settle for "good enough." This motivational state involves boldness and willingness to pull up stakes (not to get stuck at one level) and to leave one's comfort zone in order to grow and reach one's full potential. This idea is consistent with research showing that responsive support provision is associated with a greater willingness to engage in autonomous exploration (Feeney, 2007).

Situation-Relevant Behaviors and Outcomes

SOS Support

Receiving SOS support should result in positive immediate coping and better self-regulation (i.e., the ability to control one's behavior and emotions; the ability to develop, implement, and flexibly maintain planned behavior; W. R. Miller & Brown, 1991; Muraven, Tice, & Baumeister, 1998), as well as problem resolution (i.e., alleviation of the problem or reduction of its severity; e.g., Lakey & Heller, 1988; Winstead, Derlega, Lewis, Sanchez-Hucles, & Clarke, 1992). Additional immediate outcomes of SOS support include changes in one's circumstances or outcomes of those circumstances, successful rebuilding (i.e., replacing prior aspects of one's life associated with the adversity with new and improved features), and learning from the adverse experience.

RC Support

Receiving RC support should result in successful engagement in and persistence at the life opportunity, goal accomplishment/progress, opened doors for additional opportunities (made possible through engaging in the current opportunity), and the production of a high-quality result (if engagement in a life opportunity culminated in a product). This includes approaching the activity with greater focus, more energy, and a propensity to navigate the challenges more collaboratively or socially than one might otherwise. Recipients of RC support are also likely to learn something from their engagement in the life opportunity (e.g., how to perform a task, new places to explore). Although these proposed links have not been tested directly with regard to RC support, there is evidence indicating that components of RC support are associated with recipients' greater persistence at and better performance on a laboratory exploration activity (Feeney & Thrush, 2010), and greater autonomous functioning with regard to personal goal-strivings (e.g., confident exploration of independent goals; Feeney, 2007).

Relational Outcomes, Attitudes, and Expectations

SOS Support

Immediate relational outcomes of receiving SOS support include a state of trust in the partner's caring and commitment (Murray, 2005); feelings of emotional closeness as a result of feeling understood, validated, and cared for despite one's vulnerabilities (Reis & Shaver, 1988); and beliefs that seeking support from the partner and showing vulnerability are beneficial and met with compassionate responses. Additional immediate relational outcomes include feelings of social acceptance and social connection, feelings of being loved and valued, confidence in the supporting partner's availability and goodwill, and feelings of unconditional positive regard from the supporting partner. Although these proposed links have not been tested specifically with regard to SOS support, there is evidence indicating that acts of caring from a partner result in immediate increases in relationship perceptions of feeling loved, valued, accepted, and happy in one's relationship (Collins et al., 2012; Kane et al., 2012).

RC Support

Immediate relational outcomes of receiving RC support include the formation of new social connections (e.g., meeting new people as a result of engaging in the opportunity), feelings of social acceptance and social connection (from the support provider and others with whom one engages during the opportunity), and feelings of being valued and cared for. Additional immediate relational outcomes include views that the support provider believes in one's abilities; self-expansion in terms of including one's partner in the self (Aron & Aron, 1986); a healthy interdependence with relationship partners (vs. overdependence or underdependence); and beliefs that sharing one's experiences when pursuing life opportunities with the partner, capitalizing on the experiences, and seeking support for them are beneficial (Gable et al., 2006, 2004; Reis et al., 2010).

Neural Activation and Physiological Functioning

SOS Support

There is research indicating that neural regions associated with threat (amygdala, dorsal anterior cingulate cortex, anterior insula, and periaqueductal gray) can trigger physiological responses that have health implications, and that the experience of social connections can turn off this neural alarm system (Eisenberger & Cole, 2012). Thus, deactivation of neural areas associated with threat and increased activation of reward-related neural areas (ventromedial prefrontal cortex and the posterior cingulate cortex) associated with safety (Eisenberger & Cole, 2012) are expected to be immediate outcomes of receiving SOS support. On the physiological level, adaptive immune, endocrine, and cardiovascular functioning should also be immediate outcomes of receiving SOS support. This includes reduced cortisol and stress reactivity, as well as reduced cardiovascular threat response (which occurs when individuals evaluate their resources as being outweighed by situational task demands; Blascovich, 2008), physiological hardiness (which buffers the physical effects of stress on the body; Šolcová & Sýkora, 1995), and faster cardiovascular recovery. Increased oxytocin, which has been linked with positive social interactions and wound healing (Marazziti et al., 2006), may be an additional immediate consequence of receiving SOS support.

RC Support

In contrast to SOS support, an immediate outcome of the receipt of RC support should be increased activation of neural areas associated with reward, positive affect, positive challenge, representation of goals, decision making, and dopamine release (i.e., the striatum, orbitofrontal cortex, medial prefrontal cortex, ventral tegmental area, and amygdala; Aron et al., 2005; Forbes & Dahl, 2005; Spanagel & Weiss, 1999). These activations should be linked, on the physiological level, with adaptive immune, endocrine, and cardiovascular functioning associated with positive affect and positive challenge. In contrast to SOS support, RC support is likely to generate more "activated" forms of positive emotions (e.g., excitement); thus, this support function may lead to increased cardiovascular responding (Pressman & Cohen, 2005), which may reflect a challenge versus threat cardiovascular pattern (Blascovich, 2008). Increases in anabolic processes (that involve the buildup of substances and require the expenditure of energy in the process, including the growth and mineralization of bone and increases in muscle mass) are also physiological outcomes likely to result from receiving support for the pursuit of life opportunities. Finally, because of RC support's proposed effect on positive emotion, and because positive emotion has been linked with lower levels of stress hormones and adaptive immune functioning in some studies (see Pressman & Cohen, 2005, for a review), these physiological outcomes are expected to be important immediate consequences of receiving RC support.

Lifestyle Behaviors

SOS Support

Immediate changes in lifestyle behaviors are also likely to result from the receipt of SOS support. These include a healthier diet (e.g., no stress-induced eating); better sleep quality (as sleep is not inhibited by feelings of distress or rumination on adversity); decreased use of alcohol, smoking, or other addictive substances as a means of coping with stress; and adherence to medical regimens (which is particularly important if the adversity involves an illness). This may also involve being more organized in one's daily life as a strategy for reducing stress, incorporating restorative activities that allow one to decompress, and educating oneself (seeking knowledge) on factors related to overcoming the adversity.

RC Support

Immediate changes in lifestyle behaviors likely to result from the receipt of RC support also include better sleep, diet, and engagement in restorative activities. However, increased physical and mental activity/exercise is especially likely to be influenced by support that encourages one to embrace life opportunities for growth. This is consistent with research showing that positive affect (an important predicted outcome of receiving RC support) is associated with improved sleep quality (Bardwell, Berry, Ancoli-Israel, & Dimsdale, 1999), more exercise (Ryff, Singer, & Dienberg Love, 2004), greater engagement in restorative activities (Smith & Baum, 2003), and more intake of dietary zinc (Cohen et al., 2003; for a review, see Pressman & Cohen, 2005).

MECHANISMS INFLUENCING THRIVING OUTCOMES

The mechanisms we have discussed, which we view as immediate outcomes of receiving SOS and RC support, over many interactions, should make independent contributions to the prediction of the 10 indicators of long-term thriving. Our perspective considers immediate outcomes of social support interactions to be important because they have a cumulative impact on long-term outcomes. For example, because even daily hassles have cumulative, long-term effects that can equal those of major life events (DeLongis, Folkman, & Lazarus, 1988), it is important to examine the immediate solutions to life's adversities and determine the ways in which immediate solutions may, over time, have serious long-term consequences for thriving. If an individual experiences increased hope/optimism, reduced fear/anxiety, reduced autonomic reactivity to stress, increased feelings of security, positive coping, problem resolution, and increased trust/closeness after receiving SOS support from a close relationship partner when distressed, then these positive support experiences should, over time, contribute to thriving in terms of relationship growth/prosperity, enhanced prospects for good mental and physical health, a positive self-concept, a positive orientation toward others, accumulation of wisdom, the development of core strength, the development of skills/talents, the discovery of self and life purpose, and movement toward one's full potential. Likewise, if an individual experiences felt enthusiasm/excitement, a release from guilt and failure concerns, increased confidence/empowerment/self-esteem, successful engagement in life opportunities, adaptive physiological responses to challenge, and healthy interdependence after receiving RC support from a close relationship partner, then these support experiences should, over time, make important contributions to thriving above and beyond contributions made by SOS processes.

CONCLUDING STATEMENT

Our goal for this chapter was to highlight aspects of our theoretical perspective on how individuals can thrive through their relationships. We have done this by (a) outlining a conceptualization of what it means to thrive, (b) describing two support functions that work together to promote thriving, and (c) describing mechanisms through which relational support may have its effect on thriving. It is especially important to note that this perspective considers support for thriving within a life context (i.e., engagement in life opportunities) that has been neglected during decades of research on social support, it considers support for thriving in a life context (i.e., dealing with adversity) that has historically focused on buffering negative effects instead of promoting positive ones, and it provides an integrative framework for considering the joint functioning of SOS and RC support in promoting thriving. We hope that this framework will induce researchers to take a new look at social support and that it will facilitate the development of new programs of research on thriving through relationships.

REFERENCES

Aron, A., & Aron, E. N. (1986). Love and the expansion of self: Understanding attraction and satisfaction. New York, NY: Hemisphere.

Aron, A., Fisher, H., Mashek, D. J., Strong, G., Li, H., & Brown, L. L. (2005). Reward, motivation, and emotion systems associated with early-stage intense romantic love. Journal of Neurophysiology, 94, 327–337. doi:10.1152/jn.00838.2004

Bardwell, W. A., Berry, C. C., Ancoli-Israel, S., & Dimsdale, J. E. (1999). Psychological correlates of sleep apnea. Journal of Psychosomatic Research, 47, 583–596. doi:10.1016/S0022-3999(99)00062-8

Baumeister, R. F., & Vohs, K. D. (Eds.). (2004). Handbook of self-regulation: Research, theory, and applications. New York, NY: Guilford Press.

Berkman, L. F., & Syme, S. L. (1979). Social networks, host resistance, and mortality: A nine year follow-up study of Alameda County residents. American Journal of Epidemiology, 109, 186–204.

Blascovich, J. (2008). Challenge, threat, and health. In J. Y. Shah & W. L. Gardner (Eds.), *Handbook of motivation science* (pp. 481–493). New York, NY: Guilford Press.

Bowlby, J. (1973). *Attachment and loss: Vol. 2. Separation: Anxiety and anger.* New York, NY: Basic Books.

Bowlby, J. (1982). *Attachment and loss: Vol. 1. Attachment* (2nd ed.). New York, NY: Basic Books.

Bowlby, J. (1988). *A secure base: Clinical applications of attachment theory.* New York, NY: Basic Books.

Bundick, M. J., Yeager, D. S., King, P. E., & Damon, W. (2010). Thriving across the life span. In W. F. Overton (Ed.), *The handbook of life-span development: Vol. 1. Cognition, biology, and methods* (pp. 882–923). Hoboken, NJ: Wiley. doi:10.1002/9780470880166.hlsd001024

Carver, C. S. (1998). Resilience and thriving: Issues, models, and linkages. *Journal of Social Issues, 54,* 245–266. doi:10.1111/j.1540-4560.1998.tb01217.x

Clark, M. S., & Mills, J. R. (2012). A theory of communal (and exchange) relationships. In P. A. M. Van Lange, A. W. Kruglanski, & E. T. Higgins (Eds.), *Handbook of theories of social psychology* (Vol. 2, pp. 232–250). Thousand Oaks, CA: Sage.

Cohen, S. (2004). Social relationships and health. *American Psychologist, 59,* 676–684. doi:10.1037/0003-066X.59.8.676

Cohen, S., Doyle, W. J., Turner, R., Alper, C. M., & Skoner, D. P. (2003). Sociability and susceptibility to the common cold. *Psychological Science, 14,* 389–395. doi:10.1111/1467-9280.01452

Collins, N. L., & Feeney, B. C. (2000). A safe haven: An attachment theory perspective on support-seeking and caregiving in adult romantic relationships. *Journal of Personality and Social Psychology, 78,* 1053–1073. doi:10.1037/0022-3514.78.6.1053

Collins, N. L., & Feeney, B. C. (2004). An attachment theory perspective on closeness and intimacy. In D. J. Mashek & A. P. Aron (Eds.), *Handbook of closeness and intimacy* (pp. 163–187). Mahwah, NJ: Erlbaum.

Collins, N. L., Jaremka, L. M., & Kane, H. S. (2012). *Social support during a stressful task reduces cortisol reactivity, promotes emotional recovery, and builds caring relationships.* Unpublished manuscript, University of California, Santa Barbara.

Cutrona, C. E. (1996a). Social support as a determinant of marital quality: The interplay of negative and supportive behaviors. In G. R. Pierce, B. R. Sarason, & I. G. Sarason (Eds.), *Handbook of social support and the family* (pp. 173–194). New York, NY: Plenum Press.

Cutrona, C. E. (1996b). *Social support in couples: Marriage as a resource in times of stress.* Thousand Oaks, CA: Sage.

Deci, E. L., & Ryan, R. M. (2000). The "what" and "why" of goal pursuits: Human needs and the self-determination of behavior. *Psychological Inquiry, 11,* 227–268. doi:10.1207/S15327965PLI1104_01

DeLongis, A., Folkman, S., & Lazarus, R. S. (1988). The impact of daily stress on health and mood: Psychological and social resources as mediators. *Journal of Personality and Social Psychology, 54,* 486–495. doi:10.1037/0022-3514.54.3.486

DeLongis, A., & Holtzman, S. (2005). Coping in context: The role of stress, social support, and personality in coping. *Journal of Personality, 73,* 1633–1656. doi:10.1111/j.1467-6494.2005.00361.x

Dolbier, C. L, Cocke, R. R., Leiferman, J. A., Steinhardt, M. A., Schapiro, S. J., Nehete, P. N., . . . Sastry, J. (2001). Differences in functional immune responses of high vs. low hardy healthy individuals. *Journal of Behavioral Medicine, 24,* 219–229. doi:10.1023/A:1010762606006

Drigotas, S. M., Rusbult, C. E., Wieselquist, J., & Whitton, S. W. (1999). Close partner as sculptor of the ideal self: Behavioral affirmation and the Michelangelo phenomenon. *Journal of Personality and Social Psychology, 77,* 293–323. doi:10.1037/0022-3514.77.2.293

Eisenberger, N. I., & Cole, S. W. (2012). Social neuroscience and health: Neurophysiological mechanisms linking social ties with physical health. *Nature Neuroscience, 15,* 669–674. doi:10.1038/nn.3086

Elliot, A. J., & Covington, M. V. (2001). Approach and avoidance motivation. *Educational Psychology Review, 13,* 73–92. doi:10.1023/A:1009009018235

Emmons, R. A. (1991). Personal strivings, daily life events, and psychological and physical well-being. *Journal of Personality, 59,* 453–472. doi:10.1111/j.1467-6494.1991.tb00256.x

Eschleman, K. J., Bowling, N. A., & Alarcon, G. M. (2010). A meta-analytic examination of hardiness. *International Journal of Stress Management, 17,* 277–307. doi:10.1037/a0020476

Feeney, B. C. (2004). A secure base: Responsive support of goal strivings and exploration in adult intimate relationships. *Journal of Personality and Social Psychology, 87,* 631–648. doi:10.1037/0022-3514.87.5.631

Feeney, B. C. (2007). The dependency paradox in close relationships: Accepting dependence promotes independence. *Journal of Personality and Social Psychology, 92,* 268–285. doi:10.1037/0022-3514.92.2.268

Feeney, B. C., & Collins, N. L. (2012). *A new look at social support: A theory of thriving through relationships.* Manuscript submitted for publication.

Feeney, B. C., & Thrush, R. L. (2010). Relationship influences on exploration in adulthood: The characteristics and function of a secure base. *Journal of Personality and Social Psychology, 98,* 57–76. doi:10.1037/a0016961

Forbes, E. E., & Dahl, R. E. (2005). Neural systems of positive affect: Relevance to understanding child and adolescent depression? *Development and Psychopathology, 17,* 827–850. doi:10.1017/S095457940505039X

Fredrickson, B. L. (2001). The role of positive emotions in positive psychology: The broaden-and-build theory of positive emotions. *American Psychologist, 56,* 218–226. doi:10.1037/0003-066X.56.3.218

Gable, S. L., Gonzaga, G. C., & Strachman, A. (2006). Will you be there for me when things go right? Supportive responses to positive event disclosures. *Journal of Personality and Social Psychology, 91*, 904–917. doi:10.1037/0022-3514.91.5.904

Gable, S. L., Reis, H. T., Impett, E. A., & Asher, E. R. (2004). What do you do when things go right? The intrapersonal and interpersonal benefits of sharing positive events. *Journal of Personality and Social Psychology, 87*, 228–245. doi:10.1037/0022-3514.87.2.228

Hawkley, L. C., & Cacioppo, J. T. (2003). Loneliness and pathways to disease. *Brain, Behavior, and Immunity, 17*, S98–S105. doi:10.1016/S0889-1591(02)00073-9

Holt-Lunstad, J., & Smith, T. B. (2012). Social relationships and mortality. *Social and Personality Psychology Compass, 6*, 41–53. doi:10.1111/j.1751-9004.2011.00406.x

Kane, H. S., McCall, C., Collins, N. L., & Blascovich, J. A. (2012). Mere presence is not enough: Responsive support in a virtual world. *Journal of Experimental Social Psychology, 48*, 37–44. doi:10.1016/j.jesp.2011.07.001

Lakey, B., & Heller, K. (1988). Social support from a friend, perceived support, and social problem solving. *American Journal of Community Psychology, 16*, 811–824. doi:10.1007/BF00930894

Lazarus, R. S., & Folkman, S. (1984). *Stress, appraisal, and coping.* New York, NY: Springer.

Lerner, R. M., von Eye, A., Lerner, J. V., Lewin-Bizan, S., & Bowers, E. P. (2010). Special issue introduction: The meaning and measurement of thriving: A view of the issues. *Journal of Youth and Adolescence, 39*, 707–719. doi:10.1007/s10964-010-9531-8

Maddi, S. R. (2006). Hardiness: The courage to grow from stresses. *Journal of Positive Psychology, 1*, 160–168. doi:10.1080/17439760600619609

Marazziti, D., Bani, A., Casamassima, F., Catena, M., Consoli, G., Gesi, C., . . . Scarpellini, P. (2006). Oxytocin: An old hormone for new avenues. *Clinical Neuropsychiatry, 3*, 302–321.

McCrae, R. R. (1987). Creativity, divergent thinking, and openness to experience. *Journal of Personality and Social Psychology, 52*, 1258–1265. doi:10.1037/0022-3514.52.6.1258

Mikulincer, M., & Shaver, P. R. (2007). *Attachment in adulthood: Structure, dynamics, and change.* New York, NY: Guilford Press.

Miller, T. Q., Smith, T. W., Turner, C. W., Guijarro, M. L., & Hallet, A. J. (1996). Meta-analytic review of research on hostility and physical health. *Psychological Bulletin, 119*, 322–348. doi:10.1037/0033-2909.119.2.322

Miller, W. R., & Brown, J. M. (1991). Self-regulation as a conceptual basis for the prevention and treatment of addictive behaviours. In N. Heather, W. R. Miller, & J. Greeley (Eds.), *Self-control and the addictive behaviours* (pp. 3–79). Sydney, Australia: Maxwell Macmillan.

Morrison, M., & Roese, N. J. (2011). Regrets of the typical American: Findings from a nationally representative sample. *Social Psychological and Personality Science, 2*, 576–583. doi:10.1177/1948550611401756

Muraven, M., Tice, D. M., & Baumeister, R. F. (1998). Self-control as a limited resource: Regulatory depletion patterns. *Journal of Personality and Social Psychology, 74*, 774–789. doi:10.1037/0022-3514.74.3.774

Murray, S. L. (2005). Regulating the risks of closeness: A relationship-specific sense of felt security. *Current Directions in Psychological Science, 14*, 74–78. doi:10.1111/j.0963-7214.2005.00338.x

Newsom, J. T., Mahan, T. L., Rook, K. S., & Krause, N. (2008). Stable negative social exchanges and health. *Health Psychology, 27*, 78–86. doi:10.1037/0278-6133.27.1.78

Pressman, S. D., & Cohen, S. (2005). Does positive affect influence health? *Psychological Bulletin, 131*, 925–971. doi:10.1037/0033-2909.131.6.925

Pressman, S. D., Cohen, S., Miller, G. E., Barkin, A., Rabin, B. S., & Treanor, J. J. (2005). Loneliness, social network size, and immune response to influenza vaccination in college freshmen. *Health Psychology, 24*, 297–306. doi:10.1037/0278-6133.24.3.297

Reis, H. T., & Shaver, P. (1988). Intimacy as an interpersonal process. In S. Duck, D. F. Hay, S. E. Hobfoll, W. Ickes, & B. M. Montgomery (Eds.), *Handbook of personal relationships: Theory, research, and interventions* (pp. 367–389). Chichester, England: Wiley.

Reis, H. T., Smith, S. M, Carmichael, C. L., Caprariello, P. A., Tsai, F.-F., Rodrigues, A., & Maniaci, M. R. (2010). Are you happy for me? How sharing positive events with others provides personal and interpersonal benefits. *Journal of Personality and Social Psychology, 99*, 311–329. doi:10.1037/a0018344

Rook, K. S. (1984). The negative side of social interaction: Impact on psychological well-being. *Journal of Personality and Social Psychology, 46*, 1097–1108. doi:10.1037/0022-3514.46.5.1097

Ryff, C. D., & Singer, B. (1998). The contours of positive human health. *Psychological Inquiry, 9*, 1–28. doi:10.1207/s15327965pli0901_1

Ryff, C. D., & Singer, B. (2003). Thriving in the face of challenge: The integrative science of human resilience. In F. Kessel, P. L. Rosenfield, & N. B. Anderson (Eds.), *Expanding the boundaries of health and social science: Case studies in interdisciplinary innovation* (pp. 181–205). New York, NY: Oxford University Press.

Ryff, C. D., & Singer, B. H. (2008). Know thyself and become what you are: A eudaimonic approach to psychological well-being. *Journal of Happiness Studies, 9*, 13–39. doi:10.1007/s10902-006-9019-0

Ryff, C. D., Singer, B. H., & Dienberg Love, G. (2004). Positive health: Connecting well-being with biology. *Philosophical Transactions of the Royal Society of London: Series B. Biological Sciences, 359*, 1383–1394. doi:10.1098/rstb.2004.1521

Scheier, M. F., & Carver, C. S. (1992). Effects of optimism on psychological and physical well-being: Theoretical overview and empirical update. *Cognitive Therapy and Research, 16*, 201–228. doi:10.1007/BF01173489

Schulz, R., Beach, S. R., Ives, D. G., Martire, L. M., Ariyo, A. A., & Kop, W. J. (2000). Association between depression and mortality in older adults: The Cardiovascular

Health Study. *Archives of Internal Medicine, 160,* 1761–1768. doi:10.1001/archinte. 160.12.1761

Seery, M. D., Holman, E. A., & Silver, R. C. (2010). Whatever does not kill us: Cumulative lifetime adversity, vulnerability, and resilience. *Journal of Personality and Social Psychology, 99,* 1025–1041. doi:10.1037/a0021344

Simpson, J. A., Rholes, W. S., & Nelligan, J. S. (1992). Support seeking and support giving within couples in an anxiety-provoking situation: The role of attachment styles. *Journal of Personality and Social Psychology, 62,* 434–446. doi:10.1037/ 0022-3514.62.3.434

Smith, A. W., & Baum, A. (2003). The influence of psychological factors on restorative function in health and illness. In J. Suls & K. A. Wallston (Eds.), *Social psychological foundations of health and illness* (pp. 431–457). Malden, MA: Blackwell. doi:10.1002/9780470753552.ch16

Šolcová, I., & Sýkora, J. (1995). Relation between psychological hardiness and physiological response. *Homeostasis in Health and Disease, 36,* 30–34.

Spanagel, R., & Weiss, F. (1999). The dopamine hypothesis of reward: Past and current status. *Trends in Neurosciences, 22,* 521–527. doi:10.1016/S0166-2236 (99)01447-2

Sroufe, L. A., & Waters, E. (1977). Attachment as an organizational construct. *Child Development, 48,* 1184–1199. doi:10.2307/1128475

Warburton, D. E. R., Nicol, C. W., & Bredin, S. S. D. (2006). Health benefits of physical activity: The evidence. *Canadian Medical Association Journal, 174,* 801–809. doi:10.1503/cmaj.051351

Winstead, B. A., & Derlega, V. J. (1985). Benefits of same-sex friendships in a stressful situation. *Journal of Social and Clinical Psychology, 3,* 378–384. doi:10.1521/jscp. 1985.3.3.378

Winstead, B. A., Derlega, V. J., Lewis, R. J., Sanchez-Hucles, J., & Clarke, E. (1992). Friendship, social interaction, and coping with stress. *Communication Research, 19,* 193–211. doi:10.1177/009365092019002004

Wrosch, C., Scheier, M. F., Miller, G. E., Schulz, R., & Carver, C. S. (2003). Adaptive self-regulation of unattainable goals: Goal disengagement, goal reengagement, and subjective well-being. *Personality and Social Psychology Bulletin, 29,* 1494–1508. doi:10.1177/0146167203256921

17

SEXY BUILDING BLOCKS: THE CONTRIBUTION OF THE SEXUAL SYSTEM TO ATTACHMENT FORMATION AND MAINTENANCE

GURIT E. BIRNBAUM

Sexual mating and attachment are governed by separate motivational systems that arose during human evolution (Fisher, 1998; Fisher, Aron, Mashek, Li, & Brown, 2002). Thus, the processes underlying sexual desire and affectional bonding are functionally distinct (motivating reproductive acts vs. keeping partners attached to each other, respectively), and their behavioral manifestations can occur in isolation (Diamond, 2003). For example, sexual acts often occur outside the context of romantic relationships (e.g., one-night stands, short-term extradyadic copulations), and as such, they may be devoid of affectional bonding and be used for the sole purpose of immediate physical gratification. Still, in adulthood, joint operation of these two systems is typical of ongoing romantic relationships, in which partners function simultaneously as sexual partners and attachment figures (Hazan & Zeifman, 1994; see also Chapter 15, this volume).

Within the context of romantic relationships, sex has the potential for eliciting intensely meaningful experiences that may serve as a powerful motivational force across different stages of relationship development. Sexual

http://dx.doi.org/10.1037/14250-018
Mechanisms of Social Connection: From Brain to Group, M. Mikulincer and P. R. Shaver (Editors)
Copyright © 2014 by the American Psychological Association. All rights reserved.

attraction is often what brings potential partners together to begin with, and it helps to determine whether subsequent interactions will or will not take place (Berscheid & Reis, 1998). In later stages, as relationships progress from initial encounters to serious dating, sexual desire may provide the magnetism that holds partners together long enough for an attachment bond to form and then help to keep partners together in a committed relationship (Hazan & Zeifman, 1994, 1999). Yet, toward the end of a weakening relationship, sex may be what causes partners to grow apart, such as when sexual indifference motivates them to seek resolution of their relational problems by looking for a more suitable partner (Birnbaum & Reis, 2006).

In this chapter, I focus mainly on the role of sex as a promoter of emotional bonds between partners, and I discuss the role of attachment processes in the association between sexuality and relationship quality. The chapter begins with a brief overview of the literature on the contribution of intimate contact to attachment formation. I then describe potential mechanisms that promote proximity seeking and extended contact, and I review published evidence that indicates that sexual desire may serve as such a mechanism. Next, I discuss the role of sex in enhancing the emotional bond between sexual partners and present findings from studies on sex-related motives and cognitions that provide support for the proposed link between sex and attachment. I also introduce a model of the functional significance of sex that has guided most of my research on sexuality in romantic relationships. In doing so, I review findings that show how individual differences in attachment orientation help to explain variations in the role sex plays in attachment formation and maintenance across different stages of relationship development. I conclude by discussing promising directions for future research.

INTIMATE CONTACT AND ATTACHMENT FORMATION

From an attachment-theoretical perspective, sexual behaviors are regulated by an inborn sexual behavioral system, a species-universal neural program (Bowlby, 1969, 1982; Shaver, Hazan, & Bradshaw, 1988) that evolved to encourage the passing of one's genes to the next generation (via pregnancy or impregnation; Buss & Kenrick, 1998). The primary strategy for achieving this goal is to approach a potentially fertile partner, convince him or her to have sex, and engage in genital intercourse. However, impregnation is generally not sufficient for the survival of human offspring, who are vulnerable throughout an exceptionally prolonged development. Sexual partners therefore need to stay together long enough to jointly care for their offspring during the period of maximum vulnerability, thereby increasing the offspring's chances of survival and future reproductive success (Fisher, 1998; Hazan &

Zeifman, 1994; Mellen, 1981). Over the course of human evolution, selection pressures have produced mechanisms that keep sexual partners attached to each other for an extended period and motivate them to remain in a committed relationship and engage in coparenting behaviors following an offspring's birth (Birnbaum & Gillath, 2006; Birnbaum & Reis, 2006).

These selection pressures presumably enhanced proximity-seeking behaviors, including joint occurrence of prolonged mutually ventral contact, cuddling, nuzzling, and kissing, which characterize attachment bonds and distinguish them from other types of social relationships (e.g., affiliative relationships). This complex constellation of affectionate and soothing contact is a key determinant in the formation of both infant–caregiver and romantic relationships (Hazan & Zeifman, 1994, 1999; see also Chapter 3, this volume). Hence, mechanisms that encourage physical proximity and intimate contact are likely to contribute to the formation and maintenance of attachment bonds at any age. Nevertheless, the predominant motivations promoting closeness are likely to be different in infancy and adulthood. In infancy, security needs are likely to be the main driving motivation behind proximity seeking (Bowlby, 1982). In adulthood, sexual needs (or more specifically, sexual desire) are likely to provide the primary motivating force for such extended contact, increasing the likelihood that sexual partners become attached to each other (Berscheid, 1988; Diamond, 2004).

UNIQUE FEATURES OF HUMAN SEXUALITY AND PAIR-BONDING

Several unique characteristics of human reproductive physiology, anatomy, and behavior encourage physical proximity and intimate contact, implying that the sexual behavioral system may play a major role in motivating partners to stay attached to each other by strengthening and maintaining the emotional bond between them (Gonzaga, Keltner, Londahl, & Smith, 2001; Hazan & Zeifman, 1994, 1999). For example, the vaginal angle in human females has shifted over evolutionary time in such a way as to make penetration easier in the mutually ventral position (Ford & Beach, 1951), which allows face-to-face, belly-to-belly contact, and extended mutual gazing, and increases the chances of female orgasm (Short, 1979). This prevalent and preferred copulatory position, along with humans' tendencies to have sex in private and to sleep together after intercourse (Ford & Beach, 1951), is likely to enhance intimacy and emotional bonding between sexual partners.

Studies have also shown an increase in levels of serum oxytocin (OT) and vasopressin in humans during foreplay (e.g., kissing, caressing, breast and nipple stimulation), during sexual intercourse, and in the moments preceding orgasm (e.g., Carmichael et al., 1987; Carter, 1992; Filippi et al., 2003; Murphy,

Seckl, Burton, Checkley, & Lightman, 1987). These neuropeptides facilitate social approach, parental bonding, and pair-bonding behaviors among humans and other highly social species (e.g., Carter et al., 2005; Ditzen et al., 2009; K. A. Young, Gobrogge, Liu, & Wang, 2011; see also Chapters 1, 3, and 8, this volume) and are apparently involved in mediating the rewarding aspects of attachment (see Chapter 2). Together, the growing body of research on OT, vasopressin, and their attachment-promoting effects suggests that sexual activities may activate the hormone-mediated mechanisms underlying attachment formation.

It is interesting that some of the distinctive characteristics of human sexuality may further increase the release of OT and vasopressin during sexual intercourse and amplify their emotional bonding effects. For example, most mammalian species confine sexual activity to a brief estrus period around the advertised time of ovulation. In contrast, humans may have sex on any day of the menstrual cycle, thereby experiencing an extended release of OT and vasopressin. Additionally, humans are the only species whose females show permanent breast enlargement that is independent of lactation. This potential sexual appendage may serve to encourage nipple stimulation during sexual activity, resulting in heightened release of OT. Humans' tendency to engage in regular sexual activity that frequently involves nipple stimulation may thus reinforce sexual bonding and, over time, promote enduring attachment bonds between sexual partners (L. J. Young & Wang, 2004).

THE MOTIVATIONAL AND COGNITIVE MAKEUP OF THE SEX-ATTACHMENT LINKAGE

Another line of evidence for the proposed link between sex and attachment comes from studies focusing on people's accounts of their motives for having sex. There is a broad array of potential reasons that motivate people to engage in sexual intercourse, ranging from self-focused concerns (e.g., "I wanted to improve my sexual skills") to other-focused concerns (e.g., "I wanted the person to feel good about himself or herself"), as well as from approach related (e.g., "for pleasure and enjoyment") to avoidance related (e.g., "So I could relieve stress"; Cooper, Shapiro, & Powers, 1998; Hill & Preston, 1996; Meston & Buss, 2007). These reasons may vary across individuals, contexts, and partners (e.g., Birnbaum, Mikulincer, & Austerlitz, 2012; Birnbaum, Weisberg, & Simpson, 2011). For example, reasons for engaging in sex with a casual sex partner or an extradyadic partner (e.g., the desire to experience sexual variety; Symons, 1979) may differ from those that motivate sex in the context of an ongoing romantic relationship (e.g., deterring the partner from seeking sexual gratification elsewhere; Buss & Shackelford,

1997). Still, some of the most frequently endorsed reasons for having sex among both men and women reflect relationship-related motives, such as the desire for emotional closeness and the desire to intensify the relationship and to enhance the emotional bond (e.g., Meston & Buss, 2007).

Studies assessing mental representations of the sexual aspect of romantic relationships provide similar support for the theorized link between sex and attachment. In these studies, participants have been asked to describe the meanings they attach to sexual intercourse (Birnbaum, 2003) and their feelings, expectations, and beliefs about sexual activity with a romantic partner (Birnbaum & Gillath, 2006; Birnbaum & Reis, 2006). Findings indicate that beliefs that sexual activity promotes closeness between partners (e.g., "To me, sex is an important part of becoming really close to my partner") and enhances their emotional bond (e.g., "To me, sexual activity is a way of forming an affectionate relationship") are common among both men and women. However, although these studies suggest that sex is associated with the motivation to form and maintain close relationships, they do not provide evidence for the hypothesized causal pathway from activation of the sexual system to attachment maintenance.

Such experimental evidence has been presented in a series of laboratory studies showing that randomly assigning study participants to conditions that activate sexual desires and related thoughts leads to heightened relationship-promoting tendencies (Gillath, Mikulincer, Birnbaum, & Shaver, 2008). Specifically, in a series of five laboratory experiments, participants were subliminally exposed to erotic words or pictures (vs. neutral words or pictures). Results revealed that subliminal exposure to sexually arousing stimuli heightened accessibility of intimacy-related thoughts in a lexical-decision task (e.g., faster reaction times to intimacy-related words). Moreover, this sexual exposure, as compared to neutral primes, increased tendencies to initiate new relationships (as assessed by willingness to self-disclose intimate information to a potential romantic partner) and to strengthen existing ones (as assessed by willingness to sacrifice for a romantic partner or relationship and by preference for constructive conflict resolution strategies during conflictual interactions with a romantic partner). These findings suggest that sexual arousal may cause people to become more inclined to employ strategies that allow them to get closer to a potential new partner or to maintain a relationship with a current partner.

THE FUNCTIONAL SIGNIFICANCE OF SEX IN DIFFERENT RELATIONSHIP PHASES

As reviewed above, activation of the sexual system automatically facilitates both relationship initiation and relationship maintenance strategies (Gillath et al., 2008) and is therefore likely to affect attachment processes across all relationship phases. Nevertheless, the underlying function of sex may change as the relationship develops due to corresponding changes in the emotional bonding process (e.g., transformation from preattachment to a full-blown attachment relationship). The model presented here offers an initial theoretical framework for explaining the significance of sex for attachment processes in emerging and established relationships. In particular, this model illustrates how the functional significance of sex may change as relationships progress from initial encounters to long-term commitments.

In the proposed model, I identify six potential roles that sex may play in attachment formation and maintenance, and these roles correspond roughly to the various relationship phases: (a) motivating the pursuit of either short-term or long-term mating opportunities with potential sexual partners; (b) serving as a means of evaluating the suitability and compatibility of a newly met potential partner and as a gatekeeper ensuring that only suitable partners will be pursued; (c) motivating relationship initiation with a suitable potential partner; (d) promoting intimacy, trust, and commitment; (e) serving as a means of reevaluating the suitability and compatibility of a current long-term partner; and (f) motivating people to solve relational problems or pursue an alternative, more suitable partner.

Pursuit and Evaluation of a Potential Partner

Initially, the desire for sex may motivate people to look for either short-term or long-term mating opportunities with potential sexual partners (e.g., Fisher et al., 2002). Once a potential partner is identified, sexual responses to this new acquaintance may serve as a diagnostic test of his or her mate value and suitability (Birnbaum & Reis, 2006), determining whether future interactions with this partner will occur (Berscheid & Reis, 1998). Increased sexual desire for a potential partner may signify suitability and is therefore likely to motivate a person to pursue this desirable partner, whereas a lack of sexual desire may signal relationship incompatibility and therefore may motivate withdrawal from future interactions with this person (Birnbaum & Reis, 2006). If so, partner traits that signal mate value, such as those that are theorized to promote reproductive success via good investment or "good genes" (e.g., beauty, warmth–trustworthiness, attractiveness–vitality, status resources; Eastwick & Finkel, 2008; Fletcher, Simpson, Thomas, & Giles, 1999), may encourage sexual attraction to potential partners and increase the desire to bond with them (Lemay, Clark, & Greenberg, 2010). And yet, people may desire such traits in potential relationship partners only to the extent that these traits are anticipated to fulfill personal and interpersonal goals (Cottrell, Neuberg, & Li, 2007; Holmes & Johnson, 2009).

Indirect support for this claim comes from a recent series of three studies examining the contribution of perceived partner responsiveness (i.e., the belief that a relationship partner understands, values, and supports important aspects of oneself; Reis, Clark, & Holmes, 2004; see also Chapter 14, this volume) to sexual desire in initial acquaintanceships (Birnbaum & Reis, 2012). Because responsiveness is a key intimacy-building behavior geared toward promoting a partner's welfare, it is likely to be particularly valued in a potential long-term relationship partner (Clark & Lemay, 2010). Not all people, however, react to a stranger's expressions of intimacy in the same way. Some people may perceive a responsive stranger as a potentially desirable mate who is likely to invest resources in the relationship. Others may feel uncomfortable about a new acquaintance who is perceived as wanting to be close, and such feelings may impair sexual attraction to this person. It is thus reasonable that perceived responsiveness, whether desirable in a potential partner or not, affects the results of the sexual attraction "test" described above (i.e., sexual attractiveness of a potential partner).

For us to evaluate this notion, participants in all three studies discussed a negative event with an unfamiliar, opposite-sex partner and then rated how responsive this partner had been during the interaction and their desire for sex with him or her. Study 1 examined the association between perceived partner responsiveness and sexual desire in randomly paired strangers during face-to-face conversations, while allowing interactions to unfold in a natural, spontaneous way. Studies 2 and 3 were experiments, manipulating partner responsiveness to examine its effect on sexual desire. In Study 2, participants exchanged Instant Messages with a confederate who sent them either responsive (e.g., "You must have gone through a very difficult time," "I completely understand what you have been through") or unresponsive (e.g., "Doesn't sound so bad to me," "Are you sure that's the worst thing you can think of?") standardized messages. In Study 3, participants interacted face-to-face with either a responsive or an unresponsive confederate interviewer. Results indicated that perceiving a new acquaintance as responsive increased the desire for sex among men and among participants who were relatively low on attachment-related avoidance (i.e., the tendency to maintain emotional distance from a partner and avoid intimacy and interdependence; see Chapters 15 and 19). In contrast, perceiving a new acquaintance as responsive decreased sexual desire among women and more dispositionally avoidant participants.

These initial findings point to the possibility that whether responsiveness increases or decreases sexual interest in a potential partner varies across individuals and may depend on the interpretation of responsiveness in the context of initial encounters (e.g., potential sexual receptivity vs. inappropriate eagerness) and on the nature of a person's interpersonal goals (intimacy promotion vs. intimacy avoidance). Responsiveness may be valued as an asset in a potential partner by people who typically pursue intimacy goals. However, some people, such as those high in attachment-related avoidance, are more likely to pursue goals related to independence rather than intimacy both in and outside the bedroom (e.g., Birnbaum, 2010; Mikulincer & Shaver, 2007). For them, responsiveness may be threatening because it suggests emotional closeness, as well as the possibility of revealing vulnerability and feelings of dependence. Overall, this research implies that sexual desire may serve as a gatekeeper in initial encounters, ensuring that only suitable partners will be pursued. Whether a responsive potential partner will be allowed to "pass through the gate" depends on the meaning assigned to the observed responsiveness, which is affected by relationship goals and gender-specific mating strategies (e.g., perceived sexual availability versus selectivity; Buss & Schmitt, 1993).

Promoting Intimacy in Emerging Relationships

Once a suitable partner is found, sexual desire for him or her may motivate a person to form a relationship that extends beyond a single sexual episode (Birnbaum & Gillath, 2006). Then, as the relationship progresses from initial encounters to steady dating, desiring one's partner and the resulting frequent sexual activity may serve as a binding force that fosters emotional bonding between sexual partners and strengthens their emerging relationship. This proposed sequence of psychological events received support from a recent longitudinal study conducted by Mizrahi, Birnbaum, Hirschberger, Mikulincer, and Szepsenwol (2012). In this 8-month study of a community sample of 83 newly dating couples, Mizrahi et al. examined the contribution of various aspects of sexual functioning to attachment processes within the formation stage of romantic relationships. Both members of couples who had been dating for less than 4 months completed measures of sexual desire, frequency of sexual intercourse, and relationship-specific attachment avoidance and anxiety at three points in time: at the beginning of the study, after 4 months, and after 8 months.

Analyses revealed that both relationship-specific attachment avoidance (wishes for distance and self-reliance and discomfort with interdependence and closeness) and relationship-specific attachment anxiety (intense wishes for closeness and strong fear of abandonment) declined over time. However, among both men and women, this decline was moderated by a participant's reported levels of sexual desire and frequency of sexual intercourse. In particular, attachment-related avoidance declined only among participants who reported relatively high levels of sexual desire. Similarly, attachment anxiety declined mainly among participants who reported a relatively high frequency of sexual intercourse. Attachment anxiety also declined among women whose partners reported relatively high levels of sexual desire, possibly reflecting women's sensitivity to cues connoting partners' intentions and their tendency to react with a congruent increase (or decrease) in perceived relationship quality (Birnbaum & Reis, 2006). Taken as a whole, these findings indicate that sexual desire and the resulting sexual activity reduce attachment worries and defenses over time, pointing to the psychological processes by which sexuality contributes to attachment formation in the early stages of dating.

The results of this study add to previous findings suggesting that sexual desire is particularly important in the initial phase of relationships (e.g., Berscheid, 1984; Sprecher & Regan, 1998). For example, lack of sexual desire for a romantic partner has been found to be positively related to the frequency of thoughts of ending a current dating relationship and seeking alternative partners (Regan, 2000). In later phases of relationship development, processes related to the provision of mutual support, warmth, responsiveness, and interdependence may contribute more than sexual desire does to relationship maintenance (Kotler, 1985; Reedy, Birren, & Schaie, 1981; Sternberg, 1986). Nevertheless, engaging in sex may still be a common maintenance strategy among more firmly established couples (e.g., Bell, Daly, & Gonzalez, 1987), and the absence of sexual desire, although not necessarily leading to relationship dissolution, may deprive the relationship of intimacy and vitality (McCarthy, Bodnar, & Handal, 2004).

Relationship Maintenance and Deterioration

Smooth functioning of the sexual system has, indeed, long been considered in both the clinical and basic scientific literature to contribute to the quality and stability of most romantic relationships (see the review by Sprecher & Cate, 2004). Sexual encounters in which both partners gratify their sexual needs and enjoy rewarding experiences increase closeness, produce feelings of mutual love, and promote feelings of being desired and valued (Shaver & Mikulincer, 2006). In the same vein, sexual dysfunction and the resulting frustration are likely to generate relationship conflict and reduce relationship satisfaction (e.g., Birnbaum, 2007; Hartman, 1983; Hassebrauck & Fehr, 2002). Correspondingly, successful sex therapy may increase relationship satisfaction (Wright, Perrault, & Mathieu, 1977). In all, this literature implies that sex may affect, beneficially or adversely, relationship quality and stability. Even so, many of the existing studies suffer from methodological problems (e.g., cross-sectional and retrospective designs) that prevent valid assessment of the association between sex and relationship quality (Sprecher & Cate, 2004).

A deeper understanding of the potentially beneficial (and adverse) effects of sexual experiences on relationship quality can be gained through relatively recent studies based on more rigorous research designs. One of these studies examined how passion and intimacy vary on a daily basis within romantic contexts over a 3-week period (Rubin & Campbell, 2012). In this diary study, both members of heterosexual couples completed daily measures of intimacy, passion, and sexual satisfaction. Results showed that passion and intimacy operated in a bidirectional causal pattern over time: Daily increases in intimacy reported by both romantic partners predicted higher relationship passion, a higher probability of having sex, and more sexual satisfaction; moreover, daily increases in self-reported passion predicted greater intimacy. These findings suggest that just as there may be a favorable self-amplifying cycle of increasing passion and escalating intimacy that contributes to relationship quality, there may also be a vicious self-exacerbating cycle of decreased passion and deficient intimacy that reinforce each other and lead to further relational difficulties.

Other studies have illustrated the complex role of sex in attachment processes by investigating when, for whom, and how sex affects relationship quality in established relationships. One early example was a dyadic diary study that revealed that the potential contribution of sex to relationship maintenance and deterioration was moderated by attachment-related worries and defenses (Birnbaum, Reis, Mikulincer, Gillath, & Orpaz, 2006). In this study, both members of heterosexual cohabiting couples reported on their attachment orientations and provided daily diary measures of relationship quality and sexual activity for a period of 42 consecutive days. In addition, each time they had sex, participants were asked to report on their feelings and cognitions during that sexual episode (e.g., "During or after sexual intercourse, I felt some frustration and disappointment," "During sexual intercourse, I felt passionately attracted to my partner").

In this study, attachment anxiety amplified the effects of positive and negative sexual experiences on relationship quality. In particular, the daily relationship quality of couples with more anxiously attached partners was more affected by daily fluctuations in sexual experiences than that of couples with less anxiously attached partners, suggesting that sex may be most beneficial, but also most detrimental, to these couples' relationships. In contrast, avoidant attachment inhibited the effects of sexual experiences on daily relationship interactions. That is, the quality of daily relationship interactions of couples with more avoidant partners was less affected by sexual experiences than that of couples with less avoidant partners, suggesting that these couples neither enjoy the beneficial effects of positive sexual experiences nor suffer the adverse effects of bad experiences. These findings suggest that optimal functioning of the attachment system (in the case of securely attached partners) involves neither high nor low levels of dependence between sex and relationship quality. Instead, among established couples, intermediate levels of interdependence between sex and relationship quality may be a more adaptive relationship maintenance mechanism.

Somewhat surprisingly, findings from a subsequent diary study of newly-wed couples indicate that in a nonthreatening relationship context, more frequent and satisfying sex may benefit not only the relationships of anxiously attached spouses but also those of avoidant spouses (Little, McNulty, & Russell, 2010). Specifically, associations between attachment insecurities and marital dissatisfaction were attenuated among couples who reported engaging in highly frequent and satisfying sexual activity. These effects were mediated by positive expectancies for partner availability, implying that frequent and gratifying sex can make insecurely attached spouses feel more satisfied in their marriages by helping them expect their partners to be more available and responsive. Additional studies show that frequent sexual activity can buffer against the detrimental relational implications of other personality traits of romantic partners (e.g., neuroticism; Russell & McNulty, 2011) or deficits in nonsexual relational dimensions. For example, a study of married couples found that sexual satisfaction was positively associated with marital satisfaction mainly in couples characterized by poor communication (Litzinger & Gordon, 2005). Together these findings suggest that the intimacy inherent in sexual inter-actions may compensate for relationship deficiencies by providing an alternative route for satisfying otherwise unmet attachment needs for support, security, and love.

Corroborating this conclusion, recent studies have shown that sex-related cognitions may serve attachment-related goals, primarily in conditions that pose a threat to the relationship and call for distress regulation and proximity seeking. For example, in two series of experiments, participants imagined relationship-threatening scenes (e.g., a partner considering breaking up, a partner's infidelity) or nonrelationship-threatening scenes (failure on an exam) and then rated or described their desire to have sex, reasons for engaging in sex (Birnbaum et al., 2011), and what sexual activities they would like to engage in, that is, their sexual fantasies (Birnbaum, Svitelman, Bar-Shalom, & Porat, 2008). Birnbaum et al. (2008) found that relationship threat prompted prorelationship motives (e.g., engaging in sex to nurture one's partner) and attachment-related themes (e.g., perceiving the self and the objects of one's fantasies as more affectionate and pleasing), suggesting that people may use sex to repair mental representa-tions of a threatened relationship.

Nevertheless, although engaging in sex following relational threat has the potential for improving a relationship, there are cases in which relation-ship restoration may not be viewed as feasible (e.g., an inextricable conflict). In these cases, sexual feelings about one's partner (e.g., decreased sexual desire) may serve as a diagnostic marker of relational incompatibility, thereby moti-vating an individual to seek resolution of the relational problems either with the current partner or by detaching from the current partner and looking for a more suitable one (Birnbaum & Reis, 2006). Considering this dual role of sex as a potent relationship maintenance mechanism and as a force motivating people to pursue alternative sexual partners may offer additional insight into the underlying function of sex in established relationships.

Several studies have delineated some of the conditions that encourage the pursuit of these seemingly conflicting goals. For example, a recent study revealed that women's desire for intimacy-promoting sex during the fertile phase of their menstrual cycle depends on the strength of the attachment bonds with their romantic partner (Eastwick & Finkel, 2012). Particularly, and in line with the documented increase in extrapair desires near ovulation (e.g., Pillsworth & Haselton, 2006), women who were not strongly attached to their long-term partner were less likely to desire sexual intimacy with him when fertile than when nonfertile. In contrast, women who were strongly attached to their partner were more likely to desire sexual intimacy with him when fertile than when nonfertile (Eastwick & Finkel, 2012). These findings suggest that activation of attachment processes can inhibit sexual strategies (e.g., extradyadic mating efforts with men who possess indicators of "good genes") that otherwise threaten a long-term romantic relationship. A similar conclusion may be drawn from a study of married men that found that investment in one's spouse was associated with lower testosterone levels (Gray, Kahlenberg, Barrett, Lipson, & Ellison, 2002). This finding suggests that men who have the most to lose from engaging in extrapair sex have relatively lower levels of the hormone that may foster this relationship-threatening tendency.

CONCLUDING REMARKS

The sexual behavioral system evolved to motivate reproductive acts. The evidence reviewed here supports the argument that this system has also been "exploited" by evolutionary processes to promote enduring bonds between adult romantic partners (Eastwick & Finkel, 2012). Specifically, it suggests that sex may affect the future of a potential or current relationship, beginning before it is even established, through the onset of the attachment bonding process to its consolidation, and on through potential detachment and dissolution. Still, the effects of sex on relationship quality and longevity are not uniform and may depend on changes in the functional significance of sex across different stages of relationship development. In particular, these effects may be especially pronounced when the attachment relationship is more vulnerable (e.g., in the early stages of emerging relationships or during conflicts that endanger a relationship). In these phases, sex may serve attachment-based goals and thereby reduce attachment insecurities.

The functional significance of sex may also vary across individuals and contexts. It may depend on mental representations of self and other, developed from early interpersonal experiences that each person carries forward to adult interactions (see Chapter 12). These early experiences may determine the kinds of desires that people wish to satisfy, the type of relationship they seek, and what they perceive to be sexually desirable in potential and current partners. And yet, sex may be most beneficial (and detrimental) to the relationship of most people in anxiety-provoking situations, when attachment-related goals of proximity seeking are particularly prominent. On the whole, the person-by-context interactive framework offered in this chapter can deepen our understanding of the role of sex in relationships by clarifying in which contexts, why, and for whom sex may contribute to relationship quality. More research is needed to establish the validity of the proposed model and further clarify the aversive and appetitive processes underlying the connections between sexuality and attachment in each stage of relationship development in both same- and opposite-sex relationships.

REFERENCES

Bell, R. A., Daly, J. A., & Gonzalez, C. (1987). Affinity-maintenance in marriage and its relationship to women's marital satisfaction. *Journal of Marriage and the Family, 49,* 445–454. doi:10.2307/352313

Berscheid, E. (1984). Interpersonal attraction. In G. Lindzey & E. Aronson (Eds.), *Handbook of social psychology* (3rd ed., Vol. 2, pp. 413–484). Reading, MA: Addison-Wesley.

Berscheid, E. (1988). Some comments on love's anatomy: Or, whatever happened to old-fashioned lust? In R. J. Sternberg & M. L. Barnes (Eds.), *The psychology of love* (pp. 359–374). New Haven, CT: Yale University Press.

Berscheid, E., & Reis, H. T. (1998). Attraction and close relationships. In D. T. Gilbert, S. T. Fiske, & G. Lindzey (Eds.), *The handbook of social psychology* (4th ed., Vol. 2, pp. 193–281). New York, NY: McGraw-Hill.

Birnbaum, G. E. (2003). The meaning of heterosexual intercourse among women with female orgasmic disorder. *Archives of Sexual Behavior, 32,* 61–71. doi:10.1023/A:1021845513448

Birnbaum, G. E. (2007). Attachment orientations, sexual functioning, and relationship satisfaction in a community sample of women. *Journal of Social and Personal Relationships, 24,* 21–35. doi:10.1177/0265407507072576

Birnbaum, G. E. (2010). Bound to interact: The divergent goals and complex interplay of attachment and sex within romantic relationships. *Journal of Social and Personal Relationships, 27,* 245–252. doi:10.1177/0265407509360902

Birnbaum, G. E., & Gillath, O. (2006). Measuring subgoals of the sexual behavioral system: What is sex good for? *Journal of Social and Personal Relationships, 23,* 675–701. doi:10.1177/0265407506065992

Birnbaum, G. E., Mikulincer, M., & Austerlitz, M. (2012). A fiery conflict: Attachment orientations and the effects of relational conflict on sexual motivation. *Personal Relationships*. Advance online publication. doi:10.1111/j.1475-6811. 2012.01413.x

Birnbaum, G. E., & Reis, H. T. (2006). Women's sexual working models: An evolutionary-attachment perspective. *Journal of Sex Research, 43*, 328–342. doi:10.1080/00224490609552332

Birnbaum, G. E., & Reis, H. T. (2012). When does responsiveness pique sexual interest? Attachment and sexual desire in initial acquaintanceships. *Personality and Social Psychology Bulletin, 38*, 946–958. doi:10.1177/0146167212441028

Birnbaum, G. E., Reis, H. T., Mikulincer, M., Gillath, O., & Orpaz, A. (2006). When sex is more than just sex: Attachment orientations, sexual experience, and relationship quality. *Journal of Personality and Social Psychology, 91*, 929–943. doi:10.1037/0022-3514.91.5.929

Birnbaum, G. E., Svitelman, N., Bar-Shalom, A., & Porat, O. (2008). The thin line between reality and imagination: Attachment orientations and the effects of relationship threats on sexual fantasies. *Personality and Social Psychology Bulletin, 34*, 1185–1199. doi:10.1177/0146167208319692

Birnbaum, G. E., Weisberg, Y. J., & Simpson, J. A. (2011). Desire under attack: Attachment orientations and the effects of relationship threat on sexual motivations. *Journal of Social and Personal Relationships, 28*, 448–468. doi:10.1177/ 0265407510381932

Bowlby, J. (1969). *Attachment and loss: Vol. 1. Attachment.* New York, NY: Basic Books.

Bowlby, J. (1982). *Attachment and loss: Vol. 1. Attachment* (2nd ed.). New York, NY: Basic Books.

Buss, D. M., & Kenrick, D. T. (1998). Evolutionary social psychology. In D. T. Gilbert, S. T. Fiske, & G. Lindzey (Eds.), *The handbook of social psychology* (4th ed., Vol. 2, pp. 982–1026). New York, NY: McGraw-Hill.

Buss, D. M., & Schmitt, D. P. (1993). Sexual strategies theory: An evolutionary perspective on human mating. *Psychological Review, 100*, 204–232. doi:10.1037/ 0033-295X.100.2.204

Buss, D. M., & Shackelford, T. K. (1997). From vigilance to violence: Mate retention tactics in married couples. *Journal of Personality and Social Psychology, 72*, 346–361. doi:10.1037/0022-3514.72.2.346

Carmichael, M. S., Humbert, R., Dixen, J., Palmisano, G., Greenleaf, W., & Davidson, J. M. (1987). Plasma oxytocin increases in the human sexual response. *Journal of Clinical Endocrinology and Metabolism, 64*, 27–31. doi:10.1210/jcem-64-1-27

Carter, C. S. (1992). Oxytocin and sexual behavior. *Neuroscience and Biobehavioral Reviews, 16*, 131–144. doi:10.1016/S0149-7634(05)80176-9

Carter, C. S., Ahnert, L., Grossmann, K. E., Hrdy, S. B., Lamb, M. E., Porges, S. W., & Sachser, N. (Eds.). (2005). *Attachment and bonding: A new synthesis.* Cambridge, MA: MIT Press.

Clark, M. S., & Lemay, E. P., Jr. (2010). Close relationships. In S. T. Fiske, D. T. Gilbert, & G. Lindzey (Eds.), *Handbook of social psychology* (5th ed., Vol. 2, pp. 898–940). New York, NY: Wiley

Cooper, M. L., Shapiro, C. M., & Powers, A. M. (1998). Motivations for sex and risky sexual behavior among adolescents and young adults: A functional perspective. *Journal of Personality and Social Psychology, 75,* 1528–1558. doi:10.1037/0022-3514. 75.6.1528

Cottrell, C. A., Neuberg, S. L., & Li, N. P. (2007). What do people desire in others? A sociofunctional perspective on the importance of different valued characteristics. *Journal of Personality and Social Psychology, 92,* 208–231. doi:10.1037/ 0022-3514.92.2.208

Diamond, L. M. (2003). What does sexual orientation orient? A biobehavioral model distinguishing romantic love and sexual desire. *Psychological Review, 110,* 173–192. doi:10.1037/0033-295X.110.1.173

Diamond, L. M. (2004). Emerging perspectives on distinctions between romantic love and sexual desire. *Current Directions in Psychological Science, 13,* 116–119. doi:10.1111/j.0963-7214.2004.00287.x

Ditzen, B., Schaer, M., Gabriel, B., Bodenmann, G., Ehlert, U., & Heinrichs, M. (2009). Intranasal oxytocin increases positive communication and reduces cortisol levels during couple conflict. *Biological Psychiatry, 65,* 728–731. doi:10.1016/ j.biopsych.2008.10.011

Eastwick, P. W., & Finkel, E. J. (2008). Sex differences in mate preferences revisited: Do people know what they initially desire in a romantic partner? *Journal of Personality and Social Psychology, 94,* 245–264. doi:10.1037/0022-3514.94.2.245

Eastwick, P. W., & Finkel, E. J. (2012). The evolutionary armistice: Attachment bonds moderate the function of ovulatory cycle adaptations. *Personality and Social Psychology Bulletin, 38,* 174–184. doi:10.1177/0146167211422366

Filippi, S., Vignozzi, L., Vannelli, G. B., Ledda, F., Forti, G., & Maggi, M. (2003). Role of oxytocin in the ejaculatory process. *Journal of Endocrinological Investigation, 26,* 82–86.

Fisher, H. E. (1998). Lust, attraction, and attachment in mammalian reproduction. *Human Nature, 9,* 23–52. doi:10.1007/s12110-998-1010-5

Fisher, H. E., Aron, A., Mashek, D., Li, H., & Brown, L. L. (2002). Defining the brain systems of lust, romantic attraction, and attachment. *Archives of Sexual Behavior, 31,* 413–419. doi:10.1023/A:1019888024255

Fletcher, G. J. O., Simpson, J. A., Thomas, G., & Giles, L. (1999). Ideals in intimate relationships. *Journal of Personality and Social Psychology, 76,* 72–89. doi:10.1037/ 0022-3514.76.1.72

Ford, C. S., & Beach, F. A. (1951). *Patterns of sexual behavior.* New York, NY: Harper & Row.

Gillath, O., Mikulincer, M., Birnbaum, G. E., & Shaver, P. R. (2008). When sex primes love: Subliminal sexual priming motivates relational goal pursuit. *Personality and Social Psychology Bulletin, 34,* 1057–1069. doi:10.1177/0146167208318141

Gonzaga, G. C., Keltner, D., Londahl, E. A., & Smith, M. D. (2001). Love and the commitment problems in romantic relations and friendship. *Journal of Personality and Social Psychology, 81*, 247–262. doi:10.1037/0022-3514.81.2.247

Gray, P. B., Kahlenberg, S. M., Barrett, E. S., Lipson, S. F., & Ellison, P. T. (2002). Marriage and fatherhood are associated with lower testosterone in males. *Evolution and Human Behavior, 23*, 193–201. doi:10.1016/S1090-5138(01)00101-5

Hartman, L. M. (1983). Effects of sex and marital therapy on sexual interaction and marital happiness. *Journal of Sex & Marital Therapy, 9*, 137–151. doi:10.1080/00926238308405841

Hassebrauck, M., & Fehr, B. (2002). Dimensions of relationship quality. *Personal Relationships, 9*, 253–270. doi:10.1111/1475-6811.00017

Hazan, C., & Zeifman, D. (1994). Sex and the psychological tether. In K. Bartholomew & D. Perlman (Eds.), *Advances in personal relationships: Vol. 5. Attachment processes in adulthood* (pp. 151–178). London, England: Kingsley.

Hazan, C., & Zeifman, D. (1999). Pair-bonds as attachments: Evaluating the evidence. In J. Cassidy & P. R. Shaver (Eds.), *Handbook of attachment: Theory, research, and clinical applications* (pp. 336–354). New York, NY: Guilford Press.

Hill, C. A., & Preston, L. K. (1996). Individual differences in the experience of sexual motivation: Theory and measurement of dispositional sexual motives. *Journal of Sex Research, 33*, 27–45. doi:10.1080/00224499609551812

Holmes, B. M., & Johnson, K. R. (2009). Adult attachment and romantic partner preference: A review. *Journal of Social and Personal Relationships, 26*, 833–852. doi:10.1177/0265407509345653

Kotler, T. (1985). Security and autonomy within marriage. *Human Relations, 38*, 299–321. doi:10.1177/001872678503800402

Lemay, E. P., Jr., Clark, M. S., & Greenberg, A. (2010). What is beautiful is good because what is beautiful is desired: Physical attractiveness stereotyping as projection of interpersonal goals. *Personality and Social Psychology Bulletin, 36*, 339–353. doi:10.1177/0146167209359700

Little, K. C., McNulty, J. K., & Russell, V. M. (2010). Sex buffers intimates against the negative implications of attachment insecurity. *Personality and Social Psychology Bulletin, 36*, 484–498. doi:10.1177/0146167209352494

Litzinger, S., & Gordon, K. C. (2005). Exploring relationships among communication, sexual satisfaction, and marital satisfaction. *Journal of Sex & Marital Therapy, 31*, 409–424. doi:10.1080/00926230591006719

McCarthy, B. W., Bodnar, L. E., & Handal, M. (2004). Integrating sex therapy and couple therapy. In J. H. Harvey, A. Wenzel, & S. Sprecher (Eds.), *The handbook of sexuality in close relationships* (pp. 573–593). Mahwah, NJ: Erlbaum.

Mellen, S. L. W. (1981). *The evolution of love*. Oxford, England: Freeman.

Meston, C. M., & Buss, D. M. (2007). Why humans have sex. *Archives of Sexual Behavior, 36*, 477–507. doi:10.1007/s10508-007-9175-2

Mikulincer, M., & Shaver, P. R. (2007). *Attachment in adulthood: Structure, dynamics, and change*. New York, NY: Guilford Press.

Mizrahi, M., Birnbaum, G. E., Hirschberger, G., Mikulincer, M., & Szepsenwol, O. (2012). *Sexual healing: Can sex repair attachment insecurities?* Manuscript in preparation.

Murphy, M. R., Seckl, J. R., Burton, S., Checkley, S. A., & Lightman, S. L. (1987). Changes in oxytocin and vasopressin secretion during sexual activity in men. *Journal of Clinical Endocrinology and Metabolism, 65,* 738–741. doi:10.1210/jcem-65-4-738

Pillsworth, E. G., & Haselton, M. G. (2006). Women's sexual strategies: The evolution of long-term bonds and extra-pair sex. *Annual Review of Sex Research, 17,* 59–100.

Reedy, M. N., Birren, J. E., & Schaie, K. W. (1981). Age and sex differences in satisfying love relationships across the adult life span. *Human Development, 24,* 52–66. doi:10.1159/000272625

Regan, P. C. (2000). The role of sexual desire and sexual activity in dating relationships. *Social Behavior and Personality, 28,* 51–59. doi:10.2224/sbp.2000.28.1.51

Reis, H. T., Clark, M. S., & Holmes, J. G. (2004). Perceived partner responsiveness as an organizing construct in the study of intimacy and closeness. In D. J. Mashek & A. P. Aron (Eds.), *Handbook of closeness and intimacy* (pp. 201–225). Mahwah, NJ: Erlbaum.

Rubin, H., & Campbell, L. (2012). Day-to-day changes in intimacy predict heightened relationship passion, sexual occurrence, and sexual satisfaction: A dyadic diary analysis. *Social Psychological and Personality Science, 3,* 224–231. doi:10.1177/1948550611416520

Russell, V. M., & McNulty, J. K. (2011). Frequent sex protects intimates from the negative implications of neuroticism. *Social Psychological and Personality Science, 2,* 220–227. doi:10.1177/1948550610387162

Shaver, P., Hazan, C., & Bradshaw, D. (1988). Love as attachment: The integration of three behavioral systems. In R. J. Sternberg & M. L. Barnes (Eds.), *The psychology of love* (pp. 68–99). New Haven, CT: Yale University Press.

Shaver, P. R., & Mikulincer, M. (2006). A behavioral systems approach to romantic love relationships: Attachment, caregiving, and sex. In R. J. Sternberg & K. Weis (Eds.), *The new psychology of love* (pp. 35–64). New Haven, CT: Yale University Press.

Short, R. V. (1979). Sexual selection and its component parts, somatic and genital selection, as illustrated in man and the great apes. In J. S. Rosenblatt, R. A. Hinde, C. Beer, & M.-C. Busnel (Eds.), *Advances in the study of behavior* (Vol. 9, pp. 131–158). New York, NY: Academic Press. doi:10.1016/S0065-3454(08)60035-2

Sprecher, S., & Cate, R. M. (2004). Sexual satisfaction and sexual expression as predictors of relationship satisfaction and stability. In J. H. Harvey, A. Wenzel, & S. Sprecher (Eds.), *The handbook of sexuality in close relationships* (pp. 235–256). Mahwah, NJ: Erlbaum.

Sprecher, S., & Regan, P. C. (1998). Passionate and companionate love in courting and young married couples. *Sociological Inquiry, 68*, 163–185. doi:10.1111/j.1475-682X.1998.tb00459.x

Sternberg, R. J. (1986). A triangular theory of love. *Psychological Review, 93*, 119–135. doi:10.1037/0033-295X.93.2.119

Symons, D. (1979). *The evolution of human sexuality.* New York, NY: Oxford University Press.

Wright, J., Perrault, R., & Mathieu, M. (1977). The treatment of sexual dysfunction: A review. *Archives of General Psychiatry, 34*, 881–890. doi:10.1001/archpsyc.1977.01770200019001

Young, K. A., Gobrogge, K. L., Liu, Y., & Wang, Z. X. (2011). The neurobiology of pair bonding: Insights from a socially monogamous rodent. *Frontiers in Neuroendocrinology, 32*, 53–69. doi:10.1016/j.yfrne.2010.07.006

Young, L. J., & Wang, Z. (2004). The neurobiology of pair-bonding. *Nature Neuroscience, 7*, 1048–1054. doi:10.1038/nn1327

IV

GROUP

18

EVOLUTION OF THE SOCIAL BRAIN: PSYCHOLOGICAL ADAPTATIONS FOR GROUP LIVING

MARK VAN VUGT AND TATSUYA KAMEDA

"Humans are social animals." It is an often-used phrase, but what does it mean? It conveys that humans are an animal species, and more specifically, a member of the primate family, which includes the chimpanzee and bonobo, with which we share a common ancestor going back some 5 million to 7 million years. It also means that our bodies, brains, and behaviors are subject to the same laws of natural selection as those of all other animals on this planet—in fact, these laws apply to all living matter. Finally, humans are an extremely social species in the sense that we easily form close social connections with other humans and cooperate in small and large groups of kin and (genetic) strangers.

These insights were first articulated by Charles Darwin and Alfred Wallace, who were the first scientists to come up with a mechanism—natural selection—that could explain how species emerged and evolved over time. Until then it was assumed that God had created each species individually and put its members in a landscape that suited them best. By showing that

http://dx.doi.org/10.1037/14250-019
Mechanisms of Social Connection: From Brain to Group, M. Mikulincer and P. R. Shaver (Editors)

species emerge and evolve through a process of competition, in which individuals that are better adjusted to their environment survive, prosper, and pass on their traits—survival of the fittest—Darwin and Wallace provided an all-encompassing scientific theory (the theory of evolution through natural selection) that explained how all living things on earth are related. It was unavoidable that this theory would one day be applied to understand humans and human social nature. In his book *The Descent of Man*, Charles Darwin (1871) wrote: "With those animals which were benefited by living in close association, the individuals which took the greatest pleasure in society would best escape various dangers; whilst those that cared least for their comrades, and lived solitary, would perish in greater numbers" (p. 105).

In this chapter we review the evidence that human sociality is a biological adaptation. For humans, group living is an adaptive strategy because it enabled them to cope better with the various threats and opportunities provided by the world in which they evolved. First, we discuss some key assumptions underlying an evolutionary perspective on human sociality. Then we discuss the various adaptive challenges associated with group living for humans, most notably problems pertaining to social coordination, cooperation, status, cohesion, group decision making, and intergroup relations. We provide short reviews of the social psychological literature to demonstrate that for meeting each of these social challenges humans have evolved a set of cognitive adaptations. We conclude by addressing some conceptual and practical implications of a new evolutionary science of group dynamics and the human social mind.

AN EVOLUTIONARY PERSPECTIVE
ON THE HUMAN SOCIAL BRAIN

An evolutionary approach to the study of human sociality assumes that the physiological, neurological, and psychological processes involved in producing social behaviors are products of evolution through natural selection. Evolutionary theory contains three premises. First, there is variation in traits among individuals—for example, some people are loners, whereas others (joiners) like to be in groups. Second, some traits enable individuals possessing them to compete more successfully—for example, joiners can help each other by pooling their resources—and have more children. Finally, some of these traits are heritable—for example, joiners (loners) are more likely to have children with joiner (loner) genes. Repeated over time, the continuing process of variation, selection, and retention produces organisms and species that are well adapted to the environment in which they live. In the case of our species, modern humans are the descendants of individuals who preferred living in groups rather than leading a solitary life. Thus, our minds are to some extent social minds.

This claim rests on a number of key assumptions. First, there have been selective pressures on the human mind to acquire mechanisms that facilitate social interaction and group living. The social brain hypothesis (Dunbar, 2004) assumes that humans evolved large brains (i.e., neocortices) to be able to live in large, socially complex groups. Comparative studies have found a positive correlation between the size of the prefrontal cortex and average social network size, comparing humans with other primates and comparing primates with other mammals. Humans have a relatively large prefrontal cortex and typical social network size. The brain data suggest an average network size for humans of around 150 individuals, corresponding roughly to the size of a small village or neighborhood that is held together through informal social control.

Second, social traits can be the result of adaptations to the natural or the social environment or a combination of the two (Nesse, 2007). A specific case of social selection is sexual selection (Darwin, 1871). Sexually selected traits emerge if they increase the chances of an organism finding a sexual mate. Some conspicuous human social displays such as public generosity or social laughter have come about through sexual selection, because they make people more attractive to the opposite sex (Griskevicius, Goldstein, Mortensen, Cialdini, & Kenrick, 2006; Iredale, van Vugt, & Dunbar, 2008). Social traits evolve either because they benefit individuals directly or indirectly via the group to which these individuals belong (Caporael, 1997; Wilson, van Vugt, & O'Gorman, 2008). The latter is called *group selection*. After some fierce objection to the concept of group selection, evolutionary scientists are increasingly considering it useful for understanding the origins of human sociality.

Third, social adaptations come in many different forms, and many contain a mixture of physiological, neurological, psychological, and behavioral elements. Language is a biological adaptation that enables humans to transmit information efficiently. It requires both physical structures such as Broca's area and psychological mechanisms such as a theory of mind. If humans can talk but chimpanzees cannot, it is because these two species differ in their evolved physiology and psychology. Any social behavior is regulated by a combination of psychological mechanisms (e.g., emotions, cognitions) and neurophysiological mechanisms (e.g., brain activity, hormones, neurotransmitters), each having emerged through natural selection.

Fourth, social adaptations can best be regarded as conditional ("if–then") decision rules, automatically activated in appropriate conditions. Because a social environment is complex, humans likely possess a broad repertoire of conditional decision rules to make adaptive choices under different conditions. A rule such as "I will cooperate only if my partner cooperates, but otherwise I will defect" enables people to maximize their payoffs across a range of social situations (Axelrod, 1984). This conditional rule is much better than "I will cooperate regardless of what my partner does."

Furthermore, such conditional rules are likely to be domain specific. They exist in the form they do because they solved a specific social problem in our human ancestral environment. For instance, social exclusion can be described in many different ways. An evolutionary approach suggests hypotheses concerning the different evolved functions of social exclusion and proposes at least three functions: (a) excluding individuals who are free-riders, (b) excluding individuals who behave unpredictably, and (c) excluding individuals who constitute a contagion risk (Kurzban & Leary, 2001). Each of these functions has a unique underlying social psychology, is triggered by different stimuli, and produces different responses. Individuals display aggression toward free-riders yet avoid people who carry a disease threat (Kerr & Levine, 2008; Schaller, Park, & Faulkner, 2003; van Vugt & Park, 2009).

Finally, because evolution through natural selection is a painstakingly slow process, spanning many generations, social adaptations may not always produce behaviors that are adaptive (fitness maximizing) in the modern world. Most social interactions among early humans were with kin, and so our social psychology may not be fine-tuned in interactions with strangers (cf. mismatch theory; van Vugt, Hogan, & Kaiser, 2008). This explains why we are more likely to trust strangers who elicit kinship cues such as facial similarity or coresidence (Park, Schaller, & van Vugt, 2008).

Thus, understanding the human social mind requires a good understanding of evolutionary theory and the concept of an adaptation. Note that evolutionary-minded social psychologists are not seeking to test evolutionary theory per se, because evolution and natural selection are already scientific facts. What we are testing is specific predictions, derived from hypotheses generated by middle-range evolutionary theories (Buss, 1995). The theory of indirect reciprocity assumes, for instance, that individuals cooperate because it benefits their reputation (Nowak & Sigmund, 2005). The hypothesis that follows from this theory is that when people's actions are public, they cooperate more, leading to the specific prediction that in public conditions they help more than in private conditions. This prediction has received substantial support in laboratory and field research (Bateson, Nettle, & Roberts, 2006; Hardy & van Vugt, 2006).

KEY PSYCHOLOGICAL ADAPTATIONS FOR HUMAN SOCIALITY

What were the key adaptive challenges that early humans faced in forming social connections and living in groups, and what mechanisms could have evolved to address these challenges? On the basis of the evolutionary and social psychological literatures, we identify six key challenges associated with adopting a group-living strategy: coordinating joint activities, solving social exchange problems, negotiating status hierarchies, maintaining group cohesion, collective decision making, and managing intergroup relations. The list is neither exhaustive nor mutually exclusive, but it is a good starting point for developing evolutionary-based hypotheses about human sociality. Each adaptive challenge likely contains a set of subproblems that need to be solved to produce a good outcome. Coordinating on a new location for a campsite, for example, requires identifying an appropriate location to move to, deciding when to move and for how long, assessing which individuals possess the specific leadership expertise for the task, motivating individuals to follow, keeping the group together while on the move, replacing ineffective leaders, and setting up contingency plans (van Vugt et al., 2008).

To our knowledge, none of these six social challenges have been fully analyzed with an evolutionary framework. Yet various research programs have provided data and support for the existence of various psychological mechanisms enabling humans to solve these particular social challenges. In the remainder of the chapter, we offer a selected set of findings from different research programs that speak to the function and form of key adaptive social strategies to navigate these challenges.

Social Coordination

To form social connections and function in groups, early humans would have had to solve problems associated with coordinating tasks in sometimes very large groups. For instance, when gathering food, they would have had to divide up activities such as hunting and gathering, make decisions regarding which individuals should join these parties and which should stay at the camp, how much food to gather, and how long to be away from camp. This would have required specialized decision rules for identifying situations as requiring social coordination, assessing coordination potential in others, developing rules for how best to achieve coordination, and carrying out these rules.

One likely evolved mechanism facilitating social coordination is leadership. There are multiple indications that leadership might be a social adaptation. Game theory models show that leadership—where one individual takes the initiative and others follow—is a powerful solution in coordination games. Consider, for instance, Pat and James, who are thirsty and must find a water hole. They must stay together as a form of protection, but how do they decide which water hole to go to? It is highly adaptive for one individual to take the initiative to go to a particular water hole, which leaves the other no option but to follow. Coordinating on the same water hole is the equilibrium solution to this game, which suggests at least the possibility that leadership and followership are evolved strategies (van Vugt et al., 2008). An implication of this evolutionary analysis is that leadership–follower interaction emerges automatically. The emergence of leadership has been documented across many different animal species that face functionally important coordination problems, including teaching in ants, selecting foraging sites in honey bees (the famous waggle dance performed by scout bees, which is discussed in more detail later in this chapter), movement in stickleback fish, and peacekeeping in nonhuman primates (King, Johnson, & van Vugt, 2009). Among humans, leadership has been found in all societies and cultures, suggesting that it is hardwired (Brown, 1991).

Of course, the exact leadership structure varies across situations and cultures, and there is evidence for both highly democratic and highly despotic leadership structures in humans (Bass, 2008). These likely represent different cultural solutions to different local environmental conditions—for instance, dictatorial leadership might emerge in response to immediate external crises such as wars (van Vugt, 2009). This underlying evolutionary logic also yields hypotheses about evolved decision rules concerning who we appoint as leaders. We hypothesize that humans have cognitive mechanisms for identifying people—leader prototypes—who are most appropriate for solving a given adaptive problem. Recent studies suggest that warfare elicits a preference for a physically strong and masculine-looking leader (Little, Burris, Jones, & Roberts, 2007; van Vugt & Spisak, 2008).

Another evolved cognitive mechanism to facilitate social coordination is the division of labor—for example, through a transactive memory system. Such a system enhances the ability to divide up tasks among group members. Cognitive cooperation is common in social insects. One famous example is the waggle dance of the honey bee, a device for selecting foraging sites (Seeley, 1995). Research on humans suggests that members working in the same group specialize in different areas, and group members are very quick to recognize who knows what in the group (Littlepage, Hollingshead, Drake, & Littlepage, 2008). A set of experiments showed that teams performed better on a group task to the extent that the team members divided their cognitive tasks better. Furthermore, members of teams with better transactive memory systems also trusted each other's expertise more (Moreland, Argote, & Krishnan, 1996). Not surprisingly, groups outperform individuals, especially at more complex cognitive tasks (Wilson, Timmel, & Miller, 2004).

Behavioral synchrony through mimicry is another example of an evolved psychological mechanism for social coordination. In this case, individuals imitate each other's actions, expressions, or postures. Mimicry is a highly automated process—it is sometimes referred to as the chameleon effect (Chartrand & Bargh, 1999)—and its main function is to smooth coordination between interaction partners. Mimicry is possible in humans because of the evolution of sophisticated cognitive capacities such as theory of mind and empathy, which likely emerged late in human evolution (around 50,000 years ago). Research suggests that mimicry and other forms of behavioral synchrony (e.g., making the same moves while dancing) increase people's liking for each other and their willingness to help each other (Chartrand & Bargh, 1999).

In addition to leadership, division of labor, and mimicry, there are other psychological adaptations that facilitate coordination between humans, such as language, gaze cuing, joint attention seeking, and the use of various coordination rules. These need exploring.

Solving Cooperation Problems

Social exchange—cooperation for mutual benefit—is a pervasive and cross-culturally universal feature of human group life. Exchanging vital resources with others is fundamental for any social species, yet humans are unique in being able to establish large-scale cooperation with genetically unrelated individuals. What adaptive decision rules make social exchange possible? To engage in social exchange requires mechanisms for assessing the value of what is being exchanged, identifying likely coalition partners, and remembering past interactions with other individuals.

Evolutionary models suggest that for social exchanges with nonkin members to persist stably, individuals must be able to detect "cheaters" who fail to reciprocate (Axelrod, 1984; Trivers, 1971). Cosmides (1989) argued that humans have an evolved cognitive mechanism specialized for cheater detection. A brain-imaging study with a patient who had bilateral limbic system damage provided some evidence for this thesis. Using Wason's four-card selection task, Stone, Cosmides, Tooby, Kroll, and Knight (2002) showed that compared with normal controls, the patient's performance was impaired only when the logical reasoning task was framed as detecting violators of social contracts. The performance remained intact when the task was framed as detecting violators of noncontractual rules. This dissociation suggests that cheating (violations of social contracts) may be processed by our brains separately from other types of social violations.

The evolution of large-scale human cooperation would have been impossible in the absence of social norms. Humans indeed spontaneously follow social norms. An example is the norm of conditional cooperation (Fehr & Fischbacher, 2004), which dictates that an individual should cooperate if other group members cooperate but be allowed not to cooperate if the others defect. Fischbacher, Gächter, and Fehr (2001) examined participants' willingness to contribute in a one-shot public-good experiment as a function of the average contribution of the other group members. Despite the economic incentives to free-ride (contribute nothing), 50% of the participants matched their contributions with the average contribution of other members.

The evolutionary perspective suggests novel hypotheses about psychological mechanisms supporting the enforcement of cooperation. Given that cooperation occurs mainly within groups, violation of cooperation norms should be more dangerous to one's survival if committed by an ingroup member than if committed by an outgroup member. Thus, noncooperative behavior by ingroup members should be punished more severely than noncooperative behavior by outgroup members. Using a third-party punishment paradigm, Shinada, Yamagishi, and Ohmura (2004) confirmed this prediction. Such selective sanctioning includes not only physical punishment but also social exclusion—collectively denying the violator's access to interpersonal relations in a group. Research reveals that social exclusion can provoke strong negative emotional responses in the excluded individuals, including intense anger, pain, and depression (Eisenberger, Lieberman, & Williams, 2003).

To foster cooperation, humans have also evolved norms concerning how resources should be distributed (Fehr & Schmidt, 1999; Kameda, Takezawa, Ohtsubo, & Hastie, 2010). Results from one-shot ultimatum game experiments indicate that modal offers made by a proposer vary around 40% to 50%, and that offers in this range are rarely rejected (Camerer, 2003). Although there are cultural differences, extremely small offers (1%–10%) are rarely seen in ultimatum bargaining experiments conducted in a wide range of societies, including more traditional and more industrialized ones (Henrich et al., 2004). Egalitarian sharing is a core feature of hunter–gatherer life. Compared with other food resources such as cassava, hunted meat is often the target of communal sharing. Kaplan and Hill (1985) argued that sharing norms function as a collective risk reduction device. Acquisition of meat is a highly variable, uncertain event, and by including many individuals in the sharing group, the variance in meat supply decreases exponentially (Gurven, 2004). Kameda, Takezawa, and Hastie (2003) conducted a series of evolutionary computer simulations to test the robustness of communal sharing as a risk-pooling system. Their simulation results show that egalitarian sharing evolves robustly under uncertainty and can overcome the free-rider problem. This implies that human minds are built to be highly sensitive to cues of uncertainty in resource sharing.

Thus, humans likely possess specialized cognitive mechanisms for solving social exchange problems, from identifying potential cheaters to finding suitable coalition partners and adhering to social norms prescribing cooperation.

Status Seeking

As humans were living in increasingly larger and more socially complex groups, there would have been intense competition for scarce resources such as food, water, and sexual mates (Dunbar, 2004). This competition paved the way for the emergence of status hierarchies, whereby people's status would determine their access to reproductively relevant resources. Negotiating an individual's position in a group hierarchy requires specialized decision rules for assessing one's status in the group and the status of relevant others, as well as mechanisms for identifying ways to climb the group hierarchy and, once a desired status is obtained, to maintain a high-status ranking.

Humans have likely evolved a set of adaptations to signal their relative status to others. For instance, they display nonverbal signals such as a firm handshake or a poised posture to let others know that they hold a high-status position and deserve respect. High-status individuals walk faster and are more likely to tell other people what to do (Forsyth, 2010). When people seek status they speak clearly and loudly, take more initiatives in conversations, and focus attention on their personal achievements. Just like their primate cousins, high-status humans have attention-holding power, meaning that they are the focus of attention in groups (Keltner, Gruenfeld, & Anderson, 2000). Along with other primates, humans have differentiated behavioral patterns for interacting with other individuals of higher or lower status than they possess. High-status competitors are treated with respect, whereas low-status competitors are treated in ways that force or encourage them to be submissive (Brosnan & de Waal, 2003; Brosnan, Newton-Fisher, & van Vugt, 2009).

Humans have also likely evolved different kinds of emotions to signal a status gain or loss (emotions are evolved decision rules). When people experience a status gain, such as winning an award, they tend to feel pride, and when they experience a loss in status, such as making a stupid remark, they tend to feel shame (Tracy & Robins, 2004). Similarly, people can feel a vicarious sense of pride or shame when the group or team that they identify with experiences a status gain or loss—for example, winning or losing a sports competition. Such emotional experiences are likely to be accompanied by hormonal fluctuations in testosterone, a physiological status marker. In a study of chess players, the winners experienced an increase in testosterone, whereas the losers experienced a decrease (Mazur, Booth, & Dabbs, 1992).

Humans also possess mechanisms for monitoring their status position, and self-esteem may be an internal gauge of an individual's relative status. When people feel valued by their peers, their self-esteem goes up, and when they feel devalued or ostracized, their self-esteem goes down (Williams, 2009). Self-esteem likely functions as a "sociometer" that monitors people's standing in a group and motivates action when people feel their status is being threatened (Baumeister & Leary, 1995). When people find themselves in a low-status position without having the resources to climb the hierarchy, they may become depressed. Depression can be thought of as an adaptive response to avoid status competitions with dominant peers.

From an evolutionary perspective it would be useful to draw a distinction between different forms of self-esteem that reflect different status problems (Kirkpatrick & Ellis, 2004). For example, concerns about one's standing as a potential sexual mate might be quite independent from concerns about being a respected group member or concerns about the standing of one's group (cf. individual vs. collective self-esteem).

In humans, an adaptive strategy to increase one's status is to help others. This strategy is called *competitive altruism* (Roberts, 1998). Experimental research suggests that cooperative individuals receive more status than selfish individuals and are preferred as group leaders (Hardy & van Vugt, 2006). Computer simulations show that when agents can freely interact with each other and each individual gets a status score (an image score)—indicating whether he or she cooperated or defected in previous interactions—cooperation becomes the norm (Nowak & Sigmund, 2005). Evidence for competitive altruism has been found in several nonhuman primate species as well (Brosnan et al., 2009).

Competitive altruism requires psychological mechanisms for monitoring one's relative status and mechanisms for improving it. Research suggests that when people think they are being watched by others (i.e., their status is being assessed), they are more generous (Bateson et al., 2006; Hardy & van Vugt, 2006). In fact, even a pair of eyes on a computer screen makes people behave more generously (Haley & Fessler, 2005). In addition, status concerns increase people's willing to preserve the environment and engage in bystander helping (Griskevicius, Cantú, & van Vugt, 2012). Men become especially generous when being observed by an attractive female (Iredale et al., 2008).

Thus, a critical challenge for any group-living animal is to improve one's position in the hierarchy of the group. In humans this has given rise to a number of psychological adaptations to assess one's relative status position and develop strategies to increase status.

Maintaining Cohesion in Social Networks

Another key challenge for early humans was to maintain cohesion in increasingly large groups (Dunbar, 2004). *Cohesion* is sometimes defined as "resultant of all the forces acting on the members to remain in the group" (Festinger, 1950, p. 274). In light of the importance of staying together in a hostile (savannah) environment, humans needed special devices to preserve group cohesion. Furthermore, as human social networks increased drastically in size over the course of human evolution, we would expect these "bonding" mechanisms to have become increasingly sophisticated. To preserve cohesion requires specialized mechanisms to recognize oneself and others as belonging to the same tribal group, as well as mechanisms to become emotionally immersed within the group. Here we discuss a few such adaptive cohesion strategies.

Thinking of people who are not necessarily around all the time as belonging to your group requires the capacity for symbolic thought whereby symbols such as language or rituals become markers of shared group membership. A symbolic social identity allowed our ancestors to connect with a large network of individuals who were spread around a particular area, and this may have been quite helpful in sharing resources as well as in competing with other groups. Research shows that human social identity is highly tribal and that people spontaneously make "us versus them" categorizations even when group membership is based on a trivial criterion (Tajfel & Turner, 1979). Groups with highly identifying members tend to be more cohesive (Jetten, Spears, & Manstead, 1996). Preserving group cohesion also requires a sense of group loyalty whereby individuals signal that they are prepared to forgo attractive alternatives in favor of staying with the current group. Loyalty is deeply ingrained in human social psychology, and disloyal group members are strongly disliked, especially in highly cohesive groups (van Vugt & Hart, 2004).

Human groups have various specialized mechanisms to foster group cohesion that may have deep evolutionary roots. Religions, and the associated rituals, are an effective method to promote cohesion between strangers and mobilize them for joint collective action (Atran, 2002; Atran & Norenzayan, 2004). Dance, music, and sports may have similar evolved functions. Dance, music, and spectator sports may have evolved as adaptations for connecting large networks of genetic strangers (Dunbar, 2004). Finally, a potent mechanism for fostering group cohesion is laughter, which likely predates language on an evolutionary timescale. Laughter is a highly automatic and contagious phenomenon that quickly spreads positive emotions through a crowd and increases endorphin levels, causing people to feel good and, possibly, more connected (Dunbar et al., 2011; Gervais & Wilson, 2005).

In sum, preserving group cohesion requires specialized cognitive mechanisms for assessing cohesion threats as well as devices to socially interconnect large groups of strangers. We have identified religion, rituals, dance, music, and laughter as evolved mechanisms to promote group identity and loyalty in increasingly diverse social groups.

Adaptations for Group Decision Making

Supported by language, humans have evolved to be good at making collective decisions in groups—employing the wisdom of crowds. Mechanisms that support collective decision making are also found in other social species and do not necessarily require language (Conradt & List, 2009). Seeley (1995) provided a summary of group decision making in honeybees. In late spring or early summer, when a colony of bees divides to find a new nest, several hundred bees fly out as "scouts" to inspect potential nest sites. Upon returning to the current nest, these scout bees perform waggle dances to advertise any good sites they have discovered and their locations; the duration of the dance depends on the scouts' perception of the site's quality (the better the site, the longer the dance). Because other bees are more likely to visit and inspect the sites advertised by scout bees, high-quality sites receive more subsequent visits and advertisements. Such a positive feedback loop eventually leads to a "group consensus" about the best site.

What simple evolved decision rules enable collective wisdom in honey bees, humans, and many other animals? Two contrasting rules are despotism (one individual deciding for all) and democracy (all individuals decide). Using a game theory model, researchers have shown that democratic decisions, on average, yield better outcomes than despotic decisions. It pays groups to accept the despot's decision only when the group size is small and the despot has critical information that other members do not have (Conradt & Roper, 2003). Conradt and Roper (2003) argued that democratic decisions are more beneficial "primarily because they tend to produce less extreme decisions, rather than because each individual has an influence on the decision per se" (p. 155).

Hastie and Kameda (2005) extended these ideas to human group decision making. Natural environments present large statistical uncertainties that affect many key group decisions, including the choice of foraging/nest sites, choice of travel routes, monitoring of predators, and so on (Kameda & Nakanishi, 2002). Given that no single individual (despot) can handle these uncertainties alone, the best decision rule is democratic. By aggregating members' opinions, random errors in individual perceptions under uncertainty are cancelled collectively (Surowiecki, 2004). Hastie and Kameda compared despotic and democratic decision rules. Results from computer simulations and laboratory experiments showed that the democratic rule outperformed the despotic rule and fared well compared with much more computationally taxing rules. These results indicate that despite their computational simplicity, democratic rules can achieve surprisingly high levels of performance, which makes this rule system a likely candidate for an evolutionary adaptation. We see the popularity of democratic rules across the full spectrum of human groups from hunter–gatherer and tribal societies (Boehm, 1996) to modern industrial democracies (Davis, 1973; Kerr & Tindale, 2004).

Thus, simple decision rules have emerged as adaptations to support group decision making in humans and nonhumans. Under conditions that were prominent in human evolution, a democratic decision rule seems to work better than a despotic rule. More work on these decision-making rules is needed.

Managing Intergroup Relations

A final persistent problem that early humans faced was how to deal with individuals belonging to groups other than their own. As population densities increased during the late Pleistocene, so did competition for scarce resources, and human groups increasingly came into contact with members of other groups. On the one hand, relations with outgroups provided opportunities for sharing resources such as food, water holes, information, and sexual mates. On the other hand, intergroup relations could be a source of tension and conflict over these resources. As a consequence, humans likely possess highly specialized decision rules that enable them to reap the benefits of intergroup relations while avoiding the costs.

As part of this evolved intergroup psychology, humans are on average relatively suspicious and even fearful of strangers. Fear of strangers occurs spontaneously in very young children. Social psychological research shows that fear is strongest toward outgroup males, presumably because they constituted the greatest threat in ancestral times (McDonald, Navarrete, & van Vugt, 2012). Members of outgroups posed not only a significant physical threat but also a disease threat—think of the way infectious diseases spread. Hence, fear of strangers might also serve the function of avoiding pathogens. A recent study, informed by an evolutionary analysis, showed that ethnocentrism is strongest among women who are in the early stage of pregnancy, presumably because they (and their fetus) are most at risk of catching a disease (Navarrete, Fessler, & Eng, 2007).

Another evolved decision rule in managing intergroup relations is choosing to engage in violence against members of outgroups when there is a low risk of retaliation. Intergroup aggression is common across human societies, and is also found in nonhuman primates, including chimpanzees, as well as nonprimates such as dolphins and hyenas, suggesting adaptation (Brosnan et al., 2009). Humans and chimpanzees use coalitional aggression to gain access to reproductively relevant resources such as territories and sexual mates. In both species, fighting coalitions consist of males, arguably because they have more to gain, and less to lose, by engaging in organized violence—the "male warrior hypothesis" (van Vugt, De Cremer, & Janssen, 2007). Research on the male warrior hypothesis supports it. Relative to women, men have stronger "tribal" attitudes, are more aggressive in intergroup encounters, and infrahumanize members of outgroups more (van Vugt, 2009). Men also increase their group contributions when in competition with other groups (van Vugt et al., 2007).

Intergroup relations provided opportunities for trading, and humans have also likely evolved cognitive mechanisms for establishing peaceful interactions with other groups, provided that these groups do not pose a physical or disease threat. Members of high-status groups readily offer help to members of low-status outgroups, particularly when intergroup helping reaffirms the status difference between the groups (Nadler, 2002). People are also more forgiving of moral transgressions from outgroup members than from ingroup members (Stürmer & Snyder, 2010) because the latter constitutes a cohesion threat. Even after a lethal intergroup conflict, such as the Rwandan genocide, reconciliation efforts between the groups involved—the Hutus and Tutsis—seemed to bear fruit (Paluck, 2009). An evolutionary hypothesis that requires testing is whether women play an important role in peacemaking and reconciliation efforts between groups after conflict (van Vugt, 2006).

Taken together, intergroup competition has been a selection force in human history, leading to various adaptations to engage in and emerge victoriously from deadly intergroup conflict. Given the importance of expanding social networks, humans may also have evolved specialized strategies for reconciliation, peacemaking, and peacekeeping between groups.

THE PROMISE OF EVOLUTIONARY SOCIAL PSYCHOLOGY

An evolutionary approach to questions about human social interaction and group processes can be fruitful in at least four ways. First, an evolutionary perspective can provide a more complete understanding of particular social phenomenon by asking fundamental questions about the functions, origins, and evolution of these phenomena—for example, what is the function of group cohesion? A more complete account inevitably follows from rigorous attempts to establish conceptual linkages between evolutionary processes operating on ancestral populations and social psychological processes operating within contemporary groups.

Second, an evolutionary perspective can help overcome biases and blind spots in the study of group and intergroup dynamics. It strikes us as odd that the social psychological literature on group decision making often focuses on what is wrong with groups, disregarding the fact that the group is the natural environment for humans (Caporael, 1997; Wilson et al., 2008). Examples include research on groupthink, brainstorming, group polarization, and information sharing. A cursory reading of these literatures all too easily suggests that people are poor group decision makers (Wilson et al., 2008). Any such conclusion is inaccurate—or, at the very least, overly simplistic—and we believe that an evolutionary perspective can produce more sophisticated and accurate conclusions about group decision making (Kameda & Tindale, 2006).

Third, an evolutionary approach is useful in yielding novel hypotheses about well-established social psychological phenomena. Kenrick, Griskevicius,

Schaller, and colleagues have applied evolutionary reasoning to produce a number of new hypotheses about group phenomena such as status, conformity, prejudice, and social influence that are unlikely to have been stimulated by other theoretical frameworks (Griskevicius et al., 2006; Kenrick, Li, & Butner, 2003; Sundie, Cialdini, Griskevicius, & Kenrick, 2006).

Finally, evolutionary thinking about the social brain can expand the boundaries of scientific inquiry on human sociality by suggesting important group phenomena that have received little if any attention from group researchers. Laughter, language, gossip, dance, music, rituals, sports, culture, and religion are increasingly being understood as social adaptations, that is, as manifestations of evolved psychological processes that connect individuals in large and diverse social networks, and these insights have benefited from evolution-informed inquiries (Atran & Norenzyan, 2004; Dunbar, 2004; Dunbar et al., 2011; Gervais & Wilson, 2005).

In short, an evolutionary perspective reinforces our awareness that the study of the human social brain is an inevitable aspect of social psychology. An evolutionary social psychology provides a set of conceptual and empirical tools that can be used to understand and describe human sociality more completely and accurately.

REFERENCES

Atran, S. (2002). *In gods we trust: The evolutionary landscape of religion*. Oxford, England: Oxford University Press.

Atran, S., & Norenzayan, A. (2004). Religion's evolutionary landscape: Counter-intuition, commitment, compassion, communion. *Behavioral and Brain Sciences*, *27*, 713–730. doi:10.1017/S0140525X04000172

Axelrod, R. (1984). *The evolution of cooperation*. New York, NY: Basic Books.

Bass, B. M. (with Bass, R.). (2008). *The Bass handbook of leadership: Theory, research, and managerial applications* (4th ed.). New York, NY: Free Press.

Bateson, M., Nettle, D., & Roberts, G. (2006). Cues of being watched enhance cooperation in a real-world setting. *Biology Letters*, *2*, 412–414. doi:10.1098/rsbl.2006.0509

Baumeister, R. F., & Leary, M. (1995). The need to belong: Desire for interpersonal attachments as a fundamental human motivation. *Psychological Bulletin*, *117*, 497–529. doi:10.1037/0033-2909.117.3.497

Boehm, C. (1996). Emergency decisions, cultural-selection mechanics, and group selection. *Current Anthropology*, *37*, 763–793. doi:10.1086/204561

Brosnan, S. F., & de Waal, F. B. M. (2003, September 18). Monkeys reject unequal pay [Letter]. *Nature*, *425*, 297–299. doi:10.1038/nature01963

Brosnan, S. F., Newton-Fisher, N. E., & van Vugt, M. (2009). A melding of minds: When primatology meets personality and social psychology. *Personality and Social Psychology Review, 13,* 129–147. doi:10.1177/1088868309335127

Brown, D. (1991). *Human universals.* Boston, MA: McGraw-Hill.

Buss, D. M. (1995). Evolutionary psychology: A new paradigm for psychological science. *Psychological Inquiry, 6,* 1–30. doi:10.1207/s15327965pli0601_1

Camerer, C. F. (2003). *Behavioral game theory: Experiments in strategic interaction.* Princeton, NJ: Princeton University Press.

Caporael, L. R. (1997). The evolution of truly social cognition: The core configurations model. *Personality and Social Psychology Review, 1,* 276–298. doi:10.1207/s15327957pspr0104_1

Chartrand, T. L., & Bargh, J. A. (1999). The chameleon effect: The perception–behavior link and social interaction. *Journal of Personality and Social Psychology, 76,* 893–910. doi:10.1037/0022-3514.76.6.893

Conradt, L., & List, C. (2009). Group decision making in humans and animals. *Philosophical Transactions of the Royal Society of London: Series B. Biological Sciences, 364,* 719–752. doi:10.1098/rstb.2008.0276

Conradt, L., & Roper, T. J. (2003, January 9). Group decision-making in animals [Letter]. *Nature, 421,* 155–158. doi:10.1038/nature01294

Cosmides, L. (1989). The logic of social exchange: Has natural selection shaped how humans reason? Studies with the Wason selection task. *Cognition, 31,* 187–276. doi:10.1016/0010-0277(89)90023-1

Darwin, C. (1871). *The descent of man, and selection in relation to sex.* London, England: Murray.

Davis, J. H. (1973). Group decision and social interaction: A theory of social decision schemes. *Psychological Review, 80,* 97–125. doi:10.1037/h0033951

Dunbar, R. I. M. (2004). *Grooming, gossip, and the evolution of language.* London, England: Faber & Faber.

Dunbar, R. I. M., Baron, R., Frangou, A., Pearce, E., van Leeuwen, E. J. C., Stow, J., . . . van Vugt, M. (2011). Social laughter is correlated with an elevated pain threshold. *Proceedings of the Royal Society: Series B. Biological Sciences, 279,* 1161–1167. doi:10.1098/rspb.2011.1373

Eisenberger, N. I., Lieberman, M. D., & Williams, K. D. (2003, October 10). Does rejection hurt: An fMRI study of social exclusion. *Science, 302,* 290–292. doi:10.1126/science.1089134

Fehr, E., & Fischbacher, U. (2004). Third-party sanctions and social norms. *Evolution and Human Behavior, 25,* 63–87. doi:10.1016/S1090-5138(04)00005-4

Fehr, E., & Schmidt, K. M. (1999). A theory of fairness, competition, and cooperation. *Quarterly Journal of Economics, 114,* 817–868. doi:10.1162/003355399556151

Festinger, L. (1950). Informal social communication. *Psychological Review, 57,* 271–282. doi:10.1037/h0056932

Fischbacher, U., Gächter, S., & Fehr, E. (2001). Are people conditionally cooperative? Evidence from a public goods experiment. *Economics Letters*, *71*, 397–404. doi:10.1016/S0165-1765(01)00394-9

Forsyth, D. R. (2010). *Group dynamics* (5th ed.). Belmont, CA: Wadsworth.

Gervais, M., & Wilson, D. S. (2005). The evolution and functions of laughter and humor: A synthetic approach. *Quarterly Review of Biology*, *80*, 395–430. doi:10.1086/498281

Griskevicius, V., Cantú, S. M., & van Vugt, M. (2012). The evolutionary bases for sustainable behavior: Implications for marketing, policy, and social entrepreneurship. *Journal of Public Policy & Marketing*, *31*, 115–128. doi:10.1509/jppm.11.040

Griskevicius, V., Goldstein, N. J., Mortensen, C. R., Cialdini, R. B., & Kenrick, D. T. (2006). Going along versus going alone: When fundamental motives facilitate strategic (non)conformity. *Journal of Personality and Social Psychology*, *91*, 281–294. doi:10.1037/0022-3514.91.2.281

Gurven, M. (2004). To give or not to give: An evolutionary ecology of human food transfers. *Behavioral and Brain Sciences*, *27*, 543–559. doi:10.1017/S0140525X04000123

Haley, K. J., & Fessler, D. M. T. (2005). Nobody's watching? Subtle cues affect generosity in an anonymous economic game. *Evolution and Human Behavior*, *26*, 245–256. doi:10.1016/j.evolhumbehav.2005.01.002

Hardy, C. L., & van Vugt, M. (2006). Nice guys finish first: The competitive altruism hypothesis. *Personality and Social Psychology Bulletin*, *32*, 1402–1413. doi:10.1177/0146167206291006

Hastie, R., & Kameda, T. (2005). The robust beauty of majority rules in group decisions. *Psychological Review*, *112*, 494–508. doi:10.1037/0033-295X.112.2.494

Henrich, J., Boyd, R., Bowles, S., Camerer, C., Fehr, E., & Gintis, H. (Eds.). (2004). *Foundations of human sociality: Economic experiments and ethnographic evidence from fifteen small-scale societies*. Oxford, England: Oxford University Press.

Iredale, W., van Vugt, M., & Dunbar, R. (2008). Showing off in humans: Male generosity as mate signal. *Evolutionary Psychology*, *6*, 386–392.

Jetten, J., Spears, R., & Manstead, A. S. R. (1996). Intergroup norms and intergroup discrimination: Distinctive self-categorization and social identity effects. *Journal of Personality and Social Psychology*, *71*, 1222–1233. doi:10.1037/0022-3514.71.6.1222

Kameda, T., & Nakanishi, D. (2002). Cost–benefit analysis of social/cultural learning in a nonstationary uncertain environment: An evolutionary simulation and an experiment with human subjects. *Evolution and Human Behavior*, *23*, 373–393. doi:10.1016/S1090-5138(02)00101-0

Kameda, T., Takezawa, M., & Hastie, R. (2003). The logic of social sharing: An evolutionary game analysis of adaptive norm development. *Personality and Social Psychology Review*, *7*, 2–19. doi:10.1207/S15327957PSPR0701_1

Kameda, T., Takezawa, M., Ohtsubo, Y., & Hastie, R. (2010). Are our minds fundamentally egalitarian? Adaptive bases of different sociocultural models about distributive justice. In M. Schaller, A. Norenzayan, S. J. Heine, T. Yamagishi, & T. Kameda (Eds.), *Evolution, culture, and the human mind* (pp.151–163). New York, NY: Psychology Press.

Kameda, T., Takezawa, M., Tindale, R. S., & Smith, C. M. (2002). Social sharing and risk reduction: Exploring a computational algorithm for the psychology of windfall gains. *Evolution and Human Behavior, 23*, 11–33. doi:10.1016/S1090-5138(01)00086-1

Kameda, T., & Tindale, R. S. (2006). Groups as adaptive devices: Human docility and group aggregation mechanisms in evolutionary context. In M. Schaller, J. A. Simpson, & D. T. Kenrick (Eds.), *Evolution and social psychology* (pp. 317–341). New York, NY: Psychology Press.

Kaplan, H., & Hill, K. (1985). Food sharing among Ache foragers: Tests of explanatory hypotheses. *Current Anthropology, 26*, 223–246. doi:10.1086/203251

Keltner, D., Gruenfeld, D. H., & Anderson, C. (2000). Power, approach, and inhibition. *Psychological Review, 110*, 265–284. doi:10.1037/0033-295X.110.2.265

Kenrick, D. T., Li, N. P., & Butner, J. (2003). Dynamical evolutionary psychology: Individual decision rules and emergent social norms. *Psychological Review, 110*, 3–28. doi:10.1037/0033-295X.110.1.3

Kerr, N. L., & Levine, J. M. (2008). The detection of social exclusion: Evolution and beyond. *Group Dynamics: Theory, Research, and Practice, 12*, 39–52. doi:10.1037/1089-2699.12.1.39

Kerr, N. L., & Tindale, R. S. (2004). Group performance and decision making. *Annual Review of Psychology, 55*, 623–655. doi:10.1146/annurev.psych.55.090902.142009

King, A. J., Johnson, D. D. P., & van Vugt, M. (2009). The origins and evolution of leadership. *Current Biology, 19*, R911–R916. doi:10.1016/j.cub.2009.07.027

Kirkpatrick, L. A., & Ellis, B. J. (2004). An evolutionary psychological approach to self-esteem: Multiple domains and multiple functions. In M. Brewer & M. Hewstone (Eds.), *Self and social identity* (pp. 52–77). Oxford, England: Blackwell.

Kurzban, R., & Leary, M. R. (2001). Evolutionary origins of stigmatization: The functions of social exclusion. *Psychological Bulletin, 127*, 187–208. doi:10.1037/0033-2909.127.2.187

Little, A. C., Burris, R. P., Jones, B. C., & Roberts, S. C. (2007). Facial appearance affects voting decisions. *Evolution and Human Behavior, 28*, 18–27. doi:10.1016/j.evolhumbehav.2006.09.002

Littlepage, G. E., Hollingshead, A. B., Drake, L. R., & Littlepage, A. M. (2008). Transactive memory and performance in work groups: Specificity, communication, ability differences, and work allocation. *Group Dynamics, 12*, 223–241. doi:10.1037/1089-2699.12.3.223

Mazur, A., Booth, A., & Dabbs, J. M. (1992). Testosterone and chess competition. *Social Psychology Quarterly, 55,* 70–77. doi:10.2307/2786687

McDonald, M. M., Navarrete, C. D., & van Vugt, M. (2012). Evolution and the psychology of intergroup conflict: The male warrior hypothesis. *Philosophical Transactions of the Royal Society: Series B. Biological Sciences, 367,* 670–679. doi:10.1098/rstb.2011.0301

Moreland, R. L., Argote, L., & Krishnan, R. (1996). Socially shared cognition at work: Transactive memory and group performance. In J. L. Nye & A. M. Brower (Eds.), *What's social about social cognition? Research on socially shared cognition in small groups* (pp. 57–84). Thousand Oaks, CA: Sage.

Nadler, A. (2002). Inter-group helping relations as power relations: Maintaining or challenging social dominance between groups through helping. *Journal of Social Issues, 58,* 487–502. doi:10.1111/1540-4560.00272

Navarrete, C. D., Fessler, D. M. T., & Eng, S. J. (2007). Elevated ethnocentrism in the first trimester of pregnancy. *Evolution and Human Behavior, 28,* 60–65. doi:10.1016/j.evolhumbehav.2006.06.002

Nesse, R. (2007). Runaway selection for displays of partner value and altruism. *Biological Theory, 2,* 143–155. doi:10.1162/biot.2007.2.2.143

Nowak, M. A., & Sigmund, K. (2005, October 27). Evolution of indirect reciprocity. *Nature, 437,* 1291–1298. doi:10.1038/nature04131

Paluck, E. L. (2009). Reducing intergroup prejudice and conflict using mass media: A field experiment in Rwanda. *Journal of Personality and Social Psychology, 96,* 574–587. doi:10.1037/a0011989

Park, J. H., Schaller, M., & van Vugt, M. (2008). The psychology of human kin recognition: Heuristic cues, erroneous inferences, and their implications. *Review of General Psychology, 12,* 215–235. doi:10.1037/1089-2680.12.3.215

Roberts, G. (1998). Competitive altruism: From reciprocity to the handicap principle. *Proceedings of the Royal Society: Series B. Biological Sciences, 265,* 427–431. doi:10.1098/rspb.1998.0312

Schaller, M., Park, J. H., & Faulkner, J. (2003). Prehistoric dangers and contemporary prejudices. *European Review of Social Psychology, 14,* 105–137. doi:10.1080/10463280340000036

Seeley, T. D. (1995). *The wisdom of the hive: The social physiology of honey bee colonies.* Cambridge, MA: Harvard University Press.

Shinada, M., Yamagishi, T., & Ohmura, Y. (2004). False friends are worse than bitter enemies: "Altruistic" punishment of in-group members. *Evolution and Human Behavior, 25,* 379–393. doi:10.1016/j.evolhumbehav.2004.08.001

Stone, V. E., Cosmides, L., Tooby, J., Kroll, N., & Knight, R. T. (2002). Selective impairment of reasoning about social exchange in a patient with bilateral limbic system damage. *Proceedings of the National Academy of Sciences of the United States of America, 99,* 11531–11536. doi:10.1073/pnas.122352699

Stürmer, S. & Snyder, M. (Eds.). (2010). *The psychology of prosocial behavior: Group processes, intergroup relations, and helping.* London, England: Wiley-Blackwell.

Sundie, J. M., Cialdini, R. B., Griskevicius, V., & Kenrick, D. T. (2006). Evolutionary social influence. In M. Schaller, J. A. Simpson, & D. T. Kenrick (Eds.), *Evolution and social psychology* (pp. 287–316). New York, NY: Psychology Press.

Surowiecki, J. (2004). *The wisdom of crowds: Why the many are smarter than the few and how collective wisdom shapes business, economies, societies and nations.* New York, NY: Doubleday.

Tajfel, H., & Turner, J. C. (1979). An integrative theory of intergroup conflict. In W. G. Austin & S. Worchel (Eds.), *The social psychology of intergroup relations* (pp. 33–47). Monterey, CA: Brooks/Cole.

Tracy, J. L., & Robins, R. W. (2004). Show your pride: Evidence for a discrete emotion expression. *Psychological Science, 15,* 194–197. doi:10.1111/j.0956-7976.2004.01503008.x

Trivers, R. L. (1971). The evolution of reciprocal altruism. *Quarterly Review of Biology, 46,* 35–57. doi:10.1086/406755

van Vugt, M. (2006). Evolutionary origins of leadership and followership. *Personality and Social Psychology Review, 10,* 354–371. doi:10.1207/s15327957pspr1004_5

van Vugt, M. (2009). Despotism, democracy, and the evolutionary dynamics of leadership and followership. *American Psychologist, 64,* 54–56. doi:10.1037/a0014178

van Vugt, M., De Cremer, D., & Janssen, D. P. (2007). Gender differences in cooperation and competition: The male-warrior hypothesis. *Psychological Science, 18,* 19–23. doi:10.1111/j.1467-9280.2007.01842.x

van Vugt, M., & Hart, C. M. (2004). Social identity as social glue: The origins of group loyalty. *Journal of Personality and Social Psychology, 86,* 585–598. doi:10.1037/0022-3514.86.4.585

van Vugt, M., Hogan, R., & Kaiser, R. B. (2008). Leadership, followership, and evolution: Some lessons from the past. *American Psychologist, 63,* 182–196. doi:10.1037/0003-066X.63.3.182

van Vugt, M., & Park, J. H. (2009). Guns, germs, and sex: How evolution shaped our intergroup psychology. *Social and Personality Psychology Compass, 3,* 927–938. doi:10.1111/j.1751-9004.2009.00221.x

van Vugt, M., & Spisak, B. R. (2008). Sex differences in leadership emergence during competitions within and between groups. *Psychological Science, 19,* 854–858. doi:10.1111/j.1467-9280.2008.02168.x

Williams, K. D. (2009). Ostracism: A temporal need-threat model. In M. P. Zanna (Ed.), *Advances in experimental social psychology* (Vol. 41, pp. 275–314).

Amsterdam, the Netherlands: Academic Press. doi:10.1016/S0065-2601(08)00406-1

Wilson, D. S., Timmel, J. J., & Miller, R. R. (2004). Cognitive cooperation: When the going gets tough, think as a group. *Human Nature, 15*, 225–250. doi:10.1007/s12110-004-1007-7

Wilson, D. S., van Vugt, M., & O'Gorman, R. (2008). Multi-level selection theory and major evolutionary transitions: Implications for psychological science. *Current Directions in Psychological Science, 17*, 6–9. doi:10.1111/j.1467-8721.2008.00538.x

19

SOCIAL DEFENSE THEORY: HOW A MIXTURE OF PERSONALITY TRAITS IN GROUP CONTEXTS MAY PROMOTE OUR SURVIVAL

TSACHI EIN-DOR

When God looked upon man, he or she concluded that "it is not good for the man to be alone" (Genesis, 2:18). Theory and research have indeed indicated that in the course of evolution, humans lived in small, highly interactive groups of kin and formed complex social relationships that are unique among mammals. Because social solutions to adaptive challenges were so crucial for human survival, many of our psychological mechanisms undoubtedly evolved to support this aspect of human existence (Buss, 1995). Brewer and Caporael (1990) as well as other scholars (e.g., Alexander, 1987; Axelrod, 1984; Cosmides, 1989; Gazzaniga, 2008) have argued that living in cooperative groups was the primary survival strategy for humans. Nevertheless, most of the research on human reactions to threats focuses on the individual level of analysis and examines mental processes such as threat perception and coping (e.g., Brandtstädter & Rothermund, 2004) or immediate self-preservation responses such as fight or flight (e.g., Brown, 1954). There is good reason to believe, however, that psychological reactions to threats should be understood

http://dx.doi.org/10.1037/14250-020
Mechanisms of Social Connection: From Brain to Group, M. Mikulincer and P. R. Shaver (Editors)

357

within the social context in which they are produced, including the groups in which people find themselves.

In the present chapter, I present social defense theory (SDT; Ein-Dor, Mikulincer, Doron, & Shaver, 2010), which is based on the assertion that the value of a person's responses to threat, which are based partly on dispositional variables, should be understood at the group level. Some individuals are chronically hypervigilant and constantly alert to potential threats and dangers. Other individuals, once alerted to a threat, are self-reliant and likely to take protective actions rapidly and effectively. Still other individuals are relationship oriented and likely to be leaders, coordinators, and managers of collective efforts. Because each of these response patterns contributes to effective reactions in times of danger, I hypothesized that groups containing all three kinds of people will be more effective when dealing with threats and dangers (early detection, rapid response, and effective cooperation) than less heterogeneous groups. In the initial outline of SDT (Ein-Dor et al., 2010), these response patterns were viewed as cognitive and behavioral manifestations of people's attachment orientations (see Chapters 7, 10, 11, 15, and 17, this volume, for further perspectives on attachment theory and research).

ATTACHMENT THEORY

Bowlby's (1973, 1980, 1982) attachment theory proposes that human beings possess an innate psychobiological system (the *attachment behavioral system*) that motivates them to seek the aid of others—a socially based solution—when they need protection from threats and dangers. When people experience their caregivers as responsive and supportive, they develop a sense of attachment security, along with constructive strategies (e.g., support seeking) for coping with threats and regulating emotions (see Chapter 7). Conversely, when caregivers are perceived as unavailable or unreliable, a person tends to develop an insecure attachment orientation marked by either attachment-system deactivating strategies for regulating emotions and social behavior (avoidant attachment) or attachment-system hyperactivating strategies (attachment anxiety). These orientations are measurable in infancy, childhood, and adulthood, and their causes and psychological consequences have been extensively studied (for recent reviews, see Cassidy & Shaver, 2008; Mikulincer & Shaver, 2007).

Social and personality psychologists generally conceptualize adult attachment patterns as regions in a continuous two-dimensional space (e.g., Brennan, Clark, & Shaver, 1998). One dimension, attachment-related *avoidance*, reflects the extent to which a person distrusts relationship partners' goodwill, strives to maintain independence, and relies on deactivating strategies for dealing with threats and negative emotions. Avoidant people cope with threats by deemphasizing distress and vulnerability and by attempting to cope independently, without seeking others' help (e.g., Fraley & Shaver, 1997). The second dimension, attachment-related *anxiety*, reflects the extent to which a person worries that others will not be available or helpful in times of need. People high on attachment anxiety exaggerate their sense of vulnerability and insistently call on others for help and care, sometimes to the point of being intrusive (e.g., J. A. Feeney & Noller, 1990).

Attachment security is defined by low scores on both anxiety and avoidance. Secure people generally cope with threats by relying on internal resources developed with the help of security-enhancing attachment figures or by effectively seeking support from others or collaborating with them (Shaver & Mikulincer, 2002). Secure individuals generally have high self-esteem, trust other people, and perceive the world as a relatively safe place (see Mikulincer & Shaver, 2007, for a review).

According to both theory and research, attachment security confers adaptive advantages in a variety of social, emotional, and behavioral domains (Mikulincer & Shaver, 2007). For example, secure individuals tend to have more lasting and satisfying close relationships as well as fewer psychological problems. They are also viewed by others as more ideal relationship partners (e.g., Klohnen & Luo, 2003). These benefits of security caused researchers to wonder why a substantial portion of all large samples studied in various countries are insecure with respect to attachment. Belsky, Steinberg, Houts, and Halpern-Felsher (2010) were the first to argue that under certain conditions attachment insecurity has adaptive benefits, because it is associated with earlier menarche in females and earlier reproduction in environments where waiting for better conditions might result in failing to reproduce.

Theory and research also suggest that survival and coping with threats might be the major reason for the emergence of the attachment behavioral system during mammalian, especially primate, evolution (Cassidy & Shaver, 2008; Ein-Dor et al., 2010). Indeed, minimal signs of danger or threats have been found to automatically activate attachment-related mental representations in adulthood (e.g., Mikulincer, Birnbaum, Woddis, & Nachmias, 2000; Mikulincer, Gillath, & Shaver, 2002). Therefore, my colleagues and I (Ein-Dor et al., 2010) proposed SDT, arguing that each of the major attachment orientations (secure, anxious, and avoidant) confers unique adaptive advantages that increase the *inclusive fitness* (see Hamilton, 1964a, 1964b) of members of groups that include insecure as well as secure attachment patterns. These advantages might also contribute to group-level selection (e.g., D. S. Wilson, Vugt, & O'Gorman, 2008; E. O. Wilson, 2012), although group-level selection remains controversial (Ein-Dor et al., 2010).

SOCIAL DEFENSE THEORY

According to SDT (Ein-Dor et al., 2010), each of the three major attachment patterns—secure, anxious, and avoidant—confers special adaptive advantages that tend to increase the inclusive fitness of people in groups that contain members of all three kinds. Each pattern also has distinct disadvantages, which may decrease inclusive fitness if they are not complemented by contributions from people with different attachment orientations. This view is in line with Nettle's (2006) argument that personality variations can be understood in terms of trade-offs among fitness costs and benefits: "Behavioral alternatives can be considered as trade-offs, with a particular trait producing not unalloyed advantage but a mixture of costs and benefits such that the optimal value for fitness may depend on very specific local circumstances" (p. 625).

Advantages and Disadvantages of Secure Individuals

Attachment research has shown that secure individuals benefit the groups to which they belong. For example, they are generally better than insecure people at leading and coordinating group activities (e.g., Davidovitz, Mikulincer, Shaver, Ijzak, & Popper, 2007), and they work more effectively with other group members when solving problems (e.g., Rom & Mikulincer, 2003; Smith, Murphy, & Coats, 1999). According to Mikulincer and Shaver's (2003, 2007) literature reviews, these advantages stem from a sense of security rooted in past supportive experiences with attachment figures. This sense of security is closely associated with core beliefs, such as the belief that the world is a safe place, especially when significant others are present. These optimistic, comforting mental representations promote self-soothing reappraisals of threats, which help secure individuals perform better than insecure ones in many challenging situations (for reviews, see Cassidy & Shaver, 2008; Mikulincer & Shaver, 2007).

What attachment researchers call *felt security* (Sroufe & Waters, 1977), however, does not always reflect actual physical security. In times of danger, a sense of felt security can be maladaptive if it hinders rapid recognition of a threat or retards assembly of a rapid, effective response. For example, Mawson (1978, 1980, 2005) showed that the typical human response to danger is to seek the proximity of familiar people and places, even if this means remaining in or even approaching a dangerous situation (see also Baker & Chapman, 1962; Henderson, 1977; Kinston & Rosser, 1974). Therefore, secure individuals may activate schemas and scripts that promote seeking proximity to others (e.g., Mikulincer et al., 2002; Mikulincer, Shaver, Sapir-Lavid, & Avihou-Kanza, 2009; Waters & Waters, 2006), even though this is sometimes not the safest strategy. Such proximity seeking in cases of actual danger may have two disadvantages: (a) slower identification of early signs of danger and (b) slower activation of defensive behavior.

Sime (1983, 1985) examined these disadvantages in a retrospective study of reactions to a fire in a large coastal resort on the Isle of Man, Great Britain, in 1973. He found that people who were physically closer to significant others (e.g., family members) were less likely to react to ambiguous cues of danger, such as noises and shouts, which occurred during the early stages of the fire. They reacted only later, when unambiguous cues of danger, such as smoke, flames, and people running while holding fire extinguishers, occurred. Subsequent studies of survivors' behavior during disasters also suggest that people who were together with familiar others were slow to perceive that they were in danger (Aguirre, Wenger, & Vigo, 1998; Fitzpatrick & Mileti, 1991; Perry, 1994; Proulx, 2002, 2003). According to SDT, this tendency might result from secure people's sense of safety and optimistic threat appraisals.

Research examining reactions to real or imagined dangers also provides indirect support for the hypothesis that securely attached people react in nonoptimal way to signs of danger. For example, Bowlby (1973) noted that during and after disasters, "no member of a family is content, or indeed able to do anything else, until all members of the family are gathered together" (p. 91). Studies of behavior during fires also show that people tend to converge and cluster (Bryan, 1985, 2002; Sime, 1983, 1985). Governments and trained professionals have great difficulty getting people to evacuate before and during disasters, because "traditional family ties often keep individual members in the danger zone until it is too late" (Hill & Hansen, 1962, p. 217).

Taken together, the evidence suggests that although people who are secure with respect to attachment are better at leading and coordinating group activities, these advantages are partially offset by their slower identification of actual and imminent dangers and their sometimes nonoptimal reactions to danger because of their wish to stay close to other people. This suggests that the tendency of secure people to focus on an ongoing project irrespective of mounting danger may sometimes hamper their survival and the survival of their group. Vigilance to danger and a quick fight-or-flight response are sometimes necessary to avert disaster. Being high on either attachment anxiety or attachment avoidance might confer these abilities.

Advantages and Disadvantages of People High on Attachment Anxiety

Compared with people who are secure with respect to attachment, those who score relatively high on anxious attachment often perform relatively poorly in groups (e.g., Rom & Mikulincer, 2003). They may take the work less seriously, make fewer or poorer quality contributions to a team, and have lower expectations of contributing to the team effort. Nevertheless, the strategies characteristically used by anxious people to deal with threats may be of benefit to group members in certain kinds of threatening situations. Anxious people are vigilant in monitoring the environment for threats and are emotionally expressive and desirous of support when a threat is detected (e.g., Cassidy & Kobak, 1988; J. A. Feeney & Noller, 1990). They may benefit other people in their social surroundings by reacting quickly and vocally to early, perhaps ambiguous, cues of danger, a reaction that Ein-Dor et al. (2010) called *sentinel behavior*.

According to SDT, this behavior stems from a particular kind of self-schema regarding ways to cope with threats—a sentinel schema. In Rumelhart's (1980) terms, self-schemas consist of a number of "placeholders" that supply default behaviors for certain kinds of situations. Possessing this kind of schema helps a person respond quickly to relevant situations, and if the situation provides insufficiently detailed information about how to respond, the default strategy can be quickly adopted. According to SDT, the schemas of people high on attachment anxiety contain default placeholders that cause them (a) to remain vigilant with respect to possible threats, especially in unfamiliar or ambiguous situations; (b) to react quickly and strongly to early, perhaps unclear cues of danger (e.g., unusual noises, shuffling feet, shouts); (c) to alert others about the imminent danger; (d) if others are not immediately supportive, to heighten efforts to get them to provide support; and (e) to minimize distance from others when coping with a threat (Ein-Dor, Mikulincer, & Shaver, 2011a).

Many species of animals benefit from having sentinels in their midst. For instance, various mammals (e.g., Fichtel, 2004) and primates (e.g., Coss, Ramakrishnan, & Schank, 2005; Riede, Bronson, Hatzikirou, & Zuberbühler, 2005) produce shrill alarm signals when they detect a potential threat. In similar ways, human group members can benefit from anxious individuals' hyperactivating strategies.

In support of this notion, Ein-Dor et al. (2011a) found that attachment anxiety was associated with high access to core components of the sentinel schema (noticing danger before other people do, warning others about the danger) when writing a story about threatening events. More anxious participants remembered (i.e., recognized) more recently encountered sentinel-schema information, reacted quicker than their more secure counterparts to sentinel-related information, and were prone to "recall" schema-biased false memories. Moreover, after reading a sentinel-related vignette, participants who scored higher on attachment anxiety were more likely to generate more inferences and conjectures than people low on attachment anxiety. These effects were not explained by individual differences in attachment-unrelated verbal and memory abilities, speed of recognizing attachment-irrelevant information, or attachment-unrelated inference skills. Also, the findings were not explained by general personality traits (e.g., neuroticism, extraversion) or by scores on a measure of socially desirable responding.

In a second research project, Ein-Dor, Mikulincer, and Shaver (2011b) examined whether attachment anxiety is associated with actual sentinel-related behaviors. Specifically, they examined whether in threatening situations, people who score high on attachment anxiety may react emotionally and thereby alert other group members to the danger and the need for protection or escape. To test these predictions, 46 groups of three people were unobtrusively observed in a threatening laboratory situation: a room gradually filling up with smoke, apparently because of a malfunctioning computer. In line with predictions, attachment anxiety was associated with quicker detection of the smoke in the room and with greater group effectiveness in dealing with the threat. The results remained significant even when extraversion and neuroticism, two possible confounds, were statistically controlled.

More recently, Ein-Dor and Orgad (2012) extended these results and examined whether people high on attachment anxiety also share a heightened tendency to deliver a warning message without delay following threat detection. Participants were led to believe that they accidently activated a computer virus that erased the experimenter's computer. They were then asked to alert the department's computer technicians about the incident. On their way, participants were presented with four decision points at which they could choose either to delay their warning or to continue directly to the technicians' office. Specifically, upon their exit from the laboratory room (on their way to the dean's assistant manager), a confederate stopped them and pleaded them to answer a short survey (Decision Point 1). After their arrival to the dean's assistant manager, they were told to contact the laboratory's manager, who sits at the other end of the corridor. They were asked, however, to aid the dean's assistant manager in photocopying an important report before they leave (Decision Point 2). Next, on the door of the laboratory's manager's room was a sign that read "I'll be right back." Participants chose either to wait or to seek further guidance (Decision Point 3). Finally, a confederate directed the participants to the computer technicians, and while they went down the staircase to the technicians' room, another confederate dropped sheets of paper; participants chose whether to help the confederate or go directly to the technicians' room (Decision Point 4). Upon their arrival to the technicians' room, they were thanked and debriefed.

Participants' willingness to delay their warning was coded on a 5-point scale ranging from 0 to 4. For each situation in which the participants chose to delay, they received one point of delay. For example, a participant who answered the survey, photocopied the report, waited more than 1 minute by the laboratory's manager's door, and helped to pick up the sheets of paper, and received a score of 4 on the delay scale. Results indicated that attachment anxious individuals were less willing to be delayed on their way to deliver a warning message than their more secure counterparts. This result remained significant when attachment-related avoidance, extroversion, and neuroticism were statistically controlled. Thus, research has supported SDT's premise that attachment anxiety is associated with sentinel-related cognitions and behaviors.

Advantages and Disadvantages of People High on Attachment-Related Avoidance

Avoidant people tend to dismiss threats, pain, and vulnerability and to cognitively or behaviorally withdraw from sources of stress and distress (e.g., Fraley & Shaver, 1997). Therefore, they might be less vigilant to threat and perceive that they are in danger later than others. They also do not perform well as teammates and have lower expectations of contributing to a team effort (e.g., Rom & Mikulincer, 2003). In times of need, in fact, they tend to look out for their own interests and take care of themselves, even if this sometimes occurs at other people's expense (e.g., B. C. Feeney & Collins, 2001). Thus, they may be more likely to rely on self-protective fight-or-flight responses in times of danger, without hesitating or needing to deliberate with other group members, a reaction that Ein-Dor et al. (2010) called *rapid fight-or-flight behavior*. As a result, avoidant individuals' primary motivation to save themselves may allow them to quickly discover a way to effectively deal with a threat. Meanwhile, anxiously and securely attached individuals may focus much of their attention on the whereabouts and welfare of close associates without focusing quickly and fully on how to escape.

Imagine an avoidant person in the presence of a dangerous fire. While taking quick protective action, the person may find an escape route or take effective action to put out the fire or seal a door to keep the fire outside. Moreover, avoidant people may be personally effective because they are not overwhelmed by emotion when drastic action is required. Although there are obvious moral dangers in behaving this way, there is little doubt that it can increase an avoidant person's survival chances while sometimes saving other people's lives, including the lives of group members about whom the avoidant individual may not care very deeply.

Evidence for the influence of a few group members' early decisions to flee a dangerous situation can be found in studies conducted in war-related and natural disasters. One of the most alarming sights for human beings is other people running from danger (e.g., Mawson, 1980). As Marshall (1947) eloquently stated in writing about military behavior during World War II,

> It can be laid down as a rule that nothing is more likely to collapse a line of infantry in combat than the sight of a few of its number in full and unexplained flight to the rear. . . . One or two or more men made a sudden run to the rear which others in the vicinity did not understand. . . . [I]n every case the testimony of all witnesses clearly [indicated] that those who started the run . . . had a legitimate or at least a reasonable excuse for the action. (pp. 145–146)

It is also known that in dangerous situations people tend to follow the route they see others taking (Mawson, 1980).

Individuals who flee first (those who, according to SDT, are likely to be disproportionately avoidant) often clear a way by opening emergency doors, breaking a window, or finding a safer place to hide. When their escape route is identified and cleared, others can follow and take advantage of the escape route. Thus, avoidant individuals may increase their own and their group members' chances of survival under emergency conditions.

According to SDT, this behavior stems from a particular kind of schema regarding ways to cope with threats: a rapid fight-or-flight schema. SDT contends that the schemas of people high on attachment avoidance contain something like the following placeholders: (a) minimize the importance of threatening stimuli; (b) when danger is clearly imminent, take quick self-protective action, either by escaping the situation or by taking action against the danger; and (c) at such times, do not worry about coordinating one's efforts with those of other people.

In support of this notion, Ein-Dor et al. (2011a) found that attachment-related avoidance was associated with ready mental access to core components of the rapid fight-or-flight schema when writing a story about threatening events. This schema comprised five components: (a) escaping a situation without helping others, (b) acting without receiving help from others, (c) reacting quickly without depending on other people's actions, (d) lack of cooperation with others, and (e) lack of deliberation with others. In addition, more avoidant participants recognized more recently encountered rapid fight-or-flight-schema information, reacted quicker than people low on attachment avoidance to rapid fight-or-flight–related information, and were prone to recall schema-biased false memories. Finally, after reading a vignette relevant to rapid fight or flight, participants who scored higher on avoidance were likely to generate more inferences and conjectures than people low on avoidance. Across all studies, avoidance scores were not associated with processing threat-*irrelevant* information. Moreover, the effects of attachment-related avoidance were not explained by individual differences in attachment-unrelated verbal and memory abilities, speed of recognizing attachment-irrelevant information, or attachment-unrelated inference skills. Also, the findings were not explained by general personality traits (e.g., neuroticism, extraversion) or by scores on a measure of socially desirable responding.

Ein-Dor et al. (2011b) also examined whether attachment-related avoidance was associated with rapid fight-or-flight behaviors. Specifically, they examined whether, in threatening situations, people who score high on attachment avoidance would respond quickly to a detected threat (a room gradually filling up with smoke, apparently because of a malfunctioning computer); and this quick reaction might increase the survival chances of all group members. In line with predictions, avoidance was associated with speedier escape responses once a threat was detected and with greater group effectiveness in dealing with the danger. Findings remained significant even when extraversion and neuroticism were statistically controlled. Thus, research has supported SDT's premise that attachment-related avoidance is associated with rapid fight-or-flight cognitions and behaviors.

More recently, Ein-Dor et al. (2012) examined whether the rapid fight-or-flight responses of avoidant people are associated with specific metabolic processes. Socially oriented people can manage their physical energy more efficiently (Beckes & Coan, 2011; see also Chapter 5, this volume) because they can share with other people the care of young children (e.g., Ehrenberg, Gearing-Small, Hunter, & Small, 2001), provide and receive support in times of need (e.g., Townsend & Franks, 1995), share resources (e.g., Rogers & DeBoer, 2001), and contribute to the detection of potential threats (Davis, 2004; Ein-Dor et al., 2011a). Because avoidant people do not share the cost of many of life's metabolically expensive activities with others (Beckes & Coan, 2011), they might need to maintain greater metabolic resources to make decisions, engage in problem solving, and respond effectively to potential threats. In other words, people high on attachment avoidance might maintain a higher resting basal glucose level (glucose being a human being's metabolic fuel; Vannucci & Vannucci, 2000) in order to have a sufficient reservoir of energy for dealing with daily life circumstances.

In one study conducted with young adult women in the United States, Ein-Dor et al. (2012) found a positive association between avoidant attachment and resting basal glucose level. In a second study, this association was replicated in an Israeli sample of older men and women with a different measure of avoidant attachment. Thus, the association between avoidant attachment and basal glucose level seems robust. Importantly, these findings were not explained by elevated signs of stress and distress, which had been found to be related to both heightened levels of basal glucose (e.g., Armario, Marti, Molina, de Pablo, & Valdes, 1996) and avoidant attachment (see Mikulincer & Shaver, 2007, for a review). Specifically, the association between attachment-related avoidance and basal glucose level remained significant even after controlling for three sensitive indicators of tension and distress: self-rated anxiety, hypertension disorder, and dehydroepiandrosterone level (which has been repeatedly associated with stress and distress; see Goodyer, Park, Netherton, & Herbert, 2001, for a review).

Group Composition and Its Association With Effectiveness When Dealing With Threat

According to SDT, secure and insecure attachment orientations may have both unique adaptive advantages (which increase the fitness of group members) and disadvantages (which decrease inclusive fitness), and hence may have different benefits for group members under threatening conditions. Therefore, a group that contains people with different attachment patterns—secure, anxious, and avoidant—might be superior to other groups in dealing with threats and survival problems. Groups marked by a diversity of attachment orientations should detect potential problems and threats quickly (with anxious members acting as sentinels); act quickly without much deliberation, negotiation, or compromise (with avoidant members serving as models of rapid self-protection); and manage complex social tasks (with secure members acting as leaders and coordinators of the group).

To date, this proposition has been directly tested in only one study, by Ein-Dor et al. (2011b). They observed groups of three people in a room gradually filling up with smoke, apparently because of a malfunctioning computer. In line with predictions, findings indicated that the more diverse a group was in terms of attachment orientations, the more effective in dealing with the threat the group was rated by external observers. Pending replications of this finding, the study suggests the potentially adaptive aspects of certain group compositions based on attachment orientations.

CONCLUDING COMMENTS

SDT was devised to account for the social nature of group reactions to threats. It is based on the premise that people with different attachment patterns—secure, anxious, and avoidant members—bring different abilities to a group in which they find themselves, and thus can render it superior to other groups in dealing with threats and survival problems. Research indicates that people high on attachment anxiety may act as sentinels who detect potential problems and threats quickly and alert others to those threats (Ein-Dor et al., 2011a, 2011b; Ein-Dor & Orgad, 2012). People who score high on measures of attachment-related avoidance may act quickly without much hesitation, thereby contributing to group effectiveness and promoting their own survival and that of people around them (Ein-Dor et al., 2011a, 2011b). Research has also indicated that avoidant people may have elevated levels of metabolic fuel to support self-reliant responses (Ein-Dor et al., 2012). Finally, more secure individuals (those low on both attachment anxiety and avoidance) manage complex social tasks better than their more insecure counterparts (Rom & Mikulincer, 2003) and cooperate better with teammates. If SDT continues to receive empirical support, it may have important implications for theory and research concerning group processes, threat detection, and the adaptive benefits of personality diversity.

REFERENCES

Aguirre, B. E., Wenger, D., & Vigo, G. (1998). A test of the emergent norm theory of collective behavior. *Sociological Forum*, *13*, 301–320. doi:10.1023/A:1022145900928

Alexander, R. D. (1987). *The biology of moral systems*. New York, NY: Aldine de Gruyter.

Armario, A., Marti, O., Molina, T., de Pablo, J., & Valdes, M. (1996). Acute stress markers in humans: Response of plasma glucose, cortisol and prolactin to two examinations differing in the anxiety they provoke. *Psychoneuroendocrinology*, *21*, 17–24. doi:10.1016/0306-4530(95)00048-8

Axelrod, R. (1984). *The evolution of cooperation*. New York, NY: Basic Books.

Baker, G. W., & Chapman, D. W. (1962). *Man and society in disaster*. New York, NY: Basic Books.

Beckes, L., & Coan, J. A. (2011). Social baseline theory: The role of social proximity in emotion and economy of action. *Social and Personality Psychology Compass*, *5*, 976–988. doi:10.1111/j.1751-9004.2011.00400.x

Belsky, J., Steinberg, L., Houts, R. M., & Halpern-Felsher, B. L. (2010). The development of reproductive strategy in females: Early maternal harshness → earlier menarche → increased sexual risk taking. *Developmental Psychology*, *46*, 120–128. doi:10.1037/a0015549

Bowlby, J. (1973). *Attachment and loss: Vol. 2. Separation: Anxiety and anger*. New York, NY: Basic Books.

Bowlby, J. (1980). *Attachment and loss: Vol. 3. Sadness and depression*. New York, NY: Basic Books.

Bowlby, J. (1982). *Attachment and loss: Vol. 1. Attachment* (2nd ed.). New York, NY: Basic Books.

Brandtstädter, J., Voss, A., & Rothermund, K. (2004). Perception of danger signals: The role of control. *Experimental Psychology*, *51*, 24–32. doi:10.1027/1618-3169.51.1.24

Brennan, K. A., Clark, C. L., & Shaver, P. R. (1998). Self-report measurement of adult romantic attachment: An integrative overview. In J. A. Simpson & W. S.

Rholes (Eds.), *Attachment theory and close relationships* (pp. 46–76). New York, NY: Guilford Press.

Brewer, M. B., & Caporael, L. R. (1990). Selfish genes vs. selfish people: Sociobiology as origin myth. *Motivation and Emotion, 14*, 237–243. doi:10.1007/BF00996182

Brown, R. W. (1954). Mass phenomena. In G. Lindzey (Ed.), *Handbook of social psychology: Vol. 2. Special fields and applications* (pp. 833–876). Reading, MA: Addison-Wesley.

Bryan, J. L. (1985). Convergence clusters: A phenomenon of human behavior seen in selected high-rise building fires. *Fire Journal, 79*(6), 27–30, 86–90.

Bryan, J. L. (2002). A selected historical review of human behavior in fire. *Fire Protection Engineering, 2002*(16), 4–10.

Buss, D. M. (1995). Evolutionary psychology: A new paradigm for psychological science. *Psychological Inquiry, 6*, 1–30. doi:10.1207/s15327965pli0601_1

Cassidy, J., & Kobak, R. R. (1988). Avoidance and its relationship with other defensive processes. In J. Belsky & T. Nezworski (Eds.), *Clinical implications of attachment* (pp. 300–323). Hillsdale, NJ: Erlbaum.

Cassidy, J., & Shaver, P. R. (Eds.). (2008). *Handbook of attachment: Theory, research, and clinical applications* (2nd ed.). New York, NY: Guilford Press.

Cosmides, L. (1989). The logic of social exchange: Has natural selection shaped how humans reason? Studies with the Wason selection task. *Cognition, 31*, 187–276. doi:10.1016/0010-0277(89)90023-1

Coss, R. G., Ramakrishnan, U., & Schank, J. (2005). Recognition of partially concealed leopards by wild bonnet macaques (*Macaca radiata*): The role of the spotted coat. *Behavioural Processes, 68*, 145–163. doi:10.1016/j.beproc.2004.12.004

Davidovitz, R., Mikulincer, M., Shaver, P. R., Ijzak, R., & Popper, M. (2007). Leaders as attachment figures: Their attachment orientations predict leadership-related mental representations and followers' performance and mental health. *Journal of Personality and Social Psychology, 93*, 632–650. doi:10.1037/0022-3514.93.4.632

Davis, L. S. (2004). Alarm calling in Richardson's ground squirrels (*Spermophilus richardsonii*). *Zeitschrift für Tierpsychologie* [Magazine for Animal Psychology], 66, 152–164. doi:10.1111/j.1439-0310. 1984.tb01362.x

Ehrenberg, M. F., Gearing-Small, M., Hunter, M. A., & Small, B. J. (2001). Childcare task division and shared parenting attitudes in dual-earner families with young children. *Family Relations, 50*, 143–153. doi:10.1111/j.1741-3729.2001.00143.x

Ein-Dor, T., Coan, J. A., Reizer, A., Gross, E. B., Dahan, D., Wegener, M. A., . . . Zohar, A. H. (2012). *Sugarcoated isolation: Evidence that social avoidance is linked to higher basal glucose levels.* Manuscript submitted for publication.

Ein-Dor, T., Mikulincer, M., Doron, G., & Shaver, P. R. (2010). The attachment paradox: How can so many of us (the insecure ones) have no adaptive advantages? *Perspectives on Psychological Science, 5*, 123–141. doi:10.1177/1745691610362349

Ein-Dor, T., Mikulincer, M., & Shaver, P. R. (2011a). Attachment insecurities and the processing of threat-related information: Studying the scripts involved in insecure people's coping strategies. *Journal of Personality and Social Psychology, 101*, 78–93. doi:10.1037/a0022503

Ein-Dor, T., Mikulincer, M., & Shaver, P. R. (2011b). Effective reaction to danger: Attachment insecurities predict behavioral reactions to an experimentally induced threat above and beyond general personality traits. *Social Psychological and Personality Science, 2*, 467–473. doi:10.1177/1948550610397843

Ein-Dor, T., & Orgad, T. (2012). Scared saviors: Evidence that people high in attachment anxiety are more effective in alerting others to threat. *European Journal of Social Psychology, 42*, 667–671. doi:10.1002/ejsp.1895

Feeney, B. C., & Collins, N. L. (2001). Predictors of caregiving in adult intimate relationships: An attachment theoretical perspective. *Journal of Personality and Social Psychology, 80*, 972–994. doi:10.1037/0022-3514.80.6.972

Feeney, J. A., & Noller, P. (1990). Attachment style as a predictor of adult romantic relationships. *Journal of Personality and Social Psychology, 58*, 281–291. doi:10.1037/0022-3514.58.2.281

Fichtel, C. (2004). Reciprocal recognition in sifaka (*Propithecus verreauxi verreauxi*) and redfronted lemur (*Eulemur fulvus rufus*) alarm calls. *Animal Cognition, 7*, 45–52. doi:10.1007/s10071-003-0180-0

Fitzpatrick, C., & Mileti, D. S. (1991). Motivating public evacuation. *International Journal of Mass Emergencies and Disasters, 9*, 137–152.

Fraley, R. C., & Shaver, P. R. (1997). Adult attachment and the suppression of unwanted thoughts. *Journal of Personality and Social Psychology, 73*, 1080–1091. doi:10.1037/0022-3514.73.5.1080

Gazzaniga, M. S. (2008). *Human: The science behind what makes us unique*. New York, NY: Harper Collins.

Goodyer, I. M., Park, R. J., Netherton, C. M., & Herbert, J. (2001). Possible role of cortisol and dehydroepiandrosterone in human development and psychopathology. *British Journal of Psychiatry, 179*, 243–249. doi:10.1192/bjp.179.3.243

Hamilton, W. D. (1964a). The genetical evolution of social behaviour: I. *Journal of Theoretical Biology, 7*, 1–16. doi:10.1016/0022-5193(64)90038-4

Hamilton, W. D. (1964b). The genetical evolution of social behaviour: II. *Journal of Theoretical Biology, 7*, 17–52. doi:10.1016/0022-5193(64)90039-6

Henderson, S. (1977). The social network, support and neurosis: The function of attachment in adult life. *British Journal of Psychiatry, 131*, 185–191. doi:10.1192/bjp.131.2.185

Hill, R., & Hansen, D. A. (1962). Families in disaster. In G. W. Baker & D. W. Chapman (Eds.), *Man and society in disaster* (pp. 185–221). New York, NY: Basic Books.

Kinston, W., & Rosser, R. (1974). Disasters: Effects on mental and physical health. *Journal of Psychosomatic Research, 18*, 437–456. doi:10.1016/0022-3999(74)90035-X

Klohnen, E. C., & Luo, S. (2003). Interpersonal attraction and personality: What is attractive—Self similarity, ideal similarity, complementarity, or attachment security? *Journal of Personality and Social Psychology, 85,* 709–722. doi:10.1037/0022-3514.85.4.709

Marshall, S. L. A. (1947). *Men against fire: The problem of battle command in future war.* New York, NY: Morrow.

Mawson, A. R. (1978). *Panic behavior: A review and a new hypothesis.* Paper presented at the Ninth World Congress of Sociology, Uppsala, Sweden.

Mawson, A. R. (1980). Is the concept of panic useful for study purposes? In B. Levin (Ed.), *Behavior in fires* (National Bureau of Standards Report NBSIR-802070). Washington, DC: U.S. Department of Commerce.

Mawson, A. R. (2005). Understanding mass panic and other collective responses to threat and disaster. *Psychiatry: Interpersonal and Biological Processes, 68,* 95–113. doi:10.1521/psyc.2005.68.2.95

Mikulincer, M., Birnbaum, G., Woddis, D., & Nachmias, O. (2000). Stress and accessibility of proximity-related thoughts: Exploring the normative and intra-individual components of attachment theory. *Journal of Personality and Social Psychology, 78,* 509–523. doi:10.1037/0022-3514.78.3.509

Mikulincer, M., Gillath, O., & Shaver, P. R. (2002). Activation of the attachment system in adulthood: Threat-related primes increase the accessibility of mental representations of attachment figures. *Journal of Personality and Social Psychology, 83,* 881–895. doi:10.1037/0022-3514.83.4.881

Mikulincer, M., & Shaver, P. R. (2003). The attachment behavioral system in adulthood: Activation, psychodynamics, and interpersonal processes. In M. P. Zanna (Ed.), *Advances in experimental social psychology* (Vol. 35, pp. 53–152). New York, NY: Academic Press. doi:10.1016/S0065-2601(03)01002-5

Mikulincer, M., & Shaver, P. R. (2007). *Attachment in adulthood: Structure, dynamics, and change.* New York, NY: Guilford Press.

Mikulincer, M., Shaver, P. R., Sapir-Lavid, Y., & Avihou-Kanza, N. (2009). What's inside the minds of securely and insecurely attached people? The secure-base script and its associations with attachment-style dimensions. *Journal of Personality and Social Psychology, 97,* 615–633. doi:10.1037/a0015649

Nettle, D. (2006). The evolution of personality variation in humans and other animals. *American Psychologist, 61,* 622–631. doi:10.1037/0003-066X.61.6.622

Perry, R. W. (1994). A model of evacuation compliance behavior. In R. R. Dynes & K. J. Tierney (Eds.), *Disasters, collective behavior, and social organization* (pp. 85–98). Newark: University of Delaware Press.

Proulx, G. (2002). *Understanding human behavior in stressful situations.* Paper presented at the Workshop to Identify Innovative Research Needs to Foster Improved Fire Safety in the United States, National Academy of Sciences, Washington, DC.

Proulx, G. (2003). Researchers learn from World Trade Center survivors' accounts. *Construction Innovation, 8*(1), 1–3.

Riede, T., Bronson, E., Hatzikirou, B., & Zuberbühler, K. (2005). Vocal production mechanisms in a non-human primate: Morphological data and a model. *Journal of Human Evolution, 48,* 85–96. doi:10.1016/j.jhevol.2004.10.002

Rogers, S. J., & DeBoer, D. D. (2001). Changes in wives' incomes: Effects on marital happiness, psychological well-being, and the risk of divorce. *Journal of Marriage and Family, 63,* 458–472. doi:10.1111/j.1741-3737.2001.00458.x

Rom, E., & Mikulincer, M. (2003). Attachment theory and group processes: The association between attachment style and group-related representations, goals, memories, and functioning. *Journal of Personality and Social Psychology, 84,* 1220–1235. doi:10.1037/0022-3514.84.6.1220

Rumelhart, D. E. (1980). Schemata: The building blocks of cognition. In R. J. Spiro, B. C. Bruce, & W. F. Brewer (Eds.), *Theoretical issues in reading comprehension: Perspectives from cognitive psychology, linguistics, artificial intelligence, and education* (pp. 33–58). Hillsdale, NJ: Erlbaum.

Shaver, P. R., & Mikulincer, M. (2002). Attachment-related psychodynamics. *Attachment & Human Development, 4,* 133–161. doi:10.1080/14616730210154171

Sime, J. D. (1983). Affiliative behaviour during escape to building exits. *Journal of Environmental Psychology, 3,* 21–41. doi:10.1016/S0272-4944(83)80019-X

Sime, J. D. (1985). Movement toward the familiar: Person and place affiliation in a fire entrapment setting. *Environment and Behavior, 17,* 697–724. doi:10.1177/0013916585176003

Smith, E. R., Murphy, J., & Coats, S. (1999). Attachment to groups: Theory and management. *Journal of Personality and Social Psychology, 77,* 94–110. doi:10.1037/0022-3514.77.1.94

Sroufe, L. A., & Waters, E. (1977). Attachment as an organizational construct. *Child Development, 48,* 1184–1199. doi:10.2307/1128475

Townsend, A. L., & Franks, M. M. (1995). Binding ties: Closeness and conflict in adult children's caregiving relationships. *Psychology and Aging, 10,* 343–351. doi:10.1037/0882-7974.10.3.343

Vannucci, R. C., & Vannucci, S. J. (2000). Glucose metabolism in the developing brain. *Seminars in Perinatology, 24,* 107–115. doi:10.1053/sp.2000.6361

Waters, H. S., & Waters, E. (2006). The attachment working models concept: Among other things, we build script-like representations of secure base experiences. *Attachment & Human Development, 8,* 185–197. doi:10.1080/14616730600856016

Wilson, D. S., van Vugt, M., & O'Gorman, R. (2008). Multilevel selection theory and major evolutionary transitions: Implications for psychological science. *Current Directions in Psychological Science, 17,* 6–9. doi:10.1111/j.1467-8721.2008.00538.x

Wilson, E. O. (2012). *The social conquest of Earth.* New York, NY: Norton.

20

IT'S ALL IN THE MIND: HOW SOCIAL IDENTIFICATION PROCESSES AFFECT NEUROBIOLOGICAL RESPONSES

NAOMI ELLEMERS, FÉLICE VAN NUNSPEET, AND DAAN SCHEEPERS

In many situations, people think of themselves and others not as separate individuals but as representatives of social groups. As a result of shared group memberships, the characteristics and actions of other group members also affect the image of oneself in one's own eyes and in the eyes of others—one's *social identity*. Social identification processes—the tendency to associate oneself with particular others or groups—can be seen as indicating a specific mind-set. People can think in terms of shared identities even in the absence of instrumental interdependence or interpersonal similarity concerns, and different identities can become salient in different contexts. In this chapter, we examine the impact of social identification processes on neurobiological responses of individuals in group contexts. We first explain how social identification processes can result in a group-level conception of

The research reported in this article was made possible by an Academy Merian Prize, awarded by the Royal Netherlands Academy of Arts and Sciences, and a Spinoza Prize, awarded by the Netherlands Organisation for Scientific Research (NWO) to the first author, and by an early career grant (NWO-VENI) awarded to the third author.

http://dx.doi.org/10.1037/14250-021
Mechanisms of Social Connection: From Brain to Group, M. Mikulincer and P. R. Shaver (Editors)

self and affect the cognitive, emotional, and behavioral responses individuals display. We then specify the methodological challenges associated with the empirical examination of these processes, before we review recent research using measures of cardiovascular and brain activity to illustrate the different ways in which group memberships are active in people's minds.

THE GROUP SELF

The self is a central construct in human psychology. The way people think about themselves affects how they feel, the goals they pursue, and the information they communicate to others. An implicit assumption underlying most theory and research on the self is that individuals can be understood as separate entities guided by their own personal concerns, needs, and goals. Although this approach helps to explain many aspects of human behavior, it does not fully take into account the fact that people rarely operate in isolation because they are essentially social animals living together in groups. Indeed, more often than not, people primarily perceive themselves and others as representing distinct social groups. This has important implications for their behavior and is a key factor in the emergence of contemporary societal problems that occur when relations between groups are more important than interindividual similarities or interpersonal liking (Ellemers, 2012). These problems run the gamut from soccer hooliganism to interethnic and religious tensions, to hate crimes against homosexuals. Approaching people conceptually as group members helps us to understand a wide variety of day-to-day problems concerning communication, motivation, cooperation, and effective leadership at work (Haslam, van Knippenberg, Platow, & Ellemers, 2003).

In the 1970s, to better understand these issues, Tajfel and Turner (1979) developed what later became known as social identity theory (see also Postmes & Branscombe, 2010), to complement insights derived from individual-level explanations of the self. This theoretical approach specifies when the group self becomes more important than the individual self, and it explains how this transformation affects the cognitive, emotional, and behavioral responses of individual group members (Turner, 1987). The theory specifies *social categorization, social comparison,* and *social identification* as key elements in this process. It details conditions under which either the individual self or the group self is likely to become primary, and it predicts how people are likely to respond when the group self is under threat (see also Ellemers & Haslam, 2011).

Social categorization is a cognitive process used to organize and understand social information by clustering individuals into specific groups. This process of placing the self and others into distinct categories tends to enhance perceived differences between members of different groups while emphasizing similarities between members of a particular group. Social comparisons between members of different groups are used to understand the value implications of group membership. Evaluating how specific features of a particular group compare with the characteristics of other groups helps people to assess the distinctive value of a group and informs expectations about behaviors that can typically be expected from members of that group. Social identification captures the crucial difference between social categories as compared with object categories. Thinking of humans in terms of groups always has implications for the self because it is not possible to conceive of a certain class of individuals without immediately being aware of whether the self is included in or excluded from this group.

In principle, each of us can be considered in terms of multiple cross-cutting or overlapping groups (Ellemers & Rink, 2005). Which of these group selves is activated at a particular moment has important implications for the way we see ourselves and relate to others. For instance, the authors of this chapter (NE, FvN, DS) can classify ourselves in terms of a common identity: We are all Dutch psychologists. However, we may just as well focus on the differences between us, when we consider women (NE and FvN) versus men (DS), parents (NE and DS) versus nonparents (FvN), or computer whizzes (FvN and DS) versus computer dummies (NE). Depending on which of these group selves becomes important, we may think of ourselves as being similar or different, feel good or bad about ourselves, or communicate differently with each other. These effects of the group self may influence the way we relate to each other, even if our individual preferences and features, "objective" similarities or interdependencies, or feelings of interpersonal liking and appreciation remain the same.

The social identity approach provides a framework that specifies the processes through which the individual self is transformed to the group level, thereby helping us to understand human behavior in group contexts. The theory specifies conditions under which the group self can become the primary source of self-definition, self-reference, and self-esteem. An essential feature of this approach is that social identification processes literally make people *think differently*, as they consider themselves and others in group terms rather than in individual terms.

Research in support of this view (for overviews, see Ellemers, Spears, & Doosje, 1999, 2002) has established that emphasizing the importance of group affiliations affects cognitive processes relevant to social judgment. Different features are considered as prototypical for the group depending on how the group compares with other relevant groups in that context (Turner, Oakes, Haslam, & McGarty, 1994). For instance, psychology students see themselves as quite creative but not so analytical when compared with phys-ics students, whereas they think of themselves as being less creative but quite analytical when compared with arts students (Spears, Doosje, & Ellemers, 1997). Likewise, the same features, group products, or outcomes are evaluated differently depending on whether these are associated with members of one's own group (the ingroup) or members of another group (the outgroup).

Group affiliations also affect reported emotions. For instance, when confronted with previous misdeeds of their group (e.g., in the history of colo-nization) individuals experience feelings of guilt and shame, even if these mis-deeds were perpetrated before they were born (Branscombe & Doosje, 2004). Likewise, sports fans can experience pride at the successes of their home team, even if they personally were not involved and might not think of themselves as being responsible for this outcome in any way (Cialdini et al., 1976).

Behavioral responses, too, are affected by the group self. People gener-ally try to achieve outcomes that may help their group stand out from other groups, preferably in a positive sense. As a result, they may exert themselves to help their group outperform other groups, or they may sacrifice their own physical safety or well-being to achieve collective goals by enforcing political change or working toward the improvement of the rights of or outcomes for their group (Ouwerkerk, Ellemers, & de Gilder, 1999).

In support of a social identity account, all of these responses have been found to be more pronounced when individuals feel stronger ties with a group—their subjective identification as group members (Ellemers et al., 1999, 2002). This is consistent with the notion that a definition of the self at the group level implies a different conception of self and others, which is associated with different emotional and behavioral responses. Nevertheless, based on a common assumption that the individual self tends to have primacy over the group self (Gaertner, Sedikides, & Graetz, 1999), other theorists have offered alternative explanations for the observed effects based on the operation of individual-level goals (the desire to affiliate with others who are liked or similar to oneself), concerns (desire for self-esteem), or outcomes (interdependence between self and other ingroup members).

To examine the validity of such alternative explanations, researchers have sought to disentangle the subjective importance of group membership for self-definition from more objective ties between the individual and the group, such as whether formal group inclusion criteria are met or whether group members depend on each other to achieve desired outcomes. Most notable in this respect are the so-called minimal group studies, in which social interactions are simulated in a laboratory context, while individuals are randomly assigned to experimental groups, have no interpersonal knowledge of each other, and have no way to monitor each other's behavior or influ-ence reciprocal outcome allocations (Diehl, 1990). Any effects of differential group membership observed under such controlled circumstances indicate the operation of social identification processes, as these cannot be explained by differential interdependencies or familiarity with ingroup versus outgroup members, nor by greater interpersonal similarity to or a priori liking for other ingroup members compared with outgroup members.

As another way to exclude alternative explanations, researchers have compared public and private displays of individuals' willingness to commit to a group. Different effects have been observed when individuals are confronted with different (e.g., ingroup vs. outgroup) audiences, making clear that impression management plays a role (Ellemers, van Dyck, Hinkle, & Jacobs, 2000). In addition, it has been established that people may be willing to sacrifice pursuit of their own personal goals to benefit the group. That is, when their subjective feelings of identification with the group are sufficiently strong, group members display commitment to the group and its norms, even when their responses are anonymous (Barreto & Ellemers, 2000).

METHODOLOGICAL CHALLENGES

The research reviewed in the previous section has been taken as initial evidence that the group self affects people's responses in ways that cannot be explained in terms of outcome interdependence, interpersonal similarity and liking, or impression management tendencies. Nevertheless, this work has not yielded conclusive results because (a) the measures that were used do not allow for the direct examination of social identification processes, (b) they have addressed specific group types, and (c) they have focused on the way people perceive others as a result of intergroup differences, instead of examining implications of self-involvement.

Measures

It is difficult, if not impossible, to assess whether overt statements about characteristic properties of a group or ratings of its value should be interpreted as reflecting perceived properties of the social context or indicative of an adaptive way of coping with the realities of this context. For instance, when members of underperforming groups fail to acknowledge their group's inferior position, does this indicate lack of awareness of the group's current outcomes, perceived irrelevance of this particular comparative context, or a desire to convey confidence in the group's ability to improve in the future? Prior discussions about the relative primacy of the individual versus group self (Gaertner et al., 1999) have suffered from this interpretational ambiguity: Some have argued that the maintenance of high self-esteem under group-based threat indicates the primacy of the individual self over the group self, whereas others interpret these same findings as indicating a strong motivation to defend the group self.

Triangulating self-reports and behavioral responses that may stem from strategic or defensive concerns with measures of responses that are less easily monitored or controlled may help to resolve such disagreements. The recent introduction of alternative measures such as cortisol elevations, cardiovascular indicators of stress and coping responses, and measures of brain activity has the potential to move the field forward (Derks, Scheepers, & Ellemers, in press). These physiological responses have relevance beyond their analytical value as unobtrusive indicators of social identification processes, as they are known to have specific and potentially far-reaching consequences, for instance, for physical health. As an additional advantage, several of these measures can be taken continuously, so that they can be used to document how people's responses develop and change over time.

Group Types

Researchers have begun to include neurobiological measures to examine implications of the group self, but so far this work has focused mainly on real social groups rather than groups created in a laboratory (e.g., Amodio, 2009). An important advantage is that ethnic, gender, or racial group identities are immediately visible from facial features, making it possible to examine responses to ingroup and outgroup representatives in research paradigms that require large numbers (sometimes hundreds) of participant responses (e.g., to pictures of different faces) for reliable measurement. A drawback of this approach is that the reliance on existing group memberships makes it difficult to rule out alternative explanations for differential responses to ingroup versus outgroup members, for instance, due to genetic overlap, ethnic or cultural similarity, familiarity, or liking.

Additionally, some of these naturalistic research paradigms invoke reminders of actual physical danger represented by members of another group. A case in point are the so-called shooter studies, in which research participants have to quickly decide whether or not a Black or White target individual carries a gun (Correll, Park, Judd, & Wittenbrink, 2002). Although there is a lot to say for such methodologies in the sense that they capture some of the real decision making that people encounter in day-to-day intergroup encounters, they make it more difficult to determine whether the observed effects stem from ingroup–outgroup differentiation or from alternative considerations (e.g., concern for personal safety). Ideally, an investigation of social identification processes would rule out these alternative explanations. This could be done either by examining whether similar results are obtained with minimal groups or by tapping into existing group affiliations that have acquired meaning at a psychological level but are not indicated by specific genetic or physical features nor represent an actual physical danger in everyday life.

Self-Involvement

Another common characteristic of prior research using neurobiological indicators to examine group processes is that it has focused mainly on issues having to do with stereotyping and discrimination. An important implication of this research focus is that the available data mainly reveal how people respond to others depending on whether or not they are ingroup or outgroup members. Although this work has made important contributions to understanding how social evaluations depend on group affiliations, it does not reveal much about how group affiliations influence people's views of themselves. From a social identity perspective, an important goal would be to directly examine the extent to which the self is involved when different group memberships become salient.

In our research reviewed in this chapter, we have sought to meet all three challenges. We report studies using different neurobiological indicators across a range of group types to examine how people respond to group-level information that might implicate the self or to situations in which their own reputation as a proper group member is at stake. Our work incorporates a variety of measures, including cortisol elevations, cardiovascular indicators of threat versus challenge, and brain activity assessed with event-related potential (ERP) measures. We examine natural groups, experimental groups, and minimal groups. For studies involving immediate visibility of group membership, we use pictures of women wearing a headscarf, which identifies them as members of a group that is highly relevant in Dutch society. The headscarves identify the women as members of what native Dutch participants are likely to view as an outgroup on the basis of the different moral/religious value system they represent. Thus, the women in headscarves represent a threat to social identity rather than a threat to physical safety. Finally, our research focuses on the implications of self-involvement. We examine how people respond to information that is relevant to social identity either because it speaks to the position of their group compared with another group or because it is likely to have implications for their own acceptance and inclusion by other ingroup members.

THE GROUP-LEVEL SELF ELICITS CARDIOVASCULAR AROUSAL

As an unobtrusive way to tap identity implications at a physiological level, in some of our studies we assessed cardiovascular indicators specified in the biopsychosocial model of stress developed by Blascovich and coworkers

(Blascovich, 2008; Blascovich & Tomaka, 1996). Based on a threat-and-coping account, this model distinguishes between more benign arousal (*challenge*) and more maladaptive arousal (*threat*) to indicate different responses to situational demands. Challenge is characterized by increased blood volumes pumped out by the heart (increased cardiac output) accompanied by dilation of peripheral blood vessels (decreased total peripheral resistance). This facilitates the transportation of oxygenated blood throughout the body, physically preparing an individual to address and cope with the situation at hand. Threat emerges when individuals feel unable to cope with situational demands. In terms of cardiovascular responses, this is marked by constriction of peripheral blood vessels (increased total peripheral resistance) and as a consequence lower cardiac output. This cardiovascular pattern, which is typically accompanied by high levels of blood pressure, indicates a maladaptive stress response that is associated with the development of cardiovascular diseases over time. In our research, we have included cardiovascular indicators to examine how individuals respond to information that is relevant to social identity.

A first study (Scheepers & Ellemers, 2005) assessed whether people experience the same objective situation differently depending on its implications for the position of their group. Research participants were classified into minimal groups, after which they performed different rounds of a group task. The feedback they received suggested either that their group had outperformed another group (high-status ingroup) or that their group's performance was inferior to the other group's performance (low-status ingroup). When confronted with this information, participants displayed elevated blood pressure indicating threat when they thought their group had low status. However, when the experimenter announced a second round of the task, in which performance differences between the groups might be changed, participants in the high-status group displayed cardiovascular evidence of threat at the prospect that their group might lose its superior standing. These results indicate a direct connection between individual-level responses and group-level realities, suggesting the activation of a group self through social identification processes. That is, individual autonomous responses are directly affected by group-level information about intergroup comparisons as well as conditions implying the potential for changes in current relations between groups.

Another set of studies further examined the occurrence of threat due to social identity considerations (Scheepers, Ellemers, & Sintemaartensdijk, 2009). To rule out the possibility that the experience of threat stems from reminding people of their experiences with stigma or social disadvantage, we assessed high-status groups only. We induced social identity concerns by making salient the possibility that a participant's group might lose its privileged position in the future. One study was based on existing group memberships and examined the responses of male participants who discussed exchanging gender relations in society with women. Another study examined experimentally created groups that had acquired high status but were faced with the possibility of future status loss (Scheepers et al., 2009). In both studies, we observed increased blood pressure, indicating the emergence of threat, when social identity was at stake, because one's group might lose its privileged position. These results offer further evidence that the salience of membership in social groups activates a conception of self at the group level, which causes group-relevant information to affect very basic autonomic responses, even in situations that are in themselves not directly threatening or dangerous in a material way.

A final study in this series examined whether members of advantaged social groups might respond differently to the prospect of social change depending on how this change was communicated (Does, Derks, Ellemers, & Scheepers, 2012). As an improvement on our initial studies, where we relied on blood pressure as an indicator of threat, we measured threat and challenge cardiovascular profiles more directly by measuring cardiac output and total peripheral resistance. In this study, native Dutch participants were reminded of the privileged position of their group in the labor market. Subsequently, they were asked whether they would support measures for affirmative action. However, the prospect of equal opportunities was described either as a moral obligation that native Dutch would have to meet in order not to fail as a group or as a moral ideal they might aim to achieve to improve themselves as a group. Here, too, individual physiological responses to the group's prospects suggest that group-level realities directly affect the self. That is, the possibility that the group might fail to meet moral obligations induced a cardiovascular pattern indicating threat, whereas the prospect of being able to achieve moral ideals was accompanied by cardiovascular indicators of challenge.

LEVELS OF SELF-DEFINITION AND COPING RESPONSES

In a further set of studies, we addressed how personal and social self-conceptions affect people's involuntary responses during social interactions and task performance. In a first study, White male Dutch participants anticipated having to work together on a task with a woman with Moroccan features, wearing a headscarf (Bijleveld, Scheepers, & Ellemers, 2012). After having completed an alleged test of their preferred work style, participants were informed that their work style was either similar to or different from the style preferred by their interaction partner (i.e., the woman wearing a headscarf). Cortisol levels were monitored, and agreement with statements indicating (blatant and subtle) prejudice against Moroccan immigrants was assessed. The results showed that when interpersonal dissimilarity led participants to construe the situation as an intergroup context, cortisol elevations in anticipation of the joint task predicted self-stated degree of prejudice. That is, participants who experienced stress due to the prospect of having to collaborate with a woman wearing a headscarf were more likely to endorse negative views of the group she represented. However, no such effect was observed when participants were led to believe they preferred a working style similar to that of their collaborative partner. Presumably this was the case because realizing that the other was similar to the self caused participants to construe the situation at an interpersonal level, so that cortisol elevations in anticipation of the interaction did not affect their group-level judgments.

A second study examined responses of female participants who were asked to parallel-park a car in a computer simulation (Derks, Scheepers, Van Laar, & Ellemers, 2011). Social identity threat was induced by emphasizing gender differences in car parking ability. Participants were then provided with the possibility to affirm their feelings of self-worth either at the individual level (by reassuring them of their individual abilities) or at the group level (by reassuring them of their group's abilities), to cope with this threat. The cardiovascular indicators we monitored revealed that participants responded differently to these experimental manipulations depending on the extent to which they identified with their gender group. Whereas low-gender-identified women showed a pattern indicating challenge after individual self-affirmation, cardiovascular responses of high-gender-identified women indicated challenge after group-level affirmation. This study offers further evidence that subjective conceptions of self at the individual or group level result in different autonomic responses to otherwise identical situations. That is, physiological processes are affected by psychological realities.

THE THREAT AND CHALLENGE OF GROUP MEMBERSHIP

So far, we have considered mainly studies investigating how information about the position of one's group reflects upon oneself. However, another crucial implication of conceiving of individuals in terms of their social identities is that we should also be concerned about the way our own characteristic features, achievements, and behavioral choices are regarded by other members of our group. Notably, the tendency to think of oneself as a member of a social group elicits the desire to be respected by others and included as a "good" group member.

We know from prior research that shared moral values are the essence of people's shared identity (Kouzakova, Ellemers, Harinck, & Scheepers, 2012b), whereas diverging moral values are experienced as a threat to the self—as is evident from cardiovascular indicators (Kouzakova, Ellemers, Harinck, &

Scheepers, 2012a). On the basis of this knowledge, we devised an experimental procedure in which research participants were asked to reveal personal information to their fellow participants, allegedly as part of the process of getting acquainted with their prospective teammates. Subsequently, they were informed how their teammates evaluated their prior behavior in terms of competence or morality.

A first study in this series revealed that being considered as lacking in morality raised more of a cardiovascular threat response than being seen as deficient in terms of one's competencies (van der Lee, Ellemers, & Scheepers, 2012). In a second study, the moral and competent behavior of a fellow ingroup member was evaluated by one's teammates (van der Lee et al., 2012). This study revealed that having someone else in the group who is lacking in morality is as threatening as having one's own moral behavior devalued. That is, when moral evaluations pertained to another ingroup member, research participants also displayed a cardiovascular response indicative of threat. However, they showed evidence of being challenged when a fellow ingroup member was criticized for lacking competence.

Together these studies indicate that social identifications cause people not only to experience concern about the way they are evaluated by their fellow group members but also to respond to criticism concerning other members of the group as if it pertained to themselves. Again, the facts that we obtain these effects with experimentally created groups and find evidence for the operation of social identification in cardiovascular responses support the notion that the psychological meaning of the relation between different individuals changes depending on how they conceptualize themselves in relation to their group.

SOCIAL CATEGORIZATION IN THE BRAIN

Prior studies that included measures of brain activity focused mainly on the processes underlying people's automatic tendency to differentiate ingroup from outgroup members. Studies using ERPs to record the time course of person perception have revealed that the social categorization of ingroup and outgroup members occurs within hundreds of milliseconds when viewing a face (as indexed, for example, by the N100, P200, and N200 potentials—the number standing for the time in milliseconds after stimulus presentation that the positive [P] or negative [N] potential occurs; e.g., Ito & Urland, 2003, 2005; Kubota & Ito, 2007). Studies focused on racial groups have revealed that the differentiation between own-race and other-race faces, as well as early increased attention to other-race faces, is evident in both light- and dark-skinned individuals (e.g., Dickter & Bartholow, 2007). These studies also produced evidence that these brain correlates of social categorization are associated with intergroup differentiation in the form of ingroup favoritism and outgroup derogation.

Some studies have yielded evidence for differential brain activity with category dimensions that are less directly associated with physical or genetic differences than race, such as age (e.g., Wiese, 2012) and gender (e.g., Ito & Urland, 2005). Converging results were obtained even in research addressing a categorization that cut across racial differences. Here participants were presented with same-race or other-race individuals who were either students at the same university as the participant or from another university. Results revealed that both types of social categorization (according to race and university) resulted in increased brain activity on the N200 (Hehman, Stanley, Gaertner, & Simons, 2011).

Converging evidence for differential brain activity due to the mere group membership of target individuals was obtained in studies using functional magnetic resonance imaging (fMRI) to examine activity in the fusiform gyrus (which is associated with face recognition). This brain area shows more activation when viewing ingroup faces rather than outgroup or unknown faces. These results were obtained with groups of mixed race, again showing that these responses emerge because people think differently about ingroup compared with outgroup members, not because they are more similar to them (Van Bavel, Packer, & Cunningham, 2011). Likewise, research with minimal groups showed that a brain network consisting of the amygdala, fusiform gyri, orbitofrontal cortex, and dorsal striatum is more activated when viewing novel ingroup compared with novel outgroup faces (Van Bavel, Packer, & Cunningham, 2008).

Other indicators provide further evidence for intergroup differentiation and social identity formation. Gutsell and Inzlicht (2010) used electro-encephalography to show that brain activity in the motor cortex—indicating the coupling of perception and action—was evident in participants while they observed actions of (racial) ingroup but not outgroup members. This phenomenon is referred to as *motor resonance* and thought to involve activation of the mirror neuron system (see Chapter 4, this volume), which also plays a role in facial mimicry. Research using facial electromyography has shown that people are more likely to mimic negative emotions when these are displayed by ingroup rather than outgroup members. Again, the groups used in these studies rule out the possibility that alternative explanations in terms of interpersonal liking or physical similarity play a role, as these effects were obtained not only with native versus immigrant targets, but also with outwardly similar targets said to represent a favored versus nonfavored political party or students with different majors (Bourgeois & Hess, 2008; van der Schalk et al., 2011). In fact, rather than interpersonal liking or familiarity predicting differential mimicry of ingroup versus outgroup targets, the reverse relation was shown. That is, facial mimicry was found to increase liking for ingroup compared with outgroup members (van der Schalk et al., 2011).

Like mimicry, empathic concerns for others are thought to differentiate between in- and outgroup members. For example, fMRI research has shown that activation in the anterior cingulate cortex (a brain structure that is part of the network involved in the experience of physical pain) is increased when viewing painful stimulation applied to racial ingroup members compared with outgroup members (Xu, Zuo, Wang, & Han, 2009). Furthermore, reassurance by an ingroup member concerning the pain induced during an experiment is more effective than reassurance by an outgroup member, as was indicated by reduced physiological arousal (measured by galvanic skin responses; Platow et al., 2007).

SOCIAL IDENTIFICATION AND RESPONSE MONITORING

For our own research purposes (van Nunspeet, Ellemers, Derks, & Nieuwenhuis, 2012), we developed a new version of an implicit association test to assess brain activity associated with social identity threat. In this test, pictures of women with a headscarf and women without a headscarf were associated with positive and negative images. When the target pictures were rated as separate individuals by non-Muslim participants, the women with a headscarf were perceived as equally kind, trustworthy, and intelligent as the women without a headscarf. However, when participants were instructed to classify the same target pictures into two groups, the results of the implicit association test revealed a significant negative bias against women with a headscarf. Additionally, ERP measures taken while performing the task revealed evidence of enhanced social categorization (as indexed by the N100 and P200) when viewing the pictures of the women with a headscarf (van Nunspeet et al., 2012).

We used this paradigm to study how people monitor their responses when being aware that others can evaluate their performance. We increased the social implications of the experimental task by leading participants to believe that their performance reflected on their morality (or their competence). This was inspired by our prior research showing that people are more inclined to adapt their behavioral choices to accommodate to moral (compared with competence) ingroup norms (Ellemers, Pagliaro, Barreto, & Leach, 2008). Indeed, participants in our prior studies indicated that they thought they would earn intragroup respect and be considered a "good" group member when they adhered to moral ingroup norms (Pagliaro, Ellemers, & Barreto, 2011).

Building on this knowledge, we hypothesized that people would be more inclined to monitor their performance on a moral task than a competence task. However, we argued that they should be more motivated to monitor and control their moral task performance when being evaluated by an ingroup member compared with an outgroup member. We used a minimal group paradigm, leading participants to believe that they were categorized according to their preferred style of problem solving (P-style vs. O-style). Participants in all conditions were shown the same video stills of a woman who would allegedly evaluate their performance on the implicit association task. Group membership was manipulated by referring to this person as representing an ingroup member (P-type) or an outgroup member (O-type; group labels P- vs. O-type were counterbalanced across experimental conditions). This procedure enabled us to rule out the possibility that participants would attend to an ingroup rather than an outgroup evaluator for reasons other than social identification with the ingroup. After each trial of the task, the computer screen displayed a picture of this woman, who was presented either as an ingroup or as an outgroup member, depending on experimental condition. She smiled and showed a thumbs-up gesture after a correct response, and frowned and showed a thumbs-down gesture after an incorrect responses or a failure to respond on time. We conducted two studies with this methodology, to examine behavioral responses as well as ERP data.

Both studies confirmed that participants who thought they were being evaluated by an ingroup member were more inclined to control their behavior (i.e., they showed less negative bias toward the women with a headscarf on the implicit association task) when the test was said to assess their moral values rather than their competence. Importantly, participants who thought they were being evaluated by an outgroup member did not show increased response monitoring when reminded of the moral implications of their task performance. Additionally, the ERP results revealed that the emphasis on the moral implications of the test was associated with increased perceptual attention and response monitoring during the implicit association test. This was especially the case when participants were being evaluated by an ingroup compared with an outgroup member (van Nunspeet, Derks, Ellemers, & Nieuwenhuis, 2012). In sum, procedures that enhanced the social identity implications of one's task performance (because the task was said to indicate one's morality, and because responses were allegedly monitored by an ingroup) resulted in increased attention and response monitoring. This was evident from a reduction in displays of behavioral bias as well as from brain activity indicated by ERP measures. At the same time, both the stimulus materials we used (pictures of women with or without a headscarf) and the social categorization that was made salient (referring to minimal groups in the laboratory) enabled us to rule out alternative explanations for these findings.

CONCLUSION

In this chapter, we introduced the social identity approach to thinking about and examining the group-level self. Prior research had suggested that thinking of the self and others as group representatives can alter the way people think, feel, and behave. We outlined a number of empirical challenges faced by researchers in this domain and explained how recent research incorporating neurobiological measures can address such challenges. Results from research with natural groups as well as more controlled minimal groups indicate that invoking people's social identities affects how they feel about themselves and how they respond to others depending on whether they are viewed as ingroup or outgroup members. Empirical data indicate that making people aware of different group memberships can literally change the way they think about themselves and others, in responses that occur at very early stages of information processing and emerge autonomously. This suggests that social identification processes and the psychological implications of social realities these imply have real implications at a neurobiological level.

REFERENCES

Amodio, D. M. (2009). The social neuroscience of intergroup relations. *European Review of Social Psychology, 19,* 1–54. doi:10.1080/10463280801927937

Barreto, M., & Ellemers, N. (2000). You can't always do what you want: Social identity and self-presentational determinants of the choice to work for a low-status group. *Personality and Social Psychology Bulletin, 26,* 891–906. doi:10.1177/0146167 2002610001

Bijleveld, E., Scheepers, D., & Ellemers, N. (2012). The cortisol response to anticipated intergroup interactions predicts self-reported prejudice. *PLoS ONE, 7,* e33681. doi:10.1371/journal.pone.0033681

Blascovich, J. (2008). Challenge and threat. In A. J. Elliot (Ed.), *Handbook of approach and avoidance motivation* (pp. 431–445). Mahwah, NJ: Erlbaum.

Blascovich, J., & Tomaka, J. (1996). The biopsychosocial model of arousal regulation. In M. Zanna (Ed.), *Advances in experimental social psychology* (Vol. 28, pp. 1–51). New York, NY: Academic Press. doi:10.1016/S0065-2601(08)60235-X

Bourgeois, P., & Hess, U. (2008). The impact of social context on mimicry. *Biological Psychology, 77,* 343–352. doi:10.1016/j.biopsycho.2007.11.008

Branscombe, N. R., & Doosje, B. J. (Eds.). (2004). *Collective guilt: International perspectives.* Cambridge, England: Cambridge University Press.

Cialdini, R. B., Borden, R. J., Thorne, A., Walker, M. R., Freeman, S., & Sloan, L. R. (1976). Basking in reflected glory: Three (football) field studies. *Journal of Personality and Social Psychology, 34,* 366–375. doi:10.1037/0022-3514.34.3.366

Correll, J., Park, B., Judd, C. M., & Wittenbrink, B. (2002). The police officer's dilemma: Using ethnicity to disambiguate potentially threatening individuals. *Journal of Personality and Social Psychology, 83,* 1314–1329. doi:10.1037/0022-3514.83.6.1314

Derks, B., Scheepers, D., & Ellemers, N. (in press). *The neuroscience of prejudice and intergroup relations.* Oxford, England: Psychology Press.

Derks, B., Scheepers, D., Van Laar, C., & Ellemers, N. (2011). The threat vs. challenge of car parking for women: How self- and group affirmation affect cardiovascular responses. *Journal of Experimental Social Psychology, 47,* 178–183. doi:10.1016/j.jesp.2010.08.016

Dickter, C. L., & Bartholow, B. D. (2007). Racial ingroup and outgroup attention biases revealed by event-related brain potentials. *Social Cognitive and Affective Neuroscience, 2,* 189–198. doi:10.1093/scan/nsm012

Diehl, M. (1990). The minimal group paradigm: Theoretical explanations and empirical findings. *European Review of Social Psychology, 1,* 263–292. doi:10.1080/14792779108401864

Does, S., Derks, B., Ellemers, N., & Scheepers, D. (2012). At the heart of egalitarianism: How morality framing shapes cardiovascular challenge versus threat in Whites. *Social Psychological and Personality Science, 3,* 747–753. doi:10.1177/1948550612438924

Ellemers, N. (2012). The group self. *Science, 336,* 848–852. doi:10.1126/science.1220987

Ellemers, N., & Haslam, S. A. (2011). Social identity theory. In P. A. M. Van Lange, A. W. Kruglanski, & E. T. Higgins (Eds.), *Handbook of theories of social psychology* (Vol. 2, pp. 379–398). London, England: Sage.

Ellemers, N., Pagliaro, S., Barreto, M., & Leach, C. W. (2008). Is it better to be moral than smart? The effects of morality and competence norms on the decision to work at group status improvement. *Journal of Personality and Social Psychology, 95,* 1397–1410. doi:10.1037/a0012628

Ellemers, N., & Rink, F. (2005). Identity in work groups: The beneficial and detrimental consequences of multiple identities and group norms for collaboration and group performance. In S. R. Thye & E. J. Lawler (Eds.), *Advances in group processes: Vol. 22. Social identification in groups* (pp. 1–41). Amsterdam, the Netherlands: Elsevier. doi:10.1016/S0882-6145(05)22001-5

Ellemers, N., Spears, R., & Doosje, B. (Eds.). (1999). *Social identity: Context, commitment, content.* Oxford, England: Blackwell.

Ellemers, N., Spears, R., & Doosje, B. (2002). Self and social identity. *Annual Review of Psychology, 53,* 161–186. doi:10.1146/annurev.psych.53.100901.135228

Ellemers, N., van Dyck, C., Hinkle, S., & Jacobs, A. (2000). Intergroup differentiation in social context: Identity needs versus audience constraints. *Social Psychology Quarterly, 63,* 60–74. doi:10.2307/2695881

Gaertner, L., Sedikides, C., & Graetz, K. (1999). In search of self-definition: Motivational primacy of the individual self, motivational primacy of the collective self, or contextual primacy? *Journal of Personality and Social Psychology, 76,* 5–18. doi:10.1037/0022-3514.76.1.5

Gutsell, J. N., & Inzlicht, M. (2010). Empathy constrained: Prejudice predicts reduced mental stimulation of actions during observation of outgroups. *Journal of Experimental Social Psychology, 46*, 841–845. doi:10.1016/j.jesp.2010.03.011

Haslam, S. A., van Knippenberg, D., Platow, M. J., & Ellemers, N. (Eds.). (2003). *Social identity at work: Developing theory for organizational practice.* New York, NY: Psychology Press.

Hehman, E., Stanley, E. M., Gaertner, S. L., & Simons, R. F. (2011). Multiple group membership influences face-recognition: Recall and neurological evidence. *Journal of Experimental Social Psychology, 47*, 1262–1268. doi:10.1016/j.jesp.2011.05.014

Ito, T. A., & Urland, G. R. (2003). Race and gender on the brain: Electrocortical measures of attention to the race and gender of multiply categorizable individuals. *Journal of Personality and Social Psychology, 85*, 616–626. doi:10.1037/0022-3514.85.4.616

Ito, T. A., & Urland, G. R. (2005). The influence of processing objectives on the perception of faces: An ERP study of race and gender perception. *Cognitive, Affective & Behavioral Neuroscience, 5*, 21–36. doi:10.3758/CABN.5.1.21

Kouzakova, M., Ellemers, N., Harinck, F., & Scheepers, D. (2012a). *At the heart of a conflict: Cardiovascular and self-regulation responses to value vs. resource conflicts.* Manuscript submitted for publication.

Kouzakova, M., Ellemers, N., Harinck, F., & Scheepers, D. (2012b). The implications of value conflict: How disagreement on values affects self-involvement and perceived common ground. *Personality and Social Psychology Bulletin, 38*, 798–807. doi:10.1177/0146167211436320

Kubota, J. T., & Ito, T. A. (2007). Multiple cues in social perception: The time course of processing race and facial expression. *Journal of Experimental Social Psychology, 43*, 738–752. doi:10.1016/j.jesp.2006.10.023

Ouwerkerk, J. W., Ellemers, N., & de Gilder, D. (1999). Group commitment and individual effort in experimental and organizational contexts. In N. Ellemers, R. Spears, & B. Doosje (Eds.), *Social identity: Context, commitment, content* (pp. 184–204). Oxford, England: Blackwell.

Pagliaro, S., Ellemers, N., & Barreto, M. (2011). Sharing moral values: Anticipated ingroup respect as a determinant of adherence to morality-based (but not competence-based) group norms. *Personality and Social Psychology Bulletin, 37*, 1117–1129. doi:10.1177/0146167211406906

Platow, M. J., Voudouris, N. J., Coulson, M., Gilford, N., Jamieson, R., Najdovski, L., . . . Terry, L. (2007). In-group reassurance in a pain setting produces lower levels of physiological arousal: Direct support for a self-categorization analysis of social influence. *European Journal of Social Psychology, 37*, 649–660. doi:10.1002/ejsp.381

Postmes, T., & Branscombe, N. R. (Eds.). (2010). *Rediscovering social identity.* New York, NY: Psychology Press.

Scheepers, D., & Ellemers, N. (2005). When the pressure is up: The assessment of social identity threat in low and high status groups. *Journal of Experimental Social Psychology, 41*, 192–200. doi:10.1016/j.jesp.2004.06.002

Scheepers, D., Ellemers, N., & Sintemaartensdijk, N. (2009). Suffering from the possibility of status loss: Physiological responses to social identity threat in high status groups. *European Journal of Social Psychology*, 39, 1075–1092. doi:10.1002/ejsp.609

Spears, R., Doosje, B., & Ellemers, N. (1997). Self-stereotyping in the face of threats to group status and distinctiveness: The role of group identification. *Personality and Social Psychology Bulletin*, 23, 538–553. doi:10.1177/0146167297235009

Tajfel, H., & Turner, J. C. (1979). An integrative theory of intergroup conflict. In W. G. Austin & S. Worchel (Eds.), *The social psychology of intergroup relations* (pp. 33–47). Monterey, CA: Brooks/Cole.

Turner, J. C. (1987). A self-categorization theory. In J. C. Turner, M. A. Hogg, P. J. Oakes, S. D. Reicher, & M. S. Wetherell (Eds.), *Rediscovering the social group: A self-categorization theory* (pp. 42–67). Oxford, England: Basil Blackwell

Turner, J. C., Oakes, P. J., Haslam, S. A., & McGarty, C. (1994). Self and collective: Cognition and social context. *Personality and Social Psychology Bulletin*, 20, 454–463. doi:10.1177/0146167294205002

Van Bavel, J. J., Packer, D. J., & Cunningham, W. A. (2008). The neural substrates of in-group bias: A functional magnetic resonance imaging investigation. *Psychological Science*, 19, 1131–1139. doi:10.1111/j.1467-9280.2008.02214.x

Van Bavel, J. J., Packer, D. J., & Cunningham, W. A. (2011). Modulation of the fusiform face area following minimal exposure to motivationally relevant faces: Evidence of in-group enhancement (not out-group disregard). *Journal of Cognitive Neuroscience*, 23, 3343–3354. doi:10.1162/jocn_a_00016

van der Lee, R., Ellemers, N., & Scheepers, D. (2012). *The threat of a moral identity: Cardiovascular reactivity during intragroup morality (vs. competence) evaluations*. Manuscript in preparation.

van der Schalk, J., Fischer, A., Doosje, B., Wigboldus, D., Hawk, S., Rotteveel, M., & Hess, U. (2011). Convergent and divergent responses to emotional displays of ingroup and outgroup. *Emotion*, 11, 286–298. doi:10.1037/a0022582

van Nunspeet, F., Derks, B., Ellemers, N. & Nieuwenhuis, S. (2012). *Morality in intergroup relations: How social evaluation influences performance and response-monitoring on a moral implicit association test*. Manuscript in preparation.

van Nunspeet, F., Ellemers, N., Derks, B., & Nieuwenhuis, S. (2012). Moral concerns increase attention and response monitoring during IAT performance: ERP evidence. *Social Cognitive and Affective Neuroscience*. Advance online publication. doi:10.1093/scan/nss118

Wiese, H. (2012). The role of age and ethnic group in face recognition memory: ERP evidence from a combined own-age and own-race bias study. *Biological Psychology*, 89, 137–147. doi:10.1016/j.biopsycho.2011.10.002

Xu, X., Zuo, X., Wang, X., & Han, S. (2009). Do you feel my pain? Racial group membership modulates empathic neural responses. *Journal of Neuroscience*, 29, 8525–8529. doi:10.1523/JNEUROSCI.2418-09.2009

21

OXYTOCINERGIC CIRCUITRY
MOTIVATES GROUP LOYALTY

CARSTEN K. W. DE DREU

Humans empathize with others (Batson, 1998), form long-term attach-ments to close others (see Chapter 1, this volume), and sacrifice their imme-diate self-interests to promote the overarching interests of the groups and communities they belong to (Dawes, 1980; Komorita & Parks, 1995; Ostrom, 1998; see also Chapter 19, this volume). These and related tendencies indi-cate that humans are a cooperative species (Bowles & Gintis, 2011; Nowak, Tarnita, & Wilson, 2010) and fit the idea that throughout evolution, proso-cial behavior promotes the functioning of the individual's ingroup, which in turn provides for levels of security and prosperity well beyond what individu-als could possibly achieve alone (Darwin, 1873; Henrich & Henrich, 2007; Wilson, 2012). If these claims about humans' sociality are true, it stands to reason that group affiliation has its roots in evolved neurobiological systems

Preparation of this work was supported by the Research Priority Grant on Affect Regulation of the University of Amsterdam Faculty of Social and Behavioral Sciences and by Grant 432-08-002 of the Netherlands Science Foundation. The author declares no conflict of interest.

http://dx.doi.org/10.1037/14250-022
Mechanisms of Social Connection: From Brain to Group, M. Mikulincer and P. R. Shaver (Editors)

and circuitries. Here I pursue this possibility by focusing on emerging streams of research, from my own laboratory and those of others, on the role of brain oxytocin (OT).

OT is a nine-amino-acid neuropeptide that functions as both a hormone and a neurotransmitter (Donaldson & Young, 2008; see also Chapters 1, 3, and 8, this volume) and has a well-documented role in reproduction and pair-bond formation (e.g., Carter, Grippo, Pournajafi-Nazarloo, Ruscio, & Porges, 2008). Here I argue and show that its functions are broader and include a range of social behaviors that promote the functioning of an individual's group, including the tendency to protect the ingroup through competitive reactions to threatening outsiders. The starting point is a model (De Dreu, 2012a) delineating how hypothalamic release of OT modulates two critical functions underlying parochial cooperation, namely, ingroup trust and concern for (members of) the ingroup. Subsequent sections review the research evidence for these propositions and the implication that OT also motivates noncooperation toward rival outgroups. The final section summarizes the main conclusions and identifies avenues for new research into the link between OT and the regulation of intra- and intergroup relations.

HUMANS ARE PAROCHIAL COOPERATORS

A common assumption in behavioral economics, psychology, and biology is that most group settings contain incentives for individual members to compete with others so as to defend and promote immediate self-interest (e.g., personal gains and status), and incentives to cooperate with others so as to establish well-functioning long-term relationships that provide greater benefit to all than mutual competition (e.g., Axelrod & Hamilton, 1981; Camerer & Fehr, 2006; Deutsch, 1973; Kelley & Thibaut, 1978). Often these competitive and cooperative incentives are structured so that (a) each member serves his or her personal interests best by opting for noncooperation, and (b) when all members opt for noncooperation, each is worse off than if all had opted for cooperation (Bornstein, 2003; Dawes, 1980; De Dreu, Nijstad, & van Knippenberg, 2008; Komorita & Parks, 1995). Individuals are therefore expected to sacrifice immediate self-interest and to cooperate only when they experience (a) *trust*, the positive expectation that others will reciprocate one's cooperative efforts (Pruitt & Kimmel, 1977), and (b) *other-concern*—care for others' outcomes, interests, and well-being, including a desire for fairness and motivation to benefit the collective rather than only oneself (Carnevale & Pruitt, 1992; De Dreu, Weingart, & Kwon, 2000; Pruitt & Kimmel, 1977; Weber, Kopelman, & Messick, 2004).

In general, trust and other-concern tend to be stronger when a person likes and feels close to others, shares common goals and values with them, anticipates future interactions, or shares group membership (e.g., Batson, 1998; De Dreu, 2010; Komorita & Parks, 1995; Pruitt & Kimmel, 1977; Weber et al., 2004). Put differently, human trust and other-concern, and concomitant tendencies to cooperate, are parochial; that is, people more readily cooperate with members of their ingroup than with members of more or less competing outgroups (Bernhard, Fischbacher, & Fehr, 2006; Choi & Bowles, 2007; Darwin, 1873; Hammond & Axelrod, 2006; Wit & Kerr, 2002).

Parochialism serves individual and group survival in both ancestral and contemporary societies (Darwin, 1873), and it appears to depend upon three interrelated psychological mechanisms: (a) social categorization of others as ingroup or versus not ingroup, (b) a tendency to trust people categorized as ingroup more than those viewed as not ingroup, and (c) a tendency to develop other-concern primarily for those categorized as ingroup rather than those categorized as not ingroup. Importantly, when the ingroup competes with rival outgroups, parochialism may manifest itself not only in ingroup cooperation but also in competitive behavior toward the outgroup (Bowles & Gintis, 2011; Choi & Bowles, 2007; De Dreu, 2010). Such competition with outgroups may be driven by a desire to increase the ingroup's relative status and power and/or by the vigilant desire to defend and protect the ingroup against real or perceived outgroup threats. Either way, this competitive reaction to outgroups constitutes (indirect) cooperation toward one's own group, and it is often honored and publicly recognized by ingroup leaders as heroic, loyal, and patriotic. In addition to reviewing evidence that OT up-regulates ingroup trust, loyalty, and cooperation, I will discuss research indicating that OT may also up-regulate outgroup derogation and competition.

OXYTOCIN MODULATES SOCIAL CATEGORIZATION

Humans quickly classify others into ingroup versus outgroup categories (Allport, 1954; Brewer, 1999; Kurzban, Tooby, & Cosmides, 2001; Tajfel & Turner, 1979; see also Chapter 20, this volume), and such social discrimination may be modulated by OT. For example, when a bond is formed between sexual partners in monogamous species, or between a mother and her offspring, an olfactory memory is forged in the olfactory bulb of the brain. During initial social interactions (e.g., following parturition), OT released in the brain helps to establish the olfactory signatures of the sexual partner or offspring as memorable (Brennan & Kendrick, 2006). Research has shown that male rodents engineered to lack (forebrain) OT receptors do not discriminate between familiar and unfamiliar females; compared with normal rodents, these knockout rodents spent equal time investigating female rodents with whom they had shared a cage for several days, but less time investigating novel females (Ferguson et al., 2000; Ferguson, Young, & Insel, 2002; Macbeth, Lee, Edds, & Young, 2009).

The role of OT in social categorization in humans is poorly understood, but there is some indirect evidence. Rimmele, Hediger, Heinrichs, and Klaver (2009) gave participants intranasal OT or placebo and showed them a series of pictures of faces. One day later, participants returned to the laboratory and were given a surprise recognition task in which they had to indicate for a series of pictures whether they had seen each one before. Participants who had been exposed to pictures of faces under the influence of OT performed better 1 day later than those who had been exposed to the pictures after treatment with a placebo. Thus, OT makes a face more memorable. Familiarity in turn is a key driver of social categorization (Mateo, 2004; Tang-Martinez, 2001), with familiar others being more likely than unfamiliar others to be categorized as ingroup (e.g., Castelli & Zogmeister, 2000).

Humans categorize other not only on the basis of familiarity but also on that of perceptual and cognitive cues such as physical appearance, native language similarity, and attitude similarity (Dovidio & Gaertner, 2010; Yzerbyt & Demoulin, 2010). Research is needed to test the proposition that OT guides social discrimination in humans, and to uncover whether and how OT modulates the neural circuitries involved in classifying others into ingroup versus outgroup on the basis of perceptual and/or auditory cues. Research is also needed to distinguish clearly between mere categorization and the motivation to treat ingroup others more positively than outgroup others, a possibility I return to below.

OXYTOCIN MODULATES BETRAYAL AVERSION AND PAROCHIAL COOPERATION

For trust to develop, humans need to down-regulate fear and betrayal aversion. The role of OT in these processes is rather well established. OT's targets include the amygdala, hippocampus, and regions of the spinal cord that regulate the parasympathetic branch of the autonomic nervous system (Ludwig & Leng, 2006; Neumann, 2008; see also Chapter 1, this volume). OT interacts with the hypothalamic–pituitary–adrenal axis to attenuate stress responses, and this has a pervasive influence throughout both the body and the brain (Neumann, 2008; Rodrigues & Sapolsky, 2009). Specifically, OT reduces cortisol levels after exposure to stressors (Heinrichs, Baumgartner, Kirschbaum, & Ehlert, 2003), and it also inhibits cardiovascular stress responses (Uvnäs-Moberg, 1998). A pioneering neuroimaging study by Kirsch et al.

(2005) provided the most direct evidence for these claims. These researchers gave participants either an intranasal dose of OT or a placebo and showed them fearful or neutral stimuli while brain activity was measured. Results showed that OT reduced the activation of the amygdala and attenuated its coupling to brainstem centers responsible for autonomic and behavioral components of fear.

Fearful, anxiety-provoking stimuli and situations typically motivate an immediate and automatic fight-or-flight response (LeDoux, 2000; Phelps, 2006). However, because of its anxiolytic effects at both the physiological and neurological levels, OT may allow an individual to consider alternatives to fight-or-flight, including prosocial approach (Heinrichs, von Dawans, & Domes, 2009; Lim & Young, 2006; Taylor et al., 2000). This was the key hypothesis tested by Kosfeld, Heinrichs, Zak, Fischbacher, and Fehr (2005) using a trust game in which Player 1 (henceforth labeled *investor*) is asked to choose an amount to be transferred to Player 2 (henceforth *trustee*), knowing that it will be tripled before the trustee is asked to choose an amount to back-transfer to the investor. Both players understand that the back-transfer will not be tripled, and only the final amounts in the two accounts will be paid. In this game, the main reason for investors to transfer is trust—that is, expecting the trustee to reciprocate and transfer back a fair amount. To trustees, the main reason to back-transfer is other-concern. Kosfeld et al. observed that investors given OT rather than placebo made larger average transfers, indicating greater trust in their trustee.

A follow-up study by Baumgartner, Heinrichs, Vonlanthen, Fischbacher, and Fehr (2008) considered investor transfers both before and after they learned about their trustee's back-transfer (set at a constant 50% back-transfer in six trials of the trust game). Intranasal OT did not influence prefeedback transfers by investors. However, after investors learned that trustees back-transferred in 50% of the trials, investors given OT continued to make substantial transfers, whereas those given placebo significantly decreased their transfers. Thus, OT inoculated against betrayal aversion among investors (also see De Dreu, 2012b; Kéri & Kiss, 2011; Mikolajczak et al., 2010; Rilling et al., 2012).

In sum, there is evidence that OT is involved in the social categorization of others as familiar versus unfamiliar, and I conjecture that OT facilitates the classification of self and others into ingroup and outgroup categories. Importantly, perception of ingroup members is associated with reduced amygdala activation and betrayal aversion, and with greater trust. Encountering outgroup members, in contrast, has been linked to increased activation in the amygdala, increased vigilance, and reduced trust (Beer et al., 2008; Hein, Silani, Preuschoff, Batson, & Singer, 2010; Van Bavel, Packer, & Cummingham, 2008). Accordingly, hypothalamic release (or infusion) of OT has effects on the amygdala and on trust that are also common when perceiving ingroup members; the perception of outgroup members triggers neural and behavioral tendencies that go against those elicited by OT. Put differently, effects of OT on trust and cooperation should be stronger when an interaction partner is categorized as ingroup rather than outgroup; thus, OT's effects on trust and cooperation are parochial.

Studies following up the pioneering finding by Kosfeld et al. (2005) have indeed revealed that the effects of OT on (reduced) betrayal aversion and (increased) trust emerge especially when the protagonist is familiar rather than a stranger or when additional information reveals that the other party is not untrustworthy (De Dreu, 2012a). For example, Declerck, Boone, and Kiyonari (2010) studied cooperation in an assurance game wherein the only reason not to cooperate is distrust. They found that individuals given OT expected more cooperation and cooperated more, but only when they had familiarized themselves with their protagonist. Absent such positive prior interaction, OT actually led to *less* cooperation than placebo.

Direct evidence for the notion that OT up-regulates parochial altruism was provided by a series of experiments reported in De Dreu et al. (2010). In two experiments, males self-administered, in nasal spray, 24 international units of OT or placebo. Forty minutes later they were, on the basis of a trivial criterion, categorized into two three-person groups and engaged in the intergroup prisoner's dilemma–maximizing difference game (Halevy, Bornstein, & Sagiv, 2008). In this game, participants were split into two three-person groups and each individual was given a personal endowment (e.g., $10) that they were allowed to keep. They were also allowed to invest in a within-group pool, so that each dollar invested generated 50 cents to each ingroup member, the investor included. The within-group pool had the structure of a social dilemma: Each ingroup member was better off when others invested and he or she did not, yet all were worse off when no one invested, compared to when all ingroup members invested. Investments in the within-group pool reflected trust and self-costly cooperation (cf. ingroup love, ingroup favoritism; Brewer, 1999). In addition to the within-group pool, however, participants could also invest in a between-group pool. Each dollar invested now would yield a return of 50 cents to the ingroup (as with the within-group pool), yet it would also cost each outgroup member 50 cents. Contributing to the between-group pool could thus be motivated only by spite—the desire to hurt the outgroup (cf. outgroup hate, outgroup derogation; Brewer, 1999).

Across the two experiments, De Dreu et al. (2010) found that OT increased contributions to the within-group pool and did not significantly affect contributions to the between-group pool. Put differently, OT motivated ingroup love and did not motivate outgroup hate. Furthermore, it appeared that males given OT expected more ingroup love from their fellow ingroup members—that is, they seemed to experience higher ingroup trust—than those given placebo. With regard to outgroup expectations, treatment had no effect. From these results it follows that OT motivates parochial altruism.

OXYTOCIN MOTIVATES OTHER-CONCERN AND INGROUP FAVORITISM

The second core pathway through which cooperation develops as a function of OT runs through empathic concern and its neurobiological substrates. Concern for others is mediated by neural circuits involved in empathy and reward processing, including the inferior frontal gyrus and the inferior parietal lobe, which are necessary for emotion recognition and contagion, as well as the ventromedial prefrontal cortex, the temporoparietal junction, and the medial temporal lobe (Shamay-Tsoory, 2011). *Empathy* refers to an individual's capacity to experience affective reactions to the observed or anticipated experiences of another individual, and to take another individual's perspective (Batson, 1998). There is evidence that participants given OT rather than placebo have increased sensitivity to others' fear (Fischer-Shofty, Shamay-Tsoory, Harari, & Levkovitz, 2010), rate images of neutral faces as more trustworthy and attractive (Theodoridou, Rowe, Pentok-Voak, & Rogers, 2009), and more accurately infer emotions expressed by others (e.g., Domes, Heinrichs, Michel, Berger, & Herpertz, 2007). In the trust game discussed above, higher levels of blood plasma OT correlated with increased back-transfers, reflecting increased trustworthiness and other-concern (Morhenn, Park, Piper, & Zak, 2008; Zak, Kurzban, & Matzner, 2005).

Empathy is evoked more readily when individuals are exposed to ingroup rather than outgroup members (Harris & Fiske, 2007; Hein et al., 2010; Van Bavel et al., 2008), suggesting that OT's effects on empathy more easily come about when targets are classified as ingroup rather than outgroup. This proposition was tested in De Dreu, Greer, Van Kleef, Shalvi, and Handgraaf (2011a). On the basis of the well-established finding that humans value ingroup members and tend to evaluate them favorably (henceforth *ingroup favoritism*), and sometimes negatively evaluate outgroup members (henceforth *outgroup derogation*; Dovidio & Gaertner, 2010; Yzerbyt & Demoulin, 2010), De Dreu et al. (2011a) hypothesized that OT motivates ingroup favoritism and, perhaps, outgroup derogation. In five experiments, indigenous Dutch males received OT or placebo in a double-blind, randomized between-subjects design and, after 40 minutes, were exposed to images of ingroup targets (Dutch males) or outgroup targets (males from Middle Eastern descent or, in other experiments, Germans). Using different methods, De Dreu et al. (2011a) found, as hypothesized, that OT motivated stronger ingroup favoritism; that is, ingroup targets elicited stronger positive associations when participants received OT rather than placebo. Weak and inconclusive effects were found for outgroup derogation. These results suggest that OT up-regulates empathy for ingroup members but does not create more benevolent views of others generally, which would have resulted in more positive views and evaluations of ingroup and outgroup members alike. This has not happened in any studies (De Dreu et al., 2011a; De Dreu, Greer, Van Kleef, Shalvi, & Handgraaf, 2011b; see also Chen, Kumstra, & Heinrichs, 2011).

OXYTOCIN MOTIVATES COMPETITION TOWARD RIVAL OUTGROUPS

As noted at the outset, when the ingroup competes with rival outgroups, parochialism manifests itself not only in increased levels of ingroup trust, loyalty, and cooperation but also in tendencies to compete against the rival outgroups (Bowles, 2009; Choi & Bowles, 2007). In the previous sections, it was shown that OT did not increase outgroup derogation or hatred of outgroups. These results do not necessarily rule out defensive competitiveness toward rival outgroups. In fact, one key reason to attack rivals is to preempt outgroup attacks and to diminish or even neutralize outgroup threats (Arrow, 2007; Bacharach & Lawler, 1981; De Dreu, 1995; Jervis, 1976). In such cases, OT may play a more important role in augmenting negative reactions. Animal studies have shown that lactating female Wistar rats selectively bred for high-anxiety-related behavior show more aggression toward a virgin intruder compared to female Wistar rats bred for low-anxiety-related behavior (Bosch, Meddle, Beiderbeck, Douglas, & Neumann, 2005), an effect mediated by OT. Bosch et al. (2005) concluded that maternal aggression serves to protect offspring, and from this study it thus follows that OT may up-regulate defensive aggression (for an illustration of this effect in humans, see Hahn-Holbrook, Holt-Lunstad, Holbrook, Coyne, & Lawson, 2011).

To test the possibility that OT motivates not only ingroup love but also defensive negativity toward rival outgroups, De Dreu et al. (2010) conducted a third experiment in which participants played a prisoner's dilemma game between their own ingroup and a three-person outgroup. They decided between cooperation and noncooperation, with the outcome affecting the resources of the ingroup (including the decision maker). The payoffs of the prisoner's dilemma game were manipulated so that a competitive stance on the part of the outgroup (rather than cooperation) had either strong or weak negative effects on ingroup outcomes. Thus, to prevent negative effects of possible competition from the outgroup, individuals should have chosen the noncooperative rather than the cooperative alternative themselves. Results showed that the variation in outgroup threat interacted with whether participants received intranasal OT or placebo. Under low outgroup threat, treatment had no effect on noncooperation toward the outgroup, in line with the studies reviewed earlier; but when outgroup threat was high, group members were significantly more noncooperative toward the outgroup when they had been given OT rather than placebo. From these results, De Dreu et al. (2010) concluded that OT motivates humans to adopt a more competitive approach to rival outgroups, especially when the outgroup threatens the welfare of the ingroup.

In a recent follow-up study, De Dreu, Shalvi, Greer, Van Kleef, and Handgraaf (2012) replicated these findings. Through further manipulations of payoffs, the follow-up study showed that OT produced similar levels of competition when self-interest was at stake (i.e., one was personally vulnerable to outgroup competition). When the outgroup threatened the outcomes of one's fellow ingroup members (high ingroup vulnerability), but not one's own outcomes, males given placebo substantially reduced their competitive approach, whereas those given OT slightly increased their competitive tendencies. From this it follows that individuals influenced by OT behave like the proverbial "Mamma Bear" who, though not being endangered herself, lashes out to protect her cubs from a threatening predator.

Taken together, these studies suggest that OT induces a "tend-and-defend" response in intergroup competitions and conflicts: Individuals given OT relate to their ingroup with enhanced trust, ingroup favoritism, and self-sacrifice, and they relate more competitively toward rival outgroups (De Dreu, 2012a; De Dreu et al., 2010). One implication of this tend-and-defend tendency is that individuals in intergroup competition may be motivated to ally with strong, otherwise combative others who may be able to protect the ingroup against an outside threat. To test this possible implication, De Dreu, Greer, Shalvi, Handgraaf, and Van Kleef (2012) engaged participants in an intergroup competition and then asked them to select allies. Participants were shown faces of potential allies that were morphed into either a high-threat demeanor (low on trustworthiness and high on dominance) or a low-threat demeanor (high on trustworthiness and low on dominance; see, e.g., Oosterhof & Todorov, 2008). Males given OT rather than placebo selected more high-threat than low-threat allies, and rated these high-threat individuals as more useful. Usefulness ratings mediated the effect of OT on ally selection. De Dreu et al. (2012) therefore concluded that in intergroup competition, OT motivates humans to select allies that have high threat potential and appear aggressive rather than friendly, presumably to make their ingroup a stronger and more threatening competitor against rival outgroups.

FROM TEND-AND-DEFEND TO GROUP LOYALTY

The studies reviewed so far suggest that OT plays an important role in sustaining, maintaining, and improving social life within one's ingroup. To date, research has focused almost exclusively on either social-cognitive measures of facial recognition and liking or behavioral measures of trust and cooperation. However, if OT serves as a single neurohormonal mechanism underlying these and related forms of within-group cooperation, many more social behaviors may be affected by OT (Madden & Clutton-Brock, 2011). Elsewhere I have proposed that OT may modulate a broad array of group maintenance behaviors, including norm compliance and enforcement, information sharing, and perhaps even group problem solving and creativity (De Dreu, 2012a). New research is needed to substantiate this proposal.

OXYTOCIN'S "DARK SIDE"

The studies reviewed here strongly suggest that OT motivates ingroup favoritism and within-group but not between-group trust and cooperation. Moreover, OT stimulates a competitive approach to a rival outgroup when the outgroup presents an imminent threat to the ingroup. Together these studies suggest that OT may contribute, albeit indirectly, to intergroup competition and conflict. First, ingroup favoritism alone or in combination with outgroup derogation creates intergroup bias: Ingroup members get relatively better treatment and receive benefits more readily than outgroup members (Dovidio & Gaertner, 2010). Such unfair treatment triggers negative emotions, violent protests, and aggression on the part of disfavored and excluded individuals (Hewstone, Rubin, & Willis, 2002). Accordingly, by stimulating ingroup favoritism, OT could trigger a chain reaction leading to intense between-group conflict. Second, through its effects on within-group cooperation, OT contributes to making the ingroup strong and effective, not only in absolute terms but also relative to rival outgroups. Perceiving such effective and relatively strong groups may trigger preemptive aggressive strikes from rival outgroups (Bacharach & Lawler, 1981; De Dreu, 2010; Deutsch, 1973; Jervis, 1976). Again, OT's effects on within-group cooperation may, inadvertently, contribute to elevated levels of intergroup tension, competition, and conflict.

That OT is involved in, and may even indirectly promote, intergroup tension and conflict needs further examination. First, in studies of humans, OT motivated intergroup competition when outgroup threat was high but not when outgroup threat was low (De Dreu et al., 2010). In nursing rats, OT motivated aggression against intruders when rats were bred for high anxiety; among those bred for low anxiety, OT actually reduced aggression against intruders (Bosch et al., 2005). Thus, there may be important individual differences and contextual factors that temper or even reverse effects of OT on intergroup competition, and research is needed to uncover and delineate these moderators. Second, current evidence is limited to one-shot interactions, and although one would expect escalatory spirals set in motion by OT-induced ingroup favoritism and parochial cooperation, research is needed to document the unfolding of cooperation and aggression over time.

CONCLUSION

The research I have reviewed here shows that hypothalamic release (or infusion) of OT (a) down-regulates fear and anxiety, and enables trust to develop, especially with individuals who are familiar and/or categorized as ingroup members; (b) motivates empathic other-concern, ingroup favoritism, and parochial cooperation; and (c) motivates noncooperation toward potentially threatening outgroups. These conclusions fit with the emerging insight that OT-induced goodwill (empathy, trust, cooperation) is far from indiscriminate and is highly contingent on the perceived features and characteristics of the potential targets of goodwill (Bartz et al., 2010; Chen et al., 2011; De Dreu et al., 2011a, 2011b). This conclusion also fits well with the Darwinian insight that human self-sacrifice and cooperation serve ingroup functions and thereby enhance individual prosperity and survival (Wilson, 2012). Oxytocinergic circuitry may have evolved to sustain within-group cooperation, ingroup protection, and, if needed, competition toward rival outgroups. In addition to assisting reproduction and pair-bond formation, oxytocinergic circuitry serves to tend-and-defend the ingroup, and in the process it promotes ingroup loyalty.

REFERENCES

Allport, G. W. (1954). *The nature of prejudice*. Cambridge, England: Addison-Wesley.

Arrow, H. (2007, October 26). The sharp end of altruism. *Science, 318*, 581–582. doi:10.1126/science.1150316

Axelrod, R., & Hamilton, W. D. (1981, March 27). The evolution of cooperation. *Science, 211*, 1390–1396. doi:10.1126/science.7466396

Bacharach, S. B., & Lawler, E. J. (1981). *Bargaining: Power, tactics, and outcomes*. San Francisco, CA: Jossey-Bass.

Bartz, J. A., Zaki, J., Bolger, N., Hollander, E., Ludwig, N. N., Kolevzon, A., & Ochsner, K. N. (2010). Oxytocin selectively improves empathic accuracy. *Psychological Science, 21*, 1426–1428. doi:10.1177/0956797610383439

Batson, C. D. (1998). Altruism and prosocial behavior. In D. T. Gilbert, S. T. Fiske, & G. Lindzey (Eds.), *The handbook of social psychology* (4th ed., Vol. 2, pp. 282–316). New York, NY: McGraw-Hill.

Baumgartner, T., Heinrichs, M., Vonlanthen, A., Fischbacher, U., & Fehr, E. (2008). Oxytocin shapes the neural circuitry of trust and trust adaptation in humans. *Neuron, 58,* 639–650. doi:10.1016/j.neuron.2008.04.009

Beer, J. S., Stallen, M., Lombardo, M. V., Gonsalkorale, K., Cunningham, W. A., & Sherman, J. W. (2008). The quadruple process model approach to examining the neural underpinnings of prejudice. *NeuroImage, 43,* 775–783. doi:10.1016/j.neuroimage.2008.08.033

Bernhard, H., Fischbacher, U., & Fehr, E. (2006, August 24). Parochial altruism in humans. *Nature, 442,* 912–915. doi:10.1038/nature04981

Bornstein, G. (2003). Intergroup conflict: Individual, group, and collective interests. *Personality and Social Psychology Review, 7,* 129–145. doi:10.1207/S15327957PSPR0702_129-145

Bosch, O. J., Meddle, S. L., Beiderbeck, D. I., Douglas, A. J., & Neumann, I. D. (2005). Brain oxytocin correlates with maternal aggression: Link to anxiety. *Journal of Neuroscience, 25,* 6807–6815. doi:10.1523/JNEUROSCI.1342-05.2005

Bowles, S. (2009). Did warfare among ancestral hunter–gathers affect the evolution of human social behaviors? *Science, 324,* 1293–1298. doi:10.1126/Science.1168112

Bowles, S., & Gintis, H. (2011). *A cooperative species: Human reciprocity and its evolution.* Princeton, NJ: Princeton University Press.

Brennan, P. A., & Kendrick, K. M. (2006). Mammalian social odours: Attraction and individual recognition. *Philosophical Transactions of the Royal Society: Series B. Biological Sciences, 361,* 2061–2078. doi:10.1098/rstb.2006.1931

Brewer, M. B. (1999). The psychology of prejudice: Ingroup love or outgroup hate? *Journal of Social Issues, 55,* 429–444. doi:10.1111/0022-4537.00126

Camerer, C. F., & Fehr, E. (2006). When does "economic man" dominate social behavior? *Science, 311,* 47–52. doi:10.1126/science.1110600

Carnevale, P. J., & Pruitt, D. G. (1992). Negotiation and mediation. *Annual Review of Psychology, 43,* 531–582. doi:10.1146/annurev.ps.43.020192.002531

Carter, C. S., Grippo, A. J., Pournajafi-Nazarloo, H., Ruscio, M. G., & Porges, S. W. (2008). Oxytocin, vasopressin and sociality. *Progress in Brain Research, 170,* 331–336. doi:10.1016/S0079-6123(08)00427-5

Castelli, L., & Zogmeister, C. (2000). The role of familiarity in implicit memory effects: The case of exemplar activation. *European Journal of Social Psychology, 30,* 223–234. doi:10.1002/(SICI)1099-0992(200003/04)30:2<223::AID-EJSP989>3.0.CO;2-W

Chen, F. S., Kumstra, R., & Heinrichs, M. (2011). Oxytocin-induced goodwill is not a fixed pie. *Proceedings of the National Academy of Sciences of the United States of America, 108,* E45. doi:10.1073/pnas.1101633108

Choi, J.-K., & Bowles, S. (2007). The coevolution of parochial altruism and war. *Science, 318,* 636–640. doi:10.1126/science.1144237

Darwin, C. (1873). *The descent of man, and selection in relation to sex.* New York, NY: Appleton.

Dawes, R. M. (1980). Social dilemmas. *Annual Review of Psychology, 31,* 169–193. doi:10.1146/annurev.ps.31.020180.001125

Declerck, C. H., Boone, C., & Kiyonari, T. (2010). Oxytocin and cooperation under conditions of uncertainty: The modulating role of incentives and social information. *Hormones and Behavior, 57,* 368–374. doi:10.1016/j.yhbeh.2010.01.006

De Dreu, C. K. W. (1995). Coercive power and concession making in bilateral negotiation. *Journal of Conflict Resolution, 39,* 646–670. doi:10.1177/0022002795039004003

De Dreu, C. K. W. (2010). Social conflict: The emergence and consequences of struggle and negotiation. In S. T. Fiske, D. T. Gilbert, & G. Lindzey (Eds.), *Handbook of social psychology* (5th ed., Vol. 2, pp. 983–1023). New York, NY: Wiley.

De Dreu, C. K. W. (2012a). Oxytocin modulates cooperation within and competition between groups: An integrative review and research agenda. *Hormones and Behavior, 61,* 419–428. doi:10.1016/j.yhbeh.2011.12.009

De Dreu, C. K. W. (2012b). Oxytocin modulates the link between adult attachment and cooperation through reduced betrayal aversion. *Psychoneuroendocrinology, 37,* 871–880. doi:10.1016/j.psyneuen.2011.10.003

De Dreu, C. K. W., Greer, L. L., Handgraaf, M. J. J., Shalvi, S., Van Kleef, G. A., Baas, M., . . . Feith, S. W. W. (2010). The neuropeptide oxytocin regulates parochial altruism in intergroup conflict among humans. *Science, 328,* 1408–1411. doi:10.1126/science.1189047

De Dreu, C. K. W., Greer, L. L., Shalvi, S., Handgraaf, M. J. J., & Van Kleef, G. A. (2012). Oxytocin modulates the selection of allies in intergroup conflict. *Proceedings of the Royal Society: Series B. Biological Sciences, 279,* 1150–1154. doi:10.1098/rspb.2011.1444

De Dreu, C. K. W., Greer, L. L., Van Kleef, G. A., Shalvi, S., & Handgraaf, M. J. J. (2011a). Oxytocin promotes human ethnocentrism. *Proceedings of the National Academy of Sciences of the United States of America, 108,* 1262–1266. doi:10.1073/pnas.1015316108

De Dreu, C. K. W., Greer, L. L., Van Kleef, G. A., Shalvi, S., & Handgraaf, M. J. J. (2011b). Reply to Chen et al.: Perhaps goodwill is unlimited, but oxytocin-induced goodwill is not. *Proceedings of the National Academy of Sciences of the United States of America, 108,* E46. doi:10.1073/pnas.1102269108

De Dreu, C. K. W., Nijstad, B. A., & van Knippenberg, D. (2008). Motivated information processing in group judgment and decision making. *Personality and Social Psychology Review, 12,* 22–49. doi:10.1177/1088868307304092

De Dreu, C. K. W., Shalvi, S., Greer, L. L., Van Kleef, G. A., & Handgraaf, M. J. J. (2012). *Oxytocin motivates non-cooperation in intergroup relations to protect vulnerable in-group members.* PLoS One, 7, E46751. doi:10.1371/journal.pone.0046751

De Dreu, C. K. W., Weingart, L. R., & Kwon, S. (2000). Influence of social motives on integrative negotiation: A meta-analytic review and test of two theories.

Journal of Personality and Social Psychology, 78, 889–905. doi:10.1037/0022-3514.78.5.889

Deutsch, M. (1973). *The resolution of conflict: Constructive and destructive processes.* New Haven, CT: Yale University Press.

Domes, G., Heinrichs, M., Michel, A., Berger, C., & Herpertz, S. C. (2007). Oxytocin improves "mind-reading" in humans. *Biological Psychiatry, 61,* 731–733. doi:10.1016/j.biopsych.2006.07.015

Donaldson, Z. R., & Young, L. J. (2008, November 7). Oxytocin, vasopressin, and the neurogenetics of sociality. *Science, 322,* 900–904. doi:10.1126/science.1158668

Dovidio, J. F., & Gaertner, S. L. (2010). Intergroup bias. In S. T. Fiske, D. T. Gilbert, & G. Lindzey (Eds.), *Handbook of social psychology* (5th ed., Vol. 2, pp. 1084–1121). New York, NY: Wiley.

Ferguson, J. N., Young, L. J., Hearn, E. F., Matzuk, M. M., Insel, T. R., & Winslow, J. T. (2000). Social amnesia in mice lacking the oxytocin gene. *Nature Genetics, 25,* 284–288. doi:10.1038/77040

Ferguson, J. N., Young, L. J., & Insel, T. R. (2002). The neuroendocrine basis of social recognition. *Frontiers in Neuroendocrinology, 23,* 200–224. doi:10.1006/frne.2002.0229

Fischer-Shofty, M., Shamay-Tsoory, S. G., Harari, H., & Levkovitz, Y. (2010). The effect of intranasal administration of oxytocin on fear recognition. *Neuropsychologia, 48,* 179–184. doi:10.1016/j.neuropsychologia.2009.09.003

Hahn-Holbrook, J., Holt-Lunstad, J., Holbrook, C., Coyne, S. M., & Lawson, E. T. (2011). Maternal defense: Breast feeding increases aggression by decreasing stress. *Psychological Science, 22,* 1288–1295. doi:10.1177/0956797611420729

Halevy, N., Bornstein, G., & Sagiv, L. (2008). "In-group love" and "out-group hate" as motives for individual participation in intergroup conflict: A new game paradigm. *Psychological Science, 19,* 405–411. doi:10.1111/j.1467-9280.2008.02100.x

Hammond, R. A., & Axelrod, R. (2006). The evolution of ethnocentrism. *Journal of Conflict Resolution, 50,* 926–936. doi:10.1177/0022002706293470

Harris, L. T., & Fiske, S. T. (2007). Social groups that elicit disgust are differentially processed in mPFC. *Social Cognitive and Affective Neuroscience, 2,* 45–51. doi:10.1093/scan/nsl037

Hein, G., Silani, G., Preuschoff, K., Batson, C. D., & Singer, T. (2010). Neural responses to ingroup and outgroup members' suffering predict individual differences in costly helping. *Neuron, 68,* 149–160. doi:10.1016/j.neuron.2010.09.003

Henrich, N., & Henrich, J. (2007). *Why humans cooperate: A cultural and evolutionary explanation.* Oxford, England: Oxford University Press.

Heinrichs, M., Baumgartner, T., Kirschbaum, C., & Ehlert, U. (2003). Social support and oxytocin interact to suppress cortisol and subjective responses to psychological stress. *Biological Psychiatry, 54,* 1389–1398. doi:10.1016/S0006-3223(03)00465-7

Heinrichs, M., von Dawans, B., & Domes, G. (2009). Oxytocin, vasopressin, and human social behavior. *Frontiers in Neuroendocrinology, 30*, 548–557. doi:10.1016/j.yfrne.2009.05.005

Hewstone, M., Rubin, M., & Willis, H. (2002). Intergroup bias. *Annual Review of Psychology, 53*, 575–604. doi:10.1146/annurev.psych.53.100901.135109

Jervis, R. (1976). *Perception and misperception in international politics*. Princeton, NJ: Princeton University Press.

Kelley, H. H., & Thibaut, J. (1978). *Interpersonal relations: A theory of interdependence*. New York, NY: Academic Press.

Kéri, S., & Kiss, I. (2011). Oxytocin response in a trust game and habituation of arousal. *Physiology & Behavior, 102*, 221–224. doi:10.1016/j.physbeh.2010.11.011

Kirsch, P., Esslinger, C., Chen, Q., Mier, D., Lis, S., Siddhanti, S., . . . Meyer-Lindenberg, A. (2005). Oxytocin modulates neural circuitry for social cognition and fear in humans. *Journal of Neuroscience, 25*, 11489–11493. doi:10.1523/JNEUROSCI.3984-05.2005

Komorita, S. S., & Parks, C. D. (1995). Interpersonal relations: Mixed-motive interaction. *Annual Review of Psychology, 46*, 183–207. doi:10.1146/annurev.ps.46.020195.001151

Kosfeld, M., Heinrichs, M., Zak, P. J., Fischbacher, U., & Fehr, E. (2005, June 2). Oxytocin increases trust in humans. *Nature, 435*, 673–676. doi:10.1038/nature03701

Kurzban, R., Tooby, J., & Cosmides, L. (2001). Can race be erased? Coalitional computation and categorization. *Proceedings of the National Academy of Sciences of the United States of America, 98*, 15387–15392. doi:10.1073/pnas.251541498

LeDoux, J. E. (2000). Emotion circuits in the brain. *Annual Review of Neuroscience, 23*, 155–184. doi:10.1146/annurev.neuro.23.1.155

Lim, M. M., & Young, L. J. (2006). Neuropeptic regulation of affiliative behavior and social bonding in animals. *Hormones and Behavior, 50*, 506–517. doi:10.1016/j.yhbeh.2006.06.028

Ludwig, M., & Leng, G. (2006). Dendritic peptide release and peptide-dependent behaviors. *Nature Reviews Neuroscience, 7*, 126–136. doi:10.1038/nrn1845

Macbeth, A. H., Lee, H.-J., Edds, J., & Young, W. S., III. (2009). Oxytocin and the oxytocin receptor underlie intrastrain, but not interstrain, social cognition. *Genes, Brain and Behavior, 8*, 558–567. doi:10.1111/j.1601-183X.2009.00506.x

Madden, J. R., & Clutton-Brock, T. H. (2011). Experimental peripheral administration of oxytocin elevates a suite of cooperative behaviors in a wild social animal. *Proceedings of the Royal Society: Series B. Biological Sciences, 278*, 1189–1194. doi:10.1098/rspb.2010.1675

Mateo, J. M. (2004). Recognition systems and biological organization: The perception component of social recognition. *Annales Zoologici Fennici, 41*, 729–745.

Mikolajczak, M., Gross, J. J., Lane, A., Corneille, O., de Timary, P., & Luminet, O. (2010). Oxytocin makes people trusting, not gullible. *Psychological Science, 21*, 1072–1074. doi:10.1177/0956797610377343

Morhenn, V. B., Park, J. W., Piper, E., & Zak, P. J. (2008). Monetary sacrifice among strangers is mediated by endogenous oxytocin release after physical contact. *Evolution and Human Behavior, 29,* 375–383. doi:10.1016/j.evolhumbehav. 2008.04.004

Neumann, I. D. (2008). Brain oxytocin: A key regulator of emotional and social behaviours in both females and males. *Journal of Neuroendocrinology, 20,* 858–865. doi:10.1111/j.1365-2826.2008.01726.x

Nowak, M. A., Tarnita, C. E., & Wilson, E. O. (2010, August 26). The evolution of eusociality. *Nature, 466,* 1057–1062. doi:10.1038/nature09205

Oosterhof, N. N., & Todorov, A. (2008). The functional basis of face evaluation. *Proceedings of the National Academy of Sciences of the United States of America, 105,* 11087–11092. doi:10.1073/pnas.0805664105

Ostrom, E. (1998). A behavioral approach to the rational choice theory in collective action. *American Political Science Review, 92,* 1–22. doi:10.2307/2585925

Phelps, E. A. (2006). Emotion and cognition: Insights from studies of the human amygdala. *Annual Review of Psychology, 57,* 27–53. doi:10.1146/annurev. psych.56.091103.070234

Pruitt, D. G., & Kimmel, M. J. (1977). Twenty years of experimental gaming: Critique, synthesis, and suggestions for the future. *Annual Review of Psychology, 28,* 363–392. doi:10.1146/annurev.ps.28.020177.002051

Rilling, J. K., DeMarco, A. C., Hackett, P. D., Thompson, R., Ditzen, B., Patel, R., & Pagnoni, G. (2012). Effects of intranasal oxytocin and vasopressin on cooperative behavior and associated brain activity in men. *Psychoneuroendocrinology, 37,* 447–461. doi:10.1016/j.psyneuen.2011.07.013

Rimmele, U., Hediger, K., Heinrichs, M., & Klaver, P. (2009). Oxytocin makes a face in memory more familiar. *Journal of Neuroscience, 29,* 38–42. doi:10.1523/ JNEUROSCI.4260-08.2009

Rodrigues, S. M., & Sapolsky, R. M. (2009). Disruption of fear memory through dual-hormone gene therapy. *Biological Psychiatry, 65,* 441–444. doi:10.1016/ j.biopsych.2008.09.003

Shamay-Tsoory, S. G. (2011). The neural bases for empathy. *Neuroscientist, 17,* 18–24. doi:10.1177/1073858410379268

Tajfel, H., & Turner, J. C. (1979). An integrative theory of intergroup conflict. In W. G. Austin & S. Worchel (Eds.), *The social psychology of intergroup relations* (pp. 33–47). Monterey, CA: Brooks/Cole.

Tang-Martinez, Z. (2001). The mechanisms of kin discrimination and the evolution of kin recognition in vertebrates: A critical re-evaluation. *Behavioural Processes, 53,* 21–40. doi:10.1016/S0376-6357(00)00148-0

Taylor, S. E., Klein, L. C., Lewis, B. P., Gruenewald, T. L., Gurung, R. A. R., & Updegraff, J. A. (2000). Biobehavioral responses to stress in females: Tend-and-befriend, not fight-or-flight. *Psychological Review, 107,* 411–429. doi:10.1037/ 0033-295X.107.3.411

Theodoridou, A., Rowe, A. C., Pentok-Voak, I. S., & Rogers, P. J. (2009). Oxytocin and social perception: Oxytocin increases perceived facial trustworthiness and attractiveness. *Hormones and Behavior*, *56*, 128–132. doi:10.1016/j.yhbeh.2009.03.019

Uvnäs-Moberg, K. (1998). Oxytocin may mediate the benefits of positive social interaction and emotions. *Psychoneuroendocrinology*, *23*, 819–835. doi:10.1016/S0306-4530(98)00056-0

Van Bavel, J. J., Packer, D. J., & Cummingham, W. A. (2008). The neural substrates of in-group bias: A functional magnetic resonance imaging investigation. *Psychological Science*, *19*, 1131–1139. doi:10.1111/j.1467-9280.2008.02214.x

Weber, J. M., Kopelman, S., & Messick, D. M. (2004). A conceptual review of decision making in social dilemmas: Applying a logic of appropriateness. *Personality and Social Psychology Review*, *8*, 281–307. doi:10.1207/s15327957pspr0803_4

Wilson, E. O. (2012). *The social conquest of Earth*. New York, NY: Norton.

Wit, A. P., & Kerr, N. L. (2002). "Me versus just us versus us all" categorization and cooperation in nested social dilemmas. *Journal of Personality and Social Psychology*, *83*, 616–637. doi:10.1037/0022-3514.83.3.616

Yzerbyt, V., & Demoulin, S. (2010). Intergroup relations. In S. T. Fiske, D. T. Gilbert, & G. Lindzey (Eds.), *Handbook of social psychology* (5th ed., Vol. 2, pp. 1024–1083). New York, NY: Wiley.

Zak, P. J., Kurzban, R., & Matzner, W. T. (2005). Oxytocin is associated with human trustworthiness. *Hormones and Behavior*, *48*, 522–527. doi:10.1016/j.yhbeh.2005.07.009

INDEX

and representational models, 125, 126, 129–130
on the secure base, 281
and working models of self, 227–228
Bradshaw, D., 273
Brain development, 62–63
Brain lesions
in areas controlling vicarious activity, 75, 78–79, 81
and moral cognition, 114
Brain responses, 157–159
Breakups, relationship, 57, 58
Broadly congruent mirror neurons, 73
Broca's area, 80–81
Brodmann areas (BAs), 76–78
Bronfman, E., 209
Brooks, R., 171, 173, 174, 176–178
Brosnan, S. F., 108
Brown, L. L., 61
Buprenorphine, 40, 43
Buss, K., 134

Camaioni, L., 170
Campa, M. I., 279
Cape mole rat (*Georychus capensis*), 19
Capitalization (interpersonal process), 261–264
Caprariello, P. A., 260
Capuchin monkey, 108
Cardiovascular arousal, 379–381, 394
CARE (primary process), 33, 36, 37, 46
Caregiving
association between insightfulness and, 210–211
and insightfulness, 208
quality of, 223
Caring (perceived partner responsiveness), 257, 258, 260
Caudate, 59–60
CD38 genes, 153–154
Central oxytocin, 153–154
Central premotor cortex, 74
Change, mechanisms of, 177–178
Chatterjee, N., 280
Cheating, detection of, 341
Childbirth, 15
Child–parent attachment, 125–139. *See also* Biobehavioral synchrony
evolutionary underpinnings of, 134–135

history of research on, 125–126
as influence on Insightfulness Assessment, 208–210
mother–child emotion dialogues in, 213
physiology of, 130–134
representational and nonrepresentational processes in, 135–138
representational models in, 125, 129–130
secure base/safe haven construct in, 126–128
Child–parent dialogues, 205–206, 211–217
empirical research on, 213–216
level of organization in, 216–217
as part of secure base, 211–213
Children, 111–112. *See also* Infants
Chimpanzees, 347
Church, R. M., 80
Clark, M. S., 266
Coan, J. A., 280
Cocaine, 61–62
Cocreativity, 191
Cognition
and attachment, 137
moral, 108
social, 189, 243
and vicarious brain activity, 72, 81–83
Cognitive–behavioral regulatory strategies, 38
Cognitive–behavioral therapy, 91
Cohesion, social, 344–345
Collective decision making, 345–346, 348
Collins, M. L., 281
Collins, N. L., 279–281, 292
Collins, W. A., 226, 256
Commitment, in relationships, 265, 266, 295
Communal need satisfaction, 257
Communication
embodied circles of, 194–196
kinesthetic, 193–194
mis-, 191
preverbal, 187–189
Competition
as evolutionary strategy, 343
and oxytocin, 392, 398–399

Functional magnetic resonance imaging
(fMRI) research
on moral behavior and cognition,
112–114
on romantic love, 56–58, 60–61
on social categorization, 384, 385
on social regulation, 92–93
on vicarious brain activity, 74, 78, 79
Fusiform gyri, 384

Gächter, S., 341
Gainer, P., 80
Gallese, V., 189
Game theory, 339–340, 346
Gaze following, 167–180
conceptual issues in, 171–172
defined, 171
joint engagement with, 169–170
and "like me" developmental theory,
168–169, 178–180
mechanisms of change with, 177–178
role of pointing in, 170–171
and salience of eyes, 172–173
tests of, 173–176
in triadic exchanges, 167–168
Genetics, 82, 231
Glutamatergic drive, 39
GLYX-13, 44
Goal-directed behavior, 59
Grafton, S. T., 57
Granger, D. A., 134
Green, J. D., 283
Greer, L. L., 397, 399
Griffin, D. W., 239–240
Griskevicius, V., 349
Group affiliation. See Social affiliation
Group decision making, 345–346, 348
Group living, 336, 339
Group loyalty, 400
Group membership, 382–383
Group selection, 337
Group self, 374–377
Growing movement (parental embodied
mentalizing), 196
Guichard, A. C., 280, 281
Gump, B. B., 279
Gunnar, M., 134
Gutsell, J. N., 384

Habituation, 192
Haidt, J., 107
Halpern-Felsher, B. L., 359
Hamilton, A. F., 57
Handgraaf, M. J. J., 397, 399
Haptics, 78–79
Harlow, H. F., 138, 145
Hastie, R., 342, 346
Haven of safety. See Secure base/safe
haven
Hazan, C., 273, 277–279
Health, 296–297
Hebbian learning, 72, 82
Heinrichs, M., 395
Hereditary traits, 336
Herzliya Symposium on Personality and
Social Psychology, xvi
Heterosexual relationships, 57
Hibel, L. C., 134
Hierarchy of attachment figures, 276
Hill, K., 342
Hinde, R., 126, 135
Hippocampus
oxytocin's effects on, 394
and romantic love, 58
Hirschberger, G., 279, 322
Hofer, M., 130–131, 137, 138, 146
Honeybees, 340, 345–346
Hormones, 151–157
Hostility, marital, 159–160
Houts, R. M., 359
Hunger, 62
Hunter–gatherer activities, 342
Husserl, E., 161
Hutman, T., 210
Hypothalamic–pituitary–adrenal axis
activity, 89, 133–134, 151, 394
Hypothalamus, 98

IFO (insula and frontal operculum),
80–81
IGF-1 (insulin-like growth factor-1),
45
Immune modulators, 41
Immunological systems, 151
Impulsive trust, 250–251
Inclusive fitness, 359
Indirect reciprocity, theory of, 338

Individual differences
   in sex and attachment, 326–327
   social advantages of, 336
Infant–mother bonds. *See* Mother–infant
      bonds
Infant–parent attachment. *See* Child–
      parent attachment
Infants
   and biobehavioral synchrony,
      149–150
   development of regulatory abilities
      in, 97
   gaze following by. *See* Gaze following
   preference for social stimuli, 109–110
   preverbal communication by,
      187–189. *See also* Parental
      embodied mentalizing
   sensitivity to others' emotional
      expressions, 112
Infant stress reactivity, 134–135
Inferior parietal lobule, 76
Ingroup favoritism, 345, 384–385,
      397–398
Insecure–ambivalent attachment,
      208–209
Insecure–anxious attachment
   characteristics of, 275
   with death of a spouse, 285
   effects on romantic relationships, 242
   expression of, 225
Insecure attachment. *See also specific styles*
   and caregiver availability/
      responsiveness, 130
   conflict recovery with, 226, 227
   defined, 129
   effects of, 275
   and romantic relationships, 225
Insecure–avoidant attachment
   characteristics of, 275
   with death of a spouse, 285
   with disengaged parents, 209
   expression of, 225
Insecure–disorganized attachment, 209
Insight, 207. *See also* Parental
      insightfulness
Insightfulness Assessment, 186, 206–208
Insula, 77
Insulin-like growth factor-1 (IGF-1), 45
Intelligence, 209

Interdependence, 255–256, 295. *See also*
      Perceived partner responsiveness
Intergroup conflict, 400
Intergroup differentiation, 384
Intergroup relations, 347–348
Internal representational models, 125,
      129–130
Internal working models, 125. *See also*
      Internal representational models
Interpersonal experiences' impact on
      romantic relationships. *See* Early
      interpersonal experiences' impact
      on romantic relationships
Interpersonal pathways, 226
Interpersonal processes, 257–258
Interpersonal space (parental embodied
      mentalizing), 195
Intersubjectivity, 189
Intimacy, 295, 322–323
Intimacy process model, 257
Intranasal oxytocin, 16, 17, 19–21, 395
Intraparietal sulcus, 76
Inzlicht, M., 384

Jaremka, L. M., 281
Jerga, C., 285
Joint engagement (gaze following),
      169–170

Kamarck, T. W., 279
Kameda, T., 342, 346
Kane, H., 280, 281
Kaplan, H., 342
Kelley, H. H., 255, 264
Kenrick, D. T., 348–349
Kesebir, S., 107
Kinesthetic communication, 193–194
Kirsch, P., 98, 394–395
Kohlberg, L., 111
Koren-Karie, N., 187
Kosfeld, M., 395, 396
Kumashiro, M., 266
Kuo, S. I., 226

Labor, division of, 340
Language
   as biological adaptation, 337
   links between gaze following and,
      176

ABOUT THE EDITORS

Mario Mikulincer, PhD, is a professor of psychology and dean of the New School of Psychology at the Interdisciplinary Center in Herzliya, Israel. He has published five books and more than 280 scholarly journal articles and book chapters. Dr. Mikulincer's main research interests are attachment theory, terror management theory, personality processes in interpersonal relationships, coping with stress and trauma, grief-related processes, and prosocial motives and behavior. He is a member of the editorial boards of several scientific journals, including the *Journal of Personality and Social Psychology*, *Psychological Inquiry*, and *Personality and Social Psychology Review*, and he has served as associate editor of two journals, the *Journal of Personality and Social Psychology* and *Personal Relationships*. Recently, he was elected to serve as chief editor of the *Journal of Social and Personal Relationships*. He received the EMET Prize in Social Science for his contributions to psychology and the Berscheid-Hatfield Award for Distinguished Mid-Career Achievement from the International Association for Relationship Research.

Phillip R. Shaver, PhD, a social and personality psychologist, is Distinguished Professor of Psychology at the University of California, Davis. Before moving there, he served on the faculties of Columbia University, New York

University, University of Denver, and State University of New York at Buffalo. He has coauthored and coedited numerous books and has published over 250 scholarly articles and book chapters. Dr. Shaver's research focuses on attachment, human motivation and emotion, close relationships, personality development, and the effects of meditation on behavior and the brain. He is a member of the editorial boards of *Attachment and Human Development*, *Personal Relationships*, the *Journal of Personality and Social Psychology*, and *Emotion*, and he has served on grant review panels for the National Institutes of Health and the National Science Foundation. He has been executive officer of the Society of Experimental Social Psychology (SESP) and president of the International Association for Relationship Research (IARR). He has received a Distinguished Career Award and a Mentoring Award from the IARR, a Scientific Influence Award from SESP, and a Career Contribution award from the Society for Personality and Social Psychology.